DATE DUE

3/24/97			
AP 07 '97			
OCT 24 '09			
NOV 10 '09			
NOV			

Demco, Inc. 38-293

FUTURES MARKETS

DANIEL R. SIEGEL
NORTHWESTERN UNIVERSITY

DIANE F. SIEGEL

The Dryden Press
Chicago Fort Worth San Francisco Philadelphia
Montreal Toronto London Sydney Tokyo

Acquisitions Editor: Ann Heath
Developmental Editor: Judy Sarwark
Project Editor: Karen Steib
Assistant Project Editor: Sarah Russell
Design Manager: Jeanne Calabrese
Production Manager: Barb Bahnsen
Director of Editing, Design, and Production: Jane Perkins

Text and Cover Designer: Shriver/Waterhouse Design, Inc.
Copy Editor: Nancy Maybloom
Text Type: 10.5/12 Times Roman

Library of Congress Cataloging-in-Publication Data
Siegel, Daniel Richard.
    Futures markets / Daniel R. Siegel, Diane F. Siegel.
        p.   cm.
    Includes bibliographies and index.
    ISBN 0-03-025294-6
    1. Futures market.   I. Siegel, Diane.   II. Title.
HG6024.A3S54   1990
332.64'5—dc20   89-12062

Printed in the United States of America
901-118-987654321

Address orders:
The Dryden Press
Orlando, FL 32887

Address editorial correspondence:
The Dryden Press
908 N. Elm Street
Hinsdale, IL 60521

The Dryden Press
Holt, Rinehart and Winston
Saunders College Publishing

To our parents, Barry and Jetta Siegel and Peter and Marilyn Freeman.

The Dryden Press Series in Finance

Preface

The explosive growth of the futures and options markets over the past decade has been accompanied by a rapid increase in the number of courses that cover these markets. Several years ago, courses on options and futures were considered somewhat exotic offerings for a few advanced graduate students and usually were taught from a reading list of academic articles. However, as options and futures have entered into the mainstream of the financial marketplace, such courses have attracted a much broader group of students.

This book evolved from lecture notes that one of the authors began compiling for courses on futures and options markets at Northwestern University. We have since added material developed for various executive programs on futures and options given at Northwestern.

This book is designed for a quarter or semester course on futures markets or futures and options markets at the advanced undergraduate or master's level. It is organized so as to allow an instructor with limited time to concentrate on the markets in which he or she is most interested. The book can be combined with one of several options books currently available for courses on futures and options.

The book assumes only basic knowledge of finance. Students should be familiar with the concepts of the time value of money and the Capital Asset Pricing Model. They should also be comfortable with college-level algebra and be acquainted with basic statistics through regression analysis. No calculus is required.

Organization and Philosophy

The book is organized so that students first acquire a general theoretical foundations and then apply the concepts to specific markets. Chapter 1 provides an overview of the futures markets and introduces the mechanics and institutional details of these markets. Chapter 2 develops the theory of the pricing of futures contracts, concentrating on arbitrage and risk-and-return considerations. Chapter 3 develops the theory of risk management and discusses the strategic role of hedging within the firm. Together these three chapters offer the student a unified framework within which to study the various futures markets. The examples in these chapters use only a small number of contracts, allowing students to concentrate on the concepts rather than on the specific markets.

Chapters 4 through 8 apply the material covered in the first three chapters to specific markets. Chapter 4 discusses stock index futures markets and includes material on program trading and market-timing strategies. Chapter 5 covers short-term interest rate futures markets, particularly the Eurodollar and Treasury bill contracts. Chapter 6 discusses long-term interest rate futures markets; topics include bond pricing, duration, Treasury bonds, and municipal bonds. Chapter 7 covers foreign exchange futures markets, including forward markets and covered interest rate parity. Chapter 8 discusses agricultural, energy, and metal commodity futures markets. All of the applied chapters present the institutional details students need to understand the uses of the futures markets.

Chapters 9 and 10 cover the options and swap markets, respectively. They emphasize the relationship between these markets and the futures markets.

We believe that the concepts of pricing, arbitrage, and risk management are essentially the same for all futures markets. This may seem obvious, but a trader who operates a foreign exchange arbitrage desk likely would be lost if transferred to a government security arbitrage desk. This book will give students the flexibility needed to move easily among a number of different markets.

Special Features

One of our major goals in writing this book was to include both theory and institutional detail. We believe that theory and institutional detail are complementary. Theory is crucial for understanding topics such as pricing and risk management, and we have devoted considerable space to theory. However, a purely theoretical presentation is hardly optimal. Only by including a generous amount of institutional detail does the theory come sufficiently alive to interest students and be useful to them. Conversely, institutional detail without a theoretical framework is of only limited use.

An important aspect of enlivening the theory is a serious treatment of transactions costs. We are convinced that transactions costs, such as bid-ask spreads, differential borrowing and lending rates, and brokerage fees, play a central role in any futures strategy. Because of differential transactions costs among various parties, a futures strategy appropriate for one institution may be unsuitable for another, even if the institutions have similar objectives. We develop a systematic technique for determining how transactions costs affect futures strategies and demonstrate it throughout the book using actual price data.

Our focus on transactions costs has also led us to reconsider the role of arbitrage in setting futures prices. Most academic treatments of arbitrage examine pure arbitrage, in which the arbitrageur starts with a zero net position and makes profits by going long and short essentially identical positions. However, this rarely happens in real-life markets, because pure arbitrageurs face high transactions costs. Arbitrage is more often performed by those engaging in quasi-arbitrage, in which an investor replaces an existing position with a synthetic strategy that includes futures contracts. For example, a portfolio manager may replace his or her T-bills with synthetic T-bills. Throughout the book, we provide examples of quasi-arbitrage and demonstrate the impact of this activity on futures pricing.

We have also enriched the theoretical material with numerous examples, discussions of current events, and summaries of academic research. Where possible, the examples represent situations faced by market participants and use real data. The discussions of current events include such topics as program trading and the market break of October 1987. Throughout the book, we refer to both theoretical and empirical research.

Finally, we have provided end-of-chapter problems to reinforce the concepts developed in the book. Most of these problems use actual data. Some require the use of a spreadsheet program such as Lotus 1-2-3®. The solutions are available in a separate *Instructor's Manual* and on a disk, where appropriate.

Acknowledgments

Many individuals have contributed to the writing of this book. As a result of an early survey and the formal reviewing process, we made substantial improvements and are grateful for the generous effort expended by the following reviewers: Andrew Chen (Southern Methodist University), Richard Dowen (Northern Illinois University), Dennis Draper (University of Southern California), Jerome Duncan (Hofstra University), Paul Farris (Purdue University), Peggy Fletcher (Northeastern University), Virginia France (University of Illinois), Theoharry Grammatikos (University of Wisconsin), Shantaram Hegde (University of Notre Dame), Patrick Hess (University of Minnesota), David Hirshleifer (U.C.L.A.), Avaraham Kamara (University of Washington), Paul Koch (Kansas State University), Nalin Kulatilaka (Boston University), Cheng-few Lee (Rutgers University), Robert McLeod (University of Alabama), Stephen Mahle (University of Iowa), Alan Marcus (Boston University), Margaret Monroe (University of Illinois, Chicago), James Moser (Michigan State University), Hun Park (University of Illinois), George Racette (University of Oregon), Bruce Resnick (Indiana University), and A. J. Senchack, Jr. (University of Texas). In addition, Douglas Breeden (Duke University), Virginia France (University of Illinois), Pat Hess (University of Minnesota), Ravi Jagannathan (University of Minnesota), Juan Ketterer (Carnegie-Mellon University), Nalin Kulatilaka (Boston University), and Robert McDonald (Northwestern University) used the manuscript in class and provided many useful comments and suggestions. We also extend our gratitude to Robert McLeod who reviewed all the end-of-chapter problems and solutions.

Several generations of master's and Ph.D. students at Northwestern contributed to this project through their suggestions and support. Oded Ben-Ezer, Luca Celati, Antonio Dominguez, Ronen Israel, Maureen O'Toole, Randy Paulson, Pete Roche, Thierry Thaure, and Ross Vaisburd deserve special mention.

We also wish to thank Joseph Cole (Drexel Burnham Lambert), Eric Klusman (Federal Reserve Bank of Chicago), Roger Rutz (Chicago Board of Trade Clearing Corporation), Gary Schirr (Prudential-Bache), and Leslie Wurman

(Chicago Mercantile Exchange) for providing materials that enhanced the realism of many of the examples.

Finally, we wish to express our appreciation to The Dryden Press, especially Ann Heath, Judy Sarwark, Bill Schoof, Karen Steib, Sarah Russell, Barb Bahnsen, Beth Olson, and Sandy Lopez for their continuing support in bringing the book to completion.

Dan Siegel
Diane Siegel

October 1989

Contents

Introduction to Futures Contracting

A **futures contract** is an agreement between two parties that commits one to sell a commodity or security to the other at a given price and on a specified future date. Futures contracts are traded in centralized exchanges in the United States and throughout the world.

People trade futures for several reasons. Many businesses use futures to protect themselves, or **hedge**, against future changes in commodity prices, security prices, interest rates, or exchange rates. **Speculators** trade in futures in the hope of profiting from future price movements. **Arbitrageurs** trade simultaneously in futures and the futures' underlying commodities or securities to profit from price discrepancies between the futures and cash markets.

Formal futures markets have been operating in North America since the mid-nineteenth century. Up until the 1970s, trading was concentrated in agricultural commodities such as wheat, corn, and soybeans and precious metals such as gold and silver. During the 1970s and early 1980s, futures markets were revolutionized by the introduction of contracts on financial instruments such as foreign currencies, U.S. Treasury bills and bonds, stock indices, Eurodollar time deposits, and mortgage-backed securities. The new financial contracts were very popular from the first and today are the most rapidly growing segment of the futures market. Another major new area of futures trading opened up in 1978 with the introduction of a contract on heating oil. Other contracts on petroleum and petroleum products were introduced in the early 1980s, and some have become very widely traded.

Figure 1.1 charts the increase in annual U.S. futures trading volume from 3.9 million contracts in 1960 to 245.9 million contracts in 1988. Figure 1.2 shows the shift in futures trading toward the new contract areas. Financial futures increased their share of futures trading volume from 38 percent in 1983 to 57 percent in 1988. This increase was due largely to the very rapid growth of interest rate futures. Energy futures grew from a 2 percent market share in 1983 to an 11 percent share in 1988. Futures on agricultural commodities and metals, in contrast, lost market share over this period.

Figure 1.1   Volume of Futures Trading in United States, 1960–1988

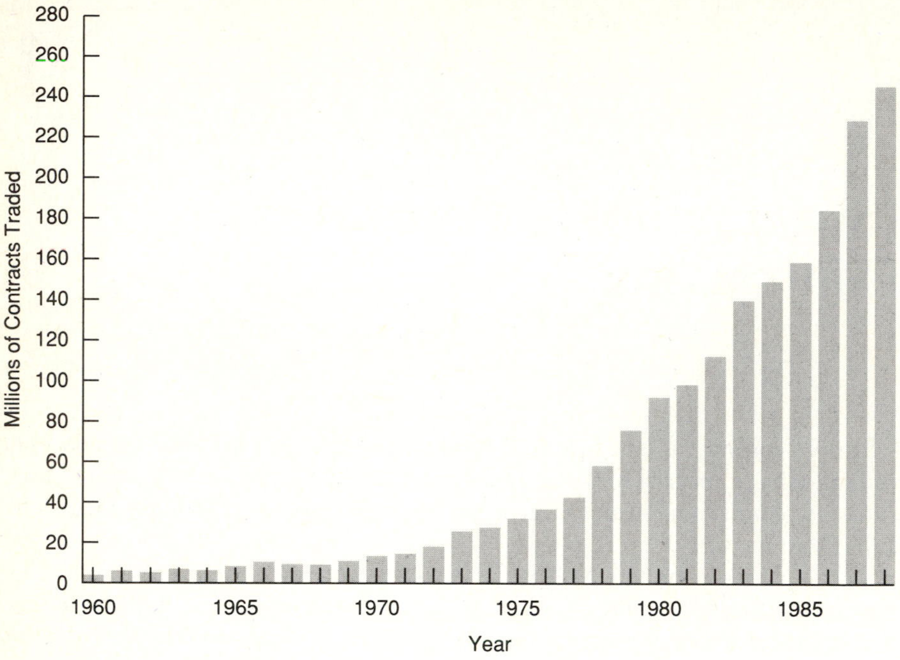

Source: Futures Industry Association.

The recent innovation and growth in the futures markets have created a very diverse futures marketplace. Table 1.1 lists all the contracts now traded on U.S. futures exchanges. Table 1.2 shows the 10 contracts with the highest trading volume in 1988. The Treasury bond contract at the Chicago Board of Trade is by far the most popular. Five of the top ten contracts are on financial instruments or indices, three on agricultural commodities, one on gold, and one on crude oil. The Chicago Board of Trade has the highest trading volume of the exchanges, followed by the Chicago Mercantile Exchange. The New York Mercantile Exchange and the Commodity Exchange are also major futures exchanges in the United States.[1]

The current explosion in futures trading is due largely to economic changes in the late 1960s and early 1970s that created an environment particularly receptive to futures trading, especially in the new contract areas. Turmoil in the financial and energy markets during these years increased interest in hedging and opportunities for speculation and arbitrage. The many new futures contracts proved very useful instruments for the growing number of institutions and individuals who wished to pursue such strategies.

[1] See Carleton [1984] for a discussion of the development of futures trading.

Figure 1.2 Share of Futures Trading by Contract Type, 1983 and 1988

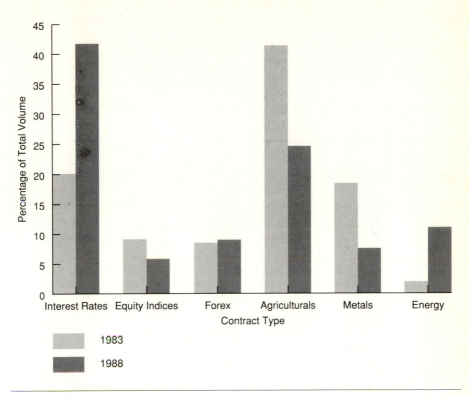

Source: Futures Industry Association.

The financial changes began as the Johnson administration, in an attempt to fund both the Great Society programs and the Vietnam War, followed monetary and fiscal policies that increased inflation. The higher inflation was accompanied by increased price volatility. As a result, both the level and the volatility of interest rates rose dramatically.

These trends led to instability in foreign exchange markets. It became more difficult for governments to keep their exchange rates in line with the Bretton Woods fixed-exchange-rate system that had been in effect since 1945. In 1971, President Nixon withdrew the United States from the Bretton Woods agreement. The fixed-rate system eventually fell apart, and a more or less flexible exchange rate system took its place.

Faced with a more volatile financial environment, firms turned to the new financial futures contracts to hedge against future adverse changes in financial conditions. The contracts on foreign exchange supplemented the foreign exchange interbank market in allowing firms to hedge exchange rate risk. The contracts on Treasury bills and bonds and on Eurodollar time deposits allowed firms to hedge interest rate risk. Individual and institutional investors used the stock index futures to hedge their portfolios against stock market declines and to carry out their trading

Table 1.1 Contracts Traded on U.S. Futures Exchanges

Exchange	Futures Contract Commodities/Instruments
Chicago Board of Trade	Corn, oats, soybeans, soybean meal, soybean oil, wheat, gold, silver, GNMA passthroughs, Treasury bonds, Treasury notes, municipal bonds, Major Market Index, 30-day interest rates, CBOE 250 Index
Chicago Mercantile Exchange	Feeder cattle, live cattle, live hogs, pork bellies, lumber
International Monetary Market Division of CME	Eurodollar time deposits, foreign exchange, Treasury bills
Index and Option Market Division of CME	Standard and Poor's 500 Stock Index
Chicago Rice and Cotton Exchange	Rough rice
Coffee, Sugar and Cocoa Exchange Inc.	Cocoa, coffee, sugar, consumer price index
Commodity Exchange Inc.	Aluminum, copper, gold, silver
Kansas City Board of Trade	Wheat, Value Line Stock Index, sorghum
MidAmerica Commodity Exchange	Corn, live cattle, live hogs, oats, soybeans, soybean meal, wheat, gold, platinum, silver, foreign exchange, Treasury bills, Treasury bonds, Treasury notes
Minneapolis Grain Exchange	Wheat, oats
New York Cotton Exchange	Cotton
Citrus Associates of New York Cotton Exchange	Orange juice
Financial Instrument Exchange Division of New York Cotton Exchange	European Currency Unit, Treasury notes, U.S. Dollar Index
New York Futures Exchange	CRB Futures Price Index, NYSE Composite Stock Index
New York Mercantile Exchange	Palladium, platinum, crude oil, heating oil, propane, unleaded gasoline

Source: Futures Industry Association.

strategies. Arbitrageurs and speculators used the new futures contracts to trade on the expanded profit opportunities that the uncertain financial climate offered.

The 1970s and early 1980s also saw major turbulence in the worldwide energy markets. The 1973 Arab oil embargo and the 1979 Iranian revolution threatened worldwide supply shortages and caused oil prices to shoot up. OPEC consolidated its power over world oil prices in the 1970s, only to see its effectiveness wane in the 1980s as the OPEC member countries disagreed over pricing policy and the energy markets entered a period of oversupply and falling prices. Futures contracts on petroleum and petroleum products were introduced to meet the growing interest in hedging and trading for profit in the more volatile energy

Table 1.2 Top 10 Contracts Traded on U.S. Exchanges: 1988 Volume of Contracts Traded

Contract/Exchange	1988 Volume	Percent of Total U.S. Volume
1 Treasury bond (CBOT)	70,307,872	28.60
2 Eurodollar (CME)	21,705,223	8.83
3 Crude oil (NYMEX)	18,858,948	7.67
4 Soybeans (CBOT)	12,497,096	5.08
5 S&P 500 Stock Index (CME)	11,353,898	4.62
6 Corn (CBOT)	11,105,516	4.52
7 Gold (COMEX)	9,496,402	3.86
8 Japanese yen (CME)	6,433,132	2.62
9 Sugar (#11) (CSC)	5,819,121	2.37
10 Deutsche mark (CME)	5,662,109	2.30

Note:
CBOT   = Chicago Board of Trade
CME   = Chicago Mercantile Exchange
COMEX = Commodity Exchange Inc.
CSC   = Coffee, Sugar & Cocoa Exchange
NYMEX = New York Mercantile Exchange

Source: Futures Industry Association.

markets. Today the energy futures area is one of the fastest-growing segments of the futures markets.

The futures markets have also participated in the trend toward greater internationalization of business. Foreign exchanges now trade U.S. futures contracts and offer their own domestic contracts. This has created an international linkage among markets and a 24-hour trading day. Table 1.3 presents some of the contracts traded on exchanges outside the United States. Some of these contracts are very active. For instance, the yen-denominated 10-year bond futures contract on the Tokyo Stock Exchange has the largest dollar volume of any contract in the world.

Futures trading is likely to continue growing, especially in the financial areas, as more contracts are introduced, more uses for the contracts are found, and more firms and individuals become skilled in futures trading techniques. Because price and rate volatility are likely to persist, the need to manage business risks of all kinds should continue. Virtually unlimited numbers of firms could become interested in hedging exchange and interest rate risks. Continued volatility will also encourage futures speculation, especially in the financial markets, where many speculators have expertise in and opinions about exchange and interest rates.

This book offers a comprehensive study of the futures markets. It presents the mechanics of futures trading; the theory of futures pricing; futures trading strategies used for arbitrage, hedging, and speculation; and descriptions of all the major futures contracts. This chapter begins by describing how futures contracts are structured and traded.

Table 1.3 Contracts Traded on Foreign Futures Exchanges

Exchange	Futures Contract Commodities/Instruments
Australia:	
Sydney Futures Exchange	Live cattle, wool, gold, Australian dollar, Australian 10-year bond, Australian 3-year bond, Eurodollar time deposit, 90-day bank-accepted bills, U.S. Treasury bonds, All Ordinaries Share Price Index
Brazil:	
Bolsa Mercantil & De Futuros	Broilers, live cattle, live hogs, U.S. dollar, Brazilian Treasury bond, domestic CDs, gold, São Paulo Stock Exchange Index, coffee
Canada:	
Montreal Exchange	Canadian bankers' acceptance
Toronto Futures Exchange	TSE 35 Index
Toronto Stock Exchange	Toronto 35 Index
Winnipeg Commodity Exchange	Barley, rapeseed, oats, wheat, flaxseed, rye
France:	
Lille Potato Futures Market	Potatoes
Marché A Terme des Instruments Financiers	French government notional bond, French Treasury 90-day bill
Paris Futures Exchange	Cocoa beans, cocoa butter, coffee, sugar
Great Britain:	
Baltic Futures Exchange	Baltic freight index
London Grain Futures Market	Barley, wheat
London Meat Futures Market	Live cattle, pigs
London Potato Futures Market	Potatoes
Soya Bean Meal Futures Association	Soybean meal
International Petroleum Exchange of London	Gas oil, Brent crude oil
London Futures and Options Exchange	Cocoa, coffee, raw sugar, refined sugar
London International Financial Futures Exchange	British pound, Deutsche mark, Japanese yen, Swiss franc, U.S. dollar-Deutsche mark, Eurodollar TD, German government bond, Japanese government bond, long gilt, medium gilt, short gilt, sterling three-month, U.S. Treasury bond, Financial Times Stock Exchange 100 Index
London Metal Exchange	Aluminum, copper, lead, nickel, silver, zinc

Source: Diamond and Kollar [1989].

Forward Contracting

Futures contracting is easier to understand if one first learns about **forward contracting**, a similar but conceptually simpler form of financial agreement. Forward contracts are important financial instruments in their own right. Many foreign exchange speculators and hedgers operate through the forward markets, and a growing number of banks and investment firms are making markets in interest rate forward contracts.

Table 1.3 (continued)

Exchange	Futures Contract Commodities/Instruments
Hong Kong:	
Hong Kong Futures Exchange	Soybeans, sugar, gold, Hang Seng Index
Japan:	
Osaka Securities Exchange	Nikkei Stock Average, Osaka Stock Futures 50
Tokyo Commodity Exchange	Gold, platinum, silver, rubber, cotton yarn, woolen yarn
Tokyo Grain Exchange	American soybeans, Chinese soybeans, Japanese soybeans, red beans, white beans, potato starch
Tokyo Stock Exchange	Japanese 10-year government bond, Japanese 20-year government bond, Tokyo Stock Price Index
Malaysia:	
Kuala Lumpur Commodity Exchange	Cocoa, crude palm oil, rubber, tin
The Netherlands:	
Financiele Termijnmarkt Amsterdam N.V.	Guilder bond
New Zealand:	
New Zealand Futures Exchange	New Zealand dollar, U.S. dollar, 5-year government bond, 90-day bank-accepted bills, Barclays Share Price Index
Singapore:	
Singapore International Monetary Exchange	British pound, Deutsche mark, Japanese yen, Eurodollar 90-day TD, Nikkei Stock Average
Sweden:	
Swedish Options and Futures Exchange	SX 16 Stock Index

A **forward contract** is an agreement between a buyer and seller that has the following characteristics:

1. It specifies a quantity and type of commodity or security to be bought or sold at a prespecified future date.

2. It specifies a delivery place.

3. It specifies a price.

4. It obligates the seller to sell to the buyer subject to conditions 1, 2, and 3, and it obligates the buyer to buy.

5. No money changes hands until the sale date except, perhaps, for a small service fee.

The two parties to the deal negotiate the terms of the forward contract. Each side must trust that the other will not default on the contract. Often one or both parties will perform a credit check on the other party before entering into the contract.

Forward (and futures) contracting employs some special terminology. The party who agrees to buy in the future is said to hold a **long position** in the contract. The party who agrees to sell in the future holds a **short position** in the contract. The **forward price** is the agreed-upon price at which the parties will transact when the contract expires. The **underlying commodity or security** of the contract is the asset that will be bought and sold when the contract expires. For example, a party who holds a long forward position in gold has agreed to buy a given amount of gold at some point in the future at the forward price.

The **spot price** of the underlying commodity or security is the purchase price for immediate delivery. The spot price of the underlying asset when the contract expires is called the **future spot price**, because it is the market price that will prevail at some future date.

Our discussion of forward contracting will use the following notation and time line:

$f_{t,T}$ = forward price at time t of a contract that expires at time T

P_t = spot price at t

P_T = future spot price (at expiration of contract)

The profit or loss on a forward (and futures) position is determined by the future spot price, P_T. Those holding long forward positions profit if the spot price at time T rises above the forward price. This is because the market price is higher than the price at which the longs have contracted to buy. Those holding short forward positions profit if the spot price at time T falls below the forward price. Then the market price of the underlying commodity or security is lower than the price at which the shorts have agreed to sell. Example 1.1 describes a forward contract on gold and illustrates the earnings of forward positions under different price scenarios.

▪ **Example 1.1: Gold Forward Contract**   Suppose that on April 1, two parties enter into a forward contract for delivery of 100 troy ounces of gold on July 1 at a price of $450 per ounce. Thus,

t   = April 1

T   = July 1

$f_{t,T}$ = $450

Let's see what happens to the long and short positions in this contract when the spot price of gold on July 1 (the future spot price) turns out to be both higher and lower than the forward price.

Suppose the future spot price at T rises above the forward price to $500 per ounce. The long forward position will experience the following cash flows when the contract expires on July 1:

Buy 100 ounces at $f_{t,T} = \$450$ (contract)	−$45,000
Sell 100 ounces at $P_T = \$500$ (spot)	50,000
Gain	$ 5,000

The long position gains by having purchased gold worth $500 per ounce at the forward price of $450 per ounce. This gain is $50 per ounce, or $5,000 for 100 ounces. In general:

Gain to long position (per contract)
= (Number of units)(Future spot price − Forward price)
= (Number of units)$(P_T - f_{t,T})$,

where the number of units is per contract.

We have assumed that the party who holds the long position sold the gold immediately on July 1 (time T). But what if the party wants to keep the gold instead? There will still be a $5,000 profit; the price of obtaining gold from the spot market on July 1 is $500 per ounce. But for the person who entered into the long forward position on April 1 (time t), the cost of obtaining the gold on July 1 is only $450. That person therefore receives an opportunity gain of $50 per ounce from the long forward position.

The party holding the short position will experience the following cash flows when the contract expires on July 1:

Buy 100 ounces at $P_T = \$500$ (spot)	−$50,000
Sell 100 ounces at $f_{t,T} = \$450$ (contract)	45,000
Loss	−$ 5,000

The short position loses by being obligated to sell gold worth $500 per ounce at the forward price of $450 per ounce. This loss is $50 per ounce, or $5,000 for 100 ounces. In general,

Gain to short position (per contract)
= (Number of units)(Forward price − Future spot price)
= (Number of units)$(f_{t,T} - P_T)$.

We have assumed that the party holding the short position had to purchase the gold on the spot market in order to deliver into the forward contract. But what if the party already owns the gold? There will still be a $5,000 loss. The alternative selling price for the gold in the spot market on July 1 (time T) is $500 per ounce. For the party who entered into a short forward position on April 1 (time t), the proceeds from selling the gold on

July 1 are only $450. Thus, there is an opportunity loss of $50 per ounce on the position.

The $50-per-ounce gain to the long position exactly offsets the $50-per-ounce loss to the short position. Since the two parties in a forward (and futures) contract agree to a specific forward (and futures) price, the gain to one party will be a loss to the other.

Now suppose the future spot price falls to $425 per ounce on July 1. The long position will experience a loss:

> Gain to long position
> = (Number of units)(Future spot price – Forward price)
> = (Number of units)$(P_T - f_{t,T})$
> = $(100)($425 – $450) = –$2,500$.

The short position will experience a gain:

> Gain to short position
> = (Number of units)(Forward price – Future spot price)
> = (Number of units)$(f_{t,T} - P_T)$
> = $(100)($450 – $425) = $2,500$.

The long party loses by being forced to purchase gold at $450 when it is worth only $425. The short party gains by being able to sell gold worth only $425 at $450. This example illustrates the general rule that those holding long positions benefit if spot prices rise and those holding short positions benefit if spot prices fall. ∎

Getting Out of a Forward Position

Up to this point, we have examined what happens when a party enters into a forward contract and holds that position until delivery. The individual bears risk until the contract expires, because profits depend only on the future spot price of the underlying commodity or security. Next we will see that it is possible to limit the risk associated with a forward position by effectively getting out of the position before the expiration date. Since one cannot unilaterally back out of a contract, one gets out of it by entering into another forward position that is exactly opposite the original position. This strategy is called **offsetting the forward contract**.

Example 1.2 demonstrates how to offset a forward position.

▪ **Example 1.2: Getting out of a Forward Position**   Suppose that on April 1, A enters into a forward contract with B in which he agrees to buy 100 ounces of gold on July 1 (time T) for $f_{t,T} = 450 per ounce. On May 1 (which we will label time t1), A decides to get out of his position. He enters into a forward contract with C in which he agrees to sell 100 ounces of gold on July 1 for $f_{t1,T} = 475 per ounce.

Consider the following time line:

	t	t1	T
	April 1	May 1	July 1
	Enter long	Enter short	Long contract
	forward contract	forward contract	and short contract
	expiring July 1	expiring July 1	expire

Let's see what happens on July 1:

A's Account

Transaction	Cash Flow on July 1
Take delivery from B at $450 per ounce	−$45,000
Deliver to C at $475 per ounce	47,500
Gain	$ 2,500

A's gain is exactly equal to the increase in the forward price between April 1 and May 1 multiplied by the number of units. It does not depend on the future spot price on July 1; that is, after May 1 A is no longer subject to risk from changing gold prices. Our general notation illustrates that A's gain or loss is now completely determined by forward prices:

A's Account

Transaction	Cash Flow on July 1
Gain from April long position	$(P_T - f_{t,T})$ per ounce
Gain from May short position	$(f_{t1,T} - P_T)$ per ounce
Gain	$(f_{t1,T} - f_{t,T})$ per ounce

∎

The profits or losses from offsetting a forward contract before the expiration date can be expressed generally.

A long position entered into at time t and offset at time t1 yields a profit on the expiration date, T, of

$$(\text{Number of units})(f_{t1,T} - f_{t,T}).$$

Thus, long positions gain if forward prices increase after the forward contract is signed.

A short position entered into at time t and offset at time t1 yields a profit on the expiration date, T, of

$$(\text{Number of units})(f_{t,T} - f_{t1,T}).$$

Thus, short positions gain if forward prices fall.

Movements in forward prices generate paper gains and losses for those holding forward positions. By taking an offsetting position, the holder of a forward contract locks in the change in the forward price that has occurred since the contract was signed at time t. This gain or loss is not realized until expiration at time T.

Once the position is offset, the party holding the forward position is subject to no further gains or losses.

While it is possible to effectively get out of a forward position, the procedure can be cumbersome. An offsetting party must carry two contracts on his or her books until the contract expiration date. To enter into an offsetting forward contract, the party must find an opposite party. However, because entering into a forward contract can require a credit check, this may be hard to accomplish quickly with a third party. Going to the original party is certainly possible, but it may place one at a competitive disadvantage.

Futures Contracting

Futures contracts are fundamentally similar to forward contracts in that they too establish a price today for a transaction that will take place in the future. However, there are some important differences between the two types of contracts. Futures contracts specify standardized quantities and delivery dates, while forward contracts are customized to meet the needs of the two parties. Futures contracts are traded in centralized and established exchanges, while forward contracts are traded between dealers who are not necessarily in the same location. Futures contracts allow participants to realize gains and losses daily, while forward contracts are settled only at delivery. To enter into a futures contract, one must simply put a certain percentage of the face value into an account, called a margin account, with a broker; to enter into a forward contract, one must usually set up a credit line with the dealer. Finally, futures contracts are regulated, while forward contracts are unregulated. We will now discuss each of these differences in more detail.

Standardization

Futures contracts have standardized terms set by the exchanges on which they are traded. Each futures exchange allows trading in a limited number of futures contracts. For example, the only gold futures contract traded at the Commodity Exchange Inc. (COMEX) in New York has the following specifications:

Contract:	Gold
Exchange:	Commodity Exchange, Inc.
Quantity:	100 troy ounces
Delivery months:	Current month, next two months, and any February, April, June, August, October, and December within a 23-month period from present month
Delivery specifications:	95 to 105 ounces, fineness above 995, delivery during delivery month
*Minimum price movement (also called a **tick**):*	$10.00 per contract, or $0.10 per ounce

Figure 1.3 Futures Transactions Prices, May 23, 1989

	Open	High	Low	Settle	Chg	High	Low	Open Interest
\multicolumn{9}{c}{—METALS & PETROLEUM—}								

COPPER-STANDARD (CMX)—25,000 lbs.; cents per lb.

	Open	High	Low	Settle	Chg	High	Low	Open Interest
May	111.00	112.00	109.00	109.30	− 2.05	146.00	73.15	964
June	....	....	....	110.00	− 2.25	137.70	115.50	123
July	112.00	113.00	109.00	110.60	− 1.95	138.50	76.00	20,279
Sept	111.90	112.50	109.00	109.80	− 2.45	131.50	76.00	5,689
Dec	111.00	111.00	108.50	109.60	− 1.65	126.00	77.45	2,787

Est vol 7,000; vol Mon 10,814; open int 29,842, −462.

GOLD (CMX)—100 troy oz.; $ per troy oz.

	Open	High	Low	Settle	Chg	High	Low	Open Interest
May	....	....	....	363.80	+ .60	384.20	369.50	21
June	365.50	367.50	363.80	364.30	+ .60	570.00	360.60	54,552
Aug	369.00	370.50	367.00	367.20	+ .50	575.00	363.80	35,339
Oct	372.00	373.80	370.90	370.80	+ .50	575.50	367.70	6,512
Dec	375.50	377.50	374.10	374.40	+ .50	514.50	371.00	31,351
Fb90	379.50	379.50	378.10	378.00	+ .50	516.00	375.50	7,987
Apr	383.80	384.50	382.50	381.80	+ .60	525.80	379.00	10,567
June	365.50	389.50	385.50	385.70	+ .70	497.00	382.00	10,987
Aug	391.40	391.40	389.50	389.60	+ .80	487.00	389.50	6,690
Oct	....	....	....	393.60	+ .90	472.00	400.50	2,420
Dec	401.00	401.00	401.00	397.70	+ 1.00	455.00	395.50	7,050
Fb91	404.00	404.00	402.00	401.80	+ 1.10	450.00	397.50	8,444

Est vol 50,000; vol Mon 52,224; open int 181,920, −2,696.

PLATINUM (NYM)—50 troy oz.; $ per troy oz.

	Open	High	Low	Settle	Chg	High	Low	Open Interest
July	500.00	502.00	482.50	489.20	− 9.10	640.00	482.50	11,689
Oct	498.50	501.50	484.00	489.50	− 8.80	609.00	484.00	6,570
Ja90	503.00	503.00	489.00	491.20	− 8.80	646.00	489.00	3,356

Source: *The Wall Street Journal*, May 24, 1989.

One advantage of standardized specifications is that trading is concentrated in just a few contracts, so the markets for those contracts are quite **liquid**.[2] If, for example, the delivery dates were not standardized, there could be a futures contract that expires every day of the year. There would be little trading in each contract; thus, someone who wished to trade a given contract might have difficulty finding another party to take the opposite position.

Standardization of futures contracts also makes it easier to compare futures prices. If futures contracts on a given underlying commodity or security had different delivery dates and quantities, the prices of various trades could not be compared.

The excerpt from *The Wall Street Journal* in Figure 1.3 shows futures trading prices for a given day. It quotes four prices for each futures contract for each of the standardized expiration months.

Three of the quotes are from actual trades that occurred during the day. The **open** quote gives the price of the first trade of the day. The **high** and **low** quotes are the highest and lowest prices, respectively, at which the contract traded that day.

The **settlement price** is the price the exchanges use to compute the gains and losses on the contracts each day. Every day, at the close of trading, a **settlement committee** composed of exchange members meets to establish a settlement price

---

[2] Liquid markets allow traders to trade large amounts while changing prices minimally.

for each contract. The committee examines the trading in the contract around the close of the market. Often it chooses the price of the closing trade of the day as the settlement price. If no trade occurred at the close, the committee uses the average of the offered purchase and sale prices—the **bid** and **ask** prices, respectively—to determine the settlement price. If there was a rush of trading around the close so that no particular trade stands out as the final one, the committee computes an average price for the settlement price.

Following the settlement price is the **settlement change**, the change in settlement price from the previous trading day. The next two columns give the high and low prices that have occurred since trading in each contract began.

The final column shows the open interest for each contract. **Open interest** is the number of total positions that remain open at the end of the day and are carried into the next trading day. Because each long position must have a short position opposite it, open interest also represents the number of long (or short) positions remaining open.

Aggregate data on futures trading in each commodity follow the price quotes. The first number gives the current day's **trading volume** and the second number the previous day's volume. The last two numbers report the total open interest and the change in total open interest from the previous day. The relationship between the trading volume and the change in open interest depends on who trades the contracts. If a trade involves two new parties entering into a contract with each other, open interest will rise. If a trade involves one party closing out a position by trading with a new party, open interest will remain unchanged. Finally, if a trade involves two opposite positions that offset each other, open interest will fall. The net effect of each day's trading volume on open interest depends on the composition of these three types of trades.[3]

Example 1.3 shows how to read the price information given in *The Wall Street Journal* excerpt in Figure 1.3 for a single gold futures contract.

▪ **Example 1.3: Reading a Futures Quotation**   Consider the Tuesday, May 23, 1989, *Wall Street Journal* quotations for the August 1989 gold contract at the COMEX shown in Figure 1.3. They represent the prices for delivery of 100 troy ounces of gold. The opening trade on that day had a price of $369. The highest-priced trade was at $370.50 per ounce, and the lowest was at $367.00 per ounce. The settlement price was $367.20, up from $366.70 the previous day. Up until this date, the August 1989 gold contract had traded at no more than $575.00 and no less than $363.80. At the close of trading there were 35,339 open August 1989 gold contracts, representing 3,533,900 troy ounces of gold. Estimated volume for all COMEX gold futures contracts was 50,000 contracts, down 2,224 from the previous day. Finally, open interest at the end of the day

---

[3] We will discuss how futures contracts are offset shortly.

for all of the gold futures contracts was 181,920, down 2,696 from the previous day. ■

Centralized Markets

The futures and forward markets have very different trading systems. Since forward contracts are customized agreements between two parties, they are traded among a loose conglomeration of market makers who may specialize in particular commodities or securities. This system is called a **dealer market**. Usually market makers do not work in the same locations. A person who wishes to enter into a forward contract typically will call a number of dealers and take the most competitive quote. Often not all of the dealers called are willing to trade in the particular contract.

Futures contracts are traded in centralized exchanges. The traders congregate by type of contract in **trading pits** on the floors of the exchanges. The exchange determines who may trade by conferring membership on individuals. Membership entails obtaining approval of the exchange and purchasing a trading seat. Only a limited number of seats exist, but at any given time there is an active market in the seats.[4] Investors who do not belong to the exchange must have members trade for them.

The classical style of trading in futures markets is called the **open outcry** system. A trader who wishes to enter into a futures contract declares the proposed trade to the entire pit using both voice and hand signals. The other traders in the pit can agree to the trade or offer alternative terms. A trade is consummated when two traders agree to take opposite sides at a given price for a specified quantity.

Some exchanges are experimenting with computerized trading systems. The Chicago Mercantile Exchange is working with Reuters, an electronic information company, to develop a system called GLOBEX, which will match the proposed trades of buyers and sellers over a computer network. The Swiss Options and Futures Exchange (SOFEX) is a fully computerized exchange. The Tokyo Stock Exchange trades its successful 10-year yen bond contract via computers. Several other European and Asian exchanges are also developing such systems. At this writing, it is too early to tell whether computers will replace pit trading. However, in early 1989, the Federal Bureau of Investigation made public a broad investigation of corrupt trading practices at the Chicago Board of Trade and the Chicago Mercantile Exchange. It seems likely that these investigations will accelerate the movement of the futures industry to computerized trading.

Daily Settlement and the Clearinghouse

Gains and losses are realized differently under a futures contract than under a forward contract. The gains or losses on a forward contract are realized when the contract expires. Even if one offsets a forward position with an opposite position,

---

[4] See Chiang, Gay, and Kolb [1987] for a discussion of the price of trading seats.

the gain or loss locked in by the offset is not realized until both positions are settled at expiration. With futures contracts, on the other hand, market participants realize their gains and losses on a daily basis. The system of daily settlement in the futures markets is called **marking to market** and is carried out through an intermediary body called the futures **clearinghouse**.[5]

When one enters into a forward position, the contract with the other party is intact until it expires. In a futures contract, in contrast, the relationship between the two parties is severed immediately after the contract is written, because the clearinghouse steps in to take a position opposite each party. For example, suppose A goes long a gold futures contract with B. As soon as the transaction is completed, the clearinghouse creates a short position for itself opposite A and a long position opposite B. The clearinghouse thus is both long and short, and its net position is always zero.

The clearinghouse settles up the gains and losses on each position every day. In our example, the clearinghouse will pay A if his position incurs a gain during the day, and A will pay the clearinghouse if his position loses. All gains and losses are figured by looking at the difference between the previous and current days' settlement prices. As with forward contracts, the gains from a long position are exactly opposite the gains from a short position. As long as all parties make good on their contracts, the gains the clearinghouse pays to a winning position will be provided by a losing position, because the clearinghouse is long as many contracts as it is short.

Example 1.4 illustrates the daily settlement system.

▪ **Example 1.4: Daily Settlement**   Suppose that at 10:00 a.m. on April 1, A enters into a futures contract with B in which he agrees to buy 100 ounces of gold on July 1 at $450 per ounce. Immediately after the transaction is completed, the clearinghouse severs the relationship between A and B. It takes a short position opposite A and a long position opposite B. Thus, the clearinghouse serves as a third party in both trades.

Now suppose that the April 1 futures settlement price for July 1 delivery of 100 ounces of gold is $452. The clearinghouse replaces A's $450 long futures contract with a $452 long futures contract. It also replaces B's $450 short futures contract with a $452 short futures contract. This, of course, hurts A and benefits B, because it is more advantageous to take delivery of gold at $450 than at $452. To compensate A, the clearinghouse pays him $2 per ounce, or $200 for 100 ounces. The clearinghouse obtains the $200 from B.

$$\begin{array}{ccccc} & \$200 & & \$200 & \\ B & \rightarrow & \text{Clearinghouse} & \rightarrow & A \end{array}$$

---

[5] See Edwards [1984] for a detailed discussion of the role of the clearinghouse in facilitating trading of futures contracts.

Another way to interpret these transactions is to say that A takes his $200 gain and B takes her $200 loss on the day they occur. Their positions are thereby marked to market.

Now suppose that on April 2, the futures settlement price for the July 1 gold contract is $451 per ounce. Again A's and B's positions are marked to market. A must pay the clearinghouse $1 per ounce, or $100, because his long position has lost. B receives $1 per ounce, or $100, from the clearinghouse, because her short position has gained. Both parties receive new contracts with a price of $451. ∎

While it may seem cumbersome, futures contracting with marking to market offers several advantages over the forward contracting system. First, a party entering into a futures position need not worry about the creditworthiness of the party who initially takes the opposite position, because the clearinghouse must meet the obligations of the opposite position. The clearinghouse maintains reserves for this purpose.

Second, because losses are paid as they accrue, the clearinghouse can keep track of any party who suffers large losses and close this party out of the contract if he or she cannot meet the payments. A loser in a forward position need not pay losses until the contract expires. At that point, the losses may be huge and the party insolvent.

Third, it is easy to close out a futures position under the marking-to-market system. As we saw earlier, getting out of a forward contract is cumbersome. One must hold two positions until expiration and cannot receive any locked-in gains until that time. With futures contracting, the gains or losses have already been realized. A party who enters into an offsetting futures position will therefore have no net cash flow. The clearinghouse recognizes this and simply closes out a party who holds both a long and a short position.

Offsetting is extremely common in the futures markets. Usually only 1 to 2 percent of all contracts are held to expiration. Often a party will offset by trading with another party who is offsetting an opposite position. In this case, both parties are removed from the clearinghouse's books and open interest is reduced. Figure 1.4 demonstrates this for the June 1987 COMEX gold futures contract. Open interest builds gradually until the weeks before June 1987, when it increases rapidly. Then it drops dramatically just before the contract expires as the parties offset their contracts with each other.

Delivery Date Convergence   The daily gains and losses earned on a futures contract are determined by the daily movements in the futures price. Over the life of the contract, these price movements will bring the futures price closer to the spot price of the underlying commodity or security until, at expiration, the futures and spot price are equal. This occurs because a futures contract that expires immediately is exactly the same as a spot transaction. There is no "future" for such a contract, so the price for immediate delivery through the futures contract must be the same as that for immediate delivery on the spot market. This movement of the futures price to the spot price is called **delivery date convergence**.

Figure 1.4 Open Interest for Gold, June '87 Futures

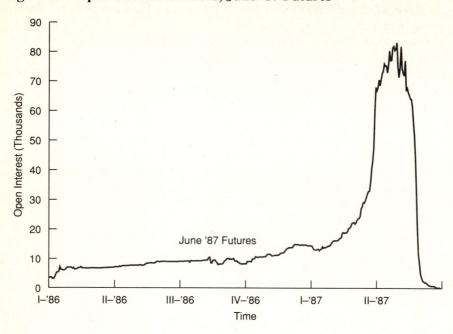

Source: Commodity Exchange Inc.

The delivery date convergence condition can be expressed formally. The futures price notation used is very similar to that used for the forward markets:

$F_{t,T}$ = futures price at time t of a futures contract that expires at time T

When a futures contract expires at T, the delivery date convergence condition is

Futures price for immediate delivery = Spot price
$$F_{T,T} = P_T.$$

The difference between the spot price and the futures price is called the **spot-futures basis:**[6]

Basis = Spot − Futures
$$= P_t − F_{t,T}.$$

---

[6] Often one uses simply the word *basis*. This may refer to the spot-futures basis or, sometimes, to the futures-spot basis.

Figure 1.5 Futures-Spot Gold Basis, June '87 Futures

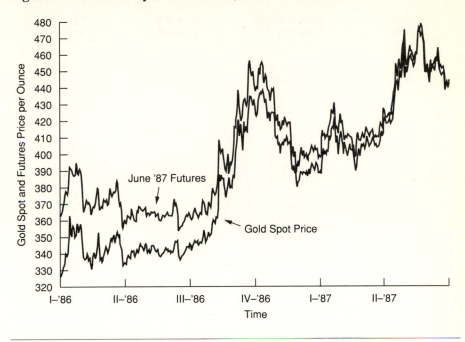

Source: Commodity Exchange Inc.

When a contract expires at T, delivery date convergence ensures that the basis is equal to zero:[7]

$$\text{Basis at } T = P_T - F_{T,T}$$
$$= 0.$$

Figure 1.5 illustrates the movement of the futures price to the spot price for a gold futures contract.

Even though gains and losses are settled daily over the life of a futures contract, delivery date convergence ensures that the total gain or loss on an expiring contract is simply the difference between the initial futures price and the future spot price at expiration. Example 1.5 shows how delivery date convergence makes it possible to calculate the gain or loss on a futures position that is held to expiration.

▪ **Example 1.5: Marking to Market and the Profit from a Futures Position**
Suppose that on June 14, A enters into a long futures contract and a long forward contract that are both for delivery of 100 ounces of gold on July 1. Both the futures

---

[7] Of course, the same will be true for a forward contract.

Table 1.4 Cash Flows for A's Forward and Futures Positions

Date	Forward and Futures Price	Forward Account	Futures Account
6/14	$450.00	$ 0.00	$ 0.00
6/15	449.00	0.00	−100.00
6/16	455.00	0.00	600.00
6/17	450.00	0.00	−500.00
6/20	452.00	0.00	200.00
6/21	449.00	0.00	−300.00
6/22	445.00	0.00	−400.00
6/23	440.00	0.00	−500.00
6/24	445.00	0.00	500.00
6/27	450.00	0.00	500.00
6/28	460.00	0.00	1,000.00
6/29	465.00	0.00	500.00
6/30	470.00	0.00	500.00
7/1	475.00	2,500.00	500.00
Net gain	$ 25.00	$2,500.00	$2,500.00

Note: Number of ounces = 100

and forward prices on June 14 are $450 per ounce. Table 1.4 presents the cash flows for the futures and forward positions. To simplify matters, this example assumes the futures and forward prices are always identical. We discuss this assumption further in Chapter 3.

There are daily cash flows for the futures position but no cash flows for the forward position until the contracts expire. On July 1, the final futures settlement price equals the spot price due to delivery date convergence of spot and futures prices. If we add up all of the daily gains and losses of the futures position and for the moment ignore the interest on gains and losses, the sum exactly equals the gain of the forward position. In fact, the gains from the futures position, per unit, are

$$\text{Gain to long futures} = \text{Expiration spot price} - \text{Initial futures price}$$
$$= P_T - F_{t,T} = F_{T,T} - F_{t,T}.$$

$$\text{Gain to short futures} = \text{Initial futures price} - \text{Expiration spot price}$$
$$= F_{t,T} - P_T = F_{t,T} - F_{T,T}.$$

In this example, a long futures position entered into on June 14 at $450 per ounce and held to expiration makes $25 per ounce in profit, because the futures price moves from $450 to the $475 spot price at expiration on July 1. On June 30, the day before expiration, the futures price is $470 and all positions are marked to market. If A holds his long position one more day until expiration, he takes delivery of the gold at $475 per ounce, but he gets $5 per ounce as his position is marked to market for a final time. Even though A originally contracted to take delivery of

100 ounces of gold on July 1 at $450 per ounce, he actually pays $475 per ounce on July 1. However, with the $25-per-ounce futures profit, the futures position has produced a hedged price of

$$\text{Hedged price} = \text{Actual delivery price} - \text{Futures profit}$$
$$= \$475 - \$25 = \$450$$
$$= \text{Initial futures price} = F_{t,T}.$$

A has *effectively* locked in a price of $F_{t,T} = \$450$ on July 1. Further, in this simple example, the $25 per ounce that A gains on his futures position equals the gain on the forward position:

$$\text{Gain to long forward position} = \text{Spot price at expiration} - \text{Forward price}$$
$$= P_T - f_{t,T}$$
$$= \$475 - \$450 = \$25 \text{ per ounce.}$$

Thus, when figuring the gain or loss on a futures position, we can treat the contract *as if it were a forward position*. For most purposes, this is a reasonable approach. However, it is not quite correct. The $25-per-ounce gain on the forward position comes at the expiration of the contract on July 1. The $25 gain on the futures position is earned in daily increments as the futures price moves from $450 to $475 over the life of the contract. Because of the time value of money, A is better off if he receives his profits earlier and incurs his losses later.

Columns 2 and 3 of Table 1.5 consider the time value of money for the futures gains and losses of A's position. We assume an interest rate of 10 percent per annum. If A borrows to pay any futures losses and invests any futures gains, the total futures profit on July 1 will be the sum of the *future values* of the daily profits. For example, on June 15 he has a futures loss of $100. If he borrows to pay this, on July 1 he must pay[8]

$$\text{Future value of June 15 loss} = (\$100)\left[1 + \left(0.10 \times \frac{16}{360}\right)\right]$$
$$= \$100.44.$$

Thus, when we account for the time value of money, we see that the gains and losses on the position have a future value of $2,500.56.

Columns 4 and 5 in Table 1.5 show the futures gains and losses under a different scenario for the path of prices between June 15 and July 1. Notice that the initial price is still $450 and the closing price is still $475, so the overall change in the futures price is still $25 per ounce. However, because this position suffers

---

[8] As we will see in Chapter 5, the industry convention is to use a 360-day year in these kinds of calculations.

Table 1.5   Impact of Interest on Marking to Market

Date	Original Scenario		Second Scenario	
	Futures Price	Futures Account	Futures Price	Futures Account
6/14	$450.00	$ 0.00	$450.00	$ 0.00
6/15	449.00	−100.44	445.00	−502.22
6/16	455.00	602.50	440.00	−502.08
6/17	450.00	−501.94	435.00	−501.94
6/20	452.00	200.61	430.00	−501.53
6/21	449.00	−300.83	425.00	−501.39
6/22	445.00	−401.00	420.00	−501.25
6/23	440.00	−501.11	415.00	−501.11
6/24	445.00	500.97	420.00	500.97
6/27	450.00	500.56	425.00	500.56
6/28	460.00	1,000.83	430.00	500.42
6/29	465.00	500.28	435.00	500.28
6/30	470.00	500.14	450.00	1,500.42
7/1	475.00	500.00	475.00	2,500.00
Net Gain	$ 25.00	$2,500.56	$ 25.00	$2,491.11

Note: Interest rate = 10%.

large early losses that are later reversed, the future value of the futures profit of $2,491.11 is less than in the previous case.

In most cases, the effect of time value is small, so we can approximate the gain or loss on a futures position by assuming it is all incurred when the contract expires. If the futures position is large, however, accuracy might be considerably improved by accounting for the time value of money when computing the total gain or loss. We discuss this issue in detail in Chapter 3. ∎

Margins

A person who enters into a futures contract is required to put up funds called a **margin**. This margin is placed in an account with a broker, who uses it to ensure that the individual can make good on his or her losses. The exchanges set minimum margins, but brokers may require larger margins if they are concerned about an individual's financial situation, for they are ultimately responsible for their clients' losses.[9, 10]

[9] Brokers, in turn, must deposit margins with the clearinghouse. However, they may net out offsetting customer positions and must place margins reflecting only their overall exposures. For example, a broker who has clients with two long December gold contracts and one short December contract must post a margin only for one long December contract. This margin is called the **net margin** and is set by the clearinghouse.

[10] See Telser [1981], Figlewski [1984a], Kahl, Rutz, and Sinquefield [1985], Fishe and Goldberg [1986], Hartzmark [1986a, b], and Hunter [1986] for a detailed discussion of margins and the controversies surrounding them.

The margin account may or may not earn interest. Large, good customers of brokers often put up Treasury securities as margins. Alternatively, their brokers may simply pay them money market interest rates on their margin accounts. Most individual investors, however, earn no interest. This loss of interest is the cost of the margin requirement. The margin money itself is not a payment to enter into a futures contract; rather, it is collateral that is returned (often with interest for commercial traders) when the contract is closed out. Therefore, it costs nothing to enter into a futures contract if the margin account balance earns a market rate of interest.

Futures margins are very different from the margins put up to purchase stock. The margin in a stock transaction is actually a down payment and is therefore a cost of buying the stock. This difference between futures and stock margins is little understood. Many investors and brokers consider the futures margin, not the interest forgone on the margin money, to be the cost of entering into a futures contract.

Margins and Settlement   The margin account is used to settle the day-to-day changes in a futures position. It would be inconvenient for an individual to pay money in or take it out of the margin account every day. Therefore, the broker usually adds to the margin account when futures prices move favorably for a client and subtracts from the margin account when prices move against the client.

There are two types of margins. The **initial margin** is the original amount that must be put into an account to establish a futures position. To determine the initial margin, the exchange considers the sizes of past futures price movements. Then it sets the initial margin so that the clearinghouse can cover losses on the position from the margin account even if a large price movement against the position occurs. If it appears that the volatility of the market has increased, the exchange typically will increase the size of the initial margin.[11] The **maintenance margin** is the minimum amount that can be kept in a margin account—usually about 75 percent of the initial margin. If prices move against a client so that the margin account falls below the maintenance margin, the broker will make a margin call—that is, ask the client to replenish the margin account (by paying **variation margin**)—often up to the level of the initial margin. Failure to act promptly may lead the broker to unilaterally close out the account by entering into an offsetting futures position.

Example 1.6 illustrates the interplay between the margin account and the daily marking to market of futures positions.

▪ **Example 1.6: Margins and Marking to Market**   Assume that on June 14, A establishes a long position in 100 ounces of July 1 gold at a futures price of $450 per ounce. The initial margin for the contract is $2,000, and the maintenance margin is $1,500. Table 1.6 follows A's account and shows the transactions

---

[11] The initial margin usually quoted is for "speculative positions." If an investor can demonstrate that he or she is a bona fide hedger, a somewhat lower initial margin will be imposed.

Table 1.6 Margins and Marking to Market for A

Date	Futures Price	Futures Amount	Beginning Margin	Cash Withdrawal	Ending Margin
6/14	$450.00	$ 0.00	$ 0.00	$–2,000.00	$2,000.00
6/15	449.00	–100.00	1,900.00	0.00	1,900.00
6/16	455.00	600.00	2,500.00	500.00	2,000.00
6/17	450.00	–500.00	1,500.00	–500.00	2,000.00
6/20	452.00	200.00	2,200.00	200.00	2,000.00
6/21	449.00	–300.00	1,700.00	0.00	1,700.00
6/22	445.00	–400.00	1,300.00	–700.00	2,000.00
6/23	440.00	–500.00	1,500.00	–500.00	2,000.00
6/24	445.00	500.00	2,500.00	500.00	2,000.00
6/27	450.00	500.00	2,500.00	500.00	2,000.00
6/28	460.00	1,000.00	3,000.00	1,000.00	2,000.00
6/29	465.00	500.00	2,500.00	500.00	2,000.00
6/30	470.00	500.00	2,500.00	500.00	2,000.00
7/1	475.00	500.00	2,500.00	2,500.00	0.00
Net gain	$ 25.00	$2,500.00		$ 2,500.00	

Notes:
Number of ounces = 100
Initial margin = $2,000
Maintenance margin = $1,500

necessary to keep his position alive, ignoring the interest on the margin discussed earlier.

On June 14, A establishes the initial margin by paying in $2,000. On June 16 the margin account rises to $2,500, so A may make a $500 cash withdrawal if he chooses. On June 17 the margin account falls to $1,500, so there is a margin call of $500 to reestablish the $2,000 initial margin. On June 20 the margin account rises to $2,200, so A may make a $200 withdrawal. There are two additional margin calls of $700 and $500 on June 22 and June 23, respectively. Prices go up over the period from June 24 through June 30, allowing A to withdraw from his margin account. A closes out his account by liquidating his position and withdrawing the money in the margin account on July 1.[12]

The gain from the position, ($475 – $450)(100) = $2,500, exactly equals the net cash withdrawal from the margin account. A gets back his initial margin plus any gain or less any loss in his position. In reality, he may receive interest on the funds kept in his margin account while the position was open. ∎

An investor who takes a short position opposite A will have the same initial and maintenance margins. The short position's risk is similar to that of the long position, since gold prices could move up as well as down.

[12] Had A taken delivery, his cash flows would be identical.

Some futures positions, called *spreads,* have lower risk than simple long or short positions. **Spreads** are created by combining short and long positions so that much of what is lost on one position is gained back on the opposite position. For this reason, spread positions require much smaller margin deposits than do individual positions. Example 1.7 illustrates a spread position in gold futures contracts.

▪ **Example 1.7: A Gold Spread**   Suppose A takes a spread position by combining a short position in June gold at $460 per ounce and a long position in October gold at $470 per ounce. Now suppose the demand for gold increases after A establishes his spread and the futures prices of June and October contracts rise to $465 and $474, respectively. A's short June position will lose $5 per ounce, and his long October position will make $4 per ounce. His spread position has a loss of $1, because the futures price for the long contract increases less than the futures price for the short contract.

A's experience shows that the profit on a spread is determined by the movements of the short and long contracts relative to each other. Before the price move, the June-October spread was $470 − $460 = $10. After the price move, the spread is $474 − $465 = $9. The spread position loses $1. In general, the profit on a short T1 − long T2 spread is

t	t1	T1	T2

$$\text{Spread profit} = (F_{t1,T2} - F_{t,T2}) + (F_{t,T1} - F_{t1,T1})$$
$$= (F_{t1,T2} - F_{t1,T1}) - (F_{t,T2} - F_{t,T1})$$
$$= \text{Closing spread} - \text{Initial spread,}$$

where

t   = date position is established

t1   = date position is closed out

T1 = expiration date of the nearby contract

T2 = expiration date of the far contract

▪

Figure 1.6 presents prices for the June 1987 and October 1987 COMEX gold futures contracts. The value of the June-October spread is equal to the difference between the two prices. Clearly, the two futures prices move almost in tandem, because both are driven by the market's beliefs about the price of gold. Thus, the June-October spread position is much less risky than either the June or October contract by itself. As a result, the initial margin for a gold spread may be only $150 as opposed to $2,000 for either a June or October position.

Figure 1.6 Gold Spread, June '87–October '87

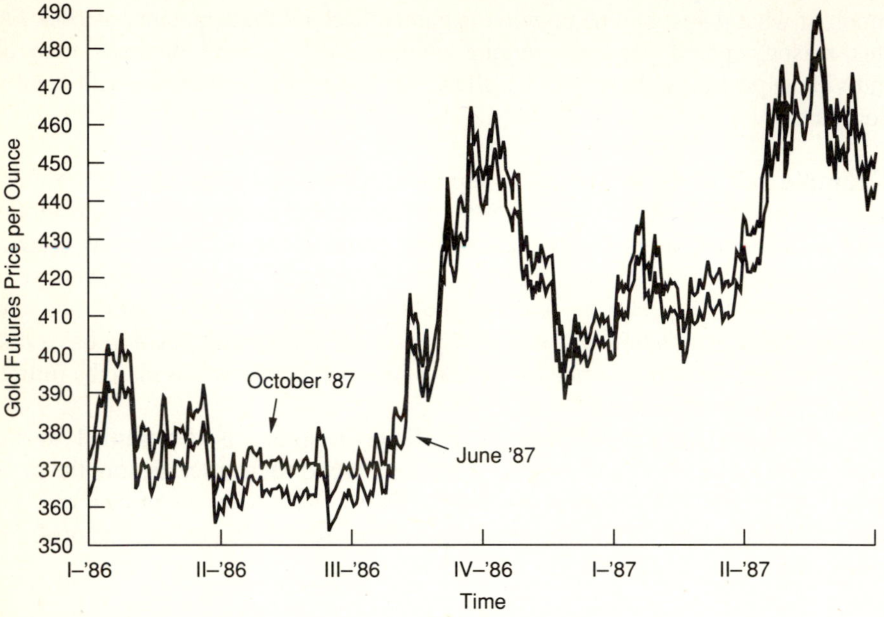

Source: Commodity Exchange Inc.

Regulation

Another major difference between the futures and forward markets is that the futures markets are regulated while the forward markets are not. The futures markets are regulated at three levels: by the clearinghouses and the exchanges; by the National Futures Association (NFA), a self-regulatory industry group; and by the Commodity Futures Trading Commission (CFTC), a government agency. The regulation by the exchanges, the clearinghouses, and the National Futures Association has two major functions: (1) to ensure that futures trading is conducted fairly and to convince potential users that this is so and (2) to preempt explicit government regulation. The primary purposes of government regulation are to ensure that futures trading serves a valuable economic purpose and to protect futures contract users.[13]

Regulation by the Clearinghouse and the Exchanges   The restrictions on futures trading imposed by the clearinghouses and the exchanges make up the first

[13] See Edwards [1981], Stone [1981], and Koppenhaver [1987] for a discussion of futures market regulation.

level of futures regulation.[14] So far we have seen that the clearinghouse sets minimum margins and the exchanges determine contract specifications, the hours of trading, and who may trade. The exchanges also set **position limits**, which specify how many contracts a party can hold at one time, and **price movement limits**, which restrict how far prices on certain contracts can move each day.

The practice of imposing price limits developed in response to the view long held by many that futures trading may allow irrational behavior to induce volatility in spot prices. The purpose of the limits is to allow a "cooling-off" period after large price movements so that traders can reconsider whether such extreme movements are warranted.[15] The price limits operate simply by prohibiting trading at prices that exceed or fall below the limit prices. For example, suppose yesterday's closing price for July gold was $450 per ounce and the daily limit is $25 per ounce.[16] Then the July gold futures contracts cannot trade at a price below $425 or above $475 today. If the price hits $425, the contract is said to be **down limit**; if it hits $475, the contract is said to be **up limit**.

This is not to say that trading is suspended if the market is up or down limit. A down-limit market in our example merely means that no one is willing to go long at $425 because the equilibrium futures price is below $425. Similarly, if the market is up limit, no one is willing to go short at $475 because the equilibrium price is above $475. If the equilibrium price changes so that people again wish to trade within the limits, they may certainly do so.

The exchanges do not always enforce the price limits. If a price hits its limit several days in a row, the exchange may increase or remove the limit. The exchanges often remove limits on contracts that are close to delivery, because impediments to trade can hamper offsetting and the delivery process.

Limits do not really provide protection against large price movements. It is of little comfort to someone trying to offset a long position that the price decline has been checked at $425 if it is not possible to find another party willing to go long at that price. Limits may stop trading if a short-term mania sets in, but they also severely restrain legitimate market moves.

Self-Regulation Associations   The **National Futures Association (NFA)** began operation as the futures industry's self-regulatory body in 1982. Its role is to establish and enforce standards of professional conduct in U.S. futures markets. It regulates the futures industry by requiring widespread membership of futures professionals and imposing eligibility and conduct rules on its members.

---

[14] See Edwards [1983] for a discussion of the trade-offs between government and self-regulation and Saloner [1984] for a discussion of the behavior of a self-regulating futures exchange.

[15] An alternative justification for price limits is given in Brennan [1986], who proposes that the limits keep losers from reneging on their contracts because the losers cannot observe the extent of their losses after a limit move. See also Khoury and Jones [1983] and Ma, Rao, and Sears [1989].

[16] The COMEX has removed its price movement limits on the gold contract; thus, this is a hypothetical example.

Membership in the NFA is mandatory for all futures professionals except floor traders and floor brokers. No NFA member may accept a futures order from a party, other than a direct customer, who is not also an NFA member.

The NFA has four major functions. First, it screens and examines potential futures professionals when they apply for CFTC registration and NFA membership. Second, it enforces compliance with CFTC regulations and NFA rules; it monitors its members' financial condition and recordkeeping practices to ensure that they conform to NFA standards and also surveys advertising and sales practices for fairness and honesty. Third, the NFA arbitrates disputes between futures markets participants. Fourth, it provides educational services for its own members, for law enforcement officials involved in investigating off-exchange futures fraud, and for the investing public.

Government Regulation   In 1974, Congress created the **Commodity Futures Trading Commission (CFTC)** to regulate the futures markets. The CFTC regulates primarily by screening new contracts and approving all aspects of new-contract trading, including the margins and price movement limits. Consideration of a new-contract proposal is a lengthy process, often lasting more than a year.[17] One of the main functions of the research departments at the futures exchanges is to prepare supportive materials for such proposals to the CFTC.[18] The CFTC is quite stringent about allowing exchanges to trade new contracts. The commission, by statute, is required to consider at least two factors before approving a new-contract proposal:

1.   *Does it serve a social purpose?* The CFTC examines each new- futures-contract proposal to determine whether it serves two social purposes. First, the CFTC considers whether the proposed contract will help market participants ascertain what the future spot price of a commodity or security will be. This is called the contract's **price discovery** function. Second, the CFTC tries to determine whether the contract will facilitate hedging by allowing some parties to reduce their risk. This is the **risk transfer** social purpose of the contract.[19]

2.   *Can the contract be manipulated?* Perhaps the greatest concern of the founders of the CFTC was the prevention of new contracts that could easily be manipulated. Manipulation occurs when individuals profit or attempt to profit by pushing prices away from the levels set by normal supply and demand conditions. We do not usually consider this much of a problem,

---

[17] See Fischel [1986] for a critique of this screening process.

[18] See Sandor [1973] for a case study of how a futures contract is developed by an exchange economics department. See Silber [1981] for a discussion of new-contract design competition among exchanges.

[19] These are the traditional social purposes emphasized in previous literature. In Chapter 2, we will see that a perhaps more important social function of futures contracts is that they allow society to conserve on transactions costs.

because other traders normally can make profits by driving prices back into line.[20] It is possible, however, that by cleverly combining positions in futures and cash markets, a manipulator will earn excess profits. Of course, those on the opposite side of the manipulator can sustain great losses.

The most important (and feared) type of manipulation is the corner. To construct a **corner**, a trader goes long futures in excess of the immediately deliverable supply and then exploits the resulting monopoly position. By keeping the long positions open, the manipulator eventually will acquire all of the deliverable commodity. However, some shorts still will be contractually required to deliver the commodity. The manipulator can then extract a high price for providing the commodity, because the shorts are obligated to buy. Alternatively, the manipulator can agree to let the shorts offset at a high price. Either way, the manipulator wins. In fact, the manipulator need not play out this scenario to the end, because the shortage of the deliverable commodity will become apparent well before delivery, driving the futures and spot prices up.

■ **Example 1.8: A Corner**   Suppose John McHunt knows there are only 1 million ounces of deliverable gold in New York. He enters into long positions representing 2 million ounces. The delivery month arrives, and shorts holding contracts representing 1 million ounces purchase gold and deliver it to McHunt. McHunt now owns all of the deliverable gold in New York, but shorts holding contracts representing 1 million ounces still must fulfill their contracts.

McHunt now has the shorts over a barrel. He can refuse to close out his long positions. It is unlikely that any of the shorts will find someone with whom they can offset. Anyone going short at this point would be in the same position as the original unfortunate shorts. McHunt can then demand a high cash price for gold so that the shorts will pay dearly to fulfill their contracts. Alternatively, McHunt can force the shorts to close out their contracts at a high futures price, allowing him to gain on all of his remaining long positions. ■

Manipulation of futures and cash markets is very bad for markets, and the possibility of manipulation has led to demands for regulation. However, several factors aside from regulation make profiting from this kind of manipulation difficult. If others realize that manipulation is under way, they will also try to profit and thereby steal the advantage from the manipulator. This works in three ways. First, speculators also will enter into long positions, taking away the manipulator's leverage and increasing the price at which the manipulator must contract. Second, potential shorts will not trade, which will also increase the futures price. Finally, speculators will increase the deliverable supply.

[20] See Chichilnisky [1984], Kyle [1984], Newbery [1984], and Easterbrook [1986] for a variety of opinions on the importance of manipulation in futures markets.

An increase in deliverable supply blocked a manipulation attempt in a spectacular way in 1897– 1898.[21] An investor named Joseph Leiter entered into large long positions in wheat and shipped a great deal of wheat out of Chicago. Unfortunately for him, a rival named Philip Armour kept shipping wheat into Chicago, using dynamite to keep frozen waterways open, and Leiter lost millions. A similar phenomenon occurred more recently when the Hunt brothers tried to corner the silver markets in late 1979 and early 1980. As the silver price rose, people began selling their silver tea sets, antique coins, and even hospital X-rays for the silver content.

A corner that fails can be very costly for the manipulator. He or she probably paid a premium to enter into so many long contracts but then must dispose of large amounts of the commodity at nonmanipulated prices once the corner fails. This problem is especially acute for agricultural commodities. It is really feasible to corner such a market only toward the end of the harvest, when stocks are low. However, the manipulator may be forced to dispose of the commodity after the harvest, when prices tend to be lowest.

Corners are difficult to pull off, for good market reasons; also, regulations prevent them. The exchanges can suspend trading and require settlement at a price of their choosing (as in the Hunts's case). They can also designate additional grades of a commodity as deliverable or allow other delivery points. Manipulators can be taken to court in civil and criminal suits. Finally, position limits specify maximum positions that an individual may take. These may not be effective, however, against conspiratorial behavior.

Other CFTC Regulation   In addition to its primary function of approving new contracts, the CFTC regulates the trading of existing contracts. To prevent investors from unfair treatment by unscrupulous professionals, the commission has set strict requirements concerning the training of brokers and the information they must disseminate to prospective and actual clients. It requires the exchanges to provide detailed prospectuses that outline the risks and uses of every contract. These prospectuses must be given to every potential client. It also requires the exchanges to provide data on prices and trading volume in a timely manner. The traders must notify pit clerks after each trade. This information then goes out to the world over the wires.

The CFTC also monitors trading and can require the exchanges to change contract specifications such as margins and price movement limits. The commission has broad powers to intervene in the market. It can close trading or even place restrictions on individual traders.

Uses of Futures Contracts

There are three motives for entering into futures transactions: to speculate, to hedge against some type of risk, and to make an arbitrage profit. While a futures

---

[21] See Hieronymous [1971] for a further description of this incident.

position may be established for more than one of these reasons, it is useful to study them separately.

Speculation

A speculator is an investor willing to take on the risk of a futures position in the hope of making a profit. One type of speculator uses fundamental analysis of economic conditions to decide which futures position to take. The typical **fundamental analyst** forecasts futures prices based on the economics of the spot market and takes a position that will yield a profit if the forecast is realized. For example, suppose an analyst has examined the gold market and expects the spot price of gold to be $460 per ounce in three months. If the current gold futures price for delivery in three months is $450, this speculator can take a long futures position in gold and expect to make a profit of $10 per ounce. This expected profit is associated with risk. If, for example, the spot price of gold in three months turns out to be $430, the speculator will lose $20 per ounce. Fundamental analysts often speculate in spreads when they believe relative prices are out of line.

Another type of speculator tries to predict how futures prices will move based on their past history. Such a speculator is called a **technical analyst**. Of course, technical analysts are also subject to the substantial risk that prices will not move as predicted. Technical analysts use similar techniques to try to predict spreads.

A speculator who owns a seat on an exchange and trades for his or her own account is called a **local**. This type of speculator provides liquidity for outside traders. Locals fall roughly into three categories: scalpers, pit traders, and floor traders.[22]

Scalpers   **Scalpers** try to profit from positions held for short periods of time. They often work on the principle that although there is a generally stable equilibrium price, matching orders do not come in from the outside at precisely the same instant. Scalpers bridge the gap between outside orders by filling orders that come in to brokers in return for slight price concessions. They hold their positions until opposite orders come in, hoping to extract other price concessions from the new brokers.

Example 1.9 demonstrates a trade that a scalper might make.

▪ **Example 1.9: Scalping**   Suppose the prevailing futures price for gold is $450 per ounce. A large market sell order comes in, and a scalper (or several scalpers together) offers to "take the hit" at $449.75. When a buy order comes in, the scalper offers to fill it for $450.25. The scalper's profit comes from the $0.50 difference. In return for this differential, the scalper offers the brokers liquidity, that is, the ability to get in and out of positions quickly. ▪

---

[22] This typography comes from Hieronymous [1971].

This strategy is not a riskless money pump for the scalpers. Several factors work against them. First, competition among scalpers is likely to drive the price concessions they receive down to a bare minimum. Most liquid markets have one- or two-tick (minimum price movement) bid-ask spreads, evidence that competition among scalpers keeps spreads quite low. Second, scalpers can lose big if a fundamental move in the equilibrium market price occurs. In Example 1.9, if the first sell order is followed by many others and the equilibrium price drops, the scalper will lose. Scalpers typically do not hold positions overnight.

Pit Traders   **Pit traders** are simply speculators who act like scalpers but take bigger positions and hold them longer. They are more likely to consider outside news than are scalpers, because they do not move as quickly. Also, pit traders usually do not hold overnight positions.

Floor Traders   **Floor traders** are speculators who try to exploit cases in which intercommodity price relationships seem out of line. They must be **full members** who can trade in any pit on their exchanges. Floor traders often watch outside news carefully and hold positions overnight or longer.

Hedging

A **hedger** uses futures markets to reduce risk caused by movements in commodity prices, security prices, exchange rates, or interest rates. A hedger may take a futures position with risk that is *opposite* a risk to which he or she is exposed. This strategy reduces or eliminates the hedger's overall risk. Example 1.10 demonstrates a simple hedge.

▪ **Example 1.10: Using Gold Futures to Hedge a Gold Purchase**   Suppose a wire manufacturer has contracted to sell gold wire at a fixed price at some point in the future. To produce the wire, the manufacturer must purchase 100 ounces of gold in February. Clearly, if the price of gold rises before this purchase, the manufacturer will suffer a loss in profitability. The manufacturer can hedge against such a loss by taking a long futures position in gold. If gold prices rise, the futures position will profit and offset the manufacturer's loss due to higher supply costs.

Assume the manufacturer goes long 100 ounces of gold at the current futures price of $450 per ounce. We will see how the manufacturer's profits are affected under scenarios in which the gold price rises and falls.

Suppose that in February the gold price is $470 per ounce, which is higher than the initial futures price of the manufacturer's contract. The manufacturer's net gold cost will be:

$$
\begin{array}{lll}
\text{Cost of gold purchase} = (\$470)(100) & = & \$47{,}000 \\
-\text{Long futures profit} = (\$470 - \$450)(100) & = & \underline{2{,}000} \\
\text{Hedged cost } = & & \$45{,}000
\end{array}
$$

The futures price when the contract expires in February is $470 because of the convergence of the futures and spot prices. The long futures position earned

$2,000 as the futures price moved from $450 to $470. The hedged cost to the manufacturer is the $47,000 for the gold less the $2,000 futures profit. The gain on the futures offsets the loss from paying higher gold prices on the spot market.

Now suppose that in February the cost of gold is $420 per ounce, which is lower than the manufacturer's initial futures price. The manufacturer's hedged gold cost will now be:

$$
\begin{array}{lrl}
\text{Cost of gold purchase} = (\$420)(100) & = & \$42,000 \\
-\text{Long futures profit} = (\$420 - \$450)(100) & = & -3,000 \\
\hline
\text{Hedged cost} = & & \$45,000
\end{array}
$$

The futures price at expiration is $420, again because of the convergence of the futures and spot prices. Thus, the futures position loses $3,000. The hedged cost to the manufacturer is the $42,000 for the actual gold plus the $3,000 futures loss. The lower gold purchase price is offset by the futures loss.

No matter what the price of gold in February, the wire manufacturer has locked in the initial futures price of $450 per ounce. Notice that the wire manufacturer would obtain essentially the same result with a forward contract.[23] ∎

The hedge in Example 1.10 is a **perfect hedge**, because it completely eliminates the gold price risk. Many hedges are not perfect, but all have the goal of reducing the risk associated with movements in prices or rates by taking futures positions with opposing risks.

Arbitrage

An arbitrageur is a trader who attempts to profit from discrepancies between futures and spot prices and among different futures prices. We have already discussed one such case. The convergence of the spot and futures prices at the expiration of a futures contract is brought about by the trading of arbitrageurs. If these prices differ, arbitrageurs make easy profits.

For example, suppose that at the expiration of the gold futures contract, the futures price is $470 but the spot price is $469. An arbitrageur could buy the gold at $469, go short a futures contract that expires immediately, and deliver the gold for $470 to generate an immediate, sure profit of $1. Such arbitrage trading drives the spot price up and the futures price down until the prices converge.

This example demonstrates a very simple type of arbitrage. We will explore other arbitrages in Chapter 2 and will see that arbitrage trading ties the spot and futures markets together. Further, we will see that many firms and portfolio managers can use arbitrage to reduce their costs of doing business.

---

[23] Again, since the timing of the cash flows differs under a forward and futures contract, the two instruments would not yield exactly the same hedge.

Mechanics of Trading

All trading in futures contracts is carried out by the members who own trading seats on the futures exchanges. A member can enter into a trade simply by finding a party willing to take the other side. The member must establish a margin with the clearinghouse and pay a fee to the clearinghouse for the trade.

A nonmember may establish a futures position by placing an order through a member. If the transaction is consummated, the party who placed the order must establish a margin account with the member, who in turn establishes a margin with the clearinghouse. The member, who is often a broker, will also charge a brokerage fee, which usually is quite moderate. For example, a discount broker will enter a customer into a 100-ounce gold futures contract at the COMEX for around $25. This fee is called a **round-trip fee**, because it enables the customer to both enter and exit a position.

An investor can place several types of orders with a broker.[24] A **market order** instructs the broker to enter into a futures position as soon as possible at the prevailing market price. A variant of the market order is the **take-your-time (T.Y.T.)**, or **not-held**, **order**, which allows the broker to exercise some judgment regarding when to fill the order. Also, the customer can state a specific time for an order to be filled.

A **limit order** restricts the price at which a broker may enter a customer into a futures position. Such an order will be filled only at the limit price or at a price that is even more advantageous to the customer. For example, one might place a limit order to go long gold futures at a price no higher than $450 per ounce.

A limit order can go unfilled after the market touches the limit price if the broker cannot obtain a price at the limit or better. Suppose, for example, that the above floor broker is for some reason unable to fill his order at $450 even though there was a trade at that price. Suppose he is able to trade only at a price of $450.25. He will not be able to fill the limit order even though the market has reached the limit price.

A **stop order** instructs the broker to trade at any price once the market price has reached a certain level. At that point, the broker will execute the order regardless of whether the price he or she can get is above, below, or equal to the stop price. Thus, unlike a limit order, a stop order is sure to be executed once the stop price has been reached.

Stop orders are used to limit losses, preserve profits, and take new positions. Buy stop orders usually specify stop prices above the current market price, and sell stop orders typically specify stop prices below the current price. For example, someone who has gone long gold at a price of $440 may limit his or her potential loss on the position with a stop order to enter into an offsetting short position if the futures price drops to $435 per ounce.

A **stop limit order** is like a stop order in that it charges the broker to enter into a position after the market price has reached a certain level. However, instead

---

[24] This discussion relies heavily on Teweles and Jones [1987].

of allowing the order to be filled at any price once the stop level is reached, it places a limit on the price of the transaction. The limit price may or may not equal the stop price. For example, the person who entered the long gold position at $440 may instruct the broker to sell if the futures price falls to $435 but to accept no less than $434.

A **market-if-touched (M.I.T.) order** also directs a broker to trade at whatever price can be obtained once the market has reached a certain level. However, as with a limit order, the specified price level is below the current price for a buy order and above the current price for a sell order. The M.I.T. order is commonly used by technical analysts who believe the market will reach an extreme price before turning and wish to trade as soon as that price is reached. By using M.I.T. instead of limit orders, they can be sure their orders will be filled.

A customer who wants to make two orders but wants only one to be filled will use an **alternative order**, which limits the potential profit or loss. For example, the customer who entered a long gold position at $440 may instruct the broker to sell if the price either rises to $450 or falls to $435.

A trader who wishes to enter or offset a position as the market follows a rising or falling course may use a **scale order**, in which he or she specifies successive positions to take if the market price moves up or down by certain increments. For example, a trader may instruct a broker to go long 100 ounces of gold futures if the market price falls by $1, then go long another 100 ounces if the price falls another $1, and so on.

A **contingent order** tells the broker to take a certain position if the price of another contract reaches a given level. A trader may place an order to go long October gold futures if the December gold futures price reaches $445.

A **spread order** instructs the broker to take a spread position composed of opposite positions in similar contracts. An **intracommodity spread** consists of opposite positions in the same commodity that have different expiration dates. In Example 1.7, A took a spread position by entering a spread order for a short position in June gold and a long position in October gold. An **intercommodity spread** involves opposite positions in similar commodities. For example, one may enter an order for a long position in December gold and a short position in December silver. Spread orders may require a certain difference between the prices of the opposing contracts rather than specific prices for them. Futures traders commonly make markets in spreads, so spread orders often can be filled in only one transaction.

Delivery Issues

So far we have simplified our discussion by assuming that futures contracts are written for delivery of a certain commodity or security at the close of a particular day. This is a fairly accurate description of the delivery process for some contracts. However, many contracts allow for variation in the delivery date and in the grade of commodity or security delivered. Other contracts do not even require actual delivery of the underlying asset.

Delivery Periods

While some futures contracts require delivery on a specific day, many permit a **delivery period** during which delivery can occur. The delivery period for many of the agricultural, metals, and financial contracts can last up to a month (as in the case of COMEX gold). During the delivery period, the person holding the *short* position determines when delivery will occur simply by informing the clearinghouse of his or her intention to deliver. In this case, we say that the short position has the **seller's option** to decide the delivery date.

Once the short exercises the seller's option, the clearinghouse finds a party with an outstanding long position (usually the longest outstanding long position) and informs that person that delivery will occur. Actual delivery takes place shortly thereafter. The short party delivers the commodity or security to the clearinghouse, and the clearinghouse invoices the long party at the closing futures price for the day the short declared the intention to deliver. The clearinghouse then passes the delivered commodity or security on to the long party and forwards payment to the short party.

Example 1.11 illustrates the delivery process for the COMEX gold futures contract.

▪ **Example 1.11: Delivery in the COMEX Gold Contract**   Delivery in the COMEX gold futures contract follows a three-day process. On the **presentation date**, a short party announces the intention to deliver at the closing futures settlement price for that day. The next day is the **notice date**, when the clearinghouse informs a party with a long position that delivery will occur. The following day is the **delivery date**, when the gold is transferred from the short to the long and the long must pay the short. The first possible presentation date is the second-to-last business day of the month before the contract expires. The last possible presentation date is the third-to-last business day of the month in which the contract expires. ▪

Multiple Deliverable Grades

Many futures contracts also allow some variation in the quality of the commodity or security acceptable for delivery. If any commodity grade or security issue is typically in small supply, the exchange will specify several grades or issues that can be delivered to satisfy the terms of the futures contract. Such contracts also specify adjustments to the futures settlement price for delivery of the various grades or issues. Delivering more valuable grades or issues brings the short a higher adjusted price than does delivering less valuable ones. This choice of grade or issue is another aspect of the seller's option.[25]

---

[25] See Kilcollin [1982] for a detailed discussion of how exchanges adjust their contracts to allow for multiple deliverable grades and how these adjustments affect the futures price.

To see how this process works, consider a futures contract that specifies n deliverable grades and expires at date T. Usually one grade is specified as the **par grade**, and delivery payments for other grades are determined in relation to this grade. Suppose that grade 1 is the par. The short party that delivers grade 1 receives an **invoice price** (IP_1) equal to the quoted futures settlement price at the expiration of the contract:

$$IP_1 = QF_{T,T},$$

where $QF_{T,T}$ is the quoted futures price at time T.[26]

Under many contracts, delivering one of the other grades ($i = 2, \ldots, n$) yields an invoice price of:

$$IP_i = c_i QF_{T,T},$$

where the c_i's are **conversion factors** specified in the futures contract to adjust the settlement price for different grades. Grades that are more valuable than the par grade have conversion factors greater than 1, and grades that are less valuable have conversion factors less than 1. Because we multiply the quoted futures price by a conversion factor, we call this adjustment a **multiplicative grade adjustment**. The widely traded Treasury bond and Treasury note contracts at the Chicago Board of Trade use a multiplicative grade adjustment.

Another type of adjustment for multiple deliverable grades is the **additive grade adjustment**. In this case, delivering a grade other than the par grade yields an invoice price of

$$IP_i = QF_{T,T} + a_i,$$

where the a_i's are **adjustment factors** specified in the futures contract. Grades that are more valuable than the par grade have adjustment factors greater than zero, and grades that are less valuable have adjustment factors less than zero. Many of the agricultural futures contracts use additive grade adjustment.

Multiplicative Grade Adjustment   Example 1.12 demonstrates how multiplicative grade adjustment works under the COMEX gold contract.

▪ **Example 1.12: Conversion Factors for the COMEX Gold Contract**   The COMEX gold futures contract allows delivery of 95 to 105 ounces of gold with a fineness of 99.5 percent or greater. The invoice price the short party receives for delivery of gold within these quantity and quality limits is

$$\text{Invoice price} = (\text{Weight})(\text{Fineness})(QF_{T,T}).$$

---

[26] As we will see in Chapter 6, the invoice price for the T-bond futures contract also includes accrued interest. However, the cash price also includes accrued interest, so the effect is offsetting.

On a per-ounce basis, the invoice price equals the fineness of the gold times the quoted futures price, and the par grade is 100 percent fine. The conversion factor of a given grade is simply its fineness. A short party who delivers 99.5 percent fine gold receives only 99.5 percent of the price he or she would get for delivery of the same quantity of 100 percent fine gold.

The conversion factors clearly are intended to equalize the relative costs of delivering different grades and quantities of gold. If a short party delivers gold that is 99.5 instead of 100 percent fine, he or she is delivering a less valuable commodity and therefore receives a lower invoice price.

The conversion factors do not, however, account perfectly for the variation in value of different grades. Suppose, for example, that the spot prices of 99.5 percent and 100 percent fine gold are $497 and $500 per ounce at time T, respectively. The ratio of these prices is:

$$\frac{P_T(100\%)}{P_T(99.5\%)} = \frac{\$500}{\$497} = 1.006.$$

The 100 percent fine gold is 0.6 percent more valuable than 99.5 percent fine gold. If the short party decides to deliver gold of 100 rather than 99.5 percent fineness, he or she must determine whether the greater invoice price of the 100 percent fine gold is high enough to justify delivering the more valuable grade. The ratio of the invoice prices of the two grades is

$$\frac{IP(100\%)}{IP(99.5\%)} = \frac{(1.000)(QF_{T,T})}{(0.995)(QF_{T,T})}$$
$$= \frac{1.000}{0.995}$$
$$= 1.005.$$

This is just the ratio of the conversion factors. No matter what the quoted futures settlement price at time T, the 100 percent fine gold yields an invoice price 0.5 percent higher than the invoice price of the 99.5 percent fine gold. If the short delivers the 100 percent fine gold instead of the 99.5 percent fine gold, he or she gives up a commodity worth 0.6 percent more but receives an invoice price only 0.5 percent higher. Clearly it is more advantageous to deliver the 99.5 percent fine gold. ■

Example 1.12 demonstrates that we can determine the best grade to deliver by comparing the ratios of the various grades' spot prices at time T with the ratios of their invoice prices. We have seen that the invoice price ratios are equal to the ratios of the conversion factors. Therefore, we would choose to deliver the grade whose conversion factor ratios relative to other grades exceed its price ratios relative to other grades in all cases. This guarantees that we will choose the grade that yields the greatest compensation relative to value given up.

We can easily express this choice in equation form. Let P_T^i be the spot price of grade i at time T. Then we should choose to deliver the grade j that satisfies the following condition:

$$\frac{P_T^j}{P_T^i} < \frac{c_j}{c_i} \tag{1.1}$$

for all other grades i. We can rewrite this as

$$\frac{P_T^j}{c_j} < \frac{P_T^i}{c_i} \tag{1.2}$$

for all i.

Equation 1.2 provides a very simple rule for choosing the most advantageous grade to deliver. We divide the spot price of each grade at time T by its conversion factor, as shown in Equation 1.2, to get the **delivery-adjusted spot price** for each grade. The best grade to deliver is thus the grade with the minimum delivery-adjusted spot price. This is called the **cheapest deliverable grade**. Since this grade will be delivered, it will be subject to the delivery date convergence condition, so the price the short part receives will equal the value he or she gives up. The quoted futures settlement price will adjust such that the invoice price equals the spot price for grade j at expiration:

$$IP_j = c_j QF_{T,T} = P_T^j, \tag{1.3}$$

or

$$QF_{T,T} = \frac{P_T^j}{c_j}. \tag{1.4}$$

The quoted futures price thus equals the delivery-adjusted spot price of the cheapest deliverable grade. It will not be advantageous to deliver any other grade i, because

$$QF_{T,T} = \frac{P_T^j}{c_j} < \frac{P_T^i}{c_i}, \tag{1.5}$$

or

$$IP_i = c_i QF_{T,T} < P_T^i, \tag{1.6}$$

so the invoice price is lower than the value of the grade delivered.

We can see how this rule for choosing the cheapest grade to deliver works by applying it to Example 1.12. Suppose that 99.5 percent and 100 percent fine gold are the only two grades available for delivery. The delivery-adjusted spot prices of these two grades are

$$\frac{P_T(99.5\%)}{c(99.5\%)} = \frac{\$497}{0.995}$$
$$= \$499.50$$

$$\frac{P_T(100\%)}{c(100\%)} = \frac{\$500}{1.000}$$
$$= \$500.00.$$

The 99.5 percent fine gold has the lowest delivery-adjusted spot price, so it is the cheapest grade to deliver, as we saw in Example 1.12. The quoted futures settlement price will be \$499.50, the delivery-adjusted spot price of the 99.5 percent fine grade.

However, the cheapest deliverable grade is not always the one with the lowest spot price, as in Example 1.12. Suppose the spot price of 99.5 percent fine gold at expiration is \$498. The delivery-adjusted spot price for this grade is then \$498/0.995 = \$500.50. The 100 percent fine gold is the cheapest grade, and the quoted futures settlement price will equal \$500.

Clearly, choosing the cheapest grade to deliver when there is multiplicative grade adjustment is necessary only if the market price ratios of various grades differ from the ratios of their conversion factors. We will see in Chapter 6 that this is a big issue for futures on Treasury bonds and Treasury notes, because the conversion factor adjustments for delivery of different Treasury issues often diverge greatly from the differences in their market values.

Additive Grade Adjustment   Choosing the cheapest deliverable grade for contracts with additive grade adjustment is a very similar process. The problem is to find the grade whose adjustment to the invoice price is more favorable than its differential in market values. We want to find grade j for which

$$IP_j - IP_i > P_T^j - P_T^i. \tag{1.7}$$

Since the invoice price is simply the quoted futures price plus the adjustment factor, we can rewrite this as

$$QF_{T,T} + a_j - [QF_{T,T} + a_i] > P_T^j - P_T^i, \tag{1.8}$$

or

$$P_T^i - a_i > P_T^j - a_j. \tag{1.9}$$

If we define

$$\text{Delivery-adjusted spot price} = P_T^i - a_i,$$

the cheapest deliverable grade is again the one with the lowest delivery-adjusted spot price. The quoted futures price will equal this price because of delivery date convergence. In Chapter 8, we will study examples of additive grade adjustment for agricultural futures.

Cash Settlement

Some futures contracts do not require that the underlying commodity or security actually be delivered when the contract expires. These are called **cash settlement** contracts. When a cash settlement contract expires, the exchange sets its final settlement price equal to the spot price of the underlying asset on that day. The contract is closed out at the final settlement price, but the underlying commodity or security does not change hands.[27]

Since cash settlement contracts are settled at the spot price, their futures prices are forced to converge to the underlying spot prices. Thus, at expiration, the prices of cash settlement contracts behave just like the prices of delivery contracts.

The major cash settlement contracts include the Eurodollar time deposit and feeder cattle contracts at the Chicago Mercantile Exchange, the stock index futures contracts traded at various exchanges, and the municipal bond contract at the Chicago Board of Trade. Cash settlement is most desirable when spot prices are well specified and easily obtained and when actual physical delivery would be very costly. The latter consideration is most important with futures contracts on broad indices, such as stock index futures.

Exchange of Futures for Physicals

In some cases, a party who holds a futures contract may wish to deliver or take delivery on terms that differ from those the exchange offers. For example, a party with a long gold futures position may wish to take delivery in Los Angeles rather than in New York, as the COMEX contract specifies. Or a party with a short gold position may wish to deliver outside of the normal trading hours of the futures exchange. The exchanges allow people to deliver under noncontract terms such as these through alternative trades called **exchanges of futures for physicals (EFPs)**.[28] The EFP system allows a party to exchange a futures position for a cash position that meets the party's delivery preferences. Unlike all other futures transactions, an EFP allows people to trade their futures positions without going through the trading pits.

For example, the above party with the long gold position could use an EFP to trade his or her futures position for a long position in cash gold that will be delivered in Los Angeles. The party must, of course, find another party willing to make the trade. Once this is accomplished and the two parties have agreed to the

---

[27] One social advantage of the cash settlement contracts is that they save their users the costs of delivery. See Jones [1982] and Garbade and Silber [1983] for a further discussion of cash settlement.

[28] See *Report on Exchanges of Futures for Physicals,* Commodity Futures Trading Commission, October 1, 1987, for a complete discussion of EFPs.

EFP trade, the futures clearinghouse removes the original party from its books and gives the long position to the counterparty. The price at which the original party is closed out and the new party is entered into the clearinghouse's books is mutually agreed upon by the two parties, as is the price of the cash transaction. Typically, the clearinghouse will guarantee performance on the futures trade but not on the physical trade.

Example 1.13 demonstrates delivery under an EFP.

■ **Example 1.13: Delivery Using an Exchange of Futures for Physicals**
Suppose A is holding a long June COMEX gold futures contract and B is holding a short June COMEX gold futures contract. Both A and B live in Los Angeles and prefer to close out their futures positions with delivery in Los Angeles rather than in New York as specified in the COMEX gold contract. They make an agreement that A will transfer his long futures position to B at a price of $450 per ounce. Then their brokers submit an EFP order with this information to COMEX. At the same time, B agrees to sell A 100 ounces of gold in Los Angeles at a price of $450 per ounce.

At this point, the clearinghouse marks A's position to market at $450 per ounce and closes him out. B now holds both a long and a short futures position, so the clearinghouse closes her out as well, marking her short position to market at $450 per ounce. The net result of these transactions is that B has delivered 100 ounces of gold to A in Los Angeles at a price of $450 per ounce. ■

A and B could use their EFP to adjust their delivery in other ways. B could deliver the 100 ounces of gold to A at 2:00 a.m. if both parties wished. In this case, the transaction would be recorded with the exchange the following morning. The two parties could set different prices for closing out the futures positions and for transferring the physical gold. Or they could agree to transfer a grade of gold that is not specified in the COMEX contract.

EFPs can also provide more efficient delivery in some cases by allowing parties to choose their delivery partners. If two parties already have a relationship and can transfer a commodity cheaply, delivery under an EFP can be superior to a match arranged by a clearinghouse. Two such parties may save delivery costs and be more confident that the delivery will go smoothly.

EFPs have become increasingly popular in recent years. They are most prevalent in the markets for energy futures. For example, 94 percent of the deliveries under the New York Mercantile Exchange August 1987 crude oil contract were arranged through EFPs. Likewise, EFPs accounted for 92 and 78 percent of the deliveries under the August 1987 heating oil and unleaded gasoline contracts, respectively.

Summary

The futures industry began in the mid-nineteenth century with contracts on agricultural products. In the 1970s, futures contracts on financial instruments were introduced, and the futures markets experienced very rapid growth.

Futures contracts establish the price and quantity of a commodity or security to be sold at a prespecified future date. The contracts have standardized specifications and are traded in centralized exchanges. Some futures contracts are settled with delivery of the underlying asset. Others, called *cash settlement* contracts, are closed out without delivery at the futures settlement price on the expiration day. Under either system, the futures price converges to the spot price of the underlying asset at expiration. Futures positions are marked to market every day, so gains and losses are realized daily.

Futures contracts are used for several purposes. One is to hedge the risks that individuals and businesses face due to changing market prices of commodities or securities. Speculators use them to gamble on future price movements and arbitrageurs to profit on the differences between prices in the futures and spot markets.

If the financial and business environments continue to be as volatile as they have been over the past two decades, futures contracting will serve more and more uses and trading in futures markets should continue to grow.

Problems

1. Explain the circumstances in which
    a.   a futures trade will increase open interest.
    b.   a futures trade will decrease open interest.
    c.   a futures trade will leave open interest unchanged.

2. Suppose you enter into a long position in a gold futures contract for 100 ounces, expiring in 120 days, at a price of $400 per ounce. Suppose further that you can borrow and lend at 9 percent per annum. Finally, suppose you borrow to pay any marking-to-market losses and lend any marking-to-market gains. Assume a 360-day year for calculating interest.
    a.   If the gold futures price stays at $400 for 119 days and then jumps to $421 just as the contract expires, what will your futures profits be at the expiration of the contract?
    b.   If the gold futures price immediately jumps to $421 and stays there until the contract expires, what will your futures profits be at the expiration date?
    c.   If the gold futures price immediately drops to $370, stays there, and then jumps to $421 just as the contract expires, what will be your futures profits at the expiration of the contract?
    d.   Why do you get a different answer in each case even though the initial futures price is $400 and the futures price at the contract's expiration is $421?

3. In financial markets, we define the *bid price* as the price at which one can sell an asset or the price at which one can go short a futures contract. We define the *ask price* as the price at which one can buy an asset or the price at which one can go long a futures contract.
    a.   Suppose that on March 15, we observe the following futures prices, per ounce:

	Bid	Ask
August gold futures	$425.10	$425.20
December gold futures	453.50	453.65

Why would we expect the bid prices to always be below the ask prices?

b.   Now suppose we decide to enter into a long August–short December spread for five contracts. On June 13, the futures prices, per ounce, are

	Bid	Ask
August gold futures	$413.40	$413.45
December gold futures	445.60	445.70

We decide to close out our spread by taking offsetting positions. What are the net profits from these transactions?

c.   Now suppose that on June 13, the futures prices, per ounce, are

	Bid	Ask
August gold futures	$433.40	$433.45
December gold futures	465.60	465.70

We decide to close out our spread by taking offsetting positions. What are the net profits from these transactions?

d.   What is the relationship between the net profits in parts b and c? Explain.

4.   Reproduce Table 1.4 on Lotus. Try "what-if" analyses with 200 and 300 ounces of gold.

5.   Reproduce Table 1.5 on Lotus. Try "what-if" analyses with interest rates of 8 and 12 percent. How does a change in the interest rate affect the importance of marking to market?

6.   Reproduce Table 1.6 on Lotus. Try "what-if" analyses with an initial margin of $5,000 and a maintenance margin of $4,000. Does the final cash flow change? Why or why not? (Hint: This is a hard problem. You will need to use the @IF function extensively.)

7.   Suppose there is a strawberry contract that allows one to deliver four grades of strawberries to satisfy the contract specifications: grades A, B, C, and D. This contract uses multiplicative invoice price adjustments. You observe the following spot prices, per flat of strawberries, at the expiration of the futures contract, and the grades have the following conversion factors:

Grade	Conversion Factor	Price at Expiration
A	1.05	$4.50
B	1.00	4.00
C	0.95	3.70
D	0.80	3.65

a.   Which grade will be delivered?

    b.   What will be the quoted futures price at the expiration of the contract?

    c.   How much will the short receive for delivering 5,000 flats of the delivered grade?

    d.   Suppose that instead of a seller's option there is a buyer's option that gives the long the right to determine which grade will be delivered. Which grade will be delivered, and what will be the quoted futures price at the contract's expiration?

8.   Suppose there is a raspberry contract that allows one to deliver four grades of raspberries to satisfy the contract specifications: grades A, B, C, and D. This contract uses additive invoice price adjustments. You observe the following spot prices, per flat of raspberries, at the expiration of the futures contract, and the grades have the following adjustment factors:

Grade	Adjustment Factor	Price at Expiration
A	$0.05	$2.46
B	0.00	2.44
C	−0.05	2.38
D	−0.10	2.33

    a.   Which grade will be delivered?

    b.   What will be the quoted futures price at the expiration of the contract?

    c.   How much will the short receive for delivering 5,000 flats of the delivered grade?

9.   Suppose a jewelry manufacturer needs to purchase 1,000 ounces of silver in August. The current futures price for delivery of silver in August is $6 per ounce. Consider the following two scenarios for the spot price of silver in August: (1) $5 per ounce and (2) $7 per ounce. The manufacturer goes long one 1,000-ounce contract of silver futures. For each of the two scenarios, answer the following questions:

    a.   What will the futures price be in August?

    b.   What will the profits on the long futures position be?

    c.   If the manufacturer takes delivery of silver in August, at what price will he do so?

    d.   What is the net cost of the silver to the manufacturer?

    e.   Suppose that instead of taking delivery of silver in August, the manufacturer closes out his futures position and buys silver on the spot market. What will be the net cost of the silver?

10.   Suppose a gold dealer has an inventory of 500,000 ounces of 99.5 percent fineness of gold. She is sure that this grade will be cheapest to deliver at the expiration of the December gold futures contract on December 28. Suppose she wishes to hedge the price at which she will be able to sell her gold on December 28. The current COMEX gold futures price is $435 per ounce.

    a.   Should the dealer go long or short COMEX gold futures contracts? How many contracts should she use?

b.   Show the dealer's unhedged revenues, futures profits, and hedged revenues for two scenarios for the December 28 gold spot price for 99.5 percent fineness of gold: (1) $415 per ounce and (2) $460 per ounce.

c.   What per-ounce price has the dealer locked in by hedging? How does this compare with the initial COMEX gold futures price?

(Hint: Try 500,000 ounces, then $0.995 \times 500,000$.)

The Pricing of Futures Contracts

Futures markets are useful to hedgers and speculators only if futures prices reflect information about the prices of the underlying commodities or securities. Therefore, to understand how futures markets work, we must understand how the prices of futures contracts relate to the spot prices of the underlying assets. In Chapter 1, we saw that the delivery date arbitrage condition drives futures and spot prices together upon expiration of a futures contract. In this chapter, we will see how the market forces of arbitrage and capital market equilibrium forge relationships between futures and spot prices well before the contract expiration date.

The market force that most strongly affects the pricing of futures contracts is arbitrage. Arbitrageurs look for profits offered by the differences between futures and spot prices and among futures prices of contracts with different maturity dates. As arbitrageurs trade between the futures and spot markets and among futures contracts with different maturities, prices will adjust until such profit opportunities are eliminated. By observing the arbitrageurs' behavior, we can derive the pricing relationships that should prevail.

Arbitrage trading strategies can be useful to *all* market participants, not just those in trading rooms on Wall Street. In many cases, managers of firms who are not involved in arbitrage as a primary business can don the arbitrageur's hat to improve their firms' performances.

Futures prices are also strongly influenced by the flow of investment funds among instruments that offer different levels of risk and expected return. The trading activity of investors pressures futures prices to adjust until the risk-return trade-offs offered in the futures markets are the same as those offered in other markets. Standard models of risk and return, such as the Capital Asset Pricing Model, can yield insights into the equilibrium relationship between the current futures price and the expected future spot price of the underlying commodity or security. We will see that the standard investment strategies that allow investors to profit from abnormal returns in spot commodities and securities markets can also be used in futures markets.

An Introduction to Arbitrage

The S&P 1 Contract

Arbitrageurs use several strategies to capture profits by trading between the spot and futures markets. To simplify our presentation of these strategies, we will illustrate them with a hypothetical futures contract written on one share of IBM stock. The long position in this contract has an obligation to buy one share of IBM stock at the futures price, and the short position is obligated to sell one share of IBM. This contract is like the futures contract on the Standard and Poor's (S&P) 500 Index traded at the Chicago Mercantile Exchange except that it has only 1 stock in its index instead of 500.[1] We will call our hypothetical contract the S&P 1 futures contract. We will study the S&P 500 contract and other major stock index futures contracts in detail in Chapter 4.

Cash-and-Carry Arbitrage

One technique arbitrageurs use to trade between the futures and spot markets is called the **cash-and-carry strategy**. As its name suggests, this strategy involves buying the underlying asset of a futures contract in the spot market and holding (carrying) it for the duration of the arbitrage. Example 2.1 illustrates a cash-and-carry trade using the hypothetical S&P 1 futures contract.

▪ **Example 2.1: S&P 1 Cash-and-Carry Trade**   Suppose an arbitrageur discovers that IBM stock is selling for $140 per share and the current S&P 1 futures price for delivery of one share of IBM in exactly one year is $155 per share. For simplicity, we will assume that IBM will pay no dividends over the next year and that trading involves no transactions costs. (Later we will see how dividends and transactions costs affect arbitrage trading strategies.)

The arbitrageur could invest in the following cash-and-carry:

1.   Purchase 1 million shares of IBM stock at $140 per share.

2.   Go short, at $155 per share, 1 million S&P 1 futures contracts that expire in exactly one year.

3.   Hold the stock for one year and deliver it at the expiration of the futures contracts.

---

[1] As we will discuss in Chapter 4, the Standard and Poor's 500 contract is a cash settlement contract, while our hypothetical Standard and Poor's 1 contract is a delivery contract. However, this is not an important distinction.

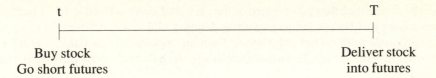

t   T

Buy stock   Deliver stock
Go short futures   into futures

This strategy costs $140 million today and will yield $155 million upon delivery in one year. The rate of return over the year is

$$\text{Rate of return} = \frac{\text{Cash inflow at T} - \text{Cash outflow at t}}{\text{Cash outflow at t}}$$

$$= \frac{\$155 \text{ million} - \$140 \text{ million}}{\$140 \text{ million}}$$

$$= 10.71\%.$$

                                                    ∎

Example 2.1 illustrates the basic steps of the cash-and-carry trading strategy:

1.   Buy the underlying spot asset.

2.   Go short the futures.

3.   Deliver into the futures contract with the spot asset.

By entering into the cash-and-carry trade shown in Example 2.1, the arbitrageur creates an investment that acts like a one-year discount bond with a face value of $155 million and a current cost of $140 million. The arbitrageur pays a set amount for the stock today and uses the short futures position to lock in the sale price one year from now. If there is no possibility that the futures clearinghouse will default, the arbitrageur in effect has a riskless discount bond, much like a Treasury bill (T-bill). We call this cash-and-carry investment a **synthetic T-bill**, because it has exactly the same cash flows as a T-bill.[2] We also say the arbitrageur has made a **synthetic loan**, because he or she has effectively lent out money that will be received back with interest, just as if a T-bill had been purchased outright. The rate of return earned on the loan is the **cash-and-carry synthetic lending rate**.

Pure Arbitrage

In Example 2.1, we saw that the arbitrageur can earn a 10.71 percent return by lending synthetically through the cash-and-carry strategy. Now suppose the arbitrageur can borrow the $140 million required for the cash-and-carry trade at a 10

---

[2] Of course, this comparison of a cash-and-carry with a discount bond ignores the marking to market on the futures position. We will discuss how to manage the cash flows from marking to market in Chapter 3.

percent rate. Since the rate of return on the cash-and-carry is fixed at 10.71 percent, this strategy of borrowing and synthetic lending allows the arbitrageur to earn a certain profit with no net investment. Such an opportunity for riskless profit on zero net investment is called a **pure arbitrage**. A **cash-and-carry pure arbitrage** exists if

Cash-and-carry synthetic lending rate > Borrowing rate.

As no net investment is required, the arbitrageur can continually add to his or her earnings by repeating the cash-and-carry arbitrage. Such arbitrage activity will have an immediate impact on market prices:

1. The price of IBM stock will rise due to buying pressure from those engaging in the cash-and-carry arbitrage.

2. The futures price for the S&P 1 contracts that expire in one year will fall due to selling pressure from those engaging in the cash-and-carry strategy.

3. The cost of borrowing will rise as arbitrageurs demand to borrow more.

Arbitrageurs should continue to trade until the price adjustment eliminates the opportunity for pure arbitrage profits. Later we will derive the relationships between spot and futures prices and the cost of credit that will prevail once this adjustment has run its course.

Reverse Cash-and-Carry Arbitrage

The cash-and-carry strategy combines positions in the futures and spot markets to create a synthetic lending position in a T-bill. It is also possible to use futures and spot positions to mimic a short, or borrowing, position in a T-bill. The trading strategy used in this case is called a **reverse cash-and-carry**. As its name implies, this strategy involves taking the opposite sides of the positions in a cash-and-carry strategy.

Short Positions   An investor takes a **short** position in a spot instrument such as a T-bill or a stock by borrowing the instrument and promising to return it at some point in the future. For example, suppose we want a short position in a $1 million, one-year T-bill with a current price of $900,000. We borrow the T-bill today and sell it immediately for $900,000. One year from now, we must buy the same T-bill and return it to the person from whom we borrowed it. Since the bill expires at that point, this will cost exactly $1 million. The net result of this short position is that we have a $900,000 cash inflow today and a $1 million cash outflow in one year. This is equivalent to borrowing $900,000 for one year. The interest is

$$
\begin{aligned}
\text{Interest} &= \text{Cash outflow at T} - \text{Cash inflow at t} \\
&= \$1,000,000 - \$900,000 \\
&= \$100,000.
\end{aligned}
$$

The interest rate is

$$\text{Interest rate} = \frac{\text{Interest}}{\text{Cash inflow at t}}$$
$$= \frac{\$100,000}{\$900,000}$$
$$= 11.11\%.$$

Thus, taking a short position in a security is equivalent to *borrowing*, while taking a long position in (buying) a security is equivalent to *lending*. If we sell a stock short, we borrow it and sell it immediately. At some future point, we must repurchase the stock to return it to the lender. For now, we assume it is as easy to go short a security as it is to buy it. Later we will see how arbitrage trading strategies are affected when short sales are costly or impossible.

Reverse Strategies   In many ways, a short position is the exact opposite of a long position. We saw earlier that one can create a synthetic long position in a T-bill using the cash-and-carry strategy of buying IBM stock and going short the S&P 1 futures contract. The reverse cash-and-carry strategy creates a synthetic short T-bill position by taking the opposite side of each step of the cash-and-carry strategy. In Example 2.1, this would involve the following steps:

1.   Instead of buying 1 million shares of IBM stock at $140 per share, we sell short 1 million shares of IBM stock at that price. This will bring in $140 million today.

2.   Instead of going short 1 million shares of the S&P 1 futures contract at $155 per share, we go long 1 million shares at that price.

3.   One year from now, we take delivery of 1 million shares of IBM on the futures market at the locked-in price of $155 million and return the borrowed shares.

In effect, we borrow $140 million today and must repay exactly $155 million in one year. Since we know the amount to be paid back in the future with certainty at the outset, this is equivalent to taking a short position in a T-bill that matures in one year. Thus, this reverse cash-and-carry strategy creates a synthetic borrowing at the **reverse cash-and-carry synthetic borrowing rate**.

Like the cash-and-carry strategy, a reverse cash-and-carry strategy can be used for pure arbitrage. A **reverse cash-and-carry pure arbitrage** is available if funds can be obtained cheaply by borrowing through the reverse cash-and-carry and then lent out at a higher rate, that is, if

Reverse cash-and-carry synthetic borrowing rate < Lending rate.

In our example, the reverse cash-and-carry synthetic borrowing rate is 10.71 percent, because we borrow $140 million and pay back $155 million. If an arbitrageur can lend at a rate higher than 10.71 percent, a reverse cash-and-carry pure arbitrage opportunity exists.

As with a cash-and-carry pure arbitrage, market prices will respond as traders rush to profit from a reverse cash-and-carry pure arbitrage opportunity. Selling pressure will drive the spot stock price down. Buying pressure will drive the futures price up. This will increase the reverse cash-and-carry synthetic borrowing rate and make synthetic borrowing less attractive. Lending rates will fall as arbitrageurs increase the supply of loanable funds. Such price adjustments will continue until the reverse cash-and-carry pure arbitrage opportunity disappears.

Implied Repo and Implied Reverse Repo Rates   Some special terminology applies for the synthetic lending and borrowing rates earned and paid through cash-and-carry and reverse cash-and-carry strategies. The rate of return earned from a cash-and-carry strategy is called the **implied repo rate**. This term comes from arbitrage in the government securities market, where arbitrageurs compare this implied repo rate with a borrowing rate called the **repo rate**. We will discuss the government securities market in detail in Chapter 5. For now, we will simply consider the implied repo rate as a term for the cash-and-carry synthetic lending rate. Similarly, the reverse cash-and-carry synthetic borrowing rate is called the **implied reverse repo rate**. These terms are used for all cash-and-carry strategies, not just those performed in the government securities markets.

No-Arbitrage Equilibrium

A cash-and-carry pure arbitrage exists if the implied repo rate exceeds the market borrowing rate. A reverse cash-and-carry arbitrage is available if the implied reverse repo rate is less than the market lending rate. No arbitrages are available if the implied repo rate is less than or equal to the borrowing rate and the implied reverse repo rate is greater than or equal to the lending rate. In equilibrium, prices will reach levels that allow no further arbitrage opportunities. In the next section, we will derive the relationship among futures prices, spot prices, and interest rates that prevails in equilibrium.

The Fundamental No-Arbitrage Equation

Arbitrageurs will follow a given strategy of trading between spot and futures markets as long as they can make riskless profits with no net investment. Their repeated trading will cause prices in both markets to adjust until each opportunity for pure arbitrage profit disappears. In this way, market forces constantly maintain relationships between spot and futures prices. In this section, we will develop a general theory of futures pricing based on the activity of arbitrageurs in the marketplace. We will derive the relationships between futures and spot prices that result as arbitrageurs repeatedly follow the cash-and-carry and reverse cash-and-carry strategies.

Arbitrage with No Payouts

The equilibrium relationship between futures and spot market prices is equivalent to the relationship that holds when there are no opportunities to earn arbitrage profits, for if prices diverge from the no-arbitrage relationship at any point, they will be quickly driven back by arbitrage trading.

The no-arbitrage pricing relationship is most easily derived for futures contracts written on very simple commodities or securities. Consider a futures contract on an asset with the following characteristics:

1. The asset can be bought or sold in a spot market without transactions costs. (It is of deliverable grade.)

2. Except for the opportunity cost of funds, the asset can be held without cost. (There are no warehousing, insurance, or spoilage costs.)

3. The asset can be sold short, with full use of proceeds. (The short-seller can sell the borrowed commodity or security.)

4. The asset has no payouts, such as dividends or coupons.

The hypothetical S&P 1 futures contract comes very close to this ideal.[3] Futures on T-bills are another good example. Futures on Treasury bonds and dividend-paying stocks do not fit into this category. We will consider these and other more complicated instruments in later sections.

We also assume that

5. The arbitrageur can borrow and lend at the same rate between times t and T.

The interest rate paid or received between t and T (on a nonannualized basis) is denoted by $r_{t,T}$. The relationship between $r_{t,T}$ and the annualized rate, r, is given by

$$r = r_{t,T}\left(\frac{1}{T-t}\right), \tag{2.1}$$

where $T-t$ is measured in years. Thus, if the time between t and T is three months, we annualize $r_{t,T}$, the three-month rate (one quarter of a year), by multiplying it by 4. While this method of annualizing, called the **bond equivalent yield**, ignores compounding, it is market practice. In fact, there are several ways to annualize rates. Because of this ambiguity, we will work with *nonannualized* rates. Thus, we will compare only rates that can be earned over a specific time period, such as from t to T.

Earlier we saw that with a cash-and-carry synthetic lending, an arbitrageur buys the underlying asset at t for P_t and locks in a sale price at T of $F_{t,T}$. The implied repo rate that an arbitrageur can earn on a cash-and-carry is

---

[3] Recall that for now we have assumed IBM pays no dividend.

$$\frac{F_{t,T} - P_t}{P_t} = \frac{\text{Cash inflow at T} - \text{Cash outflow at t}}{\text{Cash outflow at t}}. \tag{2.2}$$

With a reverse cash-and-carry synthetic borrowing, an arbitrageur borrows (goes short) the underlying asset and sells it for P_t. Then the arbitrageur locks in a purchase price at T of $F_{t,T}$ so that he or she can return the underlying asset to the lender. The implied reverse repo rate at which the arbitrageur can borrow using a reverse cash-and-carry is

$$\frac{F_{t,T} - P_t}{P_t} = \frac{\text{Cash outflow at T} - \text{Cash inflow at t}}{\text{Cash inflow at t}}. \tag{2.2a}$$

Together Equations 2.2 and 2.2a show that the synthetic borrowing rate equals the synthetic lending rate, because we have assumed that the underlying asset can be sold short without cost. This will not be true when we consider transactions costs.

Earlier we saw that arbitrage opportunities exist if the implied repo rate (synthetic lending rate) exceeds the borrowing rate or if the implied reverse repo rate (synthetic borrowing rate) is less than the lending rate. Recall that we have assumed the actual borrowing and lending rates are identical. Similarly, from Equations 2.2 and 2.2a, the implied repo and implied reverse repo rates are identical. Thus, if there are no arbitrage opportunities,

Implied reverse repo rate = Implied repo rate
= Borrowing and lending rate.

In mathematical terms, this condition is

$$\frac{F_{t,T} - P_t}{P_t} = r_{t,T}. \tag{2.3}$$

We can rearrange Equation 2.3 to express the relationship between futures prices and spot market prices when no arbitrage profits are available. This relationship is called the **fundamental no-arbitrage relationship**:

$$F_{t,T} = P_t(1 + r_{t,T}). \tag{2.4}$$

Futures price = Spot price + Interest.

Market forces will always drive the relationship between spot and futures prices toward this fundamental no-arbitrage equation. It is therefore the relationship that will prevail in equilibrium. We can demonstrate this by showing how arbitrageurs will react if the relationship does not hold.

Suppose our simple futures contract violates the no-arbitrage relationship in the following way:

$$F_{t,T} > P_t(1 + r_{t,T}) \tag{2.5}$$

or

$$\frac{F_{t,T} - P_t}{P_t} > r_{t,T} \, .$$

Pure arbitrage profits can be earned by borrowing to follow the cash-and-carry strategy of buying the underlying asset and locking in a selling price with the futures contract:

Arbitrage Strategy

Transaction	t	T
Borrow P_t (dollars)	P_t	$-P_t(1 + r_{t,T})$
Buy spot	$-P_t$	$F_{T,T} = P_T$ (from delivery)
Go short futures	0	$F_{t,T} - F_{T,T}$
Net	0	$F_{t,T} - P_t(1 + r_{t,T}) > 0$

This strategy requires no net investment at time t, yet there is a positive cash flow at T as the proceeds from delivery to the futures market exceed the cost of paying back the loan. If this were a cash settlement futures contract, the arbitrageur would sell the commodity or security for P_T instead of delivering it at the futures price of $F_{T,T}$. As these two prices are equal, the result would be the same.

We can tell that the cash-and-carry strategy is appropriate simply by looking at the futures price relative to the spot price. Notice that in Equation 2.5, the futures price is high relative to the spot price (compared with the no-arbitrage relationship in Equation 2.4). The futures is said to be *expensive* relative to the cash. We always want to sell what is relatively overpriced and buy what is relatively underpriced, that is, buy low and sell high. Buying the spot and going short the futures accomplish this. The arbitrageurs' rush into the cash-and-carry strategy will drive the futures price down and the spot price up until the fundamental no-arbitrage relationship (Equation 2.4) is restored.

Notice that the arbitrageur does not care if the absolute spot and futures prices are too high or too low. The arbitrageur is concerned only with relative prices. This is why arbitrage ties the spot and futures markets together.

Example 2.2 illustrates the profit opportunity presented by this violation of the no-arbitrage relationship, continuing our S&P 1 example.

▪ **Example 2.2: A Cash-and-Carry Pure Arbitrage**   Recall that

$$P_t \quad = \$140$$
$$F_{t,T} \quad = \$155$$
$$r_{t,T} \quad = 10\%$$
$$T - t = 1 \text{ year}$$

The fundamental no-arbitrage equation in this case is

$$F_{t,T} = \$155 > P_t(1 + r_{t,T})$$
$$= \$140(1.10)$$
$$= \$154.$$

The futures price is greater than the no-arbitrage price, so a cash-and-carry arbitrage strategy is appropriate:

Arbitrage Strategy

Transaction	Today	One Year From Now
Borrow	\$140	$-\$140(1.10) = -\$154$
Buy spot	$-\$140$	$F_{T,T}$ (from delivery)
Go short futures	0	$\$155 - F_{T,T}$
Net	0	$\$155 - \$154 = \$1$

The arbitrageur has locked in the \$1 profit no matter what the price of IBM stock is one year from now. Since no investment is required to earn this certain profit, arbitrageurs can make unlimited amounts by repeating this trade over and over. Eventually the pressure of their trading will cause the futures price to fall and the spot price to rise so that the profit drops to zero and the fundamental no-arbitrage relationship is restored.

Notice that the \$1 profit is exactly 0.71 percent of \$140. This is because the implied repo rate exceeds the borrowing rate by 0.71 percent. However, we cannot say that the rate of return on the arbitrage is 0.71 percent, because the \$1 profit is received on zero net investment.[4] ∎

Now suppose the no-arbitrage equation is violated in the opposite direction so that

$$F_{t,T} < P_t(1 + r_{t,T}) \tag{2.6}$$

or

$$\frac{F_{t,T} - P_t}{P_t} < r_{t,T}.$$

The futures price is now less than the no-arbitrage price, and pure arbitrage profits can be earned by following the reverse cash-and-carry strategy. The arbitrageur will go long (buy) the futures and go short (sell) the spot commodity or security:

---

[4] It is more appropriate to think of the rate of return from arbitrage as the arbitrage profits earned over a given time period divided by the cost of running the arbitrage operation over the same period. These costs can be substantial, because they include compensation to the traders and the physical costs of trading.

Arbitrage Strategy

Transaction	t	T
Short spot	P_t	$-F_{T,T}$ (taking delivery)
Lend P_t	$-P_t$	$P_t(1 + r_{t,T})$
Go long futures	0	$F_{T,T} - F_{t,T}$
Net	0	$P_t(1 + r_{t,T}) - F_{t,T} > 0$

There is zero cash outlay at time t; yet at time T, the proceeds received on the loan more than cover the locked-in price for taking delivery of the spot commodity or security to pay back the short-sale borrowing. The arbitrage process will drive the futures price up and the spot price down, bringing them back into the fundamental no-arbitrage relationship (Equation 2.4). Later we will discuss how this analysis is affected if the commodity or security cannot be sold short costlessly.

Futures and spot prices may not always behave as the fundamental no-arbitrage relationship predicts. For example, buyers and sellers may not move into the two markets at the same rate. However, arbitrageurs make sure that the futures and spot prices are not out of line for very long. They can profit from mispricing, and their activity will bring prices back into line.[5]

Implied Rates and the Fundamental No-Arbitrage Equation   We have introduced two ways to identify pure arbitrage opportunities. The first is to compare the implied repo rate or the implied reverse repo rate with the appropriate alternative borrowing or lending rate. The second is to use the fundamental no-arbitrage relationship to indicate when futures and spot prices are relatively out of line. Equations 2.5 and 2.6 show that these two approaches are exactly the same. Table 2.1 sums up the rules for determining whether an arbitrage opportunity exists.

Next, we will see how the no-arbitrage pricing relationship changes when we relax some of our assumptions.

Arbitrage with Payouts

Many commodities and securities have associated payouts. Some, such as dividends for stocks and coupons for bonds, are positive. Others, such as the costs of storage and spoilage for commodities such as corn and wheat, are negative. These payouts change the fundamental no-arbitrage equation in a straightforward way.

---

[5] One might think that the existence of arbitrage opportunities is evidence against the **efficient market hypothesis**. Under this hypothesis, market forces move so quickly that there are no excess profits to be earned. In fact, it is the pressure on prices applied by arbitrageurs acting on arbitrage opportunities that *keeps* the markets efficient.

Table 2.1 Arbitrage Opportunities

Cash-and-Carry Arbitrage

- Futures expensive relative to cash
- Implied repo rate exceeds financing rate
- Long cash–short futures arbitrage profitable

Reverse Cash-and-Carry Arbitrage

- Cash expensive relative to futures
- Implied reverse repo rate less than lending rate
- Short cash–long futures arbitrage profitable

Suppose the underlying commodity or security has a payout of C_1 at time t1, where t1 occurs before the futures contract expires at time T:

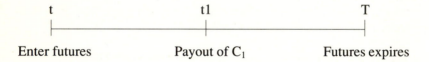

t	t1	T
Enter futures	Payout of C_1	Futures expires

Then the fundamental no-arbitrage equation, Equation 2.4, becomes

$$F_{t,T} = P_t (1 + r_{t,T}) - C_1 (1 + r_{t1,T}), \qquad (2.7)$$

where $r_{t1,T}$ is the interest (not annualized) earned between t1 and T. For simplicity, we assume this rate is known at t; otherwise, Equation 2.7 could be only an approximation. To show that this is an equilibrium relationship, we again demonstrate that arbitrage profits are available if it does not hold.

Cash-and-carry arbitrage opportunities exist in this case if

$$F_{t,T} > P_t(1 + r_{t,T}) - C_1(1 + r_{t1,T}). \qquad (2.8)$$

Arbitrage Strategy

Transaction	t	t1	T
Borrow P_t	P_t		$-P_t(1 + r_{t,T})$
Buy spot	$-P_t$	C_1	$F_{T,T} = P_T$ (from delivery)
Lend payout		$-C_1$	$C_1(1 + r_{t1,T})$
Go short futures	0		$F_{t,T} - F_{T,T}$
Net	0	0	$F_{t,T} - P_t(1 + r_{t,T}) + C_1(1 + r_{t1,T}) > 0$

Reverse cash-and-carry arbitrage opportunities exist if

$$F_{t,T} < P_t(1 + r_{t,T}) - C_1(1 + r_{t1,T}). \qquad (2.9)$$

Arbitrage Strategy

Transaction	t	t1	T
Short spot	P_t	$-C_1$	$-F_{T,T}$ (take delivery)
Lend P_t	$-P_t$		$P_t(1 + r_{t,T})$
Borrow payout		C_1	$-C1(1 + r_{t1,T})$
Go long futures	0		$F_{T,T} - F_{t,T}$
Net	0	0	$P_t(1 + r_{t,T}) - C_1(1 + r_{t1,T}) - F_{t,T} > 0$

Notice that part of the reverse cash-and-carry strategy is to borrow the amount of the payout that will be made at time t1. This is because a short-seller must refund positive payouts to the party who lends the commodity or security.[6]

These two arbitrage strategies will drive futures and spot prices back into line according to Equation 2.7. With more than one payout between t and T, the fundamental no-arbitrage equation becomes

$$F_{t,T} = P_t(1 + r_{t,T}) - FV_T(\text{Payouts between t and T}), \qquad (2.7a)$$

where FV_T refers to the future value as of the contract expiration date, T.[7] Positive payouts reduce the equilibrium futures price, and negative payouts increase it. The implied repo and reverse repo rates can be easily adjusted to account for such payouts by including the future value of the payouts in the cash inflow or cash outflow at time T. Alternatively, by dividing Equation 2.7a by P_t and rearranging, we get

$$\frac{F_{t,T} - P_t}{P_t} = r_{t,T} - \left(\frac{FV_T(\text{Payouts between t and T})}{P_t} \right), \qquad (2.7b)$$

which says that the percentage differential between the futures and spot prices equals the short-term interest rate less the nonannualized payout rate.

Example 2.3 uses the S&P 1 futures contract to show how payouts can affect arbitrage strategies when dividends are paid on IBM stock.

▪ **Example 2.3: S&P 1 Arbitrage with Dividends**   Suppose IBM stock is selling for $140 per share and IBM pays a $1 dividend quarterly, with the next payout due in three months. Suppose also that the S&P 1 futures price for delivery

---

[6] If the payout is negative, such as cost of storage, the lender should be willing to refund the cost to the borrower. This is because the lender saves on storage costs. Competition among those lending for purposes of a short sale will ensure that the borrower receives this saving of storage costs. Thus, an arbitrageur who performs a reverse cash-and-carry strategy will receive a cash inflow at time t1 that can be lent out. We will return to this point later in the chapter.

[7] The future value of a payment is that payment plus any interest earned by investing it. For example, if the interest rate is 10 percent, the future value of $100 three years from now is $100(1.10)^3 = 133.10.

in one year is $148 and that an arbitrageur can borrow and lend at a 10 percent annual rate.[8] Is there an arbitrage opportunity?

We will check for arbitrage opportunities by determining whether the fundamental no-arbitrage equation holds. Ignoring compounding, the future value of the dividends in one year is

Future value of payouts

$$= \$1\left(1 + \frac{9}{12} \times 0.10\right) + \$1\left(1 + \frac{6}{12} \times 0.10\right) + \$1\left(1 + \frac{3}{12} \times 0.10\right) + \$1$$

$$= \$1(1.075) + \$1(1.050) + \$1(1.025) + \$1$$

$$= \$4.15.$$

Therefore, the no-arbitrage equation is

Spot price + Interest − Future value of payouts
$$= \$140 + (0.10)\$140 − \$4.15$$
$$= \$149.85 > \$148$$
$$= \text{Futures price.}$$

Because the futures price is less than the no-arbitrage spot price, the arbitrageur should perform a reverse cash-and-carry arbitrage:

Arbitrage Strategy

Transaction	t	t → T	T
Short IBM stock	$140	Pay $1 per quarter	$-F_{T,T}$ (take delivery)
Borrow dividend		Borrow $1 per quarter	$-\$4.15$
Buy short-term securities (lend)	$-\$140$		$140(1.10) = \$154$
Go long futures	0		$F_{T,T} - \$148$
Net	0	0	$1.85

At time t, the arbitrageur goes long the relatively underpriced futures and sells short the relatively overpriced stock. At the end of the year, he or she takes delivery in the futures market to obtain the IBM stock. The arbitrageur returns this stock to the party from whom he or she initially borrowed it. By borrowing $1 each quarter, the arbitrageur can pay the $1-per-quarter dividend to the lender of the stock. With zero outlay, the arbitrageur has guaranteed a profit of $1.85 per share in one year.

We get the same result by comparing the arbitrageur's synthetic borrowing rate with his or her 10 percent lending rate. The synthetic borrowing rate from a reverse cash-and-carry is

---

[8] In the next section, we will relax the assumption that the borrowing and lending rates are equal.

$$\text{Implied reverse repo rate} = \frac{\text{Cash outflow at T} - \text{Cash inflow at t}}{\text{Cash inflow at t}}$$

$$= \frac{(\$148 + \$4.15) - \$140}{\$140}$$

$$= 8.68\% < 10\%.$$

■

Net Carry   One implication of Equation 2.7a is that the relationship between the futures price and the spot price depends on the difference between the interest cost and the future value of the payouts. This difference represents the interest cost of carrying the underlying asset less any payouts to the holder of the asset. It is known as the **net carry** and is usually expressed as a percentage of the price:

$$\text{Net carry} = \frac{\text{Interest} - \text{Future value of payouts}}{P_t}$$

$$= r_{t,T} - \left(\frac{FV_T(\text{Payouts between t and T})}{P_t} \right).$$

Thus, we can rewrite Equation 2.7a as[9]

$$F_{t,T} = P_t + (\text{Net carry})(P_t). \tag{2.7c}$$

Equation 2.7c shows that the spot price can exceed the futures price if the net carry is negative. If the payout from holding an underlying asset is negative, the future value of the payout will be negative and the net carry must be positive. In this case, the futures price must exceed the spot price in equilibrium. This is typical for most physical commodities, which require the payment of physical storage costs and return no payouts to the owner.

Example 2.4 demonstrates how dividends affect the price of the Standard and Poor's 500 stock index futures contract.

▪ **Example 2.4: Arbitrage Pricing of the Standard and Poor's 500 Contract**
We can see how expected dividends affect futures prices by examining the prices of the Standard and Poor's 500 futures contract on May 23, 1989. Recall that the S&P 500 contract is very similar to the hypothetical S&P 1 contract we have been illustrating in this chapter except that it is written on an index of 500 stocks instead of 1. We will examine the S&P 500 contract in detail in Chapter 4.

The excerpt from *The Wall Street Journal* shown in Figure 2.1 quotes the prices of the spot S&P 500 Index and the S&P 500 futures contracts and the Treasury bill yields at the close of markets on May 23, 1989. The closing spot index

---

[9] See Working [1948] for one of the original presentations of this equation.

Figure 2.1 Transactions on Spot S&P 500 Index, Stock Index Futures Contracts, and Treasury Bill Yields, May 23, 1989

U.S. Treas. Bills				Mat. date	Bid	Asked	Yield
Mat. date	Bid	Asked	Yield				
		Discount					
-1989-				9-21	8.33	8.29	8.64
5-25	7.41	7.19	7.29	9-28	8.32	8.28	8.65
6- 1	8.31	8.19	8.32	10- 5	8.31	8.27	8.65
6- 8	8.56	8.49	8.64	10-12	8.31	8.27	8.67
6-15	8.26	8.19	8.35	10-19	8.32	8.28	8.69
6-22	8.30	8.23	8.40	10-26	8.36	8.32	8.75
6-29	8.35	8.28	8.47	11- 2	8.31	8.28	8.72
7- 6	8.38	8.34	8.54	11- 9	8.33	8.29	8.75
7-13	8.37	8.33	8.54	11-16	8.32	8.29	8.76
7-20	8.37	8.34	8.57	11-24	8.32	8.28	8.76
7-27	8.37	8.33	8.57	12-21	8.23	8.19	8.67
8- 3	8.41	8.37	8.63				
8-10	8.35	8.32	8.59	-1990-			
8-17	8.35	8.31	8.59	1-18	8.20	8.14	8.64
8-24	8.29	8.25	8.54	2-15	8.22	8.16	8.69
8-31	8.29	8.25	8.56	3-15	8.20	8.16	8.72
9- 7	8.31	8.27	8.59	4-12	8.18	8.14	8.74
9-14	8.30	8.26	8.60	5-10	8.17	8.14	8.78

S&P 500 INDEX (CME) 500 times index

	Open	High	Low	Settle	Chg	High	Low	Open Interest
June	322.60	322.85	319.75	320.10	− 3.50	325.00	263.80	123,884
Sept	327.00	327.25	324.15	324.45	− 3.55	329.40	271.50	17,286
Dec	331.40	331.40	328.30	328.65	− 3.60	333.60	298.90	1,295

Est vol 47,059; vol Mon 53,670; open int 142,466, +813.
Indx prelim High 321.98; Low 318.20; Close 318.30−3.66

NYSE COMPOSITE INDEX (NYFE) 500 times index

	Open	High	Low	Settle	Chg	High	Low	Open Interest
June	179.75	179.90	178.35	178.50	− 1.75	181.05	149.60	5,407
Sept	182.15	182.25	180.80	180.85	− 1.80	183.50	153.90	1,342
Dec	184.50	184.50	183.95	183.20	− 1.90	185.70	161.10	415

Est vol 6,890; vol Mon5,900; open int 7,223, +16.
The index: High 179.34; Low 177.56; Close 177.61 −1.73

MAJOR MKT INDEX (CBT) $250 times index

	Open	High	Low	Settle	Chg	High	Low	Open Interest
June	491.90	492.20	488.00	488.60	− 4.85	496.40	442.50	2,285
July	495.00	495.20	491.50	491.80	− 4.90	499.60	469.10	564

Est vol 4,000; vol Mon 2,472; open int 2,849, −12,563.
The index: High 491.49; Low 485.58; Close 486.14 −5.35

KC VALUE LINE INDEX (KC) 500 times index

	Open	High	Low	Settle	Chg	High	Low	Open Interest
June	283.80	283.85	282.20	282.60	− 1.90	285.60	245.65	1,264
Sept	287.65	287.65	286.60	286.80	− 1.90	289.10	267.40	133

Est vol 105; vol Mon 181; open int 1,400, −1.
The index: High 281.93; Low 280.60; Close 280.67 −1.23

CRB INDEX (NYFE) 500 times Index

	Open	High	Low	Settle	Chg	High	Low	Open Interest
July	233.15	234.45	232.60	232.65	− .10	250.50	232.60	1,409
Sept	234.90	235.50	234.15	234.20	− .30	249.10	234.15	247
Dec	235.50	235.50	235.15	234.70	− .30	245.25	235.15	278

Est vol 822; vol Mon1,095; open int 1,984, +228.
The index: High 234.08; Low 232.45; Close 232.45 −.87

−OTHER INDEX FUTURES−

Settlement price of selected contract. Volume and open interest of all contract months.

KC Mini Value Line (KC) 100 times Index
Jun 282.60 −1.90; Est. vol. 15; Open Int. 104

CBT−Chicago Board of Trade. CME−Chicago Mercantile Exchange. KC−Kansas City Board of Trade. NYFE−New York Futures Exchange, a unit of the New York Stock Exchange.

Source: *The Wall Street Journal,* May 24, 1989.

value for the S&P 500 was 318.30. The futures settlement price for the contract with a September 15 expiration date was 324.45.[10] The annualized yield on T-bills due to expire on September 14 was 8.60 percent.[11] As there were 115 days between May 23 and September 15 in 1989, the nonannualized 115-day riskless rate was approximately $(8.60\%)(115/360) = 2.75\%$.

Equation 2.7b shows that the nonannualized payout rate implied by the futures and spot prices was:

$$\text{Payout rate} = 2.75\% - \frac{324.45 - 318.30}{318.30}$$
$$= 2.75\% - 1.93\%$$
$$= 0.82\% \text{ for 115 days}$$
$$= 2.57\% \text{ annualized.}$$

Thus, the market expected that the S&P 500 Index would pay dividends at an annual rate of 2.57% between May 23 and September 15. The net carry was

$$\text{Net carry} = r_{t,T} - \left(\frac{FV_T(\text{Dividends between } t \text{ and } T)}{P_t} \right)$$
$$= 2.75\% - 0.82\%$$
$$= 1.93\% \text{ for 115 days}$$
$$= 6.04\% \text{ annualized.}$$

Calendar Spreads and Arbitrage

We have demonstrated how arbitrage trading maintains the fundamental no-arbitrage relationship between futures and spot prices. Arbitrage strategies also drive the pricing relationships among different-maturity futures contracts written on the same asset.

For simplicity, consider a futures contract on a commodity or security that has no payouts. Suppose we wish to compare the futures prices at time t on contracts that expire at times T1 and T2, where T2 is later than T1:

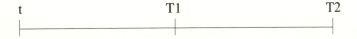

We denote the prices of these futures contracts as

$F_{t,T1}$ = futures price at t for contracts that expire at T1

$F_{t,T2}$ = futures price at t for contracts that expire at T2

The fundamental no-arbitrage pricing relationship between these futures contracts is

$$F_{t,T2} = F_{t,T1}(1 + r_{T1,T2}), \tag{2.10}$$

where we assume that one can borrow and lend between T1 and T2 at a (non-annualized) interest rate of $r_{T1,T2}$. Arbitrageurs can make profits if Equation 2.10 does not hold. For example, if

$$F_{t,T2} > F_{t,T1}(1 + r_{T1,T2}), \tag{2.11}$$

the following strategy will yield a riskless arbitrage profit:

Arbitrage Strategy

Transaction	t	T1	T2
Go long T1 futures	0	$F_{T1,T1} - F_{t,T1}$	
Go short T2 futures	0		$F_{t,T2} - F_{T2,T2}$
Borrow $F_{t,T1}$ at T1		$F_{t,T1}$	$-F_{t,T1}(1 + r_{T1,T2})$
Take delivery at T1		$-F_{T1,T1} = -P_{T1}$	
Deliver at T2			$F_{T2,T2} = P_{T2}$
Net	0	0	$F_{t,T2} - F_{t,T1}(1 + r_{T1,T2}) > 0$

We call this strategy a **forward cash-and-carry arbitrage**. It is similar to a cash-and-carry arbitrage, except that it is performed between times T1 and T2, rather than between times t and T. By going long the T1 contract, the arbitrageur locks in the price of purchasing the commodity or security at T1. By going short the T2 contract, the arbitrageur locks in a selling price at T2. This strategy ensures a positive profit at time T2 with no net investment at times t and T1. The borrowing rate $r_{T1,T2}$ between T1 and T2 must be known at time t to determine whether such an arbitrage opportunity exists.[12] Later we will see that one can lock in this rate using interest rate futures.

Such forward cash-and-carry arbitrages will drive futures prices across time back into line with one another. Buying pressure will force $F_{t,T1}$ up, and selling pressure will force $F_{t,T2}$ down.

We can also discover the forward cash-and-carry arbitrage opportunity by computing the rate of return locked in by a forward cash-and-carry between T1 and T2. This strategy effectively locks in an arrangement to lend $F_{t,T1}$ at T1 and receive $F_{t,T2}$ at T2. The **forward implied repo rate** earned is

$$\frac{F_{t,T2} - F_{t,T1}}{F_{t,T1}} = \frac{\text{Cash inflow at T2} - \text{Cash outflow at T1}}{\text{Cash outflow at T1}} \tag{2.12}$$

---

[12] The arbitrageur's borrowing of $F_{t,T1}$ at time T1 will cover both the cost of buying the commodity or security at time T1 and any futures gains or losses.

There is a forward cash-and-carry arbitrage if

Forward implied repo rate > Borrowing rate from T1 to T2.

Thus, there is an exact analog between a cash-and-carry arbitrage and a forward cash-and-carry arbitrage.

Example 2.5 illustrates a forward cash-and-carry arbitrage with a gold futures contract.

▪ **Example 2.5: Forward Cash-and-Carry Arbitrage with Gold**   Suppose a trader observes the following prices on June 15:

Futures price of gold for September 15 delivery	$450 per ounce
Futures price of gold for December 15 delivery	$460 per ounce
Borrowing and lending rate	6% per annum

In this case, $T2 - T1 = 3$ months, or 0.25 years. Ignoring compounding, the nonannualized interest rate is

$$r_{T1,T2} = 6\%(0.25) = 1.5\% \text{ over 3 months.}$$

The fundamental no-arbitrage equation shows that a forward cash-and-carry arbitrage opportunity exists:

$$F_{t,T2} = \$460 > \$450(1.015)$$
$$= \$456.75$$
$$= F_{t,T1}(1 + r_{T1,T2}).$$

The forward cash-and-carry arbitrage strategy entails the following steps:

1. On June 15, go long September 15 futures and go short December 15 futures.

2. On September 15, borrow $450 and buy an ounce of gold at the $450 net price locked in by the long futures position. No cash outflow will be required. Hold the gold until December 15.

3. On December 15, deliver the gold and receive the $460 locked in by the short futures position. Pay back the $456.75 owed on the loan taken out on September 15.

The arbitrage profit is $460 - $456.75 = $3.25 per ounce.

We can also demonstrate this arbitrage opportunity by looking at the forward implied repo rate:

$$\text{Forward implied repo rate} = \frac{\$460 - \$450}{\$450}$$
$$= 2.22\%.$$

This synthetic forward lending rate exceeds the quarterly borrowing rate of 1.5 percent, so a forward cash-and-carry arbitrage clearly is available. ▪

A forward arbitrage opportunity also exists if

$$F_{t,T2} < F_{t,T1}(1 + r_{T1,T2}).$$

(2.13)

The appropriate strategy in this case is

| | | Arbitrage Strategy | |
Transaction	t	T1	T2
Go short T1 futures	0	$F_{t,T1} - F_{T1,T1}$	
Go long T2 futures	0		$F_{T2,T2} - F_{t,T2}$
Borrow asset and deliver		$F_{T1,T1} = P_{T1}$	
Lend proceeds		$-F_{t,T1}$	$F_{t,T1}(1 + r_{T1,T2})$
Take delivery and pay back on short sale			$-F_{T2,T2} = -P_{T2}$
Net	0	0	$-F_{t,T2} + F_{t,T1}(1 + r_{T1,T2}) > 0$

This strategy is a **forward reverse cash-and-carry arbitrage**. It is similar to a reverse cash-and-carry arbitrage except that it is performed between times T1 and T2 rather than between times t and T. By going short futures that expire at T1, the arbitrageur locks in the price received for short-selling the commodity or security at T1. The arbitrageur effectively borrows $F_{t,T1}$ at T1 and pays back $F_{t,T2}$ at T2. A forward reverse cash-and-carry arbitrage occurs when

Forward implied reverse repo rate < Lending rate from T1 and T2.

Commodities or Securities with Payouts   The fundamental no-arbitrage equation must be modified if payouts between times T1 and T2 are associated with the underlying commodity or security. In such a case, the fundamental no-arbitrage equation becomes

$$F_{t,T2} = F_{t,T1}(1 + r_{T1,T2}) - FV_{T2}(\text{Payouts between T1 and T2}),$$

(2.14)

where FV_{T2}(Payouts between T1 and T2) is the future value of the payouts as of time T2. Thus, the appropriate future value for a payout of C_1 at time t1, where T1 < t1 < T2, is

$$FV_{T2}(C_1) = C_1(1 + r_{t1,T2}).$$

Transactions Costs and Arbitrage

Up to this point, we have assumed that pure arbitrageurs can trade without incurring transactions costs. Of course, this clearly is not the case in the real world. The costs of trading in the futures and spot markets will affect the fundamental no-arbitrage relationships. In this section, we will adjust the no-arbitrage equation to account for such costs.

Types of Transactions Costs

Several types of transactions costs affect opportunities for arbitrage.

Bid-Ask Spreads   When trading in commodities, securities, or futures, one pays a higher price to buy than one receives to sell. For example, to buy a share of IBM stock, one might pay an **ask** price of $140.125; yet selling a share of IBM stock might bring in a **bid** price of only $139.875. The difference between the bid price and the ask price is called the **bid-ask spread**. Similarly, the price at which one can go long a futures contract (the ask) is higher than the price at which one can go short (the bid).[13]

Margins and Short-Selling Costs   A trader who enters into a cash-and-carry pure arbitrage must borrow to finance the purchase of the commodity or security. The amount one can borrow against such a purchase often is restricted. For example, an individual investor can borrow only 50 percent of the cost of buying a stock from a broker. A financial institution such as an investment bank typically can borrow somewhat more depending on its overall borrowing position.

There are also restrictions and transactions costs associated with short-selling. One must wait until an "uptick" to perform a short sale. The proceeds from a short sale often must be lent back at a penalty rate to the firm that originally lent out the commodity or security. This penalty rate may be around 80 percent of the market lending rate. The lender of the asset may also require a small additional margin.

Differential Borrowing and Lending Rates   Market participants typically pay rates for borrowing that are higher than those they receive for lending. Otherwise, there would be an obvious arbitrage.

Transactions Fees   One must pay a broker's fee when buying or selling commodities and securities or entering into futures positions. The total brokerage fee paid for buying and selling a futures contract is called the **round-trip fee**. One can also incur transactions fees when borrowing or lending. For example, buying or selling a T-bill may require payment of a brokerage fee.

Notice that we use the term *transactions fees* to refer to the specific charges levied on traders who buy and sell. The term *transactions costs* refers to all costs traders encounter in the marketplace, including transactions fees, bid-ask spreads, margins, short-selling costs, and differential borrowing and lending rates.

---

[13] The terms *bid* and *ask* come from the dealer's view of the transaction. When an investor wishes to sell a security, he or receives what the dealer bids. When an investor wishes to buy a security, he or she pays what the dealer asks.

Cash-and-Carry and Reverse Cash-and-Carry Arbitrage

Transactions costs in the futures and spot markets affect arbitrage trading through their influence on implied repo and reverse repo rates and borrowing and lending rates. We will include transactions costs in our discussion of arbitrage by altering the formulas for these rates with the following notation (for simplicity we will ignore payouts for now):

P_t^b = bid price for spot commodity or security

P_t^a = ask price for spot commodity or security

$F_{t,T}^b$ = bid price for futures contract (price for going short)

$F_{t,T}^a$ = ask price for futures contract (price for going long)

TF = total transactions fees

$r_{t,T}^b$ = borrowing rate between t and T

$r_{t,T}^l$ = lending rate between t and T

When transactions costs are included, the cash-and-carry strategy is to buy the spot commodity or security at the ask price and lock in a sales price at the futures bid price. We take transactions fees to be the *future value* of any fees as of time T.[14] For convenience, we will consolidate all transactions fees in our calculation of the implied repo rate:[15]

$$\text{Implied repo rate} = \frac{\text{Cash inflow at T} - \text{Cash outflow at t}}{\text{Cash outflow at t}} \quad \quad \textbf{(2.15)}$$

$$= \frac{(F_{t,T}^b - TF) - P_t^a}{P_t^a}.$$

In a reverse cash-and-carry with transactions costs, the arbitrageur sells the spot commodity or security short at the bid price and covers the short position by locking in a purchase price equal to the futures ask price. The implied reverse repo rate paid on this strategy is

[14] We use the future value of transactions fees purely for convenience. We would get the same answer if we worked with the present value of transactions fees. In that case, we would subtract the transactions fees from the denominator of Equation 2.15.

[15] Alternatively, we could account for borrowing and lending transactions fees through the borrowing and lending rate. Later we will see why it is useful to consolidate all transactions fees in the implied repo rate calculation.

$$\text{Implied reverse repo rate} = \frac{\text{Cash outflow at T} - \text{Cash inflow at t}}{\text{Cash inflow at t}} \qquad (2.16)$$

$$= \frac{(F^a_{t,T} + TF) - P^b_t}{P^b_t}.$$

The transactions fees enter negatively into the numerator of the implied repo rate because they are deducted from the amount received upon selling the commodity or security. They enter positively into the numerator of the implied reverse repo rate because they are added to the cost of obtaining the commodity or security to cover the short position.

From Equations 2.15 and 2.16, we see that

Implied reverse repo rate > Implied repo rate
Synthetic borrowing rate > Synthetic lending rate.

This is because bid prices are below ask prices and transactions fees are positive. Thus, the denominator of Equation 2.15 is greater than that of the denominator of Equation 2.16, and the numerator of Equation 2.15 is less than the numerator of Equation 2.16. If the inequality went the other way so that the implied repo rate exceeded the implied reverse repo rate, we could borrow synthetically at a lower rate than we could lend synthetically. This would be an immediate arbitrage.

Transactions costs affect the fundamental no-arbitrage futures price because they affect opportunities for pure arbitrage. If there are to be no arbitrage opportunities, the implied repo rate must be less than the borrowing rate. This implies that

$$\frac{F^b_{t,T} - TF - P^a_t}{P^a_t} \leq r^b_{t,T} \qquad (2.17)$$

or

$$F^b_{t,T} \leq P^a_t(1 + r^b_{t,T}) + TF.$$

Similarly, the implied reverse repo rate must be greater than the lending rate. This implies that

$$\frac{F^a_{t,T} + TF - P^b_t}{P^b_t} \geq r^l_{t,T} \qquad (2.18)$$

or

$$F^a_{t,T} \geq P^b_t(1 + r^l_{t,T}) - TF.$$

In most futures markets, the difference between the futures bid and ask prices is very small, usually one "tick." So, if we let $F_{t,T} = F^a_{t,T} = F^b_{t,T}$ and combine Equations 2.17 and 2.18, we get

$$P_t^b(1 + r_{t,T}^l) - TF \le F_{t,T} \le P_t^a(1 + r_{t,T}^b) + TF. \tag{2.19}$$

Thus, the futures price is not determined exactly as in Equation 2.4, our simplest no-arbitrage relationship. The transactions costs of performing arbitrages introduce some "play" into futures prices. We call the left-hand side of Equation 2.19 the **no-arbitrage lower bound** and the right-hand side the **no-arbitrage upper bound**. No arbitrage opportunities exist when the futures price is between these price bounds, for the inflows from arbitrage strategies do not cover the transactions costs incurred.

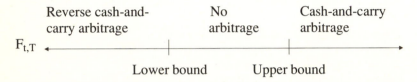

Example 2.6 demonstrates the effects of transactions costs on futures prices using the S&P 1 futures contract.

- **Example 2.6: Transactions Costs and Arbitrage with the S&P 1 Futures Contract**   Suppose an arbitrageur observes the following prices and rates:

Bid price on IBM stock	$139.90
Ask price on IBM stock	$140.10
S&P 1 futures bid price	$154.90
S&P 1 futures ask price	$155.10
Bid price on a $1-million-face-value 1-year T-bill	$908,678.00
Ask price on a $1-million-face-value 1-year T-bill	$909,504.00
Broker call rate	10.50%
Arbitrageur's normal borrowing rate	11.00%
Transactions fees (per share basis):	$0.015
−Stocks	$0.008
−Futures	$0.002
−Borrowing or lending	$0.005

The arbitrageur wishes to determine if there is an opportunity for pure arbitrage in this situation. (For simplicity, we will ignore dividends for now.) First, he will check for cash-and-carry arbitrage opportunities. A cash-and-carry strategy would involve purchasing the stock at the ask price of $140.10 and going short the futures at the bid price of $154.90. This would yield an implied repo rate of

$$\text{Implied repo rate} = \frac{\$154.90 - \$0.015 - \$140.10}{\$140.10}$$

$$= 10.55\%.$$

Suppose margin requirements allow borrowing of only 50 percent of the cost of the stock at the broker call rate. The arbitrageur must obtain the remaining 50 percent at the normal borrowing rate. Thus, the borrowing rate for the arbitrageur is

$$\text{Borrowing rate} = (0.50)(10.50\%) + (0.50)(11.00\%)$$
$$= 10.75\%.$$

There appears to be no cash-and-carry arbitrage, because the arbitrageur is able to borrow at only 10.75 percent and lend synthetically at the implied repo rate of 10.55 percent.

The implied reverse repo rate paid on a reverse cash-and-carry in this situation would be

$$\text{Implied reverse repo rate} = \frac{\$155.10 + \$0.015 - \$139.90}{\$139.90}$$
$$= 10.88\%.$$

When the arbitrageur shorts IBM stock in this reverse cash-and-carry, he must place the short-sale proceeds with the party who lent the stock. The rate this party pays typically is about 80 percent of the broker call rate.[16] The arbitrageur's lending rate is, therefore,

$$\text{Lending rate} = (0.80)(10.50\%)$$
$$= 8.40\%.$$

There appears to be no reverse cash-and-carry arbitrage either, because the arbitrageur is able to borrow synthetically only at 10.88 percent and lend at 8.40 percent.

We can also tell that there are no arbitrages by computing the price bounds in Equation 2.19:

$$\text{Lower bound} = P_t^b(1 + r_{t,T}^l) - TF$$
$$= \$139.90(1.0840) - \$0.015$$
$$= \$151.64.$$
$$\text{Upper bound} = P_t^a(1 + r_{t,T}^b) + TF$$
$$= \$140.10(1.1075) + \$0.015$$
$$= \$155.18.$$

Both the futures bid price of $154.90 and the futures ask price of $155.10 lie between the upper and lower bound, so clearly no arbitrage opportunity exists. ∎

The difference between the lower and upper bounds on the futures price in Example 2.6 appears quite large. In the next section, we will see how market participants who have lower transactions costs than do pure arbitrageurs can tighten the no-arbitrage bounds considerably.

---

[16] In addition, the arbitrageur must put up around 102 percent of the funds received. This margin of around 2 percent slightly reduces the effective lending rate.

Quasi-Arbitrage

Pure arbitrageurs are not the only financial market participants who can benefit by trading between the spot and futures markets and among futures contracts with different maturities. A corporation that is planning to lend might be able to earn a higher return by doing so through a cash-and-carry strategy. Likewise, someone who wants to borrow might be able to do so more cheaply through a reverse cash-and-carry. In these examples, cash-and-carry and reverse cash-and-carry strategies are used as alternative methods of establishing desired positions. This approach is called **quasi-arbitrage**.

In this section, we show how financial market participants can take a variety of positions by using futures to create those positions synthetically. We also show how to use the concepts of cash-and-carry and reverse cash-and-carry arbitrage to determine whether it is preferable to establish a position directly or through a synthetic alternative offered by a futures strategy.

Creating Synthetic Securities

In our discussion of pure arbitrage, we saw that one can create synthetic long and short T-bill positions through arbitrage trades in the futures and spot markets. This approach can be varied to create synthetic positions in the underlying assets of futures contracts and in the futures contracts themselves as well.

Recall that an investor can create a synthetic long T-bill position through the cash-and-carry strategy of buying the underlying commodity or security and going short the futures. The following simple equation summarizes this strategy:

$$\text{Spot} - \text{Futures} = \text{Synthetic T-bill} \qquad \textbf{I.}$$

where a minus sign indicates a short position.

This equation can be rewritten to show how to create other synthetic positions. For example, it shows that we can buy the underlying asset synthetically by purchasing a T-bill and going long the futures:

$$\text{T-bill} + \text{Futures} = \text{Synthetic spot.} \qquad \textbf{II.}$$

We can see how this strategy creates a synthetic spot position by examining its cash flows:

Transaction	t	T
Buy T-bills	$-P_t$	$P_t(1 + r_{t,T})$
Long futures		$F_{T,T} - F_{t,T}$
Net	$-P_t$	$F_{T,T} - F_{t,T} + P_t(1 + r_{t,T})$ $= P_T - [F_{t,T} - P_t(1 + r_{t,T})]$ $= P_T - \Omega$

In this strategy,

$$\Omega = F_{t,T} - P_t(1 + r_{t,T})$$

indicates whether the futures is cheap or expensive relative to the spot market.

At time t, the strategy involves buying T-bills in an amount equal to the desired holdings of the synthetic spot asset. In the above table, this means buying P_t worth of T-bills where P_t is the price of one unit of the spot asset. The face value of this T-bill purchase is $P_t(1 + r_{t,T})$. Thus, at time t, there is a net outflow equal to the price of the spot asset.

At time T, the T-bill matures and the futures contract expires. The total profit or loss on the futures contract is $F_{T,T} - F_{t,T}$. By the delivery date arbitrage condition, the futures price at time T is equal to the current spot price of the underlying asset, P_T. Therefore, the net cash flow at time T is $P_T - \Omega$. If the fundamental no-arbitrage condition holds, $\Omega = 0$ and the net cash flow at time T is P_T. The net cash flows of this strategy are thus exactly the same as if the spot asset were bought at time t and held until time T. We have created a synthetic spot asset position.

If $\Omega < 0$, the return is greater on the synthetic spot asset position than on the actual spot asset. The futures contract is cheap relative to the spot asset, so a synthetic position that utilizes a long futures position is superior to the spot asset position. If $\Omega > 0$, the spot asset has a higher yield than the synthetic position, because the futures is expensive relative to the spot asset. Since Ω is known at time t, it is easy to determine whether or not a synthetic spot position is advantageous.

Our simple equation also shows that we can create a synthetic long futures position by buying the underlying asset and going short a T-bill:

Spot – T-bill = Synthetic futures.   **III.**

We can see how this strategy creates a synthetic futures position by examining its cash flows:

Transaction	t	T
Short T-bills	P_t	$-P_t(1 + r_{t,T})$
Buy spot	$-P_t$	P_T
Net	0	$P_T - P_t(1 + r_{t,T})$ $= F_{T,T} - P_t(1 + r_{t,T})$ $= F_{T,T} - F_{t,T} + \Omega$

The position requires no net outflow at time t. At time T, it returns the market price of the asset less the face value of the T-bill position, $P_t(1 + r_{t,T})$. After some rearranging, we can see that this cash inflow is identical to the return from a long futures position plus the remainder, Ω. Thus, when the fundamental no-arbitrage condition holds and $\Omega = 0$, this strategy is equivalent to a long futures position. In this case, creating a long futures position is exactly the same as borrowing to buy a commodity or security. If $\Omega > 0$, the futures is expensive relative to the spot. It pays to use the alternative strategy that replicates the long futures with a synthetic position that involves a spot purchase. If $\Omega < 0$, the original long futures position is superior.

Our simple relationship among spot, futures, and T-bill positions also shows that synthetic short positions can be created by taking opposite positions in each of the relationship's components. For example, a reverse cash-and-carry involves simply taking the opposite positions of a cash-and-carry (case I):

$$-\text{Spot} + \text{Futures} = -\text{Synthetic T-bill.}\qquad\qquad\textbf{IV.}$$

Similarly, we can create synthetic short spot positions and synthetic short futures positions by taking the opposite positions in cases II and III.

Synthetic Forward Securities   Just as it is possible to use cash-and-carry and reverse cash-and-carry strategies to create synthetic positions, it is possible to use forward strategies to create synthetic forward positions. The forward cash-and-carry strategy can be summarized as a simple equation:

T1 Futures + Spot between T1 and T2 – T2 Futures
    = Synthetic T-bill between T1 and T2,

where "Spot between T1 and T2" refers to purchasing the spot asset at time T1 and carrying it until time T2.

As with the synthetic positions described earlier, the permutations of this equation show how to create a variety of synthetic forward positions. One example is a synthetic forward spot position:

T2 Futures – T1 Futures + T-bill between T1 and T2
    = Synthetic spot between T1 and T2.

Another example is a synthetic borrowing position between T1 and T2:

T2 Futures – T1 Futures – Spot between T1 and T2
    = –Synthetic T-bill between T1 and T2.

The latter position is simply a forward reverse cash-and-carry.

Using the Fundamental No-Arbitrage Equation

We have just seen how quasi-arbitrageurs can create synthetic T-bill, spot, and futures positions. Their choice between taking a position synthetically or directly depends on

$$\Omega = F_{t,T} - P_t(1 + r_{t,T}).\qquad\qquad(2.20)$$

This is exactly the same equation the pure arbitrageur examines to determine whether or not a pure arbitrage exists. If $\Omega > 0$, the pure arbitrageur uses a cash-and-carry pure arbitrage and Ω represents the profit per futures contract. If $\Omega < 0$, he or she uses a reverse cash-and-carry pure arbitrage and $-\Omega$ represents the profit per futures contract. If $\Omega = 0$, the futures is priced appropriately and there is no pure arbitrage. Thus, if there were no transactions costs and pure arbitrageurs traded until $\Omega = 0$, neither a synthetic nor direct strategy would be preferable to the other.

Since in the real world pure and quasi-arbitrageurs face transactions costs, they must include such costs in their calculations of Ω before they can determine whether arbitrage opportunities exist. As cash-and-carry and reverse cash-and-carry strategies have different transactions costs, Ω differs depending on which type of arbitrage is being considered. An arbitrageur who suspects there is a cash-and-carry arbitrage will examine:[17]

$$\Omega^c = F_{t,T} - [P_t(1 + r_{t,T}) + TF], \qquad (2.21)$$

where the prices, interest rate, and transactions fees are all appropriate for a cash-and-carry strategy. Notice that the transactions fees are added to the grossed-up spot price in Equation 2.21. This is because a cash-and-carry arbitrage exists only if the futures price locked in by the short futures position covers both the cost of carrying the underlying asset and the fees incurred by engaging in the arbitrage. Therefore, a cash-and-carry arbitrage opportunity exists if $\Omega^c > 0$.

An arbitrageur in search of a reverse cash-and-carry arbitrage will compute:[18]

$$\Omega^r = F_{t,T} - [P_t(1 + r_{t,T}) - TF], \qquad (2.22)$$

where all the variables are appropriate for a reverse cash-and-carry. In this case, the transactions fees are subtracted from the grossed-up spot price. A reverse cash-and-carry arbitrage opportunity exists only if the grossed-up proceeds from the short sale of the underlying asset minus the fees incurred by entering into the arbitrage exceed the futures purchase price locked in by the long futures position. Therefore, a reverse cash-and-carry arbitrage opportunity exists if $\Omega^r < 0$.

When we include transactions costs in this way, we find that opportunities for quasi-arbitrage sometimes may exist when opportunities for pure arbitrage do not. This is because many financial market participants can trade at lower cost than pure arbitrageurs can. Example 2.7 illustrates such a case.

▪ **Example 2.7: Choosing between Synthetic and Actual T-Bills**   Suppose a corporate treasurer has $500 million that she wishes to invest in a riskless instrument that matures in one year. Assume also that the bid and ask prices for one-year T-bills and the futures and stock prices are the same as in Example 2.6. The standard practice in such a situation is to invest in one-year T-bills. To do this, the treasurer must buy the T-bills at the ask price. Over the year, the T-bills will yield

$$\text{T-bill rate earned} = \frac{\$1,000,000 - \$909,504}{\$909,504}$$
$$= 9.95\%.$$

---

[17] The arbitrageur will examine $\Omega^c = F_{t,T} - [P_t(1 + r_{t,T}) - FV(\text{Payouts}) + TF]$ if there are payouts.

[18] The arbitrageur will examine $\Omega^r = F_{t,T} - [P_t(1 + r_{t,T}) - FV(\text{Payouts}) - TF]$ if there are payouts.

The treasurer is also considering the alternative strategy of using a cash-and-carry to create a *synthetic* T-bill. The pure arbitrageur in Example 2.6 can earn an implied repo rate of 10.55 percent on a cash-and-carry. But the corporate treasurer can do slightly better, because she has to pay fewer transactions fees. The pure arbitrageur must pay transactions fees when buying the stock, going short futures, and borrowing. The corporate treasurer also pays transactions fees when buying the stock and going short futures. However, she *saves* the transactions fees she would have had to pay had she purchased T-bills directly. *Relative to her benchmark,* it is as if she received a rebate of the cost of purchasing T-bills directly. Her total transactions fees, including the savings from not choosing the direct T-bill investment, are

TF = Stock brokerage fees + Futures brokerage fees
     − Transactions fees for T-bills
  = $0.008 + $0.002 − $0.005
  = $0.005,

and her implied repo rate is

$$\text{Implied repo rate} = \frac{\$154.90 - \$0.005 - \$140.10}{\$140.10}$$
$$= 10.56\%.$$

The cash-and-carry synthetic T-bill obviously is preferable to the direct T-bill investment, because its rate of return exceeds the 9.95 percent return on an actual T-bill. The treasurer has a cash-and-carry quasi-arbitrage opportunity, because she can increase her profits by using a cash-and-carry synthetic lending to replace lending in the spot market.

The cash-and-carry quasi-arbitrage exists because

Implied repo rate > Alternative lending rate

or

$$\frac{F_{t,T}^b - TF - P_t^a}{P_t^a} > \hat{r}_{t,T} \tag{2.23}$$

or

$$F_{t,T}^b > P_t^a(1 + \hat{r}_{t,T}) + TF,$$

where

$\hat{r}_{t,T}$ = alternative lending rate between times t and T (not annualized).

We saw in Equation 2.17 that a cash-and-carry pure arbitrage is profitable if

$$F_{t,T}^b > P_t^a(1 + r_{t,T}^b) + TF. \tag{2.24}$$

Equations 2.23 and 2.24 show that the conditions necessary for a cash-and-carry quasi-arbitrage to exist are similar to those for a cash-and-carry pure arbitrage; that is, the futures should be expensive relative to the cash. The major difference is that the pure arbitrageur compares the implied repo rate to the borrowing rate, $r_{t,T}^b$, while the treasurer compares the implied repo rate to the lower alternative lending rate, $\hat{r}_{t,T}$. Further, as we have seen, the quasi-arbitrageur has lower transactions fees. Therefore, the "fair futures price" the pure arbitrageur uses to determine whether the futures is overpriced is higher than the one the corporate treasurer uses.

Because of these differences, a cash-and-carry quasi-arbitrage opportunity exists even though there is no cash-and-carry pure arbitrage. Recall that in Example 2.6 no pure arbitrage opportunity exists because the arbitrageur's implied repo rate of 10.55 percent is less than his 10.75 percent borrowing rate.

The fundamental no-arbitrage equation also demonstrates the difference between the pure and quasi-arbitrage opportunities. For the pure arbitrageur, Ω^c is

$$\Omega^c = F_{t,T}^b - [P_t^a(1 + r_{t,T}^b) + TF] \tag{2.25}$$
$$= \$154.90 - [\$140.10(1.1075) + \$0.015]$$
$$= \$154.90 - \$155.18 = -\$0.28 < 0.$$

For the corporate treasurer, Ω^c is

$$\Omega^c = F_{t,T}^b - [P_t^a(1 + \hat{r}_{t,T}) + TF] \tag{2.26}$$
$$= \$154.90 - [\$140.10(1.0995) + \$0.005]$$
$$= \$154.90 - \$154.04 = \$0.86 > 0.$$

■

Like pure arbitrage, quasi-arbitrage tends to move prices back into equilibrium. In the cash-and-carry quasi-arbitrage in Example 2.7, the treasurer buys the stock, goes short the futures, and reduces the demand for T-bills. These actions will decrease the implied repo rate and increase the T-bill rate, reducing the value of the quasi-arbitrage opportunity.

Pure arbitrage opportunities tend to disappear more quickly than quasi-arbitrage opportunities. Since pure arbitrageurs make riskless profits with no net investment, they can perform the arbitrage an unlimited number of times. Their repeated trading will cause the pure arbitrage to disappear very rapidly. Trading on quasi-arbitrages, in contrast, can occur at a slower pace. Unlike pure arbitrageurs, quasi-arbitrageurs actually take on net positions. They will perform the quasi-arbitrage only until they attain their desired positions. In Example 2.7, the treasurer can perform the cash-and-carry quasi-arbitrage on only $500 million worth of IBM stock—the amount she would have invested in T-bills.

Finding Quasi-Arbitrage Opportunities

We have seen that both pure and quasi-arbitrageurs use Ω, the difference between the futures price and the "fair," or no-arbitrage, price, to determine whether an arbitrage opportunity is present. While Ω has the same form for pure and quasi-arbitrageurs, as in Equations 2.25 and 2.26 in Example 2.7, it may have different values for each, as in Example 2.7, because the prices, interest rates, and transactions fees involved in the two types of arbitrage differ. In this section, we will develop a systematic approach that determines exactly which prices, interest rates, and transactions fees a given market participant should use to determine the value of the potential arbitrage profit, Ω.

Pure Arbitrage versus Quasi-Arbitrage   The major difference between pure and quasi-arbitrage is that the pure arbitrageur has no initial net position, while the quasi-arbitrageur moves from an initial to a synthetic position. However, we will show that despite this difference, these two kinds of arbitrage are conceptually the same and thus it is useful to think of them as the same.

Consider the pure and quasi-arbitrage strategies in Examples 2.6 and 2.7. The arbitrageur in Example 2.6 could perform a pure cash-and-carry arbitrage by

1.   Buying the future's underlying asset

2.   Going short the futures

3.   Borrowing

The corporate treasurer in Example 2.7 could perform a cash-and-carry quasi-arbitrage by

1.   Buying the future's underlying asset

2.   Going short the futures

3.   Refraining from buying T-bills

The two arbitrages differ in the third step only. However, this step is essentially the same in both cases. The alternative lending rate the quasi-arbitrageur forgoes in the third step can be interpreted as an **effective borrowing rate**, similar to the borrowing rate the pure arbitrageur pays in the third step. The quasi-arbitrageur—the corporate treasurer—is initially a *net lender*. She finances the stock purchase in the first step of the quasi-arbitrage by *reducing* the firm's lending position. In effect, the firm borrows from itself to buy the stock. The cost of such borrowing is the opportunity cost of not lending, or the alternative lending rate. Thus, we say that

Alternative lending rate = Effective borrowing rate,

and we can think of the quasi-arbitrageur as comparing a synthetic lending rate with a borrowing rate, just as the pure arbitrageur does. While this approach to

Table 2.2 Cash-and-Carry Quasi-Arbitrage Table for Corporate Treasurer

Benchmark position: intended investment in T-bills

Cash-and-Carry Pure Arbitrage Components	Cash-and-Carry Quasi-Arbitrage Components	Relevant Price or Rate
1. Buy spot	Buy spot	Ask
2. Short futures	Short futures	Bid
3. Borrow	Refrain from T-bill purchase	T-bill ask

Resulting position: investment in synthetic T-bills

Transactions fees: $TF = TF_1 + TF_2 - TF_3$
1. Pay TF_1
2. Pay TF_2
3. Save TF_3

quasi-arbitrage may seem cumbersome, we will soon see that it actually greatly simplifies the problem of searching for quasi-arbitrage opportunities.

Table 2.2 presents a technique for organizing the transactions in a quasi-arbitrage and comparing them to the transactions in a pure arbitrage. We call Table 2.2 a **quasi-arbitrage table**, and from now on we will use such a table whenever we discuss a quasi-arbitrage. The first column lists the three components of a pure arbitrage. The second column shows the corresponding transactions of a *specific* quasi-arbitrage, which in this case is the quasi-arbitrage from Example 2.7. The third column lists the prices or rates the quasi-arbitrageur uses in each transaction.

The three transactions of a cash-and-carry or a reverse cash-and-carry pure arbitrage are always the same. The corresponding transactions in a quasi-arbitrage depend on the quasi-arbitrageur's initial, or **benchmark**, position. The firm's benchmark position can be an actual or a potential position. Movements away from the benchmark position are used to execute one or more of the three quasi-arbitrage transactions. In Example 2.7, the corporate treasurer's benchmark is an intended position in T-bills. She performs the borrowing component of the cash-and-carry arbitrage by moving away from the benchmark and refraining from buying T-bills. Her effective borrowing cost is the return forgone on the T-bills and is computed from the T-bill ask price as shown in Table 2.2. The treasurer completes the quasi-arbitrage by actually going short futures and buying the spot underlying asset.

We also use the quasi-arbitrage table to compute the effect of transactions fees on quasi-arbitrage. The variables TF_1, TF_2, and TF_3 represent the transactions fees associated with the three arbitrage steps, respectively. The treasurer in Example 2.7 saves the transactions fees associated with buying T-bills. She thus saves the fees associated with the third arbitrage step in Table 2.2 and *subtracts* TF_3 from her total transactions fees. However, because she actually buys the IBM stock and goes short futures, she *adds* TF_1 and TF_2 to her total transactions fees. Therefore, her total transactions fees are

Table 2.3 Cash-and-Carry Quasi-Arbitrage Table for Portfolio Manager

Benchmark position: investment in T-bills

Cash-and-Carry Pure Arbitrage Components	Cash-and-Carry Quasi-Arbitrage Components	Relevant Price or Rate
1. Buy spot	Buy spot	Ask
2. Short futures	Short futures	Bid
3. Borrow	Sell T-bills	T-bill bid

Resulting position: investment in synthetic T-bills

Transactions fees: $TF = TF_1 + TF_2 + TF_3$
1. Pay TF_1
2. Pay TF_2
3. Pay TF_3

$$TF = TF_1 + TF_2 - TF_3.$$

Thus, a quasi-arbitrage table such as Table 2.2 clearly shows the relevant prices, rates, and transactions fees for each component of the quasi-arbitrage under consideration. This information can be used to compute Ω to see if a quasi-arbitrage opportunity—in this case, a cash-and-carry—actually exists. In the next section, we will study an example in which a quasi-arbitrage table is used to evaluate a reverse cash-and-carry quasi-arbitrage.

Further, the quasi-arbitrage table format illustrates what actually occurs in quasi-arbitrage. Recall that pure arbitrage involves a zero net position because it includes both borrowing and lending. In a quasi-arbitrage, we move from a benchmark to a synthetic position using the three components of a pure arbitrage, so the resulting position must be a synthetic version of the benchmark position. The treasurer in Example 2.7 moves from a benchmark position of an intended purchase of T-bills to a purchase of synthetic T-bills.

Quasi-arbitrages can differ subtly if there are slight variations in the benchmark position. Let's compare the treasurer in Example 2.7, whose benchmark is an intended purchase of T-bills, with a portfolio manager who already owns T-bills and wishes to use a cash-and-carry to replace them with synthetic T-bills. Table 2.3 presents the portfolio manager's cash-and-carry quasi-arbitrage table.

The portfolio manager finances his synthetic T-bill purchase by selling from an existing T-bill position, while the corporate treasurer finances her synthetic T-bill purchase by refraining from purchasing T-bills. Thus, the portfolio manager figures his effective borrowing rate from the T-bill bid price, while the corporate treasurer figures her effective borrowing rate from the T-bill ask price. The effective borrowing rate for the manager, therefore, is

$$\text{Effective borrowing rate} = \frac{\$1,000,000 - \$908,678}{\$908,678}$$
$$= 10.05\%.$$

Further, while the corporate treasurer saves the transactions fees associated with buying a T-bill, the portfolio manager must pay the transactions fees associated with selling a T-bill. The manager's Ω^c, therefore, is

$$\Omega^c = F_{t,T}^b - [P_t^a(1 + r_{t,T}) + TF]$$
$$= \$154.90 - [\$140.10(1.1005) + \$0.015]$$
$$= \$154.90 - \$154.20 = \$0.70 > 0.$$

The bid-ask spread and the transactions fees the portfolio manager incurs by selling T-bills clearly make the quasi-arbitrage less profitable for him than for the corporate treasurer, whose Ω^c is \$0.86.

Reverse Cash-and-Carry Quasi-Arbitrage   We have seen that it is possible to interpret a cash-and-carry quasi-arbitrage as a move from a benchmark position to a synthetic position via the three components of a cash-and-carry pure arbitrage. Likewise, we can interpret a reverse cash-and-carry quasi-arbitrage as a move from a benchmark position to a synthetic position via the three components of a reverse cash-and-carry pure arbitrage. Again we can easily keep track of the relevant costs and rates by using a quasi-arbitrage table. Example 2.8 demonstrates a reverse cash-and-carry quasi-arbitrage.

- **Example 2.8: Choosing between Actual and Synthetic Stock Positions** Consider a portfolio manager who holds \$500 million worth of IBM stock and is considering a move to a synthetic stock position. Suppose she faces the same prices and rates as in Example 2.6 except that the bid and ask prices for the one-year T-bills are

Bid price on \$1-million-face-value 1-year T-bill	\$902,120.00
Ask price on \$1-million-face-value 1-year T-bill	902,935.00

The manager's benchmark position is her current position in IBM stock. Table 2.4 presents the reverse cash-and-carry quasi-arbitrage that will move her from the benchmark to a synthetic stock position.

The first step of the reverse cash-and-carry pure arbitrage is to short-sell the stock. The portfolio manager effectively accomplishes this by selling off her holdings of IBM. Relative to the benchmark of owning stock, selling stock is the same as retaining the stock and going short. Both transactions yield a zero net position in the stock. However, the portfolio manager has a natural advantage over the pure arbitrageur, because she is free to invest all of the stock sale proceeds in T-bills and she is not subject to uptick rules.

The manager carries out the second step of the reverse cash-and-carry as a pure arbitrageur would by taking a long futures position. The futures position locks in the price at which the manager will repurchase her stock, just as it would lock in the price at which a pure arbitrageur would acquire the stock to pay back the stock lender in the short sale. Thus, the manager essentially borrows the stock from herself for her effective short sale.

Table 2.4 Reverse Cash-and-Carry Quasi-Arbitrage Table for Portfolio Manager

Benchmark position: investment in stock

Reverse Cash-and-Carry Pure Arbitrage Components	Reverse Cash-and-Carry Quasi-Arbitrage Components	Relevant Price or Rate
1. Short spot	Sell spot	Bid
2. Go long futures	Go long futures	Ask
3. Lend	Buy T-bills	T-bill ask

Resulting position: investment in synthetic stock

Transactions fees: $TF = TF_1 + TF_2 + TF_3$
1. Pay TF_1
2. Pay TF_2
3. Pay TF_3

In the third step, the manager lends as a pure arbitrageur might by buying T-bills. She will purchase the bills at the ask price, so her rate of return will be

$$\text{Lending rate} = \frac{\$1,000,000 - \$902,935}{\$902,935}$$
$$= 10.75\%.$$

The portfolio manager must pay transactions fees on all three components of the quasi-arbitrage. Therefore, her implied reverse repo rate is exactly the same as that paid by the pure arbitrageur in Example 2.6:

$$\text{Implied reverse repo rate} = \frac{\$155.10 + \$0.015 - \$139.90}{\$139.90}$$
$$= 10.88\%.$$

Since this exceeds the manager's lending rate, there is no reverse cash-and-carry quasi-arbitrage and the manager is better off holding the stock.

We can also see this by computing Ω^r:

$$\Omega^r = F^a_{t,T} - [P^b_t(1 + r_{t,T}) - TF]$$
$$= \$155.10 - [\$139.90(1.1075) - \$0.015]$$
$$= \$155.10 - \$154.92 = \$0.18 > 0.$$

The positive Ω^r indicates there is no reverse cash-and-carry quasi-arbitrage.[19]

---

[19] Recall that a positive Ω^r does not necessarily indicate that there is a cash-and-carry quasi-arbitrage, because the relevant prices and rates differ for the components of that quasi-arbitrage. Further, transactions fees for Ω^c enter in the opposite way from that for Ω^r.

A third way to demonstrate the absence of a quasi-arbitrage opportunity is to compare the manager's cash flows from the benchmark position with those from the quasi-arbitrage:

Benchmark Position

Transaction	Today	One Year from Now
Keep stock	0	Position in stock
Net	0	Position in stock

Quasi-Arbitrage Strategy

Transaction	Today	One Year from Now
Sell stock	$139.90	$-P_T = -F_{T,T}$ (Buy back stock)
Invest in T-bills	$-$139.90	$139.90(1.1075) = $154.94
Go long futures	0	$F_{T,T} - $155.10
Pay transactions fees	0	$-$0.015
Net	0	Position in stock $- $0.18

The portfolio manager's position if she undertakes the quasi-arbitrage is the same as if she had retained her IBM stock position, except that she loses $0.18 on the quasi-arbitrage. ∎

As with a cash-and-carry quasi-arbitrage, the profitability of a reverse cash-and-carry quasi-arbitrage can change if the benchmark position changes. Example 2.9 demonstrates such a case.

■ **Example 2.9: Asset Allocation and Quasi-Arbitrage**   Suppose that another portfolio manager, who also faces the prices in Example 2.8, wishes to sell T-bills and buy IBM stock. This type of transaction is known as **asset allocation**, because it changes the composition of a portfolio. The quasi-arbitrage table in Table 2.5 shows that the manager could make his desired change synthetically through a reverse cash-and-carry strategy.

In the first step of the quasi-arbitrage, the manager effectively sells the stock short by not buying it. To see that this is an effective short sale, consider what happens if he buys stock according to his benchmark plan and then sells it short: He ends up with a zero net position. By refraining from the benchmark stock purchase in the first place, he also establishes a zero net position. Thus, he accomplishes the first leg of the arbitrage by moving away from his benchmark position. The appropriate price of this effective short sale is the ask, for it is the price at which he would have purchased stock under his benchmark plan.

The manager carries out the second step in the reverse cash-and-carry by going long futures, just as a pure arbitrageur would do. To execute the third step, he effectively lends by not carrying out his benchmark plan to sell T-bills. The appropriate price for computing the rate on this effective lending rate is the bid price at which the manager would have sold T-bills. The effective lending rate is

Table 2.5 Reverse Cash-and-Carry Quasi-Arbitrage Table for Portfolio Manager

Benchmark position: sale of T-bills and purchase of stock

Reverse Cash-and-Carry Pure Arbitrage Components	Reverse Cash-and-Carry Quasi-Arbitrage Components	Relevant Price or Rate
1. Short spot	Refrain from buying stock	Ask
2. Go long futures	Go long futures	Ask
3. Lend	Refrain from selling T-bills	T-bill bid

Resulting position: investment in synthetic stock

Transactions fees: $TF = -TF_1 + TF_2 - TF_3$
1. Save TF_1
2. Pay TF_2
3. Save TF_3

$$\text{Effective lending rate} = \frac{\$1,000,000 - \$902,120}{\$902,120}$$
$$= 10.85\%.$$

The manager has lower transactions fees under the quasi-arbitrage than he would under his benchmark strategy. While the manager pays the fees associated with going long futures, he saves the fees associated with his benchmark plan to buy stock and sell T-bills. His overall transactions fees are thus

$$TF = -TF_1 + TF_2 - TF_3$$
$$= -\$0.008 + \$0.002 - \$0.005$$
$$= -\$0.011.$$

The synthetic asset allocation offers an effective rebate of $0.011, because the transactions fees from going long futures are much lower than the combined fees for buying the stock and selling the T-bills.

The savings on transactions fees make it more likely that there is a quasi-arbitrage opportunity in this case. We can check whether the futures strategy is profitable by computing Ω^r:

$$\Omega^r = F_{t,T}^a - [P_t^a(1 + r_{t,T}) - TF]$$
$$= \$155.10 - [\$140.10(1.1085) - (-\$0.011)]$$
$$= \$155.10 - \$155.31 = -\$0.21 < 0.$$

The negative Ω^r indicates that a reverse cash-and-carry quasi-arbitrage opportunity exists for the portfolio manager. ∎

Steps in Constructing a Quasi-Arbitrage Table   We have presented several examples that use a quasi-arbitrage table to help locate quasi-arbitrage opportunities. In each case, we follow four steps:

1.   We determine whether the potential quasi-arbitrage is a cash-and-carry or a reverse cash-and-carry and establish which of the three arbitrage components we can perform by moving away from the benchmark position. In Table 2.2, a move away from a benchmark intention to invest in T-bills is equivalent to the borrowing in the third component of a cash-and-carry. In Table 2.4, a move away from a benchmark investment in stock is equivalent to shorting stock in the first component of a reverse cash-and-carry.

2.   We list the remaining arbitrage components that are performed directly. In Table 2.2, the quasi-arbitrageur literally buys the spot asset and goes short futures as is done in a pure cash-and-carry arbitrage. In Table 2.4, the quasi-arbitrageur literally goes long futures and lends.

3.   We compute the effective transactions fees. Any steps performed directly require payment of a transactions fee; any steps saved result in transactions fee rebates. Thus, effective transactions fees can be negative as in Example 2.9.

4.   We identify the appropriate price or rate for each component and compute Ω^c or Ω^r. We add transactions fees to the grossed-up spot price for a cash-and-carry and subtract transactions fees from the grossed-up spot price for a reverse cash-and-carry. If $\Omega^c > 0$, a potential cash-and-carry quasi-arbitrage will be profitable. If $\Omega^r < 0$, a potential reverse cash-and-carry quasi-arbitrage will be profitable.

Trading and Pricing Implications of Quasi-Arbitrage   We have seen that quasi-arbitrageurs often can perform cash-and-carry and reverse cash-and-carry arbitrages more cheaply than can pure arbitrageurs. For example, compare the costs faced by the pure arbitrageur in Example 2.6, the portfolio manager who holds stocks in Example 2.8, and the portfolio manager who undertakes an asset allocation in Example 2.9 as they all perform a reverse cash-and-carry arbitrage. The pure arbitrageur in Example 2.6 must pay full transactions fees and the bid-ask spread on both the stock and the futures and can lend only at a penalty rate. The portfolio manager in Example 2.8 also must pay full transactions fees and the bid-ask spread on the stock, the futures, and the T-bills, but she can earn the full T-bill rate. The portfolio manager in Example 2.9 pays only the bid-ask spread on the futures. He saves the bid-ask spread on the stock and the T-bills and the transactions fees associated with his benchmark plan to buy stock and sell T-bills. Clearly these three market participants face different no-arbitrage prices.

   The fact that some financial market participants have a comparative advantage over others in performing arbitrages has two important implications for futures trading and pricing. First, pure arbitrageurs are not the only ones who should search for arbitrage opportunities; in many cases, they are the least-advantaged traders. Second, competition should drive the futures price toward the no-arbitrage price of the parties with the lowest overall costs of performing the arbitrage (quasi or pure). The relative benchmark positions of the various parties in the market determine which parties are the lowest-cost traders. As Example 2.10 demonstrates, this convergence of the futures price toward the lowest-cost no-arbitrage price can lead to transactions costs savings for society.

▪ **Example 2.10: Cost Savings from Futures Trading**   Suppose a portfolio manager who holds an inventory of IBM stock is thinking of using a reverse cash-and-carry quasi-arbitrage with S&P 1 futures to replace her stock with a synthetic stock position. Suppose also that she faces the same stock prices, T-bill prices, and transactions fees as in Example 2.8.

Table 2.4 in Example 2.8 shows that the transactions fees on that manager's strategy are

$$TF = TF_1 + TF_2 + TF_3$$
$$= \$0.008 + \$0.002 + \$0.005$$
$$= \$0.015,$$

so the quasi-arbitrage lower-bound price for the manager's reverse cash-and-carry is

$$\text{Lower bound} = P_t^b(1 + r_{t,T}) - TF$$
$$= \$139.90(1.1075) - \$0.015$$
$$= \$154.94 - \$0.015$$
$$= \$154.925.$$

Thus, the portfolio manager is willing to go long the S&P 1 futures at any price below $154.925. She will perform this reverse cash-and-carry arbitrage until it disappears or she runs out of IBM stock in her inventory. We assume that she has large holdings of IBM, so the futures price should move quickly to $154.925.

Now suppose that a second portfolio manager wishes to sell his IBM stock and buy T-bills. This manager trades much less frequently in the stock market and thus faces much higher transactions fees for buying and selling stock. Suppose his fees are $0.060 per share instead of the $0.008 the first portfolio manager faces. While it may seem unlikely that the discrepancy between the transactions fees paid by the two portfolio managers would be so large, we will see when we study stock index futures in Chapter 4 that such a difference can exist when trading stock *portfolios*.

The second manager could buy T-bills synthetically by retaining the IBM stock and going short futures. Table 2.6 is a quasi-arbitrage table for this cash-and-carry strategy. It shows that the transactions fees of the cash-and-carry are

$$TF = -TF_1 + TF_2 - TF_3$$
$$= -\$0.060 + \$0.002 - \$0.005$$
$$= -\$0.063,$$

Table 2.6 Cash-and-Carry Quasi-Arbitrage Table for Portfolio Manager

Benchmark position: sale of stock and purchase of T-bills

Cash-and-Carry Pure Arbitrage Components	Cash-and-Carry Quasi-Arbitrage Components	Relevant Price or Rate
1. Buy spot	Refrain from selling spot	Bid
2. Short futures	Short futures	Bid
3. Borrow	Refrain from buying T-bills	T-bill ask

Resulting position: short futures position

Transactions fees: $TF = -TF_1 + TF_2 - TF_3$
1. Save TF_1
2. Pay TF_2
3. Save TF_3

---

so the quasi-arbitrage upper-bound price for the second portfolio manager's cash-and-carry is

$$\text{Upper bound} = P_t^b(1 + r_{t,T}) + TF$$
$$= \$139.90(1.1075) + (-\$0.063)$$
$$= \$154.94 - \$0.063$$
$$= \$154.877.$$

Thus, the second portfolio manager is willing to go short the S&P 1 futures at any price above $154.877. If the first (low-cost) portfolio manager has driven the futures price to $154.925, the second manager receives a cash-and-carry quasi-arbitrage profit of [20]

$$\Omega^c = \$154.925 - \$154.877$$
$$= \$0.048.$$

This profit represents the $0.052 ($0.060 – $0.008) cost advantage the first portfolio manager has over the second portfolio manager in selling stocks less the $0.004 (2 × $0.002) futures transactions fees paid by both parties. For even though the second (high-cost) manager desires the stock sale and T-bill purchase, the actual sale of stock and purchase of T-bills is performed by the first (low-cost) manager. In this way, the second manager is able to "piggyback" on the low trading costs of the first manager. The cost of this is the participation by both parties in the futures market.

---

[20] Of course, it is possible that the low-cost portfolio manager will earn some of this profit. Competition among low-cost portfolio managers makes this unlikely, however.

Thus, the futures trading of the two portfolio managers has yielded a real efficiency gain. This example shows how quasi-arbitrage allows those with the lowest transactions costs to perform the actual trades. This lowers the total trading costs paid by market participants and therefore provides a net cost saving to society. ■

Traditional discussions of the economic purposes of futures markets have concentrated on how futures allow market participants to reduce risk (hedge) and forecast future spot prices (price discovery). Our discussion of quasi-arbitrage shows that another economic purpose of futures markets is to reduce transactions costs. Thus, market participants are just as likely to use futures contracts to increase risk as they are to decrease it if doing so will reduce their transactions costs. A portfolio manager who performs asset allocation may be just as likely to create a synthetic stock position by going long futures and buying T-bills as he or she is to create a synthetic T-bill (i.e., "hedge") by going short futures and holding a stock portfolio. The role of futures in both cases is to reduce transactions costs by facilitating the creation of synthetic positions for parties with high trading costs.

Understanding how futures trading can lower transactions costs augments our understanding of the price discovery role of the futures markets. Those who receive information about prices may trade in the futures markets first, because the costs of transacting there are lower. Then low-transactions-cost arbitrageurs will bring the spot market into line with the new futures prices. Since the trading occurs first in the futures market, futures prices at any given time may be the best indicators of *current* market values.

Futures Pricing under Impediments to Short Sales

The no-arbitrage futures pricing relationship requires that investors be able to perform cash-and-carry and reverse cash-and-carry arbitrage easily so that pure and quasi-arbitrage trading can force futures prices to their no-arbitrage levels. However, in many cases, reverse cash-and-carry arbitrage cannot be performed easily because it is difficult and costly to sell the underlying futures asset short. Sometimes technical trading factors such as uptick rules, penalty rates, short-selling margins, or the seller's option can impede short-selling. To see how the seller's option, for example, can hinder short sales, recall that in a reverse cash-and-carry arbitrage the arbitrageur covers a short position at date T with the asset delivered in the futures market. But because of the seller's option, the arbitrageur may not know exactly which asset grade will be delivered or when it will be delivered.[21]

---

[21] Even if the arbitrageur decides to close out the arbitrage by making a spot purchase at time T, the invoice price will not necessarily converge to the price of the grade of the asset the arbitrageur must purchase. Thus, the arbitrageur will not have locked in a price.

This problem clearly is greater for commodities and securities with considerable latitude in their deliverable grades and delivery dates.[22]

Often the very nature of the underlying asset markets poses even greater impediments to short-selling. In many markets, people hold the underlying assets for reasons other than pure investment. They derive some unique benefits from holding the assets and therefore are reluctant to lend them out for short sales. Reverse cash-and-carry arbitrage can be very costly in markets that severely restrict lending for short sales. In this section, we will examine how the no-arbitrage pricing relationship behaves in such markets.

Pure Assets and Convenience Assets

The major difference between assets that are readily lent out for short sales and those that are not lies in the reasons the investor holds the assets in the first place. Recall that in a short sale, the lender gives up a commodity or security now and receives it back intact in the future. The borrower is required to compensate the lender for any explicit payouts, such as dividends or coupons, associated with holding the asset. As long as the lender does not need the asset for any reason during the duration of the short sale, lending for a short sale is equivalent to holding the asset over the same period.

Brokers who lend out stock in fact view short-selling in this way. They have clients who will be holding stocks for given periods. If a broker lends a client's stock out and later receives it back plus explicit payouts, the client's position will not be affected. It will be as though the client had held the stock for the entire period.

Thus, the following general principle about short-selling holds: *It is possible to sell an underlying asset short at no cost between dates t and T only if someone is willing to hold the commodity or security between those dates purely for investment purposes, that is, to earn capital gains and explicit payouts.* We call such assets **pure assets**. The owners of pure assets need not physically have the assets in their possession to earn their investment returns. Financial securities are an obvious example of pure assets.

Many assets are held for the physical services they offer as well as for their potential investment returns. These are called **convenience assets**, and their owners are unlikely to lend them out for short sale without receiving some compensation. Commodities frequently are held as convenience assets. For example, consider the reasons for holding corn. Corn prices tend to rise before a harvest and fall after it. An investor who buys corn just before a harvest and holds it until just after will most likely suffer a capital loss. Further, he or she must pay storage costs and will receive no payouts. Thus, investors are unlikely to hold corn through a harvest for pure investment purposes. However, they might hold it for other reasons. A corn processor, for example, might hold corn to avoid having to shut

---

[22] This usually is not a problem for cash settlement futures contracts, because the commodity or security grade and the expiration date are fixed. Arbitrageurs can cover their short positions by purchasing the underlying commodity or security in the spot market at T.

the plant down in the event of a temporary corn shortage. We call the value of such potential uses the corn's **convenience value**.[23]

Just as holders of IBM stock are willing to lend their stock out for short sale only if they are compensated for lost dividends, holders of convenience assets are willing to lend their assets only if they are compensated for the convenience value they give up. The corn processor who is willing to hold corn over a harvest will lend out the corn only if the borrower compensates him or her for potential shortage losses. Thus, in many ways a convenience value is similar to a dividend or a coupon. However, two important differences between convenience value and payments such as dividends and coupons make short-selling much more costly in convenience-asset markets. First, a dividend is explicit and observable, but a convenience value is not. Short-sellers of pure assets can compensate their lenders for forgone dividends much more easily than short-sellers of convenience assets can compensate their lenders for forgone convenience value. This is why we do not tend to see formal markets for selling convenience assets short. Second, anyone who holds, say, IBM stock gets the same dividend, but the convenience value of corn differs for different holders. In equilibrium, we expect those with the *lowest* convenience value, or the **marginal convenience value**, to lend convenience assets.[24] Because the lender of a convenience asset saves physical storage costs, the compensation he or she receives for lending will be net of storage costs (see footnote 6).

Full-Carry versus Non-Full-Carry Markets

We have just seen that one can interpret the convenience value as a kind of "implicit dividend" for holding a convenience asset. This has implications for the pricing of futures contracts on convenience assets. Those performing cash-and-carry arbitrage will receive the convenience value of holding the assets.[25] Those performing reverse cash-and-carry arbitrage must compensate the asset lenders for lost convenience value. Thus, the fundamental no-arbitrage equation in convenience-asset markets is

$$F_{t,T} = P_t(1 + r_{t,T}) - FV_T(\text{Payouts between t to T}) - CV_{t,T}, \qquad (2.27)$$

where $CV_{t,T}$ is the future value of the marginal convenience value between t and T and the future value of payouts is negative if it represents physical storage costs.[26] We can also express Equation 2.27 in percentage terms:

---

[23] Convenience values were first discussed by Kaldor [1939], Working [1949], and Brennan [1958].

[24] In Chapter 8, we will discuss models that show how the marginal convenience value varies over time and with the quantity of the asset being stored.

[25] Thus, we expect cash-and-carry arbitrages to be performed by those who derive convenience from holding the assets.

[26] Of course, a convenience value reflects any risk premium due to systematic risk of convenience.

$$\frac{F_{t,T} - P_t}{P_t} = r_{t,T} - \left(\frac{FV_T(\text{Payouts between t and T})}{P_t}\right) - \left(\frac{CV_{t,T}}{P_t}\right), \qquad \textbf{(2.27a)}$$

where $CV_{t,T}/P_t$ is called the unannualized **convenience yield**.

Similarly, the fundamental no-arbitrage equation between futures prices with different expiration dates is

$$F_{t,T2} \qquad \qquad \textbf{(2.28)}$$
$$= F_{t,T1}(1 + r_{T1,T2}) - FV_{T2}(\text{Payouts between T1 and T2}) - CV_{T1,T2}.$$

We define a **full-carry market** as one in which the marginal convenience value is equal to zero. The fundamental no-arbitrage equations, 2.7 and 2.14, hold with equality in such markets. Investors in a full-carry market are willing to hold the underlying asset for pure investment purposes. The futures prices reflect the full observable net carry cost for the asset. A **non-full-carry market** has a positive marginal convenience value. In this case, the futures price is less than the value given by Equations 2.7 and 2.14 and thus does not reflect the full observable net carry for the asset.

Example 2.11 demonstrates the difference between full-carry and non-full-carry markets by comparing the markets for gold and copper.

▪ **Example 2.11: Full-Carry and Non-Full-Carry Metals Futures Markets**
In this example, we show how to determine whether metals futures markets are at full carry by studying the gold and copper markets as they were on October 12, 1988. While gold has important industrial uses, many people hold it purely for investment purposes. Thus, gold is most likely a pure asset with zero marginal convenience value.[27] The gold futures market should be at full carry. Copper, on the other hand, typically is held in inventory for industrial purposes, such as ensuring a smooth supply. Thus, we expect copper to be a convenience asset with a positive marginal convenience value.[28] The copper futures market should be at less than full carry.

Figure 2.2 presents the gold and copper futures prices on October 12, 1988, as given in *The Wall Street Journal*. To determine whether these futures prices were full-carry prices, we must first compute the interest and noninterest carrying costs in the two markets. The three-month Treasury bill rate implied by the October 12, 1988, December T-bill futures contract was 7.36 percent.[29] We will use this as a measure of the riskless rate of interest. Information from the Commodity Exchange Inc. shows that storage costs at this time were $6 per month plus a $14

---

[27] Sometimes there does appear to be a very small convenience yield on gold, but this is quite rare. An example of this situation appears in Figure 1.3. (On May 23, 1989, short-term interest rates exceeded 8 percent.)

[28] In Chapter 9, we will see that copper can become a pure asset in times of glut.

[29] We will show how to compute the interest rates implied by T-bill futures contracts in Chapter 5.

Figure 2.2 Commodity Futures Transactions Prices, October 12, 1988

	Open	High	Low	Settle	Change	Lifetime High	Low	Open Interest
—METALS & PETROLEUM—								
COPPER-STANDARD (CMX) – 25,000 lbs.; cents per lb.								
Oct	128.50	129.40	128.50	129.30	– .20	129.50	108.00	513
Dec	120.90	121.80	118.80	120.30	+ .20	121.80	64.70	25,439
Mr89	107.50	108.60	105.80	107.00	– .20	108.60	66.50	7,023
May	103.70	103.90	102.00	102.50	– .30	103.90	73.15	1,058
July	100.70	100.70	98.60	99.40	– .30	100.70	76.00	567
Sept	99.20	99.20	98.50	97.80	– .40	99.20	76.00	343
Dec	97.00	98.00	95.90	96.30	– .40	98.00	77.45	537
Est vol 6,000; vol Tues 7,171; open int 35,533, –230.								
GOLD (CMX) – 100 troy oz.; $ per troy oz.								
Oct	405.50	409.00	405.50	408.40	+ 4.00	533.50	391.80	502
Dec	409.50	416.00	409.50	412.20	+ 3.80	546.00	395.50	82,456
Fb89	415.00	421.00	414.70	417.40	+ 3.80	549.50	401.00	12,966
Apr	420.50	426.50	420.50	422.60	+ 3.90	550.00	407.00	9,108
June	424.80	431.20	424.80	427.80	+ 3.90	570.00	412.00	16,147
Aug	....	....	....	433.20	+ 4.00	575.00	419.30	6,994
Oct	....	....	....	438.80	+ 4.10	575.50	423.00	8,851
Dec	441.50	446.50	441.50	444.30	+ 4.30	514.50	428.00	9,125
Fb90	....	....	....	449.90	+ 4.40	516.00	439.70	4,121
Apr	....	....	....	455.50	+ 4.50	525.80	443.00	3,021
June	....	....	....	461.30	+ 4.60	497.00	447.00	2,168
Aug	470.50	470.50	470.50	467.30	+ 4.70	470.50	453.00	665
Est vol 40,000; vol Tues 31,552; open int 156,124, –2,235.								

Source: *The Wall Street Journal,* October 13, 1988.

one-time transfer fee for the gold covered by each gold contract and $1.95 per month plus a $3.95 one-time transfer fee for the copper covered by each copper contract. The one-time transfer fees had to be paid even if the metals were held only for a short time. We assume that all these costs would have been paid when the metal was taken out of storage. This simplifies our cost calculations and puts them on a future-value basis.

We test to see if the gold futures market was at full carry by examining the relationship on October 12, 1988, between the December 1988 and February 1989 gold futures settlement prices. The cost of storing gold between December 1988 and February 1989 was expected to be

> Two-month gold storage cost
> = (Monthly charge)(Number of months) + One-time cost
> = ($6)(2) + $14
> = $26 for 100 ounces (one contract)
> = $0.26 per ounce.

Using Equation 2.28, the equilibrium February 1989 gold futures price, $F_{t,T2}$, if the market was at full carry was[30]

---

[30] Following market practice, we compute two months of interest by multiplying the annualized rate by 2/12.

$$F_{t,T2} = \$412.20[1 + (2/12)(0.0736)] + \$0.26$$
$$= \$417.52.$$

The actual February 1989 futures price of $417.40 was extremely close to the equilibrium price predicted using the T-bill yield. The difference of $0.12 amounted to only 0.03 percent of the December 1988 futures price. This evidence supports our hypothesis that gold is a pure asset and that the gold futures market was at full carry.

We get a similar result by determining the forward implied repo rate for gold:

$$\text{Forward implied repo rate} = \frac{F_{t,T2} - \text{FV(Storage cost)} - F_{t,T1}}{F_{t,T1}}$$

$$= \frac{\$417.40 - \$0.26 - \$412.20}{\$412.20}$$

$$= 1.20\% \text{ for 2 months.}$$

This was very close to the $(2/12)(7.36\%) = 1.23\%$ T-bill rate over the two months. Had gold been a convenience asset, the forward implied repo rate would have been significantly lower than the market interest rate because gold would have provided convenience value as well as investment return.

Next, we tested to see if the copper futures market was at full carry by studying the relationship between the December 1988 and March 1989 copper futures settlement prices. The cost of storing copper over the three months from December 1988 to March 1989 was expected to be

Three-month copper storage cost
  = (Monthly charge)(Number of months) + One-time cost
  = ($1.95)(3) + $3.95
  = $9.80 per ton
  = $0.0049 per pound.

We calculate the full-carry March 1989 futures price for copper using the T-bill rate implied by the futures:

$$F_{t,T2} = \$1.2030[1 + (3/12)(0.0736)] + \$0.0049$$
$$= \$1.2300.$$

This futures price is well above the actual March 1989 copper futures price of $1.0700 per pound. This indicates that the copper futures market was at less than full carry and that copper was a convenience asset at this time, as we expected. We know that if the futures contract was fairly priced, the future value of the marginal convenience value was $1.23 – $1.07 = $0.16 per pound over the three months.

We get the same result by determining the forward implied repo rate for copper:

Table 2.7 Reverse Cash-and-Carry Quasi-Arbitrage Table for Holder of Convenience Asset

Benchmark position: holding of asset

Reverse Cash-and-Carry Pure Arbitrage Components	Reverse Cash-and-Carry Quasi-Arbitrage Components	Relevant Price or Rate
1. Short spot	Sell asset	Bid
Refund payout	Lose convenience value and save storage costs	
2. Go long futures	Go long futures	Ask
3. Lend	Buy T-bills	T-bill ask

Resulting position: investment in synthetic asset

Transactions fees: $TF = TF_1 + TF_2 + TF_3$
1. Pay TF_1
2. Pay TF_2
3. Pay TF_3

$$\text{Forward implied repo rate} = \frac{F_{t,T2} - FV(\text{Storage cost}) - F_{t,T1}}{F_{t,T1}}$$

$$= \frac{\$1.0700 - \$0.0049 - \$1.2030}{\$1.2030}$$

$$= -11.46\% \text{ for 3 months.}$$

Obviously this was well below the T-bill rate of $(3/12)(7.36\%) = 1.84\%$ over the three months. While this situation seemed to offer a reverse cash-and-carry arbitrage (because the forward implied repo rate should have been close to the forward implied reverse repo rate), we could not have reaped the arbitrage profit because copper was a convenience asset and could not have been sold short without compensating the lender. ■

Quasi-Arbitrage

We already have seen that a large portion of arbitrage trading is really quasi-arbitrage. Quasi-arbitrage is especially prevalent in markets for convenience assets. As mentioned earlier, there are few formal markets for short-selling convenience assets because convenience value is unobservable and varies across different holders of the asset. Thus, most short-selling of convenience assets is actually *effective* short-selling. Table 2.7 shows how a holder of a convenience asset can perform a reverse cash-and-carry through quasi-arbitrage.

In the first step of the quasi-arbitrage, the holder of the convenience asset effectively sells the asset short by borrowing it from himself or herself and selling it. In the second two steps, the asset holder replaces the actual asset with a synthetic asset consisting of T-bills and a long futures position. He or she loses the

Table 2.8 Cash-and-Carry Quasi-Arbitrage Table for Holder of Convenience Asset

Benchmark position: sale of asset

Cash-and-Carry Pure Arbitrage Components	Cash-and-Carry Quasi-Arbitrage Components	Relevant Price or Rate
1. Buy spot	Refrain from selling	Bid
Receive payouts	Receive convenience value and pay physical storage	
2. Short futures	Short futures	Bid
3. Borrow	Borrow	Borrowing rate

Resulting position: synthetic sale of asset

Transactions fees: $TF = -TF_1 + TF_2 + TF_3$
1. Save TF_1
2. Pay TF_2
3. Pay TF_3

convenience value the asset provides but saves on storage costs. This is worth doing as long as the futures price is less than the right-hand side of Equation 2.27.

Cash-and-carry quasi-arbitrage is likely to be performed in convenience asset markets by those who are planning to sell some of their convenience-asset stocks. Table 2.8 demonstrates this quasi-arbitrage strategy. The potential seller of the asset replaces an actual sale with a synthetic sale that consists of borrowing and a short futures position. He or she receives the convenience value that would have been lost from the sale but pays the storage costs that would have been saved. This is worth doing as long as the futures price is greater than the right-hand side of Equation 2.27.

Thus, quasi-arbitrage is a strong force leading the market to consistency with Equations 2.27 and 2.28.

Risk and the Pricing of Futures Contracts

We have seen that the relationships between *today's* spot and futures prices can be determined in many cases by observing the trading opportunities open to arbitrageurs.[31] Many market participants, especially those using futures markets to hedge, would also like to understand how today's futures prices are related to market *expectations* about *future* spot commodity and security prices. For example, suppose there is a general expectation that the price of gold next July 1 will be

---

[31] When futures contracts can be priced by arbitrage considerations, we need not know anything about investors' preferences for taking risk. In this section, we will show how investors' preferences enter the pricing of futures contracts.

$450 per ounce. The futures price today for delivery of gold on July 1 must somehow reflect this expectation. If today's futures price is $445, going long futures will yield an expected profit of

Expected futures profit = Expected July 1 futures − Initial futures
                      = Expected July 1 spot − Initial futures
                      = $450 − $445
                      = $5 per ounce.

Similarly, going short futures will lead to an expected loss of $5 per ounce.

Telser [1958] hypothesized that in equilibrium, one cannot *expect* to make a profit or a loss on a futures position. He contended that any expected profits that did exist would be bid away as traders rushed to capture them. Under this hypothesis, if markets are operating properly,

Current futures price = Expected future spot price
$$F_{t,T} = E_t(P_T),$$

where $E_t(P_T)$ is the market expectation at time t of the spot price at T. In our example, the futures price today for July 1 delivery of gold would be $450 per ounce. There would then be an expected profit of zero for those entering into both long and short futures positions.

The theory that futures prices should equal expected future spot prices is called the **hypothesis of unbiased futures pricing**. It suggests that the futures price is an unbiased predictor of the future spot price because *on average* the futures price today will forecast the future spot price correctly. A great deal of empirical work has tested this hypothesis, including Cootner [1960], Bodie and Rosansky [1980], Raynauld and Tessier [1984], Chang [1985], and Hodrick and Srivastava [1987]. These studies used varying methodologies, but all have found evidence against the unbiasedness hypothesis.[32]

Two explanations for the differences between futures prices and expected future spot prices have been put forward. The first is that holders of futures positions bear risk and must be compensated for that risk just as stockholders must be compensated for bearing risk. The expected return demanded by holders of futures positions is reflected in the difference between futures prices and expected future spot prices. In this view, we can derive the relationship between the futures price and the expected future spot price with the risk-return models that are used for other assets such as stocks and bonds. In all the standard risk-return models, such as the Capital Asset Pricing Model (CAPM), investors are compensated only for nondiversifiable or **systematic risk**. Therefore, we will call this explanation for the divergence between futures prices and expected future spot prices the **systematic-risk explanation**.

The alternative view is that futures prices differ from expected future spot prices even after adjusting for systematic risk because of unevenly distributed

---

[32] For a further discussion of this large body of literature, see Khoury [1983].

demand by hedgers for futures positions. For example, if hedgers are predominantly on the short side of the market, investors who are willing to go long opposite them will receive an expected profit in addition to any systematic-risk premium. We call this theory the **hedging-pressure explanation**. While the systematic-risk and hedging-pressure explanations are not mutually exclusive, there is an unresolved debate as to the importance of the latter.[33]

In this section, we will explore the systematic-risk explanation and show how standard portfolio theory can yield insights into the relationship between futures prices and expected future spot prices. We will then discuss the debate over the hedging-pressure explanation.

Systematic-Risk Explanation

The first step in understanding the systematic-risk explanation is to see how systematic fluctuation in futures prices can cause futures prices to differ from expected future spot prices. Example 2.12 uses our understanding of arbitrage to demonstrate this.

▪ **Example 2.12: Bias in the S&P 1 Contract Futures Price**   Suppose the current price of IBM stock is $140 per share and the T-bill rate is 10 percent per year. For simplicity, assume IBM pays no dividend. Arbitrageurs will guarantee that the current S&P 1 futures price for delivery in one year is

$$F_{t,T} = P_t(1 + r_{t,T})$$
$$= \$140(1.10)$$
$$= \$154.$$

How does this price compare with the spot price expected for IBM stock one year from now? If the unbiasedness hypothesis holds, the expected future spot price should be $154. Under this scenario, IBM stock will have a 10 percent expected rate of return just like the T-bills despite the fact that the stock is a riskier investment. It is more likely that IBM stock will, on average, earn a higher rate of return than the bills will to compensate the investor for the additional risk of a

---

[33] This debate has a long history. Keynes [1930] proposed that since most hedgers are producers, they will hedge using short futures positions. These hedgers will be forced to pay speculators a premium to take the opposite long positions. Futures prices will be lower than expected future spot prices to give the speculators an expected profit. This state of affairs is called **normal backwardation** (in contrast, a situation where futures prices exceed expected future spot prices is called **contango**). Telser [1958] pointed out that if the number of potential speculators is large relative to the number of hedgers, this premium should disappear. Telser provided evidence to support his claim, but Cootner [1960] supplied conflicting evidence. This debate occurred before the development of models such as the CAPM. In a more modern framework, we would identify Keynes with the hedging-pressure explanation and Telser with the systematic-risk explanation. See also Turnovsky [1983].

stock position. If the expected return on IBM stock is 15 percent, the expected future spot price will be

$$E_t(P_T) = P_t(1 + r^*_{t,T})$$
$$= \$140(1.15)$$
$$= \$161,$$

where $r^*_{t,T}$ is the expected rate of return on IBM stock.

Thus, in this example, the futures price is less than the expected future spot price in equilibrium:

Futures price < Expected future spot price
$$F_{t,T} < E_t(P_t)$$
$$\$154 < \$161.$$

This result implies that, on average, a long futures position will yield a profit equal to $\$161 - \$154 = \$7$. We can show that this positive expected profit does *not* indicate that the futures market is operating inefficiently. We saw in an earlier section that

Synthetic stock = T-bill + Long futures.

Suppose someone follows this strategy and creates one synthetic share of IBM stock by holding $140 worth of T-bills (at the market price) and going long the futures. As this position is identical to holding one share of IBM outright, the expected return should be 15 percent, or $21, so that it equals the expected return on the stock. We know the synthetic position will earn $14 interest on the bills, so it must earn $7, on average, on the futures position as well for the total expected return to be $21. The $7 expected profit on the futures position will compensate the holder for the risk of the synthetic stock that is above the risk of the T-bills. If the stock is held outright, the owner will also earn an expected $7 premium over the T-bill rate to compensate for the additional risk of the stock. ∎

The preceding discussion implies that *the difference between the futures price and the expected future spot price is the same as the difference between the expected profits on riskless bonds and that on a pure asset with the same systematic price risk as the futures contract*. This relationship between futures and expected future spot prices must hold, because we can always create such a pure asset by holding riskless bonds and a long position in futures. Thus, we would expect that

$$\frac{E_t(P_T) - F_{t,T}}{P^*_t} \tag{2.29}$$

$$= r^*_{t,T} - r_{t,T}$$

= Premium of pure asset with same risk as futures over the riskless rate, where P_t^* is the price of a pure asset with the same price risk as the underlying asset of the futures contract and $r_{t,T}^*$ is the expected (or required) rate of return on that asset.

In Example 2.12, it is clear that the pure asset with the same price risk as the S&P 1 futures is IBM stock, because the futures contract is written on IBM stock and IBM stock is held for pure investment purposes. However, sometimes the underlying asset of a futures contract is not a pure asset and has a positive marginal convenience value. In that case, the relationship between the futures price and the expected future spot price can be derived by using a pure asset that has the same price risk as the underlying asset of the futures. The price of such a pure asset at t, P_t^*, can easily be calculated as the present value of the expected future price of the underlying asset (we will ignore payouts for simplicity):[34]

$$P_t^* = \frac{E_t(P_T)}{1 + r_{t,T}^*} . \tag{2.30}$$

If the underlying asset of a futures contract is a pure asset, as in Example 2.12, $P_t^* = P_t$. If the underlying asset is a convenience asset, $P_t^* \leq P_t$, indicating that the underlying asset is too costly to hold for pure investment purposes.

The discount rate, $r_{t,T}^*$, can be determined with a formal model of risk and return. We will use the Capital Asset Pricing Model, but later we will discuss other risk-return models we could use. For simplicity, we will omit the time subscripts from our notation.

The **Capital Asset Pricing Model (CAPM)** defines the relationship between risk and return as:[35]

$$r_i^* = r_f + \beta_i(r_m^* - r_f) \tag{2.31}$$

$$\beta_i = \frac{\rho_{im}\sigma_i}{\sigma_m} ,$$

where

r_i^* = expected (required) rate of return on a pure asset, i

r_m^* = expected (required) rate of return on the market portfolio (a portfolio including value-weighted proportions of all securities in the economy)

r_f = riskless rate of interest (essentially equal to $r_{t,T}$)

---

[34] With payouts, P_t^* must satisfy $P_t^*(1 + r_{t,T}^*) = E_t[P_T] + FV_T(\text{Payouts})$.

[35] For a more detailed discussion of the Capital Asset Pricing Model, see Brealey and Myers [1988].

ρ_{im} = correlation between rate of return on the asset and rate of return on the market portfolio

σ_i = standard deviation of rate of return on the asset

σ_m = standard deviation of rate of return on the market portfolio

The intuition behind the CAPM is that β_i represents the risk relevant to investors, that is, the **systematic risk** of an asset that cannot be diversified away in large portfolios. Investors will require an expected return above the riskless rate to compensate them for incurring this β_i risk (when $\beta_i > 0$). The expected return on each pure asset is earned from the difference between the current spot price and the expected future spot price. The CAPM shows this difference to be

$$E_t(P_T) - P_t^* = r_i^* P_t^* = r_f P_t^* + \beta_i(r_m^* - r_f)P_t^*. \tag{2.32}$$

The last term in this equation represents the differential in expected profit when the asset is held instead of riskless bonds. Our principle of futures pricing (Equation 2.29) tells us that the difference between the futures price and the expected future spot price must also equal this differential:

$$E_t(P_T) - F_{t,T} = \beta_i(r_m^* - r_f)P_t^*. \tag{2.33}$$

Equation 2.33 has an important implication for the unbiasedness hypothesis: Futures prices can be unbiased predictors of future spot prices only if the underlying commodity or security has *zero systematic risk* (that is, if $\beta_i = 0$). In this case, investors can diversify away the risk of the futures position.

In general, futures prices will reflect an equilibrium bias. If $\beta_i > 0$, holding a long futures position involves bearing *positive systematic risk* and requires an expected profit. In such a case, $F_{t,T} < E_t(P_T)$. If $\beta_i < 0$, a long futures position has *negative systematic risk*. Such a position yields an expected loss, so $F_{t,T} > E_t(P_T)$. This is perfectly consistent with the CAPM. A pure asset with a negative β_i will, on average, earn less than the riskless rate. Negative β_i pure assets have "good" risk in the sense that they rise in value when most other securities in the market fall ($\rho_{im} < 0$). In this way, they offer insurance to investors. Our principle of futures pricing implies that investors are willing to bear expected losses on long negative β_i futures positions in return for the insurance such positions provide.

Since the profit or loss on a short futures position is exactly opposite that of a long futures position, the systematic risk of a short futures position is the negative of the systematic risk of a long futures position. If $\beta_i = 0$, a short position has zero systematic risk and there is no required profit. If $\beta_i > 0$, the systematic risk of a short futures position is *negative*. A long position earns an expected gain in this case, so a short position incurs an expected loss. If $\beta_i < 0$, the systematic risk of the short futures position is *positive*. The short position requires an expected gain just as the long position requires an expected loss.

The CAPM can be used to model futures markets if futures prices are driven by the same market forces as stock prices. If Equation 2.32 does not hold for a given stock, investors can earn expected returns above the level required to compensate for the stock's systematic risk. As investors trade to take advantage of the excess expected returns, the stock's price will adjust and the CAPM relationship will be restored. The same process occurs if Equation 2.33 does not hold for a futures contract. Investors will rush to earn the excess expected returns and thereby bring the futures price back into line with the expected future spot price, as Equation 2.33 specifies. Example 2.13 demonstrates how excess profits can be earned on a futures contract that is mispriced according to the CAPM.

▪ **Example 2.13: Using the CAPM to Look for Mispriced Gold Futures Contracts**   Suppose we do some analysis that leads us to expect the price of gold to be \$455 per ounce in one year. We wish to use this information to see if the gold futures contract is mispriced. The current futures price for delivery of gold in one year is \$440 per ounce, and the spot gold price is \$400 per ounce. The β_i of gold is 0.25, the riskless rate of interest is 10 percent, and the expected rate of return on the market portfolio is 20 percent.

First, we confirm that arbitrageurs have driven the futures and spot prices to be consistent with the fundamental no-arbitrage equation:[36]

$$
\begin{aligned}
F_{t,T} &= \$440 \\
&= \$400(1.10) \\
&= P_t(1 + r_{t,T}).
\end{aligned}
$$

If we assume that gold is a pure asset, the spot price $P_t = P_t^*$. The equilibrium bias in the futures price is given by Equation 2.33:

$$
\begin{aligned}
\beta_i(r_m^* - r_f)P_t^* &= 0.25(20\% - 10\%)\$400 \\
&= \$10.
\end{aligned}
$$

The actual difference between the expected future spot price and the futures price is

$$
\begin{aligned}
E_t(P_T) - F_{t,T} &= \$455 - \$440 \\
&= \$15 > \$10.
\end{aligned}
$$

Thus, the futures price is lower than it should be in equilibrium. Investors can use this information to create a synthetic security that earns more than the CAPM indicates it should. Consider the strategy of buying T-bills with a \$400 market value and going long one futures contract. The expected rate of return on this investment will be

---

[36] For simplicity, we assume no storage costs.

$$\text{Expected return} = \frac{\text{Expected profit}}{\text{Initial investment}}$$

$$= \frac{\text{Return of T-bill} + \text{Expected futures profit}}{\text{Initial investment}}$$

$$= \frac{[(\$400)(0.10)] + \$455 - \$440}{\$400}$$

$$= 13.75\%.$$

The equilibrium expected return on a pure asset with a β_i of 0.25 is

$$r_i^* = r_f + \beta_i(r_m^* - r_f)$$
$$= 0.10 + 0.25(0.20 - 0.10)$$
$$= 12.50\% < 13.75\%.$$

The strategy of buying T-bills and going long futures yields an expected return that exceeds the equilibrium expected return. Investors will go long futures and drive up futures prices until the return on this synthetic gold strategy just equals the equilibrium return.

Investors can also capitalize on this situation by buying spot gold. The expected return on a gold investment is

$$\text{Expected return} = \frac{\$455 - \$400}{\$400}$$
$$= 13.75\%,$$

which is the same as the expected return on the synthetic futures strategy. In this case, investors will drive up the price of spot gold. Arbitrageurs will then bring the futures price into line with the new gold price. ∎

Example 2.13 shows that security analysts can use information about mispricing in the futures markets in the same way they use information about mispricing in other securities markets. If futures markets are as available to investors as other markets, they should obey the rules of risk and return that apply to other securities.

Alternatives to the Capital Asset Pricing Model   We have used the CAPM to introduce the concept of systematic risk in futures pricing because it is the most widely used model of the relationship between systematic risk and return. Dusak [1973] was the first to test whether the CAPM is appropriate for the futures markets. She estimated CAPM betas for various commodities and found they were close to zero. She also found that the expected profit from holding futures contracts was close to zero. This provided evidence that futures markets are priced according to the CAPM, for zero betas imply zero expected profits under the CAPM. In contrast, Bodie and Rosansky [1980] found evidence that futures pricing does not conform to the CAPM. They estimated betas close to zero or negative but found positive expected profits on futures contracts (indicating that futures prices are below expected future spot prices).

In recent years, other asset pricing models have been proposed to correct some of the CAPM's deficiencies. The most important alternative model was developed by Breeden [1979] to improve the measurement of systematic risk. In the CAPM, the only relevant measure of risk is how the rate of return on an asset varies relative to aggregate wealth (the market portfolio).[37] Breeden argued that wealth is relevant only because it leads to consumption. His model measures systematic risk as the degree to which an asset's rate of return varies with consumption. The betas in this model are called **consumption betas**. Breeden [1980] estimated consumption betas for various commodities and found many of them to be positive. These results suggest that the contradiction Bodie and Rosansky found between their beta estimates and the positive expected returns on futures contracts could be due to mismeasurement of the betas. If so, it might be possible to reconcile the Bodie and Rosansky results with the systematic-risk explanation of the difference between futures prices and expected future spot prices.

While debate over the best model of the relationship between systematic risk and return persists, we believe the model that applies best to other financial markets should also apply to futures markets, for investors attempt to profit from mispricings in the futures markets just as they do in other financial markets.

Hedging-Pressure Explanation

The hedging-pressure explanation for the difference between futures prices and expected future spot prices asserts that because hedgers may concentrate their demand for futures positions on one or the other side of the market, futures prices may be driven away from the systematic risk and return relationships that hold in other financial markets. Proponents of the pure systematic-risk explanation contend this cannot happen because any divergence of the futures price from Equation 2.29 will prompt a flood of investors to enter the market and drive prices back into line. Hirshleifer [1988] argued that if there are setup costs in entering the futures markets, this flood of investors will be much smaller than proponents of the pure systematic-risk explanation believe. He shows that those who do enter opposite hedgers will require an expected profit to compensate them for both the setup costs and any loss of diversification from holding a futures position. Thus, if the hedgers' net position is short, the futures price will be driven below the level given by Equation 2.29. If the hedgers' net position is long, the futures price will be driven above the level given by Equation 2.29.

---

[37] Carter, Rausser, and Schmitz [1983] and Marcus [1984] attempted to price futures contracts with the CAPM when commodities are included in the market portfolio.

To date, there is little conclusive empirical evidence about the practical importance of the hedging-pressure explanation.[38] It is not a very compelling hypothesis for financial futures contracts, because the active participants in the stock, bond, and foreign exchange markets are also heavily involved in futures and move easily between futures and spot markets. Further, we suspect that the hedging-pressure explanation has become less relevant for commodities as investors' access to futures markets has increased and the costs of this access have decreased. For instance, most investment banks now have divisions that explicitly look for investment opportunities in commodities markets. We will proceed on the assumption that the hedging-pressure effect is small.

Price Discovery

In Chapter 1, we noted that one economic purpose of futures markets is price discovery; that is, market participants can use futures prices to predict future spot prices. This purpose is most easily served if futures prices are unbiased predictors of future spot prices.[39] To the extent that risk and hedging pressure cause futures prices to deviate from expected future spot prices in unpredictable ways, futures prices will be less useful for price discovery. In later chapters, we will discuss the evidence on the ability of futures prices to forecast future spot prices.[40]

Arbitrage versus Systematic-Risk Pricing

We have developed two approaches to futures pricing. The arbitrage pricing approach shows how arbitrage processes drive futures prices into line with spot prices. The systematic-risk approach argues that futures prices are set such that investors earn an appropriate expected return to compensate for the systematic risk of their positions. We can show that these two approaches are consistent with each other. For simplicity, we will again ignore payouts.

By combining Equations 2.29 and 2.30, we see that the systematic-risk approach implies that the futures price should bear the following relationship to the expected future spot price:

$$F_{t,T} = P_t^*(1 + r_f). \tag{2.34}$$

If we add and subtract $P_t(1 + r_f)$ from the right-hand side of Equation 2.34, we get

---

[38] While Chang [1985] and others have shown a relationship between the hedging position of firms and the expected profit on a futures position, they have not corrected for systematic risk. Thus, their results do not directly support the hedging-pressure hypothesis. Jagannathan [1985] applied the Breeden consumption beta model to futures contracts. His results for the futures market were very similar to those obtained when the model was applied to other financial securities. Unfortunately, the model did not perform well in either case.

[39] However, in Chapter 3 we show that the risk premium embodied in the futures price can be useful to those making production decisions.

[40] See French [1986] and Fama and French [1987] for examples of this literature.

$$F_{t,T} = P_t(1 + r_f) - (P_t - P_t^*)(1 + r_f). \tag{2.35}$$

Now consider a futures contract written on a pure asset. In this case $P_t = P_t^*$, so Equation 2.35 becomes

$$F_{t,T} = P_t(1 + r_f) = P_t(1 + r_{t,T}) \tag{2.36}$$

which is the no-arbitrage pricing equation for a full-carry market.

Next, consider a futures contract written on a convenience asset. $P_t - P_t^*$ represents the premium that holders of the convenience asset are willing to pay over the price of a pure asset that has the same characteristics as the convenience asset but provides no convenience. Thus, the present value of the convenience must be worth at least $P_t - P_t^*$. Therefore, $(P_t - P_t^*)(1 + r_f)$ represents the future value of the marginal convenience value, and the systematic-risk equation, 2.35, is exactly the same as the fundamental no-arbitrage equation, 2.28, for convenience assets.

Summary

In this chapter, we studied arbitrage and equilibrium in the futures markets. The trading of arbitrageurs drives the relationships between prices in the futures and spot markets. We used the arbitrage trading strategies to derive the fundamental no-arbitrage relationship between futures prices and current spot prices of underlying futures assets, as well as the relationship among prices of futures contracts of different maturities. These relationships can be adjusted to include the payouts associated with certain commodities and securities and the transactions costs of trading.

Arbitrage relationships and strategies are useful not only to pure arbitrageurs; other market participants can use the same strategies to create synthetic positions that are sometimes less costly than the "real" positions. In equilibrium, we expect futures prices to be set by the trading of the market participants with the lowest transactions costs.

Futures prices are also related to current expectations about future spot prices of the underlying assets. Risk and return models such as the Capital Asset Pricing Model allow us to derive this relationship. We find that futures are priced such that investors will be compensated on an expected basis for the systematic risk they incur by taking a futures position. Thus, risk in futures markets can be viewed in the same light as risk in other markets.

Problems

1.   Suppose the current futures price for delivery of gold in 60 days is $375 per troy ounce. The current spot price of gold is $365 per troy ounce. Storing gold costs $12 per ounce per year, and the storage costs are paid when the gold is taken out of storage. The short-term interest rate is 6 percent per year. (We can borrow or lend at this rate.) Do all of the following calculations based on a 360-day year.

a.   What interest rate can we earn using a synthetic lending strategy?
b.   Is there an arbitrage? If so, how would we pursue it?
c.   What will happen to spot and futures prices as market participants pursue the arbitrage?
d.   What do the above calculations tell us about how we would expect the futures to be priced in equilibrium?

2.   Suppose the S&P 1 Index is made up solely of IBM stock. You observe the following data on March 15:

IBM stock	$125
September 15 S&P 1 futures price	$123
Borrowing and lending rate	7% per annum
Dividend on IBM (paid on the first day of February, May, August, and November)	$2.50

a.   Construct a strategy to synthetically borrow (risklessly) between March 15 and September 15.
b.   What rate do you pay on this synthetic borrowing? Is this an implied repo or implied reverse repo rate?
c.   How does the synthetic borrowing rate compare with the actual borrowing rate? Does this indicate there is an arbitrage opportunity? If so, is this a cash-and-carry or reverse cash-and-carry arbitrage opportunity?
d.   Notice that the September 15 S&P 1 futures price is below the spot price of IBM stock on March 15. Does this immediately imply that an arbitrage opportunity exists?
e.   What is the no-arbitrage price for the futures contract? Relate your answer here to that in part c.

3.   Suppose you observe the following data on March 28:

June 15 S&P 1 futures bid price	$119.90
June 15 S&P 1 futures ask price	$120.10
December 15 S&P 1 futures bid price	$119.40
December 15 S&P 1 futures ask price	$119.60
Borrowing and lending rate	7% per annum
Dividend on IBM (paid on the first day of February, May, August, and November)	$2.50

a.   What are the forward implied repo and forward implied reverse repo rates?
b.   Derive the no-arbitrage bounds for the December 15 futures price.
c.   Do the actual December 15 futures prices violate either of these bounds? If so, demonstrate that there is an arbitrage opportunity and determine the size of the arbitrage profit.

4.   Evaluate the following statement: "Using stock index futures, one can lock in the current expected rate of return on the market portfolio."

5. Suppose a portfolio manager observes the following prices and rates on April 11:

Bid price on IBM stock	$139.90
Ask price on IBM stock	$140.10
September 15 S&P 1 futures bid price	$143.60
September 15 S&P 1 futures ask price	$143.70
Bid price on a 157-day, $1-million-face-value T-bill	$959,816.00
Ask price on a 157-day, $1-million-face-value T-bill	$960,218.00
Arbitrageur overnight borrowing rate	10.50%
Arbitrageur overnight lending rate	9.00%
Transactions fees (per-share basis)	$0.020
Stocks	$0.012
Futures	$0.002
Borrowing or lending	$0.006
Dividend on IBM (paid on the first day of January, April, July, and October)	$2.50

   a.   What are the implied repo and reverse repo rates?
   b.   What are the no-arbitrage upper and lower bounds for pure arbitrage?
   c.   Is there a pure arbitrage opportunity? Examine both the no-arbitrage upper and lower bounds and the synthetic borrowing and lending rates.

6. Suppose a corporate treasurer faces the same prices and rates as those in Problem 5. On April 11, the treasurer is considering purchasing $100M face value of T-bills that expire on September 15.
   a.   What rate of return will the treasurer earn if he buys the T-bills?
   b.   What rate of return will he earn if he uses a cash-and-carry synthetic lending using IBM stock?
   c.   Construct a quasi-arbitrage table that analyzes the choice between parts a and b. Assume that buying T-bills is the benchmark position. Is this a cash-and-carry or a reverse cash-and-carry quasi-arbitrage? Compute Ω.
   d.   Now assume the cash-and-carry strategy is the benchmark position. Construct a quasi-arbitrage table. Is this a cash-and-carry or reverse cash-and-carry quasi-arbitrage? Compute Ω. How does it compare with your answer in part c?

7. Suppose a portfolio manager faces the same prices and rates as those in Problem 5. On April 11, she is considering selling stock and buying T-bills with $100M face value that expire on September 15.
   a.   What alternative strategy could the portfolio manager pursue to achieve a similar goal using futures?
   b.   Construct a quasi-arbitrage table to analyze the choice between selling stocks and buying T-bills and using a synthetic strategy. Compute Ω and determine which strategy is better.
   c.   How does the value of Ω compare with that in Problem 6? How do you explain this difference?

8.   Problems 5, 6, and 7, describe three market participants who could conceivably perform cash-and-carry arbitrages.

    a.   What is the relevant no-arbitrage upper bound for the entire market?

    b.   Which participant is likely to determine the equilibrium futures bid price?

9.   Suppose a trader observes the following prices on June 15:

Futures price of gold for September 15 delivery	$450 per ounce
Futures price of gold for December 15 delivery	$456 per ounce
Borrowing and lending rate	6% per annum

Assume the trader can short-sell gold.

    a.   What are the implied forward repo and implied forward reverse repo rates?

    b.   Is there an arbitrage opportunity?

    c.   If an arbitrage opportunity exists, describe the exact strategy and compute the arbitrage profit per ounce of gold.

Consider the extract from *The Wall Street Journal* for October 12, 1988, in answering Problems 10, 11, and 12.

	Open	High	Low	Settle	Change	Lifetime High	Lifetime Low	Open Interest
PLATINUM (NYM)—50 troy oz.; $ per troy oz.								
Oct	516.00	527.00	515.00	520.40	+ 7.30	667.50	452.00	1,269
Ja89	512.00	527.50	512.00	519.40	+ 9.30	646.00	459.00	13,937
Apr	517.00	530.00	517.00	522.90	+ 9.30	643.50	482.00	2,933
July	524.00	524.00	524.00	527.60	+ 9.30	640.00	501.00	364
Oct	526.00	535.00	526.00	533.30	+ 9.30	564.00	507.00	425
Est vol 9,739; vol Tues 5,356; open int 18,928, −534.								
PALLADIUM (NYM) 100 troy oz.; $ per troy oz.								
Dec	120.75	123.00	120.75	122.50	+ 2.40	139.50	104.50	4,074
Mr89	121.00	122.25	120.50	121.65	+ 2.40	132.00	115.50	1,513
June	119.75	119.75	119.75	120.65	+ 2.40	131.00	114.00	520
Est vol 892; vol Tues 45; open int 6,198, −28.								
GOLD (CMX)—100 troy oz.; $ per troy oz.								
Oct	405.50	409.00	405.50	408.40	+ 4.00	533.50	391.80	502
Dec	409.50	416.00	409.50	412.20	+ 3.80	546.00	395.50	82,456
Fb89	415.00	421.00	414.70	417.40	+ 3.80	549.50	401.00	12,966
Apr	420.50	426.50	420.50	422.60	+ 3.90	550.00	407.00	9,108
June	424.80	431.20	424.80	427.80	+ 3.90	570.00	412.00	16,147
Aug	....	....	....	433.20	+ 4.00	575.00	419.30	6,994
Oct	....	....	....	438.80	+ 4.10	575.50	423.00	8,851
Dec	441.50	446.50	441.50	444.30	+ 4.30	514.50	428.00	9,125
Fb90	....	....	....	449.90	+ 4.40	516.00	439.70	4,121
Apr	....	....	....	455.50	+ 4.50	525.80	443.00	3,021
June	....	....	....	461.30	+ 4.60	497.00	447.00	2,168
Aug	470.50	470.50	470.50	467.30	+ 4.70	470.50	453.00	665
Est vol 40,000; vol Tues 31,552; open int 156,124, −2,235.								
HEATING OIL NO. 2 (NYM) 42,000 gal.; $ per gal.								
Nov	.3890	.4100	.3885	.4084	+ .0176	.5140	.3700	20,781
Dec	.3975	.4180	.3975	.4167	+ .0175	.5200	.3765	33,286
Ja89	.4040	.4225	.4035	.4224	+ .0166	.5150	.3825	16,508
Feb	.4035	.4225	.4025	.4214	+ .0161	.5150	.3825	12,652
Mar	.3890	.4005	.3885	.4044	+ .0146	.5030	.3700	2,511
Apr	.3730	.3830	.3715	.3884	+ .0126	.5000	.3565	1,488
May	.3655	.3730	.3655	.3784	+ .0116	.4700	.3520	1,200
June	.3610	.3680	.3588	.3724	+ .0106	.4680	.3465	2,083
July	.3660	.3660	.3660	.3714	+ .0101	.4700	.3475	765
Aug	....	....	....	.3764	+ .0101	.4600	.3545	216
Sept	....	....	....	.3834	+ .0101	.4245	.3640	122
Dec	....	....	....	.4049	+ .0101	.4031	.3785	100
Est vol 25,992; vol Tues 16,942; open int 91,867, −81.								

10. Consider platinum and palladium. The T-bill yields for this period are approximately 7.4 percent. Storage costs for these metals are minimal. Are these metals pure assets or convenience assets? (Note that a metal can be a pure asset during part of the year and a convenience asset the rest of the year.)

11. Suppose the cost of storing gold is $6 per contract per month and $14 for a one-time transfer fee. All storage costs are paid when the gold is removed from storage. Assume that the T-bill yield is the appropriate interest rate for an arbitrageur and is the same as in Problem 10. What is the equilibrium dollar spread between the December 1988 and June 1989 gold futures prices? How does this compare with the actual spread? Express the difference as a percentage of the December 1988 futures price.

12. Consider the number 2 heating oil futures contract. Typically stocks of heating oil are held into the winter months; thus, the market tends to be at full carry November through February. Use the T-bill rate from Problem 10 to answer the following questions:
    a. What appear to be the per-month costs of storing heating oil between November and December 1988 and between December 1988 and January 1989?
    b. Which implied cost is lower? Does this make economic sense?
    c. When does heating oil appear to become a convenience asset?

13. Suppose the current spot price of copper is $1.36 per pound. The futures price for delivery in three months is $1.31 per pound. The riskless rate of interest is 8 percent per annum, and the expected rate of return on the market is 16 percent per annum. The expected future spot price of copper is $1.34, and the beta of copper is 0.50.
    a. According to the Capital Asset Pricing Model, what should be the current futures price for delivery in three months?
    b. Can you construct a strategy using the copper futures contract that will allow you to profit from the mispricing?
    c. What is the excess return from this strategy?
    d. What will drive prices back to equilibrium?
    e. Could you just as easily have simply bought the physical copper?

Risk Management

Managers often find that the profitability of their firms heavily depends on factors outside their control. Among these external influences are the many prices firms face, such as commodity prices, security prices, interest rates, and exchange rates. Futures markets can provide managers with tools to reduce and control their price risk. In the simplest cases, managers can use futures markets to completely eliminate outside price risks. However, most situations managers face are so complex that futures contracts can only partially reduce such risks.

In this chapter, we will see how futures hedges can be tailored to the peculiarities of each risk situation to eliminate as much risk as possible. We will also consider other actions firms can take to reduce risk and describe how to compare a hedge that involves futures contracts with one carried out by other means.

The Perfect Hedging Model

In a complex business environment, it usually is not possible to use futures or forward markets to completely eliminate risks due to movements in commodity prices, security prices, interest rates, or exchange rates. However, to develop the concepts of risk management, it is useful to first describe a situation in which complete elimination of such risks is possible. We discussed such a situation in Example 1.10 in Chapter 1. In that case, a wire manufacturer wants to lock in a price for purchasing gold the coming February. We saw he can do this by going long February gold futures. If gold prices rise, the increased cost of gold will be offset by the profits earned on the futures position. If gold prices fall, the saving on the gold purchase will be offset by futures losses. In either case, the net gold cost is locked in at the futures price when the manufacturer enters into the futures contract, for the futures risk is exactly opposite the risk to profits from gold price movements.

The use of a futures or forward position to completely eliminate a business risk is called a **perfect hedge**. Several conditions must be met before a perfect hedge is possible:

1.   The firm must know exactly how its profits will be affected by changes in a price or rate, and this relationship must be *linear*.[1]

2.   There must be a futures or forward contract that has the following characteristics:

   a.   It is written on the commodity or security that will affect the firm's profits.

   b.   The expiration date is the same as the date on which the firm's profits will be affected by the price or rate of the underlying asset.

   c.   It specifies a quantity equal to or evenly divisible into the quantity that will affect the firm.

The cash flows in Example 1.10 show how a perfect hedge works. Let T denote the date in February on which the wire manufacturer will purchase the gold, and let Q_T be the quantity of gold he will purchase, 100 ounces. The net cost to the manufacturer is the price of the gold less the profit on the futures position:

Gold Costs

Scenario	Gold Costs	Futures Profits	Net Gold Cost
P_T	$Q_T P_T$	$Q_T(F_{T,T} - F_{t,T})$ $= Q_T(P_T - F_{t,T})$	$Q_T F_{t,T}$

Here $P_T = F_{T,T}$ because of delivery date convergence, and

$$\text{Net gold cost} = \text{Gold costs} - \text{Futures profits}$$
$$= Q_T P_T - Q_T(P_T - F_{t,T}) = Q_T F_{t,T}.$$

This hedge meets all the requirements of a perfect hedge. The manufacturer knows that gold costs at T will be $Q_T P_T$. This cost is a linear function of the gold price, because every dollar change in the gold price will change $Q_T P_T$ by Q_T. The futures position expires precisely when the gold purchase is made at T, and it specifies the same grade and quantity of gold as the purchase.

By entering into the long futures position at time t, the manufacturer establishes that his costs at time T will be $Q_T F_{t,T}$. He thus locks in *today's futures price* for his gold purchase. Notice that this example disproves the common misperception that hedging with futures positions locks in *today's spot price* of the underlying asset.

We have ignored marking to market in our calculation of this perfect hedge's cash flows. We have computed the gains and losses on the futures position as

---

[1] The requirement that profits be linear in the commodity or security price is not strictly necessary. If the relationship is known but is nonlinear, one can hedge with dynamic hedging techniques similar to those used in option pricing. In this section, we discuss only simple, static hedges. We discuss dynamic hedges in Chapters 6 and 9. See Duffie and Jackson [1986] for a treatment of this subject.

though it were a forward position. In Chapter 1, we saw that this is a good approximation; however, later in this chapter we will see how marking to market affects hedging with futures.

The wire manufacturer example demonstrates a particular kind of hedge: It is a **long hedge**, because the manufacturer uses a long futures position to protect himself against rising prices. It is also an **anticipatory hedge**, because he is hedging a transaction that he anticipates for the future. Example 3.1 shows how a firm with a gold inventory can hedge the sale price of its gold. This hedge is a **short hedge**, because the firm will use a short futures position to protect itself against falling gold prices. It is also an **inventory hedge**, because the firm already holds the gold in inventory.

■ **Example 3.1: Hedging a Gold Inventory**   Suppose a firm has an inventory of 1,000 ounces of gold that it wishes to sell in July. Suppose also that the current spot price of gold is $450 per ounce, but the firm is worried that the price of gold will fall between now and July. To hedge itself against this possibility, the firm enters into 1,000 ounces of short positions in July gold futures at a futures price of $470 per ounce. The firm is now protected against falling gold prices, because the futures position will profit if gold prices do fall.

To see how the firm is hedged, consider what happens to the its sale revenues under two price scenarios. In the first scenario, the spot gold price rises to $500 per ounce in July; in the second scenario, the spot gold price falls to $425 per ounce in July:

	Gold Inventory Sale Revenues		
Scenario	**Gold Revenues**	**Futures Profits**	**Net Revenues**
$500	$500,000	(1,000)($470 − $500) = −$30,000	$470,000
$425	$425,000	(1,000)($470 − $425) = $45,000	$470,000

Under either scenario, the firm locks in today's futures price of $470. When gold prices rise, there will be an offsetting futures loss; when gold prices fall, an offsetting futures gain will occur. Notice that the firm does not lock in the current spot price of $450 per ounce.

This short inventory hedge can also be demonstrated in general terms:

	Gold Inventory Sale Revenues		
Scenario	**Gold Revenues**	**Futures Profits**	**Net Revenues**
P_T	$Q_T P_T$	$Q_T(F_{t,T} - F_{T,T})$ $= Q_T(F_{t,T} - P_T)$	$Q_T F_{t,T}$

We assume in this example that the firm sells its inventory gold in the spot market. The firm would get the same result if it delivered its gold into the futures market to fulfill its short position, because the futures settlement price at expiration equals the spot price, P_T. ■

Both the long anticipatory hedge and the short inventory hedge examples demonstrate the two basic steps in futures or forward hedging. First, the hedger determines how its profits are affected by movement in a commodity price, security price, interest rate, or exchange rate. Then the hedger enters into a futures or forward position with the opposite exposure. As a result, the risk is eliminated.

These hedging principles also apply to hedges in which the risk cannot be completely eliminated. Next, we will see how hedging works when the conditions required for a perfect hedge are not met.

Crosshedging

All the hedges we have discussed up to this point used futures contracts that are written on the asset whose price is to be hedged and that expire exactly when the hedge is to be lifted. In many instances, however, firms wish to hedge against price movements in a commodity or security for which there is no futures contract. We call this situation an **asset mismatch**. Many firms may also wish to hedge prices for dates on which no futures contract expires. We call this situation a **maturity mismatch**. It is no surprise that many firms face either asset or maturity mismatches. If there were futures contracts for every asset and date that people wanted to hedge, each market would be extremely illiquid.

It is still possible to hedge against price risk in such cases by using futures contracts on related commodities or securities or by using futures contracts that expire on dates other than those on which the hedges are lifted. Such hedges are called **crosshedges**. If there is an asset mismatch, an effective crosshedge requires a futures contract written on a commodity or security whose price moves very closely with the price to be hedged. If the price of the underlying asset and the price to be hedged are perfectly correlated, one can construct a perfect hedge. If the two prices are not correlated at all, one would actually add risk by taking a position in the futures. In the intermediate case, where the two prices are somewhat correlated, the crosshedge can reduce, but not completely eliminate, price risk.

The economics of each price risk situation determines which futures contracts are good candidates for a crosshedge. For example, if we wish to hedge a portfolio of gold coins, a gold futures contract will be a more effective crosshedge instrument than a silver futures contract. The gold hedge will not be perfect, however, because the price of gold coins and the price of the underlying futures asset, gold bullion with fineness of at least 99.5 percent, do not move in perfect lockstep.

Determining the appropriate futures contract is much easier for a maturity mismatch. To minimize a maturity mismatch, a crosshedge should use a futures contract whose expiration date is as close as possible to the date the hedge will be lifted.

The Crosshedge Equation

Once we have determined which contract most closely relates to the price we wish to hedge, we must determine how many contracts we need to minimize risk. One way to do this is to estimate a statistical relationship between the futures price of the contract to be used in the crosshedge and the price to be hedged. Suppose this relationship can be captured by the linear equation

$$P_{T^*} = a + bF_{T^*,T} + e_{T^*},\tag{3.1}$$

where e_{T^*} is a random error with zero mean, T is the expiration date of the futures contract, and T^* is the date the hedge will be closed out. If $T^* \neq T$, there is a maturity mismatch. The following time line demonstrates this situation:

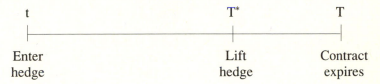

t	T^*	T
Enter hedge	Lift hedge	Contract expires

Equation 3.1 allows us to consider hedges that have both asset and maturity mismatches. We have placed the futures price on the right-hand side of Equation 3.1 for convenience only. Because the equation is purely statistical, we could just as well have specified it with the spot price on the right-hand side.

We can interpret the constant term by assuming for the moment that $b = 1$, $e_{T^*} = 0$, and $T = T^*$. Suppose the firm in Example 3.1 holds its gold inventory in Philadelphia. Suppose also that because of transportation costs, the spot price of gold in Philadelphia is always $1 per ounce more than it is in New York, the delivery location specified in the gold contract. In this case, Equation 3.1 is

$$P_T^p = a + P_T \tag{3.1a}$$
$$= 1 + F_{T,T},$$

where superscript p refers to Philadelphia. The net gold inventory revenues under the scenarios in Example 3.1 reflect the $1 difference between New York and Philadelphia prices:

Gold Inventory Sale Revenues

Scenario New York/Philadelphia	Gold Revenues	Futures Profits	Net Revenues
$500/$501	$501,000	$(1,000)($470 - $500)$ $= -$30,000$	$471,000
$425/$426	$426,000	$(1,000)($470 - $425)$ $= $45,000$	$471,000

The coefficient b in Equation 3.1 indicates that, on average, the spot price will move b dollars for every dollar move in the futures price. Thus, there is not necessarily a one-for-one correspondence between changes in the price to be hedged and changes in the futures price. A crosshedging strategy must adjust for the relationship between movements in the spot and futures prices. We do this by choosing the correct **hedge ratio**:

$$\text{Hedge ratio} = \frac{\text{Quantity of futures position}}{\text{Quantity of cash position}} \tag{3.2}$$

$$= \frac{Q_f}{Q_{T*}},$$

where we are assuming for now that Q_{T*} is fixed.

We have seen that the appropriate hedge ratio for a perfect hedge is 1, for in such cases changes in the futures price exactly offset changes in the spot price being hedged. In general, risk will be minimized if the firm hedges with a hedge ratio of [2]

$$\text{Risk-minimizing hedge ratio} = \frac{\text{Change in spot price}}{\text{Change in futures price}} \tag{3.3}$$

$$= b.$$

For example, suppose $b = 2$. If the futures price moves by \$1, the price to be hedged will move by \$2 (ignoring the error term). Since we want movements in the futures price to offset movements in the price to be hedged, we must use a futures position that covers twice the quantity we wish to hedge.

Now that we have determined the risk-minimizing hedge ratio, we can estimate the risk that will remain in a crosshedged position. For example, consider hedged revenues under a short hedge:

$$R_h = Q_{T*}P_{T*} + Q_f(F_{t,T} - F_{T*,T}). \tag{3.4}$$

The appropriate hedge ratio is

$$b = \frac{Q_f}{Q_{T*}} \tag{3.5}$$

or

$$Q_f = bQ_{T*}.$$

Thus, total revenues are

---

[2] Some have argued that the risk-minimizing hedge ratio is not the appropriate ratio to use, for it accounts only for a firm's hedging motives and ignores its speculative motives. This theory is called the **portfolio theory of hedging**. If a short hedger feels the futures price is too low relative to its "fair value," he or she might reduce the number of futures positions relative to the risk-minimizing hedge ratio. Rutledge [1972], Peck [1975], Anderson and Danthine [1981, 1983], and Benninga, Eldor, and Zilcha [1984] have discussed this approach. It is useful only if there are many instances of mispricing in the futures markets. Since there appears to be little evidence of such mispricings, we believe the risk-minimizing hedge ratio is most sensible. See Williams [1986] for other criticisms of this approach.

$$R_h = Q_{T*}P_{T*} + bQ_{T*}(F_{t,T} - F_{T*,T}) \tag{3.6}$$
$$= Q_{T*}(a + bF_{T*,T} + e_{T*}) + bQ_{T*}(F_{t,T} - F_{T*,T})$$
$$= Q_{T*}(a + bF_{t,T}) + Q_{T*}(e_{T*})$$
$$= Q_{T*}(\text{Target price} + \text{Basis error}).$$

The second line is derived by substituting Equation 3.1 for the spot price at T^*. We would achieve the same result for a long hedge.[3]

The **target price** is the price we will receive under the crosshedge if the random error is equal to zero. This target price is known and locked in at the outset. But hedged revenues usually are subject to uncertainty caused by the variability of the random, or basis, error, e_{T*}. This residual risk is called **basis risk**.[4] It is induced by the imperfect relationship between the futures price and the spot price at time T^*. Thus, crosshedging eliminates all risk except basis risk.

Equation 3.6 makes it clear that a hedge ratio of b reduces risk to the greatest extent possible, because the only risk that remains is completely random and uncontrollable. Crosshedges are more effective the higher the correlation between P_{T*} and $F_{T*,T}$, because then e_{T*} has a lower variance and the basis risk is lower.

Example 3.2 demonstrates how a crosshedge partially eliminates risk.

■ **Example 3.2: Crosshedging Gold Coins with Gold Futures**   Suppose we have a collection of 1,000 ounces of rare gold pieces and we are concerned that the value of those coins will drop over the next three months. There is no gold coin futures contract, but we know the price of gold coins is closely related to the price of gold bullion. Therefore, we consider crosshedging the value of our coin collection with a short position in COMEX gold futures expiring in three months.[5] The current COMEX gold futures price is $500 per ounce.

---

[3] We can use Equation 3.6 to show more formally that b is the correct hedge ratio. If we let HR denote the hedge ratio, per-unit hedged revenues are

$$R = P_{T*} + HR(F_{t,T} - F_{T*,T}).$$

Let Var[ ] and Cov[ ] denote variance and covariance, respectively. Then the variance of per-unit hedged revenues is

$$Var[R] = Var[P_{T*}] + (HR^2)Var[F_{T*,T}] - (2)(HR)Cov[P_{T*},F_{T*,T}],$$

because $F_{t,T}$ is known. Taking the derivative of Var[R] with respect to HR and setting it equal to zero yields the minimum-variance hedge ratio:

$$HR = \frac{Cov[P_{T*},F_{T*,T}]}{Var[P_{T*}]}.$$

A fundamental result of regression theory is that if we have an equation such as 3.1, b is exactly equal to the value for HR.

[4] The term *basis risk* is closely related to the term *basis* introduced in Chapter 1. The basis is the difference between the spot and futures prices. Basis risk refers to the difference between the spot price and the target price.

[5] See the specifications of the COMEX gold futures contract in Chapter 1.

After some analysis, we determine that the relationship between the prices of gold coins and COMEX gold futures is

$$\text{Gold coin price} = 200 + 1.20(\text{COMEX gold futures}) + e, \qquad (3.7)$$

where the error term, e, can take on values of only -10, 0, and 10 and both the gold coin price and the COMEX gold futures price are in ounces. Equation 3.7 shows us that there is an approximately linear relationship between the price of gold coins and the gold futures price. On average, the gold coin price is 20 percent more volatile than the gold futures price, because each $1 movement in the COMEX gold futures price is associated with a $1.20 movement in the gold coin price. The error term indicates that this linear relationship is not exact, because the gold coin price can differ from the relationship by as much as $10.

The 1.2 coefficient in Equation 3.7 indicates that the size of the futures position needed for the crosshedge is

$$\begin{aligned} \text{Size of futures position} &= (\text{Hedge ratio})(\text{Size of cash position}) \\ &= (1.2)(1{,}000 \text{ ounces}) \\ &= 1{,}200 \text{ ounces}. \end{aligned}$$

To see how well this crosshedge might work, we calculate the hedged value of the gold coin collection under six scenarios. We consider two values for the spot gold bullion price in three months, $450 and $550 per ounce, and the three levels of the random, or basis, error. We use Equation 3.7 to determine the price of gold coins given a gold bullion spot price and a level of basis error.

Gold Futures Price = $450

Basis Error	Gold Coin Value	Futures Profit	Hedged Value
$e = -10$	$(1,000)[200 + (1.2)(450) - 10]$ = $730,000	$(1,200)(500 - 450)$ = $60,000	$790,000
$e = 0$	$(1,000)[200 + (1.2)(450) + 0]$ = $740,000	$(1,200)(500 - 450)$ = $60,000	$800,000
$e = 10$	$(1,000)[200 + (1.2)(450) + 10]$ = $750,000	$(1,200)(500 - 450)$ = $60,000	$810,000

Gold Futures Price = $550

Basis Error	Gold Coin Value	Futures Profit	Hedged Value
$e = -10$	$(1,000)[200 + (1.2)(550) - 10]$ = $850,000	$(1,200)(500 - 550)$ = $-\$60,000$	$790,000
$e = 0$	$(1,000)[200 + (1.2)(550) + 0]$ = $860,000	$(1,200)(500 - 550)$ = $-\$60,000$	$800,000
$e = 10$	$(1,000)[200 + (1.2)(550) + 10]$ = $870,000	$(1,200)(500 - 550)$ = $-\$60,000$	$810,000

No matter what the spot price of gold bullion in three months, the hedged value of the gold coin collection equals $800,000 plus or minus $10,000. The unhedged value of the collection can range from $730,000 to $870,000. Thus, the crosshedge substantially reduces the risk of the position.

If the basis error is zero, the portfolio value is \$800 per ounce. This value is simply the target price from Equation 3.6:

$$\text{Target price} = a + bF_{t,T}$$
$$= 200 + [(1.2)(500)]$$
$$= 800.$$

If the basis error is positive, the gold coin price is higher relative to the gold bullion price, and the hedged price is higher. In this case, the basis has moved *with* the owner of the gold coins. If the basis error is negative, the gold coin price is lower relative to the gold bullion price, and the hedged price is lower. Here the basis has moved *against* the coin owner.

For a given level of basis error, the hedged value of the gold coins is the same no matter what the gold bullion spot price is in three months. Thus, the crosshedge eliminates the risk associated with overall movements in the price of gold, and only the basis risk remains. It substantially reduces the risk of the gold coin value, because the basis risk can move only plus or minus \$10 while the overall price of gold can move much more than that. ■

Example 3.2 demonstrates how we can use a statistical relationship such as Equation 3.1 to construct a crosshedge. Equation 3.1 determines the best hedge ratio and allows us to analyze the basis risk of the crosshedge. The challenge in crosshedging is to estimate Equation 3.1. There is no single way to accomplish this, however. The two major approaches are the statistical approach and the analytical approach. The **statistical approach** uses techniques such as regression analysis to estimate the parameters a and b. The **analytical approach** uses a priori knowledge about the relationship between P_{T*} and $F_{T*,T}$ to estimate a and b. We will now discuss each approach in turn.

The Statistical Approach

The most obvious way to estimate Equation 3.1 is to run a linear regression. First, we define

P_c = spot price of cash position to be hedged

P_f = spot price of asset underlying the futures contract used in the crosshedge

For simplicity, suppose $T^* = T$ in Equation 3.1 so that there is no maturity mismatch.[6] Both P_c and P_f are as of time T, so we can omit the time notation. By the delivery date arbitrage condition, the futures price when the hedge is lifted will

---

[6] If there is a maturity mismatch and $T^* < T$, we can easily adapt the analysis using concepts that we develop later in the chapter. Essentially, we will multiply the hedge ratios derived in this section by $1/(1 + r_{T*,T})$.

be exactly equal to the spot price of the asset underlying the futures, so $P_f = F_{T,T}$. Thus, we can use P_f to represent the futures price on the right-hand side of Equation 3.1:[7]

$$P_c = a + bP_f + e. \tag{3.8}$$

Next, we will examine two ways to estimate this relationship to obtain a hedge ratio.

Price Change Regression   If we let -1 denote the previous period, Equation 3.8 becomes

$$\Delta P_c = b\Delta P_f + \Delta e, \tag{3.8a}$$

where

$$\Delta P_c = P_c - P_c(-1)$$

$$\Delta P_f = P_f - P_f(-1)$$

$$\Delta e = e - e(-1)$$

We can estimate Equation 3.8a by running a linear regression which uses changes in the prices of both P_c and P_f. This is called a **price change regression**:[8, 9]

$$\Delta P_c = \alpha_\Delta + \beta_\Delta \Delta P_f + \varepsilon_\Delta. \tag{3.9}$$

The -1 price depends on the type of data used. With daily data, it is the previous day's price; with monthly data, it is the previous month's price. The subscript Δ refers to price changes. The slope term β_Δ is an estimate of the hedge ratio, b.[10] It expresses our intuitive notion of the hedge ratio very well. Recall from Equation 3.3 that the risk-minimizing hedge ratio is the ratio of the change in the

---

[7] We discuss the reasons for this substitution after we develop this argument a little further.

[8] One might wonder why we do not estimate Equation 3.8 directly. While a linear regression of the level of P_c on the level of P_f has intuitive appeal, it often yields misleading answers. If the movements in P_c and P_f do not satisfy certain statistical properties, the linear regression in the levels Equation 3.8 gives can generate unreliable estimates of the hedge ratio, b. For example, suppose both P_c and P_f follow a **random walk**. This means that the best estimates for the levels of P_c and P_f tomorrow are their levels today. Many security and commodity prices tend to follow random walks. In such cases, the sample sizes that are available usually are not large enough for the β estimated from Equation 3.8 to produce a reliable estimate of b.

[9] The hedge ratios obtained with linear regression often are called **Johnson-Stein hedge ratios**, because Johnson [1960] and Stein [1961] originally proposed the method.

[10] If the estimate of the α_Δ constant term in Equation 3.9 is very far from zero, we should reconsider whether Equation 3.1 is a useful approximation.

cash price to the change in the futures price. This is precisely the interpretation of β_Δ in Equation 3.9.

We can interpret this regression further if we note that the hedge ratio estimate is given by[11]

$$\beta_\Delta = \frac{\text{Corr}(\Delta P_c, \Delta P_f)\text{SD}(\Delta P_c)}{\text{SD}(\Delta P_f)},$$

where

$\text{Corr}(\Delta P_c, \Delta P_f)$ = correlation between ΔP_c and ΔP_f

$\text{SD}(\Delta P_c)$ = standard deviation of ΔP_c

$\text{SD}(\Delta P_f)$ = standard deviation of ΔP_f

This expression for β_Δ shows that the hedge ratio is higher the greater the correlation between changes in the price being hedged and changes in the price of the underlying futures asset. This accords with the point made earlier that it is correlation between the price to be hedged and the futures price that makes a hedge effective. We also see that the hedge ratio is higher the greater the risk of the price to be hedged, because more futures contracts are needed to hedge the greater risk. Likewise, the hedge ratio is lower the greater the risk of the underlying futures price.

It may seem odd that we do not run the regression

$$\Delta P_c = \alpha_\Delta + \beta_\Delta \Delta F + \varepsilon_\Delta, \tag{3.9a}$$

where ΔF is the change in the price of the futures contract used in the crosshedge, since our goal is to estimate the ratio of spot price changes to futures price changes. To see why it is not acceptable to use Equation 3.9a, compare its results with those of Equation 3.9 for a perfect hedge of a pure asset. In this case, we know the answer: The hedge ratio must equal 1. Equation 3.9 gives us a hedge ratio of

$$\begin{aligned}
\text{Hedge ratio} &= \frac{\Delta P_c}{\Delta P_f} \\
&= \frac{P_c - P_c(-1)}{P_c - P_c(-1)} \\
&= 1,
\end{aligned}$$

because $P_c = P_f$ in a perfect hedge. Equation 3.9a gives us a hedge ratio of

---

[11] See footnote 3 for a formal derivation of this equation. Note that $\text{Corr}[X,Y]\text{SD}[X]\text{SD}[Y] = \text{Cov}[X,Y]$.

$$\text{Hedge ratio} = \frac{\Delta P_c}{\Delta F}$$

$$= \frac{P_c - P_c(-1)}{P_c - P_c(-1)(1+r)}$$

$$\neq 1,$$

where r is the one-period interest rate and $F(-1) = P_c(-1)(1+r)$.

Using the spot price, P_f, as in Equation 3.9 gives us the correct answer, while using the futures price, F, as in Equation 3.9a gives us the wrong answer. This is because it is the relationship between P_c and F *when the hedge is lifted* that makes a crosshedge work.[12] At this point $F = P_f$, so Equation 3.9 is appropriate. Before the hedge is lifted, the futures price is affected by the cost of carry and is not equal to what it will be when the hedge is lifted.

The only way it would be correct to use the futures price to estimate the hedge ratio is to define the time periods in the regression to be the time between the expiration dates of the futures contract. Then the futures prices used in the regression would always be the prices obtained when a crosshedge might be lifted. This approach limits the sample size we could use in such regressions, for only futures prices at intervals ranging from one to three months would be acceptable. Using the spot price of the underlying futures asset, as in Equation 3.9, allows us to expand the number of observations for the statistical estimates beyond the number of expiration dates of the futures contract. In effect, we can treat each spot price as the price of a futures contract that expires immediately, because if there were a futures contract, it would have a price equal to P_f at that point.[13]

Rate-of-Change Regression   When we use the price change regression in Equation 3.9 to estimate hedge ratios, we are assuming the relationship between changes in P_c and P_f is stable. This is usually a good assumption for most commodities. However, researchers have found that this relationship is not stable for some financial instruments, such as stocks; the relationship between the *rates of change* of P_c and P_f appears more stable. In such cases, it is preferable to run a regression called a **rate-of-change regression**:

$$\frac{\Delta P_c}{P_c} = \alpha_r + \beta_r \left(\frac{\Delta P_f}{P_f} \right) + \varepsilon_r, \tag{3.10}$$

where the subscript r refers to a regression in rates of change.

To relate the slope term, β_r, to the hedge ratio b, recall that

---

[12] Recall we are assuming that $T^* = T$. If $T^* < T$, there will be an adjustment to the hedge ratio, which we discuss later.

[13] If the relationship between P_c and P_f depends on the season of the year, we can use only those observations that are from the same season as the one in which the hedge will be lifted.

$$\text{Hedge ratio} = b = \frac{\Delta P_c}{\Delta P_f} . \tag{3.11}$$

Now suppose $\alpha_r = 0$ and $\varepsilon_r = 0$ in Equation 3.10.[14] Then the slope term, β_r, is the ratio of the percentage change in P_c to the percentage change in P_f. If we multiply and divide the right-hand side of Equation 3.11 by both P_c and P_f and rearrange, we get

$$\text{Hedge ratio} = b = \frac{\left(\dfrac{P_c}{P_f}\right)\left(\dfrac{\Delta P_c}{P_c}\right)}{\dfrac{\Delta P_f}{P_f}} \tag{3.12}$$

$$= \frac{P_c}{P_f}(\beta_r).$$

Thus, we can use the current values of P_c and P_f to determine the hedge ratio from the estimate of β_r in Equation 3.10. We may need to change the hedge periodically if the ratio of P_c to P_f changes over time.

How does one choose between the price change regression and the rate-of-change regression techniques when estimating a hedge ratio?[15] There is no easy answer to this question. The analyst must ask whether the Equation 3.9 relationship or the Equation 3.10 relationship is more likely to be stable over time. As mentioned earlier, the price change regression seems to work better for commodities, while the rate-of-change regression seems more suitable for financial instruments. When in doubt, one can run statistical stability tests on the two equations.[16]

Units of Measure   The final consideration when estimating a hedge ratio concerns the units of measure for the price to be hedged and the price of the underlying futures asset, for the units of the hedge ratio must correspond to the units in which the prices are measured. For example, suppose we are again crosshedging a 1,000-ounce portfolio of gold coins with the gold futures contract, as in Example 3.2. The price of the gold coins is now per pound, and the gold futures price again is per ounce. Since there are 16 ounces in a pound, we are now hedging $1,000/16 = 62.5$ pounds of gold coins. Equation 3.7 becomes

Gold coin price (per pound)   (3.7a)
    $= (16)(200) + (16)[1.2(\text{COMEX gold futures})] + (16)(e)$
    $= 3,200 + 19.2(\text{COMEX gold futures}) + e'.$

---

[14] As with Equation 3.9, we should reconsider our specification if the constant in Equation 3.10 is not close to zero.

[15] See Witt, Schroeder, and Hayenga [1987] for a comparison of these techniques.

[16] See Judge et al. [1985] for a discussion of stability tests.

The hedge ratio is now 19.2 ounces of gold futures per pound of gold coins to be hedged. The gold futures position required by the hedge is

> Size of futures position (in ounces)
>   = (Hedge ratio)(Size of cash position in pounds)
>   = (19.20)(62.50)
>   = 1,200.

We need not make the same adjustment if we use the rate-of-change regression to estimate the hedge ratio, because rates of change are unit free.

Basis Risk   We can quantify the basis risk in a crosshedge from the error term properties of the regression used to estimate the hedge ratio. If the regression errors are highly variable, the basis risk of the crosshedge will also be high, because movements in the futures price are not greatly correlated with movements in the cash price to be hedged. This is clear from Equation 3.6.

The price change and rate-of-change regressions produce error terms with different interpretations. The error term in Equation 3.9 represents the portion of the *per-period* change in the price to be hedged that is not explained by the change in the futures price. The error term in Equation 3.10 represents the portion of the per-period percentage change in the price to be hedged that the percentage change in the futures price does not explain. The per-period price change and percentage price change basis risks must be adjusted for the number of periods over which the hedge will occur. For example, the basis risk is higher if a hedge is held in place for four weeks rather than for one week. If the price changes are computed on a weekly basis, we must adjust our calculation of the basis risk on the four-week hedge to reflect the hedge's longer period. This adjustment depends on the properties of the error terms. We will discuss this in detail later.

Example 3.3 shows how to use a price change regression to determine the hedge ratio and the level of basis risk of a crosshedge involving the New York Mercantile Exchange crude oil futures contract. We will discuss the crude oil futures contract in detail in Chapter 9.

▪ **Example 3.3: Crosshedging Brent Crude Oil with Crude Oil Futures**
Suppose a firm is holding 100,000 barrels of Brent crude oil. The spot price of Brent is $12 per barrel, so the firm's oil holdings are worth $1.2 million. The firm fears the price of Brent oil will fall and wants to hedge its oil inventories. While there is a crude oil futures contract traded at the New York Mercantile Exchange, its underlying grade is West Texas Intermediate (WTI). Thus, the firm must use a crosshedge to hedge the value of its Brent crude oil inventories.[17]

For an initial look at the relationship between Brent and WTI crude oil prices, consider Figure 3.1, which plots both prices from July 1986 through July 1987. Both prices exhibit a great deal of randomness; however, there also appears to be some comovement. Thus, an effective crosshedge may be possible.

---

[17] A Brent crude oil futures contract recently began trading on the IPE in London. Of course, if this contract became liquid, our firm would hedge with it.

Figure 3.1 WTI and Brent Crude Oil Price per Barrel

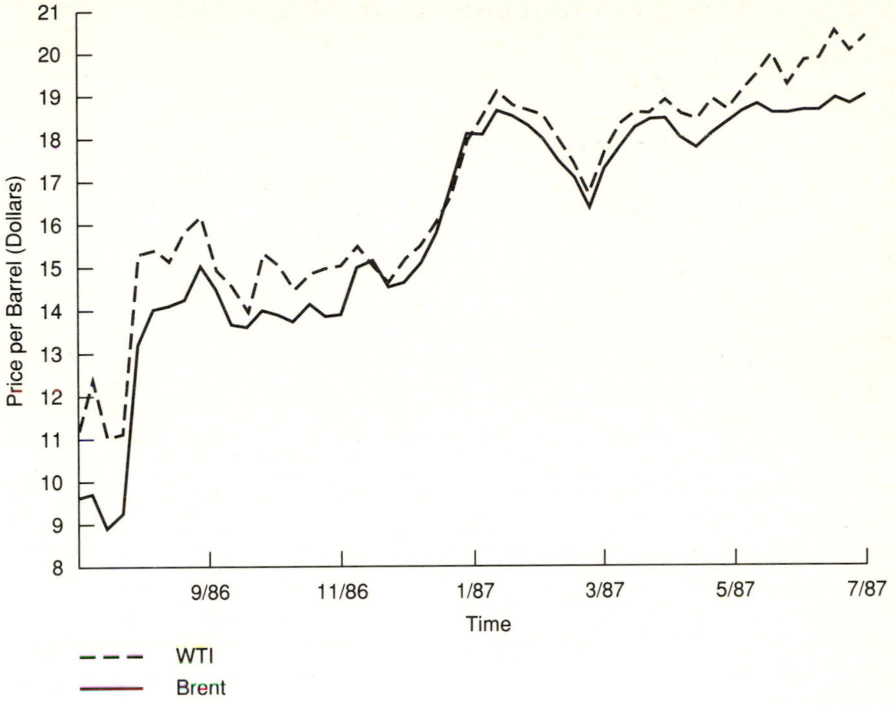

Source: Drexel Burnham Lambert.

The firm quantifies the comovement between the two prices by estimating the price change regression in Equation 3.9. It chooses the price change regression because oil is a commodity. Part A of Table 3.1 presents the results of this regression. As expected, the constant term, α_Δ, is close to zero. The estimated value of the slope is $\beta_\Delta = 0.76$. Thus, Brent appears to be less volatile than WTI. To crosshedge the 100,000-barrel Brent inventory, the firm's crude oil futures position must cover the following number of barrels:

> Number of barrels of crude oil futures
> = (Slope estimate)(Number of barrels of Brent)
> = (0.76)(100,000)
> = 76,000 barrels.

Since each crude oil futures contract represents 1,000 barrels of crude, the firm needs 76 short futures contracts.

Next, the firm examines the level of basis risk implied by the regression equation. Part B of Table 3.1 presents the variances of the weekly change in the Brent price and the basis error. **In sample** refers to the data used for the regression.

Table 3.1 Crosshedging Regression for Hedging Brent with WTI

A: Regression of Weekly Brent Price Change on Weekly WTI Price Change

Y = Weekly change in price of Brent
X = Weekly change in price of WTI

Regression Output		
Constant		0.041150
Standard error of Y estimate		0.362881
R-squared		0.753519
Number of observations		52
Degrees of freedom		50
X coefficient(s)	0.764514	
Standard error of coefficient	0.061836	

B: Variances

Variance	
In sample—Brent	0.513705
Out of sample—Brent	0.459297
In sample—residual	0.126618
Out of sample—residual	0.106552

The basis error for each observation is the unexplained portion of the change in the Brent price:

$$\text{Basis error} = \text{Brent price change} - \alpha_\Delta - \beta_\Delta(\text{WTI price change}). \qquad (3.13)$$

The ratio of the in-sample variance of the basis error to the in-sample variance of the change in the Brent price is $0.126618/0.513705 = 0.25$. Thus, changes in the WTI price can explain about 75 percent of the variance of the Brent price changes.[18]

To get an idea of the dollar consequences of the risk reduction the crosshedge offers, the firm computes the standard deviation of the portion of the change in the Brent price not explained by the price of WTI. This is simply the square root of the variance of the basis error, or $\sqrt{0.126618} = \$0.36$ per barrel. A **95 percent confidence interval** for the weekly basis error is zero plus or minus 1.96 standard deviations. Assuming the basis error comes from a normal distribution, this confidence interval indicates that 95 percent of the time the level of basis error is between

---

[18] This 75 percent is also the R-squared of the regression.

Figure 3.2 Brent Price Change versus Basis Error, Weekly per Barrel

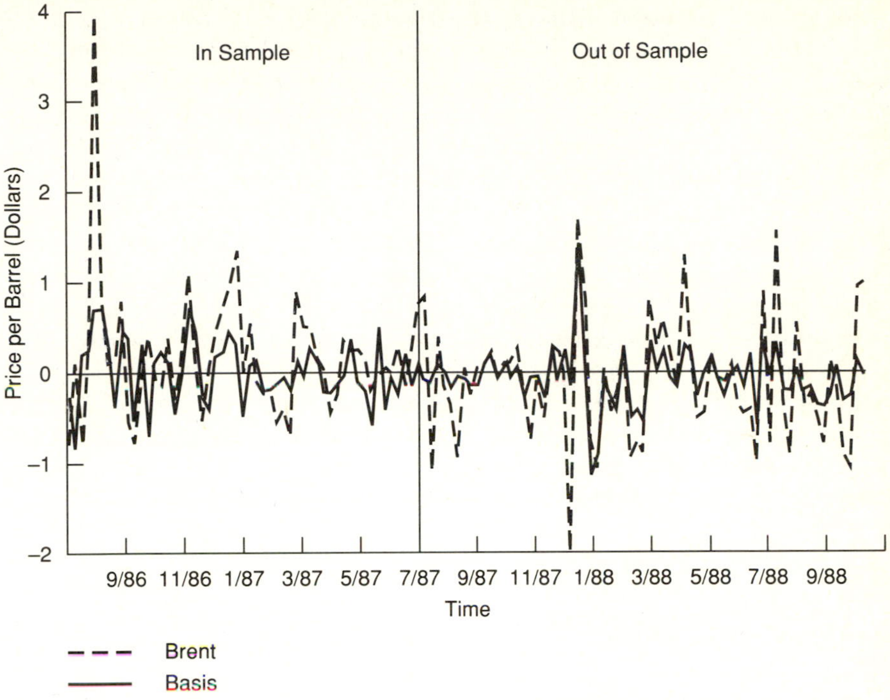

Source: Drexel Burnham Lambert.

95 percent confidence interval for weekly basis error
= ± 1.96(Total standard deviation)
= ± 1.96($0.36)(100,000)
= ± $70,560.

The firm compares this risk with the risk of an unhedged position. The standard deviation of the weekly Brent price change over the sample period is $\sqrt{0.513705} = \$0.72$ per barrel. Thus, 95 percent of the time, the weekly change in the value of the portfolio will be between

95 percent confidence interval for weekly price change
= ± 1.96($0.72)(100,000)
= ± $141,120.

Thus, although substantial basis risk remains, the crosshedge can eliminate much of the total risk. We can observe this risk reduction in Figure 3.2, which plots the basis error and the Brent price change. In sample—from July 1986 through July 1987—the basis errors clearly have lower volatility than the total changes in the Brent price. This comparison is useful if the relationship between the prices of Brent and WTI remains the same in the future. We can also examine the performance of the hedge **out of sample**—the time after July 1987 in Figure 3.2. This is a more relevant comparison, for all actual hedging is performed out of sample. The out-of-sample basis errors are computed from Equation 3.13 using the α_Δ and β_Δ estimated in sample. As is true in sample, the out-of-sample basis errors are much less volatile than the changes in the Brent price. From part B of Table 3.1, we see that the out-of-sample ratio of the basis error variance to the Brent price change variance is $0.106552/0.459297 = 0.23$. This is very close to the in-sample ratio of 0.25. Thus, the crosshedge appears to perform well both in and out of sample.

These calculations of basis risk have assumed that the firm is hedging over only one week. There will be more basis risk if the hedge covers a longer period. To measure the basis risk over a longer period, we determine the standard deviation of the basis error over that period. We use our estimates of the weekly basis error from Equation 3.13 to construct the basis errors over N-week intervals. For example, suppose $N = 4$ and our data cover 52 weeks. If we add up the basis errors for weeks 1–4, 5–8, 9–12, and so on, we will get estimates of the basis error over four-week intervals. We then take the standard deviation of these 13 (52/4) four-week basis error estimates. For the in-sample data in this example, the standard deviation is \$0.55. The 95 percent confidence interval for the basis error over four-week periods is

95 percent confidence interval for 4-week basis error
= ± 1.96(Standard deviation)
= ± 1.96(\$0.55)(100,000)
= ± \$107,800.

■

Often one can improve a crosshedge if the price of the commodity or security to be hedged is related to more than one futures contract. For example, suppose a beef purchaser believes the beef sale price is related to both the futures price of live cattle and the futures price of pork bellies (bacon). The latter relationship may pick up variations in the cost of slaughtering. The purchaser might use a crosshedge that includes both live cattle and pork belly futures contracts. To estimate the hedge ratios, he could use a regression such as

$$\Delta P_c = \alpha_\Delta + \beta_\Delta^1 \Delta P_f^1 + \beta_\Delta^2 \Delta P_f^2 + \varepsilon_\Delta, \tag{3.14}$$

where

P_f^1 = price of live cattle

P_f^2 = price of pork bellies

This hedging equation shows that the appropriate hedge ratios are[19]

---

[19] Before adding more contracts to a hedging equation, one must determine whether an additional contract will add explanatory power to the regression. See Judge et al. [1985] for a discussion of statistical tests for inclusion of variables in a regression. In general, it is better to use the minimum possible number of contracts.

$$\beta_\Delta^1 = \frac{\text{Number of units of live cattle futures}}{\text{Number of units of beef to be purchased}} \qquad \textbf{(3.15)}$$

$$\beta_\Delta^2 = \frac{\text{Number of units of pork belly futures}}{\text{Number of units of beef to be purchased}}$$

It is conceivable that some of the estimated hedge ratios will be negative. In such cases, the crosshedger should take an opposite position in futures. If the beef purchaser finds that β_Δ^1 is positive but β_Δ^2 is negative, he will go long live cattle futures and go short pork belly futures.

This type of crosshedge may be especially useful if we wish to hedge against movements in an interest rate. The best hedge might involve a combination of futures on several different financial instruments.

The Analytical Approach

The analytical approach to estimating the a and b parameters in Equation 3.1 relies on the use of some sort of a priori information about the relationship between the spot and futures prices involved in the crosshedge. Many types of information can be used in this way, and we will see a number of examples in later chapters. To introduce the approach here, we will show how we can use our knowledge of arbitrage pricing to estimate the parameters in Equation 3.1 for a maturity mismatch.

In the perfect hedging model, we assume there is a futures contract that expires on the day we want to buy or sell the underlying asset. In Example 3.1, the use of a short futures position to hedge the sale of gold inventory guarantees hedged revenues of

$$R_h = Q_T F_{t,T}. \qquad \textbf{(3.16)}$$

There is no risk because delivery date convergence ensures that any change in the underlying spot price at T (P_T) will automatically be offset by an equal change in $F_{T,T}$.

In many instances, there is no futures contract that expires on the date of the sale or purchase that a firm wishes to hedge. Consider the example of a firm with an inventory of copper, a convenience asset, that it plans to sell on date T^*. There is a copper futures contract available for the firm's hedge, but it expires on date $T > T^*$. The firm has a maturity mismatch and must perform a crosshedge with a maturity mismatch.

If the firm does not hedge, its total copper revenues from the sale, R_u, will be

$$R_u = Q_{T^*} P_{T^*}. \qquad \textbf{(3.17)}$$

If the firm hedges, its revenues will be

$$R_h = Q_{T^*} P_{T^*} + Q_f(F_{t,T} - F_{T^*,T}), \qquad \textbf{(3.18)}$$

where Q_f is the quantity of copper covered by the firm's short futures position. To derive the appropriate hedge ratio and quantify the basis risk of this crosshedge, we must determine what form Equation 3.1 takes in this situation.

Suppose for simplicity that interest rates and storage costs are known. We know from our discussion of arbitrage in Chapter 2 that in equilibrium,

$$F_{T^*,T} \leq P_{T^*}(1 + r_{T^*,T}) + SC_{T^*,T}, \tag{3.19}$$

where $SC_{T^*,T}$ is the future value of storage costs between T^* and T. The futures price at T^* can therefore be expressed as

$$F_{T^*,T} = P_{T^*}(1 + r_{T^*,T}) + SC_{T^*,T} + \varepsilon_{T^*} \tag{3.20}$$
$$= \text{Full-carry price} + \text{Error term}.$$

The **error term**, ε_{T^*}, measures the divergence of the futures price from the full-carry futures price. It equals zero if the fundamental no-arbitrage equation holds exactly and the futures market at T^* is at full carry. In Chapter 2, we saw that the error term, ε_{T^*}, can be negative if there is a positive marginal convenience value to holding copper. However, the potential for cash-and-carry arbitrage will keep it from rising too far above zero. Thus, most of the fluctuations in the error term are caused by fluctuations in the marginal convenience value.

We can divide both sides of Equation 3.20 by $1 + r_{T^*,T}$ and solve for the price P_{T^*} to get a form of the crosshedging equation, 3.1:

$$P_{T^*} = -\left(\frac{1}{1 + r_{T^*,T}}\right) SC_{T^*,T} + \left(\frac{1}{1 + r_{T^*,T}}\right) F_{T^*,T} - \left(\frac{1}{1 + r_{T^*,T}}\right) \varepsilon_{T^*} \tag{3.21}$$
$$= a + bF_{T^*,T} + e_{T^*},$$

where $a = -[1/(1 + r_{T^*,T})]SC_{T^*,T}$ is the negative of the present value of storage costs between T^* and T as of date T^*.

The hedge ratio, therefore, is[20]

---

[20] If there is a relationship between the size of the marginal convenience value and the price of the asset being hedged, this hedge ratio must be adjusted. For example, suppose the error term in Equation 3.20 is determined solely by the marginal convenience value. Then we can rewrite that equation as

$$F_{T^*,T} = P_{T^*}(1 + r_{T^*,T}) + SC_{T^*,T} - CV_{T^*,T}.$$

For example, we will see in Chapter 8 that there may be a positive correlation between the marginal convenience value and the price of copper: High copper prices occur when copper is scarce and marginal convenience values are high. Thus, if a short hedger is protecting against rising copper prices, he or she should increase the hedge ratio (relative to Equation 3.22), because any rise in the spot price of copper will not be followed by an increase in the futures price of $\Delta P_{T^*}(1 + r_{T^*,T})$. This is true because the marginal convenience value will also increase, dampening the rise in the futures price. To the extent that the difference between T^* and T is not considerable, this effect should not be large.

$$\text{Hedge ratio} = b \tag{3.22}$$

$$= \frac{1}{1 + r_{T^*,T}},$$

or

$$Q_f = bQ_{T^*} \tag{3.22a}$$

$$= \left(\frac{1}{1 + r_{T^*,T}}\right) Q_{T^*}.$$

The target price of the crosshedge is

$$\text{Target price} = a + bF_{t,T} \tag{3.23}$$

$$= -\left(\frac{1}{1 + r_{T^*,T}}\right) SC_{T^*,T} + \left(\frac{1}{1 + r_{T^*,T}}\right) F_{t,T}.$$

The target price is known at time t, so its portion of revenues is locked in when the hedged position is taken.

However, there is some uncertainty in hedged revenues because of basis risk. If we combine Equations 3.18 and 3.22a, we get

$$R_h = Q_{T^*}P_{T^*} + Q_f (F_{t,T} - F_{T^*,T}) \tag{3.24}$$

$$= Q_{T^*}P_{T^*} + Q_{T^*} \left(\frac{1}{1 + r_{T^*,T}}\right)(F_{t,T} - F_{T^*,T}).$$

If we replace $F_{T^*,T}$ with the expression in Equation 3.20, hedged revenues become

$$R_h = Q_{T^*}P_{T^*} + Q_{T^*} \left(\frac{1}{1 + r_{T^*,T}}\right)[F_{t,T} - P_{T^*}(1 + r_{T^*,T}) - SC_{T^*,T} - \varepsilon_{T^*}] \tag{3.24a}$$

$$= -Q_{T^*} \left(\frac{1}{1 + r_{T^*,T}}\right) SC_{T^*,T} + Q_{T^*} \left(\frac{1}{1 + r_{T^*,T}}\right) F_{t,T} - Q_{T^*} \left(\frac{1}{1 + r_{T^*,T}}\right) \varepsilon_{T^*}$$

$$= Q_{T^*}(\text{Target price} + \text{Basis error}).$$

When $T = T^*$, there is no maturity mismatch and $P_T = F_{T,T}$; thus, $a = 0$, $b = 1$, and $e_T = 0$ in Equation 3.21. The target price equals the futures price at t, and there is no basis risk.

Comparison of the revenues in Equations 3.17 and 3.24a shows how futures hedging can reduce total risk when there is a maturity mismatch. Unhedged revenues (Equation 3.17) are subject to the risk of movement in the commodity or security price at time T^*, while hedged revenues (Equation 3.24a) are subject to the risk of the basis error term at T^*. Price risk is usually greater than basis risk, because spot prices tend to fluctuate more than the difference between full-carry futures prices and actual futures prices. Fundamental factors that cause P_{T^*} to change are likely to cause $F_{T^*,T}$ to move in the same direction.

Example 3.4 shows how to estimate the effect of basis risk on a copper hedge with a maturity mismatch. It presents a long hedge, instead of the short hedge just discussed, to show the generality of the analysis.

▪ **Example 3.4: Maturity Mismatch in a Copper Hedge**   Suppose a manufacturer of copper roofs must purchase 2.5 million pounds of copper at the end of January. The firm wishes to hedge against increases in the price of copper by going long futures, but the nearest copper futures contract expires in March. Thus, the firm must use a crosshedge that has a two-month maturity mismatch.

The current March futures price is \$1.2000 per pound, and each contract specifies 25,000 pounds. The interest rate is 1.02 percent per month, or 2.04 percent over two months.

The appropriate hedge ratio for the firm's crosshedge is

$$\text{Hedge ratio} = \frac{1}{1 + r_{T^*,T}}$$
$$= \frac{1}{1.0204}$$
$$= 0.98,$$

so the firm's futures position must cover the following number of pounds:

$$\text{Pounds of copper futures} = (\text{Hedge ratio})(\text{Number of pounds of copper})$$
$$= (0.98)(2.5 \text{ million pounds})$$
$$= 2.45 \text{ million pounds.}$$

Therefore, since each copper contract consists of 25,000 pounds, the firm must take long positions in 98 copper futures contracts.

The firm can gauge the risk of this long hedge by specifying different reasonable scenarios for the late January (time T^*) copper spot price and error term in Equation 3.20. Suppose the firm has analyzed historical data and determined that the copper price may vary between \$0.8000 and \$1.5000 per pound by the end of January. Further, the firm believes arbitrageurs will not allow the futures price to rise more than \$0.01 above the full-carry price. It also believes the marginal convenience value of copper will never be more than \$0.10, so the futures price will not fall more than \$0.10 below the full-carry price.[21] Thus, the firm expects the error term, ε_{T^*}, to vary over the much smaller range of –\$0.10 to \$0.01. Finally, the cost of storing copper is \$2 per ton per month, plus a \$4-per-ton one-time fee. Over a two-month period, total storage costs will be \$8 per ton, or \$0.004 per pound.

[21] This example assumes the marginal convenience value is independent of the copper price level. See footnote 20.

The **sensitivity analysis**[22] in Table 3.2 shows what the firm's hedged and unhedged costs will be under these scenarios for the January spot price, P_{T^*}, and the error term, ε_{T^*}. To see how these costs are calculated, consider the scenario in which the January spot price is $0.8000 per pound and the basis error is –$0.10. The firm's unhedged copper costs in this case will be

$$\text{Unhedged copper costs} = \text{(Price per pound)(Number of pounds)}$$
$$= (\$0.8000)(2.5 \text{ million})$$
$$= \$2.000 \text{ million}.$$

The futures price will be

$$\begin{aligned} F_{T^*,T} &= \text{Full-carry price} + \text{Basis error} \\ &= P_{T^*}(1 + r_{T^*,T}) + SC_{T^*,T} + \varepsilon_{T^*} \\ &= (\$0.8000)(1.0204) + \$0.004 - \$0.10 \\ &= \$0.7203. \end{aligned}$$

The futures profit will be

$$\begin{aligned} \text{Futures profit} &= \text{(Long position)}(F_{T^*,T} - F_{t,T}) \\ &= (2.45 \text{ million})(\$0.7203 - \$1.2000) \\ &= -\$1.175 \text{ million}. \end{aligned}$$

Thus, the firm's hedged costs will be

$$\begin{aligned} \text{Hedged costs} &= \text{Unhedged costs} - \text{Futures profit} \\ &= \$2.000 \text{ million} - (-\$1.175 \text{ million}) \\ &= \$3.175 \text{ million}. \end{aligned}$$

As expected, Table 3.2 shows that hedged copper costs are much less risky than unhedged copper costs. The hedged costs vary between $2.906 million for $\varepsilon_{T^*} = \$0.01$ and $3.175 million for $\varepsilon_{T^*} = -\$0.10$. The difference is simply the $0.11-per-pound range in the basis error term times the number of futures positions. For $\varepsilon_{T^*} = 0$, the hedged cost of $2.930 million represents the $1.200 March futures price less the $0.004-per-pound storage cost, deflated by the 2.04 percent interest. If the error term is held fixed, the hedged cost will not vary as the January spot price scenario changes.

Unhedged copper costs, on the other hand, vary over a much wider range, from $2.000 million to $3.750 million. They depend only on the January spot price and are not affected by the error term. Thus, if the firm does not hedge, its costs will be subject to price risk, but if it does, its costs will be subject only to basis risk. ∎

---

[22] Sensitivity analysis is a technique that examines how robust a hedge is under various scenarios.

Table 3.2 Maturity Mismatch

	Hedged Revenues in Dollars (Basis Error)			
Spot	−0.10	−0.05	0.00	0.01
0.80	3,175,225.40	3,052,724.42	2,930,223.44	2,905,723.25
0.90	3,175,225.40	3,052,724.42	2,930,223.44	2,905,723.25
1.00	3,175,225.40	3,052,724.42	2,930,223.44	2,905,723.25
1.10	3,175,225.40	3,052,724.42	2,930,223.44	2,905,723.25
1.20	3,175,225.40	3,052,724.42	2,930,223.44	2,905,723.25
1.30	3,175,225.40	3,052,724.42	2,930,223.44	2,905,723.25
1.40	3,175,225.40	3,052,724.42	2,930,223.44	2,905,723.25
1.50	3,175,225.40	3,052,724.42	2,930,223.44	2,905,723.25

	Unhedged Revenues in Dollars (Basis Error)			
Spot	−0.10	−0.05	0.00	0.01
0.80	2,000,000.00	2,000,000.00	2,000,000.00	2,000,000.00
0.90	2,250,000.00	2,250,000.00	2,250,000.00	2,250,000.00
1.00	2,500,000.00	2,500,000.00	2,500,000.00	2,500,000.00
1.10	2,750,000.00	2,750,000.00	2,750,000.00	2,750,000.00
1.20	3,000,000.00	3,000,000.00	3,000,000.00	3,000,000.00
1.30	3,250,000.00	3,250,000.00	3,250,000.00	3,250,000.00
1.40	3,500,000.00	3,500,000.00	3,500,000.00	3,500,000.00
1.50	3,750,000.00	3,750,000.00	3,750,000.00	3,750,000.00

Note:
March futures = $1.2000
Riskless rate per month = 1.02%
Number of pounds = 2,500,000
Hedge ratio = 0.9800
Storage cost per pound = $0.0040

Example 3.4 shows that one can reduce risk even with an imperfect hedge if the error term is likely to vary less than the spot price. It also demonstrates that arbitrage concepts, such as the full-carry basis, can provide a framework for determining the hedge ratio and analyzing the risk of a crosshedge.

Crosshedging with an Asset and a Maturity Mismatch   Suppose we wish to hedge a situation involving both an asset mismatch and a maturity mismatch. To account for both mismatches, we simply estimate Equation 3.9 or 3.10 and multiply the "no-maturity mismatch" hedge ratio by $1/(1 + r_{T^*,T})$.

Crosshedging and Synthetic Spot Positions

Crosshedging can be used to partially create synthetic T-bill and spot positions. The firm with the inventory of Brent crude oil in Example 3.3 wants to turn that inventory into an investment with the characteristics of a T-bill. Thus, we can represent a short inventory crosshedge as

$$\text{Spot} - Q_f\text{Futures} = \text{T-bill} + \text{Basis risk.} \tag{3.25}$$

By rewriting Equation 3.25, we can use our crosshedging analysis to determine the optimal futures position and basis risk for the firm that wants to create a synthetic inventory of Brent oil:

$$\text{T-bill} + Q_f\text{Futures} = \text{Spot} - \text{Basis risk.} \tag{3.26}$$

A crosshedge cannot create a perfect synthetic T-bill or synthetic spot position. However, we have seen that firms often are willing to accept some basis risk in a hedge. They may also be willing to accept some basis risk when creating synthetic spot positions. In Chapter 4, we will see that portfolio managers often use stock index futures in crosshedging strategies that create synthetic stock positions. We can use the analysis developed here to evaluate the basis risk of those strategies.

Quantity Uncertainty

We have discussed how to hedge when there is no futures contract with the appropriate delivery date or on the desired commodity. Now we will make our final relaxation of the perfect hedging model and consider the hedging strategies that can be used by firms that do not know exactly how much of a commodity or security they will have to buy or sell in the future. Farmers often face this situation, for they usually do not know the size of their crops in advance. Importers may face uncertain demand for their products due to fluctuations in exchange rates. We will work through Example 3.5's description of the hedge used by a farmer who cannot predict his crop size precisely and then develop a general model of hedging under quantity uncertainty.

▪ **Example 3.5: Crop Size Uncertainty**   A farmer who wishes to hedge his revenues from corn sales faces a complicated problem. The size of his crop cannot be known precisely in advance, and it tends to be *negatively correlated* with the price he receives. If growing conditions are favorable, the quantity produced by *most* farmers will be high and the price will be low. If growing conditions are unfavorable, the quantity most farmers produce will be low and the price will be high.[23] Other factors, such as regional conditions and individual luck, also affect a farmer's quantity of corn. Prices may also be influenced by factors other than aggregate crop size, such as demand fluctuations and federal policies.

---

[23] This quantity effect may be small for farmers who irrigate their crops and thus can control their growing conditions to a certain extent.

Figure 3.3 Negative Correlation between Output and Prices

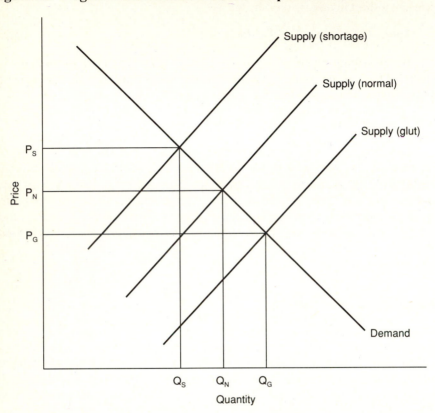

Figure 3.3 shows the overall negative correlation between a farmer's output and farm prices, which results from shifts in the supply curve as demand remains relatively stable.

   To see how the negative correlation between farm prices and crop size affects the corn farmer's hedging strategy, assume the farmer faces the following price/quantity relationship for corn:

Probability	Price per Bushel	Quantity	Revenue
.5	$3.50	100,000	$350,000
.5	$4.50	80,000	$360,000

His expected corn crop size at time T is

$$E_t(Q_T) = (.5)(100{,}000 \text{ bushels}) + (.5)(80{,}000 \text{ bushels})$$
$$= 90{,}000 \text{ bushels,}$$

and the expected price of corn is

$$E_t(P_T) = (.5)(\$3.50) + (.5)(\$4.50)$$
$$= \$4.00 \text{ per bushel,}$$

where $E_t(X)$ is the expected value or mean of X as of time t.

Now suppose for simplicity that the β of corn is zero and the CAPM holds. Then, from Chapter 2, we know that the futures price is an unbiased predictor of the future spot price:

$$F_{t,T} = E_t(P_T)$$
$$= \$4.00.$$

Suppose the farmer follows the plausible hedging strategy of entering into a short futures position on the *expected* number of bushels to be produced:

$$Q_f = E_t(Q_T)$$
$$= 90,000 \text{ bushels.}$$

He will earn the following revenues under the two price scenarios:

$$\text{Total revenue} = \text{Business revenues} + \text{Futures profits}$$
$$= Q_T P_T + Q_f(F_{t,T} - F_{T,T})$$
$$= Q_T P_T + E_t(Q_T)(F_{t,T} - P_T)$$
$$= Q_T P_T + 90,000(\$4.00 - P_T).$$

Probability	Price per Bushel	Total Revenue
.5	$3.50	$350,000 + $45,000 = $395,000
.5	$4.50	$360,000 − $45,000 = $315,000

Clearly the farmer's hedging strategy is an overkill. When the price is low, total revenues are high, and vice versa. The reason is that the higher quantity of corn partially compensates for the low per-unit price. Similarly, a high per-unit price is offset somewhat by the lower quantity. In effect, the negative correlation between quantity and price already partially hedges the farmer's revenues. The futures position $Q_f = E_t(Q_T)$ overhedges because it does not account for the partial hedging effect of the quantity variation.

The farmer can construct a more effective hedge by setting $Q_f = 10,000$ bushels:

$$\text{Total revenue} = Q_T P_T + 10,000(\$4.00 - P_T).$$

His revenues under the two scenarios will be

Probability	Price per Bushel	Total Revenue
.5	$3.50	$350,000 + $5,000 = $355,000
.5	$4.50	$360,000 − $5,000 = $355,000

His expected revenues are the same under both hedges:

Expected revenue ($Q_f = 90,000$) = .5($395,000) + .5($315,000)
$$= \$355,000$$

Expected revenue ($Q_f = 10,000$) = .5($355,000) + .5($355,000)
$$= \$355,000$$

However, the second hedge locks in the farmer's revenues no matter what the price scenario. This optimal hedging position is less than the expected crop size because the quantity variation already partially hedges corn revenues. Revenues are not nearly as variable as price because of the quantity effect. Since the farmer is trying to hedge revenues (and not price), this leads to a smaller hedge ratio. The general rule, then, is: If price and quantity are negatively correlated, a hedging futures position should be *smaller* than the expected quantity. This holds for both long and short hedges.

In some situations, a positive correlation between price and quantity exists. For example, some farmers in the Deep South of the United States raise soybeans in swampy areas. When conditions in general are dry, they experience an increase in productivity. This leads to a positive correlation between quantity and price, because overall quantity is low when conditions are dry. In such cases, a short hedger would find that when prices are low, quantity is even lower, so revenues are very low, and when prices are high, quantity is higher, so revenues are very high. The quantity uncertainty accentuates the price movements. Thus, if price and quantity are positively correlated, a hedging futures position should be *larger* than the expected quantity. This is also true for both long and short hedges. ∎

A General Formula

The optimal hedge ratio in the face of quantity uncertainty can be expressed as a general formula. Suppose the following conditions hold approximately:

1. Managers are concerned about the mean and variance of profits.

2. Futures contracts are priced according to an asset pricing model such as the CAPM.

Then the appropriate number of futures contracts for a hedge is

$$Q_f = \frac{\mathrm{Cov}[Q_T P_T, P_T]}{\mathrm{Var}[P_T]}, \tag{3.27}$$

where $\mathrm{Cov}[Q_T P_T, P_T]$ = covariance between total revenue (for a short hedge) or cost (for a long hedge) and price.[24] For the farmer in Example 3.5, $\mathrm{Cov}[Q_T P_T, P_T]$ is the covariance between revenues and price.

---

[24] See Rolfo [1980] for the development of this formula. As with the portfolio approach discussed in footnote 2, Rolfo allows for a speculative adjustment to the hedge ratio if the futures is mispriced.

It is straightforward to estimate the quantity of futures contracts Equation 3.27 requires. Suppose our corn farmer has past data on the price of corn and his total revenues. If he runs the regression

$$\text{Revenue} = \alpha + \beta(\text{Price}) + \varepsilon, \tag{3.27a}$$

the estimate of β will give the appropriate number of futures contracts.[25]

We can make several observations from Equation 3.27:

1. If Q_T is fixed, $\text{Cov}[Q_T P_T, P_T] = Q_T \text{Var}[P_T]$ and $Q_f = Q_T$.

2. Negative correlation between Q_T and P_T will reduce the covariance of total revenue or cost and price such that $Q_f < E_t[Q_T]$. This is what happened in Example 3.5.

3. Positive correlation between Q_T and P_T will increase the covariance of total revenue or cost and price such that $Q_f > E_T(P_T)$.

This quantity effect can lead to seemingly perverse results. Suppose the corn farmer in Example 3.5 now faces the following relationship between quantity and price:

Probability	Price per Bushel	Quantity	Revenue
.5	$3.50	105,000	$367,500
.5	$4.50	75,000	$337,500

Revenues and prices are inversely related, so $\text{Cov}[Q_T P_T, P_T] < 0$. According to Equation 3.27, this means that the number of futures positions should be *negative*. Instead of going short futures, the farmer should go long.

Suppose the farmer follows this strategy and sets $Q_f = -30,000$ bushels. His total revenue will be

$$\text{Total revenue} = Q_T P_T - 30{,}000(\$4.00 - P_T)$$
$$= Q_T P_T + 30{,}000(P_T - \$4.00).$$

Probability	Price per Bushel	Total Revenue
.5	$3.50	$367,500 − $15,000 = $352,500
.5	$4.50	$337,500 + $15,000 = $352,500

While it may seem strange to hedge a sale with a long position, this strategy is required merely because demand for corn in this case has an elasticity greater than 1. Clearly the quantity effect must be considered in many hedging situations.

---

[25] As we saw in Equation 3.9, with linear regression ($Y = a + bX + e$), the estimate of b is given by

$$\frac{\text{Cov}[X,Y]}{\text{Var}[X]} = \frac{\text{Corr}[X,Y]\text{SD}[Y]}{\text{SD}[X]}.$$

Tailing and Marking to Market

In our discussions of risk management and arbitrage, we have treated the payoffs from futures positions as if they were the same as those from equivalent forward positions. In Chapter 1, we saw that this is only an approximation, because there are interim cash flows under the marking-to-market system in the futures markets. This means that a party entering into a futures position is not indifferent to the path futures prices follow as they move from $F_{t,T}$ to $F_{T,T}$. Hedging positions can be adjusted to account for futures cash flow timing with a technique called **tailing**.[26] A **tail** alters a futures position such that the correspondence between the profits on forward and futures positions is reestablished.

Suppose a party constructs a hedge by entering into a long futures position at a price of $F_{t,T}$. The next day, prices move to $F_{t1,T}$. Suppose $F_{t1,T} - F_{t,T} > 0$ so the position makes a profit. Because of marking to market, the party will receive $F_{t1,T} - F_{t,T}$ from the clearinghouse to invest from t1 to T. At time T, the party will have this profit plus interest:

$$\text{Cash flow at T from t–t1 price move} = (F_{t1,T} - F_{t,T})(1 + r_{t1,T}) \qquad \textbf{(3.28)}$$

where $r_{t1,T}$ is the lending rate from t1 to T. For simplicity, assume the party can also borrow at $r_{t1,T}$. Then, if the futures price drops between t and t1, the party must pay the clearinghouse $F_{t1,T} - F_{t,T}$. If the party borrows this amount between t1 and T, the cash flow when she pays back the loan at T will also be given by Equation 3.28.

Since the party lends until time T if she makes a gain and borrows until time T if she suffers a loss, there is no cash flow at time t1; the party will have deferred the cash flows until date T, just as with a forward contract. However, unlike with a forward position, the cash flow at T is multiplied by the term $1 + r_{t1,T}$. Thus, relative to a forward position, the party with the futures position is *overhedged* due to the time value of money.

Suppose for the moment that $r_{t1,T}$ is known at time t. Then the party can correct for this difference by entering into only $1/(1 + r_{t1,T})$ futures positions at time t. Then the contribution to the time T cash flow of the first day's price move will be

(Number of contracts)(Per-contract contribution)

$$= \left(\frac{1}{1 + r_{t1,T}}\right)\left(F_{t1,T} - F_{t,T}\right)\left(1 + r_{t1,T}\right)$$

$$= F_{t1,T} - F_{t,T}.$$

---

[26] See Kawaller and Koch [1988] for a description of tailing with stock index futures and Kawaller [1986] for a description of tailing with Eurodollar futures.

The effect of marking to market is eliminated by these tailing adjustments to the hedge ratio. The adjusted futures hedging position behaves like a forward position.

Proper use of a tail requires some monitoring. As the contract moves toward expiration, the time value of money decreases, so the tail will decrease. The general rule is

$$\text{Hedge ratio at time tj} = \frac{1}{1 + r_{tj+1,T}}.$$

As tj approaches T, $r_{tj+1,T}$ approaches zero and the hedge ratio approaches 1.

Example 3.6 shows how tailing can be used in a short gold inventory hedge.

▪ **Example 3.6: Tailing a Short Gold Futures Position**   Suppose B has a 100,000-ounce gold inventory that she hedges by entering into 100,000 ounces worth of short July 1 gold futures positions on May 31. The current gold futures price is $450 per ounce. The interest rate is 10 percent per annum, on a bond-equivalent-yield basis, so the 30-day rate is (10%)(30/360) = 0.833%. Table 3.3 shows the time T cash flows for a tailed and a nontailed hedge in this case.

The $2 increase in the futures price from May 31 to June 1 causes B to lose $200,000 on her futures position. If she borrows for 30 days to pay this loss, she will owe $201,666.67 when the futures expires on July 1. With a forward position, this price move will contribute only $200,000 to the loss on July 1. To prevent overhedging with the futures position, B sets her hedge ratio equal to 1/(1 + .00833) = 0.992. If each gold contract is 100 ounces, she will go short 992 contracts on May 31. As time goes by, she will increase her hedge ratio until she is short 1,000 contracts on June 30.

By properly tailing her position, B ensures that her total futures loss by expiration on July 1 will be $2,500,000. This is exactly equal to the total $25 increase in price times 100,000 ounces. Thus, her net profit will be the same as if she had entered into a forward position. Had B not tailed her hedge, she would lose $2,503,250.00 on the futures position. ▪

Tailing is possible only if a position is large enough for one to be able to adjust the number of contracts. If B had only 10 contracts, she could not tail her hedge. The tailing adjustment is greater the longer the position will be held and the higher the interest rate, because the time value of money is more important under those circumstances.

One must, of course, consider whether the benefits of a tail are great enough to justify the transactions costs of instituting it. We have assumed the interest rate is known and the borrowing rate equals the lending rate. If rates are not very volatile, relaxation of the first assumption will not make a large practical difference. The difference between borrowing and lending rates also is not usually a problem. Most firms are either net lenders or net borrowers. Thus, at the margin, a firm's borrowing and lending rates are the same. For example, if a firm is a net

Table 3.3 B's Account: Tailing a Gold Inventory Hedge

Date	Days to Expiration	Futures Price	Time T Contribution– No Tail	Tailed Ratio	Time T Contribution– with Tail
5/31/88	31	$450.00		0.992	
6/1/88	30	452.00	$ −201,666.67	0.992	$ −200,000.00
6/2/88	29	453.00	−100,805.56	0.992	−100,000.00
6/3/88	28	455.00	−201,555.56	0.993	−200,000.00
6/6/88	25	460.00	−503,472.22	0.993	−500,000.00
6/7/88	24	465.00	−503,333.33	0.994	−500,000.00
6/8/88	23	475.00	−1,006,388.89	0.994	−1,000,000.00
6/9/88	22	460.00	1,509,166.67	0.994	1,500,000.00
6/10/88	21	455.00	502,916.67	0.995	500,000.00
6/13/88	18	452.00	301,500.00	0.995	300,000.00
6/14/88	17	450.00	200,944.44	0.996	200,000.00
6/15/88	16	449.00	100,444.44	0.996	100,000.00
6/16/88	15	455.00	−602,500.00	0.996	−600,000.00
6/17/88	14	450.00	501,944.44	0.997	500,000.00
6/20/88	11	452.00	−200,611.11	0.997	−200,000.00
6/21/88	10	449.00	300,833.33	0.998	300,000.00
6/22/88	9	445.00	401,000.00	0.998	400,000.00
6/23/88	8	440.00	501,111.11	0.998	500,000.00
6/24/88	7	445.00	−500,972.22	0.999	−500,000.00
6/27/88	5	450.00	−500,555.56	0.999	−500,000.00
6/28/88	3	460.00	−1,000,833.33	0.999	−1,000,000.00
6/29/88	2	465.00	−500,277.78	1.000	−500,000.00
6/30/88	1	470.00	−500,138.89	1.000	−500,000.00
7/1/88	0	475.00	−500,000.00		−500,000.00
Net gain		$ 25.00	$–2,503,250.00		$–2,500,000.00

Note:
Number of ounces = −100,000
Interest rate = 10.00%

lender, both its effective borrowing and lending rates are its lending rate, because it can borrow by reducing its lending.

Tailing and the Relationship between Forward and Futures Prices

We have seen that a tail can make a futures position behave like a forward position as long as one can predict at time tj the interest rate that will prevail between tj + 1 and T. If one cannot predict this rate, there will be some risk in the futures position that is not present in the forward position. This risk may or may not work to the hedger's advantage.

Consider an investor who holds a long gold futures position in an environment where interest rates cannot be accurately predicted. Further, suppose movements in the futures price of gold are positively related to changes in the interest rate. A gold futures price increase will lead to a futures profit that can be invested at a high rate of interest; a gold futures price decrease will lead to a futures loss that can be financed at a low rate of interest. Thus, the investor's overall profit on the long futures position is greater than what he or she would earn on an equivalent forward position.

The opposite occurs if gold futures price movements are negatively related to interest rate changes. If gold futures prices rise, the futures profit will be invested at a low rate of interest; if gold futures prices fall, the losses will be financed at a high rate of interest. The overall profit of the long futures position will be less than that of an equivalent forward position.

Thus, the relationship between futures price and interest rate movements can tell us something about how futures prices relate to forward prices.[27] If futures price movements are positively correlated with interest rate movements,

Forward price < Futures price
$$f_{t,T} < F_{t,T},$$

because a long futures position is more advantageous than an equivalent forward position. In equilibrium, investors will be willing to enter into a long futures position at a price higher than that of an equivalent forward position. Similarly, if futures price movements are negatively correlated with interest rate movements,

Forward price > Futures price
$$f_{t,T} > F_{t,T}.$$

Natural versus Futures Hedges

Before a firm enters into a futures hedging position, it should consider whether the risk to be hedged is offset to some degree by another aspect of the firm's business. Take, for example, the gold wire manufacturer in Chapter 1 who eliminates the risk associated with gold costs by going long futures. A crucial assumption in this case is that the price at which the wire manufacturer can sell the gold wire is fixed.

Now suppose instead that the gold wire price rises when gold prices rise. The firm is then **naturally hedged**, because while one part of profits, costs, is adversely affected by increasing gold costs, the other part, revenues, is positively affected. The farmer who faces quantity uncertainty is also naturally hedged to

---

[27] See Cox, Ingersoll, and Ross [1981], Jarrow and Oldfield [1981], and Richard and Sundaresan [1981] for theoretical discussions of the effect of correlation between short-term interest rates and futures prices on the relationship between forward and futures prices. Cornell and Reingenaum [1981], French [1983], and Park and Chen [1985] explore differences between forward and futures prices in a variety of markets. These differences appear quite small in some markets. Of course, given the different credit arrangements of forward and futures markets, it is not clear how one should interpret such differences.

some degree, for as crop size increases, farm prices decrease. Such naturally hedged firms must account for the total risk of their businesses when they determine the size of their hedging futures positions, for they could actually *induce* risk into their businesses by taking futures positions that hedge only one component of firm profits.

In many cases, firms can take actions to reduce or eliminate risk so that they become naturally hedged and need not hedge with futures positions. One important example is the floating-rate loan offered by many financial institutions. Financial intermediaries often borrow at variable short-term rates and lend at fixed long-term rates. These firms are at risk that interest rates will rise. As we discuss in Chapter 5, one way to eliminate this risk is to use interest rate futures. Another is to issue floating-rate loans. If a firm follows the second strategy, an interest rate increase will raise both its borrowing costs and its lending proceeds, and the firm's profits will not be affected. Thus, financial intermediaries have a choice between a futures hedge and a natural hedge.

In Example 3.7, a firm chooses between a futures hedge and a natural hedge for its gold inventory.

▪ **Example 3.7: Hedging a Gold Inventory**   Let's reconsider Example 3.1, in which a firm has an inventory of 1,000 ounces of gold that it wishes to sell in July. Suppose that in February the firm is considering whether to hedge this sale by entering into a short July gold futures position that covers 1,000 ounces. Suppose also that the current spot price of gold is $450 per ounce, the futures price for July delivery is $470 per ounce, the T-bill rate is 1 percent per month, and storage costs are $0.10 per ounce between February and July. For simplicity, we will ignore transactions costs.

We have seen that the firm can use a futures hedge to lock in per ounce revenues equal to the futures price for July 1 delivery. Total hedged revenues, including storage costs, will be

> (Current futures price per ounce – Storage costs per ounce)(Number of ounces)
> $= (\$470.00 - \$0.10)(1,000)$
> $= \$469,900.$

The firm could also sell its gold today and put its funds into T-bills. This is a very simple natural hedge, because the firm merely changes its cash position to eliminate risk due to the price of gold. If it sells off its gold today, the firm will receive

> Immediate gold revenues $= (\$450)(1,000)$
> $= \$450,000.$

The firm can use these proceeds to buy T-bills that expire in July and earn 1 percent per month over the five months between February and July. The face value of the bills will be

Table 3.4 Reverse Cash-and-Carry Quasi-Arbitrage Table for Firm with Gold Inventory

Benchmark position: intended short futures position

Reverse Cash-and-Carry Pure Arbitrage Components	Reverse Cash-and-Carry Quasi-Arbitrage Components	Relevant Price or Rate
1. Short spot Receive storage	Sell spot Save storage	Bid
2. Go long futures	Refrain from going short	Bid
3. Lend	Buy T-bills	T-bill ask

Resulting position: synthetic short futures position

Transactions fees: $TF = TF_1 - TF_2 + TF_3$
1. Pay TF_1
2. Save TF_2
3. Pay TF_3

$$\text{T-bill face value} = (\$450,000)(1.05)$$
$$= \$472,500.$$

The redeemed T-bills will be worth more than the $470,000 locked in with the short futures hedge. Further, because the firm sold off the gold in February, there are no storage costs. Thus, the natural hedge is superior to the futures hedge. ∎

The decision to use a natural hedge instead of a futures hedge in Example 3.7 can be viewed as a reverse cash-and-carry quasi-arbitrage, as Table 3.4 demonstrates. By choosing to use a synthetic short futures position, the firm effectively goes long the futures (by not going short), effectively goes short the spot (by selling the gold inventory), saves storage costs, and lends by buying T-bills.

The firm can determine whether the synthetic or natural hedge is better by examining the difference between the futures price and its fundamental no-arbitrage price:

$$\Omega^r = F_{t,T} - [P_t(1 + r_{t,T}) + FV(\text{Storage})]$$
$$= \$470 - [\$450(1.05) + \$0.10]$$
$$= -\$2.60 < 0.$$

The firm finds that moving from the benchmark of a futures hedge to the alternative of a natural hedge is profitable, because $\Omega^r < 0$. The futures is underpriced relative to the cash by $2.60, so the natural hedge of selling the gold and buying the T-bills is superior. As usual, this quasi-arbitrage opportunity does not imply that there is a pure arbitrage opportunity, because pure arbitrageurs do not have the special advantage of being able to sell gold out of inventory. In Chapter 5, we will see that an intermediary's decision between issuing floating-rate loans and going short interest rate futures requires the same kind of analysis.

Table 3.5 Cash-and-Carry Quasi-Arbitrage Table for Gold Wire Manufacturer

Benchmark position: intended long futures position

Cash-and-Carry Pure Arbitrage Components	Cash-and-Carry Quasi-Arbitrage Components	Relevant Price or Rate
1. Buy spot Pay storage	Buy spot Pay storage	Ask
2. Go short futures	Refrain from going long	Ask
3. Borrow	Borrow	Borrowing rate

Resulting position: synthetic long futures position

Transactions fees: $TF = TF_1 - TF_2 + TF_3$
1. Pay TF_1
2. Save TF_2
3. Pay TF_3

Table 3.5 shows that a hedger who is contemplating a long hedge can also consider a synthetic long futures position. Suppose the gold wire manufacturer in Example 1.10 in Chapter 1 wishes to hedge his future cost of gold. He could go long futures, or he could borrow and buy the gold immediately. The natural hedge is appropriate if $\Omega^c > 0$.

Why Firms Hedge

Many firms do not fully utilize the futures markets to reduce or eliminate profit risks associated with commodity and security price movements. One reason may be that they are unfamiliar with futures hedging techniques. Another may be that many firms deliberately choose not to lower or eliminate the risks they face. In this section, we will discuss the strategic issues involved in deciding whether to hedge.

Hedging is commonly considered desirable because firms supposedly can lower their cost of capital by reducing risk. In the extreme case in which the firm completely hedges all its risk, the firm's appropriate discount rate should fall to equal the riskless rate. If expected cash flows are unaffected by the hedge, the present discounted value of the firm's cash flows will increase and thereby raise the firm's value.

This logic is fundamentally flawed, however, because we can show that any decrease in a firm's cost of capital from hedging will be exactly offset by a decrease in its expected cash flows. Suppose a firm is evaluating the purchase of a gold mine. The mine has been explored and developed, so the firm knows it can extract 1 million ounces of gold. For simplicity, suppose all the gold is extracted at the end of the year. We can see whether the firm will gain by hedging by comparing the present value of hedged and unhedged gold revenues.

Present Value without Hedging   For simplicity, we will ignore costs, payouts, and convenience yields in our calculation of hedged and unhedged revenues. Further, we will suppose that futures prices are set according to the systematic-risk hypothesis discussed in Chapter 2.

   If the firm does not hedge, the per-unit present value of its gold revenues is simply the expected revenues discounted by an appropriate discount rate:

$$PV_u = \frac{E_t(P_T)}{1 + r^*} . \tag{3.29}$$

   Recall from Chapter 2 that r^* is set by the market so that the investor earns a fair rate of return on the gold (with $r^* > r_f$):

$$E_t(P_T) = (1 + r^*)P_t^*, \tag{3.30}$$

where P_t^* is the price of a marketable security with the same risk as P_T. If we combine Equations 3.29 and 3.30, we see that

$$PV_u = P_t^*. \tag{3.31}$$

This is sensible, because a financial claim at time t on the revenues at time T should have a value precisely equal to the present value of the revenues.

Present Value with Hedging   Now suppose the firm hedges its gold revenues by going short 1 million ounces' worth of futures contracts that expire in one year. This locks in the current futures price, so the discount rate should be the riskless rate, and the per-unit present value of hedged revenues is

$$PV_h = \frac{F_{t,T}}{1 + r_f} . \tag{3.32}$$

   We will now use the relationship between bias in the futures price and the risk in the spot price. From Equation 2.29 of Chapter 2, we see that

$$F_{t,T} = E_t(P_T) - (r^* - r_f)P_t^*. \tag{3.33}$$

Combining this with Equation 3.30, we get

$$F_{t,T} = (1 + r_f)P_t^*. \tag{3.34}$$

The present value of hedged revenues is therefore

$$PV_h = P_t^*, \tag{3.35}$$

which is exactly the same as the present value of unhedged revenues, $PV_u = PV_h$. Even though the required rate of return on gold mining, r^*, exceeds the riskless rate, the expected future spot gold price exceeds the futures price by just enough to outweigh the higher cost of capital of the unhedged position. Thus, hedging will not directly increase the present value of a firm's cash flows by lowering the cost of capital. We must look elsewhere to find the reasons for hedging.

Example 3.8 presents a specific case for the firm discussed above that is considering purchasing a gold mine. It demonstrates that hedging does not increase a firm's present value.

▪ **Example 3.8: Hedged versus Unhedged Gold Revenues**   Suppose the firm contemplating the purchase of a gold mine faces the following:

$$r_f \quad = 0.05$$

$$r_m^* \quad = 0.15$$

$$\beta_g \quad = 0.5$$

$$E_t(P_T) \; = \; \$495 \text{ per ounce}$$

Here β_g is the beta of gold and $E_t(P_T)$ is the expected gold price at time T.

If the CAPM holds, the required rate of return on gold is

$$r^* = r_f + \beta_g(r_m^* - r_f)$$
$$= 0.05 + 0.5(0.15 - 0.05)$$
$$= 0.10.$$

The price of a security with the same risk as gold is

$$P_t^* = \frac{E_t(P_T)}{1 + r^*}$$
$$= \frac{\$495}{1.10}$$
$$= \$450,$$

which also equals the present value, per ounce, of unhedged gold revenues.

The futures price for gold is

$$F_{t,T} = E_t(P_T) - (r^* - r_f)P_t^*$$
$$= \$495 - (0.10 - 0.05)(\$450)$$
$$= \$495 - \$22.50$$
$$= \$472.50.$$

The present value of hedged gold revenues is therefore

$$\frac{F_{t,T}}{1 + r_f} = \frac{\$472.50}{1.05}$$
$$= \$450.$$

Hedging decreases the discount rate from 10 to 5 percent. Because gold has positive systematic risk, today's futures price, $472.50, is less than the expected future spot price, $495, to yield a long gold futures position an expected profit. Thus, for the hedged firm, expected revenues and the discount rate both decrease, so the present value of revenues is unchanged. ▪

The offsetting effect of hedging on expected revenues and the discount rate is not merely fortuitous; it is an example of the famous **Modigliani-Miller propositions** concerning corporate financial policy. Modigliani and Miller [1958] showed that with perfect markets, the financial policy of a firm does not affect the firm's value. A change in dividends or capital structure cannot affect the present value of a firm's profits, for stockholders can *undo* any change in financial policy that the firm makes. For example, if the firm decides to suspend dividends but stockholders still want them, the stockholders can simply liquidate a portion of their holdings equal to the desired dividend. The firm will have the same value to the stockholders whether or not it pays dividends.

Hedging is also a kind of financial policy, and it too can be undone by stockholders in perfect markets. If the firm hedges, stockholders can unhedge by taking an opposite position in the futures market. If the firm does not hedge, stockholders themselves can take the position the firm would have to take to hedge.

Futures Prices and Capital Budgeting   We have seen that in perfect markets, the value of the hedged firm is the same as that of the unhedged firm. Thus, firms that do not hedge can use futures prices to determine their present values.

Suppose the gold-mining firm in Example 3.8 decides not to hedge but still wishes to know the value of the gold it will extract. It can simply use Equation 3.32. It need not forecast gold prices or determine a risk-adjusted discount rate as it would if it used Equation 3.29. Essentially, the firm can let the futures market do the valuation work for it.[28]

Why Do Firms Hedge?

If hedging policy is irrelevant in perfect markets, we must consider how real markets differ from perfect markets in order to find a motive for hedging. Some factors that may play a role are taxes, bankruptcy and financial distress costs, managerial contracting with imperfect information, and lack of diversification on the part of the firm's owners.[29] In this discussion, we will make the seemingly reasonable assumption that transactions costs are small relative to the gains from hedging.

---

[28] See Holthausen [1979], Feder, Just, and Schmitz [1980], Marcus and Modest [1984], Brennan and Schwartz [1985], and McDonald and Siegel [1985] for a discussion of how the same insight applies to more complicated valuations involving production investment decisions.

[29] See Stulz [1984], Smith and Stulz [1985], and Campbell and Kracaw [1987] for a detailed discussion of the effects of taxes, bankruptcy costs, and imperfect information on hedging policy.

Taxes   Taxes may provide a motive for hedging, because they do not affect firms' after-tax income in a neutral way. Firms with negative or low levels of income may be unable to take advantage of tax credits and deductions that they could use if their incomes were higher. Firms with large profits may be subject to windfall-profits taxes (such as the oil windfall-profits tax in recent years). Firms may want to reduce the variability in their before-tax incomes in order to avoid loss of tax benefits or tax payments at unfavorable rates on high income levels. Example 3.9 shows how the potential loss of a tax benefit can make hedging worthwhile.

▪ **Example 3.9: Taxes and the Gain from Hedging**   Consider an oil company whose assets consist solely of 1 million barrels of oil reserves that the firm intends to extract in one year at a cost of $25 per barrel. The current futures price for oil is $30 per barrel, and the oil price in one year has an equal chance of being $25 or $35 per barrel. For simplicity, we will assume that $\beta_{oil} = 0$ so that the oil futures price equals the expected future spot price. The firm faces a 30 percent income tax rate and has a $1 million tax credit that it can apply up to the amount of income taxes paid.

  If the firm does not hedge, its after-tax profits under each oil price scenario will be

I. $25 per Barrel

Before-tax profits = ($25 − $25)(1 million)	= $ 0.0 million
Income tax	= $ 0.0 million
After-tax profits	= $ 0.0 million

The firm pays no taxes, because its taxable income is zero. It loses the $1 million tax credit.

II. $35 per Barrel

Before-tax profits = ($35 − $25)(1 million)	= $10.0 million
Income tax = (0.30)($10 million) − $1 million	= $ 2.0 million
After-tax profits	= $ 8.0 million

The firm pays only $2 million in taxes, because it fully utilizes its tax credit of $1 million.

  The firm's expected after-tax profits in one year are

$$\text{Expected after-tax profit} = (0.5)(\$0.0 \text{ million}) + (0.5)(\$8.0 \text{ million})$$
$$= \$4.0 \text{ million}.$$

  If the firm hedges with a short position in oil futures, its after-tax profits under the two oil price scenarios will be

Before-tax profits = ($30 − $25)(1 million)	= $ 5.0 million
Income tax = (0.30)($5 million) − $1 million	= $ 0.5 million
After-tax profits	= $ 4.5 million

  The expected after-tax profits are greater for the hedged firm than for the unhedged firm. The $0.5 million difference is exactly equal to the unhedged firm's expected loss of the $1 million tax credit. The hedged firm always utilizes its tax credit fully, so its value is higher than that of the unhedged firm. ∎

In general, the effect of hedging when tax credits and deductions are available is

> Unhedged firm value
> = Hedged firm value – Expected loss of credits and deductions.

The benefit of hedging when tax benefits could be lost will be mitigated if firms can carry tax credits and deductions forward and backward in time. Further, firms that will surely have ample income to use all of their credits and deductions will gain little value from hedging due to this tax effect.

Firms whose incomes may be high enough to subject them to windfall-profits taxes may hedge to avoid such taxes. They may be willing to forgo possible high profits in order to eliminate the risk of low profits, because the windfall profits tax will reduce the value of high profits.

Bankruptcy and Financial Distress Costs   Firms with debt in their capital structure may wish to hedge because they could incur extra costs if their profits fall too low. If profits fall sufficiently low that a firm must declare bankruptcy, the firm must pay additional transactions costs as it is turned over to the bondholders. Similarly, a firm facing declining profits may violate some of its debt covenants and go into financial distress. This can constrain the firm's operations and result in lost value. In general, the benefits of hedging to such firms can be expressed as

> Unhedged firm value
> = Hedged firm value – Expected bankruptcy and distress costs.

Firms that have considerable debt can add more value by hedging than firms that are financed primarily by equity. This might lead one to wonder why bondholders do not encourage firms to hedge, perhaps by requiring hedging in their debt covenants. The reason may be that it is difficult for bondholders to tell whether a given futures transaction is a hedge or a speculation. By choosing its futures position cleverly, a firm can disguise a risk-increasing position as a hedge. Speculating in futures might be an attractive strategy for a firm that is close to bankruptcy. Most of the profits from a speculative futures position will accrue to the stockholders, because there usually is an upper bound on payments to debtholders. Most losses will be suffered by the debtholders because of the stockholders' limited liability. Thus, bondholders will encourage a firm to use futures positions only if it is easy to monitor the purpose of such positions.[30]

---

[30] This analysis is very similar to that of Myers [1977], who demonstrated that equityholders may take on risky, negative net present value projects at the expense of bondholders.

Managerial Contracting and Imperfect Information   Managers may have an incentive to hedge if their compensation is tied to their firms' performances. Performance-based compensation is popular for two reasons. First, it motivates managers to work hard in cases where the firm cannot directly observe the managers' efforts. Second, it provides incentives for the best managers to accept positions in a firm when the firm cannot accurately assess managerial talent by other means. However, performance-based compensation schemes impose risk for managers. Because managers typically dislike risk, firms may encounter problems if they burden their managers with risk that the managers cannot control by their efforts or talents. The managers may require higher base salaries and avoid potentially profitable but risky investments.

Hedging can cut down on the volatility of firm profits that is caused by factors beyond the managers' control and by the problems associated with managerial risk bearing. While managers could hedge their own positions individually, it may be more efficient to allow them to hedge through their firms as long as hedging costs are moderate.[31]

Lack of Diversification   The Modigliani-Miller-type analysis of hedging assumes that the firm is owned by well-diversified investors. Some firms are privately held by investors who have a large fraction of their wealth tied up in the firms. The family farmer is a vivid example. Such owners do not view the value of the unhedged firm to be the same as the value of the hedged firm, because their discount rates under uncertainty must account for some nonsystematic as well as systematic risk. Therefore, firms with nondiversified owners might hedge simply for the purpose of reducing risk.

Summary

Futures contracts can be used to hedge against risks caused by volatility in prices, interest rates, or exchange rates. Under ideal conditions, futures can completely eliminate price or rate risks. However, in most situations there are factors that prevent futures from providing a perfect hedge. There may be no futures contract that has the appropriate delivery date or that covers the asset whose price is causing the risk. In these cases, the firm can adjust the hedge ratio to maximize the risk reduced by the hedge. It can also adjust futures hedges to account for quantity, uncertainty, and the daily payments made under the marking-to-market system.

---

[31] If the risk to be hedged is observable, a firm can simply adjust its managers' contracts to take account of risk they cannot control. This is, in effect, the role of relative performance measurement. Hedging may be a more efficient way to protect managers from uncontrollable risks. Further, if a firm's exact exposure to commodity prices, interest rates, or exchange rates is hard to measure externally, it may make sense to encourage managers to hedge the firm.

Sometimes firms can hedge themselves naturally. A firm's choice between using a futures or a natural hedge depends on whether the fundamental no-arbitrage equation holds for it. Often this depends on the firm's initial situation.

It is not always clear why firms should hedge against price or rate risks. Stockholders can hedge on their own or undo any hedges that firms undertake. Some of the factors that might provide an incentive for firms to hedge include taxes, costs of bankruptcy and financial distress, performance-based compensation, and nondiversified owners.

Problems

1. Suppose you are a copper tubing manufacturer in Chicago. You know you will need to purchase 50,000 pounds of copper in May and want to hedge the price of copper. You know that the price of copper in Chicago moves closely with the price in New York, and the price differential is due solely to transport costs from New York to Chicago. Transport costs are variable and will be either $0.030, $0.050, or $0.070 per pound. The current futures price for May delivery of copper is $1.2000. You decide to hedge using the COMEX copper futures contract.
    a. Is your hedge a short hedge or a long hedge?
    b. Is your hedge an inventory hedge or an anticipatory hedge?
    c. Analyze your hedged costs of copper if the spot price of copper in New York is $1.0000 or $1.4500 per pound in May.
    d. How do your hedged costs relate to the current May copper futures price?

2. Suppose prices and quantities for the seller of a commodity are

Probability	P_T	Q_T
.25	$3.00	120,000
.75	$4.00	40,000

    a. If the beta of the commodity is zero and the CAPM holds, what should be the futures price?
    b. Given the futures price in part a, show what happens to total profits if a hedger enters into short contracts equal to the quantity he or she expects to sell.
    c. Should the optimal hedge be smaller or larger than the expected quantity?
    d. What hedge will result in zero risk for total profits? Briefly discuss the intuition behind your answer.

3. Suppose the current price of corn is $4.50 per bushel, the current futures price for delivery in three months is $4.60, and this contract is correctly priced. The beta of corn is 0.5, the expected rate of return on the market is 3 percent for three months, and the riskless rate of interest is 2 percent for three months. Assume storage of corn costs $0.03 per bushel per month, paid when the corn is taken out of storage. Is corn a pure asset?

4. You have at your disposal a disk with Brent and West Texas Intermediate (WTI) crude oil spot prices from the second quarter of 1986 through the end of the second quarter of 1987. This problem asks you to reproduce some of the results from Example 3.3.

    a. Reproduce the regression results from Table 3.1. Use weeks 1–52 from the data set.

    b. Calculate the unhedged risk of a one-week Brent inventory position using the price difference regression. Use weeks 1–52, then repeat for the remaining data. Determine *99* percent confidence intervals for hedged and unhedged one-week Brent positions (both in and out of sample). Plot a histogram of the in-sample basis errors. Is our assumption of normality of the errors justified?

    c. Reproduce Figure 3.2. In sample, calculate the percentage of the time that the hedged value moved more than the unhedged value.

5. This problem asks you to reproduce some of the results in Example 3.4. Suppose your firm manufactures copper roofs. You will need to purchase 2,500,000 pounds of copper at the end of January. You wish to hedge against changes in the price of copper, but the nearest copper futures contract expires in March. The current March futures price is $1.2000 per pound and each contract specifies 25,000 pounds.

    After careful study, you have determined that arbitrageurs will not allow the futures price to rise more than $0.01 above the full-carry price or fall more than $0.10 below it. Storage costs for copper are $2 per ton per month, with a $4-per-ton one-time charge. Interest rates are 1.02 percent per month.

    a. Construct a table similar to Table 3.2 that analyzes the basis risk resulting from this maturity mismatch. Suppose the spot price at the end of January can vary between $0.8000 and $1.5000 per pound. (Note: This problem will require you to master the /DATA TABLE command in Lotus.)

    b. Suppose storage costs increase to $3 per ton per month, with a $4-per-ton one-time charge. What happens to the hedge ratio? What happens to hedged revenues? Explain.

    c. Suppose (with the original storage costs) interest rates fall to 0.51 percent per month. What happens to the hedge ratio? What happens to hedged revenues? Explain.

6. Suppose we are looking at the copper futures contract and see the following information:

$r_f = 10\%$ $\beta_c = -0.2$ $T - t = 1$ year

$r_m^* = 20\%$ $E_t(P_T) = \$1.224$ $SC = \$0.014$

where SC is the annualized per-pound storage costs for copper.

    a. What is the price of a pure asset that pays off one pound of copper in one year?

b.   What is the equilibrium futures price according to the CAPM? Explain the direction of the bias intuitively.

c.   What is the present value of 50,000 pounds of copper to an unhedged firm? (Assume the firm is publicly traded.)

d.   What is the present value of 50,000 pounds of copper to a hedged firm? How does this compare with your answer in part c? Why?

▣ 7.   This problem involves running a simulation by constructing a spreadsheet that determines the net profit from holding long gold futures and forward positions. Suppose the relationship between the daily change in the price of gold and the change in the short-term interest rate is

Change in annualized rate $= \beta$(Change in gold price) $+ \varepsilon$.

Let the initial gold (futures and forward) price be $450 per ounce and the initial interest rate be 10 percent. Figure your daily gains and losses until the expiration 50 days into the future, and assume you can borrow or lend until expiration at the interest rate prevailing on the day the marking-to-market gain or loss is received.

Use the @Rand function in Lotus to construct random numbers. Each time this function is called, it generates a different random number between 0 and 1. More specifically,

a.   Assume the daily change in gold (futures and forward) price is random and is between –$10.00 and +$10.00. Assume the error is random and is between –0.0005 and +0.0005. Use the same price change for both the futures and forward prices.

b.   Assume $\beta = 0.0005$.

c.   Use a tail calculated from the current interest rate on any day.

d.   Produce a data table that performs the simulation 100 times. Calculate the minimum, maximum, and average difference between the time T cash flows from the futures and forward positions. Which is greater? Why? (Note: To produce the data table, simply create a column with numbers from 1 to 100. In the next column, copy the cash flow for the futures into the cell next to the 1. In the following column, copy the cash flow for the forward. Finally, define the data table as the three columns and use any empty cell as the input cell.)

e.   Now assume $\beta = -0.0005$. Repeat parts c and d.

f.   What does this indicate about the relationship between forward and futures prices?

8.   Suppose that at the end of March, a firm knows it will need to purchase 1,000 ounces of gold at the end of July. It notices that the spot price of gold is $450 per ounce, the futures price for expiration in July is $469, and the marginal borrowing and lending rates of the firm are each 1 percent per month. The firm is considering hedging the costs of the gold by going long July futures. Gold storage costs are minimal.

a.   Is there a natural hedge that will perform the same function?

b.   Is the choice to use a natural hedge a cash-and-carry or a reverse cash-and-carry quasi-arbitrage? Construct a quasi-arbitrage table for your analysis. Determine the net gain from using the natural hedge. Is it more worth doing the natural or the futures hedge? Interpret your answer intuitively.

9.   Suppose an oil company's sole asset is a 1-million-barrel reserve of oil. The cost of extracting the oil is $8 per barrel, and the oil must be extracted at the end of the year. The oil company is subject to a windfall-profits tax, which requires that it pay a 30 percent tax rate on profits up to $10 million and a surcharge of 10 percent on any profits above $10 million. Suppose the current futures price for crude oil, expiring in one year, is $15 per barrel. There is an equal probability that the price of oil will be $10 and $20 in one year.

a.   Calculate expected after-tax profits if the firm does not hedge.

b.   Calculate expected after-tax profits if the firm hedges.

c.   What does this difference represent?

Stock Index Futures

In the early 1980s, several futures contracts written on stock indices were introduced. These instruments have become very useful to both individual and institutional investors. Individual investors have found the stock index futures contracts to be a low-cost and efficient vehicle for trading on expectations of future general movements in the equity markets. Before the introduction of stock index futures, investors who wished to trade on broad market movements had to buy and sell large portfolios of stocks. The transactions costs of such strategies were extremely high, and execution was slow. Now investors can carry out the same trades in the stock index futures market with one simple transaction. Institutional investors have come to rely on stock index futures to hedge their portfolios and to allocate their assets among different cash, equity, and long-term debt investments.

Cash Market

In the United States, stocks are traded on exchanges, such as the New York and American Stock Exchanges, and through the decentralized over-the-counter (OTC) markets. On the exchanges, stock trades go through **specialists** who manage the flow of bids and offers; each stock is managed by a single specialist. This system of trading is called the **specialist system**. It differs from the trading on the futures exchanges, where many traders can take bids and make offers. Trading in the OTC markets more closely resembles futures trading, because many OTC dealers can take bids and make offers. However, OTC stocks are traded not on an exchange but over an electronic system known as the **National Association of Securities Dealers Automated Quotation** (NASDAQ) system.

Stock trading has undergone a major change in recent years with the introduction of computerized order routing.[1] The **Designated Order Turnaround (DOT)** system at the New York Stock Exchange (NYSE) and the **Post Execution Reporting (PER)** system at the American Stock Exchange (AMEX) allow brokers

---

[1] This material is drawn from Ruder and Adkins [1990].

off the floor to route orders to the specialists. Members of the NYSE and AMEX can use these electronic systems to submit limit and market orders of up to 30,099 and 2,000 shares, respectively. The NASDAQ system has a similar electronic order routing system, called the **Small Order Execution System (SOES),** which can take orders of up to 1,000 shares. In all cases, orders routed through these systems have priority over block trades. These systems have become an integral part of the markets. For example, on an average day the DOT system handles over 70 percent of the trading on the NYSE.

Brokers who wish to buy or sell portfolios of several hundred stocks can now do so on the NYSE using the **List Order Processing (LIST)** program of the DOT system. This program allows brokers to submit simultaneous orders of up to 3,000 shares in each of more than 450 stocks. Thus, entire portfolios can now be traded very quickly. (Before the LIST system was introduced, brokers who wanted to trade entire portfolios had to send runners to each specialist post at the same time.) As we will see, this kind of computerized stock trading facilitates arbitrage between the stock market and the stock index futures market.[2]

Indices

Long before trading in stock index futures began, followers of the stock market used stock indices to measure the general behavior of the market. The Dow Jones Industrial Average ("Dow") is one well-known stock index that is widely reported in both the print and the electronic media. In this section, we will examine the three major types of stock indices: price-equally-weighted, return-equally-weighted, and value-weighted.

Price-Equally-Weighted Index   A **price-equally-weighed index** is constructed by adding up the prices of the stocks in the index and dividing by a divisor:

$$\text{Index} = \left(\frac{1}{\text{Divisor}}\right)\left(\sum_{i=1}^{N} P_i\right), \tag{4.1}$$

where P_i is the price of stock i and N is the number of stocks comprising the index. Both the Dow Jones Industrial Average and the Major Market Index (MMI), the underlying index of the Chicago Board of Trade's stock index futures contract, are price-equally-weighted indices.

The divisor of a price-equally-weighted index can have any value. For example, when the Chicago Board of Trade originally constructed the Major Market Index, it set the divisor equal to 5. If the index is a simple average of the prices of the index stocks, the divisor is the number of stocks in the index.

Example 4.1 demonstrates the calculation of a price-equally-weighted index.

---

[2] We will also discuss the limitations on these kinds of trades imposed after the drastic stock market decline of October 1987.

▪ **Example 4.1: Determining the Value of a Price-Equally-Weighted Index**
Consider a price-equally-weighted index that covers the following three stocks
and has a divisor of 5. This index is computed as follows:

Stock	Base Period Price	Current Period Price
ABC	$ 50	$ 70
DEF	40	30
XYZ	20	40
Sum	$110	$140

Base period index value = 110/5 = 22.00
Current index value   = 140/5 = 28.00

▪

Notice that the divisor in Example 4.1 is 5 in both the base period and the
current period.

Now suppose stock XYZ undergoes a two-for-one split and its stock price
drops from $40 to $20 to reflect this. If the divisor remains the same, the value
of the index will drop to (70 + 30 + 20)/5 = 24. Such a drop will be misleading,
however, because none of the firms in the index have actually experienced a
loss in value. The divisors of price-equally-weighted indices usually are
adjusted to prevent such artificial index changes. To do this in Example 4.1,
we must find a divisor that will maintain the value of the index despite the stock
split:

Index value after split = Index value before split

$$\frac{120}{\text{New divisor}} = 28.00$$

New divisor = 4.2857.

The divisor also may change if the composition of the index changes.
Suppose stock XYZ is replaced by stock QRS, which has a price of $20. The
divisor must again be changed to 4.2857 to prevent the index value from changing.
Any event that decreases the value of the index by a technicality also necessitates
a decrease in the divisor. Similarly, any event that increases the value of the index
by a technicality necessitates an increase in the divisor.

It is easy to create a stock portfolio whose value will move with the
value of a price-equally-weighted index. The portfolio must simply contain
all the stocks of the index in equal number. If a stock split or stock dividend
occurs, or if one stock is replaced by another, the composition of the
"mimicking" portfolio must be changed (rebalanced) such that the portfolio
will continue to mimic the index. Since the index divisor will change to
preserve the market value of the index, the transactions that rebalance the
portfolio must cancel each other out, and the net cost of the rebalancing
(ignoring transactions costs) will be zero. Further, the change in the index
divisor tells us precisely how the portfolio must be rebalanced. Example 4.2
shows how such rebalancing works.

▪ **Example 4.2: Rebalancing a Portfolio That Mimics an Index**   Suppose we hold a stock portfolio whose value mimics the value of the price-equally-weighted index in Example 4.1. This portfolio contains 20,000 shares each of stocks ABC, DEF, and XYZ. These stocks have the same prices as in the current period in Example 4.1. The value of our portfolio is

> Original value of portfolio
> = (20,000 ABC)($70) + (20,000 DEF)($30) + (20,000 XYZ)($40)
> = $2.8 million.

This portfolio value is exactly 100,000 times the index value of 28.

Now suppose stock XYZ is replaced by stock QRS in the index. We must replace our holdings of XYZ with QRS such that our portfolio will continue to mimic the value of the index. However, because QRS has a lower value than XYZ, we must also increase our holdings of all three stocks such that the value of the entire portfolio will not be changed. The change in the index divisor will show us how many shares of each stock we must hold. As we saw before, the index divisor drops from 5 to 4.2857 when the price of one of the stocks falls from $40 to $20. Therefore, we must hold the following number of shares of each stock:

$$\text{New number of shares} = \left(\frac{\text{Old divisor}}{\text{New divisor}}\right)(\text{Old number of shares})$$

$$= \left(\frac{5.0}{4.2857}\right)(20,000)$$

$$= 23,333.41 \text{ shares.}$$

Thus, we must purchase 23,333.41 shares of QRS plus 3,333.41 additional shares of both ABC and DEF.

The total cost of rebalancing our portfolio in this way is

> Rebalancing cost
> = (3,333.41 ABC)($70) + (3,333.41 DEF)($30) + (23,333.41 QRS)($20)
> = $.80 million.

We finance these purchases by selling our 20,000 shares of XYZ:

> Rebalancing revenue = (20,000)($40)
> = $.80 million.

We have accomplished the rebalancing at zero net cost. The new value of the portfolio is

> Value of mimicking portfolio after rebalancing
> = (23,333.41 ABC)($70) + (23,333.41 DEF)($30) + (23,333.41 QRS)($20)
> = $2.8 million.

▪

In the case of a stock split, we must sell off some of the stock that split and increase the shares held of all other stocks. Use of the divisor to guide the rebalancing allows us to constantly maintain a portfolio that mimics the index. Of course, we must weigh the benefits of maintaining such a portfolio against the transactions costs we incur by frequent rebalancing. This rebalancing technique is important for arbitrage between stocks and stock index futures.

Price-equally-weighted indices have some disadvantages. First, changes in the dollar price of small-firm stocks have the same impact on the index as do changes in the dollar price of large-firm stocks. In Example 4.1, a \$1 increase in the price of any of the three companies would increase the value of the index by 1/Divisor = 0.20. An index cannot reflect the importance of price movements relative to the entire market unless changes in the value of heavily capitalized stocks affect it more than do changes in the value of less heavily capitalized stocks.

Second, the effect of a given percentage stock price change on a price-equally-weighted index depends on the initial price of the stock. In Example 4.1, a 10 percent move in the price of ABC will change the index by 7/Divisor = 1.40, while a 10 percent move in the price of XYZ will change the index by only 4/Divisor = 0.80. Consider two firms that are identical but have different numbers of shares outstanding. If they experience the same percentage change in value, the changes will have different impacts on a price-equally-weighted index. Similarly, if a firm's stock splits, future changes in the firm's value will be spread over a greater number of shares and thus will have less impact on the index.

Although these disadvantages can cause price-equally-weighted indices to misrepresent the importance of stock price changes, the Dow Jones Industrial Average remains the most widely quoted index.

Return-Equally-Weighted Index   A **return-equally-weighted index** is calculated by first taking the arithmetic mean of 1 plus the rate of price change of all stocks in the index. This mean is then multiplied by the previous day's index value to obtain today's index:

$$\text{Index} = \text{Index}(-1) \left(\frac{1}{N} \right) \left(\sum_{i=1}^{N} \left[\frac{P_i}{P_i(-1)} \right] \right), \tag{4.2}$$

where −1 refers to the previous day's value. Today's return-equally-weighted index is simply the previous day's index increased or decreased by the average rate of price change experienced by the stocks in the index. Because the value of a return-equally-weighted index is determined relative to its value on the previous day, the index is arbitrarily assigned a **base-period value** on a certain day in the past. For example, the index might have been given a value of 100.00 on January 1, 1975.

The Value Line Index is the best-known return-equally-weighted stock index in the United States.[3] Example 4.3 shows how to calculate return-equally-weighted indices.

▪ **Example 4.3: Determining the Value of a Return-Equally-Weighted Index** Suppose a return-equally-weighted index that contains the three stocks in our previous examples had a value of 250 yesterday. We then compute the index's value today as follows:

Stock	Previous Day's Price	Current Price	1 Plus Rate of Change
ABC	$70	$77	1.10
DEF	30	36	1.20
XYZ	40	42	1.05

Previous day's index value = 250.0
Average of one plus the rate of change = (1.10 + 1.20 + 1.05)/3 = 1.11667
Current index value = (250)(1.11667) = 279.168

▪

Because a return-equally-weighted index is computed from rates of price change, the *level* of any individual stock's price does not affect the index value as it would with a price-equally-weighted index. Two identical firms with differing numbers of shares would have the same impact on a return-equally-weighted index, because the percentage changes in their share prices would be the same.

While desirable, this characteristic of return-equally-weighted indices makes it much more difficult to maintain a portfolio that mimics a return-equally-weighted index than one that mimics a price-equally-weighted index. A portfolio that mimics a price-equally-weighted index must be rebalanced only when there is a stock split, a stock dividend, or a change in the list of stocks in the index. But a portfolio that mimics a return-equally-weighted index must be rebalanced every day, because a change in the price of one stock has the same impact on a return-equally-weighted index as the same percentage change in the price of any other stock. To duplicate this behavior with a portfolio of stocks, we must adjust the portfolio every day such that its individual stock holdings are always equal in market value. Then a percentage price change experienced by one stock will have the same impact on the portfolio value as will the same percentage price change in any other stock. Such daily rebalancing can generate substantial transactions costs.

The return-equally-weighted index shares one of the shortcomings of the price-equally-weighted index, for small firms have as much influence on the return-equally-weighted index as large firms do. A given percentage change in the price of IBM has the same impact on the value of the index as the same percentage

---

[3] The Value Line Index was a geometrically weighted index until 1988. Instead of using an arithmetic average of the component stocks' rates of price change, the index used a geometric average of the rates of change. This was abandoned because of its complexity.

change in the price of a much smaller firm does. The value-weighted index, discussed next, solves this problem.

Value-Weighted Index   A **value-weighted index** weights each of its component stocks by the stock's market value, or **capitalization**. It is constructed by dividing the current total market value of all stocks in the index by the total market value of all stocks during the base period. This ratio is then divided by a divisor such that the index is

$$\text{Index} = \left(\frac{1}{\text{Divisor}}\right)\left(\frac{\displaystyle\sum_{i=1}^{N} n_i P_i}{\displaystyle\sum_{i=1}^{M} n_i^b P_i^b}\right), \tag{4.3}$$

where n_i is the number of outstanding shares of stock i and the b superscripts refer to the base period. The number of stocks in the index at the present time, N, need not equal the number of stocks in the index during the base period, M. As with the price-equally-weighted and return-equally-weighted indices, the role of the divisor is to ensure that the index does not move simply because stocks are added to or subtracted from it. Thus, the divisor is set such that the old index equals the new index when the index composition changes.

   The best-known value-weighted indices are the Standard and Poor's (S&P) 500 and the New York Stock Exchange (NYSE) indices. Example 4.4 illustrates how a value-weighted index is computed.

▪ **Example 4.4: Determining the Value of a Value-Weighted Index**   Suppose a value-weighted index contains three stocks with the following prices and capitalization. The current index divisor is 0.10. The index value is computed as follows:

Stock	Shares Outstanding	Base Period Price	Base Period Capitalization	Current Period Price	Current Period Capitalization
ABC	1,000	$50	$50,000	$70	$ 70,000
DEF	500	40	20,000	30	15,000
XYZ	800	20	16,000	40	32,000
			$86,000		$117,000

Current divisor = 0.10
Index = (1/0.10)($117,000/$86,000) = 13.6047

▪

   The value-weighted index resembles the return-equally-weighted index in that the effect on the index of a change in a firm's equity value does not depend on the number of shares. It is irrelevant for the index whether a firm has 1,000 shares and a stock price of $70 or 2,000 shares and a stock price of $35. But the value-weighted index is unlike the return-equally-weighted index in that the effect of a change in a firm's equity value *does* depend on the market capitalization of the stock. For instance, if in Example 4.4 the price of stock ABC increased by 1 percent, the total change in the index would be

$$\text{Change in index} = \left(\frac{1}{\text{Divisor}}\right)\left(\frac{\text{Change in current value}}{\text{Base value}}\right)$$

$$= \left[\frac{1}{0.10}\right]\left[\frac{(\$0.70)(1{,}000)}{\$86{,}000}\right]$$

$$= 0.0814.$$

If the price of stock XYZ increased by 1 percent, the total change in the index would be

$$\text{Change in index} = \left[\frac{1}{0.10}\right]\left[\frac{(\$0.40)(800)}{\$86{,}000}\right]$$

$$= 0.0372.$$

Since stock ABC has a larger capitalization, a given percentage change in its equity value will have a greater impact on the index than will the same percentage change in stock XYZ's equity value. This characteristic of the value-weighted index enables the index to reflect the importance of each firm's value changes relative to the entire market.

We can create a portfolio that mimics a value-weighted index simply by holding a set percentage of the outstanding equity of all the firms in the index. For example, a mimicking portfolio in Example 4.4 could hold 1 percent of each of the three stocks in the index. This portfolio would contain 10 shares of ABC, 5 shares of DEF, and 8 shares of XYZ. Its value would always be 1 percent of the value of all the stocks in the index and therefore would match the index's performance.

This portfolio would not have to be rebalanced every day as the return-equally-weighted index would. Changes in the market value of the component stocks would, of course, be immediately incorporated into the mimicking portfolio. If a stock split or stock dividend occurred, the number of shares in the portfolio would automatically increase in proportion to the increase in the number of shares outstanding. If we added or subtracted stocks from the index, we could rebalance the portfolio at zero cost (ignoring transactions costs) because the divisor would set the market value of the new portfolio equal to that of the old portfolio.

A value-weighted index that includes a broad cross-section of stocks in the economy will be very similar to the market portfolio in the Capital Asset Pricing Model. Like a value-weighted index, the **market portfolio** holds stocks in proportion to their market capitalization. The market portfolio also does not require daily rebalancing. For these reasons, researchers often use either the Standard and Poor's 500 or the New York Stock Exchange Index as a proxy for the market portfolio.

Stock Index Futures

A **stock index futures contract** is simply a futures contract to buy or sell the face value of a stock index. The four main stock index futures contracts traded in the United States are the Standard and Poor's 500 contract at the CME, the New York Stock Exchange Index contract at the NYFE, the Major Market Index at the CBOT,[4] and the Value Line Index at the KCBT. These contracts experienced rapid growth in their early years, from a volume of 12.75 million contracts in 1983 to a peak of 25.39 million in 1986. Following the crash of 1987 (discussed later), trading in equity index futures fell to 14.35 million in 1988. Figure 4.1 shows that the Standard and Poor's 500 contract has become the dominant index futures contract.[5]

Standard and Poor's 500 Futures

In April 1982, the CME introduced the Standard and Poor's 500 futures contract written on the S&P 500 Index. The S&P 500 Index is a value-weighted index of 500 stocks, most of which are highly capitalized, blue-chip stocks. It is a broader index than the Dow, for its stocks are diversified across industries, utilities, transportation companies, and financial institutions, and it includes stocks from the NYSE, AMEX, and OTC markets. Around 95 percent of the firms represented in the index are listed on the NYSE. The market value of the stocks in the index is approximately 80 percent of the market value of all stocks listed on the NYSE.[6]

Standard and Poor's 500 Futures Contract Specifications

Contract:	Standard and Poor's 500 Index
Exchange:	Chicago Mercantile Exchange
Quantity:	$500 times the S&P 500 Index
Delivery months:	March, June, September, December
Delivery specifications:	Cash settlement according to the value of the index at the opening on the Friday after the last day of trading; if a stock does not open on Friday, its last sale price is used
Minimum price movement:	0.05 index points, or $25 per contract

The S&P 500 futures contract is valued at $500 per S&P 500 Index point. For example, see the stock index futures quotations for May 23, 1989, from *The Wall Street Journal* in Figure 4.2. The closing value of the spot S&P 500 Index on that day was 318.30, so the size of the S&P 500 contract was

---

[4] The Chicago Board of Trade has supplanted its original Major Market Index (MMI) contract with the MMI Maxi contract. In this chapter, we will refer to the current contract as the MMI.

[5] Throughout this book, 1989 figures are extrapolated from the first five months of that year.

[6] See Byrne [1987] for further details about the S&P 500 Index.

Figure 4.1 Major U.S. Stock Index Futures, Annual Volume, 1983–1989

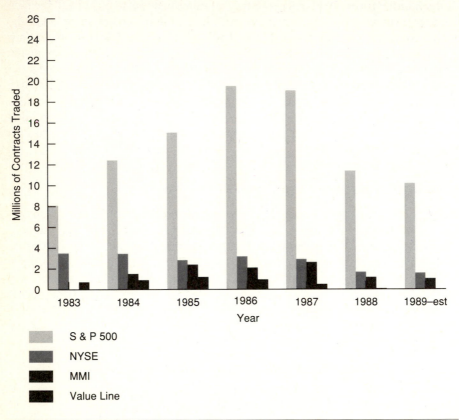

Source: Futures Industry Association.

$$\begin{aligned}
\text{Contract size} &= (\text{Index value})(\$500) \\
&= (318.30)(\$500) \\
&= \$159{,}150.
\end{aligned}$$

To see how the S&P 500 futures contract operates, suppose we enter into a futures contract on May 23, 1989, to buy the S&P 500 at 324.45 when the contract expires on September 15.[7] If the value of the index is 330.00 on September 15, the net gain from entering into the contract will be

$$\begin{aligned}
\text{Gain to long position} &= (\$500)(\text{Closing index} - \text{Initial futures}) \\
&= (\$500)(330.00 - 324.45) \\
&= \$2{,}775.
\end{aligned}$$

---

[7] While futures trading stops on Thursday, September 14, cash settlement occurs on Friday.

Figure 4.2 Stock Index Futures Transactions Prices for May 23, 1989

```
                         FUTURES
         S&P 500 INDEX (CME) 500 times index
                                                    Open
              Open  High   Low  Settle  Chg  High   Low Interest
    June    322.60 322.85 319.75 320.10 − 3.50 325.00 263.80 123,884
    Sept    327.00 327.25 324.15 324.45 − 3.55 329.40 271.50  17,286
    Dec     331.40 331.40 328.30 328.65 − 3.60 333.60 298.90   1,295
       Est vol 47,059; vol Mon 53,670; open int 142,466, +813.
       Indx prelim High 321.98; Low 318.20; Close 318.30−3.66

         NYSE COMPOSITE INDEX (NYFE) 500 times index
    June    179.75 179.90 178.35 178.50 − 1.75 181.05 149.60   5,407
    Sept    182.15 182.25 180.80 180.85 − 1.80 183.50 153.90   1,342
    Dec     184.50 184.50 183.95 183,20 − 1.90 185.70 161.10     415
       Est vol 6,890; vol Mon5,900; open int 7,223, +16.
       The index: High 179.34; Low 177.56; Close 177.61 −1.73
         MAJOR MKT INDEX (CBT) $250 times index
    June    491.90 492.20 488.00 488.60 − 4.85 496.40 442.50   2,285
    July    495.00 495.20 491.50 491.80 − 4.90 499.60 469.10     564
       Est vol 4,000; vol Mon 2,472; open int 2,849, −12,563.
       The index: High 491.49; Low 485.58; Close 486.14 −5.35
         KC VALUE LINE INDEX (KC) 500 times index
    June    283.80 283.85 282.20 282.60 − 1.90 285.60 245.65   1,264
    Sept    287.65 287.65 286.60 286.80 − 1.90 289.10 267.40     133
       Est vol 105; vol Mon 181; open int 1,400, −1.
       The index: High 281.93; Low 280.60; Close 280.67 −1.23 -
         CRB INDEX (NYFE) 500 times index
    July    233.15 234.45 232.60 232.65 −  .10 250.50 232.60   1,409
    Sept    234.90 235.50 234.15 234.20 −  .30 249.10 234.15     247
    Dec     235.50 235.50 235.15 234.70 −  .30 245.25 235.15     278
       Est vol 822; vol Mon1,095; open int 1,984, +228.
       The index: High 234.08; Low 232.45; Close 232.45 −.87

               −OTHER INDEX FUTURES−

       Settlement price of selected contract. Volume and open
    interest of all contract months.

    KC Mini Value Line (KC) 100 times index
      Jun 282.60 −1.90; Est. vol. 15; Open int. 104

       CBT−Chicago Board of Trade. CME−Chicago Mercan-
    tile Exchange. KC−Kansas City Board of Trade. NYFE−
    New York Futures Exchange, a unit of the New York Stock
    Exchange.
```

Source: *The Wall Street Journal,* May 24, 1989.

If we close out our position early, on June 1 at 320.00, the net gain will be

$$\text{Gain to long position} = (\$500)(\text{Current futures} - \text{Initial futures})$$
$$= (\$500)(320.00 - 324.45)$$
$$= -\$2,225.$$

New York Stock Exchange Composite Index Futures

The New York Stock Exchange Composite Index futures contract, introduced in May 1982 at the NYFE, is another widely traded futures contract on a value-weighted stock index. Its value is $500 times the level of the New York Stock Exchange Composite Index. The NYSE Composite Index includes all the stocks listed on the New York Stock Exchange, which currently number about 1,500. Thus, the NYSE Composite Index contains many smaller firms that are not in the S&P 500 Index. Despite this difference, however, the two indices are very highly correlated.

New York Stock Exchange Composite Index Futures Contract Specifications

---

Contract:	New York Stock Exchange Composite Index Futures
Exchange:	New York Futures Exchange
Quantity:	$500 times the NYSE Composite Index
Delivery months:	March, June, September, December
Delivery specifications:	Cash settlement according to the value of the index at the close of the last day of trading
Minimum price movement:	0.05 index points, or $25 per contract

Major Market Index Futures

The most recent entrant into the stock index futures market is the Major Market Index (MMI) contract that the CBOT introduced in July 1984. Its value is $250 times the level of the MMI, a price-equally-weighted index very similar to the Dow. For many years the CBOT sought to use the Dow for its stock futures contract, but it was blocked by Dow Jones in a legal battle. So the CBOT created the MMI. The MMI contains 20 stocks, while the Dow has 30. The MMI and the Dow are highly correlated; the correlation usually is around 0.97. Yet a big move in a stock included in one index but not the other can lower this correlation.[8] Historically, the two indices have been sufficiently correlated for the MMI futures contract to be useful to those who follow the Dow.

Major Market Index Futures Contract Specifications

Contract:	Major Market Index Futures
Exchange:	Chicago Board of Trade
Quantity:	$250 times the Major Market Index
Delivery months:	Monthly
Delivery specifications:	Cash settlement according to the value of the index at the close of the last day of trading
Minimum price movement:	0.05 index points, or $12.50 per contract

Value Line Index Futures

The Kansas City Board of Trade introduced the very first stock index futures contract in February 1982. The contract is written on the Value Line Index, and its value is $500 times the level of the index. The Value Line Index currently includes about 1,700 stocks listed on the New York Stock Exchange, the American Stock Exchange, the Toronto Stock Exchange, and the OTC markets. It provides much broader coverage of the stock markets than do the other indices, because it includes many more small-firm stocks. The index is return-equally-weighted, so the small-firm stocks have a major impact on the index value.

---

[8] Byrne [1987] points out that the drop in Union Carbide stock that followed the chemical plant disaster in Bhopal, India, caused the Dow to fall, while the MMI rallied.

Value Line Index Futures Contract Specifications

Contract:	Value Line Index Futures
Exchange:	Kansas City Board of Trade
Quantity:	$500 times the Value Line Index
Delivery months:	March, June, September, December
Delivery specifications:	Cash settlement according to the value of the index at the close of the last day of trading
Minimum price movement:	0.05 index points, or $25 per contract

The Fundamental No-Arbitrage Equation

We can easily describe the pricing of stock index futures with a no-arbitrage equation. Recall the fundamental no-arbitrage equation we derived for the fictitious S&P 1 Index futures contract in Chapter 2:

$$F_{t,T} = P_t(1 + r_{t,T}) - FV_T(\text{Dividends between t and T}). \tag{4.4}$$

We can modify this equation to apply to the actual stock index futures markets. First, we redefine P_t as the index at time t times the multiplier specified in the index futures contract. Then we redefine the term "dividends between t and T" as the dividends paid between t and T on a portfolio that mimics the index and whose value equals the dollar value of the index at time t.

This fundamental no-arbitrage equation is enforced by cash-and-carry and reverse cash-and-carry arbitrage between the stock and the stock index futures markets. Such trading strategies are known as **index arbitrage**.

If $F_{t,T} > [P_t(1 + r_{t,T}) - FV_T(\text{Dividends between t and T})]$, the following index arbitrage yields a cash-and-carry arbitrage profit:

At time t:

1. Buy the portfolio that mimics the index.

2. Borrow to finance the portfolio purchase.

3. Go short the index futures.

Between t and T:

1. Collect dividends on the portfolio and invest until time T.

At time T:

1. Sell the portfolio.

2. Repay the borrowed funds.

3. Close out the futures using cash settlement.

4. Obtain proceeds from invested dividends.

If $F_{t,T} < [P_t(1 + r_{t,T}) - FV_T(\text{Dividends between t and T})]$, the following index arbitrage yields a reverse cash-and-carry arbitrage profit:

At time t:

1.   Sell short the portfolio that mimics the index.

2.   Lend the proceeds from the portfolio sale.

3.   Go long the index futures.

Between t and T:

1.   Borrow to pay dividends on the portfolio.

At time T:

1.   Buy the portfolio and cover the short positions.

2.   Receive proceeds from the loan.

3.   Close out the futures using cash settlement.

4.   Pay back loans taken out to pay dividends.

Index arbitrages are just like the S&P 1 arbitrage strategies we studied in Chapter 2 except that they require the arbitrageurs to buy or short an entire portfolio of stocks and account for the dividends on that portfolio. Index arbitrageurs have two techniques for buying and selling stock portfolios. The first—and now less often used—approach is to design portfolios that closely mimic the index underlying the futures but include fewer stocks than the index. For instance, an investor might try to mimic the S&P 500 with a portfolio of 50 stocks. The 50 stocks would be chosen not only for their ability to match the performance of the index but also for their liquidity. Holding a small portfolio of liquid stock would cut down on transactions costs and allow the investor to move quickly to take advantage of arbitrage opportunities.

One drawback of this technique is that it introduces basis risk into the trade if the mimicking portfolio does not move directly with the index. To cut down on the basis risk problem, arbitrageurs recently have started trading their stock portfolios through the LIST program of the DOT system at the NYSE. The LIST program allows arbitrageurs to place orders in many stocks simultaneously and thus reduce the risk that only part of a portfolio will be bought or sold. Because the portfolios index arbitrageurs trade contain many different stocks, the amount traded in each stock typically is small enough to go through the DOT system. Index arbitrage with the DOT system has become the primary tool of arbitrageurs in the index futures markets. This technique is commonly known as **program trading**.

Dividends do not pose a major problem for index arbitrage, for it is fairly easy to predict the dividends on a broadly based portfolio, unlike predicting dividends on individual stocks. Several services make near-term predictions of the dividend payouts on the portfolios underlying the various stock indices. Figure 4.3 shows a dividend prediction one such service provides. It graphs the daily predicted dividends on the

Figure 4.3 Dividends on the S&P 500, in S&P Index Points

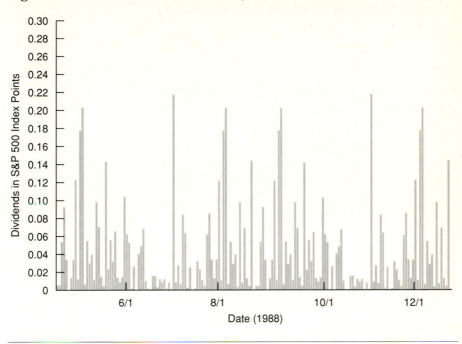

Source: Drexel Burnham Lambert.

S&P 500 portfolio in terms of S&P 500 points. Arbitrageurs can use such data to estimate the future value of dividends between t and T.

Suppose, for example, that the current level of the S&P 500 spot index is 260. The portfolio underlying the S&P 500 futures contract, then, has a value of (260)($500) = $130,000. On May 9, the expected dividend is 0.03 S&P 500 points. This represents a dollar value under the futures contract of (0.03)($500) = $15. Thus, a portfolio that mimics the S&P 500 Index and has a market value of $130,000 is expected to pay dividends of $15 on May 9.

Example 4.5 shows how predicted dividend information is used to calculate a no-arbitrage futures price in the S&P 500 futures market. This calculation can then be used to search for index arbitrage opportunities.

▪ **Example 4.5: Calculating the No-Arbitrage Price on the S&P 500 Futures**
Suppose the S&P 500 spot index is 260 on April 20. Expected dividends on the S&P 500 are as given in Table 4.1. The short-term interest rate is 8 percent per annum. We wish to calculate the no-arbitrage futures price for an S&P 500 contract that expires on June 17. Table 4.1 shows the future value of the predicted dividends, in S&P 500 points, as of June 17.[9]

---

[9] Because settlement occurs at the open on June 17, we exclude dividends for that day.

Table 4.1 Future Value of Predicted S&P 500 Dividend Stream in S&P 500 Points, 8 Percent Short-Term Interest Rate

Date	Days to Expiration	Expected Daily Dividend	Future Value as of June 17
4/20/88	58	0.005	0.005064
4/22/88	56	0.005	0.005062
4/25/88	53	0.054	0.054636
4/26/88	52	0.092	0.093063
4/27/88	51	0.034	0.034385
4/28/88	50	0.000	0.000000
4/29/88	49	0.014	0.014152
5/1/88	47	0.034	0.034355
5/2/88	46	0.122	0.123247
5/3/88	45	0.012	0.012120
5/4/88	44	0.177	0.178731
5/5/88	43	0.202	0.203930
5/6/88	42	0.007	0.007065
5/8/88	40	0.055	0.055489
5/9/88	39	0.030	0.030260
5/10/88	38	0.040	0.040338
5/11/88	37	0.012	0.012099
5/12/88	36	0.098	0.098784
5/16/88	32	0.070	0.070498
5/17/88	31	0.015	0.015103
5/18/88	30	0.005	0.005033
5/19/88	29	0.142	0.142915
5/21/88	27	0.024	0.024144
5/22/88	26	0.056	0.056324
5/23/88	25	0.033	0.033183
5/24/88	24	0.065	0.065347
5/25/88	23	0.014	0.014072
5/26/88	22	0.010	0.010049
5/27/88	21	0.015	0.015070
5/29/88	19	0.103	0.103435
6/1/88	16	0.063	0.063224
6/2/88	15	0.053	0.053177
6/3/88	14	0.002	0.002006
6/4/88	13	0.027	0.027078
6/6/88	11	0.000	0.000000
6/7/88	10	0.041	0.041091
6/8/88	9	0.049	0.049098
6/9/88	8	0.068	0.068121
6/10/88	7	0.011	0.011017
6/11/88	6	0.002	0.002003
6/13/88	4	0.001	0.001001
6/14/88	3	0.017	0.017011
6/15/88	2	0.017	0.017008
6/16/88	1	0.004	0.004001
Total			1.914

Source: Drexel Burnham Lambert.

The no-arbitrage futures price, then, is

No-arbitrage futures price

$$= (\text{Current index})\left[1 + \frac{(r)(\text{Days from t to T})}{360}\right] - FV_T(\text{Dividends})$$

$$= (260)\left[1 + \frac{(.08)(58)}{360}\right] - 1.914$$

$$= 261.437.$$

For simplicity, we have excluded transactions costs. These would be taken into account, as discussed in Chapter 2. ■

Quasi-Arbitrage   Index arbitrage is used for quasi-arbitrage as well as for pure arbitrage. Portfolio managers who hold both short-term riskless securities and diversified equity portfolios often find trading index futures a less costly way to hold their desired positions. For example, suppose the futures price is high relative to the spot index according to the no-arbitrage relationship. A portfolio manager could profit by using index arbitrage to replace some of his or her short-term riskless securities with synthetic T-bills. The manager would do this by selling some short-term riskless securities, using the proceeds to purchase a portfolio that mimicked the index, and going short the futures (T-bill = Spot – Futures). By selling the riskless securities, the manager would effectively borrow from himself or herself at a lower rate than would be available to pure arbitrageurs. Table 4.2 demonstrates this cash-and-carry quasi-arbitrage strategy.

Alternatively, if the futures price is low relative to the spot index, the portfolio manager could benefit by replacing some stocks with synthetic stocks. He or she would do this by selling some of the equity portfolio, buying short-term riskless securities, and going long futures (Spot = T-bill + Futures). The manager would avoid short-selling costs by selling off existing stock holdings and thus carry out the index arbitrage more cheaply than a pure arbitrageur could. Table 4.3 illustrates this reverse cash-and-carry quasi-arbitrage strategy.

Function of Index Arbitrage   As we saw in Chapter 2, pure and quasi-arbitrage in the stock index market can save transactions costs for society. Suppose, for example, that a portfolio manager who infrequently changes his asset allocation decides to buy a portfolio of stocks. This may be costly and time consuming if he has not established access to the LIST program of the DOT system. He must either buy each stock individually or gain access to the system. Either approach could take a great deal of time and effort. The manager might be able to buy the stocks synthetically at lower cost by buying T-bills and going long stock index futures. The futures price will reflect the costs of those portfolio

Table 4.2 Cash-and-Carry Quasi-Arbitrage Table for Portfolio Manager

Benchmark position: investment in T-bills

Cash-and-Carry Pure Arbitrage Components	Cash-and-Carry Quasi-Arbitrage Components	Relevant Price or Rate
1. Buy spot	Buy mimicking portfolio	Ask
Receive dividends	Receive dividends	
2. Short futures	Short futures	Bid
3. Borrow	Sell T-bills	T-bill bid

Resulting position: investment in synthetic T-bills

Transactions fees: TF = TF_1 + TF_2 + TF_3
1. Pay TF_1
2. Pay TF_2
3. Pay TF_3

Table 4.3 Reverse Cash-and-Carry Quasi-Arbitrage Table for Portfolio Manager

Benchmark position: holding of equity portfolio

Reverse Cash-and-Carry Pure Arbitrage Components	Reverse Cash-and-Carry Quasi-Arbitrage Components	Relevant Price or Rate
1. Short spot	Sell mimicking portfolio	Bid
Rebate dividends	Lose dividends	
2. Go long futures	Go long futures	Ask
3. Lend	Buy T-bills	T-bill ask

Resulting position: investment in synthetic equity portfolio

Transactions fees: TF = TF_1 + TF_2 + TF_3
1. Pay TF_1
2. Pay TF_2
3. Pay TF_3

managers and arbitrageurs who have quick and low-cost access to the DOT system.[10] Thus, the futures contract would offer the original portfolio manager both low costs and convenience.

Empirical Evidence on the Fundamental No-Arbitrage Equation   Many empirical studies have tried to determine whether the no-arbitrage relationship for stock index futures, Equation 4.4, holds in actual markets. Because of transactions

---

[10] As discussed in Chapter 2, it is likely that the lowest-cost arbitrageur will be a quasi-arbitrageur. Thus, gestures by investment banks after the 1987 market break to refrain from index arbitrage on their own account were somewhat empty, because the same banks agreed to perform the arbitrages on behalf of their clients.

costs, most researchers compute no-arbitrage bounds as in Equation 2.19 of Chapter 2 and then test to see if futures prices lie within these bounds.

The results of these studies are conflicting. Modest and Sundaresan [1983] examined very early S&P 500 futures contracts and generally found that the futures prices fell within the no-arbitrage bounds. Cornell and French [1983] found that the prices of futures on the S&P 500 and the NYSE Composite Index were lower than expected. However, Cornell [1985] discovered that these mispricings grew smaller over time.[11] Bailey [1989] found few arbitrage opportunities in Japanese stock index futures.

These studies have been criticized because they used closing values for the underlying stock index and the futures. The critics argue that since arbitrage occurs very quickly, the prices actually available to traders during the day are more likely to show whether arbitrage opportunities exist. Chung [1988] attempted to overcome this criticism by using actual transactions price data to see if there were arbitrage opportunities in the Major Market Index futures contract. He found that previous studies had overestimated the size and frequency of profitable arbitrage opportunities.[12] However, as in the earlier work, Chung found that the number of profitable arbitrage opportunities had declined over time.

Taken together, the empirical work to date indicates that some profitable arbitrage opportunities exist in stock index futures, but they are small in number and appear to decline over time.[13] However, we would not expect to find markets that never exhibit profitable arbitrage opportunities. If these existed, there would be no incentive to set up arbitrage operations. In equilibrium, we would expect there to be enough profitable arbitrage opportunities to cover the costs of the marginal arbitrageur.[14]

Index Arbitrage and Stock Market Volatility   Some policymakers and market participants have been concerned that trading in stock index futures and index arbitrage create excessive volatility in the stock market. The major reason for this concern is that we often observe large movements in the stock market following the execution of index arbitrage. Thus, it is common to read in the financial press that index arbitrage was responsible for a drop in the stock market.

[11] A futures price that is too low indicates that there are profitable reverse cash-and-carry arbitrages. The costs of selling stocks short may have prevented some of these arbitrages. Perhaps the entry of quasi-arbitrageurs over time eliminated such arbitrage opportunities. Chang and Loo [1987] also proposed that some "apparent" underpricing may be due to marking-to-market effects.

[12] MacKinlay and Ramaswamy [1988] also used intraday data. However, they used the value of the index rather than the individual stocks' prices. They also failed to find large mispricing

[13] Other studies include Figlewski [1984], Brennan and Schwartz [1986], Finnerty and Park [1987], Kawaller, Koch, and Koch [1987], and Stoll [1988].

[14] This argument is similar to Grossman's [1977] contention that it is impossible to have a perfectly efficient market.

Our understanding of arbitrage leads us to an alternative, and less sinister, explanation for the observed phenomenon. Suppose there is a general feeling in the market that the stock market level is too high. Investors can act on this view either by selling broad equity portfolios or by going short stock index futures. They are more likely to go short futures because of the liquidity, speed of execution, and lower costs of transacting in the futures markets.[15] A large movement of investors into short futures positions will drive stock index futures prices down relative to the stock market. Index arbitrageurs will observe that the cash stock market has become expensive relative to the futures so that there are new opportunities for reverse cash-and-carry arbitrage. The arbitrageurs will enter into reverse cash-and-carry strategies by going long stock index futures and selling broad stock portfolios. Their activity will drive the cash stock market level down until it is in line with the futures market.

To the outside observer, it may appear that the index arbitrageurs have caused the stock market to fall by selling equities. In fact, the drop in the market had already occurred when investors went short futures. Thus, it is not at all clear that index arbitrage "causes" large changes in the value of the cash stock market.

Harris [1988] examined whether the introduction of the S&P 500 futures contract has increased the volatility of the stocks in the S&P 500 Index. He found that the largest increase in the standard deviation of daily stock returns after the index futures were introduced was 0.14 percent. While Harris determined that this increase is statistically significant, it is not economically significant when compared to the roughly 2 percent typical daily standard deviation in stock returns.[16, 17]

Stock Index Futures and the October 1987 Market Break   Much of the discussion of the impact of index futures trading on stock market volatility has been prompted by the October 1987 market break. On Monday, October 19, 1987, equity markets around the world suffered a massive crash. Figure 4.4 shows that the Dow dropped 508 points, or almost 25 percent from the previous Friday's close, on that day. Other indices suffered a similar fate. Many observers felt that index futures trading contributed to the drastic market drop.

The index futures markets were very active on October 19 and 20, 1987. Many institutions went short large quantities of index futures. Some of them were

---

[15] Zeckhauser and Niederhoffer [1983], Herbst, McCormack, and West [1987], Ng [1987], Laatsch and Schwartz [1988], and Swinnerton, Curcio, and Bennett [1988] found that movements in the index futures tend to lead movements in the spot indices.

[16] Whaley [1986] and Stoll and Whaley [1987] found that stock price volatility did increase around the expiration dates of the S&P 500 futures contract. This increase was due to the "triple witching hour," when options, index options, and index futures all expire at the same time. Arbitrageurs would unwind their trades in the last few minutes on such expiration dates, leading to large (transient) price swings. The Chicago Mercantile Exchange has changed its final settlement procedures so that trading in futures now stops the day before the final settlement of the contract. This has effectively eliminated the "triple-witching-hour" problem.

[17] For other perspectives, see Rendleman [1986], Aggarwal [1988], Edwards [1988], Grossman [1988], and Stoll and Whaley [1988].

Figure 4.4 Stock Index Behavior, October 1987 Market Break

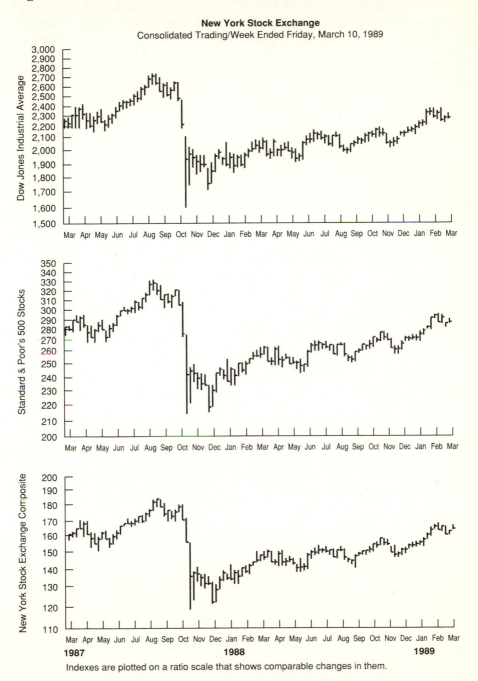

New York Stock Exchange
Consolidated Trading/Week Ended Friday, March 10, 1989

Indexes are plotted on a ratio scale that shows comparable changes in them.

Source: *The New York Times,* March 12, 1989.

using a strategy called **portfolio insurance**, which involves going short futures when the stock market starts to drop.[18] This selling of futures lowered futures prices relative to the spot stock market. Index arbitrageurs then engaged in reverse cash-and-carry arbitrages, selling stocks and going long futures. As a result, stock prices themselves fell. Gammill and Marsh [1988] documented that index arbitrageurs were among the major buyers of index futures contracts and major sellers of stocks on October 19.

While at first glance it may appear that index arbitrage caused the stock prices to fall, a more sensible interpretation is that the initial short positions in the futures were the cause. The index arbitrageurs merely provided the link between the futures and cash markets. Under this interpretation, it is not clear that the drop was even caused by the existence of index futures. In the absence of index futures, portfolio insurers could have sold the cash stocks themselves. However, they chose to use futures because of the greater liquidity, greater speed, and lower costs of transacting in futures that we discussed earlier.

There is still considerable debate over how well index arbitrage performed during the 1987 market break. It appears that S&P 500 futures traded during those few days at a huge discount relative to the S&P 500 Index. This suggests that index arbitrageurs were not effectively tying the futures and cash markets together. However, Harris [1987], Kleidon [1988], and Bassett, France, and Pliska [1989] showed that this discount is illusory, for there was so much chaos in the NYSE system for reporting prices that the reported S&P 500 cash index was essentially meaningless. Further, the NYSE effectively stopped index arbitrage activity on October 20 by requesting that members not use the DOT system for arbitrage. Thus, futures prices provided the only effective measure of the stock market level during the market break. The futures market played a very important price discovery role.

The NYSE and CME put some limitations on index arbitrage after the October 1987 market break.[19] Now if the Dow falls more than 25 points, program traders lose priority in the DOT system. A "sidecar" procedure requires that program trade orders be withheld from the market for five minutes if the S&P 500 Index moves more than 12 points.[20] These orders are held by specialists, who determine whether imbalances are present and whether they can execute these orders in a methodical manner. If not, the specialists halt trading and publicize the imbalances before reopening trading in the stock. The Securities and Exchange Commission (SEC) and the CFTC have also approved a system of "circuit breakers" for situations in which the market drops too quickly. These range from the Chicago Mercantile Exchange's policy of allowing futures trading only at

---

[18] We will discuss portfolio insurance in more detail in Chapter 10. See Stulz [1988] for a discussion of this issue.

[19] See Greenwald and Stein [1988] for a discussion of the report of the Brady Commission. President Reagan gave this commission the task of evaluating the events of the market break and recommending measures to prevent its recurrence.

[20] A 12-point drop in the S&P 500 Index corresponds to about a 75-point drop in the Dow.

higher prices if the S&P 500 Index drops more than 12 points to its halting of all trading in CME index contracts for the remainder of the day if the S&P 500 drops more than 50 points. These measures are still controversial, because many financial economists feel that closing markets can fuel panic.[21]

Stock Index Futures and Institutional Investors

Stock index futures have become a major trading tool for institutional investors such as employee benefit plans, insurance companies, institutional endowments, foundations, trust agency accounts of banks and trust companies, and investment companies. These portfolios typically consist of cash (short-term, fixed-income securities), long-term, fixed-income securities, and equities. Stock index futures are most often used in the management of the cash and equity holdings as part of two trading strategies called *market timing* and *stock picking*.

Portfolio managers who follow a **market-timing** strategy move their funds between cash and equities according to their expectations about which will perform better. A manager who thinks equities will perform well relative to short-term instruments places a higher proportion of funds into equities. A manager who believes equities will do relatively poorly moves funds from equities to cash. As discussed in Chapter 2, this trading strategy is known as *asset allocation*.

Portfolio managers who follow a **stock-picking** strategy attempt to beat the market by buying undervalued stocks and selling overvalued ones. They employ stock analysts to identify stocks that are under- or overpriced given their risk levels. In this section, we will show how stock index futures can help implement market-timing and stock-picking strategies.

Market Timing   Portfolio managers who engage in market timing may find themselves buying and selling many equities and short-term instruments. They may incur large transactions costs, such as brokerage fees and bid-ask spreads, in the process. Stock index futures provide an alternative, and perhaps less costly, method of carrying out the market-timing transactions. Stock index futures prices will reflect both brokerage fees and bid-ask spreads, but they will be the transactions costs of the lowest-cost trader. A portfolio manager who does not specialize in rapid and low-cost trading of many equities is unlikely to be the lowest-cost trader. Even if costs are low, the portfolio manager can increase his or her flexibility by following the futures prices and choosing to operate in the cheaper of the stock and index futures markets.[22]

The following two equations from Chapter 2 provide the rules for asset allocation with stock index futures:

---

[21] Fama [1989] and Roll [1989] provide arguments against the halting of trading.

[22] See Grant [1982], Figlewski and Kon [1982], and Figlewski [1984, 1985] for a discussion of using index futures in portfolio management.

Synthetic T-bill = Spot − Futures
Synthetic spot   = T-bill + Futures.

A portfolio manager who wishes to replace equity holdings with cash instruments can do so directly or keep the equities and go short index futures. We see from the above equations that the latter strategy creates a synthetic T-bill. Conversely, if the portfolio manager wishes to move from short-term securities into equities, he or she can keep the short-term securities and go long index futures. This will create a synthetic stock position.

We will assume that the fundamental no-arbitrage condition holds in our initial demonstration of market timing with stock index futures. Later we will show how portfolio managers can use divergences from the fundamental no-arbitrage relationship to their advantage.

Moving from Equities to T-Bills   Suppose a portfolio manager holds a $100 million equity portfolio that mimics the S&P 500 Index.[23] On date t1, she decides to switch her holdings to T-bills until date T. She can simply sell her equities and buy T-bills that expire on date T, or she can go short index futures and hold the equities until date T. We will assume that her futures contracts expire on date T, although we will see later that this assumption is not required for using index futures for asset allocation.

The time line for the manager's two possible strategies is

If the manager chooses to use stock index futures, she must determine the appropriate number of short futures contracts to take. She must go short one futures contract for every unit of the S&P 500 portfolio represented by her equity holdings. Therefore, her futures position will be

$$\text{Number of short futures contracts} = \frac{V_{t1}}{P_{t1}}, \qquad (4.5)$$

where V_{t1} is the value of the equities she wishes to put into T-bills and P_{t1} is the dollar (spot) value of one S&P 500 futures contract.

Assume the S&P 500 spot index has a value of 250 on date t1. Under the terms of the S&P 500 futures contract, this index value represents a portfolio of $(250)(\$500) = \$125,000$. Thus, to convert her equities to T-bills using index futures, the manager must take a short futures position of

---

[23] Suppose instead that the equity portfolio has a $\beta_e \neq 1$ with respect to the S&P 500. Then we multiply all of our hedge ratios by β_e.

$$\frac{V_{t1}}{P_{t1}} = \frac{\$100 \text{ million}}{\$125,000}$$

$$= 800 \text{ contracts.}$$

The manager essentially uses a hedge ratio of 1, just as in a simple cash-and-carry. If the fundamental no-arbitrage equation holds at both t1 and T, the natural strategy of selling the equities and buying T-bills is identical to that of keeping the equities and going short futures. Example 4.6 demonstrates the equivalence of the two strategies.

▪ **Example 4.6: Switching from Equities to T-Bills Using Index Futures**
Suppose that on March 18, 1989, a portfolio manager holds a $100 million equity portfolio that mimics the S&P 500. However, he wishes to move his funds into short-term, fixed-income securities over the 90-day period ending on June 16. The current level of the S&P 500 Index is 250, the current T-bill rate is 8 percent, and the S&P 500 is expected to pay dividends that average 0.04 S&P 500 Index points daily over a 365-day year.

The manager has two possible strategies:

1.   Sell the $100 million in equities and invest the proceeds in 8 percent T-bills. On June 16, the portfolio will be worth

$100 million + (0.08)(90/360)($100 million) = $102 million.

2.   Keep the $100 million in equities and go short S&P 500 futures contracts that expire on June 16.[24]

The value of each S&P 500 futures contract on March 18 is (250)($500) = $125,000. If, for simplicity, we ignore interest on the dividends, the dividends accrued on the portfolio over the 90 days between March 18 and June 16 are

Accrued dividends = (0.04)($500)(90)
                  = $1,800.

The fundamental no-arbitrage equation tells us that on March 18 the futures price, in dollar terms, should be

Futures price = (Index value)$(1 + r_{t1,T})$ − Accrued dividends   **(4.6)**
              = ($125,000)[1 + (0.08)(90)/360] − $1,800
              = $125,700
              = 251.40 S&P 500 Index points.

To carry out the second strategy, the manager must go short:

---

[24] While the trading of the contract ends on June 15, the final settlement occurs on June 16.

$$\frac{\$100 \text{ million}}{\$125,000} = 800 \text{ S\&P futures contracts.}$$

To see how these strategies work out, consider two scenarios for the S&P 500 Index on June 16:

I. S&P 500 = 240:

Value of stock	($100 million)(240/250)	= $ 96.00 million
Dividends	(800)($1,800)	= 1.44 million
Futures profit	(800)($500)(251.40 – 240.00)	= 4.56 million
Total value		= $102.00 million

II. S&P 500 = 280:

Value of stock	($100 million)(280/250)	= $112.00 million
Dividends	(800)($1,800)	= 1.44 million
Futures profit	(800)($500)(251.40 – 280.00)	= –11.44 million
Total value		= $102.00 million

Because there are no transactions costs, the portfolio manager's holdings on June 16 are the same as if he had sold equities and invested in short-term bonds (under each scenario). This result is not surprising, for we saw in Chapter 2 that one can create a synthetic T-bill using a spot position hedged with a short futures position. ∎

The equivalence in Example 4.6 between strategy 1, in which the manager sells equities and buys T-bills, and strategy 2, in which he holds the equities and goes short futures, occurs because the fundamental no-arbitrage equation is satisfied. If the futures price is less than 251.40, the futures profit will be lower than in the example and the manager will earn more by selling the relatively overpriced equities and buying the bills. Conversely, if the futures price is greater than 251.40, the futures profit will be higher than in the example and the manager will earn more by keeping the equities and going short the relatively overpriced futures. Thus, the choice between the two strategies depends on whether the fundamental no-arbitrage equation, 4.6, is satisfied.

It is actually quite plausible that the futures price will be above the value given by Equation 4.6. To see this, consider our portfolio manager's cash-and-carry quasi-arbitrage table in Table 4.4. The index value is determined from the bid prices of the component stocks, because the manager's benchmark position is to sell the equities and buy T-bills. Suppose the current marginal quasi-arbitrageur is another portfolio manager who is holding T-bills as in Table 4.2. For him, the relevant index value is determined by the ask prices he must pay to buy the stocks in the equity portfolio. Thus, the futures price is likely to be higher than our manager's no-arbitrage futures price.

Suppose, for example, that both the T-bill bid and ask rates are 8 percent and the ask on the index is $125,200 per S&P 500 unit. Then the fundamental no-arbitrage equation for the portfolio manager in Table 4.2 is

Table 4.4 Cash-and-Carry Quasi-Arbitrage Table for Portfolio Manager

<u>Benchmark position:</u> sale of equity portfolio and purchase of T-bills

Cash-and-Carry Pure Arbitrage Components	Cash-and-Carry Quasi-Arbitrage Components	Relevant Price or Rate
1. Buy spot Receive dividends	Refrain from selling equities Receive dividends	Bid
2. Go short futures	Go short futures	Bid
3. Borrow	Refrain from buying T-bills	T-bill ask

<u>Resulting position:</u> investment in synthetic T-bills

<u>Transactions fees:</u> $TF = -TF_1 + TF_2 - TF_3$
1. Save TF_1
2. Pay TF_2
3. Save TF_3

$$\text{Futures price} = (\text{Index value})(1 + r_{t1,T}) - \text{Accrued dividends} \qquad (4.7)$$
$$= (\$125,200)[1 + (0.08)(90)/360] - \$1,800$$
$$= \$125,904$$
$$= 251.80 \text{ S\&P 500 Index points.}$$

Under this price, the payoffs from strategy 2 for our manager are now

I. S&P 500 = 240:

Value of stock	($100 million)(240/250)	= $ 96.00 million
Dividends	(800)($1,800)	= 1.44 million
Futures profit	(800)($500)(251.80 – 240.00)	= 4.72 million
Total value		= $102.16 million

II. S&P 500 = 280:

Value of stock	($100 million)(280/250)	= $112.00 million
Dividends	(800)($1,800)	= 1.44 million
Futures profit	(800)($500)(251.80 – 280.00)	= –11.28 million
Total value		= $102.16 million

Thus, even though there is no pure arbitrage opportunity, there is a cash-and-carry quasi-arbitrage opportunity for the portfolio manager performing an asset allocation. He could earn $0.16 million more by choosing strategy 2 instead of strategy 1. This gain would equal the difference between the futures price and the fundamental no-arbitrage price for the portfolio manager:

$$\Omega^c = \text{Futures price} - \text{Portfolio manager's no-arbitrage price}$$
$$= 251.80 - 251.40$$
$$= 0.40 \text{ S\&P 500 Index points}$$
$$= (800 \text{ Contracts})(\$500)(0.40 \text{ Index points})$$
$$= \$160,000 > 0.$$

By moving from a benchmark position of selling equities and buying T-bills, the portfolio manager performing an asset allocation can effectively perform a cash-and-carry arbitrage more cheaply than the portfolio manager who is replacing T-bills with synthetic T-bills. In fact, this analysis probably understates the advantage to the manager from using strategy 2, because he may be poorly positioned to sell the equities quickly as strategy 1 requires. Further, he saves transactions fees.

Moving from T-Bills to Equities   Now suppose that on date t1, a portfolio manager who holds T-bills wishes to switch to equities until date T. One strategy is to sell the T-bills and buy equities. Another is to hold the T-bills until date T and go long index futures that expire at date T (we still assume that futures that expire on date T exist). The time line for the two strategies is

Example 4.7 shows how to use the fundamental no-arbitrage equation, 4.6, to determine which strategy is superior.

▪ **Example 4.7: Switching from T-Bills to Equities Using Index Futures**
Suppose that on March 18, 1989, a portfolio manager holds a $100 million portfolio of T-bills that expire on June 16. She wishes to sell the T-bills and move into an equity portfolio that mimics the S&P 500 Index over the 90 days until June 16. As in Example 4.6, the current level of the S&P 500 Index is 250.00, the T-bill bid rate is 8 percent, and the average daily dividend yield on the S&P 500 Index is expected to be 0.04 S&P 500 index points. The June S&P 500 futures price is 251.00. We will ignore bid-ask spreads.
The manager has two possible strategies:

1.   Sell the $100 million in T-bills and invest in equities. On June 16, the portfolio will be worth

$$(\$100 \text{ million}) \left(\frac{\text{S\&P 500 Index on June 16}}{\text{S\&P 500 Index today}} \right)$$

+ Dividends on $100 million equity portfolio.

As in Example 4.6, each S&P 500 unit accrues $1,800 worth of dividends over the 90 days between t and T. Under the two scenarios in Example 4.6, the equity portfolio will yield

Table 4.5 Reverse Cash-and-Carry Quasi-Arbitrage Table for Portfolio Manager

Benchmark position: sale of T-bills and purchase of equity portfolio

Reverse Cash-and-Carry Pure Arbitrage Components	Reverse Cash-and-Carry Quasi-Arbitrage Components	Relevant Price or Rate
1. Short spot Rebate dividends	Refrain from buying equities Forgo dividends	Ask
2. Go long futures	Go long futures	Ask
3. Lend	Refrain from selling T-bills	T-bill bid

Resulting position: investment in synthetic equity portfolio

Transactions fees: $TF = -TF_1 + TF_2 - TF_3$
1. Save TF_1
2. Pay TF_2
3. Save TF_3

I. S&P 500 = 240:

Value of stock	($100 million)(240/250)	= $96.00 million
Dividends	(800)($1,800)	= 1.44 million
Total value		= $97.44 million

II. S&P 500 = 280:

Value of stock	($100 million)(280/250)	= $112.00 million
Dividends	(800)($1,800)	= 1.44 million
Total value		= $113.44 million

2. Keep the $100 million in T-bills and go long S&P 500 futures contracts that expire on June 16. Table 4.5 presents a reverse cash-and-carry quasi-arbitrage table for this strategy. The appropriate number of long futures contracts in this case is

$$\frac{\$100 \text{ million}}{\$125,000} = 800 \text{ S\&P 500 futures contracts.}$$

Consider the results of strategy 2 under the same two scenarios for the S&P 500 Index on June 16:

I. S&P 500 = 240:

Value of T-bills	($100 million)(1.02)	= $102.00 million
Futures profit	(800)($500)(240.00 – 251.00)	= –4.40 million
Total value		= $ 97.60 million

II. S&P 500 = 280:

Value of T-bills	($100 million)(1.02)	= $102.00 million
Futures profit	(800)($500)(280.00 – 251.00)	= 11.60 million
Total value		= $113.60 million

In both the high- and low-value scenarios, the value of the synthetic equity portfolio exceeds the value of the actual equity portfolio by $0.16 million. In Equation 4.6, we saw that the no-arbitrage futures price for the portfolio manager is 251.40;[25] thus, the excess yield from the synthetic equity portfolio derives from the difference between the actual futures price of 251 and the no-arbitrage price for the portfolio manager of 251.40:

$$\Omega^r = \text{Futures price} - \text{Portfolio manager's no-arbitrage price}$$
$$= 251.00 - 251.40$$
$$= -0.40 \text{ S\&P 500 index points}$$
$$= (800 \text{ contracts})(\$500)(-0.40 \text{ index points})$$
$$= -\$160,000 < 0.$$

This indicates that there is a reverse cash-and-carry quasi-arbitrage opportunity. So again, to determine whether the natural strategy of selling T-bills and buying equities is better than the synthetic strategy of keeping the T-bills and going long futures, we must examine the pricing of the futures. When the futures is below the no-arbitrage price of the portfolio manager, the synthetic strategy is superior, because one can go long the relatively underpriced futures. If the futures is above the no-arbitrage price for the portfolio manager, it is better to buy the relatively underpriced equities directly. ∎

Additional Considerations for Asset Allocation   Up to this point, our discussion of asset allocation with index futures has been based on three simplifying assumptions. The first is that the index futures contract expires exactly when the period of the desired asset change ends. The second is that the equity portfolio we wish to trade has the same risk as the portfolio underlying the index futures. The final assumption is that we wish to adjust our portfolio by moving completely in or out of either T-bills or equities. Next, we will show how to use stock index futures in asset allocation when these three assumptions do not hold.

Maturity Mismatch   If there is no futures contract that expires exactly when we hope to move back into equities or T-bills, we have a maturity mismatch problem just like the maturity mismatch hedges we discussed in Chapter 3. Consider a

---

[25] The benchmark position of the portfolio manager is to sell T-bills and buy equit s. The manager performs two components of the arbitrage by refraining from these transactior Thus, in this case we interpret the index price in Equation 4.6 as the ask and the riskless ra   as the T-bill bid rate.

portfolio manager who uses index futures to switch from equities to T-bills at time t1 and wishes to switch back at time t2 before the futures contracts expire at T:

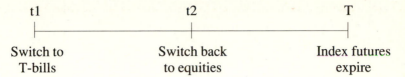

t1	t2	T
Switch to T-bills	Switch back to equities	Index futures expire

As we saw in Chapter 3, this manager must adjust his hedge ratio, for at time t2 the fundamental no-arbitrage equation is

$$F_{t2,T} = P_{t2}(1 + r_{t2,T}) - FV_T(\text{Dividends between t2 and T}).$$ **(4.8)**

Equation 4.8 shows that the futures price will be more volatile than the spot index at time t2, and the term $1/(1 + r_{t2,T})$ is the adjustment that will eliminate risk. Therefore, the appropriate number of futures contracts in this case is

$$\text{Number of futures contracts} = \left(\frac{1}{1 + r_{t2,T}}\right)\left(\frac{V_{t1}}{P_{t1}}\right).$$ **(4.9)**

Crosshedging   Suppose a portfolio manager wishes to move between short-term, fixed-income securities and a portfolio that does not mimic one of the indices underlying a stock index futures contract. If the manager uses an index futures position for such an asset allocation, she must determine the proper hedge ratio to take and analyze the basis risk of her position. Example 4.8 shows how this portfolio manager uses the S&P 500 futures contract to hedge an equity portfolio whose risks differ from those of the S&P 500 Index.

▪ **Example 4.8:   Crosshedging a Stock Portfolio with Stock Index Futures**
Suppose the above portfolio manager manages a fund of small firms (firms with low market capitalizations) and wishes to hedge her portfolio's risk by using stock index futures to convert it into a synthetic T-bill. The portfolio has a market value of $100 million and consists only of stocks with market capitalizations in the bottom quintile of NYSE and AMEX stocks. The portfolio is value weighted.

Since there is no futures contract written on small-capitalization stocks, the portfolio manager is planning to hedge the portfolio using the Standard and Poor's 500 (S&P 500) futures contract. Her first task is to determine whether the correlation between her portfolio and the S&P 500 is high enough that the S&P 500 futures contract can provide an effective crosshedge.

Figure 4.5 plots the monthly rate of return on both the small-firm portfolio and the S&P 500 from 1982 through 1988. Clearly the correlation between the portfolio and the S&P 500 is high but not perfect. Thus, the crosshedge will contain some basis risk.

The manager uses the statistical approach to determine the appropriate crosshedge ratio. Financial analysts have found that for stock returns, the most stable relationship can be estimated by running a linear regression of the monthly

Figure 4.5 Portfolio Correlations: S&P 500 versus Small-Cap Stocks

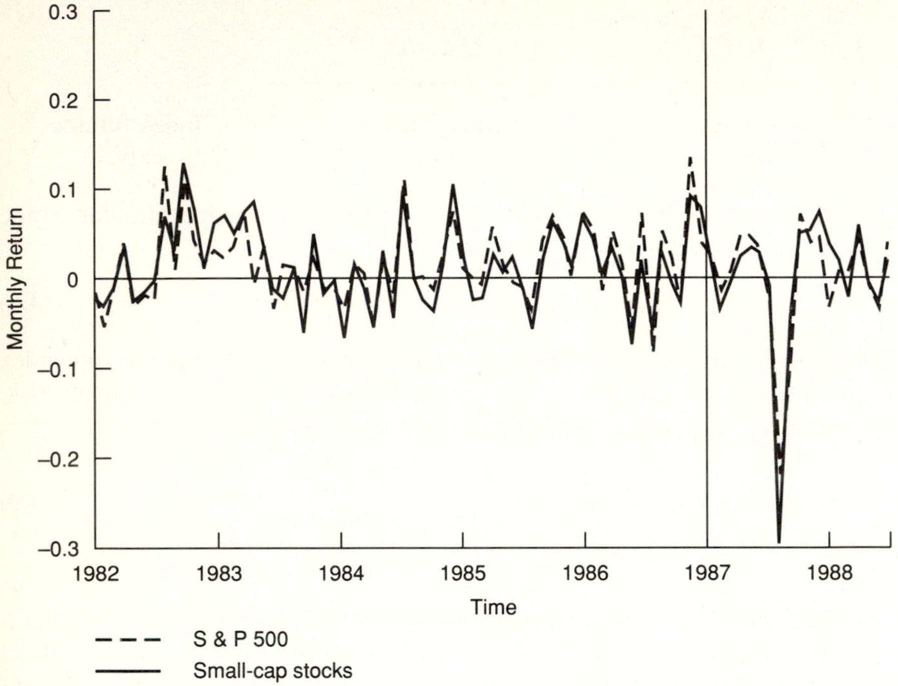

Source: Ibbotson Associates.

rate of return on the small-firm portfolio on the monthly rate of return on the S&P 500:

$$\frac{\Delta P_c}{P_c} = \alpha_r + \beta_r \left(\frac{\Delta P_f}{P_f} \right) + \varepsilon_r \,, \qquad \textbf{(4.10)}$$

where P_c is the *market* value of the small-firm portfolio and P_f is the *spot* value of the S&P 500.

Table 4.6 presents results from this regression for the period January 1982 through December 1986 using monthly returns. The R-squared statistic indicates that the rate of return on the S&P 500 Index can explain about 70 percent of the variation in the rate of return on the small-firm fund. Thus, the correlation between the two is about 84 percent,[26] certainly high enough to warrant using the S&P 500 contract in a crosshedge.

[26] For a simple regression, the R-squared statistic is the square of the correlation.

Table 4.6 Regression of Small-Firm Portfolio on S&P 500, 1982–1986

A. Rate of Return Regression

Y = monthly rate of return on small-firm portfolio
X = monthly rate of return on S&P 500

Regression Output

Constant	0.000062
Standard error of Y estimate	0.024591
R-squared	0.704819
Number of observations	60
Degrees of freedom	58

X coefficient(s)	0.889976	
Standard error of coefficient	0.075625	

B. Lagged Error Term Regression

Y = error term from regression of small-firm portfolio on S&P 500
X = lagged error term

Regression Output

Constant	0.000083
Standard error of Y estimate	0.024722
R-squared	0.005979
Number of observations	59
Degrees of freedom	57

X coefficient(s)	0.077303	
Standard error of coefficient	0.132020	

C. Variances

	Variance
In sample Small stocks	0.001980
Out of sample Small stocks	0.005888
In sample Residual	0.000584
Out of sample Residual	0.001079

The X coefficient of 0.89 indicates that the rate of return on the small-firm portfolio is less volatile than the S&P 500 Index. For every 1 percent movement in the S&P 500 Index, the small-firm fund moves only 0.89 percent. The portfolio manager therefore must adjust her hedge ratio to account for this disparity.

In Chapter 3, we saw that the appropriate hedge ratio is

$$\text{Hedge ratio} = \left(\frac{P_c}{P_f}\right)(\beta_r). \tag{4.11}$$

For example, suppose the current value of the S&P 500 *spot* index is 250, or $125,000. Then the appropriate hedge ratio is

$$\text{Hedge ratio} = \left(\frac{\$100 \text{ million}}{\$125,000}\right)(0.89) \tag{4.12}$$

$$= (800)(0.89)$$
$$= 712 \text{ S\&P 500 contracts.}$$

This hedge ratio has two components. The first adjusts for the size of the portfolio. Because each unit of the S&P 500 is worth $125,000, the manager needs 800 contracts to match her $100 million portfolio. However, because β_r differs from 1.0, she must further adjust the hedge ratio by multiplying the 800 contracts by 0.89.

The portfolio manager can use the regression results to estimate the basis risk of the crosshedge in dollar terms. The 0.025 (in-sample) standard deviation of the Y estimate is the standard deviation of the error term when the rate of return on the S&P 500 is used to explain the rate of return on the small-firm fund. Since the regression was run with monthly returns, the manager estimates that over one month the standard deviation of the unhedged part of the portfolio value is 2.5 percent of the portfolio's value:

Standard deviation of basis risk in dollar terms
   = (Rate of return risk)(Portfolio value)
   = (0.025)($100 million)
   = $2.5 million.

The 95 percent confidence interval for the basis risk, then, is

Confidence interval = ±(1.96)($2.5 million)
                = ±$4.9 million.

This may seem like a lot of risk for a hedged position. However, from part C of Table 4.6, the standard deviation of the monthly rate of return on the unhedged portfolio is about 4.4 percent ($\sqrt{0.001980}$). Thus, the 95 percent confidence interval for the unhedged portfolio value (around its average rate of return) is

Confidence interval = ±(1.96)($4.4 million)
                = ±$8.62 million.

This is almost twice the size of the 95 percent confidence interval for the basis risk of the hedged portfolio.

We can see the effect of the crosshedge on the rate of return in Figure 4.6. The figure plots the small-firm fund's total rate of return and the basis error as a

Figure 4.6   Level versus Basis Risk: Small Stocks Hedged with S&P 500

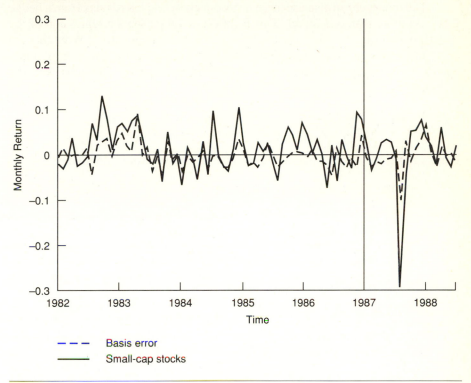

Source: Ibbotson Associates.

rate of return on the fund (the basis error rate of return).[27, 28] To validate the approach, we have added the period from January 1987 through September 1988 as an out-of-sample validation period to the in-sample period from 1982 through 1986 in Figure 4.5.

The basis error is much less variable than the rate of return on the small-firm fund, both in and out of sample. The small-firm fund exhibits large positive and negative movements that the hedge eliminates. For example, the hedge substantially reduced the losses of the small-firm portfolio during the October 1987 market break. From part C of Table 4.6, it is evident that risk is significantly reduced by the hedge out of sample. Overall, the in-sample ratio of the variance of the basis error to the variance of the rate of return on the small-firm fund (0.29) is greater

[27] The basis risk portfolio rate of return is estimated by the fitted residuals of the regression.

[28] The rate of return on the hedged portfolio should equal the riskless rate plus the basis error plotted in Figure 4.6. Because movements in the riskless rate are small, Figure 4.6 should give a reasonably accurate picture of the different risks of the hedged and unhedged portfolios.

than the same ratio out of sample (0.18). Thus, the hedge eliminates risk due to overall price movements and the portfolio manager is left with the lesser basis risk.

The manager can also use these results to analyze the basis risk from a hedge that lasts more than one month. Part B of Table 4.6 presents a regression of the (fitted) basis error rate of return on its lagged value. The results indicate that the error terms are not related over time. Thus, the basis error from month to month appears to be independent, and we can figure the basis risk for N months using the formula:

N-month basis error standard deviation
    $= (\sqrt{N})$(Monthly basis error standard deviation).

For example, for a hedge over three months, the basis error standard deviation is

3-month standard deviation of basis error $= (1.73)(\$2.5$ million)
                                                        $= \$4.33$ million.

This compares with a standard deviation of total risk of

3-month standard deviation of total portfolio value $= (1.73)(\$4.4$ million)
                                                                    $= \$7.61$ million.

However, it may be necessary to change the hedge ratio for hedges that last more than one month. After one month, the portfolio manager should compute the current ratio, P_c/P_f, and the hedge ratio prescribed by Equation 4.11 to see whether the current hedge ratio is still appropriate. ∎

Using the Beta of a Portfolio for Crosshedging   The appropriate hedge ratio for crosshedging a portfolio with index futures can be determined in another way—from the portfolio's beta. A portfolio beta has the same interpretation as the individual stock betas we discussed in Chapter 2. It measures the sensitivity of the portfolio's returns to general stock market movements. If we assume the S&P 500 Index is a good proxy for the general market, we can interpret the slope, β_r, in Equation 4.10 as the beta of the portfolio.[29] Therefore, we can derive the ratio for a crosshedge with stock index futures by substituting the portfolio beta for the β_r term in Equation 4.11.

We cannot estimate the beta of a portfolio from Equation 4.10 if the portfolio manager periodically changes the portfolio's composition, because the portfolio's past performance cannot accurately predict its future behavior. However, we can compute a portfolio beta from the individual betas of the stocks in the portfolio. A portfolio's beta is the weighted average of the betas of its component stocks, where the weights are the proportion of portfolio value contributed by each stock:

[29] One can always validate this assumption by measuring betas with respect to the S&P 500.

$$\text{Portfolio beta} = \sum_{i=1}^{N} \left(\frac{n_i P_i}{V_p} \right) (\beta_i), \qquad\qquad (4.13)$$

where

n_i = number of shares of stock i

P_i = price of stock i

β_i = beta of stock i

V_p = total value of the portfolio

Individual stock betas can be obtained from any number of services that publish "beta books." Figure 4.7 presents an example of such a book from Merrill Lynch.[30]

In Example 4.9, a portfolio's beta is estimated using the S&P 500 as a proxy for the market portfolio. Then the estimated beta is substituted into Equation 4.13 to determine the appropriate ratio for a crosshedge of the portfolio with the S&P 500 Index futures contract.

▪ **Example 4.9: Using Individual Stock Betas to Determine a Hedge Ratio**
Suppose we have a portfolio that contains the following stocks:

Stock	Shares	Price	Value	Beta	Proportion of Portfolio
ABC	100,000	$50	$ 5 million	0.95	50%
DEF	200,000	20	4 million	1.20	40
XYZ	25,000	40	1 million	1.40	10
Total			$10 million		100%

The beta of the entire portfolio is therefore

$$\text{Portfolio beta} = (0.50)(0.95) + (0.40)(1.20) + (0.10)(1.40)$$
$$= 1.095.$$

Now suppose the current value of the S&P 500 Index is 250, or $125,000. We can see from using Equation 4.11 that the appropriate hedge ratio is

$$\text{Hedge ratio} = \left(\frac{\$10 \text{ million}}{\$125,000} \right) (1.095)$$

$$= (80)(1.095)$$
$$= 87.6 \text{ S\&P } 500 \text{ contracts.}$$

---

[30] These betas should be calculated using the S&P 500 as a proxy for the market portfolio. If not, the betas must be multiplied by the ratio of the standard deviation of the rate of return on the proxy portfolio to the standard deviation of the rate of return on the S&P 500 portfolio.

Figure 4.7 Stock Betas Estimated by Merrill Lynch, Pierce, Fenner & Smith, Inc.

MLPF&S, INC.—MARKET SENSITIVITY STATISTICS

TKR SYMB	SECURITY NAME	09/86 CLOSE PRICE	BETA	ALPHA	R-SQR	RESID STD DEV-N	STD.ERR.— OF BETA	OF ALPHA	ADJUSTED BETA	NUMBER OF OBSERV
DTEI	DETROIT EDISON CO PFD CONV	93.250	.40	.56	.09	4.96	.15	.67	.60	60
DVP	DEVELOPMENT CORP AMER	12.125	1.50	-.56	.30	9.54	.29	1.28	1.33	60
DIN	DEVON RESOURCE INVS DEPOSIT A	5.875	.86	-4.68	.04	12.42	.68	3.48	.90	14
DVRY	DVRY INC	9.500	.62	-.79	.08	7.92	.33	1.43	.75	33
DLCF	DEVELCON ELECTRS LTD	3.438	.21	-4.36	.03	16.28	.69	3.11	.48	30
DWY	DEWEY ELECTRS CORP	3.750	.91	2.29	.02	19.54	.60	2.63	.94	60
DXON	DEXON INC	1.000	2.99	-.98	.12	31.64	.98	4.26	2.32	60
DEX	DEXTER CORP	29.750	.98	.01	.23	7.35	.23	.99	.99	60
DIA9	DI AN CTLS INC	1.313	.28	-.02	.01	18.11	.56	2.44	.52	60
DIG	DI GIORGIO CORP	24.375	.93	.64	.27	6.32	.19	.85	.95	60
DIGN	DIAGNON CORP	1.688	.25	-1.23	.03	20.82	.85	3.49	.50	38
DINO	DIAGNOSTIC INC	7.250	.88	7.28	.01	36.76	1.13	4.95	.92	60
DPC2	DIAGNOSTIC PRUDS CORP	23.000	1.69	.37	.31	10.35	.35	1.55	1.46	51
DRSI	DIAGNOSTIC RETRIEVAL	7.500	1.08	.40	.09	13.10	.40	1.76	1.05	60
DBH	DIAMOND BATHURST INC	16.000	2.07	1.28	.27	13.43	.55	2.28	1.71	37
DMD	DIAMOND CRYSTAL SALT CO	32.500	.37	1.76	.03	7.14	.22	.96	.58	60
DIA	DIAMOND SHAMROCK CORP	10.875	.90	-2.24	.23	6.82	.21	.92	.94	60
SLF	DIANA CORP	11.000	.56	1.48	.04	10.11	.31	1.36	.71	60
DNIC	DIASONICS INC	3.375	1.55	-4.67	.12	15.80	.61	2.50	1.36	43
DXTK	DIAGNOSTEK INC	2.063	1.27	1.67	.00	29.88	1.27	5.82	1.18	29
DBRL	DIBRELL BROS INC	25.000	.95	1.77	.16	8.77	.27	1.18	.96	60
DICN	DICEON ELECTRS INC	19.750	1.12	.13	.13	11.29	.46	2.00	1.08	34
DKJN	DICKEY-JOHN CORP	11.500	.70	-.69	.07	9.87	.30	1.33	.80	60
DCOM	DICOMED CORP	2.250	2.11	-3.22	.31	12.95	.40	1.74	1.74	60
DBD	DIEBOLD INC	39.500	.72	.24	.10	8.51	.26	1.15	.82	60
DIGI	DIGICON INC	.500	1.19	-6.22	.11	13.78	.42	1.84	1.13	60
DILD	DIGILOG INC	6.000	1.11	-.39	.06	16.44	.51	2.21	1.07	60
DEC	DIGITAL EQUIP CORP	89.875	1.21	.21	.23	8.97	.28	1.21	1.14	60
DGPD	DIGITAL PRODS CORP	2.313	.98	-1.88	.02	21.11	.65	2.84	.99	60
DGTD	DIGITECH INC	5.625	3.69	6.73	.08	45.78	1.88	8.00	2.78	35

BASED ON S&P 500 INDEX, USING STRAIGHT REGRESSION   PAGE 46

Source: Merrill Lynch, Pierce, Fenner & Smith, Inc., "Security Risk Evaluation," October 1986.

As in Example 4.8, we can interpret this hedge ratio as having two parts. First, the hedge prescribes 80 futures contracts, so that our holdings of the $125,000 S&P 500 contracts will equal our $10 million portfolio in value. Second, the hedge further adjusts the futures position by a factor of 1.095 to account for our portfolio's greater volatility relative to the S&P 500 Index. ∎

Example 4.9 showed how to crosshedge a portfolio with stock index futures when the portfolio beta is other than 1.0. There we adjusted the hedge ratio with the beta and then took the short futures position prescribed by the hedge ratio. If there is no basis risk, this hedge will create a synthetic T-bill:

Synthetic T-bill with value P_c **(4.14)**
= Equity portfolio with value P_c − (Portfolio beta)(P_c/P_f) Futures.

If we rewrite Equation 4.14, we can see how to use stock index futures to transform a T-bill portfolio into a synthetic equity portfolio with any desired beta:

Synthetic equity portfolio with value P_c **(4.15)**
= T-bill portfolio with value P_c + (Desired portfolio beta)$(P_c/\dot{P}_f)$ Futures.

We must simply take a long futures position that is adjusted by the desired beta of the synthetic equity portfolio.

Using Index Futures to Adjust the Beta of an Equity Portfolio   So far we have seen how a bearish manager can use index futures to convert equities into synthetic T-bills. We have also seen how a manager who is bullish on the stock market can use index futures to convert T-bills into synthetic equities. In many cases, portfolio managers prefer to act on their changing expectations by altering their portfolios' betas instead of moving entirely between T-bills and equities. For example, a manager who is bearish may wish to decrease the beta of the portfolio so that the portfolio will be less sensitive to market declines. Managers can easily make such adjustments to their portfolio betas using the methods of asset allocation we have developed.

We know from Equation 4.13 that the beta of a portfolio is a weighted average of the betas of the securities that make up the portfolio. For a portfolio of T-bills and equities, the beta is

Portfolio beta **(4.16)**
= (Portfolio proportion in T-bills)(T-bill beta)
+ (Portfolio proportion in equities)(Equity beta)
= (Portfolio proportion in equities)(Equity beta).

The last step eliminates the T-bill beta because riskless securities have a beta of zero.

We can use index futures to manipulate the proportion of a portfolio that is in equities. For example, suppose we are managing an equity portfolio with a beta of 1.20. If we hedge half of that portfolio with short index futures positions (using the hedge ratio given by Equation 4.11), our portfolio will be half synthetic T-bills and half equities. The beta of the new portfolio will be $(0.50)(1.20) = 0.60$. If we hedge only 25 percent of the portfolio, the beta will be $(0.75)(1.20) = 0.90$.

Similarly, suppose we are holding a T-bill portfolio but would prefer a portfolio with a beta of 0.50. Then we can create synthetic equity positions by going long futures for half of the T-bills in the portfolio. Then half of the portfolio will consist of zero-beta T-bills and half of synthetic equities with a beta of 1. The beta of the entire portfolio will be 0.50.

Using Futures for Other Types of Asset Allocation   Portfolio managers can use index futures for other asset allocation strategies in addition to the movements between equities and T-bills we have discussed. For example, suppose a portfolio manager who holds a portfolio of blue-chip stocks believes the stocks of smaller companies will outperform blue-chips in the near future. The natural strategy for the manager is to sell the blue-chip stocks and buy a portfolio that includes more small stocks. But the manager could follow an equivalent strategy using index futures:

1.   Create a synthetic T-bill by going short Major Market Index futures:

      T-bill = Stock(blue chip) – Futures(blue chip).

2.   Create a synthetic equity position by going long Value Line Index futures:

      Stock(smaller firms) = T-bill + Futures(smaller firms).

A portfolio manager who wishes to move between an equity index such as the S&P 500 and long-term bonds also may find index futures useful. The natural strategy is to sell the equities and buy long-term bonds. An equivalent strategy with index futures is to

1.   Create a synthetic T-bill by going short S&P 500 Index futures:

      T-bill = Stocks(S&P 500) – Futures(S&P 500).

2.   Create a synthetic long-term bond position by going long U.S. T-bond futures:

      T-bond = T-bill + Futures(T-bond).

Thus, because one can create synthetic spot and T-bill positions using futures, one can always use futures to move among different spot positions.

Stock Picking   Stock index futures can also be valuable to portfolio managers who engage in stock-picking investment strategies. Such managers attempt to find stocks that are under- or overpriced relative to the rest of the market. One difficulty with stock-picking strategies, however, is that the excess returns on the mispriced stocks can be swamped by general market price movements. For example, a manager who buys a stock that is underpriced by 2 percent relative to other stocks of equal risk will not profit if all stocks in the market fall by 10 percent. Stock index futures allow managers to shield their stock-picking strategies from such general market movements. In this example, managers could use them to hedge against the 10 percent general market decline and thereby permit them to realize the 2 percent gain on the underpriced stock.[31]

The following expression of the Capital Asset Pricing Model identifies the abnormal return on an under- or overvalued stock:

$$r_j = r_f + \beta_j(r_m - r_f) + \varepsilon_j + \alpha_j , \qquad (4.17)$$

where

r_j = rate of return on stock j

r_f = riskless rate

r_m = rate of return on the market portfolio

ε_j = nonsystematic error

α_j = abnormal return

Equation 4.17 divides the excess rate of return on a stock into three components. The first component, $\beta_j(r_m - r_f)$, is associated with general market movements. If the market moves up or down by 1 percent and all other influences are held constant, the stock will move up or down by β_j percent. The second component, ε_j, is risk that is unique to the firm. The third component, α_j, is the abnormal return due to mispricing. If $\alpha_j > 0$, the expected rate of return on the stock will be greater than its risk warrants and the stock will be underpriced. If $\alpha_j < 0$, the expected rate of return on the stock will be less than warranted by its risk and the stock will be overpriced.

With stock index futures, a portfolio manager can hedge against movements in the first component and profit from stock mispricing by restricting his or her excess returns to the second two components. Suppose a manager believes that stock j is underpriced at time t1. The stock-picking strategy at time t1 is to purchase V_{t1} worth of the underpriced stock and take a short index futures position with a hedge ratio of

$$\text{Hedge ratio} = \left(\frac{V_{t1}}{P_f}\right)(\beta_j) \qquad (4.18)$$

where P_f is, as usual, the value of the spot index underlying the index futures. This creates an investment similar to a synthetic T-bill except that its return is still subject to the $(\alpha_j + \varepsilon_j)$ components. Thus, at time T, the value of the investment will be

---

[31] Similarly, Dubofsky [1987] shows how to hedge against market moves when performing dividend-capture strategies.

$$V_T = V_{t1}(1 + r_f + \alpha_j + \epsilon_j).$$

If α_j and ϵ_j both equal zero, the manager has simply a synthetic T-bill. If $\alpha_j > 0$ and $\epsilon_j = 0$, the manager will earn the abnormal return on the under-valued stock. The firm-specific error term, ϵ_j, will add basis risk if it does not equal zero. However, the manager can diversify away this basis risk by holding a portfolio of many mispriced stocks.

If the stock is overpriced such that $\alpha_j < 0$, the manager can get the same result by going short V_{t1} worth of the stock and taking a long index futures position with the hedge ratio in Equation 4.18. The manager will thus hedge against increases in the market when he or she is short stock.

Once the portfolio manager has created this modified synthetic T-bill, which is still subject to basis risk and abnormal returns, he or she can use the techniques discussed earlier to adjust the portfolio's mix of equities and T-bills. This approach effectively separates the market-timing and stock-picking functions of the fund.

Summary

We have seen that individual and institutional investors can use stock index futures to carry out many of their desired market transactions. Often the index futures strategies can be executed more rapidly and at lower cost than direct transactions in the stock and debt markets. Stock index futures have a varied clientele, for even investors whose stock compositions differ from those of the index futures often can use the contracts as trading tools. Such investors simply use the crosshedging techniques we have studied to adjust their hedge ratios for the differences between their portfolios and the index futures contracts.

Problems

1.   Suppose that on a given day we observe the following prices:

Stock	Price
IBM	$120
Unisys	25
Xerox	60

A price-equally-weighted index of these stocks, the High Tech Three, has a value of 10.25.

a.   What is the current value of the divisor?

b.   Suppose each point of the index represents $500. How many shares of each stock must we hold to create a portfolio that mimics the index?

c.   Suppose IBM undergoes a three-for-one stock split and there are no other price changes. What is the new value of the divisor?

d.   How many shares of each stock must we now hold to create a portfolio that mimics the index? What is the net rebalancing cost?

2. Consider the *Wall Street Journal* extract with futures prices for May 23, 1989, in Figure 4.2. Suppose the relevant interest rate between June 1989 and September 1989 is 8.40 percent.

   a. Of the S&P 500 Index and the NYSE Composite Index, which is expected to have a higher dividend yield between June 1989 and September 1989?

   b. What are these yields on an annualized basis?

   c. Does the difference appear to be significant? Even if the expected dividend yields on the two indices are identical, why might we compute different numbers?

3. Suppose it is May 23, 1989, and prices are as quoted in Figure 4.2 for the S&P 500 Index and index futures. The dividend yield, on an annualized basis, is expected to be 2.8 percent between May 23, 1989, and the expiration of the contract on September 15, 1989. The (bond-equivalent) yield on T-bills expiring on September 14, 1989, is 8.60 percent.

   a. Consider a portfolio manager who is contemplating buying T-bills that expire on September 15, 1989. (Actual T-bills expire on September 14. Ignore this difference, and assume the manager can buy T-bills expiring on September 15 at the same rate as those expiring on September 14.) Should he buy actual T-bills or create synthetic T-bills? Construct a quasi-arbitrage table to help answer this question.

   b. Consider a portfolio manager who is contemplating buying a portfolio of equities. Should she buy actual equities or create synthetic equities? Construct a quasi-arbitrage table to help answer this question.

   c. Evaluate the following statement: "Portfolio managers prefer to use stock index futures in their portfolio transactions, because futures prices are more competitive than prices in cash markets."

4. Suppose you wish to buy a well-diversified portfolio with a beta of 1.50. You have $280 million. Construct a synthetic portfolio using T-bills and S&P 500 stock index futures.

   a. If the current S&P 500 Index value is 280, into how many futures positions should you enter?

   b. Will these be long or short positions?

   c. How does the expiration date of the futures contract relate to the expiration date of the T-bills you will purchase?

5. Suppose you currently have a portfolio with a market value of $100 million. T-bills comprise $25 million of the portfolio, and equities with a beta of 0.80 account for $75 million. The current value of the S&P 500 is 250.

   a. What is the current beta of the entire portfolio?

   b. Suppose you believe there is a good chance that the stock market will drop, so you wish to change to a portfolio that will cut your portfolio beta in half. How many S&P 500 futures contracts should you enter into? Should these be long or short positions?

■ **6.**   This problem involves replicating some of the results of the crosshedge in Example 4.8 and extending the analysis. You have at your disposal data on the monthly total returns on both a portfolio of small-firm stocks and the S&P 500 Index.

a.   Recreate Figure 4.5 by plotting the monthly return on the portfolio versus the monthly return on the S&P 500.

b.   Recreate Table 4.6.

c.   In your regression, you have assumed that the following model holds:

$$r_p = \alpha + \beta r_{sp} + \varepsilon,$$

where r_{sp} is the rate of return on the S&P 500. Now suppose you wish to evaluate how your hedge will perform in the future. Of course, you cannot observe the future, but you can simulate what might happen. From your crosshedge regression, you can compute the residuals (that is, the basis errors). If the future behaves like the past, you can simulate the future with the following procedure:

(1)   Assume the return on the S&P 500 in future months comes from a distribution that is the same as that for the previous months. Thus, randomly select a past month and suppose that the return on the S&P 500 will repeat itself in the following month.

(2)   Assume the basis error in future months comes from a distribution that is the same as that for the previous months. Thus, randomly select another past month and suppose that this residual will repeat itself in the following month.

(3)   Using the equation in part c, compute the rate of return on your portfolio that will prevail given this randomly selected return and residual.

(4)   Compute the value of two portfolios in one month's time. The first portfolio has $100 million invested in an unhedged portfolio. The second has $100 million invested in the same portfolio, but one that you hedge. Assume the current value of the S&P 500 Index is 250 and the futures contract expires in exactly one month. Calculate the number of futures positions needed.

(5)   Using a /Data/Table, repeat the same experiment 100 times. Produce a histogram that compares the various hedged and unhedged values of the portfolio. Also, compute the standard deviation and the minimum, maximum, and average hedged and unhedged portfolio values. How do you explain the differences in the averaged portfolio values?

(Notes: You will need to use the @VLOOKUP command in Lotus in combination with the @RAND command. Thus, you will create a random number between 1 and 60 that will tell you which month's S&P 500 return to use. Do the same for the residual. The /Data/Table command will allow you to simulate the same experiment 100 times with one command. Finally, assume that when you put on the hedge, the market is in no-arbitrage equilibrium. Assume also that the riskless rate is 9.00 percent per annum and the dividend yield is 3.50 percent per annum. Note that both the returns on the small firm portfolio and those on the S&P 500 include dividends, while the S&P 500 Index that you use to calculate futures gains and losses does not.)

Short-Term Interest Rate Futures

Futures contracts on Eurodollar time deposits and U.S. Treasury bills were introduced in the mid-1970s and early 1980s. These contracts can lock in short-term interest rates that will be paid in the future and thus have been very popular instruments in the volatile interest rate environment of the 1970s and 1980s. They are useful for borrowers and lenders who wish to protect themselves against movements in short-term rates. They can be used to create synthetic fixed-rate loans or to change the maturity of existing Eurodollar time deposit and T-bill holdings. And, as in other futures markets, arbitrageurs use the short-term interest rate futures contracts to pursue arbitrage profits.

The Eurodollar contract has grown to become the most successful short-term interest rate contract as the rate on Eurodollar time deposits, the London Interbank Offer Rate, has become the benchmark short-term rate for many U.S. dollar borrowers and lenders. The T-bill futures contract is also a very liquid contract because of the importance of T-bills in government finance.

In this chapter, we will study both the cash and futures markets for Eurodollar time deposits and U.S. T-bills and will see how the futures contracts are used in risk management and arbitrage.

Eurodollar Time Deposits

Cash Market

Eurodollar time deposits (TDs) are nonnegotiable, fixed-rate U.S. dollar deposits in banks that are not subject to U.S. banking regulations.[1] These banks are not located only in Europe; Eurodollar TDs are issued by many banks in the Caribbean, Asia, and South America. Further, U.S. banks can take deposits on an unregulated basis through International Banking Facilities (IBFs).

---

[1] See Goodfriend [1986] for a description of the Eurodollar market.

The rate at which major money center banks are willing to place Eurodollar time deposits at other major money center banks is called the *London Interbank Offer Rate (LIBOR)*. The LIBOR is an important benchmark rate, for U.S. banks commonly charge the LIBOR plus a certain number of basis points on their floating-rate loans. The LIBOR is quoted on an **add-on yield** basis, meaning that it is a percentage of the TD purchase amount. It is an annualized rate based on a 360-day year. So, for example, if the three-month (90-day) LIBOR is 8 percent, the interest on $1 million is

$$Interest = (0.08)(90/360)(\$1 \text{ million})$$
$$= \$20,000.$$

Settlement in the Eurodollar TD market typically takes two days. Thus, if a bank agrees to borrow $1 million on December 18, it does not receive the funds until December 20. However, banks can also arrange for immediate delivery of funds for a fee.

Futures Market

The most widely traded short-term interest rate futures contract is the contract on Eurodollar time deposits that was introduced by the Chicago Mercantile Exchange in late 1981. Figure 5.1 charts the rapid growth in trading volume of the Eurodollar contract. By 1987, it had become the second most widely traded futures contract in the United States.

The futures contract on Eurodollar TDs locks in a rate for borrowing or lending when the contract expires just as a futures contract on gold locks in a price for gold. But the Eurodollar futures contract differs from futures on metals or agricultural products in that it is not actually written on an asset that can be bought and sold. It is based on a three-month, $1 million Eurodollar time deposit, but it is a cash settlement contract, so actual delivery of a TD does not take place.

Eurodollar Futures Contract Specifications

Contract:	Eurodollar Time Deposit
Exchange:	Chicago Mercantile Exchange
Quantity:	$1 million
Delivery months:	March, June, September, December
Delivery specifications:	Cash settlement based on three-month LIBOR, expiration on third Monday of delivery month
Minimum price movement:	$25 per contract (1 basis point)

When a Eurodollar futures contract expires, the final settlement price, the **expiration futures price**, is constructed from an index of the three-month LIBOR at selected banks. The formula for the expiration futures price is

Expiration futures price = 100 − LIBOR.

Before expiration, the quoted futures price implies an interest rate of

Interest rate = 100 − Quoted futures price.

Figure 5.1 Eurodollar Time Deposit Futures Annual Volume, 1983-1989

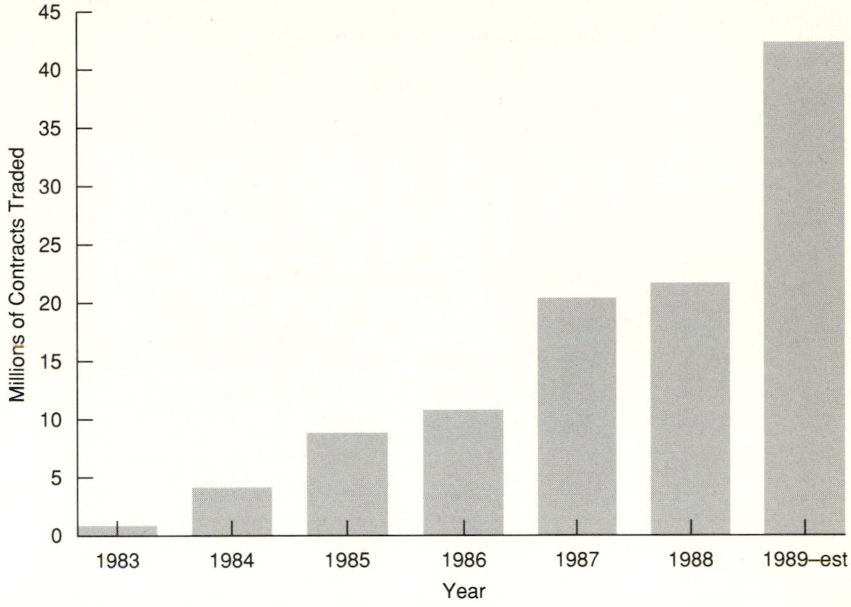

Source: Futures Industry Association.

This is the interest rate that can be locked in under the futures contract.

Figure 5.2 presents an extract from *The Wall Street Journal* that quotes the prices of Eurodollar futures contracts for May 23, 1989. The June Eurodollar futures price on that day was 90.65. This translates into an interest rate of 9.35 percent.

The expiration futures price and the quoted futures prices before expiration of the Eurodollar contract are not entirely analogous to the prices of other futures contracts. The per-unit gains and losses under other futures contracts are simply the daily changes in the quoted futures prices. But the gain or loss on a Eurodollar TD futures contract is $2,500 for each percentage move in the rate implied by the quoted futures price. Because there are 100 basis points in a percentage point, each basis point move in the quoted futures price is worth $25.

Since the Eurodollar expiration futures price is 100 minus the LIBOR, the payments under the futures contract are ultimately tied to the LIBOR at the time the contract expires. Prior to expiration, the profits and losses on a Eurodollar futures position reflect the changes in the interest rate implied by the quoted futures price. Long positions in Eurodollar futures make money when the quoted futures price rises, and short positions make money when the quoted futures price falls. Therefore, long positions gain when the implied interest rate falls, and short positions gain when the implied interest rate rises.

Figure 5.2 Eurodollar Time Deposit and Treasury Bill Futures Transactions Prices for May 23, 1989

```
EURODOLLAR (IMM)—$1 million; pts of 100%
                                        Yield        Open
        Open  High  Low Settle  Chg  Settle Chg Interest
June   90.72 90.77 90.59 90.65 + .05  9.35 − .05 209,500
Sept   91.07 91.07 90.89 91.00 + .07  9.00 − .07 226,609
Dec    91.03 91.05 90.90 91.02 + .11  8.98 − .11 106,004
Mr90   91.13 91.14 91.00 91.10 + .08  8.90 − .08  62,561
June   91.11 91.13 90.99 91.06 + .05  8.94 − .05  34,537
Sept   91.06 91.06 90.92 90.98 + .02  9.02 − .02  28,890
Dec    90.94 90.94 90.81 90.86 + .01  9.14 − .01  24,937
Mr91   90.98 91.00 90.88 90.92 + .01  9.08 − .01  16,290
June   90.95 90.99 90.87 90.91 + .01  9.09 − .01  14,103
Sept   90.95 90.96 90.86 90.90 + .01  9.10 − .01  19,281
Dec    90.89 90.92 90.80 90.85 + .01  9.15 − .01  11,940
Mr92   90.94 90.96 90.84 90.90 + .02  9.10 − .02   7,012
  Est vol 289,347; vol Mon 183,076; open int 761,664, +205.


TREASURY BILLS (IMM)—$1 mil.; pts. of 100%
                                      Discount       Open
        Open  High  Low Settle  Chg  Settle Chg Interest
June   91.88 91.89 91.74 91.80 − .02  8.20 + .02 10,320
Sept   92.38 92.38 92.23 92.30 + .04  7.70 − .04 10,622
Dec    92.40 92.41 92.28 92.38 + .06  7.62 − .06  2,527
Mr90   92.46 92.46 92.40 92.46 + .03  7.54 − .03    294
  Est vol 6,682; vol Mon 9,470; open int 23,815, +2,791.
```

Source: *The Wall Street Journal,* May 24, 1989.

Example 5.1 shows that the profits and losses on a Eurodollar futures position equal the changes in interest payments on a three-month, $1 million Eurodollar TD implied by the changes in the quoted futures price.

▪ **Example 5.1: Calculating the Profit on a Eurodollar Position**   Suppose that on May 23, 1989, we take a long position in a June Eurodollar futures contract that has a quoted price of 90.65. Then suppose that on May 30, the quoted futures price falls 100 basis points to 89.65. Since each basis point change in the quoted futures price represents a $25 gain or loss to the contract holder, our long position incurs a total loss of

$$(\$25)(100) = \$2,500.$$

This loss is exactly equal to the change in interest payments on a three-month, $1 million Eurodollar time deposit implied by the change in the quoted futures price. The initial futures price of 90.65 represents a yearly interest rate of 9.35 percent, or (ignoring compounding) a quarterly rate of 2.3375 percent. This rate implies that the quarterly interest payment on a $1 million time deposit will be

$$(0.023375)(\$1,000,000) = \$23,375.$$

The May 30 futures price of 89.65 represents a yearly interest rate of 10.35 percent, or a quarterly rate of 2.5875 percent. Therefore, the quarterly interest payment implied for a $1 million time deposit has increased to

$$(0.025875)(\$1,000,000) = \$25,875.$$

The $2,500 difference between the first and second implied interest payments is exactly equal to the loss we incur on the long position in the futures contract. Thus, the Eurodollar TD futures contract represents the dollar amount of interest on a three-month, $1 million Eurodollar time deposit. The holder of a long position will profit if this dollar amount of interest decreases, and the holder of a short position will profit if it increases. ∎

Hedging Eurodollar futures can be used to hedge against short-term interest rate changes. In Example 5.2, a firm uses a short Eurodollar futures position to protect itself against changes in borrowing rates.

▪ **Example 5.2: Locking in a Borrowing Rate** Suppose that on May 23, 1989, a firm knows it must borrow $1 million on June 19 for a period of 90 days. It will pay the 90-day LIBOR, which prevails on June 19, and will receive its funds on that date. The firm is concerned that interest rates will rise before June 19, the last day of trading for the Eurodollar futures contract. From Figure 5.2, the current Eurodollar futures price for June expiration is 90.65. The current 90-day LIBOR is 9.25 percent.

The firm can use Eurodollar futures to protect itself against an increase in interest rates between now and June 19. By going short Eurodollar futures contracts, the firm will make money if rates rise and thus offset the higher interest it must pay. The following time line shows the relevant dates of this hedge:

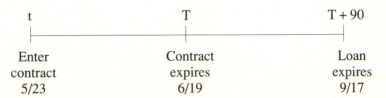

	t	T	T + 90
	Enter contract 5/23	Contract expires 6/19	Loan expires 9/17

We can see how the firm hedges itself by computing its net interest costs under scenarios in which the LIBOR falls and rises. Suppose the LIBOR falls to 7 percent by June 19. The firm's net interest costs will be the sum of the interest it pays on the loan and the loss on its futures position:

$$\text{Interest paid} = \frac{(0.07)(\$1,000,000)}{4}$$
$$= \$17,500.$$

$$\text{Futures profit} = [(\text{Initial futures price}) - (100 - \text{LIBOR})](100)(\$25)$$
$$= (90.65 - 93.00)(100)(\$25)$$
$$= (-235 \text{ basis points})(\$25)$$
$$= -\$5,875.$$

$$\text{Net interest} = \text{Interest paid} - \text{Futures profit}$$
$$= \$17,500 - (-\$5,875)$$
$$= \$23,375.$$

Now suppose the LIBOR rises to 10.5 percent by June 19. The firm's profit on its futures position will offset the increase in its interest costs. Its net interest cost is

$$\text{Interest paid} = \frac{(0.105)(\$1,000,000)}{4}$$

$$= \$26,250.$$

$$\text{Futures profit} = [(\text{Initial futures price}) - (100 - \text{LIBOR})](100)(\$25)$$
$$= (90.65 - 89.50)(100)(\$25)$$
$$= (115 \text{ basis points})(\$25)$$
$$= \$2,875.$$

$$\text{Net interest} = \text{Interest paid} - \text{Futures profit}$$
$$= \$26,250 - \$2,875$$
$$= \$23,375.$$

The firm pays $23,375 in interest under both scenarios. On an annual basis, this represents interest of

$$\text{Interest rate} = \left(\frac{\$23,375}{\$1,000,000}\right)\left(\frac{360}{90}\right)$$

$$= 0.0935$$
$$= 9.35\%$$

The firm's net rate is the 9.35 percent interest rate implicit in today's Eurodollar futures price, not today's 9.25 percent spot LIBOR. Hedging with Eurodollar futures allows the firm to lock in a borrowing rate equal to the rate implicit in the current futures price. This hedge is equivalent to futures hedges that lock in current futures prices. ∎

Firms can use long Eurodollar futures positions to lock in the lending rates implied by today's Eurodollar futures prices. In this case, a fall in the LIBOR will mean a lower lending rate for the firm, but it will also create a futures profit.

Tailing the Hedge   As we saw in Chapter 1, proper calculation of futures profits and losses should reflect the fact that futures cash flows accrue on a daily basis. In Chapter 3, we showed how a tail can adjust a futures hedge for the interest on the daily futures cash flows. A tail prescribes a hedge ratio of $1/(1 + r_{t+1,T})$ that is adjusted as t moves towards T. This ensures that the futures gains and losses will exactly offset the gains and losses on the cash position as of date T.

Tailing a Eurodollar futures hedge involves an additional complication, because the interest on a Eurodollar TD is not paid until date $T + 90$. In this case, the gains and losses on the futures position must offset those on interest paid or received at date $T + 90$. The appropriate hedge ratio with Eurodollar futures is thus

$1/(1 + r_{t+1,T+90})$.[2] As with hedges that involve other futures contracts, this ratio must be adjusted as interest rates change and t moves toward T. While this consideration applies to all of our subsequent discussions of risk management and arbitrage for both Eurodollar and T-bill futures, we will ignore it for simplicity.[3]

The Fundamental No-Arbitrage Equation: Eurodollars   The fundamental no-arbitrage equation in the Eurodollar market differs somewhat from the expression we derived for futures on commodities and other securities. As before, the no-arbitrage relationship in the Eurodollar market is driven by arbitrage trading. The basic steps in Eurodollar arbitrage are similar to those in arbitrage with futures on commodities or securities. However, the transactions differ enough that we require a separate equation to express the no-arbitrage relationship.

Eurodollar arbitrage trading strategies extend over a longer period than does arbitrage in commodities and other securities. At time t, the arbitrageur enters into a futures contract and establishes or takes in a Eurodollar time deposit; at time T, the futures contract expires; and at time T + 90, the Eurodollar TD expires. For simplicity, we will assume that Eurodollar TDs are settled immediately.

We will use the following notation to describe the arbitrage strategies in the Eurodollar TD market:

$r_{t,T+90}$ = Eurodollar TD rate between t and T + 90, set at time t

$r_{t,T}$ = borrowing and lending rate between t and T

$r_{T,T+90}^{t}$ = rate implied by the Eurodollar futures price at t, to be paid on a Eurodollar TD between T and T + 90

Given the quotation conventions of the Eurodollar contract,[4]

$$r_{T,T+90}^{t} = \frac{100 - \text{Quoted futures price at t}}{(100)(4)}.$$ **(5.1)**

---

[2] If the borrowing or lending involves two-day settlement, as with most Eurodollar TDs, the hedge ratio will be $1/(1 + r_{t+1,T+92})$, because the interest on the 90-day Eurodollar TD will be paid or received on date T + 92.

[3] In Chapter 3, we discussed the implications of a correlation between changes in short-term interest rates and changes in the futures price. With Eurodollar and T-bill futures, there is likely to be a strong negative correlation. This will make short hedges more attractive, because futures losses will be associated with lower borrowing costs and futures gains with high lending rates. The opposite will be true for long hedges. See Morgan [1981] for a theoretical discussion of this issue for T-bill futures. Chow and Brophy [1982] found the marking-to-market effect to be small.

[4] We divide by 400 because $r_{T,T+90}^{t}$ is a quarterly rate.

We will show that the fundamental no-arbitrage equation in the Eurodollar market is[5]

$$1 + r_{t,T+90} = (1 + r_{T,T+90}^t)(1 + r_{t,T}). \qquad (5.2)$$

As for futures on commodities and other securities, we will derive this equation by determining the conditions that hold if no arbitrage opportunities exist. First, we will consider the opportunities for cash-and-carry arbitrage. In the Eurodollar market, a cash-and-carry synthetic lending strategy involves the following steps:

1. At time t, establish a $[(1 + r_{T,T+90}^t)/(1 + r_{t,T+90})]$ million Eurodollar TD between t and T + 90. At time T + 90, this will yield

$$[\$(1 + r_{T,T+90}^t)/(1 + r_{t,T+90}) \text{ million}](1 + r_{t,T+90}) = \$(1 + r_{T,T+90}^t) \text{ million}.$$

2. At time t, go short a Eurodollar TD futures contract that expires at T.

3. At time T, borrow $1 million at the LIBOR and take any profits from the futures position. This locks in a borrowing rate of $r_{T,T+90}^t$, because any changes in the LIBOR between t and T are offset by the futures profit.

4. At time T + 90, use the proceeds from the original Eurodollar TD in step 1 to pay back the loan in step 3.

The net effects of the strategy are as follows:
- Time t: An outlay of $[(1 + r_{T,T+90}^t)/(1 + r_{t,T+90})]$ million
- Time T: A cash inflow of $1 million
- Time T + 90: A cash inflow of $(1 + r_{T,T+90}^t)$ million from the Eurodollar TD and an equal cash outflow of $(1 + r_{T,T+90}^t)$ million from the loan taken out at T

Like all cash-and-carry strategies, this strategy creates a synthetic T-bill. It has a price at t of $[(1 + r_{T,T+90}^t)/(1 + r_{t,T+90})]$ million and a face value at T of $1 million. No arbitrage opportunities will exist if the rate of return on this synthetic T-bill (the implied repo rate) equals the borrowing rate, $r_{t,T}$:

$$1 + \text{Synthetic return} = 1 + r_{t,T}$$

$$1/[(1 + r_{T,T+90}^t)/(1 + r_{t,T+90})] = 1 + r_{t,T}$$

$$(1 + r_{t,T+90})/(1 + r_{T,T+90}^t) = 1 + r_{t,T}.$$

---

[5] If we define t′ = t + 2 and T′ = T + 2, the fundamental no-arbitrage equation with two-day settlement is

$$(1 + r_{T',T'+90}^t)(1 + r_{t',T'}) = 1 + r_{t',T'+90},$$

where all of these rates are known at time t.

This expression gives us our fundamental no-arbitrage relationship, Equation 5.2.

An intuitive interpretation of Equation 5.2 is that the return on an investment between dates t and T + 90 $(1 + r_{t,T+90})$ must equal the return on an investment between t and T $(1 + r_{t,T})$ that is reinvested from T until T + 90 at the rate locked in by the futures contract $(1 + r_{T,T+90}^t)$.

Example 5.3 illustrates a cash-and-carry synthetic lending in the Eurodollar market.

- **Example 5.3: Eurodollar Cash-and-Carry Synthetic Lending**   Suppose an arbitrageur is considering a cash-and-carry synthetic lending in the Eurodollar market. On May 23, 1989, he observes that the June 19 Eurodollar TD futures price is 90.65, so the 90-day LIBOR implied by the futures price is 9.35 percent. There is a 9.40 percent rate on a Eurodollar TD over the 117 days from May 23 through September 17, when a three-month time deposit entered into on June 19, with funds received immediately, would expire.

In this situation, a cash-and-carry lending strategy extends over the following time line and involves the following transactions:

1. On May 23, go short one June 19 Eurodollar futures contract. This locks in a 2.3375 percent quarterly borrowing rate as of June 19.

2. On May 23, place ($1,000,000)(1.023375)/(1.03055) = $993,038 in a 117-day time deposit that earns 9.40 percent annually. The $1 million amount is grossed up by the 2.3375 percent quarterly borrowing rate that has been locked in with the futures contract. It is also deflated by the rate that will be earned on the time deposit from May 23 through September 17:

$$\text{Nonannualized TD rate} = \frac{(\text{Annual rate})(\text{Number of days})}{360}$$

$$= (9.40\%)\left(\frac{117}{360}\right)$$

$$= 3.055\%.$$

3. On June 19, borrow $1 million at the locked-in quarterly rate of 2.3375 percent, with funds received immediately.

4. On September 17, take the money out of the 117-day time deposit. This will yield

$$\text{Receipt from TD} = (\$993,038)(1.03055)$$
$$= \$1,023,375.$$

This is precisely enough to pay back the $1 million from the loan taken out on June 19.

The net result of these transactions is

- Cash outflow on May 23: $993,038
- Cash inflow on June 19: $1,000,000

Thus, the cash-and-carry is equivalent to receiving on May 23 a $1-million-face-value T-bill that expires on June 19. The rate of return on the synthetic T-bill is

$$\text{Implied repo rate} = \frac{\$1,000,000 - \$993,038}{\$993,038}$$

$$= 0.70\% \text{ for 27 days.}$$

On an annualized basis, this rate is

$$\text{Annualized rate} = (0.70\%)\left(\frac{360}{27}\right)$$

$$= 9.33\%.$$

The arbitrageur will compare this implied repo rate to his effective borrowing rate to determine whether there is a cash-and-carry pure arbitrage. ∎

We can also create a synthetic borrowing using a reverse cash-and-carry strategy. We simply perform the opposite transaction for each component of the cash-and-carry synthetic lending:

1.   At time t, borrow $[(1 + r^t_{T,T+90})/(1 + r_{t,T+90})]$ million.

2.   At time t, go long a Eurodollar TD futures contract that expires at T.

3.   At time T, establish a $1 million Eurodollar TD that extends from T until T + 90. The long Eurodollar TD futures contract we entered into at time t will lock in the rate earned.

4.   At time T + 90, use the proceeds from lending at time T to pay back the initial funds received at t.

The net result will be to receive $[(1 + r^t_{T,T+90})/(1 + r_{t,T+90})]$ million at time t and pay back $1 million at time T.

Application: Creating Synthetic Fixed-Rate Loans

The large increase in interest rate volatility that occurred in the 1970s and early 1980s created a serious problem for banks and other financial intermediaries. By tradition, many financial intermediaries offered fixed-rate, longer-term loans that were financed by shorter-term liabilities (deposits). For example, a one-year, fixed-rate loan might have been financed by rolling over four three-month Euro-dollar time deposits. While the rate earned was fixed, the rate paid was variable. As interest rates became more volatile, bank profits grew more uncertain.

Many banks responded to this situation by offering loans at interest rates that fluctuated with market rates. Then, if the rate banks paid for funds rose, the yields on the loans also would increase. The variable-rate loans were a natural hedge solution for the banks.

While the floating-rate loans reduced the banks' risk, they had some bad side effects because of the risk they imposed on the banks' customers. Some firms became reluctant to borrow because of the uncertainty over interest payments. Further, the variable-rate loans increased the risk of insolvency faced by borrowing firms. If a large increase in rates occurred, some firms would have trouble meeting their interest payments.

Eurodollar futures allowed both banks and their customers to protect themselves against interest rate risk. One way to achieve this dual protection was for the banks to lend at variable rates and the customers to hedge in the futures market. Another way was for the banks to lend at fixed rates and hedge themselves in the futures market. In the latter case, a bank would choose a futures hedge instead of the natural hedge provided by the variable-rate loans. Example 5.4 shows that these two strategies are equivalent.

▪ **Example 5.4: Hedging with Eurodollar Futures**   Suppose a firm is planning to borrow $10 million from a bank over one year beginning on September 15. It will pay interest every quarter and make a balloon payment of $10 million when the loan matures in one year. The following time line shows the dates of the interest and balloon payments:

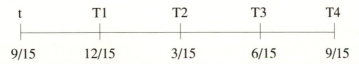

Both the firm and the bank wish to shield themselves from interest rate changes on the loan over the year. The bank may (1) offer a variable-rate loan and let the firm hedge in the Eurodollar futures market or (2) offer a fixed-rate loan and hedge itself against interest rate movements.

The Firm Hedges   Suppose the bank offers a variable-rate loan at the LIBOR for the quarter plus 100 basis points to cover its costs and credit risk. It divides this rate by 4 to yield quarterly rates. The bank funds this loan by issuing 90-day Eurodollar TDs at the LIBOR. This provides the bank with a natural hedge. Part A of Table 5.1 provides one scenario for the spot LIBOR over the life of the loan. Part B shows that the bank's spread between interest earned and borrowing costs is 100 basis points every quarter.

This variable-rate loan places the borrowing firm at risk that interest rates will rise. The firm can hedge itself against interest rate risk by taking a short futures position, because the futures price (100 – Implied interest rate) will fall if rates

Table 5.1 The Firm Hedges a Variable-Rate Loan

A: Futures Prices and Spot Rates

| Date | Spot LIBOR | Futures Prices | | |
		IMM (T1)	IMM (T2)	IMM (T3)
9/15 (t)	8.00	91.75	91.60	91.45
12/15 (T1)	9.15	90.85	90.70	90.55
3/15 (T2)	9.50	—	90.50	90.35
6/15 (T3)	10.05	—	—	89.95

B: Bank and Firm Rates

Date	Interest on Loan	Bank's Borrowing Rate	Bank's Hedged Spread
9/15 (t)	9.00	8.00	1.00
12/15 (T1)	10.15	9.15	1.00
3/15 (T2)	10.50	9.50	1.00
6/15 (T3)	11.05	10.05	1.00

C: Quarterly Net Interest Expense of Firm ($ Million)

Date	Interest	Futures Gain/Loss	Net Interest	Net Annual Rate
9/15 (t)	0.22500	—	0.22500	9.00
12/15 (T1)	0.25375	0.02250	0.23125	9.25
3/15 (T2)	0.26250	0.02750	0.23500	9.40
6/15 (T3)	0.27625	0.03750	0.23875	9.55

rise. Since the Eurodollar TD contract covers 90 days, the firm can hedge for a full year on September 15 by taking futures positions that expire on December 15, March 15, and June 15. The futures positions of each maturity lock in an interest rate for the following 90-day period, so the hedge covers the whole year.

For simplicity, we will ignore the interest on the daily futures payments and the difference between the dates when futures profits are received and interest is paid. (One could account for these factors using the tail described earlier in the chapter.) Similarly, we will ignore the difference between the length of each quarter and the 90 days specified by the futures contracts. Finally, we will assume that Eurodollar futures contracts that expire on the December 15, March 15, and June 15 do exist. Later in the chapter, we will show how to account for the last two complications.

The firm must enter into 10 contracts of each maturity to hedge its entire loan of $10 million. Thus, on September 15 the firm can hedge its interest rate risk for the coming year by taking the following futures positions:

- 10 December 15 short Eurodollar TD futures
- 10 March 15 short Eurodollar TD futures
- 10 June 15 short Eurodollar TD futures

Part C of Table 5.1 shows how the short futures positions hedge the firm against the LIBOR movements under the scenario in part A. For example, on September 15 the firm goes short 10 March futures contracts at a price of IMM(T2) = 91.60. The interest rate implied by this price is 8.4 percent. When March 15 arrives the spot LIBOR is 9.5 percent, so the firm pays an annualized rate of 10.5 percent on the loan. The futures price has moved to 90.50 by that date, so futures profits are

> Futures profit
> = Inital futures − Closing futures
> = [(91.60 − 90.50)(100 basis points)]($25 per basis point)(10 contracts)
> = $27,500.

The interest to be paid the following quarter is

> Interest payment = (Annual rate)(Principal)(90/360)
> = (0.1050)($10,000,000)(90/360)
> = $262,500.

The net interest payment is therefore

> Net interest = Interest − Futures profit
> = $262,500 − $27,500
> = $235,000.

On an annualized basis, this is

$$\text{Annualized rate} = \left(\frac{\text{Interest}}{\text{Principal}}\right)\left(\frac{360}{90}\right)$$

$$= \left(\frac{\$235,000}{\$10,000,000}\right)(4)$$

$$= 9.40\%.$$

Thus, for the quarter beginning March 15, the firm has locked in an interest rate equal to the rate implied by the March futures price on September 15 plus the 100 basis points charged by the bank over the LIBOR. The firm also locks in the implied September futures rates for the December and June quarters plus 100 basis points. This hedge allows the firm to eliminate unexpected variability in its funding cost, while the bank lowers its spread risk through a natural hedge.

The Bank Hedges   Now suppose the bank decides to offer its customers a fixed-rate loan and hedge the interest rate risk itself. To continue the same example, suppose the bank charges the firm a loan rate *fixed* at the rate implied by the September 15 futures prices for each quarter plus 100 basis points. Thus, for example, the firm knows on September 15 that it will pay 9.4 percent for the quarter

Table 5.2 The Bank Hedges Its Costs of Funding a Fixed-Rate Loan

A: Futures Prices and Spot Rates

		Futures Prices		
Date	Spot LIBOR	IMM (T1)	IMM (T2)	IMM (T3)
9/15 (t)	8.00	91.75	91.60	91.45
12/15 (T1)	9.15	90.85	90.70	90.55
3/15 (T2)	9.50	—	90.50	90.35
6/15 (T3)	10.05	—	—	89.95

B: Bank and Firm Rates

Date	Interest on Loan	Bank's Borrowing Rate	Bank's Unhedged Spread
9/15 (t)	9.00	8.00	1.00
12/15 (T1)	9.25	9.15	0.10
3/15 (T2)	9.40	9.50	–0.10
6/15 (T3)	9.55	10.05	–0.50

C: Quarterly Net Interest Earned by Bank ($ Million)

Date	Interest	Futures Gain/Loss	Net Interest	Net Annual Rate
9/15 (t)	0.22500	—	0.22500	9.00
12/15 (T1)	0.23125	0.02250	0.25375	10.15
3/15 (T2)	0.23500	0.02750	0.26250	10.50
6/15 (T3)	0.23875	0.03750	0.27625	11.05

between March 15 and June 15.[6] The bank is vulnerable to rising interest rates, because its income is fixed but its funding costs will increase if rates rise. To hedge against this risk, the bank takes the same futures positions used by the firm earlier (10 contracts per quarter).

Part B of Table 5.2 shows how the bank's unhedged spread will decline as interest rates rise. This deterioration will be exactly offset by the profits from the short hedge. Part C of Table 5.2 shows that the bank effectively receives the LIBOR plus 100 basis points on its loan no matter what course interest rates follow. Thus, its hedged spread is unaffected by interest rate changes. The firm and the bank both have the same cash flows as in the case where the firm hedged. ∎

---

[6] Typically a bank would quote the same fixed rate for each quarter. This rate would be something like the average of the four rates the bank in this example charges. However, to keep our example consistent, we assume the bank charges four different rates, each known on September 15.

In Example 5.4, it makes no difference whether the bank or the firm takes the hedged position. The risk of rate increases must be borne by one or the other, so a short futures hedge by either one is needed to reduce the risk. However, the bank may be able to hedge at a lower cost than the firm. It may have more expertise in the futures markets, and, if it has many loans, it may be able to save on managerial effort and transactions costs when it enters into its hedging positions.

Strips and Stacks   The bank in Example 5.4 hedges its interest rate risk using 10 futures contracts of each maturity. These contracts provide a perfect hedge because they expire on the dates when the bank's funding rate changes. Such a hedge is called a **strip**, because it has the same number of contracts of each maturity. Figures 5.3a and 5.3b illustrate the striplike shape of the hedge in Example 5.4.

Strips are very effective hedges for short-term loans, but they may work less well for longer-term loans. Futures contracts that expire more than three-and-one-half years in the future often are so illiquid and have such large bid-ask spreads that they cannot provide effective hedges when used in a strip. Thus, for longer-term risks, banks often use a technique called a **stack**, which relies on near-term contracts to hedge the risk of interest rate changes for distant quarters. A stack hedge, therefore, does not use the same number of futures contracts of each maturity. Example 5.5 illustrates how a stack hedge works.

■ **Example 5.5: A Stack Hedge**   Suppose the bank in Example 5.4 determines that futures contracts that expire more than six months in the future do not have enough liquidity to permit effective hedging. The bank can still hedge its fixed-rate loan over the year, however, by using shorter-term futures contracts in the following stack hedge:

On September 15:
- Go short 10 December 15 Eurodollar futures
- Go short 20 March 15 Eurodollar futures

On December 15:
- Go long 10 March 15 Eurodollar futures
- Go short 10 June 15 Eurodollar futures

Figures 5.4a and 5.4b and part D of Table 5.3 show the bank's futures positions over the year. Following each quarter's futures position in part D, we see how the gains and losses on that position will be distributed over the year to hedge the bank's interest costs.

Let's first examine the hedge provided by the September 15 position. The 10 short December contracts will hedge the bank's interest expense for the December quarter (T1). Ten of the 20 short March contracts will hedge the bank's interest for the March quarter (T2). The bank takes the 10 additional short March positions to hedge against interest rate movements for the June quarter (T3), since it does not consider the June contracts liquid enough for the hedge. The bank hopes that any news released in the first quarter that prompts an increase in June rates

Figure 5.3 Strip Hedge

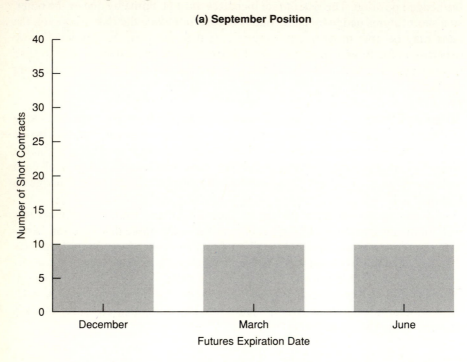

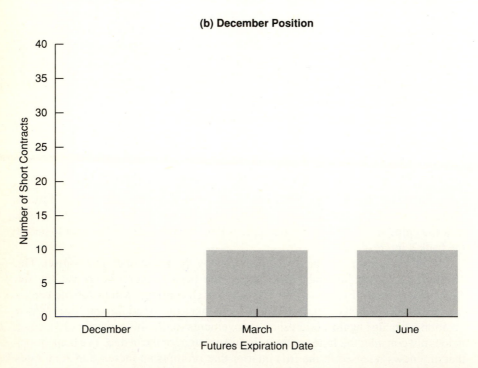

Figure 5.4 Stack Hedge

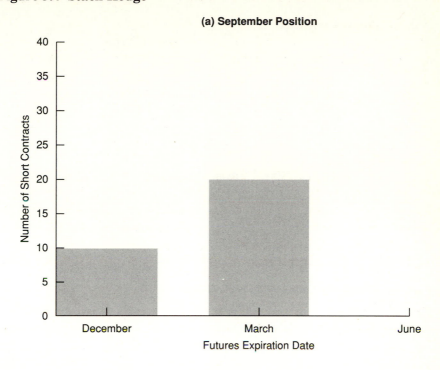

(a) September Position

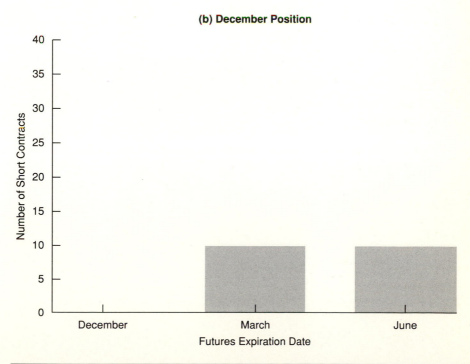

(b) December Position

Table 5.3 The Bank Hedges with a Stack

A: Futures Prices and Spot Rates

Date	Spot LIBOR	Futures Prices		
		IMM (T1)	IMM (T2)	IMM (T3)
9/15 (t)	8.00	91.75	91.60	91.45
12/15 (T1)	9.15	90.85	90.70	90.55
3/15 (T2)	9.50	—	90.50	90.35
6/15 (T3)	10.05	—	—	89.95

B: Bank and Firm Rates

Date	Interest on Loan	Bank's Borrowing Rate	Bank's Unhedged Spread
9/15 (t)	9.00	8.00	1.00
12/15 (T1)	9.25	9.15	0.10
3/15 (T2)	9.40	9.50	–0.10
6/15 (T3)	9.55	10.05	–0.50

C: Quarterly Net Interest Earned by Bank ($ Million)

Date	Interest	Futures Gain/Loss	Net Interest	Net Annual Rate
9/15 (t)	0.22500	—	0.22500	9.00
12/15 (T1)	0.23125	0.02250	0.25375	10.15
3/15 (T2)	0.23500	0.02750	0.26250	10.50
6/15 (T3)	0.23875	0.03750	0.27625	11.05

D: Bank's Futures Positions

Date	Expiration Date of Futures Contracts		
	T1	T2	T3
9/15 (t) position	–10	–20	0
Gain/loss applies to:			
T1	–10	0	0
T2	0	–10	0
T3	0	–10	0
12/15 (T1) position	—	–10	–10
Gain/loss applies to:			
T2	—	–10	0
T3	—	0	–10
3/15 (T2) position	—	—	–10
Gain/loss applies to:			
T3	—	—	–10

will have a similar effect on March rates. If so, the March 15 contract will be able to hedge the June interest rates to some extent.

When December 15 arrives, the bank moves into June futures (which now have only six months to maturity) by offsetting 10 of the March 15 contracts and going short 10 June contracts. From this point on, the bank is perfectly hedged with a strip. The 10 March contracts will hedge interest in the March quarter, and the 10 June contracts will hedge interest in the June quarter. By March 15 the bank has only the 10 June contracts left, and these, of course, are still intended to hedge its interest in the June quarter.

Now that we have charted the timing of the futures gains and losses, we can compute the bank's net interest earnings over the year as shown in part C of Table 5.3. The only complication occurs when we compute the bank's net interest for the quarter beginning in June. The futures profits that apply for that quarter are

$$
\begin{aligned}
\text{Futures Profit} \qquad\qquad\qquad\qquad\qquad\qquad\qquad\qquad & \text{(5.3)}\\
= \text{Profit earned from September to December}&\\
+ \text{Profit earned from December to March}&\\
+ \text{Profit earned from March to June}&\\
= (10 \text{ March short contracts})(91.60 - 90.70)(100)(\$25)&\\
+ (10 \text{ June short contracts})(90.55 - 90.35)(100)(\$25)&\\
+ (10 \text{ June short contracts})(90.35 - 89.95)(100)(\$25)&\\
= \$37{,}500.&
\end{aligned}
$$

The net interest earnings for the quarter beginning in June are

$$
\begin{aligned}
\text{Net interest} &= \text{Actual interest} + \text{Futures profit}\\
&= \$238{,}750 + \$37{,}500\\
&= \$276{,}250\\
&= 11.05\% \text{ annualized.}
\end{aligned}
$$

In each quarter, the gain on the futures position completely offsets the increase in the bank's borrowing costs. The bank maintains a 100-basis-point spread over its borrowing rate throughout the year. The stack provides a perfect hedge in this case, because the March and June futures prices change by the same amount from September to December. Had the bank used a strip, it would have replaced the 10 March contracts that made a profit of 90 basis points (91.60 − 90.70) per contract between September and December with 10 June contracts that also would have made a profit of 90 basis points (91.45 − 90.55) per contract. Therefore, the March futures contract used by the stack to hedge the interest for the June quarter is just as effective as a June futures contract (were it sufficiently liquid) would have been. ∎

The effectiveness of a stack hedge clearly is determined by the movement in the interest rates implied by the futures prices for various maturity dates. The bank in Example 5.5 achieved a perfect hedge by using a March contract to hedge a June LIBOR because the implied June rate rose by the same amount as the implied March rate. The relationship among the interest rates implied for future

Figure 5.5 Yield Curve Shifts, Implied 90-day LIBOR

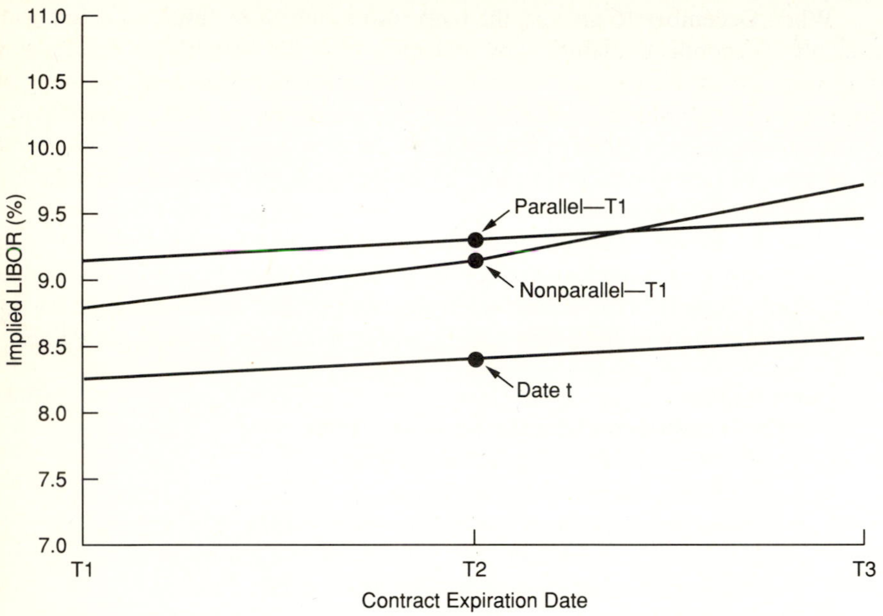

dates by current futures prices is called the **yield curve of implied futures rates**.[7] When all the rates in this yield curve rise by the same amount as in Example 5.5 and as graphed in Figure 5.5, we say that there has been a *parallel* shift in the yield curve. A stack will always provide a perfect hedge if the yield curve shifts over time in a parallel fashion.

Stacks do not provide perfect hedges if the yield curve shifts in a *nonparallel* fashion. Consider the results of our strip and stack hedges if the yield curve experiences the nonparallel shift shown in Figure 5.5 and part A of Table 5.4. From September to December, the spot LIBOR rises 55 basis points relative to the rate implied by the September 15 futures prices, the implied futures LIBOR for the March quarter rises 75 basis points, and the implied futures LIBOR for the June quarter rises 115 basis points. The results of the strip will, of course, be no different in this case because the firm is perfectly hedged, as part C of Table 5.4 demonstrates.

---

[7] This is related to, but somewhat different from, the usual yield curve, which plots the yield to maturity of discount bonds with different maturities. All of the yields plotted on the yield curve of implied futures rates are for one quarter.

Table 5.4 The Bank Hedges with a Strip —Nonparallel Shift in Yield Curve

A: Futures Prices and Spot Rates

Date	Spot LIBOR	Futures Prices		
		IMM (T1)	IMM (T2)	IMM (T3)
9/15 (t)	8.00	91.75	91.60	91.45
12/15 (T1)	8.80	91.20	90.85	90.30
3/15 (T2)	9.70	—	90.30	89.45
6/15 (T3)	10.95	—	—	89.05

B: Bank and Firm Rates

Date	Interest on Loan	Bank's Borrowing Rate	Bank's Unhedged Spread
9/15 (t)	9.00	8.00	1.00
12/15 (T1)	9.25	8.80	0.45
3/15 (T2)	9.40	9.70	−0.30
6/15 (T3)	9.55	10.95	−1.40

C: Quarterly Net Interest Earned by Bank ($ Million)

Date	Interest	Futures Gain/Loss	Net Interest	Net Annual Rate
9/15 (t)	0.22500	—	0.22500	9.00
12/15 (T1)	0.23125	0.01375	0.24500	9.80
3/15 (T2)	0.23500	0.03250	0.26750	10.70
6/15 (T3)	0.23875	0.06000	0.29875	11.95

D: Bank's Futures Positions

Date	Expiration Date of Futures Contracts		
	T1	T2	T3
9/15 (t) position	−10	−10	−10
Gain/loss applies to:			
T1	−10	0	0
T2	0	−10	0
T3	0	0	−10
12/15 (T1) position	—	−10	−10
Gain/loss applies to:			
T2	—	−10	0
T3	—	0	−10
3/15 (T2) position	—	—	−10
Gain/loss applies to:			
T3	—	—	−10

But Table 5.5 shows that the bank comes out behind if it hedges with a stack instead of a strip. Consider the futures profits applied to the interest for the quarter beginning in June:

Futures Profits   **(5.4)**
    = Profit earned from September to December
      + Profit earned from December to March
      + Profit earned from March to June
    = (10 March short contracts)(91.60 − 90.85)(100)($25)
      + (10 June short contracts)(90.30 − 89.45)(100)($25)
      + (10 June short contracts)(89.45 − 89.05)(100)($25)
    = $50,000.

The bank does gain 75 basis points on its futures position as the March futures price moves from 91.60 to 90.85, but it would have gained 115 basis points (91.45 − 90.30) had it held a June contract. This loss from the imperfect hedge shows up in the bank's hedged spread. With the strip, the bank maintains a 100-basis-point spread over its funding costs throughout the whole year (see Table 5.4). But with the stack, the bank's hedged spread is only 60 basis points in the June quarter. The loss of 40 basis points occurs because the implied LIBOR for June moved 40 basis points more than the implied LIBOR for March.

The loss produced by a stack is a kind of *basis risk*.[8] The stack hedging problem is similar to a maturity mismatch or any other kind of crosshedge. A risk is hedged with a futures contract written on an asset other than the one being hedged.

Choosing between Strips and Stacks   As we have seen, the choice between hedging with a strip and with a stack hinges primarily on the liquidity of the contracts that expire in the distant future. With an illiquid contract, the danger is that one will be unable to transact at a reasonable price. This drawback must be weighed against the basis risk of using a contract for a quarter other than the one being hedged.

Another often-suggested approach is to base this choice on one's opinion about how the yield curve will shift. We have seen that for a short hedge, a strip outperforms a stack when an upward-sloping yield curve becomes steeper, that is, when the implied rates in the more distant quarters rise relative to the near-term implied rates. A stack will outperform a strip if the upward-sloping yield curve becomes flatter, because the gains on the near-term contracts will exceed those on the more distant contracts. The opposite will be true for a long hedge. Thus, it appears plausible that once one has forecast future yield curve shifts, the choice between a stack and a strip will be clear.

This strategy may sound like an effective hedge, but it is actually just a *speculation* on yield curve shifts. Suppose the bank in Example 5.5 wishes to hedge

---

[8] The term *basis risk* in this context is unfortunate because of the possible confusion with *basis points*. The two terms relate to different concepts.

Table 5.5   The Bank Hedges with a Stack—Nonparallel Shift in Yield Curve

A: Futures Prices and Spot Rates

Date	Spot LIBOR	Futures Prices IMM (T1)	IMM (T2)	IMM (T3)
9/15 (t)	8.00	91.75	91.60	91.45
12/15 (T1)	8.80	91.20	90.85	90.30
3/15 (T2)	9.70	—	90.30	89.45
6/15 (T3)	10.95	—	—	89.05

B: Bank and Firm Rates

Date	Interest on Loan	Bank's Borrowing Rate	Bank's Unhedged Spread
9/15 (t)	9.00	8.00	1.00
12/15 (T1)	9.25	8.80	0.45
3/15 (T2)	9.40	9.70	−0.30
6/15 (T3)	9.55	10.95	−1.40

C: Net Interest Earned by Bank ($ Million)

Date	Interest	Futures Gain/Loss	Net Interest	Net Annual Rate
9/15 (t)	0.22500	—	0.22500	9.00
12/15 (T1)	0.23125	0.01375	0.24500	9.80
3/15 (T2)	0.23500	0.03250	0.26750	10.70
6/15 (T3)	0.23875	0.05000	0.28875	11.55

D: Bank's Futures Positions

Date	Expiration Date of Futures Contracts T1	T2	T3
9/15 (t) position	−10	−20	0
Gain/loss applies to:			
T1	−10	0	0
T2	0	−10	0
T3	0	−10	0
12/15 (T1) position	—	−10	−10
Gain/loss applies to:			
T2	—	−10	0
T3	—	0	−10
3/15 (T2) position	—	—	−10
Gain/loss applies to:			
T3	—	—	−10

its interest cost and to speculate that the March contract will fall relative to the June contract (or that the March rate will rise relative to the June rate) so that the yield curve flattens. We saw in Chapter 1 that the bank could use a spread position for this speculation by going short the March contract and long the June contract. If the yield curve does not flatten but instead steepens by 40 basis points as in Table 5.5, the spread will lose money:

> Profit on short March – Long June spread
> = Closing spread – Initial spread
> = (90.30 – 90.85) – (91.45 – 91.60)
> = –0.40.

The net position of the hedged bank that also speculates with the short March–long June spread is identical to a stack position:

Hedge	Speculation	Net
10 short December	0 short December	10 short December
10 short March	10 short March	20 short March
10 short June	10 long June	0 short June

Thus, the decision to use a stack instead of a strip when there is ample liquidity in contracts of distant maturities is simply a speculation, even though it is sometimes presented as a hedge.

The Effect of Hedging   We have seen how a bank can use a natural hedge (floating-rate loans) or a futures hedge to reduce the variability of the spread between interest income and funding costs for loans. This risk reduction clearly benefits the bank. However, it comes at a cost, because the bank's expected return may decline along with its risk exposure.

We can see from Example 5.4 how a bank may expect to earn a lower spread on its loan if it hedges its interest rate risk. The bank's fixed lending rate is 100 basis points plus the LIBORs implied by the prices of the Eurodollar futures contracts that expire prior to each quarter. These implied rates have an upward-sloping yield curve as shown in Figure 5.5. Such upward-sloping implied rates are thought by some to reflect a **risk premium** that compensates those issuing long-term liabilities for added risk caused by the greater interest rate sensitivity of longer-term, fixed-income securities. Thus, even though the bank's average fixed lending rate is 9.30 percent [(9.00 + 9.25 + 9.40 + 9.55)/4] over the year, it may be that *on average* the market expects the short-term LIBOR to be lower—say, 8 percent—over the following year. If so, an unhedged bank will earn, on average, a 130-basis-point spread of interest income over the 8 percent funding cost. Of course, the unhedged bank will face the risk of a large loss if the spread deteriorates as well as the possibility of a gain if the spread widens. The bank that hedges, either naturally or with futures, locks in a 100-basis-point spread. In effect, by eliminating risk, the hedged bank also eliminates the expected risk premium.

We encountered similar cases in previous chapters. In Chapter 3, we saw that a firm hedging a cash flow with positive systematic risk would suffer a drop in the expected value of that cash flow. In Chapter 4, we saw that a portfolio manager would expect to earn more than the riskless rate of interest on his or her stock holdings. However, once the manager hedges the portfolio, he or she earns only the riskless rate. In both cases, hedging reduces risk and thereby eliminates risk premia.

Hedging Interest over Periods Other Than 90 Days   So far in this chapter, we have studied examples in which Eurodollar futures are used to hedge interest paid or received over some 90-day future period. However, hedgers often wish to protect themselves from interest rate changes over periods other than 90 days. We can crosshedge with 90-day Eurodollar futures in such cases as long as the interest rate on the period in question moves closely with the rate quoted for a 90-day period. We construct the crosshedge such that changes in the Eurodollar TD futures price will offset changes in the interest on the non-90-day asset.

A hedge of the interest on a non-90-day Eurodollar TD covers the following time line, where N is other than 90:

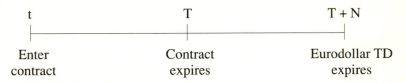

t	T	T + N
Enter contract	Contract expires	Eurodollar TD expires

For simplicity, suppose that at date T the annualized interest rate on the N-day Eurodollar TD moves one for one with the annualized interest on a 90-day Eurodollar TD. This is a reasonable assumption if N is close to 90. Thus, we know from Chapter 3 that the hedge ratio should be

$$\text{Hedge ratio} = \frac{\text{Change in interest on an N-day investment}}{\text{Change in 90-day Eurodollar futures profits}} \qquad (5.5)$$

$$= \frac{(\text{Change in annualized N-day rate})(N/360)(\text{TD size})}{(\text{Change in annualized 90-day rate})(90/360)(\text{TD size})}$$

$$= \frac{N}{90}.$$

For example, any change in the annualized rates will affect the interest on a 135-day investment 135/90 = 1.5 times as much as it will affect the interest on a 90-day investment. Because the interest paid on an N-day Eurodollar TD is N/90 times as volatile (variable) as the interest paid on a 90-day Eurodollar TD, this type of analysis is called **volatility analysis**. Example 5.6 demonstrates how volatility analysis allows us to use 90-day Eurodollar futures to hedge an N-day investment that is tied to the LIBOR.

▪ **Example 5.6: Hedging a 135-Day Investment Using Eurodollar Futures**
Suppose we know on May 23, 1989, that we will have $10 million to lend out from June 19 until November 1, as shown in the following time line:

We will earn the June 19 90-day LIBOR plus 50 basis points, with immediate settlement. The current June Eurodollar futures price is 90.65.

We wish to hedge our lending rate, so we will go long Eurodollar futures. The appropriate hedge ratio is

> Hedge ratio = (N/90)(Millions of dollars)
> = (135/90)(10)
> = 15 June long Eurodollar contracts.

To see how this crosshedge performs, consider what our net interest earnings will be if the June 19 90-day LIBOR turns out to be either 7 or 10 percent:

LIBOR = 7%

Interest received = (0.075)(135/360)($10 million)	$0.281250 million
Futures profit = (15)(93.00 − 90.65)(100)($25)	0.088125 million
Net interest received	0.369375 million

LIBOR = 10%

Interest received = (0.105)(135/360)($10 million)	$0.393750 million
Futures profit = (15)(90.00 − 90.65)(100)($25)	−0.024375 million
Net interest received	0.369375 million

The crosshedge has ensured that our net earnings will be the same in either case.

On an annualized basis, our net earnings are

$$\text{Annualized interest} = \left(\frac{\$0.369375 \text{ million}}{\$10 \text{ million}}\right)\left(\frac{360}{135}\right)$$

$$= 9.85\%.$$

This equals the 9.35 percent rate implied by the initial June futures price of 90.35 plus the 50-basis-point premium we receive over the LIBOR. ∎

Thus, to the extent that the yield curve moves in a parallel fashion, we can crosshedge N-day investments with Eurodollar futures. Any nonparallel movements in the yield curve will induce basis risk. We will see how to analyze basis risk in a similar context later in the chapter.

This technique allows us to extend the fundamental no-arbitrage equation, Equation 5.2. If we assume that the N-day LIBOR equals the 90-day LIBOR at date T, Equation 5.2 becomes

$$1 + r_{t,T+N} = (1 + r^t_{T,T+N})(1 + r_{t,T}), \tag{5.2a}$$

Figure 5.6 Treasury Bill Futures Annual Volume, 1983–1989

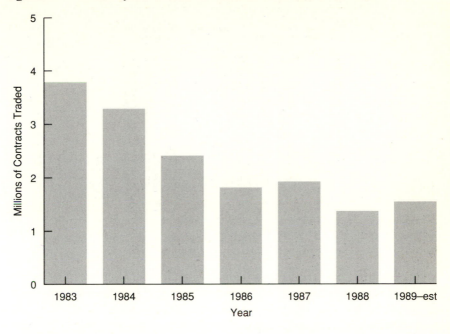

where $r^t_{T,T+N}$ is the 90-day LIBOR implied by the futures price at time t, applied for N days. If there is a constant difference between the 90-day and N-day LIBOR, we must adjust $r^t_{T,T+N}$ to reflect this.

Treasury Bills

Prior to the introduction and tremendous growth of the Eurodollar TD futures contract, the contract on 90-day U.S. Treasury bills was the major short-term interest rate futures contract. Trading in the T-bill contract began in early 1976 at the International Monetary Market at the CME. The T-bill contract still is widely traded, as Figure 5.6 shows, and thus is very liquid. To understand the T-bill futures contract, we will first examine how the T-bill cash market works.

Cash Market

Treasury bills are short-term debt instruments of the U.S. government.[9] They are discount bonds with maturities of less than one year. The U.S. Treasury sells bills

---

[9] See Cook [1986] for a description of the Treasury bill market.

Figure 5.7 T-Bill Spot Yields for May 23, 1989

U.S. Treas. Bills Mat. date	Bid	Asked	Yield Discount	Mat. date	Bid	Asked	Yield Discount
-1989-				9-21	8.33	8.29	8.64
5-25	7.41	7.19	7.29	9-28	8.32	8.28	8.65
6- 1	8.31	8.19	8.32	10- 5	8.31	8.27	8.65
6- 8	8.56	8.49	8.64	10-12	8.31	8.27	8.67
6-15	8.26	8.19	8.35	10-19	8.32	8.28	8.69
6-22	8.30	8.23	8.40	10-26	8.36	8.32	8.75
6-29	8.35	8.28	8.47	11- 2	8.31	8.28	8.72
7- 6	8.38	8.34	8.54	11- 9	8.33	8.29	8.75
7-13	8.37	8.33	8.54	11-16	8.32	8.29	8.76
7-20	8.37	8.34	8.57	11-24	8.32	8.28	8.76
7-27	8.37	8.33	8.57	12-21	8.23	8.19	8.67
8- 3	8.41	8.37	8.63				
8-10	8.35	8.32	8.59	-1990-			
8-17	8.35	8.31	8.59	1-18	8.20	8.14	8.64
8-24	8.29	8.25	8.54	2-15	8.22	8.16	8.69
8-31	8.29	8.25	8.56	3-15	8.20	8.16	8.72
9- 7	8.31	8.27	8.59	4-12	8.18	8.14	8.74
9-14	8.30	8.26	8.60	5-10	8.17	8.14	8.78

Source: *The Wall Street Journal*, May 24, 1989.

at both regularly and irregularly scheduled competitive auctions. The regular auctions occur on a weekly basis for three- and six-month bills and every fourth week for one-year bills, so there is a T-bill expiring each week. T-bills are usually settled after one day, although it is possible to obtain same-day settlement. T-bills are considered the least subject to default of all short-term instruments, because they are backed by the U.S. government. Figure 5.7 presents an excerpt from *The Wall Street Journal* that quotes the May 23, 1989, cash T-bill yields for various bills.

The quoted yield on a T-bill is called the **T-bill yield**. T-bill yields are on a **discount basis**, meaning that they give the percentage by which the T-bill price is discounted from the face value. By convention, T-bill yields are based on a 360-day year. They are therefore related to T-bill prices (per $1 million face value) by the following formula:

$$P_t = \$1,000,000 - \frac{(\$1,000,000)(\text{Yield})(\text{Number of days to maturity})}{360}. \quad (5.6)$$

Suppose we have a 180-day T-bill with an 8 percent quoted yield. The T-bill price must be

$$P_t = \$1,000,000 - \frac{(\$1,000,000)(0.08)(180)}{360}$$

$$= \$960,000.$$

The price of the bill is less than the face value by $40,000, or 4 percent, which is the 8 percent annual discount over 180 days. The actual interest rate, called the **bond yield equivalent**, on this bill is

$$\text{Bond yield} = \frac{\text{Face value} - \text{Price}}{\text{Price}}$$

$$= \frac{\$1,000,000 - \$960,000}{\$960,000}$$

$$= 4.17\% \text{ for 180 days}$$

$$= 8.34\% \text{ annualized.}$$

To be consistent, we use a 360-day year to annualize T-bill rates, although 365-day annualizations also are common.

The bond yield equivalent is always more than the T-bill yield, because the former is figured by taking the difference between the face value and the price as a percentage of the price, while the latter is calculated by taking this difference as a percentage of the face value.

Given the T-bill price, we can compute the T-bill yield by inverting Equation 5.6:

$$\text{T-bill yield} = \left(1 - \frac{P_t}{\$1,000,000}\right)\left(\frac{360}{\text{Number of days to maturity}}\right). \qquad \textbf{(5.7)}$$

Futures Market

The futures contract on T-bills is a delivery contract that has a 13-week T-bill as the deliverable grade. Either a newly issued 13-week T-bill or a T-bill that was initially issued with a longer maturity and now has 13 weeks remaining until expiration may be delivered.

U.S. Treasury Bill Futures Contract Specifications

Contract:	U.S. Treasury Bills
Exchange:	Chicago Mercantile Exchange
Quantity:	$1 million face value
Delivery months:	March, June, September, December
Delivery specifications:	Delivery of a 90-, 91-, or 92-day T-bill on three successive business days, beginning the day after the last day of trading; the last day of trading is the business day before the U.S. government issue of 13-week T-bills
Minimum price movement:	$25 per contract (1 basis point)

The **quoted T-bill futures price** is an index created by subtracting the T-bill yield from 100:[10]

Quoted futures price = 100 − T-bill yield.

---

[10] Mechanically this is very similar to the quotation convention for Eurodollar futures. However, the Eurodollar rate implied by the quoted futures price is an add-on yield, while the T-bill yield implied by the quoted futures price is on a discount basis.

This index price is simply a way of quoting the T-bill yield the market sets for delivery of a 13-week T-bill at the expiration of the futures contract. It is not the price at which T-bill futures contracts are actually traded. The quoted futures price (actually the T-bill yield implied by the quoted futures price) is related to the actual **transactions futures price**, $F_{t,T}$, by the T-bill pricing equation, 5.6, for a 13-week bill:

$$F_{t,T} = \$1,000,000 - \frac{(\$1,000,000)(100 - \text{Quoted futures price})(M)}{(360)(100)}, \qquad (5.8)$$

where M can be 90, 91, or 92 days to maturity and we divide by 100 to place the implied T-bill yield in decimal form. The variable M is the number of days to expiration of a 13-week T-bill that is issued one business day after the last day the T-bill futures is traded.

To see the relationship between the quoted and transactions futures prices, suppose M = 90 and the quoted futures price is 92.00. This quoted price represents a T-bill yield of 8 percent per annum, or 2 percent for 90 days. The transactions futures price is therefore $F_{t,T} = \$980,000$. It is the \$980,000 transactions price, not the 92.00 quoted price, that is the equivalent of the futures prices of other commodities and securities.

Under the T-bill futures contract, a 90-day T-bill is used to calculate changes in transactions value represented by movements in the futures price. The futures pricing equation, 5.8, shows that a one-basis-point move in the quoted futures price corresponds to a \$25 move in the transactions futures price.[11] This is the tick size for the contract. For example, suppose the quoted futures price increases 100 basis points, from 92.00 to 93.00. The implied T-bill yield falls from 8 to 7 percent, and the transactions futures price associated with the new yield increases by \$2,500 to

$$F_{t,T} = \$1,000,000 - \frac{(\$1,000,000)(0.07)(90)}{360}$$

$$= \$982,500.$$

Whether a 90-, 91-, or 92-day T-bill will be delivered depends on the issuing cycle of the U.S. government and on the calender. For any particular futures expiration date, there is only one T-bill maturity date that qualifies for delivery. Thus, the T-bill futures contract does not have multiple deliverable grades. The different possible maturity lengths specified in the futures contract allow for the variations in Treasury financings and the calendar.

Example 5.7 shows how the maturity length of a deliverable T-bill is determined.

---

[11] Later we show that because the price of a 91- or 92-day T-bill moves more than the price of a 90-day T-bill for a given change in T-bill yields, we must use hedge ratios of 91/90 and 92/90 to lock in prices for 91- and 92-day bills, respectively.

■ **Example 5.7: Determining the Maturity Length of a Deliverable T-Bill**
The *Wall Street Journal* excerpt in Figure 5.2 includes T-bill futures prices for May 23, 1989. The June T-bill futures price was 91.80, which represented a T-bill yield of 8.20 percent. The last day of trading for the June T-bill futures contract was May 31.[12] The contract allows delivery in any of the three business days after the last day of trading. From Figure 5.7, we see that there was a T-bill due to expire on August 31, 92 days after May 31. Thus, on June 1, the first business day after the close of trading in the June contract, a newly issued 13-week T-bill had 91 days to maturity.

A party with a short futures contract therefore would have delivered a 91-day T-bill on the first delivery day, June 1. The price received is computed from Equation 5.8 with the actual number of days to maturity of the delivered bill:

$$F_{t,T} = \$1,000,000 - \frac{(\$1,000,000)(0.0820)(91)}{360}$$

$$= \$979,272.$$

Had the short party waited until June 2 to deliver, he or she would have delivered a 90-day T-bill. However, the exchange still would have calculated the invoice price using the 91 days from the issuance date to maturity of the newly issued 13-week T-bill. Thus, we see a strong disincentive to deliver after the first delivery date, and such deliveries in fact are rare. ■

Repurchase Agreements   An integral part of trading in both cash T-bills and T-bill futures is the market for repurchase agreements,[13] which are used in much of the arbitrage trading in T-bills. In a **repurchase agreement**—also called an **RP** or **repo**—one party sells a security (in this case, a T-bill) to another party at one price and commits to repurchase the security at another price at a future date. The buyer of the T-bill in a repo is said to enter into a **reverse repurchase agreement**, or **reverse repo**. The buyer's transactions are just the opposite of the seller's. Figure 5.8 demonstrates the transactions in a repo.

A repurchase agreement effectively allows the seller to borrow from the buyer using the security as collateral. The seller receives funds today that must be paid back in the future and relinquishes the security for the duration of the agreement. The interest on the borrowing is the difference between the initial sale price and the subsequent price for repurchasing the security. The borrowing rate in a repurchase agreement is called the **repo rate**. The buyer of a reverse repurchase agreement receives a lending rate called the **reverse repo rate**. The repo market is a competitive dealer market, with quotations available for both borrowing and lending. As with all borrowing and lending rates, there is a spread between repo and reverse repo rates.

---

[12] The last day of trading for the June 1989 contract was May 31, because the first delivery date was in June.

[13] See Lumpkin [1986] for a description of the repurchase agreement market.

Figure 5.8 Transactions in a Repurchase Agreement

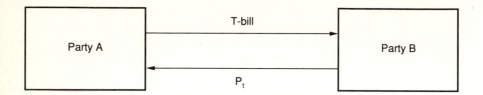

Date t

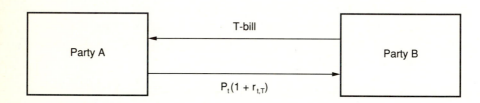

Date T

Note: $r_{t,T}$ = Unannualized repo rate.

Repo market rates are quoted on an add-on yield basis, that is, as a percentage of the security's price. For example, a four-day repurchase agreement may involve the purchase of $1 million face value of T-bills for $980,000 at a repo rate of 6 percent. In this case, the repurchase price in four days will be

Repurchase price
= [(Initial price)(Repo rate)(Number of days)/360)] + Initial price
= [($980,000)(0.06)(4/360)] + $980,000
= $980,653.33.

The amount one can borrow with a repo agreement is less than the market value of the security by a margin called a **haircut**. The size of the haircut depends on the maturity and liquidity of the security. For repos on T-bills, the haircut usually is very small, often only one-eighth of a point. But it can be as high as 5 percent for repurchase agreements on longer-term securities such as Treasury bonds and other government agency issues.

Most repos are held only overnight, so those who wish to borrow for longer periods must roll their positions over every day. However, there are some longer-term repurchase agreements, called **term repos**, that come in standardized maturities of one, two, and three weeks and one, two, three, and six months. Some other customized agreements also are traded.

In the following sections, we will see how repos are used for cash-and-carry and reverse cash-and-carry arbitrage in the T-bill futures market.

The Fundamental No-Arbitrage Equation: T-Bills   The fundamental no-arbitrage relationship is expressed somewhat differently for the T-bill market because of the quotation conventions for T-bills. It is (expressed in millions of dollars)

$$1 - \frac{(100 - I_{t,T})(M)}{(360)(100)} = \left[1 - \frac{d_{t,T+M}(\text{Days from t to T} + M)}{360} \right] (1 + r_{t,T}), \quad \textbf{(5.9)}$$

where

T   = first delivery date (i.e., first business day after last day of trading)

M   = number of days to maturity of 13-week T-bill issued at T

$I_{t,T}$ = quoted futures price at t for delivery of a T-bill at T

$d_{t,T+M}$ = T-bill discount yield at t for a T-bill that expires at T + M, in decimal form (we use d to denote "discount"); *unlike other rates, this rate is annualized*

The term $(360)(100)$ is the denominator of the left-hand side of Equation 5.9 because the quoted futures price is not on a decimal basis. For simplicity, we assume that the T + M − t maturity T-bill purchased at time t is acquired immediately.[14]

We can easily see that Equation 5.9 is the same as our familiar no-arbitrage equation:

$$F_{t,T} = P_t(1 + r_{t,T}).$$

The left-hand side of Equation 5.9 represents the futures transaction price for an M-day T-bill associated with a quoted futures price of $I_{t,T}$. The term multiplying $1 + r_{t,T}$ on the right-hand side of Equation 5.9 represents the price at t of a T-bill that expires at T + M.

We can also express the T-bill no-arbitrage equation in terms of rates as in the Eurodollar TD no-arbitrage equation, 5.2. Let

$r_{t,T+M}$ = (nonannualized) rate of return on a T-bill that expires at T + M

$r^t_{T,T+M}$ = (nonannualized) rate of return we can lock in with a futures contract at time t on a T-bill that we will purchase at T and that will expire at T + M

---

[14] If the T-bill is settled the next day, we use $t' = t + 1$ as our initial date.

Then

$$P_t = \frac{\$1{,}000{,}000}{1 + r_{t,T+M}}$$

$$F_{t,T} = \frac{\$1{,}000{,}000}{1 + r_{T,T+M}^t} \, ,$$

Thus, the fundamental no-arbitrage equation becomes

$$\frac{1}{1 + r_{T,T+M}^t} = \left(\frac{1}{1 + r_{t,T+M}} \right)(1 + r_{t,T})$$

or

$$1 + r_{t,T+M} = (1 + r_{T,T+M}^t)(1 + r_{t,T}) \, ,$$

which is exactly the same as Equation 5.2.

If Equation 5.9 (or 5.2) does not hold, a cash-and-carry or reverse cash-and-carry strategy will produce arbitrage profits.[15] In a T-bill arbitrage, the arbitrageur trades among the futures, spot, and repo markets. Example 5.8 demonstrates a T-bill cash-and-carry arbitrage.

▪ **Example 5.8: Cash-and-Carry Arbitrage with T-Bills and Repos** Suppose a pure arbitrageur observes the following prices on May 23, 1989:

▪   The ask on a 100-day T-bill that expires on August 31 is a T-bill yield of 8.25 percent.
▪   The quoted (bid) price on T-bill futures that expire on June 1 is 91.80 (the last day of trading is May 31).
▪   The repo rate for 9 days is an annualized 8.45 percent.

The arbitrageur suspects there is an opportunity for cash-and-carry arbitrage over the following period:

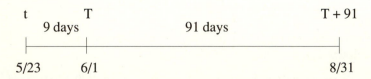

---

[15] See Capozza and Cornell [1979] and Kawaller and Koch [1984] for a discussion of cash-and-carry and reverse cash-and-carry in the T-bill futures market.

The first part of the arbitrage is to lend synthetically in the T-bill futures market. To do this, the arbitrageur must

1. Buy a 100-day T-bill on May 31 at a cost of (superscript a denotes the ask price)

$$P_t^a = \$1,000,000 - \frac{(\$1,000,000)(0.0825)(100)}{360}$$

$$= \$977,083.$$

2. Go short June T-bill futures on May 23. The transactions futures price is (superscript b denotes the bid price)[16]

$$P_{t,T}^b = \$1,000,000 - \frac{(\$1,000,000)(0.0820)(91)}{360}$$

$$= \$979,272,$$

because the T-bill yield implied by the futures price is

$$\begin{aligned} \text{T-bill yield} &= 100 - I_{t,T} \\ &= 100 - 91.80 \\ &= 8.20\%. \end{aligned}$$

3. On June 1, deliver the T-bill into the futures contract. As the T-bill now has only 91 days left until maturity, it can fulfill the delivery specifications of the futures contract.

This strategy creates a synthetic loan between May 23 and June 1. The arbitrageur pays out $977,083 on May 23 and receives $979,272 on June 1. He earns an implied repo rate of

$$\begin{aligned} \text{Implied repo rate} &= \frac{F_{t,T}^b - P_t^a}{P_t^a} \\ &= \frac{\$979,272 - \$977,083}{\$977,083} \\ &= 0.22\% \text{ for 9 days} \\ &= 8.80\% \text{ annualized.} \end{aligned}$$

The next step of the arbitrage is to finance this synthetic lending by borrowing in the repo market. The arbitrageur can borrow at a favorable rate in the repo market because he uses the T-bill he purchased for the synthetic lending to collateralize the repo loan.

---

[16] As we will see later, the appropriate hedge ratio is 91/90.

Figures 5.9 and 5.10 demonstrate the transactions used to finance the arbitrage in the repo market. The arbitrageur borrows for the cash-and-carry by selling into a repo on May 23. He obtains $977,083 from the opposite party to the repo, buys the T-bill, and gives it to the opposite party. Thus, he essentially sells the T-bill to the opposite party on May 23 for $977,083. On June 1, the arbitrageur gets the T-bill back from the opposite party, delivers it into the futures market, and uses the proceeds from the futures delivery to pay back his repo borrowing plus interest.

The interest cost to the arbitrageur is the repo rate over the nine-day period:

$$9\text{-day repo rate} = (8.45\%)\left(\frac{9}{360}\right)$$
$$= 0.21\%.$$

Therefore, the arbitrageur must pay back a total of

$$(\text{Initial sale price})(1 + \text{Repo rate}) = (\$977,083)(1.0021)$$
$$= \$979,135.$$

The arbitrageur makes a pure arbitrage profit because the $979,135 he must pay back under the repo agreement is less than the $979,272 T-bill sale price locked in by the futures contract.

The pure arbitrage profit opportunity can also be demonstrated by comparing the interest rates the arbitrageur faces. The arbitrageur can borrow at the repo rate of 0.21 percent and lend synthetically at the implied repo rate of 0.22 percent. ∎

Example 5.9 shows how arbitrageurs use reverse repo agreements in reverse cash-and-carry arbitrages.

▪ **Example 5.9: Reverse Cash-and-Carry Arbitrage with T-Bills and Reverse Repos**   Suppose a pure arbitrageur observes the following prices on May 23, 1989:

▪   The bid on a 212-day T-bill that expires on December 21 is a T-bill yield of 8.23 percent.
▪   The quoted ask price on T-bill futures that expire on September 21 is 92.30 (the last day of trading is September 20).
▪   The reverse repo rate for 121 days is an annualized 9.15 percent.

The arbitrageur suspects there is an opportunity for reverse cash-and-carry arbitrage over the following period:

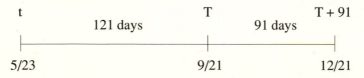

Figure 5.9 Transactions in a Cash-and-Carry Arbitrage, Date t

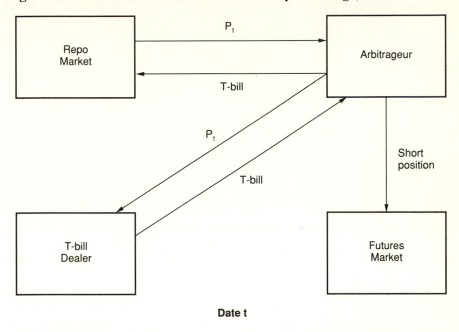

Date t

Figure 5.10 Transactions in a Cash-and-Carry Arbitrage, Date T

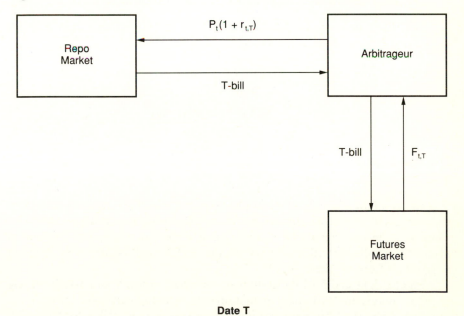

Date T

The first step of the arbitrage is to borrow synthetically through a reverse cash-and-carry as follows:

1. On May 23, sell short a 212-day T-bill with proceeds of

$$P_t^b = \$1,000,000 - \frac{(\$1,000,000)(0.0823)(212)}{360}$$

$$= \$951,534.$$

2. On May 23, go long September T-bill futures at a transactions price of

$$F_{t,T}^a = \$1,000,000 - \frac{(\$1,000,000)(0.0770)(91)}{360}$$

$$= \$980,536.$$

because the T-bill yield implied by the futures price is

$$\text{T-bill yield} = 100 - I_{t,T}$$
$$= 100 - 92.30$$
$$= 7.70\%.$$

3. On September 21, take delivery of the T-bill under the futures contract to cover the short T-bill position. The bill now has only 91 days until maturity and so is of deliverable grade under the futures contract.

With these transactions, the arbitrageur has borrowed synthetically between May 23 and September 21 at the implied reverse repo rate of

$$\text{Implied reverse repo rate} = \frac{F_{t,T}^a - P_t^b}{P_t^b}$$

$$= \frac{\$980,536 - \$951,534}{\$951,534}$$

$$= 3.05\% \text{ for 121 days}$$

$$= 9.07\% \text{ annualized.}$$

Reverse repurchase agreements play a central role in reverse cash-and-carry arbitrage just as repurchase agreements do in cash-and-carry arbitrage. With one transaction, the arbitrageur in a reverse cash and carry can use a reverse repo to execute the T-bill short sale and carry out the next step of the arbitrage: lend out the proceeds from the short sale.

Figures 5.11 and 5.12 illustrate the movement of funds and T-bills among the repo, futures, and cash markets in a reverse cash-and-carry. On May 23, the arbitrageur obtains a T-bill from the opposite party to the repo, sells it for $951,534, and deposits the proceeds with the opposite party. On September 21, she receives the $951,534 plus interest from the opposite party, uses the proceeds to take delivery in the futures market, and returns the bills to the opposite party.

Figure 5.11 Transactions in a Reverse Cash-and-Carry Arbitrage, Date t

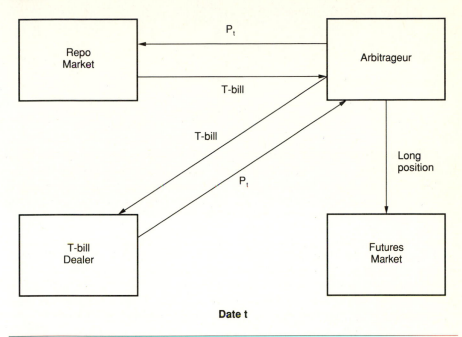

Date t

Figure 5.12 Transactions in a Reverse Cash-and-Carry Arbitrage, Date T

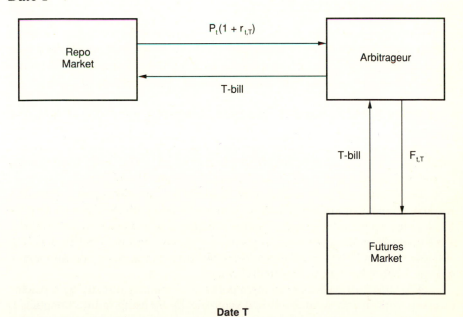

Date T

The reverse repo rate the arbitrageur earns over the 121 days is

$$\text{121-day reverse repo rate} = (9.15\%)\left(\frac{121}{360}\right)$$

$$= 3.08\%,$$

so she receives back

$$\text{(Initial purchase price)}(1 + \text{Reverse repo rate}) = (\$951{,}534)(1.0308)$$
$$= \$980{,}841.$$

The arbitrageur makes an arbitrage profit because the $980,841 she receives from the opposite party under the reverse repo agreement is greater than the $980,536 purchase price locked in under the futures contract. She borrows at the implied reverse repo rate of 3.05 percent and lends at the reverse repo rate of 3.08 percent. ∎

In both the cash-and-carry arbitrage in Example 5.8 and the reverse cash-and-carry arbitrage in Example 5.9, the arbitrageur used actual delivery in the futures markets. Because of the delivery date convergence of spot and futures prices, another way to achieve the same end is to sell or buy a T-bill in the open market and then simply close out the futures contract at expiration.

Using T-Bill Futures to Change the Maturity of a T-Bill

Portfolio managers frequently use T-bill futures contracts to change the maturities of their short-term holdings. Clearly, this can be done without futures by selling assets of one maturity and purchasing assets of another. However, T-bill futures offer an alternative approach that may be cheaper in some cases.

Shortening T-Bill Maturities   Suppose a manager of a portfolio of short-term instruments wishes to shorten the portfolio's maturity. He could sell off the instruments with the longest times to maturity and replace them with shorter-term instruments, or he could shorten the portfolio maturity with T-bill futures using transactions similar to those in a cash-and-carry synthetic lending.

In the cash-and-carry arbitrage of Example 5.8, an arbitrageur purchased a 100-day T-bill and transformed it into a synthetic 9-day T-bill by going short T-bill futures that expired after 9 days. A portfolio manager who already owns a 100-day T-bill could shorten the bill's maturity simply by going short the T-bill futures. The 100-day bill would be turned into a 9-day bill by the manager's commitment to sell the T-bill 9 days later at the futures price.

The choice between shortening a portfolio's maturity directly by replacing its assets with shorter-term assets and synthetically by using futures contracts is essentially a choice between a "natural" and a futures solution that we have encountered before. As usual, this choice depends on relative spot and futures

Table 5.6 Cash-and-Carry Quasi-Arbitrage Table for Portfolio Manager

Benchmark position: sale of 100-day T-bill and purchase of 9-day T-bill

Cash-and-Carry Pure Arbitrage Components	Cash-and-Carry Quasi-Arbitrage Components	Relevant Price or Rate
1. Buy spot	Refrain from selling 100-day T-bill	Bid
2. Short futures	Short futures that expire in 9 days	Bid
3. Borrow	Refrain from buying 9-day T-bill	Ask

Resulting position: synthetic investment in 9-day T-bill

Transactions fees: $TF = -TF_1 + TF_2 - TF_3$
1. Save TF_1
2. Pay TF_2
3. Save TF_3

prices and can be viewed as an arbitrage. Suppose the portfolio manager's *benchmark position* is an intention to reduce the maturity of his portfolio by selling the 100-day T-bill and buying a 9-day T-bill. Then, if he changes course and chooses to use a short futures position instead, he will actually be engaging in a cash-and-carry quasi-arbitrage. Table 5.6 demonstrates this strategy.

The portfolio manager's decision to use futures rather than the direct trade will depend on whether this cash-and-carry strategy will yield an arbitrage profit. The portfolio manager has several cost advantages over the pure arbitrageur in Example 5.8, so he is more likely to find an arbitrage opportunity.[17]

One of the portfolio manager's advantages is that he can effectively obtain the 100-day T-bill at a lower cost than the pure arbitrageur can. The pure arbitrageur must buy the bill at the ask price. But the manager can effectively buy the bill at the bid price by forgoing the revenue from his intended T-bill sale. Since the bid price is lower than the ask price, the manager obtains the T-bill at lower cost.

The manager can also effectively borrow to finance the cash-and-carry at a lower rate than the pure arbitrageur can. The pure arbitrageur must borrow at the market repo rate. The portfolio manager can borrow by not carrying out his original plan to buy a nine-day T-bill. He thereby effectively sells the bill short (borrows) at the ask price. Had he purchased the bill at the ask price, he would have lent out money and earned a lending rate. By retaining the funds he would have lent out, the manager effectively borrows from himself at a lending rate. Since lending rates

[17] The comparison of the 9-day implied repo rate with the 9-day T-bill rate assumes that the cash-and-carry synthetic lending is riskless. This will be true as long as the short futures position pays what is promised. Some managers may wish to build in a risk premium to account for potential clearinghouse failure.

are lower than borrowing rates, the manager borrows at a lower rate than does the pure arbitrageur.

Finally, the portfolio manager incurs lower transactions costs than the pure arbitrageur does. The pure arbitrageur pays transactions costs on every component of the arbitrage. The manager pays transactions costs only when he takes the futures position, because he can carry out the other components of the arbitrage internally. Thus, he saves the transactions fees associated with buying and selling T-bills.

The no-arbitrage equation shows how these advantages make arbitrage opportunities more likely for the manager:

$$\Omega^c = F_{t,T} - [P_t(1 + r_{t,T}) + TF].$$

The Ω^c term is more likely to be positive for the manager because, as we saw above, P_t, $r_{t,T}$, and TF are lower for him than for the pure arbitrageur.

Alternative Techniques for Shortening Maturity   So far in our discussion of maturity shortening with T-bill futures, we have required that the longer-term T-bill have a maturity date exactly 13 weeks longer than the shorter-term bill that replaces it. In such a case, the longer-term bill will have 13 weeks left until maturity when the futures contract that creates the synthetic shorter-term bill expires. Since the futures contract is written on a 13-week bill, it can lock in a sale price for the longer-term bill on that date. Therefore, this technique can shorten the maturity of a T-bill by only 13 weeks. In this section, we will study some techniques for maturity shortening with T-bill futures that can produce a wider range of results.

Crosshedging Bills with Maturities Other Than 13 Weeks   Earlier in the chapter, we showed how volatility analysis allows us to use 90-day Eurodollar futures to hedge investments with maturities other than 90 days.[18] Volatility analysis can also show us how to use futures on 13-week T-bills to shorten the maturities of T-bills whose maturities at the futures' expiration are other than 13 weeks. In such cases, we use 13-week futures to crosshedge the price of T-bills with N days to maturity at time T. This hedge will be effective as long as movements in the 13-week T-bill futures price are closely related to movements in the price of the N-day T-bill. Since yields on T-bills of similar maturities tend to move together over time, such comovement in yields is most likely if the period remaining until the bills' maturities is close to 13 weeks.[19] Under such circumstances, the futures

---

[18] For studies of hedging and crosshedging with T-bill futures, see McLeod and McCabe [1980], Cicchetti, Dale, and Vignola [1981], Parker and Daigler [1981], Hegde [1982], Senchack and Easterwood [1983], Maness and Senchack [1986], Lasser [1987], Brodt [1988], and McDonald, Peterson, and Koch [1989].

[19] Throughout this section, we will assume that the *discount yields* of the T-bills to be hedged move with the discount yield on a 13-week T-bill. Note that this is not the same as saying that bond equivalent yields move together. Practically speaking, however, this is not an important distinction.

contract can hedge, to some extent, the price of selling the T-bill in the spot market at the desired maturity date. Because this is a crosshedge, the hedged T-bill is a security other than a 13-week bill.

As with any crosshedge, we must determine the appropriate hedge ratio and account for basis risk. The appropriate hedge ratio will correct for the different price sensitivities to T-bill yield changes of a 13-week T-bill and the bill to be hedged. Since daily settlement on the 13-week T-bill futures contract is figured on a 90-day basis, we will use 90 days to represent 13 weeks. The appropriate hedge ratio is therefore

$$\text{Hedge ratio} = \frac{\text{Change in N-day T-bill price}}{\text{Change in 90-day T-bill price}} .$$

We can see from the T-bill pricing equation, Equation 5.6, that a change in the T-bill yield will cause the following change in the T-bill price (per \$1 million face value):

$$\text{Change in T-bill price} = (\$1,000,000)(\text{Yield change})(N/360), \qquad \textbf{(5.10)}$$

where N is the number of days to maturity of the bill.

Suppose we have two T-bills that are close enough in maturity that their yields always move together. If we denote their maturities as N_1 and N_2, the relative change in their prices following a yield change is

$$\text{Relative price change} = \frac{(\$1,000,000)(\text{Yield change})(N_1/360)}{(\$1,000,000)(\text{Yield change})(N_2/360)} \qquad \textbf{(5.11)}$$

$$= \frac{N_1}{N_2} .$$

This shows that when the yields on two T-bills move together, the relationship between the price changes of the two bills is determined solely by the differences in their maturities. The price of a longer-maturity T-bill changes more when the yield changes than does the price of a shorter-maturity T-bill, because it is more subject to time value. We call the sensitivity of a bill price to yield changes the **volatility** of the bill. Equation 5.11 gives the relative volatilities of bills with different maturities. We can use Equation 5.11 to derive hedge ratios that shorten the maturities of T-bills by periods other than 90 days.

One implication of this is that if one is hedging a T-bill that will have 91 days to maturity at expiration date T, one must use a hedge ratio of 91/90. Example 5.10 presents a case where changing the hedge ratio is more critical.

▪ **Example 5.10: Using Volatility Analysis for Shortening Maturity**   Suppose that on May 23, 1989, a portfolio manager buys T-bills of \$10 million face value that expire on October 5 and therefore have 135 days to maturity. Suppose also that the portfolio manager wishes to shorten the maturity of these bills to nine days. She decides to use 13-week T-bill futures contracts to lock in a price at which she can sell the bills 9 days later, on June 1. The portfolio manager's T-bills will then have 126 days left until maturity on October 5. The timing of her strategy is as follows:

For consistency and simplicity, we will assume that the 135-day bills are purchased with same-day settlement on May 23 but are then sold with 1-day settlement on May 31, one day before the portfolio manager's futures expire. This way the price she receives for her T-bills will be determined on the same date as the invoice price of the 13-week T-bills deliverable under her futures contracts.

The prices on May 23, 1989, are as follows:

- The ask on a 135-day T-bill that expires on October 5 is a T-bill yield of 8.27 percent.
- The quoted bid price on T-bill futures that expire on June 1 is 91.80 (the last day of trading is May 31).

Therefore, the portfolio manager pays the following spot price, per $1 million face value, for her 135-day T-bills:

$$P_t = \$1,000,000 - \frac{(\$1,000,000)(0.0827)(135)}{360}$$

$$= \$968,988.$$

Now assume the 13-week T-bill yield will be exactly the same as the 126-day T-bill yield on May 31, when the price for June 1 futures delivery is set.[20] As we saw earlier, this means that the difference between the prices of the 13-week and 126-day T-bills will be due solely to the difference in the bills' maturities. The portfolio manager can completely correct for this difference with the hedge ratio given by Equation 5.11; it will give her a perfect hedge with no basis risk:

$$\text{Hedge ratio} = \frac{\text{Change in spot price on 126-day T-bill}}{\text{Change in futures price on 90-day T-bill}}$$

$$= \frac{126}{90}$$

$$= 1.40.$$

For a given change in rates, the 126-day bill price will move 1.4 times as much as the 90-day bill price implied by the futures contract. To hedge the price of the 126-day bills, the portfolio manager goes short 1.4 13-week T-bill futures

---

[20] Thus, as mentioned earlier, the bond equivalent yields will not be the same.

contracts for each $1 million face value of 135-day bills. Her hedged position is therefore 14 short futures contracts that expire on June 1.

We can see how the portfolio manager's hedge works by computing the net amount she will receive for her 126-day bills on June 1 under two price scenarios. First, suppose the yield on her bills on May 31 is 7 percent. Then the price she will receive for her bills on June 1 is

$$\text{Price of 126-day T-bill} = \$1,000,000 - \frac{(\$1,000,000)(0.07)(126)}{360}$$

$$= \$975,500.$$

The profit on her short futures contracts will be

Futures profit per contract
= (Initial quoted price – Expiration quoted price)($25 per basis point)
= (91.80 – 93.00)(100)($25)
= –$3,000.

Therefore, the portfolio manager's total revenues from the sale of her T-bills will be

Hedged sales revenues = Sale revenues + Futures profit
= [(10)($975,500)] + [(14)(–$3,000)]
= $9,713,000.

For the second scenario, suppose the yield on the portfolio manager's T-bills is 10 percent on May 31. Then the price the portfolio manager will receive on June 1 for her bills is

$$\text{Price of 126-day T-bill} = \$1,000,000 - \frac{(\$1,000,000)(0.10)(126)}{360}$$

$$= \$965,000.$$

The portfolio manager will earn the following profit on her futures position:

Futures profit per contract
= (Initial quoted price – Expiration quoted price)($25 per basis point)
= (91.80 – 90.00)(100)($25)
= $4,500.

Her total revenues from the sale of her T-bills will be

Hedged sales revenues = Sale revenues + Futures profit
= [(10)($965,000)] + [(14)($4,500)]
= $9,713,000.

The portfolio manager will have locked in a price of $971,300 per $1 million face value for the 126-day bills. From Equation 5.7, we see that the T-bill yield implied by this price is

$$\text{T- yield} = \left(1 - \frac{\$971{,}300}{\$1{,}000{,}000}\right)\left(\frac{360}{126}\right)$$

$$= 8.20\%,$$

which is exactly the T-bill yield implied by the 13-week T-bill futures price of 91.80 on May 23.

By using an appropriate hedge ratio, the portfolio manager is able to hedge a 126-day bill with a 13-week T-bill futures contract and thus turn a 135-day bill into a 9-day bill. The implied repo rate for this strategy is the return from purchasing a 135-day bill for \$968,988 and locking in a sales price 9 days in the future of \$971,300:

$$\text{Implied repo rate} = \frac{\$971{,}300 - \$968{,}988}{\$968{,}988}$$

$$= 0.24\% \text{ for 9 days.}$$

∎

Example 5.10 shows that using volatility analysis, we can construct hedges that lock in rates of return on T-bills of maturities other than 90 days as long as the bill's (discount) yields move in tandem with the yield on a 13-week bill. This implies that there could be more opportunities for cash-and-carry arbitrage in the T-bill market than we have seen up to this point, for if there is no basis risk, a hedge ratio of N/90 can lock in a rate of return over the N days between T and T + N. Thus, the no-arbitrage equation, 5.2a, should hold for T-bills as well as for Eurodollar TDs.[21]

Strips and Chained Hedge Ratios   We have seen that 13-week T-bill futures can shorten T-bill maturities with little basis risk as long as the yields on the bills that are shortened move closely with the yields on 13-week bills. The yields are more likely to move together in cases where a T-bill is shortened by a period close to 90 days. Hedges that shorten T-bills by periods that greatly exceed 90 days are much more likely to suffer from substantial basis risk.

However, there is a way to extend the volatility analysis technique to shorten T-bill maturities by long periods without incurring large amounts of basis risk. This approach hedges the T-bill that is to be sold at time T by combining several 13-week T-bill futures contracts of different maturity dates. It is a modified strip hedge that uses hedge ratios called **chained hedge ratios**. We can see how this strip hedge works by considering the case of a portfolio manager who faces the following time line:

---

[21] As with Eurodollar futures, if there is a constant differential between the 13-week T-bill rate and the N-day rate, $r^t_{T,T+N}$ will include that differential.

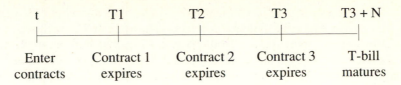

t   T1   T2   T3   T3 + N

Enter   Contract 1   Contract 2   Contract 3   T-bill
contracts   expires   expires   expires   matures

The manager has a T-bill that expires at date T3 + N and wishes to shorten its maturity so that it expires at T1. She can accomplish this by repeatedly applying the volatility analysis technique for shortening maturity. The basic strategy involves the following steps.[22]

- *Step 1:* The manager can shorten the expiration date of the T-bill from T3 + N to T3 by going short T-bill futures that mature at T3. If N does not equal 90, she uses a hedge ratio of N/90.
- *Step 2:* The manager now has a synthetic T-bill that matures at T3. She can shorten the maturity of this bill from T3 to T2 by going short T-bill futures that expire at T2. If the time between T2 and T3 is not 90 days, the manager uses a hedge ratio of (Number of days between T2 and T3)/90.
- *Step 3:* The manager now has a synthetic T-bill that matures at T2. She can shorten the maturity of this bill from T2 to T1 by going short T-bill futures that expire at T1. If the time between T1 and T2 is not 90 days, the manager uses a hedge ratio of (Number of days between T1 and T2)/90.

The effect of these transactions is to shorten the maturity date of the original T-bill from T3 + N to T1. The time between successive T-bill futures expiration dates is close to three months. If N is close to 90, there will be little basis risk in this set of transactions.

However, to complete this strategy, the hedge ratios described above must be adjusted further. They must account for the fact that the face values of the T-bills whose maturities are successively shortened are decreasing. To see this, we define the 13-week (annualized) T-bill yield implied by the quoted futures price, $I_{t,T}$, as

$$d^t_{T,T+M} = \frac{100 - I_{t,T}}{100}.$$

Now suppose the bill that matures at T3 + N has a face value of $1 million. Then, going short futures that expire at T3 yields a synthetic T-bill that expires at T3 with a face value of $1 million less the discount locked in between T3 and T3 + N by the futures contract:

Face value of T3-maturity synthetic bill   **(5.12)**

$$= \$1{,}000{,}000 - \left[\$1{,}000{,}000 \, \frac{(d^t_{T3,T3+M})(N)}{360} \right].$$

---

[22] If there are more than three contract maturities in the problem, one simply expands the analysis to include all of them.

To shorten the synthetic T3-maturity bill and create a synthetic T2-maturity bill, the manager enters into futures contracts that expire at T2 for this face value only. The futures contracts set a T-bill price at T2, per $1 million, of $1 million less the discount locked in between T2 and T3. Thus, the face value of the manager's synthetic T2-maturity T-bill will be the hedged T2 bill price times the face value of the synthetic T3-maturity bill:

Face value of T2-maturity synthetic bill   (5.13)
= (Hedged T-bill price at T2)(Face value of T3-maturity synthetic bill)

$$= \left[\$1,000,000 - \$1,000,000 \frac{(d^t_{T2,T2+M})(T3 - T2)}{360} \right] \left[\begin{matrix} \text{Face value of T3-Maturity} \\ \text{synthetic bill} \\ \text{(\$ millions)} \end{matrix} \right].$$

Finally, if the manager shortens the synthetic T2-maturity bill to a synthetic T1-maturity bill, she must enter into futures contracts that expire at T1 for the face value of the synthetic T2-maturity bill only. This will result in T1-maturity synthetic T-bills with a face value of:

Face value of T1-maturity synthetic bill   (5.14)
= (Hedged T-bill price at T1)(Face value of T2-maturity synthetic bill)

$$= \left[\$1,000,000 - \$1,000,000 \frac{(d^t_{T1,T1+M})(T2 - T1)}{360} \right] \left[\begin{matrix} \text{Face value of T2-Maturity} \\ \text{synthetic bill} \\ \text{(\$ millions)} \end{matrix} \right].$$

Thus, two factors cause the chained hedge ratios[23] to differ from 1. First, the T-bill (synthetic or actual) being hedged may not have exactly 90 days to maturity at the expiration of the futures. Second, as we have just seen, the face values of the T-bills change as we move from maturity date T3 + N to T1. Example 5.11 demonstrates the interaction between these two effects on the chained hedge ratios.

▪ **Example 5.11: Maturity Shortening and Chained Hedge Ratios for T-bills**   Suppose that on May 23, 1989, a portfolio manager is considering buying T-bills of $100 million face value that expire 185 days later, on November 24. He then intends to shorten the maturity of these T-bills to nine days. His strategy will cover the following time line:

---

[23] The use of the term *chained hedge ratio* arises because the face value of the T2-maturity synthetic bill is determined by working backward in a "chain" from the face value of the T3 + N maturity bill.

The prices on May 23, 1989, are as follows:

- The ask on a 185-day T-bill that expires on November 24 is a T-bill yield of 8.28 percent.
- The quoted bid price on T-bill futures that expire on June 1 is 91.80 (the last day of trading is May 31).
- The quoted bid price on T-bill futures that expire on September 21 is 92.30 (the last day of trading is September 20).

The manager can use the June and September futures contracts to shorten the maturity of his T-bill holdings. He will use chained hedge ratios in the following set of transactions:

Step 1:   The manager enters into a short position in September futures to hedge the price of the T-bills on September 21. We assume the yield on 13-week T-bills is the same as the yield on the 64-day T-bill on September 20. The appropriate futures position is

Face value of bills to be hedged	$100 million
Volatility hedge (64 days/90 days)	0.71
Total futures [($100 million)(0.71)]	71 September contracts

This transaction locks in a T-bill yield of 7.70 percent $(100 - 92.30)$ for the 64-day bill on September 21. The price per $1 million face value that is locked in for the 64-day bill on September 21 is

$$\text{Hedged price of 64-day T-bill} = \$1,000,000 - \$1,000,000\,\frac{(0.0770)(64)}{360}$$

$$= \$986,311.$$

The manager now holds synthetic 121-day T-bills (185 days − 64 days) that expire on September 21 at a face value of

Face value of 121-day bills
  = (Hedged price of 64-day T-bill)(Face value of 185-day T-bills)
  = ($986,311/million)($100,000,000)
  = $98,631,100.

Step 2:   The manager enters into short June T-bill futures to hedge the price of his T-bill holdings on June 1. Now we assume the yield on 13-week T-bills equals the yield on the 112-day bills on May 31. The appropriate position is

Face value of bills to be hedged	$98.63 million
Volatility hedge (112 days/90 days)	1.24
Total futures [($98.63 million)(1.24)]	122.30 June contracts

This transaction locks in an annualized yield of 8.20 percent (100 − 91.80) for the 112-day bills on June 1. The T-bill price locked in for June 1, per $1 million face value, is

$$\text{Hedged price of 112-day T-bill} = \$1,000,000 - \$1,000,000 \frac{(0.0820)(112)}{360}$$

$$= \$974,489.$$

The manager now has synthetic nine-day T-bills with a face value of

Face value of 9-day T-bills
 = (Hedged price of 112-day T-bill)(Face value of synthetic 121-day
  T-bills)
 = ($974,489/million)($98.63 million)
 = $96,113,850.

It is now straightforward to calculate the implied repo rate for this strategy. The cost of the 185-day bills purchased on May 23 is

$$\text{Cost of 185-day T-bills} = \$100,000,000 - \$100,000,000 \frac{(0.0828)(185)}{360}$$

$$= \$95,745,000.$$

Thus, the implied repo rate on the nine-day synthetic bills is

$$\text{Implied repo rate} = \frac{\$96,113,850 - \$95,745,000}{\$95,745,000}$$

$$= 0.39 \text{ for 9 days}$$

$$= 15.60\% \text{ annualized.}$$

The manager must compare this synthetic rate with the rate on an actual nine-day T-bill to determine the desirability of the synthetic strategy. Similarly, a pure arbitrageur would compare this implied repo rate to the nine-day repo rate. ∎

As we discussed earlier, this kind of hedge is very similar to the strip hedge used for Eurodollars. In Example 5.11, the September futures contract covers movements in expected rates for September through November as a result of news between May 23 and May 31. The June futures contract covers movements in expected rates for June through September as a result of news between May 23 and May 31. Thus, while we derive the appropriate hedge ratios by successively hedging shorter and shorter maturity bills, in practice the portfolio manager will sell a 176-day T-bill (185 days − 9 days) on June 1. The profits on the June and September futures positions will hedge the price of that T-bill.

Lengthening T-Bill Maturities   T-bill futures can be used to lengthen as well as shorten T-bill maturities. Suppose that at time t a portfolio manager buys a T-bill that matures at time T but wishes to extend the bill's maturity to time T + N using T-bill futures. Her strategy will cover the following time line:

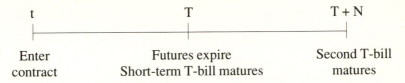

t	T	T + N
Enter contract	Futures expire Short-term T-bill matures	Second T-bill matures

At time t, the portfolio manager will enter into a long T-bill futures position that expires at time T. When her T-bill matures at T, she will reinvest the bill's proceeds in a T-bill that matures at date T + N. Her futures position has locked in the rate she will earn on the second bill between T and T + N. Thus, at time t, the portfolio manager has an investment with a known payout at T + N; it is equivalent to a T-bill that matures at T + N.

Example 5.12 shows how to set the correct hedge ratio when lengthening a T-bill's maturity with T-bill futures.

▪ **Example 5.12: Lengthening the Maturity of a T-bill**   Suppose that on May 23, 1989, our portfolio manager is contemplating buying 9-day T-bills that will mature on June 1 with a face value of $100 million and lengthening their maturity such that they will expire in 114 days, on September 14:

t	T		T + N
	9 days	105 days	
5/23	6/1		9/14

The prices on May 23, 1989, are as follows:

- The ask on a nine-day T-bill that expires on June 1 is a T-bill yield of 8.19 percent.
- The quoted ask price on T-bill futures that expire on June 1 is 91.80 (the last day of trading is May 31).

Assume, for the sake of simplicity, that the 13-week T-bill yield will equal the 105-day T-bill yield on May 31. Then the portfolio manager can use a long position in June 1 T-bill futures to lock in a T-bill yield of 8.20 percent (100 – 91.80) for 105-day bills on June 1. This yield represents a T-bill price, per $1 million face value, of

$$\text{Price of 105-day T-bill at } T = \$1,000,000 - \$1,000,000 \frac{(0.0820)(105)}{360}$$

$$= \$976,083.$$

The manager can lock in this price for June 1 with a futures hedge ratio of

$$\text{Hedge ratio} = \frac{105}{90} = 1.17.$$

When the T-bills mature on June 1, the manager will receive proceeds of $100 million. She will use these funds to buy T-bills that will expire on September 14. At the locked-in price of $976,083 per $1 million face value, she can purchase

Number of $1-million-face-value 105-day T-bills

$$= \frac{\text{Funds at date T}}{\text{Locked-in T-bill price per } \$1,000,000 \text{ face value}}$$

$$= \frac{\$100,000,000}{\$976,083}$$

$$= 102.45.$$

The total number of long futures contracts the manager needs to fully hedge this purchase is

Total long June T-bill contracts
= (Number of contracts per $1 million face value)(Number of $1,000,000-face-value T-bills)
= (1.17)(102.45)
= 119.87 contracts.

In practice, the manager would use 120 contracts.

Now that she has determined the hedge that will lengthen the maturity of her T-bills to 114 days, the portfolio manager can choose between using the futures hedge and buying 114-day T-bills directly. If she lengthens the maturity of the 9-day bills with futures, her total rate of return will come from the return on the 9-day bill and the locked-in return on the 105-day bill. The price of the nine-day bill is

$$\text{Price of 9-day T-bill} = \$1,000,000 - \$1,000,000 \frac{(0.0819)(9)}{360}$$

$$= \$997,953.$$

This represents a rate of return of

$$\text{Rate of return on 9-day T-bill} = \frac{\$1,000,000 - \$997,953}{\$997,953}$$

$$= 0.21\% \text{ for 9 days.}$$

The $976,083 price locked in for the 105-day bill on June 1 represents a rate of return of

$$\text{Rate of return on 105-day T-bill} = \frac{\$1,000,000 - \$976,083}{\$976,083}$$

$$= 2.45\% \text{ for 105 days.}$$

Thus, if $1 is invested on May 23 in a 9-day T-bill and then reinvested in a 105-day bill on June 1 at the rate locked in by a long futures position, it will return

$$\text{Value of \$1 invested for 114 days} = \$1(1.0021)(1.0245)$$
$$= \$1.0267.$$

This represents a rate of return of 2.67 percent for 114 days, or 8.43 percent annualized. The portfolio manager should compare this return to that received on a 114-day T-bill. The pure arbitrageur would compare it to the 114-day repo rate.

We can view the manager's decision to use a synthetic 114-day bill instead of purchasing an actual 114-day bill as a reverse cash-and-carry arbitrage. The manager's benchmark position is to buy a 114-day bill. By lengthening the maturity of nine-day T-bills with futures instead, the manager performs a reverse cash-and-carry quasi-arbitrage as demonstrated in Table 5.7. ∎

Lengthening Maturity with Strips   Earlier we saw that one can gain considerable latitude when shortening T-bill maturities by using a strip of T-bill futures contracts of different maturities. The same is true when one uses futures to lengthen T-bill maturities. By going long futures of successive maturities, one can lock in the rates of return earned by repeatedly reinvesting the proceeds from shorter-term bills. This yields a synthetic T-bill with a maturity equal to the sum of the maturities of the shorter-term bills. As with a strip that shortens T-bill maturities, the hedge ratios used to lengthen a T-bill's maturity must be chosen carefully.

The strip approach to lengthening maturity provides a generalization of the fundamental no-arbitrage relationship given by Equation 5.2a. That equation shows that an investment between dates t and T that is reinvested between T and T + N (at a rate locked in at t) must earn the same rate of return as an investment between t and T + N. When we lock in rates of return over several periods in the future using different futures contracts, we get a more complicated no-arbitrage equation:

$$1 + r_{t,T3+N} = (1 + r_{t,T1})(1 + r^t_{T1,T2})(1 + r^t_{T2,T3})(1 + r^t_{T3,T3+N}). \tag{5.15}$$

We can use this equation to determine whether it is preferable to lengthen the maturity of a T-bill with futures or to buy a longer-maturity T-bill directly.[24]

Example 5.13 shows how a T-bill's maturity can be lengthened with a strip of T-bill futures.

∎ **Example 5.13: Lengthening Maturity with a Strip of T-Bills**   Suppose that on May 23, 1989, a corporate treasurer has funds that he wishes to lend out for 212 days, until December 21. He is considering lengthening the maturity of a

---

[24] As in the case of maturity shortening, it is easy to expand this analysis to include more than three futures expiration dates.

Table 5.7 Reverse Cash-and-Carry Quasi-Arbitrage Table for Portfolio Manager

Benchmark position: purchase of 114-day T-bill

Reverse Cash-and-Carry Pure Arbitrage Components	Reverse Cash-and-Carry Quasi-Arbitrage Components	Relevant Price or Rate
1. Short spot	Refrain from buying 114-day T-bill	Ask
2. Go long futures	Go long futures that expire in 9 days	Ask
3. Lend	Buy 9-day T-bill	Ask

Resulting position: synthetic investment in 114-day T-bill

Transactions fees: $TF = -TF_1 + TF_2 + TF_3$
1. Save TF_1
2. Pay TF_2
3. Pay TF_3

9-day bill to 212 days bill using long positions in June and September T-bill futures contracts:

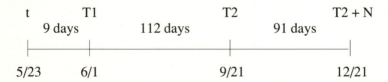

The prices on May 23, 1989, are as follows:

- The ask price on a nine-day T-bill that expires on June 1 is a T-bill yield of 8.19 percent.
- The quoted ask price on T-bill futures that expire on June 1 is 91.80 (the last day of trading is May 31).
- The quoted ask price on T-bill futures that expire on September 21 is 92.30 (the last day of trading is September 20).

If the treasurer chooses to create a 212-day T-bill synthetically, he will start by purchasing a nine-day T-bill. We saw in Example 5.12 that the price of this bill at the T-bill yield of 8.19 percent is $997,953. This implies a rate of return of 0.21 percent for nine days.

Next, the treasurer will take a long position in June 1 T-bill futures to lock in a price for a 112-day T-bill that will be purchased on June 1 and will expire on September 21. We assume the yield on 13-week T-bills will equal the yield on the 112-day bill on May 31. The price locked in by the futures position is

$$\text{Price of 112-day T-bill} = \$1,000,000 - \$1,000,000\,\frac{(0.0820)(112)}{360}$$

$$= \$974,489.$$

The rate of return implied by the time t futures price for this 112-day bill is

$$r_{T1,T2}^t = \frac{\$1,000,000 - \$974,489}{\$974,489}$$

$$= 2.62\% \text{ for 112 days.}$$

The treasurer's final step is to take a long position in September 21 futures to lock in the following price for a 91-day T-bill that will be purchased on September 21 and will expire on December 21:

$$\text{Price of 91-day T-bill} = \$1,000,000 - \$1,000,000 \frac{(0.0770)(91)}{360}$$

$$= \$980,536.$$

The rate of return implied by the time t futures price for this 91-day bill is

$$r_{T2,T2+N}^t = \frac{\$1,000,000 - \$980,536}{\$980,536}$$

$$= 1.98\% \text{ for 91 days.}$$

The treasurer has lengthened the maturity of the 9-day T-bill to 212 days. If he puts \$1 million into this synthetic T-bill, he will earn

$$\$[(1 + r_{t,T1})(1 + r_{T1,T2}^t)(1 + r_{T2,T2+N}^t)] \text{ million}$$
$$= \$[(1.0021)(1.0262)(1.0198)] \text{ million}$$
$$= \$1.0487 \text{ million.}$$

Thus, the treasurer will earn a 4.87 percent return on the synthetic T-bill for 212 days, or 8.27 percent annualized. He can then compare this rate of return to that earned on an actual 212-day T-bill. To implement this strategy, he must compute hedge ratios as in Example 5.11. ∎

Basis Risk and Maturity Lengthening   Thus far, in all our examples of hedging N-day T-bills with 13-week T-bill futures, we have assumed that the yields on N-day and 13-week bills move together over time. In such cases, the T-bill prices at time T can be perfectly hedged. The only difference between the 13-week and N-day T-bill prices is due to the differences in their maturities, and we can adjust for this completely with hedge ratios of N/90.

But if 13-week and N-day T-bill yields do not move by the same amount over time, the difference between the prices of 13-week and N-day bills at time T is not due solely to their maturity differences. Hedge ratios of N/90 cannot completely correct for the bills' price differences at time T, and such hedges will be subject to some basis risk.

To analyze the effect of basis risk on maturity lengthening with T-bill futures, suppose the yield on an N-day T-bill, $d_{T,T+N}$, is related to the yield on a 13-week T-bill, $d_{T,T+M}$, by

$$d_{T,T+N} = a + d_{T,T+M} + \varepsilon_T \, , \tag{5.16}$$

where a is an average constant differential, ε_T is random basis error, and M = 90, 91, or 92.[25] If ε_T is always equal to zero, there is no basis risk and one could use a hedge ratio of N/90 to lock in the yield implied by $I_{t,T}$, the current quoted futures price, plus the constant, a, for an N-day T-bill at time T. But with basis risk, a price cannot be completely locked in for the N-day bill at T, for the hedged yield will be a function of ε_T:

$$\text{Hedged yield on N-day bill} = d^h_{T,T+N} (\varepsilon_T) \tag{5.17}$$
$$= a + (100 - I_{t,T}) + \varepsilon_T \, .$$

Suppose an investor wishes to create a synthetic T-bill that matures at T + N by buying a T-bill that matures at T and reinvesting the bill's proceeds at T in a bill that matures at T + N. If he hedges the purchase of the second bill by going long N/90 T-bill futures, his total return between t and T + N will be

$$\text{Return on synthetic T-bill} = (1 + r_{t,T})[1 + d^h_{T,T+N}(\varepsilon_T)].$$

The only unknown factor in this hedged N-day rate is the level of basis error, ε_T.

Example 5.14 demonstrates how to evaluate a plan to lengthen T-bill maturities with T-bill futures when basis risk is present.

▪ **Example 5.14: Basis Risk and Creating a Longer-Term Synthetic T-Bill**
Suppose that on May 23, 1989, an investor is contemplating buying 121-day T-bills that will mature on September 21 at a face value of $100 million. She then plans to use T-bill futures to lengthen the bills' maturity so that they will expire in 185 days on November 24:

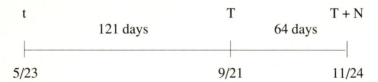

The prices on May 23, 1989, are as follows:

- The ask on 121-day T-bills that expire on September 21 is a T-bill yield of 8.29 percent.
- The ask on 185-day T-bills that expire on November 24 is a T-bill yield of 8.28 percent.
- The quoted ask price on T-bill futures that expire on September 21 is 92.30 (the last day of trading is September 20).

---

[25] Recall that even when M = 91 or 92, we use a hedge ratio of N/90 because futures profits or losses are figured using 90 days.

To create a 185-day T-bill synthetically, the investor will first buy a 121-day bill at a price of \$972,136 and earn a rate of return of 2.87 percent for the 121 days. Thus,

$$r_{t,T} = 2.87\% \text{ for 121 days.}$$

The investor's next step is to take a long futures position that will hedge the price of a 64-day T-bill on September 21. The appropriate hedge ratio is

$$\text{Hedge ratio} = \frac{64}{90} = 0.71.$$

Now suppose the investor has performed some statistical analysis and found that the constant, a, in Equation 5.17 equals −0.05 percent and the basis risk, ε_T, can vary between −0.20 and 0.20 percent. With a hedge ratio of 0.71, the investor will receive a hedged T-bill yield between T and T + 64 of

$$
\begin{aligned}
d^h_{T,T+64} &= a + (1 - I_{t,T}) + \varepsilon_T \\
&= -0.05 + (100.00 - 92.30) + \varepsilon_T \\
&= (7.65 + \varepsilon_T)\%.
\end{aligned}
$$

Clearly, this return will depend on the level of basis error. Suppose the basis error turns out to be 0.15 percent. Then

$$d^h_{T,T+64} = 7.65\% + 0.15\% = 7.80\%,$$

and the price of a \$1-million-face-value 64-day T-bill, including futures gains or losses, will be

$$\text{Hedged price of 64-day bill} = \$1,000,000 - \$1,000,000 \frac{(0.0780)(64)}{360}$$

$$= \$986,133.$$

The yield on the 64-day bill will be

$$r^t_{T,T+64}(\varepsilon_T = 0.15) = \frac{\$1,000,000 - \$986,133}{\$986,133}$$

$$= 1.406\% \text{ for 64 days.}$$

The investor's total rate of return from the synthetic 185-day T-bill will be

Rate on synthetic 185-day T-bill
$$= (1 + r_{t,T})(1 + \text{Rate on hedged 64-day T-bill}) - 1.$$

If $\varepsilon_T = 0.15$, it will be

Table 5.8 Basis Risk and Maturity Lengthening for T-bills

Date t: 5/23/89   a = –0.050%
Date T: 9/21/89
N = 64   t, T price: 0.972136
                                          t, T rate: 2.866%

T maturity rate: 8.290%
T + N maturity rate: 8.280%   t, T + N price: 0.957450
T futures price: 92.3   t, T + N rate: 4.444%

Basis Error	T, T + N Hedged Price	T, T + N Hedged rate	Synthetic t, T + N Rate
–0.200%	0.986756	1.342%	4.247%
–0.175	0.986711	1.347	4.252
–0.150	0.986667	1.351	4.256
–0.125	0.986622	1.356	4.261
–0.100	0.986578	1.360	4.266
–0.075	0.986533	1.365	4.270
–0.050	0.986489	1.370	4.275
–0.025	0.986444	1.374	4.280
0.000	0.986400	1.379	4.284
0.025	0.986356	1.383	4.289
0.050	0.986311	1.388	4.294
0.075	0.986267	1.392	4.299
0.100	0.986222	1.397	4.303
0.125	0.986178	1.402	4.308
0.150	0.986133	1.406	4.313
0.175	0.986089	1.411	4.317
0.200	0.986044	1.415	4.322

$$(1 + r_{t,T})[1 + r^t_{T,T+64}(\varepsilon_T = 0.15)] = (1.0287)(1.01406)$$
$$= 1.0431$$
$$= 4.31\% \text{ for 185 days}$$
$$= 8.39\% \text{ annualized.}$$

Table 5.8 provides a sensitivity analysis for the rate of return on the synthetic 185-day T-bill. It shows that the total rate of return ranges between 4.247 and 4.322 percent as the basis error scenario ranges between -0.20 and 0.20 percent. To determine whether the synthetic strategy is sensible, the investor must compare it to the alternative strategy of purchasing a 185-day bill directly. The price of a $1-million-face-value, 185-day bill on May 23 is

$$\text{Price of 185-day T-bill} = \$1,000,000 - \$1,000,000 \frac{(0.0828)(185)}{360}$$
$$= \$957,450.$$

The rate of return on this bill will be

$$r_{t,T+N} = \frac{\$1,000,000 - \$957,450}{\$957,450}$$

$$= 4.44\% \text{ for 185 days}$$

$$= 8.64\% \text{ annualized.}$$

Thus, even if the basis error is 0.20 percent, the actual 185-day T-bills are superior to the synthetic 185-day T-bills. ∎

Empirical Evidence on T-Bill Futures

While there has been little empirical work on Eurodollar TD futures, a number of studies have explored different aspects of the T-bill futures market. Some researchers have tested to see whether the no-arbitrage relationship holds in the T-bill markets. Others have studied whether the T-bill yields implied by T-bill futures prices can be used to predict future T-bill yields. Still others have questioned whether the introduction of T-bill futures has increased the volatility of the cash T-bill market.

Arbitrage   Rendleman and Carabini [1979] examined T-bill spot and futures prices to determine whether the T-bill no-arbitrage equation, Equation 5.9, holds in real markets. Taking account of transactions costs, they created no-arbitrage bounds (as discussed in Chapter 2) for pure arbitrage and tested to see if T-bill futures prices fell within those limits. They were unable to find any instances in which the futures price fell outside of the bounds and concluded that arbitrageurs had eliminated pure arbitrage opportunities. However, they were able to find a small number of quasi-arbitrage opportunities in the T-bill markets. Their general conclusion was that arbitrage in the T-bill markets drives prices into line very quickly.

Elton, Gruber, and Rentzler [1984] extended this line of work by studying the relationships of intraday prices instead of the closing prices examined by Rendleman and Carabini [1979]. The use of intraday prices allows the researcher to match up trades in the futures and spot markets over short time intervals and thus is a more realistic representation of the conditions arbitrageurs face.[26] By examining all T-bill futures trades between 1976 and 1982, matching the futures prices with cash prices and taking account of transactions costs, Elton, Gruber, and Rentzler identified 2,304 trades that would have produced arbitrage profits.

These results give us a very dynamic picture of arbitrage. We argued in Chapter 4 that if there were never any arbitrage opportunities, there would be no arbitrageurs. Thus, when markets operate efficiently, we would expect to observe a fair number of arbitrage opportunities that arbitrageurs quickly eliminate. This

---

[26] Even this paper did not study completely realistic conditions, because the cash T-bill quotes were taken approximately every hour.

seems to be the kind of market characterized by Elton, Gruber, and Rentzler's results. It seems very reasonable that 2,304 arbitrage opportunities might appear over a six-year period as volatile as the one between 1976 and 1982.[27,28]

Implied Yields as Predictors of Future Yields   Both Howard [1982] and Hegde and McDonald [1986] found that T-bill yields implied by futures prices have useful information about future spot T-bill yields.[29]

Spot Market Volatility   There is some disagreement about whether the introduction of T-bill futures has affected the volatility of cash T-bill prices. Dale and Workman [1981] found no increase in cash market volatility. Simpson and Ireland [1985] found that cash market volatility dropped initially after the introduction of T-bill futures and then increased as the futures market grew, albeit moderately.

The TED Spread

So far we have discussed Eurodollar TD futures and T-bill futures individually. Now we will examine the **TED spread**, which consists of opposite positions in each of these two futures contracts. Long and short positions in the TED spread are defined as follows:

Long the TED spread:
- Long T-bill futures
- Short Eurodollar TD futures

Short the TED spread:
- Short T-bill futures
- Long Eurodollar TD futures

where both contracts in the spread expire in the same month. This is possible because the Eurodollar TD and T-bill futures contracts have the same expiration months of March, June, September, and December even though they have different expiration dates.

---

[27] Kawaller and Koch [1984] provide evidence consistent with the fundamental no-arbitrage equation. Hegde and Branch [1985] and Monroe and Cohn [1986] present evidence that some arbitrage opportunities do exist in the T-bill futures market. See also Puglisi [1978] and Vignola and Dale [1980].

[28] Kane [1980] proposed that the divergences from the no-arbitrage equation exist because of market incompleteness. Similarly, Kamara [1988] proposed that there will appear to be arbitrage opportunities because of the low trading costs of T-bill futures relative to synthetic interest rate forward contracts.

[29] See also Branch [1978], Chow and Brophy [1978], Lang [1978], Poole [1978], and MacDonald and Hein [1989].

Figure 5.13 TED Spread, 1982–1988

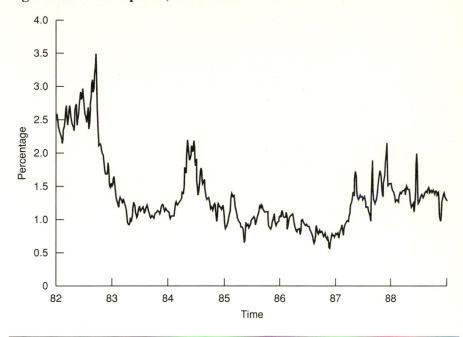

Source: Chicago Mercantile Exchange.

The TED spread for a given month is quoted as

TED spread = T-bill futures price − Eurodollar TD futures price   **(5.18)**
= (100 − Implied T-bill rate) − (100 − Implied Eurodollar rate)
= Implied Eurodollar rate − Implied T-bill rate.

We can see some actual TED spreads in Figure 5.2, which presents an extract from *The Wall Street Journal* with Eurodollar and T-bill futures prices for May 23, 1989. The June TED spread on May 23, 1989 was

June TED spread = 91.80 − 90.65
= 1.15%.

This spread would be quoted as 115 basis points. Figure 5.13 presents the TED spread from 1982 through 1988 using the nearest expiration months.

Quoted TED spreads are believed to represent the risk premium associated with holding Eurodollar TDs instead of T-bills. Because Eurodollar TDs are issued by unregulated banks that do not carry deposit insurance, their rates generally are expected to reflect a risk premium over T-bill rates. However, this interpretation of quoted TED spreads is not completely accurate, for the implied Eurodollar rates are quoted on an add-on basis and the implied T-bill rates on a discount basis. Since discount yields are lower than their associated add-on yields, quoted TED spreads will overstate any risk premium. Further, because the disparity between the discount and add-on yields increases with the T-bill yield, the risk premium overstatement is greater at higher yield levels.

The TED spread is used by investors who wish to trade on their views about the Eurodollar TD risk premium over T-bills. As a result, events that threaten the soundness of the money center banks tend to increase the TED spread. This occurred in May 1984 when Continental Illinois Bank came very close to failing. The entire banking system appeared shaky, and investors became nervous about investing in uninsured Eurodollar TDs. This increased Eurodollar TD rates relative to T-bill rates, and the TED spread increased to around 200 basis points. As it became clear that the U.S. government would not let the bank fail, the TED spread gradually fell below 100 basis points.[30]

Example 5.15 shows a case where profits are earned from a TED spread.

▪ **Example 5.15: Using a TED Spread**   Suppose that on May 23, 1989, an investor believes the world's financial system will soon enter a period of instability and the current risk premium for Eurodollar TDs over T-bills is too low. He decides to go long the June TED spread at the prices shown in Figure 5.2:

Go long June T-bills at	91.80
Go short June Eurodollars at	90.65
TED spread	= 1.15

The investor can perform this transaction in one order. His broker will tell him that the ask on the TED spread is 115, and he does not need to know the absolute level of either contract.

Now suppose that on May 30, the major money center banks reveal that their losses are larger than expected. The investor then closes out his positions at a June T-bill futures price of 90.40 and a June Eurodollar TD futures price of 88.40, as follows:

Go short June T-bills at	90.40	(Profit = 90.40 − 91.80 = −1.40)
Go long June Eurodollars at	88.40	(Profit = 90.65 − 88.40 = 2.25)
TED spread	= 2.00	(Profit = 2.25 − 1.40 = 0.85)

The investor's profit of 85 basis points is also equal to the change in the TED spread:

$$\text{Change in TED spread} = \text{Closing TED spread} - \text{Initial TED spread}$$
$$= 2.00 - 1.15$$
$$= 85 \text{ basis points.}$$

Since a one-basis-point movement in both the Eurodollar TD and T-bill futures contracts equals $25, his gain per contract is

---

[30] See Slentz [1987] for a discussion of this incident and its effect on the TED spread.

$$\text{Profit on TED spread per contract} = (\text{Change in TED spread})(\$25)$$
$$= (85)(\$25)$$
$$= \$2{,}125.$$

∎

An investor who expected the premium between Eurodollar TD and T-bill rates to fall would follow the opposite strategy of the investor in Example 5.15 and go short the TED spread.

Effect of Rising Interest Rates on the TED Spread   Investors with positions in TED spreads will be affected by rising interest rates as well as by changes in the Eurodollar TD risk premium, because the TED spreads overstate the risk premium more severely at higher interest rate levels. To see the effect of rising interest rates on the TED spread, we first show that the 90-day T-bill yields understate the bond equivalent yields (360-day basis) more sharply as interest rates increase:

T-Bill Yield	Bond Equivalent Yield
5.00%	5.06%
7.00	7.12
9.00	9.21
11.00	11.31
13.00	13.44

Now suppose the Eurodollar TD risk premium is fixed at 100 basis points over the T-bill rate. Then, if the T-bill yield is 5 percent, the Eurodollar TD rate will be $5.06\% + 1.00\% = 6.06\%$ and the quoted TED spread will be $6.06\% - 5.00\% = 106$ basis points. At a 13 percent T-bill yield, the quoted TED spread will be $14.44\% - 13.00\% = 144$ basis points. Thus, a long TED spread position will make a profit and a short TED spread position will lose money if T-bill yields rise, even if the risk premium remains constant.

Transmission of Interest Rate Changes between Markets   The TED spread can play a major role in transmitting changes in supply and demand for short-term borrowing between the Eurodollar TD and T-bill markets. From Equation 5.2, we know that when the markets are in equilibrium, the (Eurodollar or T-bill) rate, $r^t_{T,T+90}$, implied by the futures price is

$$1 + r^t_{T,T+90} = \frac{1 + r_{t,T+90}}{1 + r_{t,T}}. \tag{5.19}$$

```
t                          T                        T + 90
|--------------------------|------------------------|
```

Suppose there is an increase in the demand to hold short-term (t to T) Eurodollar TDs and a decrease in the demand to hold long-term Eurodollar TDs (t to T + 90), with no similar movement in the T-bill market. This demand change might be transferred into the T-bill market as follows:

1.   Pressure to hold short-term Eurodollar TDs will drive down the rate paid on short-term Eurodollar TDs, $r_{t,T}$, and drive up the rate paid on long-term Eurodollar TDs, $r_{t,T+90}$.

2.   As a result, the rate implied by the Eurodollar TD futures, $r^t_{T,T+90}$, will be lower than the equilibrium rate in Equation 5.19. The Eurodollar TD futures price therefore will be too high, and portfolio managers will respond by engaging in cash-and-carry quasi-arbitrages. They will replace Eurodollar TDs that extend from t to T with synthetic Eurodollar TDs over the same period that consist of Eurodollar TDs from t to T + 90 and short Eurodollar futures (as in Example 5.3). This will partially undo the movement into short-term TDs and drive down the Eurodollar futures price, thus increasing the implied $r^t_{T,T+90}$.

3.   If no change in the creditworthiness of the money center banks occurs, the increase in the T to T + 90 rate implied by the Eurodollar futures will make short TED spread positions attractive. Investors taking short TED spread positions will go short T-bill futures, driving down the T-bill futures price and boosting the rate implied by the T-bill futures for an investment between T and T + 90.

4.   The higher implied T-bill rate will make the T-bill futures price appear low to portfolio managers, and they will engage in reverse cash-and-carry quasi-arbitrages. They will sell T-bills that last from t to T + 90 and replace them with synthetic T-bills consisting of T-bills that last from t to T and long T-bill futures positions (as in Example 5.12). This will drive up the rate on T-bills that last from t to T + 90 and drive down the rate on T-bills that last from t to T.

The net result of these four steps will be the transfer of some of the demand to shorten the maturities of assets held in the Eurodollar TD market to the T-bill market. The futures markets, through quasi-arbitrage and the TED spread, will have played an integral part in this transmission of demand changes between markets.

Summary

Eurodollar and T-bill futures are very popular instruments for locking in short-term borrowing and lending rates. In this chapter, we saw that these contracts can be used for many different purposes. In one example, Eurodollar futures created a synthetic fixed-rate loan; we saw that both a bank and its borrowing customer can be protected from short-term interest rate movements by hedging with Eurodollar futures. We also saw how a stack hedge with Eurodollar futures can lock in interest rates on a longer-term loan. Finally, we learned how to shorten or lengthen Treasury bill maturities with T-bill futures.

Problems

1. Suppose an arbitrageur is considering a reverse cash-and-carry synthetic borrowing of $1 million between May 23, 1989, and June 19, 1989. On May 23, she observes that the June 19 Eurodollar TD futures price is 90.65. There is a 9.80 percent rate on a Eurodollar TD over the 117 days from May 23 through September 17, when a three-month time deposit entered into on June 19 would expire. The arbitrageur can borrow and lend at the current Eurodollar TD rates. (Assume that all funds are received immediately.)
    a.   Construct a strategy that will allow the arbitrageur to borrow synthetically between May 23 and June 19.
    b.   What rate will the arbitrageur pay on this synthetic borrowing?

◨ 2. Using Lotus, reproduce Table 5.3 and Figure 5.5. Redo both with the following replacement for part A:

   A: *Futures Prices and Spot Rates*

Date	Spot LIBOR	Futures Prices		
		IMM (T1)	IMM (T2)	IMM (T3)
9/15 (t)	8.00	91.75	91.60	91.45
12/15 (T1)	7.80	92.20	92.15	92.10
3/15 (T2)	7.60	—	92.40	92.05
6/15 (T3)	7.40	—	—	92.60

   a.   With the strip, how does the hedged result for the bank differ from the scenarios in Figure 5.3? Explain.
   b.   Did the strip or the stack perform better? Why? How do you explain the exact difference between them?

3. Suppose it is currently May 23, 1989, and you know your firm will need to borrow $100 million on June 19 until October 5. You can borrow at the prevailing 90-day LIBOR plus 150 basis points. The current June Eurodollar futures price is 90.65. (Assume that all funds are received immediately.)
    a.   Construct a hedge that will lock in your borrowing rate. What is the appropriate hedge ratio?
    b.   Suppose the 90-day LIBOR is either 7 percent or 10 percent on June 19. Show your net interest cost under both scenarios. Intuitively, why do you get this result?

4. Suppose you know you will need to borrow $10 million for 90 days 50 days from now. The rate at which you will borrow is closely tied to the LIBOR but is not perfectly correlated with it. In fact, the rate you will pay is the LIBOR plus either 90 or 110 basis points depending on market conditions, which you do not know today. The current futures price of the Eurodollar TD with expiration 50 days from now is 94.50. Analyze your net interest costs if you hedge your interest rate exposure by going short 10 Eurodollar TD contracts. Consider the two scenarios in which the LIBOR equals either 4 percent or 6 percent in 50 days. Ignore the fact that futures gains and losses come before the interest is paid. (Hint: If the LIBOR equals 4 percent, your

interest cost is either 4.90 or 5.10 percent. You need to analyze both cases. The same is true if the LIBOR equals 6 percent.)

Use Figures 5.2 and 5.7 to answer Problems 5 through 9:

5. Suppose it is currently May 23, 1989, and you wish to lend out funds until December 14 as of today. Compare the purchase of T-bills that expire on December 14 (at a discount yield of 8.22 percent) with a strategy that utilizes December T-bill futures. Which strategy is preferable? Construct a quasi-arbitrage table in making your choice.

6. Suppose it is currently May 23, 1989, and you wish to lend out funds until December 21 as of today. Compare the purchase of T-bills that expire on December 21 with a strategy that utilizes September T-bill futures. Which strategy is preferable? Construct a quasi-arbitrage table to make your decision.

7. Suppose that on May 23, 1989, a corporate treasurer is holding $250 million face value of T-bills that expire on April 12, 1990. He wishes to shorten the maturity of the investment to one that expires on September 21. How can he do this using September and December futures contracts? Assume the treasurer can lock in the yield implied by the futures even when the bill being hedged has a time to maturity other than 91 days.

8. Suppose you observe the following market prices on May 23, 1989:

T-bill discount yield ask on an August 31 T-bill	8.25%
T-bill discount yield bid on an August 31 T-bill	8.29%
Repo rate (applicable up to 14 days)	9.20%
Reverse repo rate (applicable up to 14 days)	8.40%
Round-trip transactions fees per contract	$25
Futures price for 3-month T-bill delivered June 1	91.80

   a. Is there an arbitrage opportunity? Answer this by finding no-arbitrage upper and lower bounds for the futures price. Assume that there is no bid-ask spread on the futures.
   b. What are the implied repo and implied reverse repo rates? How do these compare with the repo and reverse repo rates? Does this comparison also indicate an arbitrage opportunity?

9. Using Lotus, reproduce Table 5.8. Change the table so that the investment lasts until October 5, with a = 0.50%. Use Figure 5.7 to obtain the T-bill yield for a T-bill expiring on October 5.

Long-Term Interest Rate Futures

The most widely traded U.S. long-term interest rate futures contracts are the Chicago Board of Trade's contracts on U.S. government treasury bonds (T-bonds), U.S. government Treasury notes (T-notes), and municipal bonds (Munis).[1] These contracts were introduced in 1977, 1982, and 1985, respectively. The popularity of the T-bond and T-note contracts is due to the large size of the cash government debt market resulting from the massive deficits of the U.S. government in recent years.[2] Further, because T-bonds and T-notes are considered default-free investments, their yields are used as benchmark long-term interest rates to which other long-term rates are tied. T-bond and T-note futures thus are useful to investors in other long-term instruments.

The Muni futures contract is actively traded, because it is best suited to meet the hedging needs of investors in the large municipal bond market. Municipal bond yields behave quite differently than T-bond and T-note yields because of the bonds' tax-free status. As a result, T-bond and T-note futures do not provide good hedges for municipal bonds.

T-bond, T-note, and Muni futures are much more complicated instruments than the short-term interest rate futures contracts. They must adjust for the fact that long-term bonds pay coupons and are available in so many varieties. However, we can still apply our basic concepts of arbitrage and risk management to demonstrate how the long-term interest rate futures markets operate.

---

[1] Several other exchanges have T-bond and T-note contracts that are much less heavily traded. The MidAmerica Commodity Exchange trades a T-bond contract, and the New York Cotton Exchange trades a T-note contract. Both of these contracts were introduced in 1987. The London International Financial Futures Exchange also trades a U.S. T-bond contract. Futures trading in corporate bonds began in 1987 when the Commodity Exchange introduced a futures contract on the Moody's Corporate Bond Index.

[2] See Fabozzi [1988] for a discussion of the T-bond and T-note cash markets.

Treasury Bond and Treasury Note Cash Market

Treasury bonds and Treasury notes are long-term debt instruments issued by the U.S. government. Treasury bonds (T-bonds) have maturities of over 10 years and Treasury notes (T-notes) maturities of 10 years or less. Unlike T-bills, these long-term instruments pay coupons twice a year. Both T-bonds and T-notes are considered less subject to default than other long-term instruments because of their backing by the U.S. government.

T-bonds and T-notes are identical except for the difference in maturity. Our discussion from this point on will focus primarily on the T-bond markets. But unless specifically stated otherwise, all of the following explanation of T-bonds also applies to T-notes.

Figure 6.1 presents spot and futures T-bond and T-note transactions for May 23, 1989, from *The Wall Street Journal*. Consider the 9 percent November 2018 T-bond. That rate is the rate of the coupon payment, not the rate earned on the bond. The bond will pay coupons of $4.50 per $100 face value on November 15 and May 15 of each year until it matures on November 15, 2018. At maturity, the holder of the bond will receive $100 in principal and the last $4.50 coupon payment. Thus, a T-bond is like a combination of two securities, one an annuity and the other a discount bond. The annuity pays out the stream of coupons, and the discount bond pays out the face value of the bond at maturity. Trading in T-bonds is on a next-day settlement basis. Thus, the price on a given day is for delivery the next day.

Some bonds are **callable**, meaning that the U.S. government can retire them early by paying their face value to the bondholders. For example, in Figure 6.1 there is a February 7⅝ percent bond with an expiration given by 2002-07. This means that the first call date is February 15, 2002, and the bond expires on February 15, 2007. The U.S. government has not been issuing callable bonds in recent years.

T-Bond Yields, Pricing, and Quoting Conventions

The rate of return earned on a T-bond is computed as the **yield to maturity**, which is the internal rate of return on an investment in the bond. By convention, this internal rate of return is figured on a semiannual basis and annualized by multiplying by 2. The relationship between a T-bond's yield to maturity and its market price (per $1 face value) is[3]

$$P_t = \left[\sum_{k=1}^{N} \frac{C/2}{(1 + r/2)^{(k-1)+(tc/B)}} \right] + \left[\frac{1}{(1 + r/2)^{(N-1)+(tc/B)}} \right] \qquad (6.1)$$

= Present value (coupon annuity) + Present value (face),

---

[3] See Stigum [1983] for a detailed discussion of this formula.

Figure 6.1 Spot and Futures T-Bond and T-Note Transactions for May 23, 1989

Tuesday, May 23, 1989

Representative Over-the-Counter quotations based on transactions of $1 million or more as of 4 p.m. Eastern time.

Hyphens in bid-and-asked and bid changes represent 32nds; 101-01 means 101 1/32. a-Plus 1/64. b-Yield to call date. d-Minus 1/64. k-Nonresident aliens exempt from withholding taxes. n-Treasury notes. p-Treasury note; nonresident aliens exempt from withholding taxes.

Source: Bloomberg Financial Markets

TREASURY BONDS AND NOTES

Rate	Mat. Date	Bid	Asked	Bid Chg.	Yld.
8	1989 May p	99-30	100-01	....	6.14
7⅜	1989 Jun p	99-25	99-28	....	8.36
9⅝	1989 Jun p	100	100-03	– 01	8.38
7⅝	1989 Jul p	99-22	99-25	....	8.60
14½	1989 Jul n	100-23	100-26	– 01	8.34
7¾	1989 Aug p	99-19	99-22	....	8.78
6⅝	1989 Aug p	99-13	99-16	....	8.69
13⅞	1989 Aug n	101	101-03	– 01	8.68
8½	1989 Sep k	99-22	99-25	....	9.03
9⅜	1989 Sep p	100	100-03	....	8.98
11⅞	1989 Oct n	101	101-03	....	8.89
7⅞	1989 Oct p	99-15	99-18	....	8.87
6⅜	1989 Nov p	98-24	98-28	....	8.83
10¾	1989 Nov n	100-23	100-27	– 01	8.88
12¾	1989 Nov p	101-23	101-27	....	8.69
7¾	1989 Nov p	99-11	99-15	+ 01	8.81
7⅞	1989 Dec p	99-07	99-11	....	8.99
8⅜	1989 Dec p	99-16	99-20	– 01	9.00
7⅜	1990 Jan k	98-28	99	+ 01	8.88
10½	1990 Jan n	100-25	100-29	– 01	8.98
3½	1990 Feb	95-15	96-01	....	9.24
6½	1990 Feb k	98-06	98-10	....	8.92
7⅛	1990 Feb k	98-18	98-22	....	8.90
11	1990 Feb p	101-09	101-13	....	8.92
7¼	1990 Mar p	98-15	98-19	....	8.98
7⅜	1990 Mar p	98-19	98-23	+ 01	8.95
10½	1990 Apr n	101-06	101-10	....	8.92
7⅝	1990 Apr p	98-23	98-27	....	8.93
7⅞	1990 May k	98-29	99-01	....	8.93
8¼	1990 May	99-16	99-22	+ 02	8.59
8⅛	1990 May p	99-04	99-08	....	8.91
11⅜	1990 May p	102-03	102-07	+ 02	8.94
7¼	1990 Jun p	98-05	98-09	+ 02	8.91
8	1990 Jun p	98-29	99-01	+ 01	8.93
10¾	1990 Jul n	101-25	101-29	+ 02	8.94
8⅜	1990 Jul p	99-09	99-13	....	8.89
7⅞	1990 Aug k	98-22	98-26	....	8.90
9⅞	1990 Aug p	100-31	101-03	....	8.89
10¾	1990 Aug n	101-30	102-02	+ 02	8.92
8⅝	1990 Aug	99-18	99-22	+ 02	8.87
6¾	1990 Sep p	97-04	97-08	....	8.94
8½	1990 Sep p	99-11	99-15	+ 01	8.91
11½	1990 Oct n	103-05	103-09	+ 01	8.93
8¼	1990 Oct p	99-01	99-05	– 04	8.88
8	1990 Nov p	98-21	98-25	– 01	8.90
9⅝	1990 Nov k	100-28	101	....	8.88
13	1990 Nov n	105-14	105-18	– 01	8.89
8⅞	1990 Nov p	99-28	100	....	8.87
6⅝	1990 Dec p	96-19	96-23	....	8.86
9⅛	1990 Dec p	100-08	100-12	– 01	8.86
9	1991 Jan p	100-03	100-07	....	8.84
11¾	1991 Jan n	104-06	104-10	– 02	8.86
7⅜	1991 Feb p	97-18	97-22	+ 02	8.83
9⅛	1991 Feb k	100-10	100-14	– 03	8.83
9⅜	1991 Feb p	100-23	100-27	....	8.83
6¾	1991 Mar p	96-12	96-16	+ 01	8.83
9¾	1991 Mar p	101-11	101-15	– 01	8.86
9¼	1991 Apr p	100-21	100-25	– 01	8.80
12⅜	1991 Apr n	105-26	105-30	....	8.89
8⅛	1991 May p	98-20	98-24	– 01	8.83
14½	1991 May n	110-19	110-23	– 06	8.49
7⅞	1991 Jun n	98-05	98-09	+ 01	8.78
13¾	1991 Jul n	109-06	109-10	– 03	8.87
7½	1991 Aug p	97-09	97-13	+ 01	8.80
8¾	1991 Aug p	99-23	99-27	....	8.82
14⅞	1991 Aug n	112-13	112-17	– 01	8.56
9⅛	1991 Sep k	100-17	100-21	+ 01	8.80
12¼	1991 Oct p	107-02	107-06	– 02	8.84
6½	1991 Nov p	94-26	94-30	+ 01	8.82
8½	1991 Nov p	99-07	99-11	....	8.80
14¼	1991 Nov n	112-11	112-15	+ 01	8.55
8¼	1991 Dec k	98-19	98-23	– 02	8.81
11⅝	1992 Jan p	106-09	106-13	+ 01	8.84
6⅝	1992 Feb p	94-22	94-26	....	8.80
9⅛	1992 Feb p	100-23	100-27	+ 01	8.76
14⅝	1992 Feb n	114-13	114-17	+ 01	8.53
7⅞	1992 Mar p	97-21	97-25	....	8.76
11¾	1992 Apr	107-07	107-11	....	8.81
6⅝	1992 May k	94-12	94-16	+ 03	8.76
9	1992 May p	100-18	100-22	+ 01	8.73
13¾	1992 May n	112-17	112-21	+ 02	8.82
8¼	1992 Jun p	98-13	98-17	+ 01	8.80
10⅜	1992 Jul p	104-01	104-05	....	8.82
4¼	1987-92 Aug	96-28	97-14	+ 01	5.12
7¼	1992 Aug	95-20	95-24	+ 01	8.78
8¼	1992 Aug p	98-13	98-17	+ 04	8.77
8¾	1992 Sep p	99-26	99-30	+ 02	8.77
9¾	1992 Oct p	102-21	102-25	+ 01	8.78
8⅜	1992 Nov p	98-21	98-25	+ 01	8.79
10½	1992 Nov n	104-30	105-02	+ 01	8.78
9⅛	1992 Dec p	100-30	101-02	....	8.77
8¾	1993 Jan p	99-25	99-29	+ 01	8.77
4	1988-93 Feb	97-02	97-16	+ 01	4.74
6¾	1993 Feb	93-24	94-10	+ 01	8.56
7⅞	1993 Feb	97-02	97-07	+ 01	8.76
8¼	1993 Feb p	98-09	98-13	+ 03	8.75
10⅞	1993 Feb n	106-12	106-16	+ 01	8.78
9⅝	1993 Mar p	102-27	102-31	+ 01	8.70
7⅜	1993 Apr p	95-10	95-14	+ 01	8.78
7⅝	1993 May	96-03	96-07	+ 01	8.77
10⅛	1993 May n	104-09	104-13	+ 04	8.79
7¼	1993 Jul p	94-22	94-26	+ 02	8.77
7½	1988-93 Aug	95-18	95-22	....	8.74
8⅝	1993 Aug	99-19	99-23	+ 09	8.70
8¾	1993 Aug p	99-28	100	– 01	8.74
11⅞	1993 Aug n	110-10	110-14	....	8.85
7⅛	1993 Oct p	93-28	94	– 03	8.80
8⅝	1993 Nov	99-19	99-25	– 01	8.68
11¾	1993 Nov n	110-15	110-19	– 05	8.83
9	1993 Nov p	100-28	101	– 03	8.72
7	1994 Jan p	93-08	93-12	– 01	8.76
9	1994 Feb	101-19	101-23	– 08	8.54
8⅞	1994 Feb p	100-15	100-19	– 01	8.70
7	1994 Apr p	93	93-04	– 02	8.75
4⅛	1989-94 May	97-19	98-05	– 01	4.54
13⅛	1994 May p	117	117-04	– 01	8.80
9½	1994 May p	103-02	103-06	– 01	8.68
8	1994 Jul n	96-26	96-30	+ 01	8.75
8¾	1994 Aug	100-17	100-25	– 01	8.56
12⅝	1994 Aug p	115-24	115-28	– 01	8.77
9½	1994 Oct p	103-03	103-07	– 01	8.73
10⅛	1994 Nov	105-24	105-28	– 01	8.75
11⅝	1994 Nov	112-02	112-06	– 03	8.77
8⅝	1995 Jan p	99-14	99-18	+ 01	8.72
3	1995 Feb	98-05	98-23	– 01	3.25
10½	1995 Feb	107-21	107-25	– 01	8.74
11¼	1995 Feb p	110-29	111-01	– 02	8.75
8⅜	1995 Apr p	98-13	98-17	....	8.70
10⅜	1995 May	107-22	107-26	....	8.67
11¼	1995 May p	111-17	111-21	....	8.71
12⅝	1995 May	118-09	118-15	....	8.61
8⅞	1995 Jul p	100-25	100-29	– 02	8.68
10½	1995 Aug p	108-11	108-15	....	8.70
8⅝	1995 Oct p	99-14	99-18	– 03	8.71
9½	1995 Nov p	103-23	103-27	– 04	8.71
11½	1995 Nov	113-15	113-19	....	8.71
9¼	1996 Jan	102-24	102-28	– 03	8.67
8⅞	1996 Feb p	100-26	100-30	– 03	8.68
9⅜	1996 Apr p	103-22	103-26	– 03	8.63
7⅜	1996 May p	93	93-04	– 04	8.71
7¼	1996 Nov p	92-01	92-05	– 03	8.70
8⅝	1997 Aug k	99-13	99-17	– 05	8.70
8½	1997 May k	98-25	98-29	– 02	8.69
8⅞	1997 Nov p	100-29	101-01	– 08	8.70
8⅛	1998 Feb p	96-19	96-23	– 07	8.66
9	1998 May p	102-04	102-08	– 05	8.63
9¼	1998 Aug p	103-17	103-21	– 09	8.66
7	1993-98 May	90-30	91-02	– 04	8.44
3½	1998 Nov	99-24	100-10	+ 04	3.46
8⅞	1998 Nov p	101-11	101-15	– 04	8.64
8⅞	1999 Feb p	101-14	101-18	– 06	8.63
8½	1994-99 May	98-26	98-30	– 06	8.66
9⅛	1999 May p	103-13	103-17	– 06	8.59
7⅞	1995-00 Feb	94-09	94-13	– 08	8.68
8⅜	1995-00 Aug	97-19	97-23	– 10	8.69
11¾	2001 Feb	122-01	122-07	+ 04	8.69
13⅛	2001 May	132-06	132-12	+ 07	8.72
8	1996-01 Aug	95-03	95-09	– 05	8.63
13⅜	2001 Aug	134-05	134-11	– 05	8.74
15¾	2001 Nov	153-12	153-18	– 05	8.65
14¼	2002 Feb	142-05	142-11	– 09	8.68
11⅝	2002 Nov	122-14	122-20	– 06	8.74
10¾	2003 Feb	115-23	115-29	– 05	8.74
10¾	2003 May	115-29	116-03	– 02	8.73
11⅛	2003 Aug	118-30	119-04	– 04	8.75
11⅞	2003 Nov	125-08	125-14	– 01	8.74
12⅜	2004 May	129-19	129-25	– 05	8.77
13¾	2004 Aug	141-08	141-14	– 05	8.76
11⅝	2004 Nov k	123-30	124-04	+ 01	8.75
8¼	2000-05 May	96-05	96-11	– 05	8.68
12	2005 May k	127-17	127-23	– 02	8.75
10¾	2005 Aug k	117	117-06	– 11	8.74
9⅜	2006 Feb k	106-01	106-07	– 09	8.66
7⅝	2002-07 Feb	90-11	90-17	– 05	8.68
7⅞	2002-07 Nov	92-13	92-19	– 07	8.69
8⅜	2003-08 Aug	96-25	96-31	– 07	8.70
8¾	2003-08 Nov	100-07	100-13	– 06	8.70
9⅛	2004-09 May	103-09	103-15	– 18	8.71
10⅜	2004-09 Nov	113-01	113-07	– 02	8.79
11¾	2005-10 Feb	124-13	124-19	– 12	8.82
10	2005-10 May	110-06	110-12	– 03	8.78
12¾	2005-10 Nov	133-17	133-23	– 12	8.83
13⅞	2006-11 May	144-02	144-08	– 03	8.80
14	2006-11 Nov	145-17	145-23	– 08	8.82
10⅜	2007-12 Nov	113-29	114-03	– 12	8.82
12	2008-13 Aug	128-29	129-03	– 09	8.83
13¼	2009-14 May	141-02	141-08	– 07	8.82
12½	2009-14 Aug k	134-08	134-14	– 06	8.82
11¾	2009-14 Nov k	127-31	128-05	– 12	8.77
11¼	2015 Feb k	125-31	126-05	– 09	8.69
10⅝	2015 Aug k	119-28	120-02	– 10	8.67
9⅞	2015 Nov k	112-08	112-14	– 07	8.67
9¼	2016 Feb k	105-27	106-01	– 16	8.66
7¼	2016 May k	85-10	85-14	– 10	8.65
7½	2016 Nov k	87-26	87-30	– 14	8.66
8¾	2017 May k	100-29	101-01	– 08	8.65
8⅞	2017 Aug k	102-09	102-13	– 07	8.64
9⅛	2018 May k	104-31	105-03	– 07	8.64
9	2018 Nov k	103-24	103-28	– 03	8.63
8⅞	2019 Feb k	102-20	102-24	– 07	8.61

	Open	High	Low	Settle	Chg	Yield Settle	Yield Chg	Open Interest
TREASURY BONDS (CBT)—$100,000; pts. 32nds of 100%								
June	93-02	93-15	92-19	92-27	– 10	8.765	+ .035	201,176
Sept	92-31	93-09	92-15	92-23	– 9	8.779	+ .032	95,031
Dec	92-25	93-04	92-12	92-18	– 10	8.797	+ .036	19,538
Mr90	92-21	92-28	92-09	92-14	– 9	8.811	+ .032	6,693
June	92-22	92-22	92-04	92-10	– 8	8.825	+ .028	4,346
Sept	92-15	92-15	91-31	92-05	– 8	8.843	+ .029	1,999
Dec	....	....	....	92-00	– 7	8.861	+ .025	266
Mr91	....	....	....	91-26	– 7	8.882	+ .025	160
June	....	....	....	91-20	– 7	8.904	+ .025	206
Est vol 300,000; vol Mon 371,102; op Int 329,435, –6,668.								
TREASURY BONDS (MCE)—$50,000; pts. 32nds of 100%								
June	93-10	93-10	92-19	92-27	– 10	8.765	+ .035	6,649
Sept	93-05	93-05	92-16	92-23	– 9	8.779	+ .032	793
Est vol 4,200; vol Mon 4,473; open Int 7,508, –172.								
T–BONDS (LIFFE) U.S. $100,000; pts of 100%								
June	93-23	93-23	92-20	92-26	– 0-07	93-23	86-10	10,845
Sept	93-11	93-11	92-18	92-21	– 0-07	93-11	92-18	135
Est vol 10,580; vol Mon 16,281; open Int 10,980, +3,106.								
TREASURY NOTES (CBT)—$100,000; pts. 32nds of 100%								
June	96-03	96-11	95-25	95-30	– 8	8.614	+ .039	66,764
Sept	96-07	96-13	95-29	96-02	– 7	8.595	+ .034	23,901
Dec	....	....	....	96-02	– 7	8.595	+ .034	676
Est vol 24,000; vol Mon 29,063; open Int 91,342, +3,032.								
5 YR TREAS NOTES (CBT) $100,000; pts. 32 of 100%								
June	97-16	97-165	97-08	97-125	– 0.5	8.65	....	39,618
Sept	97-20	97-21	97-12	97-165	– 0.5	8.62	....	7,622
Est vol 9,000; vol Mon 8,113; open Int 47,242, –327.								
5 YR TREAS NOTES (FINEX) $100,000; pts. 32 of 100%								
June	97-14	97-14	97-06	97-095	– 1.0	8.68	+ .01	18,047
Sept	97-165	97-165	97-11	97-13	– 1.0	8.65	+ .01	183
Est vol 1,500; vol Mon 1,978; open Int 18,230, +855.								

Source: *The Wall Street Journal*, May 24, 1989.

where

r   = annualized yield to maturity

C = coupon rate

N = number of remaining semiannual coupons

tc = number of days until the next coupon

B = number of days between the most recent coupon and the next coupon as shown in the following time line:

Thus, just after a coupon payment, tc = B.

The convention on callable bonds is that their price or yield to maturity is determined assuming they are called on the earliest possible call date.

Another T-bond market convention is that the *quoted prices* are not the actual prices at which the bonds are traded. When a T-bond changes hands, the transaction price set by the buyer and seller compensates the seller for the fractional coupon earned, but not received, since the most recent coupon payment. This portion of the next coupon is called the **accrued interest** on the bond. Quoted T-bond prices differ from market prices, because they do not include accrued interest.

The accrued interest on a T-bond is computed as

Accrued interest   **(6.2)**

$$= \left(\frac{\text{Number of days since last coupon}}{B} \right) (\text{Semiannual coupon})$$

$$= \left(\frac{B - tc}{B} \right) (\text{Semiannual coupon}).$$

The T-bond transaction price is

$$P_t = \text{Quoted price} + \text{Accrued interest}. \qquad \textbf{(6.3)}$$

Example 6.1 shows how to calculate the quoted price, the transaction price, and the yield to maturity on an actual T-bond.

▪ **Example 6.1: T-Bond Quotation Conventions**   Consider the 9 percent November 2018 T-bond in Figure 6.1 that pays $4.50 per $100 face value on November 15 and May 15 of each year. Since T-bonds are settled the following day, the bond will actually be delivered on May 24, 1989. On that date, this T-bond is 9 days into its current coupon period and has 175 days remaining until the next coupon payment:

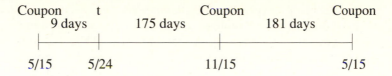

Thus, B = 184 days and tc = 175 days.

The May 23, 1989, quoted (ask) price for this bond is $103-28. The first figure in a T-bond or T-note price quotation is in dollars, and the second figure gives points out of 32. Thus, the $103-28 quoted price represents $103 plus 28/32 of a dollar. In *decimal* form, the price is $103.875.

The quoted price of this T-bond does *not* mean that one can buy a $100,000-face-value bond for $103,875; rather, the bond buyer must compensate the seller for the nine days of accrued interest the seller will forgo by giving up the bond on May 24:

$$\text{Accrued interest} = \left(\frac{9 \text{ days}}{184 \text{ days}}\right)(\$4.50)$$

$$= \$0.220 \text{ per } \$100 \text{ par value.}$$

The transaction price of this bond is therefore

$$P_t = \$103.875 + \$0.220 = \$104.095 \text{ per } \$100 \text{ par,}$$

or $104,095 per $100,000 face value.

The yield to maturity on this bond is derived by solving for r in Equation 6.1. In this case, the yield to maturity is 8.63 percent. ∎

Duration

In Chapter 5, we saw that the sensitivity of a T-bill's price to changes in T-bill yields depends solely on the length of time until the bill matures. Thus, to hedge a T-bill price with 13-week T-bill futures, we simply use the ratio of the bill's maturity to 90 days as the hedge ratio.

In this chapter, we wish to measure the sensitivity of bond prices to interest rate changes so that we can derive hedge ratios that can lock in bond prices with T-bond futures. However, price volatility is less easily measured for bonds than for bills, because bonds derive their value from coupons as well as from the length of time until maturity. The effect of interest rate changes on a bond's price depends on how the bond's coupon and face value payouts are distributed over time. Bonds with low coupon rates and long maturities will be most heavily affected by interest rate changes. Since a greater portion of their payouts comes in the distant future, the compounding effect of an interest rate change on the payouts' present value has more time to take place. Bonds with high coupons and short maturities will be least affected by interest rate changes, because a greater portion of their payouts comes early in time.

To compare the price volatility of different bonds, we use a measure, called **duration**, that collapses a bond's coupon and maturity characteristics into a single number. The duration of a bond is a weighted average of the maturities of the bond's coupon and face value cash flows. The weights are the fractions of the bond's price contributed by each cash flow. The duration is defined as[4]

$$
D(C,N) = \frac{\displaystyle\sum_{k=1}^{N} \frac{(C/2)[(k-1)+(tc/B)]}{(1+r/2)^{(k-1)+(tc/B)}} + \frac{(N-1)+(tc/B)}{(1+r/2)^{(N-1)+(tc/B)}}}{P_t}
\tag{6.4}
$$

where P_t is the market price of the bond per \$1 face value and the remaining notation is the same as in Equation 6.1.

To see how the duration weights the maturity of each cash flow, consider the first coupon payment received after tc days. The maturity of this coupon is tc/B of a full coupon period. The contribution of this first coupon to the duration measure can be written as

$$
\left[\frac{tc}{B}\right]\left[\frac{\frac{C/2}{(1+r/2)^{tc/B}}}{P_t}\right].
$$

Likewise, the second coupon has a maturity of $1 + tc/B$, and its contribution to the duration measure is

$$
\left[1+\frac{tc}{B}\right]\left[\frac{\frac{C/2}{(1+r/2)^{1+tc/B}}}{P_t}\right].
$$

In both these cases, the length of time until the coupon is paid is weighted in the duration measure by the contribution of the coupon payment to the price of the bond. This is true for every coupon payment and for the final payment of the bond's face value.

The duration is higher for bonds that receive more of their value from payments made in the distant future, for in such cases the payments with the greatest maturities have the highest weights. Bonds with low coupons or long maturities fall into this category and so have high duration measures. Bonds with high coupons and short maturities receive a greater portion of their value from near-term payments, so their durations are low. Thus, the duration measure indicates how susceptible a bond's value is to interest rate changes. In the extreme case of a discount bond such as a T-bill, the duration is equal to the maturity of the bond, because the only cash flow occurs at maturity.

---

[4] There are several different measures of duration. We use McCauley's duration, which assumes a flat term structure. For alternative measures that allow for other than flat term structures, see Bierwag [1987].

Example 6.2 demonstrates how duration incorporates both the maturity and the coupon of a two-year T-note.

▪ **Example 6.2: Computing the Duration of a T-Note**   Suppose we wish to compute the duration of a 6 percent, two-year T-note with a yield to maturity of 9 percent. Suppose also that this note has just paid a coupon and thus has four coupon payments remaining. The time remaining until the next coupon, tc, is six months—exactly equal to B, the time between the previous coupon and the next coupon. The transaction price of the note is $94.619 per $100 face value. We can calculate the duration as follows:

Number of Periods to Maturity	Cash Flow per $100 Face Value	Present Value of Cash Flow	Duration Weight	Periods × Duration Weight
1	$ 3	$ 2.871	0.0303	0.0303
2	3	2.747	0.0290	0.0580
3	3	2.629	0.0278	0.0834
4	3	2.516	0.0266	0.1064
4	100	83.856	0.8862	3.5448
Duration				3.8229

Since the coupon periods are six months long, this duration is expressed in terms of six-month periods. On an annual basis, the duration is $3.82/2 = 1.91$ years. The duration is close to the maturity of the note because most of the payments on the note come from the face value at maturity. ▪

Now that we know how to calculate the duration of a single bond, we can easily compute the duration of an entire portfolio of bonds. We simply sum the durations of all the bonds in the portfolio weighted by their shares of the portfolio's market value:

$$D_p = \sum_{i=1}^{M} p_i D_i, \qquad\qquad (6.5)$$

where

D_i = duration of a given bond i in the portfolio

p_i = proportion of the portfolio invested in bond i (at market values)

D_p = duration of the portfolio

In Example 6.3, we compute the duration of a portfolio that consists of two T-bonds.

▪ **Example 6.3: Computing the Duration of a Portfolio**   Suppose we wish to compute the duration of a portfolio that consists of 5 percent, 15-year T-bonds with a face value of $100 million and 15 percent, 30-year T-bonds with a face value of $200 million. The current yield to maturity is 6 percent. At this yield, the 5 percent bonds are worth $90.200 per $100 face value and the 15 percent bonds $224.540 per $100 face value.

First, we compute the durations of the individual bonds:

Bond	Market Price	Duration	Percentage of Portfolio
5%, 15-year	(0.9020)($100 million) = $ 90.2 million	10.4677	0.1673
15%, 30-year	(2.2454)($200 million) = $449.1 million	12.4674	0.8327
Sum	$539.3 million		

The duration of the entire portfolio is the market value weighted average of the individual bond durations:

$$\text{Portfolio duration} = D_p = (0.1673)(10.4677) + (0.8327)(12.4674)$$
$$= 12.1329.$$

Only weights based on market value can give an accurate measure of the portfolio's duration. Our results would have been very different had we used face value or book value weights to calculate the portfolio duration. ∎

Duration gives a convenient measure of the "weighted-average" maturity of a bond or portfolio. The durations of the bonds in Example 6.3 show the importance of accounting for both the coupon and the maturity, for the durations of the 5 percent, 15-year bond and the 15 percent, 30-year bond differ only by two years, even though the bonds' maturities differ by 15 years. This is because the higher 15 percent coupon on the 30-year bond causes a greater proportion of cash flows to come early in the bond's life than is the case with the 5 percent coupon on the 15-year bond.

The duration of a bond or bond portfolio measures the effect of changes in yields to maturity on the price of the bond, as Equation 6.6 demonstrates:[5]

$$D = -\frac{(1 + r)(\Delta P/P)}{\Delta r} \tag{6.6}$$

$$= -(1 + \text{Yield})\left(\frac{\text{Percentage change in price}}{\text{Change in yield}}\right).$$

Thus, coupon bonds with longer durations, like T-bills with longer maturities, are more price sensitive to changes in yields.

In the following sections, we will see how the duration measure is used to calculate hedge ratios for hedging T-bond portfolios.

---

[5] This formula comes from taking the derivative of Equation 6.1. It is literally true only when the change in the yield to maturity, Δr, is extremely small. However, we will see later that the formula works quite well even for relatively large changes in yields.

Figure 6.2 T-Bond and T-Note Futures, Annual Volume, 1983–1989

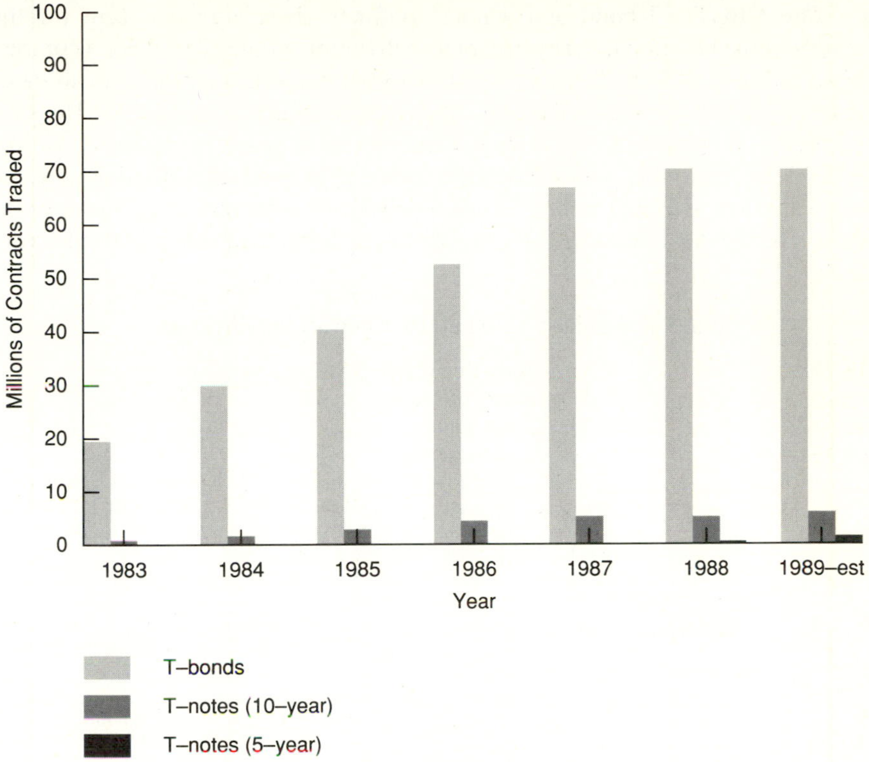

Source: Futures Industry Association.

Repurchase Agreement Markets

The repurchase agreements used in the T-bond and T-note markets are very similar to the T-bill repos we discussed in Chapter 5. The "haircut," or margin, required on T-bond or T-note repos may be higher than on T-bill repos, because the longer durations of bonds and notes make them more volatile. The bond market value, which determines how much one can borrow with a repurchase agreement, includes accrued interest as well as the quoted bond price.

Treasury Bond and Treasury Note Futures

The Chicago Board of Trade's futures contracts on T-bonds and T-notes are among the most successful futures contracts in the world today. Figure 6.2 shows the yearly volume of trading in these contracts from 1983 to 1989.[6] In 1988, the T-bond contract had the highest trading volume of any futures contract in the United States.

The CBOT's T-bond and T-note contracts are identical except for the maturity of the instruments they accept as deliverable grade. The T-bond contract accepts delivery of U.S. Treasury securities with maturities or earliest call dates at least 15 years in the future. The two T-note futures contracts accept U.S. Treasury securities with maturities of $4\frac{1}{4}$ to $5\frac{1}{4}$ and $6\frac{1}{2}$ to 10 years, respectively. Unlike the T-bill futures contract, which specifies delivery at contract expiration only, the T-bond and T-note futures contracts allow delivery at any time during the delivery month. The last day of trading is the eighth-to-the-last business day of the delivery month.

U.S. T-Bond and T-Note Futures Contract Specifications

Contract:	U.S. Treasury Bonds and U.S. Treasury Notes
Exchange:	Chicago Board of Trade
Quantity:	$100,000 face value
Delivery months:	March, June, September, December
Delivery specifications:	For the T-bond contract: delivery of U.S. T-bonds with maturity of at least 15 years if not callable and, if callable, with a first call date no earlier than 15 years from the first day of the delivery month; the last day of trading is the eighth to last business day of the delivery month; delivery can be during any business day of the delivery month
	For the 10-year T-note contract: delivery of U.S. T-notes with maturity of $6\frac{1}{2}$ to 10 years from the first day of the delivery month
	For the 5-year T-note contract: delivery of U.S. T-notes with maturity of $4\frac{1}{4}$ to $5\frac{1}{4}$ years from the first day of the delivery month
Minimum price movement:	$\frac{1}{32}$ points, or $31.25 per contract

Because T-bond and T-note futures are so similar, we will follow the example of the previous section and focus our discussion on the T-bond futures contract unless indicated otherwise. As before, the material that follows applies to T-notes as well as T-bonds.

The Delivery Sequence

As with all futures contracts, the party who holds the short position in a T-bond contract initiates delivery. The short can choose which bond to deliver and when to deliver it during the delivery month. The day he or she declares intention to deliver is called the *position day.* The short party can notify the exchange of the intention up until 8 p.m. on the position day even though the market closes at 2 p.m. On the (next) notice day, the clearinghouse matches the short with the long party who has the longest outstanding position and notifies the long that delivery will occur on the next day. The short party has until 5 p.m. on the notice day to state

---

[6] Because the five-year T-note contract is so new, Figure 6.2 shows only two years' worth of volume data.

which bond he or she intends to deliver.[7] On the delivery day, the short delivers the T-bond by wire transfer to the long, and the long makes payment to the short. The short has until 10 a.m. to make the delivery. The price the long pays to the short is determined by the settlement price on the position day.

Multiple Deliverable Grades

The multiple-deliverable-grade feature of the T-bond futures contract allows delivery of bonds with a range of coupons and maturity dates and, consequently, very different market values. Therefore, like the gold contract in Chapter 1, the T-bond contract specifies conversion factors that adjust the invoice price so that the price the short receives for delivering a more valuable bond is higher than the price he or she receives for a less valuable bond. Table 6.1 lists the 29 T-bonds that were eligible for delivery into the March 1989 T-bond futures contract, along with their conversion factors.

The invoice price received for delivering a given bond is computed as

Invoice price   **(6.7)**
= Invoice principal amount
+ Accrued interest on the delivered bond,

where

Invoice Principal Amount   **(6.8)**
= (Conversion Factor)(Decimal Futures Settlement Price)($100,000).

The **decimal futures settlement price** is the quoted futures price expressed in decimal form as a price per $1 face value. A quoted futures price of $88-10 (88 plus $10/32$s of a point) becomes a decimal futures settlement price of $0.883125 per $1 face. The accrued interest is computed as of the date the bond is delivered. Example 6.4 demonstrates how to determine the invoice price.

▪ **Example 6.4:   Determining the Invoice Price for a T-Bond**   Suppose that in March 1989, an investor is holding a short T-bond futures contract that expires in March 1989. He decides to deliver into the contract on March 9. He announces his intention to deliver on March 7, when the futures settlement price is $88-10. He chooses a $7\frac{1}{4}$ percent T-bond that expires on May 15, 2016, for the delivery. Table 6.1 shows that the conversion factor for this bond is 0.9175.

To determine the invoice price the short will receive, we must first calculate the accrued interest on the bond. The following time line shows that this bond has earned accrued interest over 114 days since the most recent coupon, on November 15, 1988:

---

[7] On the last notice day of the month, the short party must state which bond he or she intends to deliver by 3 p.m.

Table 6.1 Deliverable T-Bonds, March and June 1989

Coupon	Month	Year	March Conversion Factor	June Conversion Factor
7¼%	May	2016	0.9175	0.9176
7½	November	2016	0.9447	0.9447
8¾	May	2017	1.0833	1.0829
8⅞	August	2017	1.0972	1.0972
8⅞	February	2019	1.0986	1.0986
9	November	2018	1.1126	1.1122
9⅛	May	2004-09	1.0973	—
9⅛	May	2018	1.1262	1.1257
9¼	February	2016	1.1369	1.1367
9⅜	February	2006	1.1255	1.1248
9⅞	November	2015	1.2051	1.2042
10	May	2005-10	1.1787	1.1771
10⅜	November	2004-09	1.2089	1.2069
10⅜	November	2007-12	1.2273	1.2257
10⅝	August	2015	1.2860	1.2854
10¾	August	2005	1.2474	1.2458
11¼	February	2015	1.3521	1.3513
11⅝	November	2004	1.3188	1.3158
11¾	February	2005-10	1.3322	1.3298
11¾	November	2009-14	1.3749	1.3727
12	May	2005	1.3575	1.3544
12	August	2008-13	1.3893	1.3874
12⅜	May	2004	1.3783	—
12½	August	2009-14	1.4473	1.4453
12¾	November	2005-10	1.4310	1.4275
13¼	May	2009-14	1.5196	1.5165
13¾	August	2004	1.5011	1.4971
13⅞	May	2006-11	1.5408	1.5367
14	November	2006-11	1.5599	1.5558

Note: All bonds expire on the 15th of the month.

Source: Chicago Board of Trade.

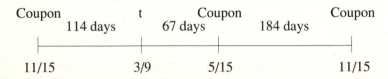

The 7¼ percent coupon rate implies an annual payment of $7,250 per $100,000 face value and, therefore, a $3,625 semiannual coupon. Thus, accrued interest is

$$\text{Accrued interest} = \left(\frac{114}{181}\right)(\$3,625)$$

$$= \$2,283.$$

Earlier we saw that the relevant decimal futures settlement price is 0.883125. Equation 6.8 shows that the invoice principal amount is

Invoice principal amount = (0.9175)(0.883125)($100,000)
= $81,027,

so the invoice price is

Invoice price = $81,027 + $2,283
= $83,310.

■

The conversion factors specified by the T-bond futures contract for bonds of different grades are simply the prices, per $1 face value, those bonds would have if the market yield to maturity were 8 percent. They are computed by using Equation 6.1 to discount the future cash flows of each bond by an 8 percent annual rate.[8]

Table 6.1 also shows that for bonds with similar maturities, the conversion factors are higher the higher the coupon rates. For example, the 11⅝ percent November 2004 bond has a conversion factor of 1.3188, while the 13¾ percent August 2004 bond has a conversion factor of 1.5011. Holding constant the maturity, a higher coupon always adds more value to a bond than does a lower coupon. Therefore, the invoice price on a bond with a high coupon must be adjusted such that it is higher than that on a bond with a low coupon. This is the function of the conversion factors.

For bonds with the same coupon, the effect of bond maturity on the conversion factors depends on whether the coupon is higher or lower than 8 percent. If the coupon is lower than 8 percent, bonds with long maturities will have lower conversion factors than bonds with short maturities, because the coupon is lower than the 8 percent discount rate. If the coupon is higher than 8 percent, longer-maturity bonds will have higher conversion factors than shorter-maturity bonds, because the coupon is higher than the discount rate. We can see the latter case in Table 6.1 by comparing the conversion factor of 1.0972 for the 8⅞ percent August 2017 bond with the conversion factor of 1.0986 for the 8⅞ percent February 2019 bond.

How well do these conversion factors bring the invoice prices into line with the market values of the delivered T-bonds? That depends on how accurately the conversion factors reflect the relationships among the market values of different bonds. If the yield curve is flat at 8 percent so that bonds of all maturities have 8 percent yields, the conversion factors will maintain the market value relationships among bonds perfectly. If the yield curve is not flat at 8 percent, the conversion factors will be unable to preserve the market value relationships among bonds.

---

[8] The conversion factors figured by the Chicago Board of Trade round the maturity of the bond to the nearest quarter.

The short parties in T-bond contracts will be imperfectly compensated for delivering different bonds, as Example 6.5 demonstrates.

▪ **Example 6.5: Adjusting for Value Differences Using Conversion Factors**
Suppose that on March 7, 1989, the short party in a T-bond futures contract is deciding which of the following two T-bonds to deliver:

Bond		Quoted Price	Yield to Maturity
7¼%	May 2016	$ 81-06 (81.18750)	9.13%
10⅜%	November 2007-12	109-13 (109.40625)	9.30%

The short will receive a higher invoice principal amount if she delivers the 10⅜ percent bond rather than the 7¼ percent bond, because the former has a higher conversion factor. Thus, she must determine whether the higher invoice principal amount will compensate her sufficiently for delivering the more valuable bond.

The profit from delivering a given bond into the T-bond futures contract is

$$\text{Profit to short} \tag{6.9}$$
$$= \text{Invoice price} - \text{Market price of delivered bond}$$
$$= (\text{Invoice principal amount} + \text{Accrued interest})$$
$$- (\text{Quoted bond price} + \text{Accrued interest}).$$

Because both the total invoice price and the total market price include the same accrued interest, we can rewrite the short's profit as

$$\text{Profit to short} = (\text{Invoice principal amount}) - (\text{Quoted bond price}). \tag{6.10}$$

Thus, in determining whether conversion factors properly compensate for delivering bonds of different values, we can ignore accrued interest on the delivered bond. We simply compare the ratio of the bonds' quoted prices with the ratio of their invoice principal amounts.

Table 6.1 shows that the conversion factor of the 10⅜ percent bond is 1.2273 and that of the 7¼ percent bond is 0.9175. The ratio of the invoice principal amount of the 10⅜ percent bond to that of the 7¼ percent bond is

$$\text{Invoice principal amount ratio} = \frac{(1.2273)(\text{Futures settlement price})}{(0.9175)(\text{Futures settlement price})}$$
$$= 1.3377.$$

The ratio of the 10⅜ percent bond's quoted price to the 7¼ percent bond's quoted price is

$$\text{Quoted price ratio} = \frac{109.40625}{81.18750}$$
$$= 1.3476.$$

Thus, if the short delivers the 10⅜ percent bond instead of the 7¼ percent bond, she will give up a bond worth 34.76 percent more but receive an invoice principal amount that is only 33.77 percent more. The conversion factors in this case cause the short party to be undercompensated for delivery of a more expensive bond, and the short will choose to deliver the cheaper bond.

The desirability of delivering one bond instead of another can change if the yields to maturity change. Suppose the yields to maturity are 6.63 percent and 6.80 percent for the 7¼ percent and 10⅜ percent bonds, respectively. Then the quoted prices of the two bonds increase to

Bond		Quoted Price	Yield to Maturity
7¼%	May 2016	$107-23 (107.72322)	6.63%
10⅜%	November 2007-12	137-15 (137.46934)	6.80%

The quoted price ratio is now

$$\text{Quoted price ratio} = \frac{137.46934}{107.72322}$$

$$= 1.2761.$$

Now if the short party delivers the 10⅜ percent bond instead of the 7¼ percent bond, she will give up a bond worth 27.61 percent more but receive an invoice principal amount that is 33.77 percent more. In this case, the conversion factors lead to overcompensation for delivery of a more expensive bond. Given the choice, the short party will deliver the more expensive bond. ∎

Example 6.5 shows that the imperfections in the conversion factors cause some T-bonds to be cheaper to deliver than others. As we saw in Chapter 1, the cheapest-to-deliver bond when a futures contract expires is the one with the lowest delivery-adjusted spot price. Example 6.6 shows how to determine the cheapest-to-deliver T-bond.

▪ **Example 6.6: Determining the Cheapest-to-Deliver T-Bond at Expiration**   Suppose that on March 7, 1989, we wish to determine which T-bond is cheapest to deliver into the March T-bond futures contract. Assume those holding short March T-bond futures positions have decided to give intention to deliver immediately. They can do this because March 7 is part of the delivery month on the March T-bond futures contract. Part A of Table 6.2 presents the bonds that are most likely to be delivered.[9] The delivery-adjusted spot prices are, as defined in Chapter 1, the spot prices divided by the conversion factors.

The 7¼ percent May 2016 bond has the lowest delivery-adjusted spot price, $88.48774 (88-16), and therefore will be delivered. If all shorts decide to deliver

---

[9] This subset of all deliverable bonds was determined by the Institutional Financial Futures and Options Division of Drexel Burnham Lambert.

Table 6.2 Determining the Cheapest-to-Deliver Bond at Expiration

A: High-Interest-Rate Scenario

Coupon	Maturity	Quoted Price	Yield to Maturity	Conversion Factor	Delivery-Adjusted Spot Price
10.375%	11/07-12	$109.40625	9.301%	1.2273	$89.14385
12.000	8/08-13	123.71875	9.332	1.3893	89.05114
12.500	8/09-14	129.06250	9.297	1.4473	89.17467
9.875	11/15	107.09375	9.157	1.2051	88.86711
9.250	2/16	101.00000	9.148	1.1369	88.83807
7.250	5/16	81.18750	9.132	0.9175	88.48774
7.500	11/16	83.62500	9.131	0.9447	88.52017
8.750	5/17	96.25000	9.120	1.0833	88.84889
8.875	8/17	97.50000	9.122	1.0972	88.86256
9.125	5/18	100.15625	9.107	1.1262	88.93292
9.000	11/18	99.03125	9.093	1.1126	89.00885
8.875	2/19	97.84375	9.085	1.0986	89.06222
				Minimum	$88.48774

B: Low-Interest-Rate Scenario

Coupon	Maturity	Quoted Price	Yield to Maturity	Conversion Factor	Delivery-Adjusted Spot Price
10.375%	11/07-12	$137.46934	6.801%	1.2273	$112.00957
12.000	8/08-13	155.13935	6.832	1.3893	111.66728
12.500	8/09-14	162.49096	6.797	1.4473	112.27179
9.875	11/15	139.89996	6.657	1.2051	116.08992
9.250	2/16	132.40988	6.648	1.1369	116.46573
7.250	5/16	107.72322	6.632	0.9175	117.40951
7.500	11/16	110.93758	6.631	0.9447	117.43154
8.750	5/17	127.02627	6.620	1.0833	117.25863
8.875	8/17	128.68023	6.622	1.0972	117.28056
9.125	5/18	132.37697	6.607	1.1262	117.54303
9.000	11/18	131.16873	6.593	1.1126	117.89388
8.875	2/19	129.76960	6.585	1.0986	118.12270
				Minimum	$111.66728

immediately, the delivery date arbitrage condition should cause the futures settlement price to adjust to yield a zero profit for them. Thus,

> Invoice principal amount for 7¼% bond
> = Quoted spot price of 7¼% bond,

or

> (Conversion factor for 7¼% bond)(Decimal futures settlement price)
> ($100,000)
> = Quoted spot price of 7¼% bond.

Therefore,

Futures Settlement Price

$$= \frac{\text{Quoted spot price of } 7\frac{1}{4}\% \text{ bond}}{\text{Conversion factor}}$$

$= \text{Delivery-adjusted spot price of } 7\frac{1}{4}\% \text{ bond}$

$= \$88\text{-}16 \text{ per } \$100 \text{ face.}$

The actual futures settlement price on March 7, 1989, was $88-10, about 0.20 percent below the futures settlement price we predicted above. Later in the chapter, we will discuss how the shorts' options to choose which bond and which date to deliver into the contract can cause this phenomenon.

A change in yields can change the bond that is cheapest to deliver. Part B of Table 6.2 presents spot prices and delivery-adjusted spot prices for yields to maturity that are 250 basis points below those in part A. The cheapest-to-deliver bond is now the 12 percent August 2008-13 bond, and the futures settlement price will be a bit above $111-21. ∎

Duration and the Cheapest-to-Deliver Bond   Participants in the T-bond futures market often use the durations of deliverable bonds to determine which bond is the cheapest to deliver. Recall that in Example 6.6, the cheapest-to-deliver bond for a March 1989 T-bond futures contract was a $7\frac{1}{4}$ percent May 2016 bond when T-bond yields were around 9 percent. When yields dropped to around 6.5 percent, a 12 percent August 2008-13 bond became the cheapest to deliver. The $7\frac{1}{4}$ percent bond has a high duration, because it has a low coupon rate and a relatively distant expiration date. Conversely, the 12 percent bond has a low duration, because it has a high coupon rate and a relatively closer expiration date. The rule of thumb commonly used by market participants is

1.   If yields are above 8 percent, the cheapest-to-deliver bond will be the eligible bond with the highest duration.

2.   If yields are below 8 percent, the cheapest-to-deliver bond will be the eligible bond with the lowest duration.

This rule of thumb requires a flat yield curve, so it is not completely accurate in all situations. However, it is often a useful approximation. It is quite difficult to prove this rule, but we can gain some insight as to why it holds by studying a somewhat different problem. Suppose for the moment that T-bonds are discount bonds. In this case, the duration of a bond equals the bond's maturity, and deliverable bonds can differ only in their maturities and face values. We assume all deliverable bonds have the same face value as they do under the T-bond futures contract.

The price of such a discount bond is

Spot price $= (\text{Face value})(e^{-rS})$,   **(6.11)**

where r is the annualized yield to maturity on the bond and S is the number of years until maturity. Of course, S is also the duration of the bond. The number e = 2.718 is used to compute the continuously compounded interest on the bond. In the notation of this book,

$$1 + r_{t,T} = e^{r(T-t)} \tag{6.12}$$

and

$$\frac{1}{1 + r_{t,T}} = e^{-r(T-t)}. \tag{6.13}$$

Suppose the conversion factors for our hypothetical discount T-bonds are the same as those under the T-bond futures contract: bond prices per $1 face value discounted at an 8 percent yield to maturity. We can express each conversion factor as

$$\text{Conversion factor} = e^{(-0.08)(S)}. \tag{6.14}$$

Now we can determine the cheapest-to-deliver bond by using Equations 6.11 and 6.14 to identify the bond with the minimum delivery-adjusted spot price, where

$$\begin{aligned}
\text{Delivery-adjusted spot price} &= \frac{\text{Spot price}}{\text{Conversion factor}} \\
&= \frac{(\text{Face value})(e^{-rS})}{e^{(-0.08)(S)}} \\
&= (\text{Face value})(e^{(0.08-r)(S)}).
\end{aligned} \tag{6.15}$$

Now suppose the yield curve is flat so that each bond has the same continuously compounded yield to maturity, r. Then the above rule of thumb for choosing the cheapest-to-deliver bond will hold:

1. If r > 8 percent, the exponent in Equation 6.15 will be negative. Therefore, the bond with the longest time to expiration (duration), S, will have the lowest delivery-adjusted spot price and will be the cheapest to deliver.

2. If r < 8 percent, the exponent in Equation 6.15 will be positive. Therefore, the bond with the shortest time to expiration (duration), S, will have the lowest delivery-adjusted spot price and will be the cheapest to deliver.

We can also express this result intuitively. Because of the way the conversion factors are structured, the invoice price the short receives drops at an 8 percent rate for each year that the maturity of the delivered bond increases. If the yield, r, is greater than 8 percent, the market value of the bond delivered by the short will decrease at an even higher rate as the maturity increases. Thus, the short gains the most by delivering the bond with the longest time to maturity. If r is less than 8 percent, the market value of the bond will drop at a lower rate than the invoice price as the maturity of the delivered bond increases. Thus, the short should deliver the bond with the shortest time to maturity. Because duration captures a bond's weighted-average time to maturity, the intuition behind the rule of thumb for actual T-bonds is very similar.

Like any rule of thumb, this one has its limitations. The main one is that it requires a flat yield curve. In practice, however, the rule of thumb seems to perform well.[10]

Fundamental No-Arbitrage Equation

The fundamental no-arbitrage equation for T-bond futures is merely an applied version of the no-arbitrage relationship for an asset with payouts (Equation 2.7a) that we derived in Chapter 2:

$$F_{t,T} = P_t(1 + r_{t,T}) - FV_T(\text{Coupons from t to T}), \tag{6.16}$$

where $F_{t,T}$ is the total invoice price and P_t is the total market price of the bond.[11]

Suppose there is just one coupon between dates t and T, as in the following time line:

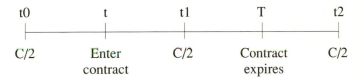

t0	t	t1	T	t2
C/2	Enter contract	C/2	Contract expires	C/2

Now we can rewrite Equation 6.16 using Equations 6.7 and 6.8 to determine a no-arbitrage (fair) quoted futures price, $QF_{t,T}$:

$$QF_{t,T} = \frac{P_t(1 + r_{t,T}) - FV_T(\text{Coupons from t to T}) - AI_{t1,T}}{\text{Conversion factor}}, \tag{6.16a}$$

where $AI_{t1,T}$ is the accrued interest on the bond as of date T.[12]

Because there are multiple deliverable grades, each deliverable bond will have a different no-arbitrage quoted futures price. Earlier we saw that the cheapest-to-deliver bond at expiration is the one that minimizes the delivery-adjusted spot price. Now we will show that the cheapest-to-deliver bond at time t, *before expiration,* is the one that minimizes the no-arbitrage quoted futures price in Equation 6.16a.

---

[10] For a more detailed discussion of this issue, see Kilcollin [1982], Livingston [1984, 1987], Meisner and Labuszewski [1984], and Jones [1985].

[11] There is also a fundamental no-arbitrage equation for the relationship among futures prices for contracts with different maturities that is analogous to those discussed in Chapter 2. See Jones [1981] and Rentzler [1986] for a discussion.

[12] Even if no coupon is paid between dates t and T, t1 is the date of the last coupon before T.

First, assume we are at expiration so that $t = T$ and the total bond price is P_T = $QP_T + AI_{t1,T}$ (where QP_T is the quoted bond price), $r_{t,T} = 0$, and FV_T(Coupons from t to T) = 0. Then the right-hand side of Equation 6.16a becomes QP_T/(Conversion factor), which is simply the delivery-adjusted spot price. Thus, when $t = T$, minimizing the delivery-adjusted spot price is the same as minimizing Equation 6.16a.

We get a similar result before expiration when $t < T$. Using Equation 6.16, we can rewrite the right-hand side of Equation 6.16a for a specific bond:

$$\frac{F_{t,T}^* - AI_{t1,T}}{\text{Conversion factor}},$$

where $F_{t,T}^*$ is the fair total futures price (from Equation 6.16), as of time t, for delivery of that bond at time T. Subtracting accrued interest from $F_{t,T}^*$ gives the fair futures price less accrued interest, $QF_{t,T}^*$. Therefore,

$$\frac{F_{t,T}^* - AI_{t1,T}}{\text{Conversion factor}} = \frac{QF_{t,T}^*}{\text{Conversion factor}}.$$

Thus, the bond with the lowest delivery-adjusted fair quoted futures price also is the bond that minimizes Equation 6.16a.[13] Hence, finding the cheapest-to-deliver bond before expiration is similar to finding the cheapest-to-deliver bond at expiration. We simply substitute the delivery-adjusted fair quoted futures price for the delivery-adjusted quoted spot price when we minimize Equation 6.16a.

Example 6.7 shows how to determine the cheapest-to-deliver bond before expiration.

▪ **Example 6.7: Determining the Cheapest-to-Deliver Bond before Expiration**   Suppose that on March 31, 1989, we wish to determine which of the T-bonds that are deliverable into a June 1989 futures contract is the cheapest to deliver. The current 30-day repo rate is 10 percent. We will use this rate as the short-term interest rate for our calculations.

Table 6.3 presents the delivery-adjusted fair quoted futures prices implied for a variety of bonds that are eligible for delivery into the June T-bond contract. We will show how these fair prices are computed by working through the calculation for the 7¼ percent May 2016 bond.

The following time line illustrates the timing of cash flows for this bond:

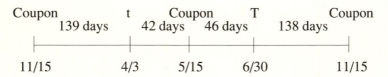

	Coupon		t	Coupon	T		Coupon
		139 days		42 days	46 days		138 days
	11/15		4/3	5/15	6/30		11/15

Table 6.3 Determining the Cheapest-to-Deliver Bond before Expiration, June 1989 T-Bond Futures

March 31, 1989, Prices
Quoted Futures Price = $88-13

Coupon	Expiration Date	Quoted Price	Delivery-Adjusted Fair Quoted Futures Price	Unannualized Implied Repo Rate	Annualized Implied Repo Rate
10.375%	11/15/2007-12	$109.18750	$89.2445	1.537%	6.286%
12.000	8/15/2008-13	123.65600	89.2314	1.530	6.260
12.500	8/15/2009-14	128.68750	89.1401	1.631	6.670
9.875	11/15/2015	106.90600	88.9958	1.803	7.376
9.250	2/15/2016	100.84375	88.9325	1.858	7.602
7.250	5/15/2016	81.12500	88.6905	2.134	8.728
7.500	11/15/2016	83.53125	88.6926	2.131	8.719
8.750	5/15/2017	96.06250	88.9537	1.848	7.561
8.875	8/15/2017	97.65625	89.2400	1.519	6.213
9.125	5/15/2018	100.00000	89.0757	1.716	7.022
9.000	11/15/2018	98.81250	89.0898	1.701	6.959
8.875	2/15/2019	97.34375	88.8349	1.966	8.044

Because March 31, 1989, is a Friday, the bond is actually received and paid for on Monday, April 3. As a result, the time period that is relevant for our calculations covers the 88 days between April 3 and expiration of the futures contract on June 30. Thus, we will assign April 3 as date t.

The first step in determining the delivery-adjusted fair quoted futures price in Equation 6.16a is to calculate the total market price of the 7¼ percent May 2016 bond on April 3. Table 6.3 shows that the quoted price is $81.125 per $100 face value. The bond has earned accrued interest over the 139 days since November 15, 1988. Because there are 181 days in the full coupon period between November 11, 1988, and May 15, 1989, the accrued interest on the bond as of April 3 is

$$\text{Accrued interest} = \left(\frac{139}{181}\right)\left(\frac{\$7.25}{2}\right)$$

$$= \$2.784 \text{ per } \$100 \text{ face.}$$

Thus, the total market price of the bond on April 3 is

$$\text{Total market price} = P_t$$

$$= \$81.125 + \$2.784$$

$$= \$83.909 \text{ per } \$100 \text{ face.}$$

The second step in calculating Equation 6.16a is to determine the future value at the futures expiration date of the coupons received by holding the T-bond. In this case, the investor will receive a coupon of $7.25/2 = $3.625 per $100 par on

May 15. The future value of this coupon as of the futures expiration on June 30 will be

$$\text{Future value of coupons} = FV_T(\text{Coupons from t to T})$$
$$= (\$3.625)[1 + (46/360)(0.10)]$$
$$= \$3.671 \text{ per } \$100 \text{ face.}$$

The third step is to compute the interest the bond will accrue over the 46 days between the coupon payment on May 15 and the futures expiration on June 30:

$$\text{Futures accrued interest} = \left(\frac{46}{184}\right)\left(\frac{\$7.25}{2}\right)$$
$$= \$0.906 \text{ per } \$100 \text{ face.}$$

The fair total futures price is therefore

$$\text{Fair total futures price} = F^*_{t,T}$$
$$= (\$83.909)[1 + (0.10)(88/360)] - \$3.671$$
$$= \$82.289 \text{ per } \$100 \text{ face.}$$

The fair quoted futures price is

$$\text{Fair quoted futures price} = QF^*_{t,T}$$
$$= \$82.289 - \$0.906$$
$$= \$81.383 \text{ per } \$100 \text{ face.}$$

Table 6.1 shows that the conversion factor of the $7\frac{1}{4}$ percent bond is 0.9176.[14] The delivery-adjusted fair quoted futures price for the $7\frac{1}{4}$ percent bond is therefore

$$\text{Delivery-adjusted fair quoted futures price} = \frac{\$81.383}{0.9176}$$
$$= \$88.69$$
$$= \$88\text{-}22 \text{ per } \$100 \text{ face.}$$

The $7\frac{1}{4}$ percent May 2016 bond has the lowest delivery-adjusted fair quoted futures price of all the eligible bonds. Thus, it is the cheapest-to-deliver bond as of March 31, 1989. ∎

---

[14] This differs slightly from the conversion factor for the $7\frac{1}{4}$ percent bond in Example 6.4, because the futures contract in that example has a March delivery date.

The actual quoted futures price of the T-bond contract in Example 6.7 is $88-13. Of all the deliverable bonds, the 7¼ percent bond has the delivery-adjusted fair quoted price ($88-22) closest to this actual price. Thus, the market seems to be pricing the futures off of the 7¼ percent bond, as we would expect for the cheapest-to-deliver bond. A similar calculation using the three-month T-bill rate of 9.22 percent as an alternative lending rate (rather than the repo rate as an arbitrageur's borrowing rate) produces a delivery-adjusted fair quoted futures price of $88-17 for the 7¼ bond, which is even closer to the actual quoted futures price.

The difference between the actual quoted futures price and the delivery-adjusted fair quoted futures price of the cheapest-to-deliver bond most likely reflects the value of the short position's options, for the seller's options tend to reduce the futures price relative to the no-arbitrage price of Equation 6.16, even for the cheapest-to-deliver bond. We can modify Equation 6.16 to include this option value:[15]

$$F_{t,T} = P_t(1 + r_{t,T}) - FV_T(\text{Coupons from t to T}) \qquad \textbf{(6.16b)}$$
$$- FV_T(\text{Seller's options}).$$

We will discuss the valuation of these options later in the chapter. For now, we can see that because of the seller's options, a futures price that is less than the no-arbitrage futures price does not necessarily indicate that a reverse cash-and-carry arbitrage opportunity exists. Since the arbitrageur in such a strategy goes long futures and thus *grants* seller's options, any arbitrage profits suggested by Equation 6.16a may be only illusory.

An Alternative Specification of the Fundamental No-Arbitrage Equation

The fundamental no-arbitrage equation, 6.16, is written in terms of the futures invoice price and the total market price of the T-bond. In practice, it is often written in terms of the quoted futures price and the quoted spot price of the underlying bond. We derive this alternative specification of the no-arbitrage relationship by first rewriting Equation 6.16 as

$$c_i QF_{t,T} + AI_{t1,T} = (QP_t + AI_{t0,t})(1 + r_{t,T}) - (C_i/2)(1 + r_{t1,T}), \qquad \textbf{(6.17)}$$

where

c_i = conversion factor for the bond

C_i = annual coupon

$t1$ = date of the coupon between t and T

$QF_{t,T}$ = quoted futures price at time t for delivery at T

---

[15] We can view the seller's options as a payout from a cash-and-carry strategy. Thus, as with other payouts, we subtract the future value of the options in the no-arbitrage equation.

QP_t = quoted spot price of the deliverable bond at t

$AI_{t1,T}$ = accrued interest on the deliverable bond at T

$AI_{t0,t}$ = accrued interest on the deliverable bond at t

The time line for the arbitrage strategy is

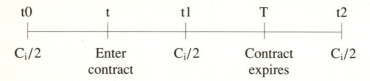

If we rearrange terms, Equation 6.17 becomes

$$QF_{t,T} \qquad\qquad\qquad\qquad\qquad\qquad\qquad\qquad\qquad\qquad (6.18)$$
$$= \frac{QP_t + (AI_{t0,t} - AI_{t1,T} - C_i/2) + QP_t r_{t,T} + AI_{t0,t} r_{t,T} - (C_i/2) r_{t1,T}}{c_i}.$$

We know from our time line that[16]

$$AI_{t0,t} - AI_{t1,T} - C_i/2 = - C_i[(\text{Days from t to T})/365], \qquad (6.19)$$

because $AI_{t0,t}$ represents the coupon between t0 and t and $C_i/2$ represents the coupon between t0 and t1. The difference between the two is therefore the negative of the coupon between t and t1. Adding this to $-AI_{t1,T}$ yields the negative of the coupon between t and T.

The last terms in the numerator of Equation 6.18 represent interest on accrued interest, and typically they are very small. In Example 6.7, for instance, the sum of these terms is \$0.02 per \$100 face value. For practical purposes, we can ignore them and rewrite Equation 6.18 as

$$QF_{t,T} = \frac{QP_t + (r - CY)[(\text{Days from t to T})/360]QP_t}{c_i}, \qquad (6.20)$$

where r is the annualized short-term interest rate and

$$CY = \left(\frac{C_i}{QP_t}\right)\left(\frac{360}{365}\right) \qquad\qquad\qquad\qquad\qquad (6.21)$$

is defined as the current yield on the bond. The **current yield** is the annual coupon (C_i) expressed as a percentage of the current quoted spot price, placed on a 360-day-year basis.

[16] For leap years, we replace 365 with 366 in the following discussion.

Equation 6.20 is the fundamental no-arbitrage relationship written in terms of T-bond quoted futures and spot prices. It demonstrates that the relationship between the quoted futures price and the quoted spot price of the deliverable bond is determined by the **net carry**,[17] defined as

$$\text{Net carry} = r - CY. \tag{6.22}$$

We now compute this alternative no-arbitrage equation for the $7\frac{1}{4}$ percent May 2016 bond of Example 6.7. The current yield for this bond as of April 3, 1989, is $(7.25/81.125)(360/365) = 8.81$ percent. This is less than the 10 percent short-term interest rate, and the net carry is 1.19 percent annualized. Equation 6.20 shows that the fair quoted futures price for the June 1989 T-bond contract in Example 6.7 is

$$\text{Quoted futures price} = \$81.125\left[\frac{1 + (0.0119)(88/360)}{0.9176}\right]$$

$$= \$88.67$$

$$= \$88\text{-}21 \text{ per } \$100 \text{ face.}$$

The positive net carry causes the fair quoted futures price to exceed the quoted spot price. This no-arbitrage price is only slightly lower than the $88-22 no-arbitrage price we derived using Equation 6.16a.

A major advantage of Equation 6.20 over the original no-arbitrage equation, 6.16, is that it uses quoted prices directly. Like Equation 6.16, Equation 6.20 is also valid in cases where there is no coupon or more than one coupon between t and T.

Implied Repo Rates   Another way we have derived no-arbitrage relationships in other markets is to compare the implied repo rates that can be earned on cash-and-carry strategies with the prevailing short-term interest rate. A cash-and-carry in the T-bond market requires the following steps:

1.   Buy spot T-bonds and collect any coupons.

2.   Go short T-bond futures.

3.   Hold the T-bond and deliver into the T-bond futures contract.

Normally a cash-and-carry strategy involves buying one unit of the underlying asset for each unit of the short futures position. But in markets with multiple deliverable grades such as the T-bond market, the delivery date arbitrage condition requires that a hedge ratio other than 1 be used in a cash-and-carry. We know from Equation 6.10 that the invoice principal amount will converge to the quoted bond

---

[17] In general, the net carry is the difference between the cost of carrying the asset and any cash inflows.

price when a T-bond futures contract expires. Since the invoice principal amount equals the term (Conversion factor)(Quoted futures price), the following will be true at expiration:

$$\frac{\text{Change in spot price}}{\text{Change in quoted futures price}} = \text{Conversion factor.} \qquad \textbf{(6.23)}$$

The appropriate hedge ratio to use in a T-bond cash-and-carry therefore is the conversion factor of the underlying T-bond. This adjustment to the cash-and-carry hedge ratio is more important in the T-bond market than in most markets with multiple deliverable grades, because the T-bond conversion factors cover an especially wide range.

As we saw in Chapter 2, the implied repo rate from the cash-and-carry strategy will be

$$\text{Implied repo rate} = \frac{F_{t,T} + FV_T(\text{Coupons from t to T}) - P_t}{P_t}, \qquad \textbf{(6.24)}$$

where P_t and $F_{t,T}$ are as defined is Equation 6.16.

Each T-bond that can be delivered into a T-bond futures contract will have an implied repo rate given by Equation 6.24. When we compute the implied repo rate for a given bond, we must adjust the invoice price, $F_{t,T}$, as though that bond were the one being held in the cash-and-carry. This means that we temporarily assume the bond in question is the one that will be delivered into the contract.

Example 6.8 shows how to compute the implied repo rate on a cash-and-carry that involves the 7¼ percent May 2016 bond and the June 1989 T-bond contract.

▪ **Example 6.8: Computing the Implied Repo Rate for T-Bond Futures**
Suppose we enter into a cash-and-carry on March 31, 1989, using the 7¼ percent May 2016 bond and the June 1989 T-bond futures contract from Example 6.7. We know that the following information holds for the 7¼ percent May 2016 bond:

P_t	= \$83.909 per \$100 face
$FV_t(\text{Coupons from t to T})$	= \$3.671 per \$100 face
$AI_{t1,T}$	= \$0.906 per \$100 face

The conversion factor for the 7¼ percent bond under the June 1989 contract is 0.9176. Therefore, the appropriate hedge ratio for this cash-and-carry is 0.9176.

The quoted futures price in Example 6.7 is \$88-13 per \$100 face value, or \$88.40625. Thus, the futures invoice price is

$$F_{t,T} = (0.9176)(\$88.40625) + \$0.906$$
$$= \$82.028 \text{ per } \$100 \text{ face.}$$

Now we can compute the implied repo rate for the 7¼ percent May 2016 bond from Equation 6.24:

$$\text{Implied repo rate} = \frac{\$82.028 + \$3.671 - \$83.909}{\$83.909}$$

$$= 2.134\% \text{ for 88 days}$$

$$= 8.73\% \text{ annualized.}$$

Thus, using the 7¼ percent May 2016 bond in a cash-and-carry synthetic lending yields an implied repo rate of 2.134 percent for 88 days, or 8.73 percent on an annualized basis. Table 6.3 shows that this bond has the highest implied repo rate of all the deliverable bonds. This suggests that futures market participants believe this bond will be cheapest to deliver when the June T-bond contract expires. This result agrees with our determination of the cheapest-to-deliver bond in Example 6.7.

Notice that this bond has an implied repo rate lower than the 10 percent repo rate and the 9.22 percent T-bill rate. This is due to the same forces—the seller's options—that drive the actual quoted future price below the fair futures price. ▪

The Yield to Maturity Implied by the Quoted Futures Price   In Chapter 5, we showed how to derive the short-term interest rates that quoted Eurodollar and T-bill futures prices imply for the expiration dates of the futures contracts. We can also compute the T-bond yields to maturity that T-bond futures prices imply will prevail as of the T-bond futures expiration dates. We have seen that except for the value of the short positions' options, a T-bond futures price tracks the bond that is expected to be the cheapest to deliver. Therefore, we can use the T-bond futures price to derive the implied yield to maturity for this bond. Example 6.9 demonstrates how to determine the yield to maturity implied by the T-bond futures contract in Example 6.7.

▪ **Example 6.9: Calculating the Yield to Maturity Implied by a Futures Price**   Suppose, as in Example 6.7, that on March 31, 1989, the quoted June T-bond futures price is $88-13. In that example, we saw that the 7¼ percent May 2016 bond is perceived as the cheapest-to-deliver bond and that its accrued interest as of June 30 is $0.906 per $100 face value. The futures contract will be priced for this bond, so the futures invoice price implied by Equation 6.7 is

$$\text{Invoice price} = (0.9176)(\$88.40625) + \$0.906$$
$$= \$82.028 \text{ per } \$100 \text{ face.}$$

This price implies that the yield to maturity on the 7¼ percent May 2016 bond will be 9.15 percent as of the futures contract's expiration on June 30, 1989. Of course, this futures invoice price is a little too low, because it does not account for the seller's options. The true implied rate should be computed relative to a slightly higher price and thus should be somewhat lower than 9.15 percent.

The omission of the seller's options makes little difference in practice. If, for example, we computed the yield implied by the no-arbitrage futures price of $88-22 derived in Example 6.7, we would get a rate of 9.12 percent. ∎

Empirical Studies of Futures Pricing   Several empirical studies have tested to see whether T-bond futures prices behave according to the fundamental no-arbitrage equation. Klemkosky and Lasser [1985] found evidence that arbitrage opportunities do exist in the T-bond markets. However, Kolb, Gay, and Jordan [1982], Resnick and Henningar [1983], and Resnick [1984] concluded that the T-bond markets generally capitalize on arbitrage opportunities quite efficiently. Testing the efficiency of the T-bond markets is particularly difficult because of the seller's options.[18]

Using T-Bond Futures to Hedge a Bond Portfolio

One of the most important uses of T-bond futures is to hedge bond portfolio values. As in all hedging problems, the primary task is to determine the hedge ratio. For T-bond hedges, we use the following version of the hedge ratio formula:

$$\text{Hedge ratio} = \frac{\text{Change in bond portfolio value}}{\text{Change in T-bond futures price}}. \qquad (6.25)$$

The T-bond hedge ratio is calculated with analysis similar to that used to determine the ratio that will hedge a T-bill portfolio with 13-week T-bill futures. In the T-bill case, we use the T-bill pricing formula to determine how the price of an N-day T-bill will move relative to the price of the 90-day bill underlying the futures when the futures expires. In the T-bond case, we use the bond pricing equation, 6.1, to determine how a yield change will affect the values of a bond portfolio and a T-bond futures contract *when the futures expires.*[19] For now, we will assume that T-bond yields for different bonds move in lockstep. We will relax this assumption later.

There are two major steps we must take to calculate T-bond hedge ratios. First, we must determine how a change in the price of the perceived cheapest-to-deliver bond will affect the futures price. Second, we must determine which T-bond yields to assume will prevail when the futures expire.

The Impact of Changes in the Cheapest-to-Deliver-Bond Price on the Futures Price   The first step in calculating the T-bond hedge ratio is to determine how a given yield change will affect the futures price. This is a three-step

---

[18] In a related study, Bortz [1984] found no evidence that the existence of T-bond futures markets destabilizes the T-bond cash market.

[19] If we wish to hedge a T-bond portfolio only until a date before the expiration of the futures contract, we have a maturity mismatch of the type discussed in Chapter 2. We must multiply our hedge ratios by $1/(1 + r_{T^*,T})$, where T^* is the date the hedge will be lifted.

process in itself. First, we determine which bond the market perceives as the cheapest to deliver, for the futures contract is priced relative to this bond. Second, we use Equation 6.1 to calculate how a given change in yields will affect the price of the cheapest-to-deliver bond. Finally, we calculate how a change in the price of the cheapest-to-deliver bond will affect the quoted futures price.[20]

Once we accomplish the first two tasks, we can see how changes in the cheapest-to-deliver bond price will affect the futures price by rewriting Equation 6.23 as

$$\frac{\text{Change in quoted futures price}}{\text{Change in CTD bond price}} = \frac{1}{\text{Conversion factor for CTD}}, \qquad (6.26)$$

where the conversion factor is for the cheapest-to-deliver (CTD) bond. Now we can rewrite the hedge ratio given in Equation 6.25 as[21]

Hedge ratio   **(6.27)**

$$= \left(\frac{\text{Change in bond portfolio value}}{\text{Change in CTD bond price}}\right)(\text{Conversion factor for CTD}).$$

Determining the Current Yield to Maturity   Now the only factor we need to know to calculate the T-bond hedge ratio in Equation 6.27 is what the yields to maturity of the bonds involved in the hedge will be when the futures expire. We must take some care in determining these yield levels, for the relationship between prices and yields in the T-bond market is not linear as it is in the T-bill market. Therefore, the price changes at T of the bonds to be hedged and the cheapest-to-deliver bond in response to a yield change depend on the initial yield levels at T.

For the cheapest-to-deliver bond, we can use the yield to maturity that the current futures price implies for time T as the base yield. We showed how to derive this yield in Example 6.9. For the bond to be hedged, we will add an assumed differential to the yield implied by the futures price for the cheapest-to-deliver bond. The most straightforward approach is to assume that the yield differential between the two bonds at the futures' expiration will be the same as the differential we observe at time t. We will discuss the case in which this is not true later.

Example 6.10 shows how T-bond futures can hedge the value of a T-bond portfolio.

---

[20] Kane and Marcus [1984, 1986] showed that because of the possibility that the cheapest-to-deliver bond will change, there will be additional risk in a hedge. For simplicity, we will ignore this effect.

[21] This hedge ratio was also presented by Arak and Goodman [1986]. These authors too showed that the common suggestion that one use the conversion factor of the bond being hedged as a hedge ratio is inappropriate.

Figure 6.3   Convexity of Bond Price: Prices versus Yield

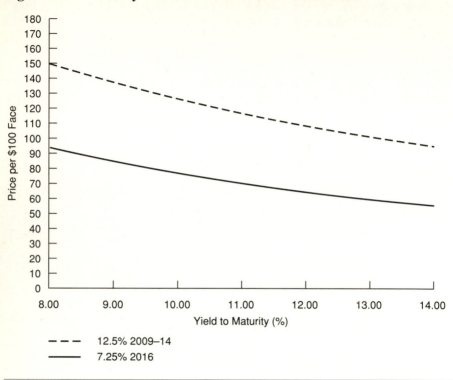

- - -   12.5% 2009–14

———   7.25% 2016

- **Example 6.10: Hedging a T-Bond Portfolio with T-Bond Futures**
Suppose that on March 31, 1989, we wish to use T-bond futures to hedge
the value of a portfolio of 12½ percent T-bonds with an expiration date of
August 2009-14. We want our hedge to last until June 30. Current T-bond
prices are as given in Table 6.3 in Example 6.7. We are concerned that
T-bond prices will fall, so we take a short position in June 1989 T-bond
futures.

Our first task is to determine how the prices of the portfolio bonds and
the cheapest-to-deliver bond underlying the futures respond to changes in
market yields. Figure 6.3 shows how prices per $100 face move as the yield
to maturity changes. It demonstrates two properties that affect the T-bond
hedge ratio. First, the prices of all the bonds fall when the yield to maturity
increases, but at different rates. Second, the relationships between prices and
yields are not linear as they are for T-bills; instead they move along *convex*
paths.

In Example 6.7, we saw that the cheapest-to-deliver bond for the June
1989 T-bond futures contract was the 7¼ percent May 2016 bond. The yields
to maturity on March 31, 1989, the date our hedge will go into effect, of this
bond and our portfolio bonds are

Current yield to maturity on 7¼% bond	9.14%
Current yield to maturity on 12½% bond	9.33
Yield to maturity implied by futures on 7¼% bond	9.15

We will use the 9.15 percent yield implied by the futures for June 30, 1989, as a base for computing changes in the price of the 7¼ percent bond. For the 12½ percent bond, we will assume that the current $(9.33 - 9.14) = 0.19$ percent difference between the yields of the two bonds will still prevail on June 30. Therefore, we project that the base yield for the 12½ percent bond on June 30 will be $9.15 + 0.19 = 9.34$ percent.

Now we can see how the prices of the two bonds could move on June 30. Suppose T-bond yields increase by 20 basis points on that date. Equation 6.1 shows us how the T-bond prices will change:

Change in price of 7¼% bond (9.15% to 9.35%)
    $= -\$1.64370$ per $100 face

Change in price of 12½% bond (9.34% to 9.54%)
    $= -\$2.17316$ per $100 face.

The hedge ratio given by Equation 6.27 is thus

$$\text{Hedge ratio} = \left(\frac{2.17316}{1.64370}\right)(0.9176)$$

$$= 1.213.$$

If we have $100 million face value of the 12½ percent bonds in our portfolio, we need 1,213 short T-bond futures contracts for our hedge. Notice that we have (for now) assumed that a 20-basis-point move in the yield on the 7¼ percent bond will be accompanied by a 20-basis-point move in the yield on the 12½ percent bond. ▪

Dynamic Hedging   Unlike a T-bill hedge, a T-bond hedge requires that the hedge ratio be updated as the yield to maturity implied by the futures price changes. Several factors produce a T-bond hedge ratio that is appropriate at a 9 percent yield, for instance, to be inappropriate at a 12 percent yield. First, because of the convex relationship between T-bond yields and prices, a given change in yields will change a bond's price differently at various yield levels. Second, as shown in Figure 6.4, bonds do not have the same convexities, so a given yield change will cause different bonds to experience different price changes. The varied convexities of T-bond prices cause the relative bond price changes that make up T-bond hedge ratios to differ at different yield levels. Figure 6.5 shows how the hedge ratio for our 12½ percent May 2009-14 bond changes as yields move from 8 to 14 percent.

A final factor that may affect T-bond hedge ratios is the possibility that the cheapest-to-deliver bond will change. If yields fall from above to below 8 percent, the cheapest-to-deliver bond will change to a lower-duration bond. Conversely,

Figure 6.4   Convexity of Change in Bond Price: Change in Price versus Yield

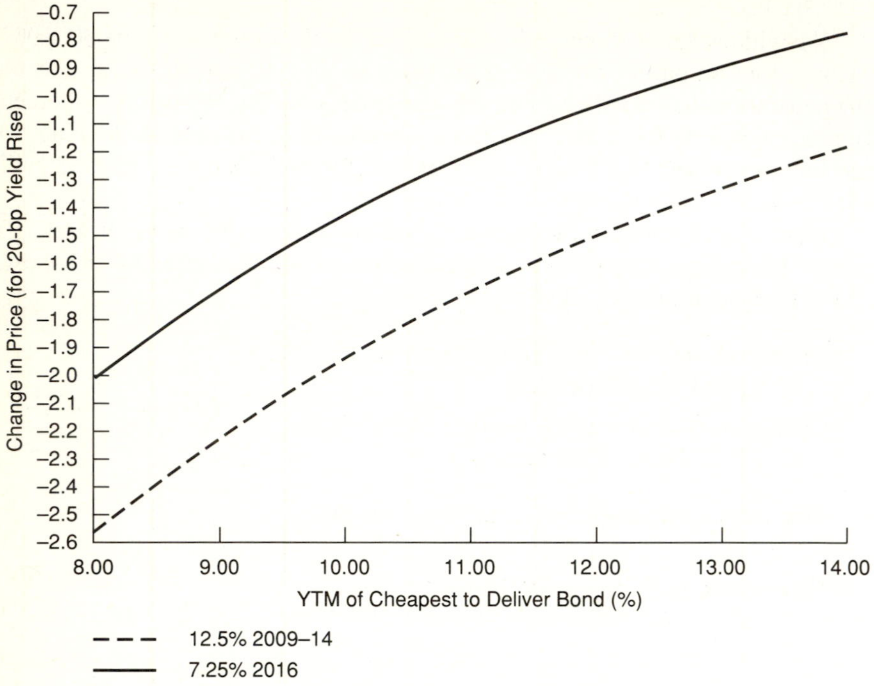

YTM of Cheapest to Deliver Bond (%)

- - - -   12.5% 2009–14

————   7.25% 2016

a yield increase that crosses the 8 percent level will cause the cheapest-to-deliver bond to change to a higher-duration bond. Changes in the shape of the yield curve can also lead to a change in the cheapest-to-deliver bond. In such cases, the hedge ratio must be recalculated relative to the new cheapest-to-deliver bond.

A hedge whose ratios experience such a revision is called a **dynamic hedge**. Dynamic hedges are required whenever the convexity of the bond being hedged differs from the convexity of the futures price.[22]

If it were costless to change futures positions, the optimal dynamic hedge would *instantaneously* adjust the hedge ratio as the current yield to maturity changed. For instance, if the yield to maturity implied by the futures price for the cheapest-to-deliver 7¼ percent bond in Example 6.10 moved from 9.15 to 10.15

---

[22] See Duffie and Jackson [1986] and Geske and Pieptea [1987] for a detailed discussion of the advantages of dynamic hedging with bond portfolios.

Figure 6.5 Hedge Ratio at Given Yields, 12½ Percent May 2009-14 Bond

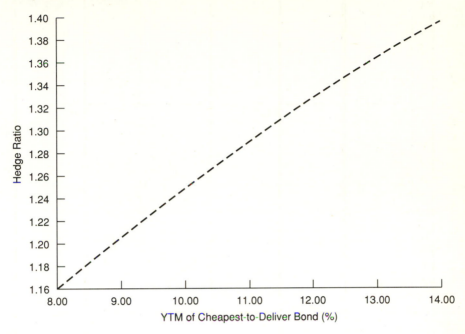

percent, an optimal dynamic hedge of the 12½ percent bond would immediately increase the number of short positions from 1.213 to 1.256 per bond. But because of the costs of monitoring a hedge and transacting in futures, the optimal strategy may be to update the hedge ratio only after large yield changes. To determine the appropriate rebalancing of the hedge ratio, we must gauge the seriousness of the hedge imperfections caused by differing convexities of hedged bonds and futures.

Figure 6.6 gives an example of the hedge imperfections that can arise when a hedge ratio is initially appropriate for the current yield to maturity. It assumes the current yield implied by the futures is 9.15 percent and the 12½ percent bond portfolio in Example 6.10 is hedged with a ratio appropriate for the 9.15 percent yield. Then it graphs the difference between the change in the value of the bond portfolio and the change in the value of the futures position for various yield movements away from 9.15 percent. This difference is the gain or loss due to the imperfections of the hedge.

If the implied futures yield falls 50 basis points from 9.15 to 8.65 percent, we see from Figure 6.4 that the 7¼ percent bond increases in value $4.3679 per $100 face and the 12½ percent bond gains $5.6995. The change in the value of our hedged position is

Figure 6.6 Imperfections of T-Bond Hedge: Appropriate Hedge Ratio, 12½ Percent May 2009-14 Bond

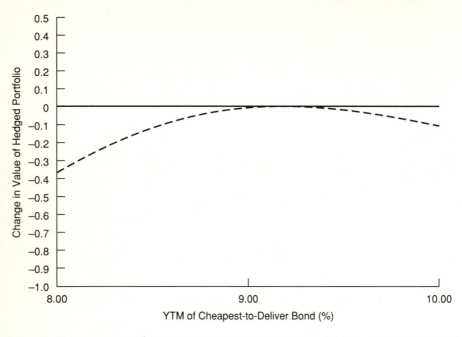

Change in Hedged Portfolio Position

> = Change in value of bond portfolio – Change in value of futures position

> = Change in value of 12½% bond

$$- \frac{(\text{Hedge ratio})(\text{Change in value of } 7\frac{1}{4}\% \text{ bond})}{\text{Conversion factor}}$$

$$= \$5.6995 - \frac{(1.213)(\$4.3679)}{0.9176}$$

$$= -\$0.075 \text{ per } \$100 \text{ face,}$$

where we compute the change in the value of the futures position using Equation 6.23. The hedged position incurs a small loss because the yield change affects the value of the bonds and the futures position slightly differently.

   We see from Figure 6.6 that no matter in which direction yields move, the hedged position loses money. We say this position has **negative convexity**. A position has **positive convexity** if the hedged value of the portfolio increases regardless of the direction in which yields move. Whether a position has positive or negative convexity depends on the relative convexities of the bond portfolio being hedged and the cheapest-to-deliver bond.

Figure 6.7 Imperfections of T-Bond Hedge: Inappropriate Hedge Ratio, 12½ Percent May 2009-14 Bond

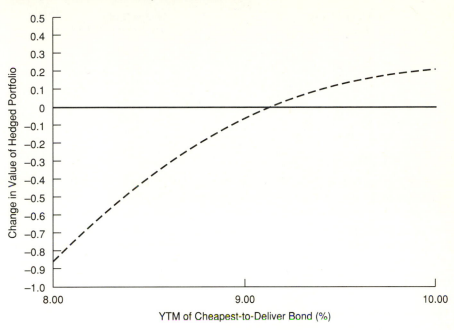

Figure 6.7 shows that the hedge imperfections are more serious, and not consistently positive or negative, if the hedge ratios initially are inappropriate for the current yield to maturity. It graphs the performance of a hedge in which the hedge ratios have been set for a 10.15 percent yield but the current yield is 9.15 percent. The bondholder in this situation has not adjusted the hedge ratio. Like Figure 6.6, Figure 6.7 graphs the differences in the value changes experienced by the bonds and the futures position if the yield moves away from 9.15 percent.

In this hypothetical experiment, the hedge ratio for the 12½ percent bond was set at 1.256 when the futures yield was 10.15 percent. If the futures yield now drops 50 basis points, from 9.15 to 8.65 percent, the net change in value of the hedged position will be

$$\text{Change in hedged portfolio position} = \$5.6995 - \frac{(1.256)(\$4.3679)}{0.9176}$$

$$= -\$0.280 \text{ per } \$100 \text{ face.}$$

This is a much larger loss than the one incurred when the hedge ratio had been set properly when the futures yield moved to 9.15 percent. The increase in potential losses from failing to adjust the hedge ratio must be weighed against the transactions and monitoring costs incurred by frequent hedge ratio adjustment. The decision to change a hedge critically depends on the relative convexities of the

Table 6.4 Hedge Ratios Calculated from Various Yield Changes, Example 6.10: Futures Yield of 9.15 Percent

Yield Change (Basis Points)	Hedge Ratio for 12½% Bond (2009-14)
5	1.2099
10	1.2110
20	1.2132
30	1.2154
40	1.2175
50	1.2197

bond being hedged and the bond underlying the futures. We will encounter dynamic hedges again when we discuss options in Chapter 9.

Duration Analysis   Up to this point, we have calculated T-bond hedge ratios by using the bond pricing equation, Equation 6.1, to determine how much a given yield change would affect the prices of the T-bond being hedged and the T-bond underlying the futures contract. In Example 6.10, we used a 20-basis-point yield increase to compute the hedge ratios, but we would have obtained similar ratios with other yield changes. Table 6.4 shows hedge ratios calculated with various yield increments for the bonds in Example 6.10.

Clearly, hedge ratios are not very sensitive to the yield changes chosen to calculate them. This method of observing how bond prices change with a given yield change is called the **basis-point-value technique**.

There is another method of computing hedge ratios that does not depend on the size of the yield increment assumed. It uses the durations of the bond to be hedged and the bond underlying the futures and is called the **relative duration technique**.[23] First, we assume that shifts in the yields of the cheapest-to-deliver bond and the bonds being hedged are the same, so there is no basis risk. If we compute a hedge ratio using the basis-point-value technique with increasingly smaller yield changes, we will get the following result:

$$\text{Hedge ratio} = \left(\frac{D_c P_c}{D_f P_f}\right)\left(\frac{1 + r_f}{1 + r_c}\right)(\text{Conversion factor of CTD}), \qquad (6.28)$$

where

P_c = price of cash bond

P_f = price of cheapest-to-deliver bond with the same face value

---

[23] See Chambers [1984], Landes, Stoffels, and Seifert [1985], Little [1985], Chance [1986], and Toevs and Jacob [1986] for a further discussion of using duration in bond hedges.

D_c = duration of bond being hedged

D_f = duration of cheapest-to-deliver bond

r_f = yield to maturity implied by the futures

r_c = yield to maturity used for bond being hedged

All of these variables are as of the futures expiration date.

This equation is derived from Equation 6.6, which can be rewritten as[24]

$$\Delta P = (-D)(\Delta r)\left(\frac{P}{1+r}\right).\tag{6.29}$$

If we apply Equation 6.29 to both ΔP_c and ΔP_f, we obtain

$$\frac{\Delta P_c}{\Delta P_f} = \left(\frac{D_c}{D_f}\right)\left(\frac{\Delta r_c}{\Delta r_f}\right)\left(\frac{1+r_f}{1+r_c}\right)\left(\frac{P_c}{P_f}\right) = \frac{\text{Change in price of cash bond}}{\text{Change in price of CTD bond}}.\tag{6.30}$$

Our assumption that changes in yield are equal implies that

$$\Delta r_c = \Delta r_f,$$

Hence, combining Equation 6.30 with Equation 6.27 gives us Equation 6.28.

Though this result is somewhat complicated mathematically, it can be understood intuitively. Duration measures the sensitivity of a bond's price to yield changes. The higher the duration of a bond, the more the bond value is affected by yield changes. Equation 6.28 states that if a high-duration bond is hedged with a futures based on a lower-duration bond, the hedge ratio must be high enough that the changes in the futures price will cover changes in the cash price.

The relative duration technique differs from the basis-point-value technique only in that it assumes very small yield changes. Hedge ratios derived from bond durations are very similar to those computed with the basis-point-value technique. The relative duration technique hedge ratio for the 12½ percent May 2009-14 bond is 1.2078. This is almost identical to the hedge ratios calculated with the basis-point-value technique shown in Table 6.4.

Using T-Bond Futures to Change the Duration of a Bond Portfolio   In Chapter 5, we learned how to change the maturity of a T-bill by taking positions in short T-bill futures. Now we will see how to use T-bond futures to change the duration of a bond portfolio.

We can lower a bond portfolio's duration by taking a short position in T-bond futures. With a properly determined hedge ratio and dynamic hedging, a short T-bond futures position can lock in a T-bond sales price for the expiration date of

---

[24] Recall that Equation 6.29 holds literally only for extremely small changes in yield.

Table 6.5 Cash-and-Carry Quasi-Arbitrage Table for T-Bond Portfolio Manager

Benchmark position: sale of T-bonds and purchase of T-bills to shorten duration

Cash-and-Carry Pure Arbitrage Components	Cash-and-Carry Quasi-Arbitrage Components	Relevant Price or Rate
1. Buy spot	Refrain from selling T-bonds	Bid
2. Short futures	Short futures	Bid
3. Borrow	Refrain from buying T-bill	Ask

Resulting position: synthetic shortening of duration

Transactions fees: $TF = -TF_1 + TF_2 - TF_3$
1. Save TF_1
2. Pay TF_2
3. Save TF_3

the futures contracts. This creates a synthetic T-bill that matures when the futures expires.[25] Since the duration of a discount bond such as a T-bill is simply the bond's maturity, the duration of a hedged bond will equal the time until expiration of the futures contract that hedges the bond. We can see from Equation 6.5 how a short hedge affects the duration of a bond portfolio:

Hedged portfolio duration   **(6.31)**
    = (Proportion of portfolio hedged)(Time to expiration of futures contract)
      + (Proportion of portfolio unhedged)(Initial duration),

where the proportions are in terms of market value. The more a portfolio is hedged, the more it becomes like a T-bill that matures when the futures expires and, therefore, the lower the portfolio's duration. T-bond futures thus give bond portfolio managers considerable flexibility in adjusting their portfolio durations.

Another way to shorten the duration of a portfolio is to replace T-bonds with T-bills. Table 6.5 shows that the choice between this natural strategy of selling off T-bonds and the futures strategy of hedging the T-bonds can be viewed as a cash-and-carry quasi-arbitrage problem.

The choice between the natural and futures strategy will depend on how the futures is priced relative to the fundamental no-arbitrage price. However, as Equation 6.16b demonstrates, the futures price typically will appear too low ($\Omega^c < 0$) if we naively use the no-arbitrage equation, 6.16, which ignores the options of those holding the short position. This suggests that there are fewer opportunities for cash-and-carry quasi-arbitrage than actually exist. Thus, determining the desirability of a futures strategy is somewhat more complicated for

---

[25] As in Example 6.8, if there is a coupon between the time the hedged position is taken and the futures expire, we include the future value of the coupon in the face value of the synthetic T-bill.

Table 6.6 Reverse Cash-and-Carry Quasi-Arbitrage Table for T-Bond Portfolio Manager

Benchmark position: sale of t-bills and purchase of T-bonds to lengthen duration

Reverse Cash-and-Carry Pure Arbitrage Components	Reverse Cash-and-Carry Quasi-Arbitrage Components	Relevant Price or Rate
1. Short spot	Refrain from buying T-bonds	Ask
2. Go long futures	Go long futures	Ask
3. Lend	Refrain from selling T-bonds	Bid

Resulting position: synthetic lengthening of duration

Transactions fees: $TF = -TF_1 + TF_2 - TF_3$
1. Save TF_1
2. Pay TF_2
3. Save TF_3

T-bonds, because we must determine whether the futures is priced correctly relative to Equation 6.16b.

Just as we can lower a T-bond portfolio's duration with short T-bond futures positions, we can lengthen portfolio duration with long T-bond futures positions. The latter strategy is made possible by the relationship

T-bond = T-bill + Futures.

The decision between going long futures and the natural strategy of selling T-bills and buying T-bonds can be viewed as a reverse cash-and-carry quasi-arbitrage problem. Table 6.6 outlines this choice. In this case, the existence of the seller's options may inflate the apparent number of reverse cash-and-carry quasi-arbitrages. Again, one must take great care to determine whether the futures is underpriced relative to Equation 6.16b rather than to Equation 6.16.

Basis Risk and Volatility Analysis   Up to this point, we have studied the basic principles of hedging T-bond prices under the simplifying assumption that the T-bond yield curve moves in a parallel fashion over time. If this is true, the yields of the bond being hedged and the bond underlying the futures contract always move in tandem, so a (dynamic) T-bond hedge is not subject to basis risk. But we must account for basis risk if we wish to use T-bond futures to hedge a bond whose yield behaves differently than that of the cheapest-to-deliver bond. This situation can occur if the hedged T-bond has a different coupon or maturity than the cheapest-to-deliver bond. Or the bond to be hedged may be a corporate or mortgage-backed bond that has a different risk than the cheapest-to-deliver T-bond. In such cases, T-bond futures are used to crosshedge the value of the bonds.[26]

---

[26] See Ederington [1979], Kuberek and Pefley [1983], Hilliard [1984], Chance, Marr, and Thompson [1986], Batkins [1987], and Lasser [1987] for a variety of crosshedges using T-bond futures. See McDonald [1986] for the implications of taxes for hedging.

In this section, we show how to account for the complications induced by different yield behavior in a T-bond crosshedge. First, we use regression analysis to estimate the relationship between changes in the yield of the bond to be hedged and changes in the yield of the bond underlying the futures. Then, to determine the hedge ratio, we calculate the price volatilities of the two bonds from the estimated relationship between their yields.[27]

We estimate the yield relationship with the following regression:

$$\Delta r_c = \alpha + \beta \Delta r_f + \varepsilon, \tag{6.32}$$

where, as before, r_f is the yield to maturity implied by the futures and r_c is the yield used for the cash bond that is to be hedged.[28] The ε term represents random error in the relationship between the cash yield and the futures yield and is the factor that induces basis risk.

Equation 6.32 shows that aside from random error, a 20-basis-point move in the yield on the bond underlying the futures will be accompanied by a $(\beta)(20)$-basis-point change in the yield on the cash bond. Our earlier assumption was that $\beta = 1$ and $\varepsilon = 0$, so that $\Delta r_c = \Delta r_f$. We obtained the hedge ratio from Equation 6.25 by computing the changes in the price of the cash bond, P_c, and the price of the cheapest-to-deliver bond, P_f, that would occur if both bonds experienced a given yield increase—say, of 20 basis points. Now, without the assumption of equal yield changes, the basis-point-value technique of computing hedge ratios must incorporate the fact that if r_f changes by 20 basis points, r_c will change by $(\beta)(20)$ basis points, on average. For example, if $\beta = 0.7$, we will calculate the numerator in Equation 6.27 with a 14-basis-point change and the denominator with the full 20-basis-point change. If $\beta < 1.0$, the hedge ratio will be smaller than the one estimated before; if $\beta > 1.0$, it will be larger. We can also use the relative duration technique to calculate the hedge ratios by noting that in Equation 6.30, $\Delta r_c / \Delta r_f = \beta$. We would multiply the relative duration hedge ratio in Equation 6.28 by β.

As before, our hedge ratio must account for the fact that the yield *levels,* r_c and r_f, may differ. We must use different yield values to compute the prices and durations of the two bonds. We will follow our earlier procedure and use the yield to maturity implied by the futures price for r_f and

$$r_c = r_f + (\text{Current } r_c - \text{Current } r_f)$$

for r_c.

Once we have computed the appropriate hedge ratio, we can determine the basis risk of the hedge from the properties of the random error, ε, in Equation 6.32.

---

[27] Usually we do not derive hedge ratios by regressing the changes in the price of the bond to be hedged on the changes in the cheapest-to-deliver T-bond price (divided by its conversion factor), for two reasons. First, the relationship will depend on the level of yields, as we saw earlier. Second, we often lack data precise enough to perform such a regression.

[28] Of course, we are assuming the relationship between changes in yield is linear.

As in Chapter 3, we use the standard deviation of ε to determine reasonable bounds for the size of ε. We can then use the bond pricing equations to determine the price effects of random errors of various magnitudes.

Example 6.11 illustrates a hedge in which the yield of the portfolio being hedged behaves differently than the yield of the bond underlying the futures.

■ **Example 6.11:   Hedging a AAA Bond with T-Bond Futures**   Suppose we have a portfolio of AAA bonds that we wish to hedge from March 31, 1989, until June 30, 1989. The portfolio has an average coupon of 10 percent and an average maturity of 23 years. We will crosshedge this portfolio with a short position in June 1989 futures. As we saw in Example 6.7, the cheapest-to-deliver bond for the June contract is the 7¼ percent May 2016 (27-year) T-bond. The market considers AAA bonds riskier than T-bonds, so their yields tend to exceed the yields on T-bonds with similar coupons and maturities. AAA and T-bond yields move together, but they do not move in lockstep, so our proposed hedge will be subject to basis risk.

Our first task is to determine whether the T-bond yield moves closely enough with the AAA portfolio yield to make a hedge feasible. Figure 6.8 attempts to represent this correlation with a plot of a weekly index of 30-year T-bond yields against a weekly index of AAA yields. As is often the case in applications, we do not have the exact data we need. In this instance, we use a 30-year bond yield to represent the yield on a 7¼ percent, 27-year T-bond, and the bonds used to calculate the AAA yield cover a variety of coupons and maturities. But the yield correlations we derive should be close enough for our purposes.

While the correlation between the two yields is not perfect, it appears that much of the change in AAA rates is associated with changes in the 30-year T-bond rate. Table 6.7 presents the results of a regression of changes in the AAA yield on changes in the 30-year T-bond yield. The R-squared statistic of 0.6556 indicates a correlation of 0.8097, which is high enough to warrant considering a crosshedge. The regression also indicates that AAA yields are less volatile than T-bond yields. For every 20-basis-point movement in the T-bond yield, the AAA yield moves only about $(0.547283)(20) = 11$ basis points. To calculate our hedge ratios, we will increase the T-bond yield by 20 basis points and the AAA yield by 11 basis points.

Determining the Correct Hedge Ratio   Now that we have an estimated relationship between AAA and 30-year T-bond yields, we must determine the base yield levels to use in calculating the hedge ratios. Suppose the current yields are

Current yield to maturity on 7¼% bond	9.14%
Current yield to maturity on 10% AAA portfolio	10.13
Yield to maturity implied by futures on 7¼% bond	9.15

We will use the 9.15 percent rate implied by the futures contract as the base yield for determining changes in the value of the T-bond futures. The current yield on the AAA portfolio is 99 basis points greater than the yield on the cheapest-to-deliver T-bond. We assume this difference will continue, on average, until the

Figure 6.8 30-Year T-Bond versus AAA Rates, 1/1986–3/1989

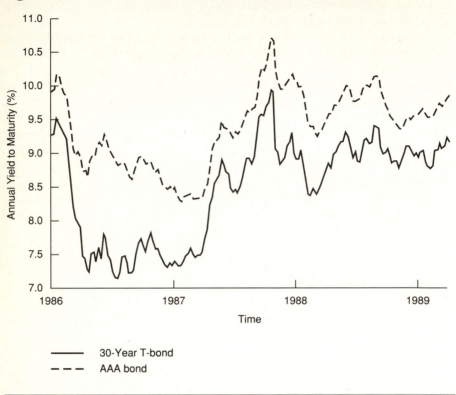

Source: Federal Reserve Bank of Chicago.

futures expire. Thus, the appropriate base yield for the AAA portfolio is the futures yield plus the differential in the cash yields, or 10.14 percent.

We can determine the hedge ratio by calculating how the values of the 7¼ percent T-bond and the 10 percent AAA portfolio respond to yield increases of 20 and 11 basis points, respectively, over the assumed base yields:

Change in 7¼% T-bond price (yield moves from 9.15% to 9.35%)
    = –$1.64370 per $100 face

Change in 10% AAA portfolio (yield moves from 10.14% to 10.25%)
    = –$0.95552 per $100 face.

The conversion factor of the 7¼ percent T-bond is 0.9176, so the hedge ratio from Equation 6.27 is

$$\text{Hedge ratio} = \left(\frac{0.95552}{1.64370}\right)(0.9176)$$

$$= 0.5334.$$

Table 6.7 Regression of Weekly Change in AAA Yield on Weekly Change in 30-Year T-Bond Yield

A. Crosshedging Equation

Y = weekly change in AAA yield
X = weekly change in 30-year T-bond yield

Regression Output

Constant	−0.00007
Standard error of Y estimate	0.060168
R-squared	0.655613
Number of observations	170
Degrees of freedom	168

X coefficient(s)	0.547283
Standard error of coefficient	0.030602

B. Residual Variance Regression

Y = squared residual from crosshedging regression
X = 30-year T-bond yield

Regression Output

Constant	0.005443
Standard error of Y estimate	0.008172
R-squared	0.000419
Number of observations	170
Degrees of freedom	168

X coefficient(s)	−0.00021
Standard error of coefficient	0.000826

C. Lagged Residual Regression

Y = residual from crosshedging regression
X = lagged residual from crosshedging regression

Regression Output

Constant	0.000119
Standard error of Y estimate	0.060260
R-squared	0.002433
Number of observations	169
Degrees of freedom	167

X coefficient(s)	0.049481
Standard error of coefficient	0.077523

Of course, the hedge ratio will change as the yield to maturity on the bonds changes. If we adjust the hedge ratio frequently, we will hedge risk from general interest rate movements. However, we must still estimate the basis risk of this hedge.

Analyzing Basis Risk   The first step in estimating the size of the basis risk is to identify how much of the movement in the AAA rate is not directly related to the movement in the 30-year T-bond rate. The regression in Table 6.7 shows that the standard deviation of the weekly unexplained component of the change in the AAA rate is 0.060168 percent, or 6.02 basis points. Thus, over a week, a 95 percent confidence interval for the unexplained movement in the AAA rate is approximately

$$95\% \text{ confidence interval} = (-2)(6.02 \text{ bp}), (2)(6.02 \text{ bp})$$
$$= -12.04 \text{ bp}, 12.04 \text{ bp}.$$

We can use this confidence interval to determine the basis risk of a hedge that lasts for one week. It tells us by how much a weekly movement in the unhedged portion of the AAA rate might change the AAA bond price. Figure 6.9 shows how a 1- or 2-standard-deviation unhedged movement in the AAA rate changes the AAA bond price at various yields implied by the T-bond futures.

At the current T-bond futures yield of 9.15 percent, the implied rate for the AAA bond is 10.14 percent. We could lock in this implied AAA rate with a dynamic hedge if there were no basis risk. However, if the unexplained portion of the movement in the AAA price were 2 standard deviations above its mean of zero, the hedged rate would be

$$\text{Hedged rate} = \text{Rate with no basis risk} + \text{Unexplained rate change}$$
$$= 10.1400\% + 0.1204\%$$
$$= 10.2604\%.$$

The price change implied by the 0.1204 percent change in the hedged rate is

Implied price change (yield moves from 10.1400% to 10.2604%)
$$= \text{Price with unexplained change} - \text{Price without unexplained change}$$
$$= -\$1.1044 \text{ per } \$100 \text{ face.}$$

Figure 6.9 indicates that an unhedged (unexplained) movement in the AAA yield will have a larger effect on the AAA price if the current yield to maturity is low than it will if it is high.[29] This is due to bond price convexity. In Figure 6.4, we see that the higher the yield to maturity of a bond, the smaller the dollar effect of a given yield change.

---

[29] One might suspect that the standard deviation of ε would increase as bond yields increase. Part B of Table 6.7 presents a regression of the squared residual on the yield levels. There appears to be no relationship.

Figure 6.9   Dollar Basis Risk of AAA Bond Hedge, 10 Percent, 23-Year Portfolio

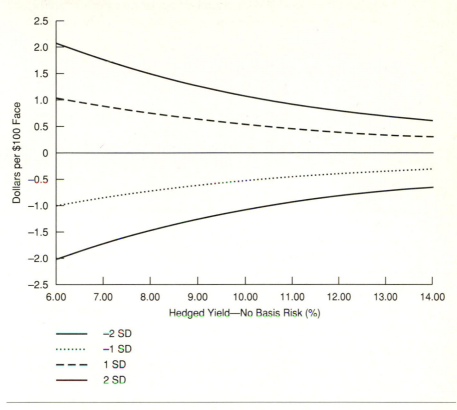

If the hedge is to be maintained for more than a week, there will clearly be a greater possibility for unhedged movement in the AAA rate. If the weekly unhedged movements are uncorrelated over time, we can use the following formula to calculate the standard deviation of unhedged AAA rate changes:

N-week standard deviation of unhedged AAA movements   **(6.33)**
= $(\sqrt{N})$(1-week standard deviation of unhedged AAA movements).

In the current case, however, the weekly unhedged movements in the AAA rate may be correlated over time. Thus, the N-week unhedged movements may be somewhat more or less risky than Equation 6.33 predicts (depending on whether the unhedged movements are positively or negatively correlated over time), and the use of Equation 6.33 may misrepresent the basis risk of an N-week hedge.

A preferable approach in this case is to calculate the standard deviation of the N-week unexplained portion of AAA rate changes directly from the estimated residuals of the regression in Table 6.7. For example, to compute the standard deviation of the unexplained rate movements over five weeks, we simply add up the estimated residuals for each consecutive five-week period and take the standard deviation of the resulting constructed variable. Thus, we would add up the residuals from weeks 1 through 5, 6 through 10, 11 through 15, and so on.

The following table shows that the standard deviation estimates are higher under this "adding-up" technique than those computed from Equation 6.33:

N-Week Standard Deviations of Unexplained Portion of AAA Rate Changes

N	Equation 6.33 Technique	Adding-up Technique
1	0.0602%	0.0602%
5	0.1346	0.1732
10	0.1904	0.2595

This indicates that the unexplained portion of the AAA rate changes reinforces itself over time, so the adding-up technique produces more accurate standard deviation estimates.[30]

Another way to examine this issue is to determine the maximum and minimum movements in the unexplained component of the AAA rate for one, five, and ten weeks:

Minimum and Maximum Movements in Unexplained Component of AAA Rate

N	Minimum	Maximum
1	–0.1967%	0.2620%
5	–0.3462	0.3978
10	–0.5075	0.4896

The growth of the maximum and minimum movements in the various time periods indicates that the AAA and T-bond yields tend to drift further apart over time.[31] This evidence supports our conclusion that in this case it would be unwise to extrapolate the one-week standard deviation to ten weeks using Equation 6.33.

Figure 6.10 plots the price basis risk for a 1-standard-deviation move in the unexplained component of the AAA rate over periods of one, five, and ten weeks. This figure quantifies the effect of the length of the hedge on the basis risk. ∎

The Seller's Options

Throughout this chapter, we have alluded to the impact on T-bond futures prices of the seller's option to choose which eligible T-bond to deliver and when to deliver it. In our discussion of the fundamental no-arbitrage equation, we found that both the quoted futures price and the implied repo rate for the cheapest-to-deliver bond (before delivery) typically appear to be too low because they do not include the value short-position holders derive from the seller's options. In this section, we

---

[30] Part C of Table 6.7 also supports the positive correlation between unhedged movements in rates.

[31] Of course, this drifting apart of rates can continue only for so long before fundamental economic forces tend to bring them back into line.

Figure 6.10 Dollar Basis Risk (One Standard Deviation) for Different Hedge Horizons

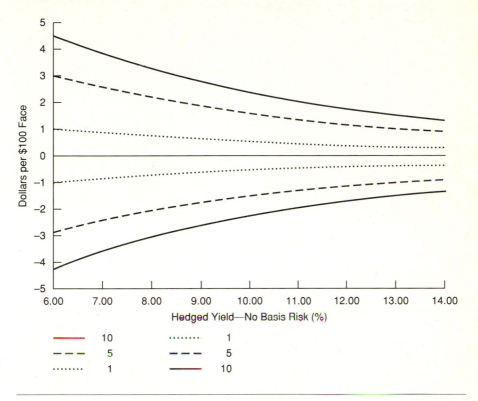

will discuss the seller's options and their influence on futures prices in much greater detail.

The seller's options fall into two categories. The **timing option** refers to the right of the short-position holder to specify when to deliver during the delivery month. The **quality option** refers to the short party's right to sell the initial cheapest-to-deliver bond to make an extra profit if another bond becomes the cheapest-to-deliver bond.

While many futures contracts have both timing and quality options, several peculiarities of T-bond futures make these options particularly valuable for the T-bond contracts. As we noted earlier, the futures settlement price used for computing the invoice price is determined at 2:00 p.m. Central Standard Time (CST) every day during the delivery period. But the short can give notice of intention to deliver at any time up until 8:00 p.m. CST. The short's flexibility in this situation is called the **wildcard option**, and it has two components. If interest rates move between 2:00 and 8:00 p.m., the short party may be able to deliver the bond he or she holds at a favorable price. If not, the short can wait until the next day. This is called the **timing option component of the wildcard**. The short also has until 5:00 p.m. the following day to choose to deliver a different bond. If interest rates move substantially between 2:00 p.m. one day and 5:00 p.m. the next, the short party may make a profit by changing the delivered bond. This is called the **quality option component of the wildcard**.

There are two other quality options. One gives the short party until the second-to-last business day of the delivery month (until 3:00 p.m.) to decide which bond to deliver even though the last day of trading is the eighth-to-last business day of the delivery month. This is called the **end-of-the-month option**. The other allows the short party to profit if the cheapest-to-deliver bond changes before expiration of the contract. All of the seller's options have significant value because the imperfections in the conversion factors create real economic differences among the choices of bonds and delivery dates.

The Timing Option Component of the Wildcard Option   The option to choose the delivery day within the delivery month is very valuable to an investor in a T-bond cash-and-carry. The futures price is fixed from 2:00 to 8:00 p.m. every day, while the cash prices of the bonds the investor holds are free to move. Changes in bond prices during this period can only help the investor, because he or she has the flexibility to act on favorable movements and wait out the unfavorable ones. Example 6.12 shows how an investor can profit from the timing option component of the wildcard option.

▪ **Example 6.12: The Timing Option**   Suppose that on March 31, 1989, an investor wishes to enter into the T-bond cash-and-carry presented in Example 6.8. He pays $83,909,000 for $100 million face value of 7¼ percent T-bonds that expire on May 15, 2016. These bonds have a conversion factor of 0.9176, so the investor completes the cash-and-carry by going short 918 T-bond futures contracts that expire in June. The futures settlement price for the June 1989 contract is $88-13, and the short-term interest rate is 10 percent.

The investor makes a small departure from the cash-and-carry in Example 6.8 by deciding to terminate his synthetic lending on June 14. The time line for his strategy is

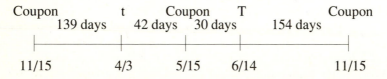

We will first compute the investor's implied repo rate under the assumption that there are no seller's options. Then we will show how the investor can gain from the timing option component of the wildcard. We know the market price of the T-bond purchased in the cash-and-carry, so the next step in computing the implied repo rate is to calculate the invoice price locked in by going short futures. The decimal futures price (per $100 face) is $88.40625, so the futures contract's invoice principal amount per $100 face is

$$\text{Invoice principal amount} = (0.9176)(\$88.40625)$$
$$= \$81.122 \text{ per } \$100 \text{ face.}$$

The underlying bond of the futures contract will accrue the following interest over the 30 days between the coupon payment on May 15 and delivery on June 14:

$$\text{Futures accrued interest} = \left(\frac{30}{184}\right)\left(\frac{\$7.25}{2}\right)$$

$$= \$0.591 \text{ per } \$100 \text{ face.}$$

Therefore, the total invoice price locked in by the futures contract is

$$\text{Total invoice price} = F_{t,T}$$
$$= \$81.122 + \$0.591$$
$$= \$81.713 \text{ per } \$100 \text{ face.}$$

Next, we determine the future value at the futures expiration date of the coupons the investor receives on his T-bond holdings. The investor will receive a coupon of $7.25/2 = $3.625 per $100 par on May 15. The future value of this coupon as of delivery on June 14 will be

$$\text{Future value of coupons} = FV_T(\text{Coupons from t to T})$$
$$= (\$3.625)[1 + (30/360)(0.10)]$$
$$= \$3.655 \text{ per } \$100 \text{ face.}$$

Now we can compute the implied repo rate for the 7¼ percent May 2016 bond from Equation 6.24:

$$\text{Implied repo rate} = \frac{\$81.713 + \$3.655 - \$83.909}{\$83.909}$$
$$= 1.74\% \text{ for 72 days}$$
$$= 8.70\% \text{ annualized.}$$

Suppose the investor commits on June 12 at 2:00 p.m. to deliver on June 14.[32] Just prior to this move, he must go short an additional $1,000 - 918 = 82$ contracts so that he holds contracts with a face value of $100 million and can deliver his entire T-bond holdings. Since he is entering into the 82 short positions at the contract's expiration, there is no gain or loss on the new contracts and they will not affect his overall profit on the cash-and-carry.

Now assume the yield to maturity on the 7¼ percent bond is 8.50 percent on June 12. Then the quoted price and total spot price for delivery of the bond on June 14 are as follows:

---

[32] The relevant quoted spot price on June 12 will be for June 14 settlement, because that is when delivery will occur.

7¼ Percent May 2016 Bond at 8.5 Percent per $100 Face

Quoted Price	Accrued Interest	Total Spot Price
$86.848	$0.591	$87.439

Because we assume there are no seller's options, the futures settlement price should converge to the delivery-adjusted spot price of the 7¼ percent bond:

$$\text{Futures settlement price (no seller's options)} = \frac{\$86.848}{0.9176}$$

$$= \$94.647 \text{ per } \$100 \text{ face.}$$

The total price received for announcing delivery is therefore

Total price received for delivery
  = (Number of contracts)(Invoice price per contract)
  = (Number of contracts)[(Conversion factor)(Quoted decimal futures)
    + (Accrued interest)]($100,000)
  = (1,000)[(0.9176)(0.94647) + 0.00591]($100,000)
  = $87.439 million.

Now let's assume the timing option component of the wildcard does exist. Suppose the investor decides not to close out his futures position at 2:00 p.m. on June 12 and does not enter into the additional 82 short positions required for immediate delivery. Suppose also that at 4:00 p.m. on June 12, the yield to maturity on the 7¼ percent bond falls 70 basis points to 7.80 percent. The bond price becomes

7¼ Percent May 2016 Bond at 7.8 Percent per $100 Face

Quoted Price	Accrued Interest	Total Spot Price
$93.838	$0.591	$94.429

The investor can now commit to deliver 918 $100,000-face-value bonds against his 918 T-bond futures positions at the 0.94647 decimal futures price that was established at 2:00 p.m. He can sell his additional 82 $100,000-face-value bonds at the current market price. This yields a total inflow of

Total proceeds
  = Proceeds from futures delivery + Proceeds from cash sale
  = (918)[(0.9176)(0.94647) + 0.00591]($100,000) + (82)($94,429)
  = $80.269 million + $7.743 million
  = $88.012 million.

The incremental profit from waiting until 4:00 to commit to delivery is

Incremental profit
  = Total proceeds from waiting – Profits from immediate notice
  = $88.012 million – $87.439 million
  = $0.573 million.

We can now calculate the incremental contribution to the implied repo rate of the investor's gain from the timing option. His additional profit as a percentage of the initial \$83.909 million investment is

$$\text{Addition to implied repo rate} = \frac{\$0.573}{\$83.909}$$
$$= 0.68\% \text{ for 72 days}$$
$$= 3.40\% \text{ per annum.}$$

His total implied repo rate earned is therefore

Total implied repo rate
= Implied repo rate without timing option
  + Incremental rate from timing option
= 8.70% + 3.40%
= 12.10% per annum.

When we did not include the timing option in our calculations, it appeared that a cash-and-carry synthetic lending would earn 130 basis points less than the 10 percent short-term interest rate (8.70% − 10.00% = −130 basis points). But we have seen that because of the timing option, the investor will actually earn an implied repo rate of 12.10 percent on the cash-and-carry—a full 210 basis points more than the short-term interest rate.

Now suppose interest rates do not fall significantly after 2:00 p.m. on June 12. Since the investor cannot profit from the timing option in this case, he might wait until the next trading day to act. He is still hedged against price changes, because he holds the appropriate short futures position. The next day, the futures price will move back into line with the cash market and the investor will have the timing option again, starting when the futures settlement price is fixed at 2:00 p.m. CST. In fact, the investor will have this option every day through the ninth-to-last trading day in the delivery month. The investor cannot lose from the timing option, because he can wait until the next day to deliver. Thus, the 8.70 percent implied repo rate we initially calculated is a *lower bound* on the rate the investor will earn. As we have seen, he may earn significantly more because of the timing option. ∎

The investor in Example 6.12 can also gain from the timing option component of the wildcard if the current cheapest-to-deliver bond has a conversion factor greater than 1 and interest rates rise between 2:00 and 8:00 p.m. Suppose the bond he holds for delivery has a conversion factor of 1.5. To hedge bonds with \$100 million face value, he must enter into 1,500 short futures positions. If rates rise after the futures settlement price is established at 2:00 p.m., the bond price will fall but the futures settlement price will stay the same. The investor will deliver the \$100-million-face-value bonds that he holds into the futures contract. He can then complete the delivery by buying bonds of \$50 million face value at the new, lower price. He will earn an extra profit on the \$50-million-face-value bonds, because the futures price cannot fall into line with the new bond price.

Because of the timing option, the futures settlement price at 2:00 will not converge to the delivery-adjusted quoted spot price of the cheapest-to-deliver bond. If it did, arbitrageurs could buy the cheapest-to-deliver bond at 2:00 and hedge themselves perfectly until the next day by going short futures. They would thus receive a free timing option. The futures settlement price must fall until this cash-and-carry becomes a fair deal. Thus, we expect the futures price at 2:00 p.m. to be somewhat below the delivery-adjusted quoted spot price of the cheapest-to-deliver bond.

The Quality Option   The quality option gives the short the opportunity to earn an additional profit if an interest rate movement causes the cheapest-to-deliver bond to change. There are three ways in which this option can work to the advantage of the short party: through the wildcard option, through the end-of-the-month option, and from additional profits to a cash-and-carry strategy simply from a change in the cheapest-to-deliver bond.

The Quality Option Component of the Wildcard Option   The quality option component of the wildcard option is very much like the timing option just described, as Example 6.13 demonstrates.

▪ **Example 6.13: The Quality Option Component of the Wildcard Option**
Suppose the investor in Example 6.12 has entered into a cash-and-carry synthetic lending strategy on March 31, 1989, by purchasing 1,000 7¼ percent May 2016 T-bonds of $100,000 face value for $83,909,000. As before, he completes the cash-and-carry by going short 918 T-bond futures contracts that expire in June 1989.

Again we assume the yield to maturity on the 7¼ percent bond is 8.50 percent on June 12. From Example 6.12, we know that the total spot price of the bond is $87.439 per $100 face. If there are no seller's options, the investor can receive $87.439 on June 14 by announcing delivery of the 7¼ percent bonds at 2:00 p.m. on June 12 and going short an additional 82 futures contracts.

Now suppose that the 7¼ percent T-bond yield rises 70 basis points to 9.20 percent between 2:00 and 8:00 p.m. and there is a flat yield curve. The price of the 7¼ percent bond moves to

7¼ Percent May 2016 Bond at 9.2 Percent per $100 Face

Quoted Price	Accrued Interest	Total Spot Price
$80.676	$0.591	$81.267

There is no profit to be made from the timing option in this case, because it would involve delivering 918 $100,000-face-value bonds into the futures contracts and selling the remaining 82 at the new, lower price of $81.267. However, the investor may be able to make a profit from the quality option. He can earn an incremental profit if the net proceeds from selling the 1,000 7¼ percent bonds, buying 918 ($100,000 face value) of a different bond, and delivering these 918 bonds exceeds the proceeds from delivering the 7¼ percent bonds at 2:00. This

Table 6.8 Delivery Proceeds from Quality Option Component of Wildcard Option, June 1989 T-Bond Futures (Yield Move from 8.50 to 9.20 Percent)

Coupon	Expiration Date	Conversion Factor	Quoted Price	Accrued Interest	Delivery Proceeds
10.375%	11/15/2007-12	1.2257	$110.31943	$0.84579	$85.72110
12.000	8/15/2008-13	1.3874	124.97838	3.94475	87.08233
12.500	8/15/2009-14	1.4453	129.99306	4.10912	87.50956
9.875	11/15/2015	1.2042	106.64030	0.80503	87.99916
9.250	2/15/2016	1.1367	100.47065	3.04075	87.79809
7.250	5/15/2016	0.9176	80.67572	0.59103	86.93310
7.500	11/15/2016	0.9447	83.07922	0.61141	87.08130
8.750	5/15/2017	1.0829	95.49238	0.71332	87.69367
8.875	8/15/2017	1.0972	96.72517	2.91747	87.80444
9.125	5/15/2018	1.1257	99.23133	0.74389	87.98003
9.000	11/15/2018	1.1122	97.96654	0.73370	87.96815
8.875	2/15/2019	1.0986	96.68979	2.91747	87.95856

strategy sometimes earns an extra profit because of the imperfections in the conversion factors.

Table 6.8 shows the net price the investor will receive from this strategy for various eligible bonds. For example, suppose he sells the 7¼ percent bonds and purchases 918 9⅞ percent, November 2015 bonds of $100,000 face value. The current price of the 9⅞ percent bonds is

9⅞ Percent November 2015 Bond at 9.2 Percent per $100 Face

Quoted Price	Accrued Interest	Total Spot Price
$106.640	$0.805	$107.445

The inflow from selling the old bonds is

$$\text{Inflow from selling } 7\tfrac{1}{4}\% \text{ bonds} = (1,000)(\$81,267)$$
$$= \$81.267 \text{ million.}$$

The outflow from buying the new bonds is

$$\text{Outflow from buying } 9\tfrac{7}{8}\% \text{ bonds} = (918)(\$107,445)$$
$$= \$98.635 \text{ million.}$$

The invoice price for delivering the 9⅞ percent bonds is determined by the $94.647-per-$100-face-value futures settlement price at 2:00 p.m. and the bonds' conversion factor of 1.2042:

$$\text{Invoice price for } 9\tfrac{7}{8}\% \text{ bonds} = (1.2042)(\$94.647) + \$0.805$$
$$= \$114.779 \text{ per } \$100 \text{ face.}$$

Therefore, the total proceeds from delivering the 918 9⅞ percent bonds are

Total proceeds from delivering 9⅞% bonds = (918)($114,779)
$$= \$105.367 \text{ million.}$$

The net proceeds from the bond swap are

Net proceeds from selling 7¼% and buying 9⅞%
= $81.267 million – $98.635 million + $105.367 million
= $87.999 million.

The incremental profit from waiting is

Incremental profit
= Total proceeds from waiting – Profits from immediate notice
= $87.999 million – $87.439 million
= $0.560 million.

The addition to the implied repo rate is

$$\text{Addition to implied repo rate} = \frac{\$0.560}{\$83.909}$$
$$= 0.67\% \text{ for 72 days}$$
$$= 3.35\% \text{ per annum.}$$

The optimal bond to swap for the 7¼ percent bond is determined by taking the maximum net proceeds from Table 6.8. In this case, the 9⅞ percent bond is best.[33] ∎

Although the effect of the quality option component of the wildcard option is very similar to that of the timing option component, the two components take on different values for different rate moves. The timing option component becomes valuable when the initial bond has a conversion factor below 1 and yields fall or when the initial bond has a conversion factor above 1 and yields rise, as we saw in Example 6.12. In Example 6.13, we saw that when the initial bond has a conversion factor below 1, the quality option component becomes valuable when yields rise. Similarly, when the initial bond has a conversion factor above 1, the quality option component becomes valuable when yields fall.[34]

The investor who wishes to exercise the quality option has two decisions to make. First, he or she must decide whether to give notice of delivery by 8:00 p.m. The investor merely renews the option by not giving notice.[35] Second, he or she has until 5:00 p.m. of the following day to decide which bond to deliver. Thus, an

---

[33] Notice that the optimal bond is not necessarily the one that minimizes the delivery-adjusted spot price.

[34] See Arak and Goodman [1987] for a theoretical discussion of this point.

[35] For simplicity, we assume the investor does not transact until the following day. Thus, all prices are for June 14 delivery.

investor who detects an advantageous move in interest rates between 2:00 and 8:00 p.m. and swaps into a new bond may profit even further if rates move again between 8:00 p.m. and 5:00 p.m. the following day.

The End-of-the-Month Option   The end-of-the-month option is very similar to the quality option component of the wildcard option. Trading in a futures contract ceases on the eighth-to-last business day of the contract's delivery month. At that point, the investor in Examples 6.12 and 6.13 will be holding 7¼ percent May 2016 bonds of $100 million face value and will be short 918 contracts. He must go short an additional 82 contracts to bring his total to the 1,000 contracts necessary for delivering his $100-million-face-value bond holdings. He need not decide which bond to deliver until 3:00 p.m. of the second-to-last business day of the month and so can take advantage of interest rate movements as in Example 6.13. However, there are two differences in the end-of-the-month situation. First, the investor is holding 1,000 short futures positions, so if he sells the 7¼ percent bonds, he must buy $100 million face value (instead of $91.8 million) of the new bonds. Second, the period over which interest rates can change is much longer.

Delivery Date Convergence   Like the timing option, both the quality option component of the wildcard option and the end-of-the month option will cause the futures settlement price to fall below the delivery-adjusted spot price of the cheapest-to-deliver bond at 2:00 p.m. Thus, on any date during the delivery month, we expect that

$$\text{Futures settlement price at 2:00 p.m.}$$
$$= \left(\frac{\text{Quoted price of cheapest-to-deliver bond}}{\text{Conversion factor of CTD bond}} \right)$$
$$- \text{Value of timing and quality options.}$$

As a result, an investor engaging in a cash-and-carry synthetic lending can increase the implied repo rate by selling the bonds at 2:00 p.m. and closing out the futures positions. This strategy is equivalent to delivering as long as the spot and futures prices converge, but it is superior to delivering when the delivery options force the futures price below the spot price. Thus, the investor can gain from the delivery options even if he or she closes out the position at 2:00 p.m. on a given day.

Changes in the Cheapest-to-Deliver Bond   We have seen how the wildcard and end-of-the month options can add to the apparent implied repo rate from a cash-and-carry synthetic lending. We will now show how changes in the cheapest-to-deliver bond can be valuable even without the other two options. Thus, for the moment we will assume there are no wildcard or end-of-the-month options.

In Example 6.8, we calculated the implied repo rate earned on a cash-and-carry under the assumption that the bond held by the short is the cheapest to deliver throughout the life of the strategy. In such a case (when there are no other delivery options), the futures invoice price will converge to the market price of the short's bond. Because the accrued interest is the same for the futures invoice price and the market price, the price relationship at expiration is

$$c_i QF_{T,T} = QP_T^i \tag{6.34}$$

or

$$QF_{T,T} = \frac{QP_T^i}{c_i},$$

where i is the cheapest-to-deliver bond, QP_T^i is the quoted T-bond price at T, c_i is the conversion factor, and $QF_{T,T}$ is the futures settlement price at T.

The profit on the short position will be

$$
\begin{aligned}
\text{Futures profit} &= (\text{Conversion factor})(QF_{t,T} - QF_{T,T}) \\
&= c_i(QF_{t,T} - QF_{T,T}) \\
&= c_i QF_{t,T} - QP_T^i,
\end{aligned}
\tag{6.35}
$$

because the appropriate hedge ratio is the conversion factor, c_i. As usual, the convergence of the invoice price to the spot price causes the investor to be indifferent between delivering the bond or selling it and closing out the futures position.

Now consider what happens if the cheapest-to-deliver bond changes after the investor enters into the cash-and-carry. The invoice price will converge to the price of the new cheapest-to-deliver bond so that

$$c_j QF_{T,T} = QP_T^j \tag{6.36}$$

or

$$QF_{T,T} = \frac{QP_T^j}{c_j}$$

and

$$c_i QF_{T,T} < QP_T^i$$

or

$$QF_{T,T} < \frac{QP_T^i}{c_i},$$

where j refers to the new cheapest-to-deliver bond. The profit on the short position will be

$$\text{Futures profit} = (\text{Conversion factor})(QF_{t,T} - QF_{T,T}) \qquad \textbf{(6.37)}$$
$$= c_i(QF_{t,T} - QF_{T,T})$$

$$= c_i QF_{t,T} - c_i\left(\frac{QP_T^j}{c_j}\right)$$

$$= c_i QF_{t,T} - QP_T^i + c_i\left(\frac{QP_T^i}{c_i} - \frac{QP_T^j}{c_j}\right).$$

If we compare this futures profit with the profit earned if bond i remains cheapest to deliver (Equation 6.35), we see there is an additional profit of

Additional profit due to change in cheapest-to-deliver bond   **(6.38)**

$$= c_i\left(\frac{QP_T^i}{c_i} - \frac{QP_T^j}{c_j}\right) > 0.$$

It is clear from Equation 6.36 that this additional profit is positive. Example 6.14 will demonstrate how the quality option can increase a short position's earnings from a cash-and-carry.

▪ **Example 6.14:   The Value of a Change in the Cheapest-to-Deliver Bond**
Suppose the investor in Example 6.12 enters into a cash-and-carry strategy on March 31, 1989. He goes short T-bond futures that expire in June 1989 and buys $100 million face value of the current cheapest-to-deliver bond, the 7¼ percent May 2016 bond, at a price of $83.909 per $100 face. We assume he will deliver on June 14. As before, the conversion factor for the bond is 0.9176, so the investor must go short 918 futures contracts to complete the cash-and-carry.

Suppose the yield to maturity is 7.80 percent when the investor closes out his position on June 12 (for delivery on June 14). We saw in Example 6.12 that at this rate the quoted spot price of the 7¼ percent bond is $93.838 and the total spot price is $94.429 per $100 face. If the 7¼ percent bond were still the cheapest to deliver, the futures price would be

$$\text{Closing futures price} = \text{Delivery-adjusted spot price}$$
$$= \frac{\text{Quoted price}}{\text{Conversion factor}}$$
$$= \frac{\$93.838}{0.9176}$$
$$= \$102.265 \text{ per } \$100 \text{ face.}$$

However, because yields have dropped below 8 percent by June 12, the high-duration 7¼ percent bond is no longer the cheapest to deliver. The cheapest-to-deliver bond is now the low-duration 12 percent August 2008-13 bond with a conversion factor of 1.3874. Its quoted and total spot prices on June 12 are as follows:

12 Percent August 2008-13 Bond at 7.8 Percent per $100 Face

Quoted Price	Accrued Interest	Total Spot Price
$141.402	$3.945	$145.347

Its delivery-adjusted spot price is

$$\text{Delivery-adjusted spot price} = \frac{\text{Quoted price}}{\text{Conversion factor}}$$

$$= \frac{\$141.402}{1.3874}$$

$$= \$101.919 \text{ per } \$100 \text{ face.}$$

The investor can profit from the quality option by selling his $7\frac{1}{4}$ percent bonds and closing out his futures positions. Equation 6.38 shows that the additional profit due to the quality option will be

$$\text{Additional profit} = (0.918)(\$102.265 - \$101.919)$$
$$= \$0.318 \text{ per } \$100 \text{ face}$$
$$= \$0.318 \text{ million.}$$

Therefore, the quality option in this case will increase the implied repo rate by

$$\text{Increment to implied repo rate} = \frac{\text{Additional profit}}{\text{Initial investment}}$$

$$= \frac{\$0.318}{\$83.909}$$

$$= 0.38\% \text{ for 72 days}$$

$$= 1.90\% \text{ per annum.}$$

■

Effect of Delivery Options upon Futures Settlement Prices   We began this section on the seller's options by observing that the quoted futures price usually appears too low relative to the fundamental no-arbitrage price, even for the cheapest-to-deliver bond. Equivalently, the implied repo rate usually appears to be less than the short-term interest rate. Now we have seen that the delivery options are most likely responsible for this discrepancy, for they can add to the value of a short position but not reduce it. As a result, investors are willing to go short at a lower price than they would if there were no seller's options. Thus, as presented earlier, the fundamental no-arbitrage equation for the cheapest-to-deliver bond is

$$F_{t,T} = P_t(1 + r_{t,T}) - FV_T(\text{Coupons from t to T}) \qquad \textbf{(6.16b)}$$
$$\qquad - FV_T(\text{Seller's options}).$$

An important implication of Equation 6.16b is that one should not necessarily avoid cash-and-carry arbitrage just because the implied repo rate appears too low relative to the short-term interest rate. Similarly, as mentioned earlier, one should not engage in reverse cash-and-carry arbitrage just because the implied reverse repo rate appears low relative to the short-term interest rate, because going long futures entails *granting* options to the short. To determine whether the futures is fairly priced according to Equation 6.16b, we must understand how the delivery options are valued.

Option Value Determination   The delivery options have more value under some conditions than others. All will add more value to a short position if interest rates are very volatile, because then the short is more likely to be able to profit from advantageous bond price moves. Hemler [1988] did find a positive relationship between the volatility of T-bond yields and the value of the seller's options (using Equation 6.16b). The wildcard option is more valuable the earlier it is in the delivery month, because there are more days to exercise the option. The value of the possibility of a change in the cheapest-to-deliver bond is greater the longer it is until the futures contract expires, because the likelihood of such a switch increases with time. Finally, the closer market yields are to 8 percent, the more likely it is that a change in the cheapest-to-deliver bond will occur and the value of the quality options will increase. As we will see in Chapter 10, these conditions are standard properties of option valuation.

Several authors have explicitly modeled the valuation and optimal exercise of the delivery options for the T-bond contract.[36] Hemler [1988] computed the value of the seller's options using Equation 6.16b. Figure 6.11 presents his estimates of the seller's option values three, six, and nine months before contract expiration. The figure makes it clear that the value to the market of such options varies considerably over time. As expected, the seller's options tend to be more valuable the further in the future the delivery month. The average option values over his sample period were $0.53, $0.98, and $1.32 per $100 face value for contracts with three, six, and nine months, respectively, to delivery. These values are somewhat comparable to the discount of $0-9/32 that we found in Example 6.7.[37]

---

[36] See, for example, Gay and Manaster [1984, 1986], Benninga and Smirlock [1985], Kane and Marcus [1986a, 1986b], Arak and Goodman [1987], Barnhill [1987], Barnhill and Seale [1988], Hemler [1988], and Boyle [1989].

[37] In Example 6.7, we found only a 4/32 value using the T-bill rate. This is somewhat lower than the values Hemler [1988] found. Note that our values are future values and are with respect to the quoted futures price. Thus, to make them comparable to those of Hemler, we would need to discount them by 10 percent for 88 days and multiply by the conversion factor of 0.9176.

Figure 6.11   Value of Delivery Options, T-Bond Futures Contract

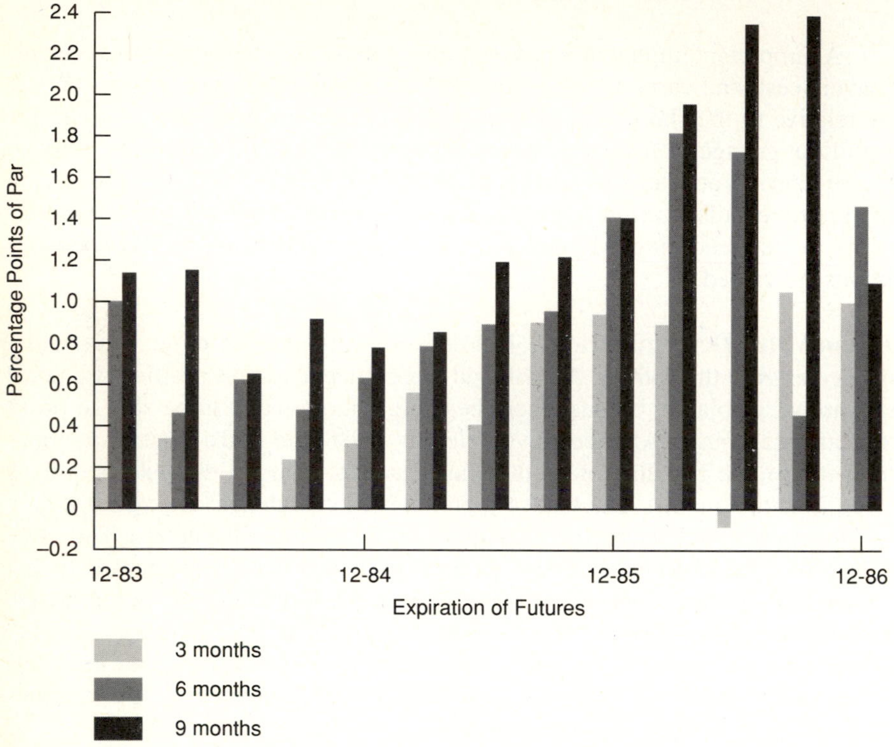

Source: Hemler [1988].

Optimal Exercise of Seller's Options   One of the complexities introduced by the seller's options for those with short positions is determining when in the delivery month to deliver. We have seen how large movements in interest rates at any time during the delivery month can lead to profits from delivering because of the wildcard option. However, when a short takes advantage of the wildcard option, he or she gives up all future wildcard options during the month as well as the end-of-the-month option. If interest rates move substantially at some point during the delivery month, we get a situation such as that in part A of Figure 6.12, in which most deliveries occur before the end of the month. In this case, the immediate profits outweigh the loss of future options. Another common situation, however, is depicted in part B of Figure 6.12. Here the short parties wait until the end of the month to maximize the value of the end-of-the-month option.[38]

---

[38] See the explicit option pricing models discussed earlier for optimal exercise strategies.

Figure 6.12 Distribution of Delivery Date

(a) December 1982 T-Bond Contract

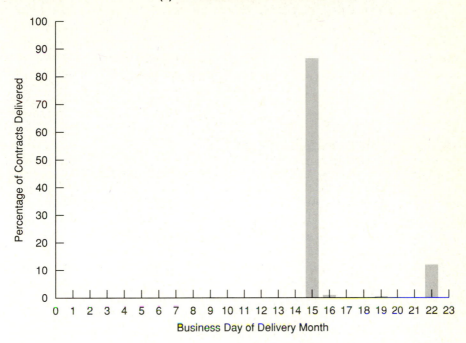

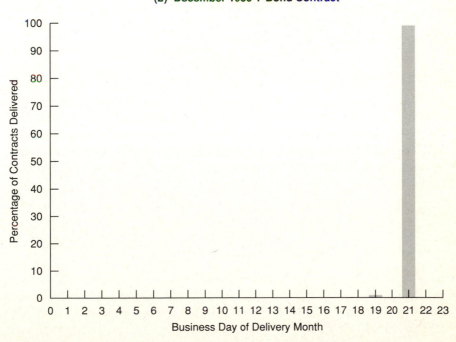

The Seller's Options and Hedging   The seller's options have several implications for hedging strategies. First, in comparing natural versus futures hedges, one must use Equation 6.16b instead of 6.16 to determine whether the T-bond futures is overpriced or underpriced. We saw this in our discussion of the use of futures to change the durations of T-bond portfolios. Second, hedgers usually find it advantageous to close out their positions before the delivery month to avoid the complex process of exercising the seller's options. Finally, even if hedgers close out their positions before the delivery month, the changing value of the seller's options can introduce some basis risk into hedges.

Municipal Bond Cash Market

Municipal bonds are long-term coupon bonds issued by municipalities, counties, states, and special districts. To keep state and local governments' borrowing costs down, the federal government does not tax the coupons on municipal bonds as it does T-bond coupons.[39] Also, T-bonds are considered virtually riskless, while municipal bonds can carry some risk. The federal government can print money to pay off its debt as a last resort, but municipal bonds are backed only by the taxing authority of the state or local government or an insurance company that insures the bonds' payments. Moody's and Standard and Poor's publish bond ratings for traded municipal bonds. These ratings are similar to those provided for corporate bonds.

Due to their tax-free status, municipal bonds usually trade at lower yields than those on taxable bonds of equivalent risk. Through these lower rates, the market equates the after-tax returns from holding taxable and nontaxable bonds. Figure 6.13 shows that municipal bond rates have been lower than 30-year T-bond rates for the past several years.[40]

Quoting Conventions and Pricing

The quoting conventions for municipal bonds are identical to those for T-bonds. The quoted coupon rates are the coupons as a percentage of the bonds' face values, and the coupons typically are semiannual. The quoted yields to maturity are on a before-tax basis, and Equation 6.1 is used to calculate total bond prices. The quoted municipal bond prices are the total bond prices less accrued interest.

---

[39] Investors are willing to accept a lower rate of return, because their coupon income is not taxed.

[40] The odd behavior of the Muni yield in mid-1986 is often attributed to uncertainty about whether Congress would retain the tax exemption for municipal bond coupon income. This uncertainty was resolved later in 1986.

Figure 6.13 30-Year T-Bond versus Municipal Bond Yields, 1/1986–3/1989

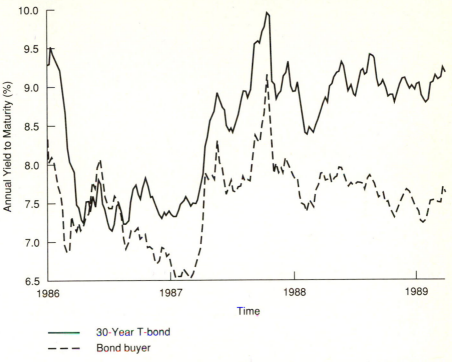

Source: Federal Reserve Bank of Chicago.

Municipal Bond Futures Market

In 1985, the Chicago Board of Trade introduced a futures contract on municipal bonds, the Muni contract, to meet the hedging needs of the many people who trade and invest in municipal bonds. Figure 6.14 shows trading volume since the contract's introduction. Figure 6.15 presents a *Wall Street Journal* excerpt with Muni futures prices for May 23, 1989.

The CBOT's primary reason for introducing the Muni contract was that the T-bond futures contract had not proven to hedge municipal bond rates effectively, for the movements in T-bond and municipal bond rates are not sufficiently correlated for crosshedging. Though the T-bond and municipal bond yield levels appear highly correlated in Figure 6.13, when we regress changes in the municipal bond rate on changes in the T-bond rate, as in Table 6.9, we find that the variability of T-bond rate movements can explain only about 30 percent of the variability in municipal bond rate movements. This implies a correlation of about 55 percent between the movements of the two

Figure 6.14 Municipal Bond Futures, Annual Volume, 1985–1989

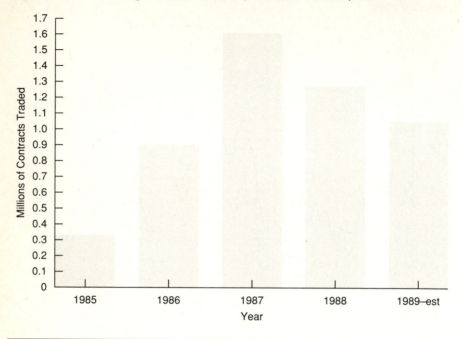

Source: Futures Industry Association.

Figure 6.15 Municipal Bonds Futures Transactions Prices for May 23, 1989

Source: *The Wall Street Journal,* May 24, 1989.

rates, which is much less than the 81 percent correlation between the changes in the AAA and T-bond rates that we saw in Table 6.7.[41]

---

[41] See Arak, Fischer, Goodman, and Darganani [1987] for a discussion of the MOB (municipals-over-bonds) trade, which uses T-bond and Muni futures to speculate on the relationship between T-bond and municipal bond yields.

Table 6.9 Regression of Weekly Change in Muni Bond Yield on Weekly Change in T-Bond Yield

Y = weekly change in Bond Buyer yield
X = weekly change in 30-year T-bond yield

Regression Output

Constant	–0.00378
Standard error of Y estimate	0.128207
R-squared	0.298938
Number of observations	170
Degrees of freedom	168

X coefficient(s)	0.551909	
Standard error of coefficient	0.065207	

The Bond Buyer 40 Index

Unlike the T-bond contract, the Muni contract is a cash settlement contract. It uses a fairly complicated municipal bond price index, called the **Bond Buyer 40 Index**, to calculate the cash settlement. The index was developed by *The Bond Buyer* and the Chicago Board of Trade specifically for the futures contract, and the former computes it daily.

Muni Futures Contract Specifications

Contract:	Municipal Bonds
Exchange:	Chicago Board of Trade
Quantity:	$100,000 face value, which is $1,000 times the Bond Buyer Municipal Bond Index
Delivery months:	March, June, September, December
Delivery specifications:	Cash settlement according to the value of the Bond Buyer Municipal Bond Index on last day of trading
Minimum price movement:	$1/32$ points, or $31.25 per contract

As its name implies, the Bond Buyer 40 Index is based on the prices of 40 municipal bonds. To be included in the index, a bond must satisfy the following criteria:

1. It must have a minimum rating of A– by Standard and Poor's or A by Moody's.

2. It must have an outstanding face value of at least $50 million ($75 million for housing issues).

3. Its remaining maturity must be at least 19 years.

4. It must be callable prior to maturity, with the first call in 7 to 16 years.

5. It must have a fixed coupon and semiannual coupon payments.

6. It must be reoffered, out of syndicate, at a price of from $95 to $105 per $100 face value.

7.   It must be publicly traded and include no extraordinary features.

These criteria are imposed to ensure that the index includes bonds that have long terms, low risk, good liquidity, and coupons close to current yields. The last feature is guaranteed by requiring that the bonds have prices within 5 percent of par.

The composition of the Bond Buyer 40 Index is changed on the fifteenth calendar day and the last business day of each month. A bond will be dropped from the index and replaced by another eligible bond if

1.   There is a default on the bond.

2.   The bond's rating drops below the required Standard and Poor's or Moody's rating.

3.   More than two bonds from the same issuer are under consideration for the index.

4.   The bond is immediately callable *and* its price was greater than or equal to 102 on the two days before the index composition change. This is to prevent inclusion of bonds that do not reflect market prices because of their provision for immediate call.

5.   The bond is not being actively traded.

The Bond Buyer 40 Index is recalculated every day. Between 1:45 p.m. and 2:00 p.m. CST, five dealer-to-dealer municipal bond brokers supply *The Bond Buyer* with price quotes on the 40 bonds in the index. For each bond, the highest and lowest prices are discarded and the remaining three prices averaged. This average price is then divided by a conversion factor to yield a **converted price**. Like the T-bond conversion factors, the municipal bond conversion factors are the bond prices, per $1 face value, that would prevail if the yield to maturity were 8 percent.

The index is then calculated by averaging the 40 converted prices and multiplying the average by a **coefficient index value** that corrects for the bi-monthly changes in the index composition. This coefficient has the same function as the divisors used in constructing the stock indices we discussed in Chapter 4. It ensures that the index will not jump as its composition changes. Such jumps do not reflect changing yields and, if not eliminated from the index, would add risk to a municipal bond futures position. The coefficient index value forces the value of the new index to equal the value of the old index at the point of revision. Thus, we can represent the value of the Bond Buyer 40 Index as

$$QP_t^B = CIV\left(\frac{1}{40}\right)\left[\sum_{i=1}^{40}\left(\frac{QP_t^i}{c_i}\right)\right] \tag{6.39}$$

$$= \sum_{i=1}^{40}\left(\frac{CIV}{40c_i}\right)\left(QP_t^i\right),$$

Table 6.10 Hypothetical Bond Buyer 2 Index with Two Bonds, 7.90 Percent Current Yield to Maturity (Prices per $100 par)

Coupon	Maturity	Issuer	Price	Conversion Factor	Converted Price
Old Index					
7.125%	20	Anytown	$92.2729	0.9134	$101.0206
7.250%	21	Middletown	93.3890	0.9243	101.0371
				Average	$101.0288
				Coefficient	0.9500
				Index value	$ 95.9774
New Index					
8.000%	22	Farm City	$101.0356	1.0000	$101.0356
7.500%	25	Chicago	95.6665	0.9463	101.0959
				Average	$101.0658
				Coefficient	0.9497
				Index value	$ 95.9774

where QP_t^B is the value of the Bond Buyer 40 Index, CIV is the coefficient index value, and c_i and QP_t^i are the conversion factor and quoted price of bond i, respectively. Thus, we can view the Bond Buyer 40 Index as representing the price of a portfolio of 40 bonds, in which each bond has a face value of $(CIV/40c_i)(\$100)$ per $100 face value.

Example 6.15 demonstrates how the index is calculated and how it behaves when a composition change occurs.

▪ **Example 6.15: Determining the Value of the Bond Buyer 40 Index**   For simplicity, suppose the Bond Buyer 40 Index includes only two bonds. On March 30, the two bonds in the index are

March 30 Index Components

7⅛%	20-year Anytown
7¼%	21-year Middletown

On March 31, the current yield to maturity is 7.90 percent and the value of the index is calculated as shown in Table 6.10. The average converted price of the two bonds is $101.0288 per $100 par. The coefficient index value is 0.9500. Therefore, the index value is

Index value = (Average converted price)(Coefficient)
= ($101.0288)(0.9500)
= $95.9774 per $100 par.

Now suppose March 31 is an index revision day. The bonds in the index must be examined to see if they meet the inclusion criteria. We find that both bonds have prices lower than $95 per $100 par, so they must be replaced. Suppose the bonds are replaced by

March 31 Index Components

8%	22-year Farm City
7½%	25-year Chicago

The new average converted price is $101.0658. If the old coefficient index value of 0.9500 were used, the value of the index would be ($101.0658)(0.9500) = $96.0125 per $100 par. The value of the index would rise simply because the component bonds had changed. To avoid this problem, a new coefficient index value is determined such that the value of the new index equals the value of the old index:

$$\text{Coefficent index value} = \frac{\text{Old index}}{\text{New average converted price}}. \qquad \textbf{(6.40)}$$

In this case, the value of the new index using the old coefficient is higher than that of the old index, so the coefficient index value must decrease:

$$\text{Coefficient index value} = \frac{\$95.9774}{\$101.0658}$$
$$= 0.9497.$$

Thus, by construction, the index value with the new bonds equals the old index value on March 31. Changes in the index therefore will reflect changes in the prices of the two bonds in the index, not changes in the index's component bonds. ∎

The components of the Bond Buyer 40 Index change quite frequently. Table 6.11 shows the number of bonds added to and deleted from the index, the coefficient index value, and the average coupon for 1986 and 1987.[42] The falling average coupon reflects the decreasing interest rates over the period.

The Fundamental No-Arbitrage Equation

Since the Muni contract is written on an index of coupon bonds, its pricing is similar to that of a T-bond futures contract. Therefore, we can derive a fundamental no-arbitrage pricing equation for the Muni contract by adapting a T-bond no-arbitrage equation to account for the Muni contract's unique features. We will use the T-bond no-arbitrage equation, 6.20, that is written in terms of quoted prices:

---

[42] The coefficient index value was set to equal 1.000 on December 12, 1983, before trading in futures began in 1985. The index has been continuously revised ever since.

Table 6.11 Biweekly Revisions to Bond Buyer Muni Bond Index

Revision Day	Number of Bonds Added/Deleted	New Value of Coefficient	Average Coupon
15-Jan-86	3	0.9710	8.99%
31-Jan-86	2	0.9705	8.96
14-Feb-86	0	0.9705	8.96
28-Feb-86	4	0.9705	8.86
14-Mar-86	6	0.9675	8.54
31-Mar-86	6	0.9674	8.34
15-Apr-86	10	0.9597	7.96
30-Apr-86	9	0.9556	7.73
15-May-86	6	0.9559	7.64
30-May-86	6	0.9513	7.60
13-Jun-86	5	0.9502	7.66
30-Jun-86	4	0.9509	7.69
15-Jul-86	8	0.9476	7.70
31-Jul-86	13	0.9432	7.64
15-Aug-86	9	0.9459	7.70
29-Aug-86	10	0.9430	7.57
15-Sep-86	3	0.9416	7.52
30-Sep-86	3	0.9418	7.51
15-Oct-86	6	0.9437	7.48
31-Oct-86	10	0.9450	7.42
14-Nov-86	13	0.9458	7.28
28-Nov-86	10	0.9493	7.28
15-Dec-86	11	0.9447	7.18
31-Dec-86	8	0.9489	7.22
15-Jan-87	1	0.9483	7.21
30-Jan-87	12	0.9448	7.08
13-Feb-87	7	0.9465	7.11
27-Feb-87	7	0.9430	7.04
13-Mar-87	11	0.9439	6.98
31-Mar-87	14	0.9468	7.05
15-Apr-87	3	0.9446	7.06
30-Apr-87	1	0.9446	7.06
15-May-87	2	0.9419	7.10
29-May-87	5	0.9349	7.25
15-Jun-87	3	0.9321	7.34
30-Jun-87	6	0.9310	7.48
15-Jul-87	1	0.9292	7.49
31-Jul-87	2	0.9260	7.53
14-Aug-87	2	0.9268	7.57
31-Aug-87	1	0.9267	7.56
15-Sep-87	0	0.9267	7.56
30-Sep-87	2	0.9267	7.60
15-Oct-87	4	0.9214	7.70
30-Oct-87	2	0.9228	7.78
13-Nov-87	3	0.9195	7.81
30-Nov-87	5	0.9191	7.80
15-Dec-87	3	0.9190	7.87
31-Dec-87	4	0.9171	7.85

Source: *The Bond Buyer.*

$$QF_{t,T} = \frac{QP_t + (r - CY)[(Days \ from \ t \ to \ T)/360]QP_t}{c_i}.$$ (6.20)

Recall that $QF_{t,T}$ is the quoted futures price, QP_t is the quoted bond price, r is the annualized short-term interest rate, $(C/QP_t)(360/365)$ is the annual current yield on the bond, and c_i is the conversion factor of the cheapest-to-deliver bond. The equation applies to the following general time line of arbitrage dates and coupon payments:

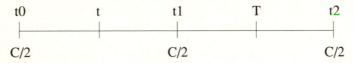

To convert Equation 6.20 so that it is appropriate for the Muni contract, we must first adjust the current yield term to reflect municipal bonds' tax-free status and the Muni contract's underlying 40-bond portfolio. The current yield in Equation 6.20 is based on a fully taxable coupon. Therefore to modify Equation 6.20 for the Muni contract, we will use a current-yield term that expresses the current yield on the contract's underlying 40-bond portfolio in a taxable form. This is the **equivalent taxable current yield (ETCY)** of the underlying index.

The second adjustment we will make to Equation 6.20 is to replace QP_t with the quoted value of the Bond Buyer 40 Index, QP_t^B. Since the Bond Buyer 40 Index divides the price of each component bond by its conversion factor, this division does not have to be made in the Muni contract's no-arbitrage equation. These adjustments to Equation 6.20 give us the following fundamental no-arbitrage equation for the Muni contract:

$$QF_{t,T} = QP_t^B + (r - ETCY)[(Days \ from \ t \ to \ T)/360]QP_t^B.$$ (6.41)

To calculate the ETCY term in Equation 6.41, we must first restate the coupons on the Muni contract's underlying bonds on a taxable basis. Investors in a municipal bond are willing to accept a nontaxable coupon as low as

$$\hat{C} = (1 - \tau)C,$$ (6.42)

where τ is the marginal tax rate, because their after-tax coupon will then be the same as if they received a fully taxable coupon of C. Turning Equation 6.42 around, we see that the following taxable coupon, C, is equivalent to a nontaxable coupon of $\hat{C}$:

$$C = \frac{\hat{C}}{1 - \tau}.$$ (6.42a)

For example, if the coupon on a nontaxable municipal bond is $10 and the marginal tax rate is 33 percent, the equivalent taxable coupon on the bond is $10/(0.67) = $14.93.

Once we know the equivalent taxable coupon on a municipal bond, we can calculate the bond's equivalent taxable current yield. It is merely the equivalent taxable coupon divided by the bond price. For each of the Muni contract's underlying bonds, the equivalent taxable current yield, on a 360-day basis, is

$$\text{Equivalent taxable current yield} = \text{ETCY} \tag{6.43}$$

$$= (360/365)(C/QP_t)$$

$$= \frac{(360/365)[\hat{C}/(1-\tau)]}{QP_t}$$

where $\hat{C}$ is now the actual coupon on a bond in the Bond Buyer 40 Index and QP_t is the current market value of the index bond. Note that QP_t differs from QP_t^B in Equation 6.41. The former is a market value, while the latter, the Bond Buyer 40 Index value, reflects the conversion factor and coefficient index value adjustments that are made to the market prices of the index bonds.

There are two ways to compute the equivalent taxable current yield for the Bond Buyer 40 Index. One approach is to sum up the actual coupons paid on all the bonds in the portfolio and divide the sum by the total market value of the portfolio. A far easier approach, which is a very close approximation (and industry practice), is to use the average coupon and average market price of the bonds in the index. Example 6.16 uses the second approach to determine the no-arbitrage price for the Muni contract.[43]

▪ **Example 6.16: Computing the No-Arbitrage Price for Muni Futures**
Suppose we wish to compute the no-arbitrage price on April 10, 1989, for a Muni futures contract that expires on June 21, 1989. We observe the following prices and rates on April 10:

Bond Buyer 40 Index	$90-20	(90.625)
June 1989 Muni futures	$89-24	(89.750)
Repo rate (30 days)	10.00%	

Table 6.12 lists the bonds included in the Bond Buyer 40 Index on April 10 (after the March 31 revision).

Instead of computing the no-arbitrage relationship with the aggregate coupon and market value of the bonds in the Bond Buyer 40 Index, we choose to use the hypothetical "average" bond of the portfolio. This average bond has the following characteristics:

Average coupon	7.61%
Average price	$98.47
Average first call date	5/27/2001
Average maturity date	2/04/2017
Coefficient index value	0.8927

---

[43] For this example, using the average coupon and price gives an answer that matches the answer using the "correct" approach to four decimal places. This is so because the yields on the component bonds of the index are, by design, quite close to one another.

Table 6.12 Composition of the Bond Buyer Index, April 10, 1989

Name	Coupon	Due	First Call	Price	Conversion Factor
Georgia Muni Elect	8.125%	1/1/2017	1/1/2000	$101.1250	1.0092
Maryland Health & Ed	7.500	7/1/2020	7/1/2002	99.0833	0.9578
Philadelphia Muni Auth	7.800	4/1/2018	4/1/2000	101.0417	0.9809
New York MAC ser 87	7.625	7/1/2008	7/1/2001	99.6250	0.9702
New York MTA	7.500	7/1/2017	7/1/2000	98.2917	0.9622
Orlando-Orange Co Expwy	7.625	7/1/2018	7/1/2000	99.5417	0.9721
NYC Muni Water	7.625	6/15/2016	6/15/2009	97.1250	0.9739
Pennsylvania Turnpike	7.625	12/1/2017	12/1/2000	99.9583	0.9716
Salt River Power	7.500	1/1/2029	1/1/2000	97.9583	0.9639
Hudson Co NJ	7.600	12/1/2021	12/1/2000	99.4583	0.9716
Piedmont Muni Power	7.400	1/1/2018	1/1/2000	97.4167	0.9548
New York MTA	8.000	7/1/2018	7/1/2000	100.2083	1.0000
Massachusetts	7.375	12/1/2008	12/1/2002	97.2500	0.9483
Oakland Calif	7.600	8/1/2021	8/1/2000	100.2500	0.9721
Port Auth NY & NJ	8.000	12/1/2023	2/2/2001	100.0417	1.0000
Los Angeles DEWAP	7.375	2/1/2029	2/1/2010	97.4167	0.9370
Dade Co Sch Dist Fla	7.375	7/1/2008	7/1/2001	96.8750	0.9516
Gainesville Fla Util	7.250	10/1/2013	10/1/2000	96.9167	0.9443
Los Angeles Convention	7.000	8/15/2020	8/15/2002	92.0750	0.9190
Los Angeles Convention	7.375	8/15/2018	8/15/2002	96.7500	0.9493
Los Angeles Co trans	7.400	7/1/2015	7/1/2001	97.0000	0.9516
Metro Atlanta Rapid Trans	7.250	7/1/2010	7/1/2000	96.0000	0.9449
NYS Energy Research Dev	7.750	1/1/2024	1/1/2000	98.0000	0.9820
Northern Minn MPA	7.250	1/1/2016	1/1/2001	95.2917	0.9434
Fairfax Econ Dev Va	7.750	2/1/2011	2/1/2002	98.7917	0.9801
Matagorda Navigation Tex	7.700	2/1/2019	2/1/2000	96.1667	0.9820
Oklahoma Turnpike Auth	7.700	1/1/2022	1/1/2003	100.3333	0.9792
Oklahoma Turnpike Auth	7.875	1/1/2021	1/1/2003	100.2500	0.9895
Puerto Rico	7.750	7/1/2017	7/1/2002	99.1250	0.9796
Texas Water Resources	7.500	8/15/2013	8/15/1999	98.2917	0.9653
Texas Water Resources	7.625	8/15/2008	8/15/1999	98.2083	0.9739
NYS Med Care	7.800	2/15/2019	2/15/2001	98.7500	0.9810
Port Auth NY & NJ	7.875	3/1/2024	5/2/2001	99.0000	0.9905
Triborough Bridge	7.700	1/1/2019	1/1/2001	99.5417	0.9810
Broward Co North	7.950	12/1/2008	12/1/2002	99.9583	1.0000
Broward Co South	7.950	12/1/2008	12/1/2002	99.9583	1.0000
Florida	7.375	7/1/2019	7/1/2003	97.8317	0.9472
Illinois Sports Fac	7.875	6/15/2010	6/15/2001	100.0000	0.9905
Los Angeles Airports	7.400	5/1/2010	5/1/1999	98.3333	0.9575
NYC Muni Water	7.625	6/15/2017	6/15/2000	99.4167	0.9729

Source: *The Bond Buyer.*

The highest marginal tax rate for investors at this time is 33 percent. Investors in this tax bracket are most likely to be holding municipal bonds, so the equivalent taxable current yield on the average bond is

$$\text{Equivalent taxable current yield} = \frac{(360/365)(7.61/0.67)}{98.47}$$

$$= 11.38\%.$$

Due to one-day settlement in the municipal bond market, the relevant interval between t and T for our calculation is the 71-day period from April 11 to June 21. From Equation 6.41, we can see that the no-arbitrage price on this Muni contract is

$$QF_{t,T} = (\$90.625)[1 + (0.10 - 0.1138)(71/360)]$$
$$= \$90.378$$
$$= \$90\text{-}12 \text{ per } \$100 \text{ face.}$$

■

The $90-12 no-arbitrage price in Example 6.16 is somewhat above the actual futures price of $89-24. This apparent underpricing cannot be explained by delivery options as in the T-bond markets, because the Muni contract is cash settled. One explanation is that short-selling of municipal bonds is uncommon in the dealer market, so reverse cash-and-carry pure arbitrages are very difficult to carry out. Quasi-arbitrage strategies that involve selling municipal bonds out of a portfolio and replacing them with T-bills and long Muni futures positions are possible. But such trades may be unable to eliminate the observed futures under-pricing, for the bid-ask spreads in the secondary municipal bond market often are as large as $16/32$. This can explain a large portion of the $20/32$ difference between the no-arbitrage price and the futures price in Example 6.16. The rest of the difference may be explained by the costs of simultaneously selling a municipal bond portfolio, going long futures, and buying T-bills.

The most profitable strategy in the presence of Muni futures underpricing is to replace an *intended* purchase of municipal bonds with a purchase of T-bills and a long position in municipal bond futures. The arbitrageur in this case does not have to pay the bid-ask spread. This strategy does not provide tax-free income as municipal bonds do, but since the futures price accounts for the tax-free coupons (see Equation 6.41), after-tax earnings are the same as they would be had the coupons been received. If this strategy grows more popular in the future, the Muni futures pricing discrepancy should decline.[44]

Hedging with Muni Futures

Municipal bond futures can be used for hedging and quasi-arbitrage in the same way that T-bond futures can. To hedge with Muni futures, we determine the appropriate hedge ratio in the usual fashion by comparing the changes in value of the Bond Buyer 40 Index and the portfolio being hedged when the bond yield

[44] See Heaton [1988].

changes. The change in value of the Bond Buyer 40 Index is calculated by aggregating the changes in value of all 40 bonds in the index (using Equation 6.39):

$$\Delta QP_t^B = CIV\left(\frac{1}{40}\right)\left[\sum_{i=1}^{40}\left(\frac{\Delta QP_t^i}{c_i}\right)\right]. \tag{6.44}$$

We can also approximate Equation 6.44 by computing the value change of the "average" bond and then multiplying this change by the coefficient index value divided by the conversion factor of the average bond. Finally, we can also use duration analysis to derive the appropriate hedge ratio. The duration of the Muni futures equals the duration of the 40-bond portfolio in the Bond Buyer 40 Index. Equation 6.5 will compute the durations of the index and the portfolio to be hedged from the durations of the individual bonds in the two portfolios. Again, we can also use the duration of the "average" bond in the Bond Buyer 40 Index.

Summary

Long-term interest rate futures are complicated to use because of the many intricate features of the contracts and their underlying instruments. Hedges with T-bond futures must account for the T-bond pricing conventions and also must be adjusted for multiple deliverable grades. To keep an effective T-bond hedge in place for some time, one must adjust the hedge ratio periodically to reflect changes in the current yield to maturity. Duration analysis can be used to set and alter T-bond futures hedge ratios. The seller's options to choose the delivery grade and date add value to short T-bond futures positions and thus affect the no-arbitrage price relationship in the T-bond market. In the Muni futures market, the pricing process and the hedging techniques are specialized to account for the tax-free status of municipal bonds and the construction of the underlying 40-bond index.

Problems

Note: For many of these calculations, you will need a financial calculator that will compute bond prices and bond yields.

1. Suppose you are examining two bonds. One expires in exactly two years and has a coupon of 14 percent. The other also expires in exactly two years but is a discount bond (i.e., pays no coupon). The yield to maturity on both bonds is 10 percent.
    a. What are the durations of the two bonds?
    b. What is the percentage change for each bond if yields rise to 11 percent?
    c. Discuss the relationship between your answers to parts a and b.

2. Consider the bonds in Problem 1. Suppose you are holding a portfolio that includes $250 million face value of the 14 percent bonds and $500 million

face value of the discount bonds. What is the duration of the portfolio if the yield to maturity on both bonds is 10 percent?

3. Suppose you are holding a short June 1989 T-bond futures contract. You are also holding a 10¾ percent T-bond expiring in August 2005. On June 12, you announce the intention to deliver this bond. Quoted futures settlement prices are

June 9	$92-30
June 12	92-15
June 13	91-24
June 14	91-30
June 15	92-00

When will you actually deliver the bond, and what invoice price will you receive? Use Table 6.1 to obtain the conversion factor.

4. Suppose only two bonds are eligible to be delivered into the June 1989 T-bond futures contract: the 9.875 percent November 2015 and the 7.250 percent May 2016. On June 12, you decide to announce intention to deliver one of these bonds.
    a. If yields to maturity for both bonds are 7 percent, which bond is cheaper to deliver? Assuming that delivery must occur immediately, what will be the futures settlement price?
    b. If yields to maturity for both bonds are 9 percent, which bond is cheaper to deliver? Assuming that delivery must occur immediately, what will be the futures settlement price?
    c. How do you explain the switch in the cheapest-to-deliver bond?

5. Suppose that on May 23, 1989, you purchase a 9⅞ November 2015 T-bond. You intend to hold the bond until June 30, at which time you will deliver the bond into a short position in the June T-bond futures contract. Using prices from Figure 6.1, what is the implied repo rate from this strategy? What hedge ratio would you use in this cash-and-carry strategy?

6. Using Lotus, reproduce Table 6.3. Inputs into the table are the quoted prices and the quoted futures price. You can obtain the conversion factors from Table 6.1. Update the table using the prices for May 23, 1989, given in Figure 6.1. (Hint: Be careful with coupons between dates t and T.)

7. Suppose we know that on May 23, 1989, the 7¼ percent May 2016 bond is cheapest to deliver. Using the information in Figure 6.1, calculate the yield to maturity implied by the June T-bond futures price. Assume the T-bond futures contract expires on June 30, and ignore any seller's options. Use Table 6.1 to obtain the conversion factor.

8. Suppose it is May 23, 1989, and you wish to hedge the value of a 10⅝ percent August 2015 T-bond as of June 30, 1989, using June T-bond futures. The 7¼ percent May 2016 bond is the cheapest to deliver. How many futures contracts per $100,000 face value should you use? (Hint: Use the yield obtained in Problem 7.) Use the basis-point-value technique with a 20-basis-point change and any data that you need from Figure 6.1.

 9.   Using Lotus, reproduce Figure 6.6. Update the figure using the prices for
      May 23, 1989, given in Figure 6.1. (Hint: Be careful with coupons between
      dates t and T. Use the yield obtained in Problem 7.)

 10. Using Lotus, reproduce Table 6.8. Update the table using a yield move from
      8.50 to 9.50 percent. As Table 6.8 does, assume a flat term structure.

 11. Assume the fundamental no-arbitrage equation holds for Muni futures
      expiring on June 21, 1989.
      a.   Using the prices from Figure 6.15, determine the equivalent taxable
           current yield (ETCY) for the bonds in the Bond Buyer 40 Index.
           Assume a short-term interest rate of 8.50 percent and a marginal tax
           rate of 33 percent.
      b.   What further information would you need to calculate the average
           coupon for the bonds comprising the index?

Foreign Exchange Futures

Trading in foreign exchange has grown tremendously with the expansion of international trade over the past several decades. In 1988, daily trading volume in the foreign exchange markets approached $300 billion.[1] Those engaged in international trade and finance use the spot foreign exchange markets to acquire the currency necessary to transact across national borders. But because the profitability of many planned projects and transactions depends on future exchange rate levels, firms are exposed to the risk of exchange rate movements. With the demise of the world's fixed exchange rate system in the early 1970s, currency risk has become substantial for many firms. These firms are increasingly turning to the foreign exchange futures and forward markets to manage their foreign exchange risk. In this chapter, we will study the foreign exchange futures and forward markets and the synthetic strategies firms can use to hedge their foreign exchange exposure.

Foreign Exchange Cash Market

The cash market in foreign exchange, like the cash markets in commodities and securities, consists of a network of dealers. The dealers, often large money center banks, make markets in different currencies. They carry out some of their transactions over the telephone and some through a computer network. Because of rapid communications technologies, foreign exchange dealers need not be in any one place and in fact are spread all over the world. Business is transacted throughout the world on a continual basis, so it is possible to trade foreign currencies 24 hours a day. The market is extremely competitive; therefore, prices from different dealers tend to be virtually identical.

The standard settlement period in the foreign exchange cash market is two days. Thus, if an investor buys Swiss francs at a price set on Monday, the actual transaction will not occur until Wednesday.

---

[1] See Summers and Summers [1990].

Quoting Conventions

By convention, exchange rates are quoted on a per-dollar basis in the United States. This means that the exchange rate for each foreign currency is stated as the dollar cost of a unit of that currency. Figure 7.1 shows the exchange rate quotes listed in *The Wall Street Journal* currencies section for Tuesday, May 23, 1989 (for settlement on Thursday, May 25, 1989). It lists the selling prices offered by Bankers Trust, one of the largest dealers in foreign exchange, at 3:00 p.m. EST. For example, we can see that Bankers Trust's offer rates (customer ask rates) for the British pound and the Swiss franc were $1.5640 and $0.5580, respectively.

We can also express these rates as the foreign currency costs of one U.S. dollar, as is the practice in Great Britain. If $1.5640 will buy one British pound, 0.6393 British pounds (1/1.5640) will buy one U.S. dollar. Similarly, if $0.5580 will buy one Swiss franc, 1.7920 Swiss francs (1/0.5580) will buy one U.S. dollar. To avoid confusion, we will list the quotation units after every exchange rate we mention in this chapter. Thus, we will write 1.5640 ($/BP) and 0.6393 (BP/$).

The prices quoted in Figure 7.1 are the ask prices at which Bankers Trust was willing to sell currencies. Banks such as Bankers Trust are also willing to buy foreign currencies at bid prices. As always, the bid prices are below the ask prices. The spread between the bid and the ask depends on who is trading and the size of the transaction. Large commercial buyers and sellers face the smallest spreads, while retail customers face the largest. A tourist who purchases British pounds from his or her local bank will find an ask rate much less favorable than that quoted by Bankers Trust. But for a given buyer or seller, the bid-ask spread usually increases with the size of the transaction.

We can also state the bid-ask spreads in terms of the foreign currency rather than the dollar. Earlier we saw that if Bankers Trust sells British pounds at its ask rate of 1.5640 ($/BP), it is also buying dollars in exchange for British pounds at a rate of 1/1.5640 = 0.6393 (BP/$). If the bank buys British pounds at a bid rate of 1.5630 ($/BP), it is also selling dollars in exchange for British pounds at a rate of 1/1.5630 = 0.6398 ($/BP). Thus, in terms of British pounds, the bid is 0.6393 ($/BP) and the ask is 0.6398 ($/BP).

Because exchange rates are the prices of currencies relative to each other, an exchange rate movement is merely the change in a currency's value relative to that of another. We say that the dollar has **depreciated** relative to another currency if it will buy fewer units of that currency than before. Suppose the price of the British pound moves from 1.5640 ($/BP) to 1.5700 ($/BP). One dollar will now buy only 1/1.5700 = 0.6369 (BP/$), while it would have bought 1/1.5640 = 0.6393 (BP/$) before. The dollar has become less valuable in terms of British pounds, and the British pound has become more valuable, or **appreciated**, in terms of dollars.

Thus, it is meaningful to talk about one currency appreciating or depreciating only in relation to another currency. Often an article in the press will say that the dollar has appreciated or depreciated without reference to another currency. The authors of such articles are implying that the dollar has moved relative to other major currencies.

Figure 7.1 Exchange Rate Quotes for May 23, 1989

EXCHANGE RATES
Tuesday, May 23, 1989

The New York foreign exchange selling rates below apply to trading among banks in amounts of $1 million and more, as quoted at 3 p.m. Eastern time by Bankers Trust Co. Retail transactions provide fewer units of foreign currency per dollar.

Country	U.S. $ equiv. Tues.	U.S. $ equiv. Mon.	Currency per U.S. $ Tues.	Currency per U.S. $ Mon.
Argentina (Austral) ...	.006666	.006211	150.00	161.00
Australia (Dollar)	.7455	.7440	1.3413	1.3440
Austria (Schilling)	.07064	.07072	14.15	14.14
Bahrain (Dinar)	2.6528	2.6528	.37695	.37695
Belgium (Franc)				
Commercial rate	.02376	.02377	42.07	42.05
Financial rate	.02369	.02370	42.20	42.18
Brazil (Cruzado)	.892857	.892857	1.1200	1.1200
Britain (Pound)	1.5640	1.5780	.6393	.6337
30-Day Forward	1.5596	1.5738	.6411	.6354
90-Day Forward	1.5498	1.5644	.6452	.6392
180-Day Forward ...	1.5333	1.5501	.6521	.6451
Canada (Dollar)	.8331	.8361	1.2003	1.1960
30-Day Forward	.8309	.8340	1.2035	1.1990
90-Day Forward	.8276	.8309	1.2083	1.2035
180-Day Forward ...	.8237	.8327	1.2139	1.2085
Chile (Official rate) ...	.0039753	.0039753	251.55	251.55
China (Yuan)	.268672	.268672	3.7220	3.7220
Colombia (Peso)	.002750	.002750	363.60	363.60
Denmark (Krone)	.1276	.1277	7.8360	7.8270
Ecuador (Sucre)				
Floating rate	.001908	.001908	524.00	524.00
Finland (Markka)	.2232	.2238	4.4800	4.4675
France (Franc)	.1468	.1469	6.8100	6.8040
30-Day Forward	.14695	.1470977	6.8050	6.7982
90-Day Forward	.1471	.1472	6.7995	6.7910
180-Day Forward ...	.1472	.1474	6.7950	6.7840
Greece (Drachma)	.005858	.005868	170.70	170.40
Hong Kong (Dollar) ...	.128369	.128592	7.7900	7.7765
India (Rupee)	.0617665	.0617665	16.19	16.19
Indonesia (Rupiah) ...	.0005694	.0005694	1756.00	1756.00
Ireland (Punt)	1.3290	1.3290	.75244	.75244
Israel (Shekel)	.5503	.5503	1.8170	1.8170
Italy (Lira)	.0006863	.0006868	1457.00	1456.00
Japan (Yen)	.007027	.007047	142.30	141.90
30-Day Forward	.007054	.007077	141.75	141.30
90-Day Forward	.007102	.007125	140.80	140.34
180-Day Forward ...	.007171	.007194	139.45	139.00
Jordan (Dinar)	1.8968	1.8968	.5272	.5272
Kuwait (Dinar)	3.3917	3.3917	.2948	.2948
Lebanon (Pound)	.001941	.001941	515.00	515.00
Malaysia (Ringgit) ...	.37140	.37140	2.6925	2.6925
Malta (Lira)	2.7816	2.7816	.3595	.3595
Mexico (Peso)				
Floating rate	.0004076	.0004076	2453.00	2453.00
Netherland(Guilder) .	.4413	.4415	2.2660	2.2650
New Zealand (Dollar)	.5990	.5935	1.6694	1.6849
Norway (Krone)	.1381	.1384	7.2400	7.2240
Pakistan (Rupee)	.04830	.04830	20.70	20.70
Peru (Inti)	.0003691	.0003691	2709.00	2709.00
Philippines (Peso)	.048543	.048543	20.60	20.60
Portugal (Escudo)	.006046	.006046	165.39	165.39
Saudi Arabia (Riyal) ..	.2665	.2665	3.7510	3.7510
Singapore (Dollar)	.5116	.5116	1.9545	1.9545
South Africa (Rand)				
Commercial rate	.3613	.3600	2.7678	2.7778
Financial rate	.2401	.2436	4.1650	4.1050
South Korea (Won) ...	.0014925	.0014925	670.00	670.00
Spain (Peseta)	.007968	.007974	125.50	125.40
Sweden (Krona)	.1480384	.1480	6.7550	6.7540
Switzerland (Franc) ..	.5580	.5581	1.7920	1.7915
30-Day Forward ...	.5589	.5591	1.7890	1.7885
90-Day Forward ...	.5605	.5606	1.7841	1.7835
180-Day Forward ...	.5628	.5628	1.7767	1.7767
Taiwan (Dollar)	.038625	.038850	25.89	25.74
Thailand (Baht)	.038910	.038910	25.70	25.70
Turkey (Lira)	.0004856	.0004856	2059.00	2059.00
United Arab(Dirham) .	.2722	.2722	3.6725	3.6725
Uruguay (New Peso)				
Financial	.001811	.001811	552.00	552.00
Venezuela (Bolivar)				
Floating rate	.02649	.02649	37.75	37.75
W. Germany (Mark) ..	.4968	.4973	2.0125	2.0105
30-Day Forward ...	.4981	.4985	2.0075	2.0057
90-Day Forward ...	.4999	.5002	2.0004	1.9989
180-Day Forward ...	.5018	.5023	1.9925	1.9905
— — —				
SDR	1.24126	1.23939	0.805636	0.806851
ECU	1.03882	1.03393	....	....

Special Drawing Rights (SDR) are based on exchange rates for the U.S., West German, British, French and Japanese currencies. Source: International Monetary Fund.

European Currency Unit (ECU) is based on a basket of community currencies. Source: European Community Commission.

Figure 7.2 Foreign Exchange Cross Rates for May 23, 1989

Key Currency Cross Rates Late New York Trading May 23, 1989

	Dollar	Pound	SFranc	Guilder	Yen	Lira	D-Mark	FFranc	CdnDlr
Canada.........	1.1996	1.8843	.66979	.52944	.00843	.00082	.59637	.17611	.....
France.........	6.8115	10.700	3.8032	3.0062	.04787	.00467	3.3863	....	5.6781
Germany.......	2.0115	3.1597	1.1231	.88777	.01414	.00138	....	.29531	1.6768
Italy...........	1457.3	2289.0	813.65	643.15	10.241	....	724.46	213.94	1214.8
Japan..........	142.30	223.52	79.453	62.803	....	.09765	70.743	20.891	118.62
Netherlands....	2.2658	3.5591	1.2651	....	.01592	.00155	1.1264	.33264	1.8888
Switzerland....	1.7910	2.8133	....	.79045	.01259	.00123	.89038	.26294	1.4930
U.K..............	.63662	....	.35545	.28097	.00447	.00044	.31649	.09346	.53069
U.S..............	....	1.5708	.55835	.44135	.00703	.00069	.49714	.14681	.83361

Source: Telerate

Source: *The Wall Street Journal*, May 24, 1989.

Cross Rates

The exchange rates of most currencies are quoted in terms of dollars, as the number of currency units per dollar, or as the number of dollars per unit of currency. However, since many international transactions are carried out without using dollars, the direct exchange rates between nondollar currencies are very important to world trade. For example, a British importer may wish to buy Swiss francs directly. The number of Swiss francs he or she can buy for each British pound is known as the **cross rate**. Figure 7.2 presents various cross rates for May 23, 1989, from *The Wall Street Journal*.

The cross rate between any two currencies must be consistent with the currencies' dollar exchange rates, or else there will be opportunities for arbitrage. We will denote the spot exchange rate between currency A and currency B at time t as $P_t(A/B)$. Thus, $P_t(A/B)$ is the number of units of currency A needed to purchase one unit of currency B. For any two currencies A and B, the equilibrium relationship between the cross rate and the dollar exchange rates is

$$P_t(A/B) = \frac{P_t(A/\$)}{P_t(B/\$)} \tag{7.1}$$

or

$$P_t(B/A) = \frac{P_t(\$/A)}{P_t(\$/B)}.$$

If this relationship does not hold, one can earn an arbitrage profit by trading between dollars and the two currencies to create an artificial transaction between currencies A and B. Suppose Equation 7.1 is violated as follows:

$$P_t(A/B) > \frac{P_t(A/\$)}{P_t(B/\$)} \qquad\qquad (7.2)$$

or

$$P_t(B/A) < \frac{P_t(\$/A)}{P_t(\$/B)} \ .$$

In this case, it is cheaper to sell currency A and buy currency B by transacting in dollars than it is to exchange A for B directly. An arbitrage profit can result from the following strategy of exchanging A for B:

1. Sell Q^A worth of currency A for dollars. The number of dollars received is

    $$Q^\$ = (Q^A)[P_t(\$/A)].$$

2. Use the dollars to buy currency B. The number of units of currency B received is

    $$\begin{aligned}
    Q^B &= (Q^\$)[P_t(B/\$)] \qquad\qquad (7.3)\\
    &= (Q^A)[P_t(\$/A)][P_t(B/\$)]\\
    &= (Q^A)\left[\frac{P_t(B/\$)}{P_t(A/\$)}\right].
    \end{aligned}$$

3. Convert currency B back into currency A using the quoted cross rate $P_t(A/B)$. The number of units of currency A received is

    $$\begin{aligned}
    \hat{Q}^A &= (Q^B)[P_t(A/B)]\\
    &= (Q^A)\left[\frac{P_t(B/\$)}{P_t(A/\$)}\right][P_t(A/B)].
    \end{aligned}$$

But we can see from Equation 7.2 that

$$\left[\frac{P_t(B/\$)}{P_t(A/\$)}\right][P_t(A/B)] > 1,$$

so the number of units of currency received, $\hat{Q}^A$, exceeds the quantity sold, Q^A.

The pressure put on the exchange rates as arbitrageurs act on this arbitrage opportunity will restore the equilibrium of Equation 7.1 as follows:

1. The arbitrageurs will buy dollars by selling currency A. This will drive up the value of the dollar relative to currency A, thereby increasing $P_t(A/\$)$.

2. The arbitrageurs will sell dollars by buying currency B. This will drive down the value of the dollar relative to currency B, thereby decreasing $P_t(B/\$)$.

3.   The arbitrageurs will sell currency B to buy currency A. This will drive up the value of currency A in terms of currency B, thereby decreasing P_t (A/B).

We can also demonstrate the arbitrage opportunity presented by Equation 7.2 if we compare the actual cross rate with the artificial rate of exchange when dollars are used as an intermediate currency to trade A for B. Equation 7.3 shows that the artificial rate of exchange between A and B is

$$\frac{Q^A}{Q^B} = \frac{P_t\,(A/\$)}{P_t\,(B/\$)} \;. \tag{7.4}$$

Under the artificial rate, currency A is expensive and currency B is cheap relative to the actual rate, P_t (A/B). Thus, as we saw from the cash flows of the arbitrage strategy, it is profitable to sell A and buy B using the synthetic transaction and then buy A and sell B using the actual cross rate. Of course, in actual transactions, the arbitrage profits must be great enough to cover transactions fees and bid-ask spreads before the strategy will be undertaken.

Example 7.1 shows a cross rate arbitrage.

▪ **Example 7.1: Cross Rate Arbitrage between British Pounds and Swiss Francs**   Suppose current spot exchange rates on May 23, 1989, are

$$
\begin{aligned}
P_t\,(\$/BP) &= 1.5640 \text{ or } P_t\,(BP/\$) &= 0.6393 \\
P_t\,(\$/SF) &= 0.5580 \text{ or } P_t\,(SF/\$) &= 1.7920 \\
P_t\,(SF/BP) &= 2.8200 \text{ or } P_t\,(BP/SF) &= 0.3546
\end{aligned}
$$

The equilibrium relationship, Equation 7.1, does not hold because[2]

$$
\begin{aligned}
\frac{P_t\,(SF/\$)}{P_t\,(BP/\$)} &= \frac{1.7920}{0.6393} \\
&= 2.8031 < 2.8200 \\
&= P_t\,(SF/BP).
\end{aligned}
$$

When denominated in Swiss francs, British pounds are relatively more expensive under the actual cross rate than under the synthetic cross rate. Thus, we will make an arbitrage profit if we use Swiss francs to buy British pounds synthetically and then sell those pounds directly for francs as follows:

1.   Suppose we sell 1 million Swiss francs for dollars. This will bring in

$$
\begin{aligned}
\text{Dollars received} &= (1,000,000 \text{ SF})[0.5580\ (\$/SF)] \\
&= \$558,000.
\end{aligned}
$$

---

[2] Note that the BP/SF cross rate in Figure 7.2 differs slightly from the synthetic rate. This is partly due to the different timing for the quotes.

2.   Next, we buy British pounds with these dollars:

British pounds received = ($558,000)[0.6393 (BP/$)]
                                    = 356,729 BP.

3.   Finally, we use the cross rate to convert these British pounds back into Swiss francs:

Swiss francs received = (356,729 BP)[2.8200 (SF/BP)]
                                 = 1,005,976 SF.

As a result of these transactions, we have sold 1,000,000 Swiss francs and received 1,005,976 Swiss francs in exchange. The 5,976-Swiss-franc difference is our arbitrage profit. ■

Now suppose the Equation 7.1 equilibrium relationship between cross rates and dollar exchange rates is violated in the opposite way so that

$$P_t(A/B) < \frac{P_t(A/\$)}{P_t(B/\$)} \tag{7.5}$$

or

$$P_t(B/A) > \frac{P_t(\$/A)}{P_t(\$/B)}.$$

If we take the reciprocal of Equation 7.5, we will get

$$P_t(B/A) > \frac{P_t(B/\$)}{P_t(A/\$)} \tag{7.6}$$

or

$$P_t(A/B) < \frac{P_t(\$/B)}{P_t(\$/A)},$$

which is exactly the same as Equation 7.2 except that currencies A and B are reversed. We can perform the same arbitrage as before simply by switching the roles of the two currencies:

1.   Sell currency B and receive dollars.

2.   Use the dollars to buy currency A.

3.   Convert currency A back into currency B using the quoted cross rate $P_t(B/A)$.

If we compare the artificial exchange rate with the direct cross rate in this case, we find that under the artificial rate currency B is expensive and currency A is cheap relative to the direct cross rate. It is therefore profitable to sell B and buy A with the synthetic transaction and then buy B and sell A using the direct cross rate.

Foreign Exchange Forward Contracts

In most financial markets, people who wish to establish prices for future delivery usually use futures contracts. However, in the foreign exchange markets, futures trading is not the dominant form of contracting for the future. Instead, the futures market functions side by side with the forward market; in fact, forward trading actually has a higher volume than futures trading. The two markets coexist harmoniously because they have very different clienteles. The forward market serves large commercial users and institutional traders who hedge forward commitments, while the futures market serves smaller commercial users and speculators. Forward and futures prices are very similar, because the two markets are tightly linked through arbitrage.[3] Thus, users of the futures market benefit fully from the liquidity of the larger forward market.

The foreign exchange forward market is also well integrated with the foreign exchange spot market. Many dealers who make markets in spot foreign exchange also make markets in foreign exchange forward contracts. Also, spot and forward contracts are traded over the same computer and phone networks.

As with all forward contracts, the sizes and expiration dates of the foreign exchange forward contracts can be tailored to meet the needs of individual customers.[4] But despite this flexibility, only large contracts are actually traded in the forward market. Further, a few contracts have become de facto standards for the market, and their prices are quoted regularly. Figure 7.1 shows that *The Wall Street Journal* publishes daily prices for the 30-, 90-, and 180-day forward contracts of the major currencies. On the date of the excerpt in Figure 7.1, the 30-day forward rate for the British pound was 1.5596 ($/BP) or 0.6411 (BP/$). Foreign exchange dealers use the rates of these few contracts as benchmarks when they determine rates for other maturities.

The clientele delineation between the foreign exchange forward and futures markets is encouraged by the different procedures for establishing and closing out forward and futures contracts. The futures market uses the clearinghouse and margining system to minimize credit risk. Since the forward market has no clearinghouse or margins, forward contract dealers must check their customers' credit and may require customers to establish a line of credit with them. This

---

[3] In Chapter 2, we saw that because of marking to market the futures price and forward price for contracts with the same expiration dates may differ somewhat. In the foreign exchange markets, these differences are so small that we will consider the futures and forward prices as virtually identical. See Cornell and Reinganum [1981].

[4] The forward contracts also relieve their holders of the inconvenience of daily marking to market.

system favors large, creditworthy customers. The difficulty of getting out of forward contracts before maturity makes the forward market more attractive to those who wish to hold their contracts to maturity. As we saw in Chapter 1, the only way to offset a forward contract is to agree to offset with the dealer or to enter into an opposite forward contract with another dealer and carry both contracts to maturity. As a result, 90 percent of the forward contracts and fewer than 1 percent of the futures contracts in foreign exchange are settled by delivery.

The rest of this chapter will focus on the foreign exchange futures market. However, the no-arbitrage condition and the hedging techniques that we derive for the futures market apply to the foreign exchange forward market as well.

Foreign Exchange Futures Market

The major foreign exchange futures market is the International Monetary Market at the Chicago Mercantile Exchange. Founded in 1972, the IMM currently trades contracts on the British pound, Canadian dollar, Deutsche mark, Japanese yen, Swiss franc, French franc, and Australian dollar. The specifications for these futures contracts are as follows:

Foreign Exchange Futures Contracts Specifications

Contract:	Foreign Exchange
Exchange	International Monetary Market (Chicago Mercantile Exchange)
Quantity:	
British pound	62,500 BP
Canadian dollar	100,000 CD
Deutsche mark	125,000 DM
Japanese yen	12,500,000 JY
Swiss franc	125,000 SF
French franc	250,000 FF
Australian dollar	100,000 AD
Delivery months:	March, June, September, December
Delivery specifications:	Delivery by wire transfer two days after the last day of trading
Minimum price movement:	
British pound	$0.0002/BP ($12.50 per contract)
Canadian dollar	$0.0001/CD ($10.00 per contract)
Deutsche mark	$0.0001/DM ($12.50 per contract)
Japanese yen	$0.000001/JY ($12.50 per contract)
Swiss franc	$0.0001/SF ($12.50 per contract)
French franc	$0.00005/FF ($12.50 per contract)
Australian dollar	$0.0001/AD ($10.00 per contract)

Figure 7.3 shows the annual trading volume from 1983 through 1989 for the five major currency contracts.[5]

The prices of the U.S. foreign exchange futures contracts are quoted as dollars per unit of the foreign currency, $/A, as are U.S. spot and forward foreign

---

[5] Trading volume in the French franc was only 3,932 contracts in 1988. Trading in the Australian dollar began in 1987, and the volume was only 75,960 contracts in 1988.

Figure 7.3 Foreign Exchange Futures Annual Volume, 1983–1989

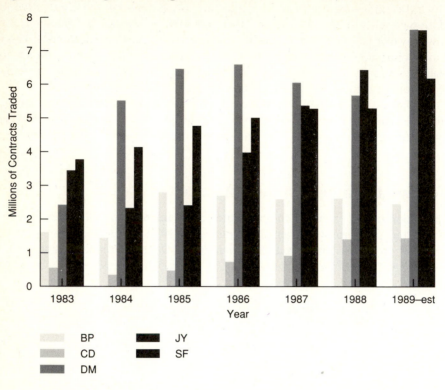

Source: Futures Industry Association.

exchange prices. Figure 7.4 presents an excerpt from The Wall Street Journal that gives futures prices on Tuesday, May 23, 1989.

The U.S. dollar futures contracts that are traded on foreign exchanges are quoted as the home currency per dollar, A/$. The London International Financial Futures Exchange, the BMF (Brazil), the New Zealand Futures Exchange, and the Sydney Futures Exchange all trade U.S. dollar contracts.

To ensure that the quotation method used in every case is clear, we will use the following notation:

$F_{t,T}$ (B/A) = futures price for currency A in units of currency B

P_t (B/A)   = spot price for currency A in units of currency B (as before)

Both the U.S. cash and futures foreign exchange markets have a two-day settlement period. The last day of trading in the CME futures contracts is two business days before the last Wednesday of the expiration month, but actual delivery does not occur until that Wednesday. In our foreign exchange pricing notation shown above, we will let t represent the date on which a transaction occurs; this will be two days after a deal is made.

Figure 7.4 Foreign Exchange Futures Transactions Prices for May 23, 1989

```
                          FUTURES
                                       Lifetime      Open
             Open  High  Low Settle Change High Low Interest
    JAPANESE YEN (IMM) 12.5 million yen; $ per yen (.00)
June      .7093 .7100 .7046 .7052 − .0018 .8485 .7046 68,966
Sept      .7162 .7172 .7118 .7123 − .0020 .8580 .7118  4,773
Dec       .7220 .7235 .7182 .7190 − .0023 .8635 .7182    741
Mr90      .7285 .7295 .7264 .7254 − .0026 .8357 .7264    188
    Est vol 40,365; vol Mon 43,848; open int 74,668, +1,721.
    W. GERMAN MARK (IMM) − 125,000 marks; $ per mark
June      .4996 .5018 .4973 .4983  ....  .5975 .4973 70,230
Sept      .5022 .5042 .4998 .5006  ....  .5977 .4998  6,260
Dec       .5045 .5065 .5025 .5028 − .0002 .5895 .5023    780
    Est vol 41,111; vol Mon 44,386; open int 77,270, +5,149.
    CANADIAN DOLLAR (IMM) − 100,000 dlrs.; $ per Can $
June      .8334 .8337 .8308 .8313 + .0006 .8440 .7670 19,965
Sept      .8285 .8290 .8262 .8267 + .0004 .8396 .7990  2,310
Dec       .8245 .8252 .8228 .8228 + .0002 .8370 .7920    679
Mr90      .8193 .8193 .8193 .8193  ....  .8322 .7890    100
June        ....  ....  .8161 − .0002 .8272 .8193       554
    Est vol 7,727; vol Mon 8,118; open int 23,608, +328.
    BRITISH POUND (IMM) − 62,500 pds.; $ per pound
June   1.5782 1.5806 1.5570 1.5608 − .0120 1.8370 1.5570 24,750
Sept   1.5636 1.5660 1.5410 1.5458 − .0124 1.8030 1.5410  1,609
Dec    1.5490 1.5500 1.5250 1.5328 − .0130 1.7450 1.5250    186
June   1.5150 1.5270 1.5090 1.5088 − .0130 1.6950 1.5090    151
    Est vol 11,843; vol Mon 10,578; open int 26,697, −344.
    SWISS FRANC (IMM) − 125,000 francs-$ per franc
June      .5617 .5636 .5582 .5590 + .0003 .7145 .5582 40,217
Sept      .5639 .5659 .5605 .5612 + .0002 .7210 .5590  3,664
Dec       .5665 .5690 .5630 .5637 − .0001 .6653 .5600    304
    Est vol 31,612; vol Mon 26,358; open int 44,185, +575.
    AUSTRALIAN DOLLAR (IMM) − 100,000 dlrs.; $ per A.$
June      .7442 .7470 .7403 .7409 + .0019 .8725 .7352  2,549
Sept      .7300 .7325 .7268 .7274 + .0024 .8000 .7210    368
    Est vol 775; vol·Mon 853; open int 2,931, +319.
    U.S. DOLLAR INDEX (FINEX) 500 times USDX
June   103.43 104.02 103.20 103.79 − .02 104.02 90.20  5,034
Sept   103.55 104.05 103.28 103.87 − .05 104.05 90.40  2,170
Dec    103.52 104.15 103.52 103.92 − .07 104.15 95.05    187
    Est vol 2,400; vol Mon 5,945; open int 7,391, +1,276.
    The index: High 104.01; Low 103.27; Close 103.94 +.18
```

Source: *The Wall Street Journal*, May 24, 1989.

Fundamental No-Arbitrage Equation

As in our discussions of other futures contracts, we will derive the fundamental no-arbitrage equation for foreign exchange futures by first studying the strategies for cash-and-carry and reverse cash-and-carry arbitrage. Then we will show the fundamental no-arbitrage equation to be the relationship that prevents these strategies from yielding arbitrage profits. We will express the relationship in terms of U.S. dollars and another currency, A; however, it will hold for any two currencies.

We can use a cash-and-carry with foreign exchange futures to create a synthetic U.S. dollar T-bill. Because of the two-day settlement in both the spot foreign exchange markets and the Eurocurrency markets, we will let time t be two days after the current date. The cash-and-carry includes the following steps:

1.   At the current time, t, we convert $Q_t^\$$ U.S. dollars into a foreign currency, A, using the current exchange rate, P_t ($/A). This will yield the following quantity of currency A at time t:

$$Q_t^A = (\text{U.S. dollars})[P_t\,(A/\$)]$$

$$= Q_t^\$\left[\frac{1}{P_t\,(\$/A)}\right].$$

2.   We hold currency A between times t and T by investing it in a riskless security, denominated in currency A, that expires at T. We denote the rate of interest on this security as $r_{t,T}^A$. At time T, it will yield an amount of currency A, Q_T^A, equal to

$$Q_T^A = Q_t^A\,(1 + r_{t,T}^A)$$

$$= Q_t^\$\left[\frac{1}{P_t\,(\$/A)}\right](1 + r_{t,T}^A).$$

3.   At time t, we enter into Q_T^A worth of short futures contracts that expire at time T. This will allow conversion of currency A into U.S. dollars at the locked-in rate of $F_{t,T}\,(\$/A)$. This will yield the following quantity of U.S. dollars at time T:

$$Q_T^\$ = Q_T^A[F_{t,T}\,(\$/A)] \tag{7.7}$$

$$= Q_t^\$\left[\frac{1}{P_t\,(\$/A)}\right](1 + r_{t,T}^A)[F_{t,T}\,(\$/A)]$$

$$= Q_t^\$\left[\frac{F_{t,T}\,(\$/A)}{P_t\,(\$/A)}\right](1 + r_{t,T}^A).$$

The net result of these transactions is that $Q_t^\$$ dollars are invested at time t and $Q_T^\$$ dollars are received at time T. The dollar inflow at T, $Q_T^\$$, is known at t because the currency-A-denominated investment is riskless and the exchange rate at time T is locked in. Thus, the cash-and-carry strategy has created a riskless synthetic U.S. dollar investment.

The implied repo rate earned on the cash-and-carry is given by

$$1 + \text{Implied repo rate} = \frac{Q_T^\$}{Q_t^\$} \tag{7.8}$$

where $Q_T^\$$ is given by Equation 7.7, so that

$$1 + \text{Implied repo rate} = \left[\frac{F_{t,T}\,(\$/A)}{P_t\,(\$/A)}\right](1 + r_{t,T}^A). \tag{7.9}$$

Example 7.2 shows how foreign exchange futures can be used to create a synthetic U.S.-dollar-denominated riskless investment. It also demonstrates how to calculate the implied repo rate on such an investment.

▪ **Example 7.2: Creating a Riskless U.S. Dollar Investment Abroad**
Suppose we observe the following prices on May 23, 1989:

Spot British pound	1.5640 ($/BP)	0.6393 (BP/$)
December 20 British pound futures	1.5328 ($/BP)	0.6524 (BP/$)
Short-term British-pound-denominated interest rate (365-day year)	12.00% per annum	

The last day of trading on the contract is December 18, but delivery occurs on December 20.

Now suppose we have $100 million that we wish to invest until December 20. One strategy is to create a synthetic riskless dollar investment with a cash-and-carry, as follows:

t   T

209 days

5/25   12/20

1. We convert the $100 million to British pounds. This will yield on May 25 (two days after May 23)

$$\text{British pounds on May 25} = (\$100,000,000)[0.6393 \ (BP/\$)]$$
$$= 63,930,000 \ BP.$$

2. We invest the 63,930,000 BP at 12 percent over the 209 days from May 25 until December 20. This will yield

$$\text{British pounds on December 20} = (63,930,000)[1 + (0.12)(209/365)]$$
$$= 68,322,779 \ BP.$$

Note that because British-pound-denominated short-term rates are quoted on a 365-day basis, we determine the 209-day nonannualized rate by multiplying the annual rate by 209/365.

3. On May 23, we take a short position in British pound futures that locks in the rate at which we can convert the pounds we will receive on December 20 into dollars:

Number of short British pound futures contracts

$$= \frac{\text{Number of BP on December 20}}{\text{BP per futures contract}}$$

$$= \frac{68,322,779}{62,500 \ \text{BP per futures contract}}$$

$$= 1,093 \ \text{BP futures contracts.}$$

This position locks in an exchange rate of 1.5328 ($/BP) on December 20 no matter what the spot exchange rate is at that time. On December 20, we will receive

Dollars received on December 20

= (Number of British pounds on December 20)[$F_{t,T}$ ($/BP)]

= (68,322,779 BP)[1.5328 ($/BP)]

= $104,725,156.

If we undertake this cash-and-carry, we will pay out $100 million on May 25 and earn $104,725,156 209 days later, on December 20. The implied repo rate on this investment is

$$\text{Implied repo rate} = \frac{\$104,725,156 - \$100,000,000}{\$100,000,000}$$

$$= 4.73\% \text{ for 209 days}$$

$$= 8.15\% \text{ per annum (360-day year).}$$

We get the same implied repo rate from Equation 7.9:

$$1 + \text{Implied repo rate} = \left(\frac{1.5328}{1.5640}\right)[1 + (0.12)(209/365)]$$

$$= 1.0473.$$

We use a 360-day year to annualize the implied repo rate, because that is the practice for U.S.-dollar-denominated money market rates. However, we use a 365-day year for the British rate, because that is the British quotation convention. ∎

We have seen that U.S. dollars can be lent out synthetically by using another currency in a cash-and-carry strategy. U.S. dollars can also be borrowed synthetically by using another currency in a reverse cash-and-carry strategy. The steps are just the opposite of those in a synthetic loan:

1. Suppose we wish to borrow $Q_t^\$$ at the current time, t. We can achieve this by borrowing Q_t^A in currency A and converting these funds into dollars using the current exchange rate, P_t ($/A), where

    Q_t^A = (Dollars to be borrowed)[P_t (A/$)]

    $$= Q_t^\$\left[\frac{1}{P_t \, (\$/A)}\right].$$

2. Between t and T, we pay interest of $r_{t,T}^A$, which is denominated in currency A. At time T, we owe Q_T^A:

    $Q_T^A = Q_t^A(1 + r_{t,T}^A)$

    $$= Q_t^\$\left[\frac{1}{P_t \, (\$/A)}\right](1 + r_{t,T}^A).$$

3. At time t, we enter into Q_T^A worth of long currency A futures that expire at time T. This allows us to convert our dollars back into currency A at a

locked-in rate of $F_{t,T}$ ($/A) when it is time to pay back the loan. At time T, the quantity of U.S. dollars needed to pay back the loan will be

$$Q_T^\$ = Q_T^A [F_{t,T} \ (\$/A)] \tag{7.10}$$

$$= Q_t^\$ \left[\frac{1}{P_t \ (\$/A)} \right] (1 + r_{t,T}^A)[F_{t,T} \ (\$/A)]$$

$$= Q_t^\$ \left[\frac{F_{t,T} \ (\$/A)}{P_t \ (\$/A)} \right] (1 + r_{t,T}^A).$$

The net result of these transactions is that we have borrowed $Q_t^\$$ dollars at time t and paid back $Q_T^\$$ dollars at time T. As $r_{t,T}^A$ is known at time t and we have locked in the exchange rate we will get at time T, we have a riskless synthetic U.S. dollar borrowing. The implied reverse repo rate on this synthetic borrowing is

$$1 + \text{Implied reverse repo rate} = \frac{Q_T^\$}{Q_t^\$}. \tag{7.11}$$

There will be opportunities for arbitrage unless the rates earned and paid on such synthetic loans and borrowings are the same as the rates for lending or borrowing directly, and at no risk, in the U.S. market. If we assume there are no transactions costs, the synthetic and direct rates will be exactly equal in equilibrium, and the no-arbitrage relationship will be

$$1 + \text{Implied repo rate} = 1 + \text{Implied reverse repo rate} \tag{7.12}$$

$$= \left[\frac{F_{t,T} \ (\$/A)}{P_t \ (\$/A)} \right] (1 + r_{t,T}^A)$$

$$= 1 + r_{t,T}^\$.$$

Rewriting Equation 7.12 yields

$$\frac{F_{t,T} \ (\$/A)}{P_t \ (\$/A)} = \frac{1 + r_{t,T}^\$}{1 + r_{t,T}^A}. \tag{7.13}$$

Thus, in equilibrium,

$$r_{t,T}^\$ < r_{t,T}^A \text{ when } F_{t,T} \ (\$/A) < P_t \ (\$/A)$$

and

$$r_{t,T}^\$ > r_{t,T}^A \text{ when } F_{t,T} \ (\$/A) > P_t \ (\$/A).$$

The relationship depicted by Equation 7.13 is known as **covered interest rate parity**, because it requires equality, or parity, between the direct and synthetic interest rates. The word *covered* refers to the fact that the synthetic strategies lock in the future rate at which currency A can be converted into U.S. dollars, and vice versa.

The no-arbitrage relationship in the foreign exchange market is the same as in other markets, because the arbitrage strategies in all futures markets are identical. In a foreign exchange cash-and-carry, we purchase the foreign currency at time t, carry it between t and T, and then sell it at time T at a price locked in at time t. This is the same as buying gold at t, holding it between time t and T, and selling it at time T at a price locked in with futures at time t.

We can show that the following rewritten version of the covered interest rate parity equation, 7.13, is nothing more than our familiar fundamental no-arbitrage equation:

$$F_{t,T} (\$/A) = [P_t (\$/A)](1 + r^{\$}_{t,T}) - [F_{t,T} (\$/A)]r^{A}_{t,T}. \qquad (7.14)$$

The first term on the right-hand side of Equation 7.14 states that the futures price for currency A must cover the interest cost of carrying the foreign currency. The second term is the future value of the payouts from the investment of currency A between t and T. This investment pays interest at the rate of $r^{A}_{t,T}$ that will be converted back into U.S. dollars at the known exchange rate of $F_{t,T}$ ($/A) at T. Thus, the covered interest rate parity relationship is no different from the other fundamental no-arbitrage equations we have developed throughout the book.

We have ignored the influence of transactions fees and bid-ask spreads in our derivation of the covered interest rate parity formula. If we consider these costs, covered interest rate parity will require equality between the direct and synthetic rates net of transactions costs. Example 7.3 shows how a synthetic borrowing works when transactions fees and bid-ask spreads are included.

▪ **Example 7.3: Borrowing U.S. Dollars Synthetically Abroad**   Suppose a firm wishes to borrow $200 million from May 25, 1989, until December 20, 1989. Suppose also that on May 23, 1989, two days before the firm wishes to receive the borrowed funds, the following prices prevail:[6]

Spot Deutsche mark:		
Bid	0.4960 ($/DM)	2.0125 (DM/$)
Ask	0.4968 ($/DM)	2.0161 (DM/$)
December 20 Deutsche mark futures:		
Bid	0.5024 ($/DM)	1.9889 (DM/$)
Ask	0.5028 ($/DM)	1.9904 (DM/$)
Riskless Deutsche-mark-denominated borrowing rate (365-day year)	7.00% per annum	
Short-term U.S.-dollar-denominated lending rate (360-day year)	8.50% per annum	
Short-term U.S.-dollar-denominated borrowing rate (360-day year)	9.90% per annum	

---

[6] Recall that when a bank quotes an ask price at which it will sell Deutsche marks, it is also quoting a bid price at which it will buy U.S. dollars.

The firm sees that it can borrow synthetically by undertaking the following transactions in the U.S. dollar and Deutsche mark markets:

1. On May 25 (using May 23 rates), the firm borrows enough Deutsche marks to yield $200 million. The firm can sell Deutsche marks for dollars at the bid rate of 0.4960 ($/DM). Equivalently, it can buy U.S. dollars with Deutsche marks at the ask rate of 2.0161 (DM/$). Therefore, the firm borrows the following quantity of Deutsche marks:

    Deutsche marks borrowed on May 25
    $= (\text{U.S. dollars desired})[P_t\,(\text{DM/\$})]$
    $= (\$200,000,000)[2.0161\,(\text{DM/\$})]$
    $= 403,220,000\ \text{DM}.$

When it receives these funds on May 25, the firm converts them to the desired sum of $200 million.

2. On December 20, 209 days after May 25, the firm must pay back the 403.22 million DM it borrowed plus interest. Its total payment will be

    Deutsche marks owed on December 20
    $= (\text{Deutsche marks borrowed on May 25})(1 + 209\text{-day rate})$
    $= (403,220,000\ \text{DM})[1 + (0.07)(209/365)]$
    $= 419.382\ \text{million DM}.$

3. On May 23, the firm also takes a long Deutsche mark futures position that locks in the rate at which it can convert U.S. dollars into Deutsche marks when it must pay off its loan on December 20. Because the firm will buy Deutsche marks, the appropriate futures price is the ask rate of 0.5028 ($/DM) or, equivalently, the bid rate of 1.9889 (DM/$). To cover its full loan payment, the firm must enter into the following number of long December Deutsche mark futures contracts:

    Number of long Deutsche mark futures contracts
    $$= \frac{\text{Number of DM on December 20}}{\text{DM per futures contract}}$$
    $$= \frac{419.382\ \text{million DM}}{125,000\ \text{DM/contract}}$$
    $= 3,355\ \text{DM futures contracts}.$

Thus, the firm's dollar cost of the Deutsche marks it needs on December 20 will be

    Dollars needed on December 20
    $= (\text{Number of Deutsche marks needed on December 20})[F_{t,T}\,(\text{\$/DM})]$
    $= (419.382\ \text{million DM})[0.5028\,(\text{\$/DM})]$
    $= \$210.865\ \text{million}.$

With this strategy, the firm borrows $200 million on May 25 and pays back $210.865 million 209 days later, on December 20. The implied reverse repo rate on this synthetic borrowing is

$$\text{Implied reverse repo rate} = \frac{\$210.865 \text{ million} - \$200 \text{ million}}{\$200 \text{ million}}$$

$$= 5.43\% \text{ for 209 days}$$

$$= 9.35\% \text{ per annum (360-year)}.$$

There is a quasi-arbitrage opportunity here, because the 9.35 percent synthetic dollar borrowing rate is less than the 9.90 percent dollar borrowing rate. But there is no pure arbitrage opportunity, because the synthetic borrowing rate exceeds the 8.50 percent dollar lending rate. ∎

Covered Interest Rate Parity and International Investment

The covered interest rate parity relationship implies that portfolio managers searching for international investments cannot simply compare interest rates across countries and invest where the rates are highest. They must consider the returns they can lock in on currencies in the futures markets as well as the interest rate differentials among countries. Example 7.4 shows how the covered interest rate parity equation can be used to compare interest rates across countries.

▪ **Example 7.4: Comparing Interest Rates across Currencies**   Suppose we wish to invest funds from May 25, 1989, until December 20, 1989, and we observe the following prices on May 23 (for simplicity, we will ignore bid-ask spreads):

Spot Swiss franc	0.5580 ($/SF)	1.7920 (SF/$)
December 20 Swiss franc futures	0.5637 ($/SF)	1.7740 (SF/$)
Short-term Swiss-franc-denominated interest rate (365-day year)	7.00% per annum	
Short-term U.S.-dollar-denominated interest rate (360-day year)	8.50% per annum	

We can earn the following nonannualized rates over the 209-day period from May 25 through December 20 by investing in Swiss francs or U.S. dollars:

209-day Swiss franc rate = (7.00%)(209/365) = 4.0082%
209-day U.S. dollar rate = (8.50%)(209/360) = 4.9347%.

At first glance, the U.S. dollar investment appears superior because it has a higher interest rate. However, we must account for the earnings offered by the discount of the spot Swiss franc rate relative to the December Swiss franc futures rate. If we invest dollars in Swiss francs through a cash-and-carry, we can receive interest *and* a locked-in appreciation in franc value. We will have a synthetic dollar investment with a total implied repo rate as given by Equation 7.9:

$$1 + \text{Implied repo rate} = \left[\frac{0.5637 \ (\$/SF)}{0.5580 \ (\$/SF)} \right] (1.040082) \qquad \textbf{(7.15)}$$

$$= 1.050706.$$

This 5.0706 percent implied repo rate on the Swiss franc investment exceeds the dollar investment rate of 4.9347 percent. Thus, the Swiss franc investment is more profitable even though the Swiss 209-day interest rate is lower than the U.S. rate.

Equation 7.15 clearly shows that this return on the synthetic dollar investment in Swiss francs consists of the short-term Swiss interest rate compounded with the Swiss franc appreciation. The Swiss franc appreciation that we can lock in over the 209 days is

$$1 + \text{Locked-in appreciation} = \frac{0.5637(\$/SF)}{0.5580(\$/SF)}$$

$$= 1.0102.$$

In Equation 7.15, this appreciation is compounded with the 4.0082 percent short-term Swiss interest rate to yield the total 5.0706 percent return on the Swiss franc investment. ■

Empirical Evidence on Covered Interest Rate Parity

Several studies have examined whether covered interest rate parity holds in practice. Frenkel and Levich [1975, 1977], McCormick [1979], and Eaker [1980] found that when there is free flow of capital between two countries, there are few arbitrage profits available from covered interest rate arbitrage between the currencies of those countries. Aliber [1973] and Dooley and Isard [1980] found that there may be deviations from covered interest rate parity if either country has currency controls or if there is a chance that currency controls will be imposed before the arbitrage is completed. This is because currency controls make it difficult to complete the transactions of the arbitrage. Germany, for example, has had periods of currency controls, and covered interest rate parity did not hold for the Deutsche mark at those times. Under the current regime of flexible exchange rates and free movement of capital, covered interest rate parity appears to hold for the currencies of the major Western industrial countries.[7]

---

[7] There are two other empirical issues. The first issue is whether the exchange rates implied by futures prices are unbiased predictors of future spot exchange rates. Hodrick and Srivastava [1987], McCurdy and Morgan [1987], and Kodres [1988] found evidence against the unbiasedness hypothesis. The second issue is how accurately forward and futures prices forecast future spot exchange rates relative to professional forecasters. Levich [1983] found that in general professional forecasters perform poorly relative to futures and forward prices.

Hedging

Like futures on other commodities and securities, foreign exchange futures are used to hedge business risks.[8] In this case, the risks are those associated with exchange rate fluctuations. We already encountered foreign exchange hedges in two of our examples. In Example 7.2, we worked through a cash-and-carry in which we purchased British pounds in the spot market and lent them out in a riskless pound-denominated investment. There was no risk as to the number of pounds we would have when this security came due. However, the number of U.S. dollars these pounds would buy in the future was uncertain, so we entered into a short British pound futures position to lock in the rate at which we could sell the pounds. Similarly, in Example 7.3, a firm borrowed Deutsche marks and converted them to dollars. The firm used a long Deutsche mark futures position to lock in the rate at which it could buy Deutsche marks when the time to pay back its loan arrived.

Corporate profits are exposed to exchange rate risk in many situations. A U.S. exporter that is paid with foreign exchange faces the risk that the U.S. dollar will appreciate, making its foreign currency revenues less valuable in terms of dollars. Such a firm can hedge against an appreciating dollar (and a depreciating foreign currency) by taking a short position in the currency it will receive. Similarly, a U.S. firm with foreign subsidiaries may wish to convert its foreign profits into dollars at some future date. It could use a short futures position to hedge this profit repatriation.

There are many potential uses for long exchange rate hedges as well. A firm that pays for imports with a foreign currency could use a long hedge to protect itself against a U.S. dollar depreciation (and a foreign currency appreciation) that would increase its foreign currency costs. A foreign firm with U.S. subsidiaries could use a long hedge to lock in the rate at which it would convert its U.S. dollar profits into its home currency.

The general rule for determining whether a long or short futures position will hedge a potential foreign exchange loss is

Loss from appreciating U.S. dollar   →   Short hedge
Loss from depreciating U.S. dollar   →   Long hedge.

Example 7.5 shows how a firm uses a long hedge to reduce currency risk.

■ **Example 7.5: Using a Long Hedge to Protect Against a Depreciating Dollar**   Suppose that on May 23, 1989, a U.S. firm agrees to buy 100,000 motorcycles from Japan on December 20 at a price of 202,350 JY each. The firm fears the U.S. dollar will depreciate before the sale date, making the yen it must buy more expensive. It decides to take a long position in December Japanese yen futures to protect itself against a falling dollar.

---

[8] See Gramatikos and Saunders [1983] for a discussion of hedging with foreign currency futures.

The prices facing the firm on May 23 are

Spot Japanese yen:
   Bid   0.007020 ($/JY)   142.30 (JY/$)
   Ask   0.007027 ($/JY)   142.45 (JY/$)

December 20 Japanese yen futures:
   Bid   0.007185 ($/JY)   139.08 (JY/$)
   Ask   0.007190 ($/JY)   139.18 (JY/$)

The total number of JY the firm will need on December 20 is

$$\text{Total JY needed} = (\text{Number of motorcycles})(\text{Price per motorcycle})$$
$$= (100{,}000)(202{,}350 \text{ JY})$$
$$= 20{,}235{,}000{,}000 \text{ JY}.$$

To hedge the price of these yen, the firm must enter into the following number of long December yen futures contracts:

Number of long Japanese yen futures contracts

$$= \frac{20{,}235{,}000{,}000 \text{ JY}}{12{,}500{,}000 \text{ JY/contract}}$$

$$= 1{,}619 \text{ JY futures contracts.}$$

As the firm is taking a long position, its futures price is the ask of 0.007190 ($/JY).

We can see how this strategy locks in the importer's dollar costs by considering two scenarios for the spot Japanese yen price on December 18 (for December 20 settlement). Note that we subtract futures profits from costs to calculate the firm's net costs.

In the first scenario, the dollar appreciates and the yen depreciates so that the spot yen rate is 0.006500 ($/JY) on December 18. The firm's hedged dollar costs of purchasing the motorcycles therefore will be

Hedged U.S. dollar December 20 costs

   = Unhedged U.S. dollar costs − Futures profit

   = (Japanese yen costs)[December 18 ($/JY)]
     − (Yen futures contracts)(Yen per contract)[December 18 ($/JY)
     − Futures ($/JY)]

   = (20,235,000,000 JY)[0.006500 ($/JY)]
     − (1,619)(12,500,000 JY)[0.006500 ($/JY) − 0.007190 ($/JY)]

   = $131.53 million − (−$13.96 million)

   = $145.49 million.

In the second scenario, the dollar depreciates and the yen appreciates so that the spot yen rate on December 18 is 0.008000 ($/JY). The firm's hedged dollar costs will be:

Hedged U.S. dollar December 20 costs

= Unhedged U.S. dollar costs − Futures profit

= (20,235,000,000 JY)[0.008000 ($/JY)]
    − (1,619)(12,500,000 JY)[0.008000 ($/JY) − 0.007190 ($/JY)]

= $161.88 million − ($16.39 million)

= $145.49 million.

The hedge has locked in the firm's dollar costs regardless of whether the dollar appreciates or depreciates relative to the yen. In both cases, the hedged costs are the yen cost of the motorcycles times the December 20 yen futures ask price on May 23:

Hedged costs = (Japanese yen costs)[Futures price ($/JY)]
            = (20,235,000,000 JY)[0.007190 ($/JY)]
            = 145.49 million.

∎

Natural Hedge

The importer in Example 7.5 was able to lock in the dollar cost of buying motorcycles from Japan by hedging with a long position in Japanese yen futures. The importer could also use a natural hedge to solve its risk management problem. From Chapter 2, we know that

Synthetic long futures = −T-bill + Underlying asset.

Thus, the importer can lock in the dollar cost of purchasing motorcycles in December by borrowing dollars and buying yen today. The steps in this natural hedge are

1. Determine the quantity of yen that, if invested today in a riskless yen instrument, will yield the amount required to pay for the motorcycles on December 20. This quantity is

$$Q_t^Y = \frac{Q_T^Y}{1 + r_{t,T}^Y},$$ (7.16)

where $r_{t,T}^Y$ is the riskless yen lending rate between t and T and Q_t^Y is simply the present value, in yen, of the yen needed at time T.

2. Determine how many dollars are needed to buy the Q_t^Y yen today. This quantity is

$$Q_t^\$ = Q_t^Y[P_t \, (\$/JY)].$$ (7.17)

The importer therefore must borrow $Q_t^\$$ dollars today, convert them to yen, and invest the yen in a riskless instrument to guarantee that it will have the required

Q_T^Y yen at time T. In this way, the importer essentially sells a T-bill short and buys the underlying yen asset as required to create the synthetic long futures position.

3.   The importer must pay back its loan of $Q_t^\$$ dollars with the following quantity of dollars at time T:

$$Q_T^\$ = Q_t^\$(1 + r_{t,T}^\$) \tag{7.18}$$
$$= Q_t^Y[P_t \, (\$/JY)](1 + r_{t,T}^\$),$$

where $r_{t,T}^\$$ is the importer's dollar borrowing rate between t and T. This payment is known to the importer at time t. Therefore, this strategy has locked in the dollar cost of the importer's future motorcycle purchase.

We can determine whether this natural hedge is superior to a futures hedge by comparing the number of dollars the two strategies require at time T. We saw that the futures strategy requires the following number of dollars at time T:

$$\text{Number of U.S. dollars needed at T} \tag{7.19}$$
$$= (\text{Number of yen needed at T})(\$/\text{yen rate implied by futures})$$
$$= Q_T^Y[F_{t,T} \, (\$/JY)]$$
$$= Q_t^Y[F_{t,T} \, (\$/JY)](1 + r_{t,T}^Y),$$

where the last equality comes from Equation 7.16. This amount is less than the dollar quantity required by the natural hedge at time T, shown in Equation 7.18, if

$$Q_t^Y[F_{t,T} \, (\$/JY)](1 + r_{t,T}^Y) < Q_t^Y[P_t \, (\$/JY)](1 + r_{t,T}^\$). \tag{7.20}$$

If we rewrite Equation 7.20, we get

$$F_{t,T} \, (\$/JY) < [P_t \, (\$/JY)](1 + r_{t,T}^\$) - [F_{t,T} \, (\$/JY)]r_{t,T}^Y \tag{7.21}$$

or

$$\Omega^c = F_{t,T} - [P_t \, (1 + r_{t,T}) - FV(\text{Payouts})] < 0. \tag{7.22}$$

Equation 7.21 is merely a statement that the fundamental no-arbitrage equation, 7.14, does not hold. Therefore, the importer should, as always, use the no-arbitrage relationship to choose between a natural and a futures hedge. If, as in Equation 7.21, the yen futures is inexpensive relative to the spot rate, a long futures position is preferable to the natural hedge. If the inequality in Equation 7.21 goes the other way, the natural hedge is superior because the spot rate is inexpensive relative to the futures rate. The quasi-arbitrage table in Table 7.1 demonstrates that the choice between the long futures hedge and the natural hedge of borrowing and buying spot yen amounts to a cash-and-carry quasi-arbitrage.[9]

---

[9] We can also consider this a reverse cash-and-carry arbitrage if we view our benchmark position as the natural hedge. However, we will get the same answer.

Table 7.1 Cash-and-Carry Quasi-Arbitrage Table for U.S. Importer

Benchmark position: long futures position, net borrower

Cash-and-Carry Pure Arbitrage Components	Cash-and-Carry Quasi-Arbitrage Components	Relevant Price or Rate
1. Buy yen	Buy yen	Ask
Invest yen	Invest yen	Lending rate
2. Short futures	Refrain from going long futures	Ask
3. Borrow dollars	Borrow dollars	Borrowing rate

Resulting position: synthetic long futures position, net borrower

Transactions fees: $TF = +TF_1 - TF_2 + TF_3$
1. Pay TF_1
2. Save TF_2
3. Pay TF_3

Example 7.6 shows how one importer chooses between a futures and a natural hedge. It also shows that this choice depends on whether the importer is a net borrower or a net lender.

- **Example 7.6: Choosing between a Futures and a Natural Hedge for an Importer**   Suppose the importing firm we met in Example 7.5 is now considering hedging its dollar cost of purchasing Japanese motorcycles with a natural hedge. Such a hedge requires the firm to borrow dollars today to buy the quantity of yen that will yield the yen cost of the motorcycles on the purchase date. We assume the firm's intended purchase of 100,000 motorcycles will still cost 20,235,000,000 JY on December 20 and the May 23 spot and futures prices are the same as in Example 7.5. In that example, we saw that the importer can use a futures hedge to lock in the following cost, in dollars, for the motorcycles on December 20:

U.S. dollar cost of motorcycles on December 20 = $145.49 million.

We assume the short-term U.S. and Japanese interest rates on May 23 (for May 25 settlement) are[10]

Short-term Japanese-yen-denominated lending rate (365-day year)	5.75% per annum
Short-term U.S.-dollar-denominated lending rate (360-day year)	8.50% per annum
Short-term U.S.-dollar-denominated borrowing rate (360-day year)	9.90% per annum

[10] Recall from Chapter 5 that the Eurodollar borrowing and lending market has a two-day settlement period just like the currency market.

To construct the natural hedge, the firm must take the following steps:[11]

1. On May 25, the firm must acquire a quantity of yen equal to the present value (at May 23 prices) of the 20,235,000,000 yen required to pay for the motorcycles on December 20. We use the Japanese short-term lending rate as the discount rate to compute this present value. Over the 209-day period from May 25 to December 20, this rate is $(209/365)(5.75\%) = 3.29\%$. Thus, the present value of the future yen outflow is

$$\text{Japanese yen needed on May 25} = \frac{20{,}235{,}000{,}000 \text{ JY}}{1.0329}$$
$$= 19{,}590.47 \text{ million JY.}$$

2. The importer must borrow, in dollars, the amount necessary to buy the required quantity of yen on May 25. The dollar cost of the yen purchase is determined by the current ask spot exchange rate ($/JY):

U.S. dollars needed on May 25
$$= (19{,}590.47 \text{ million JY})[0.007027 (\$/JY)]$$
$$= \$137.66 \text{ million.}$$

3. On December 20, the importer will pay back its dollar loan plus interest. Its borrowing rate over the 209-day period is $(209/360)(9.90\%) = 5.75\%$. The amount to be paid back is therefore

U.S. dollars needed on December 20 $= (\$137.66 \text{ million})(1.0575)$
$$= \$145.58 \text{ million.}$$

This amount exceeds the $145.49 million the importer would pay under the futures hedge, so the natural hedge is inferior to the futures hedge. The fundamental no-arbitrage equation also gives us the same result. Table 7.1 tells us that in this case, the no-arbitrage equation should be calculated with the U.S. borrowing rate, the Japanese yen lending rate, the spot ask exchange rate ($/JY), and the December ask futures exchange rate ($/JY). These rates yield the following value for Ω^c:

$$\Omega^c = [F^a_{t,T}(\$/JY)] - [P^a_t(\$/JY)](1 + r^{\$}_{t,T}) + [F^a_{t,T}(\$/JY)]r^y_{t,T}$$
$$= [0.007190 (\$/JY)] - [0.007027 (\$/JY)](1.0575)$$
$$\quad + [0.007190 (\$/JY)](0.0329)$$
$$= -0.0000045 (\$/JY) < 0.$$

This shows that the futures is relatively inexpensive and the long futures hedge is preferable to the natural hedge. This Ω^c is measured on a per-yen basis. The saving from the futures strategy on the entire hedge is

---

[11] Because of rounding error, the careful reader may find slight discrepancies in the following calculations. These disappear when the calculations are performed on a spreadsheet.

Table 7.2 Cash-and-Carry Quasi-Arbitrage Table for U.S. Importer

Benchmark position: long futures position, net lender

Cash-and-Carry Pure Arbitrage Components	Cash-and-Carry Quasi-Arbitrage Components	Relevant Price or Rate
1. Buy yen	Buy yen	Ask
Invest yen	Invest yen	Lending rate
2. Short futures	Refrain from going long futures	Ask
3. Borrow dollars	Reduce dollar lending	Lending rate

Resulting position: synthetic long futures position, net lender

Transactions fees: $TF = +TF_1 - TF_2 + TF_3$
1. Pay TF_1
2. Save TF_2
3. Pay TF_3

Total saving to futures hedge
$$= (-\Omega^c)(\text{Number of Japanese yen needed on December 20})$$
$$= [0.0000045\ (\$/\text{JY})](20,235,000,000\ \text{JY})$$
$$= \$0.09\ \text{million.}$$

This amount is exactly the difference between the $145.49 million needed for the long futures hedge and the $145.58 million needed for the natural hedge.

We have assumed the importer must borrow the dollars required for the natural hedge. Now suppose the firm is a net lender and thus can finance today's yen purchase by reducing its lending. The natural hedge will then be a quasi-arbitrage as presented in Table 7.2.

The effective borrowing rate for the firm in this case is the lending rate it gives up by reducing its lending. This rate over the 209-day period is $(209/360)(8.50\%) = 4.93\%$. Thus,

$$\Omega^c = [F^a_{t,T}\ (\$/\text{JY})] - [P^a_t\ (\$/\text{JY})](1 + r^{\$}_{t,T}) + [F^a_{t,T}\ (\$/\text{JY})]r^y_{t,T}$$
$$= [0.007190\ (\$/\text{JY})] - [0.007027\ (\$/\text{JY})](1.0493)$$
$$\quad + [0.007190\ (\$/\text{JY})](0.0329)$$
$$= 0.000052\ (\$/\text{JY}) > 0.$$

The positive Ω^c indicates that for the quasi-arbitrageur, the futures is relatively expensive and the natural hedge is preferable to the futures hedge. The quasi-arbitrageur's choice of the natural hedge over the futures hedge yields a total saving of

Total saving from natural hedge
$$= (\Omega^c)(\text{Number of Japanese yen needed on December 20})$$
$$= [0.000052\ (\$/\text{JY})](20,235,000,000\ \text{JY})$$
$$= \$1.05\ \text{million.}$$

We can also demonstrate the difference between the positions of the importer that must borrow and the importer that is a net lender by examining their cash flows under the two hedges. The importer that borrows to finance the yen purchase on May 25 must pay $137.66 million plus interest, or $145.58 million, on December 20. This amount exceeds the $145.49 million payment the firm could lock in with the futures hedge. However, the importer that is a net lender must only replace the $137.66 million plus the interest it would have earned on December 20. This amounts to

> Proceeds to importer from investing $137.66 million
> = ($137.66 million)(1.0493)
> = $144.44 million,

which is less than the $145.49 million it must pay out under the futures hedge. Clearly, the choice between a natural and futures hedge can depend on the importer's benchmark position ∎

In Examples 7.5 and 7.6, we saw how a U.S. importer can protect itself against a depreciating dollar by taking a long hedge position either in the futures market or with a natural strategy (synthetic futures). Similarly, a non-U.S. firm with U.S. investments can use a long hedge to protect the domestic value of its U.S. dollar revenues. Foreign firms that import from the United States or U.S. firms with foreign investments can follow similar strategies to protect themselves against an appreciating dollar. Suppose that on May 23, a Japanese importer is planning to purchase U.S. goods on December 20. The firm could use short December yen futures contracts to lock in the yen price of the dollars needed for the purchase on December 20. Alternatively, it could construct a natural hedge based on the following relationship:

> Synthetic short futures = T-bill − Underlying asset.

This equation shows that the firm could lock in the price it will pay for U.S. goods in December by borrowing yen, converting them into dollars, and buying a U.S. T-bill today.

The steps in this natural hedge would be as follows:

1.   The importer borrows yen on May 23 (for May 25 settlement).

2.   The firm converts its yen to dollars and buys a U.S.-dollar-denominated T-bill that expires on December 20 and whose face value just equals the number of dollars needed for the purchase on December 20.

3.   The importer pays back the yen loan on December 20.

These three transactions lock in the number of yen the Japanese importer will pay out on December 20. The quasi-arbitrage table for the choice between a natural and futures hedge in this case is shown in Table 7.3.

Table 7.3 Reverse Cash-and-Carry Quasi-Arbitrage Table for Japanese Importer

Benchmark position: short futures position

Reverse Cash-and-Carry Pure Arbitrage Components	Reverse Cash-and-Carry Quasi-Arbitrage Components	Relevant Price or Rate
1. Sell yen (buy dollars) Borrow yen	Sell yen Borrow yen	Bid Borrowing rate
2. Go long futures	Refrain from going short yen futures	Bid
3. Lend dollars	Lend dollars	Lending rate

Resulting position: synthetic short futures position

Transactions fees: $TF = +TF_1 - TF_2 + TF_3$
1. Pay TF_1
2. Save TF_2
3. Pay TF_3

Creating Synthetic Foreign-Currency-Denominated Futures Contracts

So far, our discussion of foreign exchange futures has considered only transactions that involve U.S. dollars. The U.S.-dollar-denominated futures contracts are the most liquid foreign exchange contracts in the world and therefore are an obvious choice when such a futures contract is required. In this section, we show how parties who wish to transact in currencies other than the dollar can use dollar-denominated contracts to create synthetic foreign currency futures contracts. We show how to construct both synthetic cross rate futures contracts and synthetic foreign-currency-denominated short-term interest rate futures contracts.

Synthetic Cross Rate Futures Contracts

Suppose a British importer wishes to lock in a British-pound-denominated Deutsche mark exchange rate. In other words, it wants to lock in the number of British pounds it will need to pay for a known number of Deutsche marks in the future. Currently there is no Deutsche mark futures contract denominated in pounds, but the importer can use dollar-denominated British pound and Deutsche mark futures contracts to create such a contract synthetically.

The creation of a synthetic cross rate futures contract is similar to that of synthetic spot cross exchange rates that we saw earlier in this chapter. Suppose the British importer wants to contract at time t to buy Q_T^D Deutsche marks at time T for a given number of British pounds. It can create a synthetic British-pound-denominated Deutsche mark futures contract with the following steps:

1.   At time t, the importer goes long Q_T^D worth of dollar-denominated Deutsche mark futures contracts that expire at T. The futures price of these contracts

is $F_{t,T}$ ($/DM), so at time T the importer is guaranteed Q_T^D worth of Deutsche marks at a dollar price of

$$Q_T^\$ = Q_T^D[F_{t,T}\ (\$/DM)]. \tag{7.23}$$

2.   At time t, the importer locks in the British pound price of buying the $Q_T^\$$ dollars by going short dollar-denominated pound futures contracts that expire at T. The futures price of the pound contract is $F_{t,T}$ ($/BP). To cover the planned purchase of $Q_T^\$$ dollars exactly, the importer's short pound futures position must be

$$\begin{aligned} Q_T^B &= Q_T^\$[1/F_{t,T}\ (\$/BP)] \\ &= Q_T^D[F_{t,T}\ (\$/DM)][1/F_{t,T}\ (\$/BP)]. \end{aligned} \tag{7.24}$$

The net result of these two transactions is that the importer is committed to buying Q_T^D marks for $Q_T^B = Q_T^D[F_{t,T}\ (\$/DM)][1/F_{t,T}\ (\$/BP)]$ pounds. This guarantees the importer, at time t, a British-pound-denominated time T Deutsche mark futures rate of

$$F_{t,T}\ (BP/DM) = \left[\frac{F_{t,T}\ (\$/DM)}{F_{t,T}\ (\$/BP)}\right]. \tag{7.25}$$

Example 7.7 demonstrates a hedge that uses a synthetic cross-rate futures contract.

▪ **Example 7.7: Hedging with Synthetic Cross Rate Futures Contracts**
Suppose a British importer agrees on May 23, 1989, to purchase 500,000 cases of beer from a German exporter on December 20 at a price of 10 DM per case. The importer will need the following quantity of Deutsche marks on December 20 to pay for the beer:

$$\begin{aligned} \text{Deutsche marks needed on December 20} &= (500,000)(10\ \text{DM}) \\ &= 5,000,000\ \text{DM}, \end{aligned}$$

The importer is afraid the Deutsche mark will appreciate relative to the British pound before December 20 so that its cost, in pounds, of buying the beer will increase. The firm considers hedging against a possible mark appreciation by creating a synthetic pound-denominated mark futures contract that will lock in the rate of exchange between the pound and the mark on December 20. To do this, the firm will use the existing dollar-denominated pound and mark futures contracts. On May 23, the prices of these contracts are as follows:

December 20 British pound futures:		
Bid	1.5310 ($/BP)	0.6524 (BP/$)
Ask	1.5328 ($/BP)	0.6532 (BP/$)

December 20 Deutsche mark futures:		
Bid	0.5024 ($/DM)	1.9889 (DM/$)
Ask	0.5028 ($/DM)	1.9904 (DM/$)

Earlier we saw that to create a synthetic pound-denominated mark futures contract, the importer must go long mark futures and short pound futures. Thus, the price of the synthetic futures contract is determined by the ask for the mark contract and the bid for the pound contract. Since the firm wishes to buy Deutsche marks, the price of the synthetic futures contract will be an ask price of

$$F^a_{t,T}\,(BP/DM) = \left[\frac{F^a_{t,T}\,(\$/DM)}{F^b_{t,T}\,(\$/BP)} \right] \tag{7.26}$$

$$= \frac{0.5028\;(\$/DM)}{1.5310\;(\$/BP)}$$

$$= 0.3284\;(BP/DM).$$

To obtain the required quantity of Deutsche marks for its beer purchase, the firm will take a long position in 40 mark futures contracts:

Number of long Deutsche mark futures contracts

$$= \frac{\text{Number of Deutsche marks}}{\text{Deutsche marks per contract}}$$

$$= \frac{5,000,000\;DM}{125,000\;DM/contract}$$

$$= 40\;\text{contracts.}$$

These 40 contracts will lock in a dollar cost on December 20 of

Dollars needed on December 20 = (Number of marks)$[F_{t,T}\,(\$/DM)]$
$$= (5,000,000\;DM)[0.5028\;(\$/DM)]$$
$$= \$2,514,000.$$

The firm intends to buy these dollars at the 0.6532 (BP/\$) ask price for dollars that it will lock in with the current British pound futures contract. On December 20, the importer will buy these dollars under its pound futures contracts at the following cost in pounds:

British pounds needed on December 20
$$= (\text{Number of U.S. dollars needed})[F_{t,T}\,(BP/\$)]$$
$$= (\$2,514,000)[0.6532\;(BP/\$)]$$
$$= 1,642,145\;BP.$$

To lock in this desired purchase of dollars, the firm must go short approximately 26 pound futures contracts on May 23:

Number of short British pound futures contracts

$$= \frac{\text{Number of British pounds}}{\text{British pounds per contract}}$$

$$= \frac{1,642,145}{62,500 \text{ BP/contract}}$$

$$= 26.27 \text{ contracts.}$$

Table 7.4 shows how this hedge locks in a pound-denominated mark rate for the importer. It presents the importer's unhedged and hedged costs, in pounds, of obtaining the 5 million DM on December 20 under four different price scenarios.

In scenario I, the December 18 (for December 20 settlement) dollar price of British pounds is lower than the initial futures price and the December 18 dollar price of Deutsche marks is higher than the initial futures price. The resulting cross rate of 0.5385 (BP/DM) is much higher than the cross rate of 0.3284 (BP/DM) implied by the initial futures prices. Thus, the cost of obtaining the 5 million DM in the spot market on December 20 is high:

December 20 cost of 5,000,000 DM = (5,000,000 DM)[0.5385 (BP/DM)]
$$= 2.692 \text{ million BP.}$$

This high cost is offset by the importer's gains on its futures positions. The futures profits, in dollars, are

British pound futures profit
$$= (-26.27 \text{ contracts})(62,500 \text{ BP/contract})[1.3000 \text{ ($/BP)}$$
$$- 1.5310 \text{ ($/BP)}]$$
$$= \$0.379 \text{ million.}$$

Deutsche Mark Futures Profit
$$= (40 \text{ contracts})(125,000 \text{ DM/contract})[0.7000 \text{ ($/DM)}$$
$$- 0.5028 \text{ ($/DM)}]$$
$$= \$0.986 \text{ million.}$$

At the December 18 exchange rate, the importer's futures profits, in pounds, are

British-pound-denominated futures profit
$$= (\$0.379 \text{ million} + \$0.986 \text{ million})[0.7692 \text{ (BP/$)}]$$
$$= 1.050 \text{ million BP.}$$

The hedged cost of the 5 million DM to the importer is therefore

Hedged Deutsche mark cost = Unhedged cost − Futures profit
$$= 2.692 \text{ million BP} - 1.050 \text{ million BP}$$
$$= 1.642 \text{ million BP}$$
$$= 0.3284 \text{ BP/DM.}$$

Table 7.4 British Importer's Synthetic Cross Rate Futures Contract

May 23 Futures Prices

	December British Pound Futures			December Deutsche Mark Futures	
	($/BP)	(BP/$)		($/DM)	(DM/$)
Bid	1.5310	0.6524		0.5024	1.9889
Ask	1.5328	0.6532		0.5028	1.9904

Synthetic Pound/Mark Futures Position

British Pound Contracts (62,500 BP/Contract)	Deutsche Mark Contracts (125,000 DM/Contract)	Deutsche Marks Locked in for Delivery
−26.27	40	5,000,000 DM

Synthetic Cross Rate Futures Prices

	(BP/DM)	(DM/BP)
Bid	0.3278	3.0449
Ask	0.3284	3.0510

Importer's Hedged Cost of Deutsche Marks on December 20

	Price Scenario			
	I	II	III	IV
December 18 spot pound:				
($/BP)	1.3000	1.9000	1.9000	1.3000
(BP/$)	0.7692	0.5263	0.5263	0.7692
December 18 spot mark:				
($/DM)	0.7000	0.7000	0.4000	0.4000
(DM/$)	1.4286	1.4286	2.5000	2.5000
Synthetic spot cross rates:				
(BP/DM)	0.5385	0.3684	0.2105	0.3077
(DM/BP)	1.8571	2.7143	4.7500	3.2500

Importer's Costs

	I	II	III	IV
Cost of marks (BP)	2,692,308	1,842,105	1,052,632	1,538,462
BP futures profit ($)	379,317	−605,922	−605,922	379,317
DM futures profit ($)	986,000	986,000	−514,000	−514,000
Total futures profit (BP)	1,050,244	200,041	−589,432	−103,602
Hedged cost of marks (BP)	1,642,064	1,642,064	1,642,064	1,642,064
Hedged cost per DM	0.3284	0.3284	0.3284	0.3284

This is the cross rate implied by the dollar-denominated pound and mark futures contracts on May 23. The importer gets this rate under all four price scenarios. By creating a synthetic pound-denominated mark futures contract, the firm has locked in the rate at which it will exchange pounds for marks on the date of its purchase of German beer. ■

Synthetic Foreign-Currency-Denominated Interest Rate Futures Contracts

In Chapter 5, we saw that the short-term interest rate contracts are among the most useful and widely traded of all futures contracts. The entire discussion in that chapter concerned U.S.-dollar-denominated instruments, but investors in other currencies also have many reasons to trade short-term interest rate futures contracts. In this section, we will show how to use a combination of U.S. short-term interest rate contracts and U.S. foreign currency contracts to create synthetic foreign-currency-denominated interest rate futures contracts. Market participants in countries without short-term interest rate contracts can use these synthetic contracts just as traders in the U.S. markets use U.S. short-term interest rate futures. Those who trade in countries that do have short-term interest rate contracts benefit from the liquidity added to their markets as arbitrageurs trade the synthetic contracts against the real ones.

Suppose that at date t we wish to create a synthetic interest rate futures contract that is denominated in currency A. It will expire at date T1, and its underlying instrument will have N days to maturity at T1, just like the dollar-denominated short-term interest rate futures contracts:

We can create a long position in a synthetic interest rate futures contract with the following steps:

1.   Take a short position in currency A futures to buy \$1 million at T1. This will lock in an expenditure of currency A at time T1 of

$$Q_{T1}^A = (\$1,000,000)[1/F_{t,T1} (\$/A)]. \tag{7.27}$$

The number of contracts needed to achieve the desired inflow of dollars is

Number of short T1 currency A futures contracts

$$= \frac{Q_{T1}^A}{\text{Amount of A per contract}}.$$

2.   Take a long position in Eurodollar time deposit contracts that expire at T1 and lock in the rate earned on the \$1 million between T1 and T2. In Chapter 5, we defined the rate we could lock in as $r_{T1,T2}^t$. To denote that this is a dollar rate, we now write it as $r_{T1,T2}^t (\$)$. Thus, the long futures position guarantees earnings of

$$Q_{T2}^\$ = (\$1,000,000)[1 + r_{T1,T2}^t (\$)] \tag{7.28}$$

at time T2. As we saw in Chapter 5, the hedge ratio that will lock in the $r^t_{T1,T2}$ ($) return is:

Number of long Eurodollar futures contracts $= \dfrac{N}{90}$.

3. Take a long position in currency A futures that locks in a sale of $Q^\$_{T2}$ for currency A at time T2. This position guarantees currency A proceeds at time T2 of

$$Q^A_{T2} = Q^\$_{T2}[1/F_{t,T2}\,(\$/A)] \qquad\qquad\qquad (7.29)$$
$$= (\$1{,}000{,}000)[1 + r^t_{T1,T2}\,(\$)][1/F_{t,T2}\,(\$/A)].$$

The number of currency A contracts needed to lock in a sale of exactly $Q^\$_{T2}$ dollars is

Number of long T2 currency A futures contracts

$$= \dfrac{Q^A_{T2}}{\text{Amount of A per contract}}.$$

Together these three transactions lock in an expenditure of Q^A_{T1} in currency A at T1 and receipts of Q^A_{T2} in currency A at T2. They form a synthetic futures contract that at time t locks in a rate of return between times T1 and T2 of

$$1 + \text{Synthetic currency-A-denominated rate between T1 and T2} \qquad (7.30)$$
$$= \dfrac{Q^A_{T2}}{Q^A_{T1}}.$$

Example 7.8 demonstrates how to create a long position in a synthetic short-term interest rate futures contract that is denominated in Deutsche marks.

▪ **Example 7.8: Synthetic Deutsche Mark Interest Rate Futures Contracts**
Suppose that on May 23, 1989, a German firm knows it will have 520 million DM to lend out for 91 days on September 20. It wishes to lock in the rate it will earn on this Deutsche mark investment and is considering creating a synthetic short-term interest rate futures contract to do so. The time line for its desired synthetic contract will be

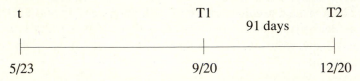

The firm observes the following futures prices at the Chicago Mercantile Exchange on May 23:[12]

September 20 Deutsche
mark futures:
Bid	0.5000 ($/DM)	1.9976 (DM/$)
Ask	0.5006 ($/DM)	2.0000 (DM/$)

December 20 Deutsche
mark futures:
Bid	0.5024 ($/DM)	1.9889 (DM/$)
Ask	0.5028 ($/DM)	1.9904 (DM/$)

September 20 Eurodollar
time deposit futures:
Bid	90.95
Ask	91.00

The firm can take the following three steps to create a contract that will lock in an interest rate between September 20 and December 20:

1. Take a short position in September Deutsche mark futures so as to lock in the bid exchange rate for its 520 million DM of 0.5000 ($/DM) on September 20. This will enable the firm to purchase the following quantity of U.S. dollars:

    U.S. Dollars Purchased on September 20
    $$= (520,000,000 \text{ DM})[0.5000 \ (\$/\text{DM})]$$
    $$= \$260 \text{ million.}$$

    The number of short futures contracts required for this purchase is

    Number of short September Deutsche mark futures contracts
    $$= \frac{520,000,000 \text{ DM}}{125,000 \text{ DM/contract}}$$
    $$= 4,160 \text{ contracts.}$$

2. Lock in the rate of return the firm will earn over the 91 days between September 20 and December 20 by taking a long position in Eurodollar time deposit contracts that expire on September 20. At the ask price of 91.00, the Eurodollar contracts will lock in an annualized rate of 9 percent, or (9%)(91/360) = 2.275% percent for 91 days. Therefore, the firm will have the following quantity of dollars on December 20:

    U.S. dollars received on December 20 = ($260.00 million)(1.02275)
    $$= \$265.91 \text{ million.}$$

---

[12] Recall from Chapter 5 that Eurodollar TD futures contracts expire on Mondays. In this case, the expiration date is September 18 but the contract is priced according to the 90-day LIBOR for a 90-day Eurodollar TD settled on September 20.

Because the Eurodollar time deposit futures contract is written on a 90-day investment of $1 million, the number of long Eurodollar contracts required to cover the firm's intended dollar holdings is

Number of long September Eurodollar futures contracts

$$= \frac{(\$260.00 \text{ million})(91/90)}{\$1 \text{ million/contract}}$$

$$= 263 \text{ Contracts.}$$

3.   Use a long position in December Deutsche mark futures to lock in the ask rate of 0.5028 ($/DM) to convert its dollar proceeds on December 20 back into marks. Such a position will guarantee the firm the following mark revenues:

Deutsche marks purchased on December 20

$$= \frac{\$265.91 \text{ million}}{0.5028 \text{ (\$/DM)}}$$

$$= 528.86 \text{ million DM.}$$

To convert its entire dollar proceeds, the firm will need the following number of long December Deutsche mark contracts:

Number of long December Deutsche mark futures contracts

$$\frac{528.86 \text{ million DM}}{125,000 \text{ DM/contract}}$$

$$= 4,231 \text{ contracts.}$$

With these three positions in U.S. futures contracts, the German firm can guarantee that it will receive 528.86 million DM on December 20 by investing 520 million DM on September 20. The rate of return on this investment is

Deutsche-mark-denominated rate of return

$$= \frac{528.86 \text{ million DM} - 520 \text{ million DM}}{520 \text{ million DM}}$$

$$= 1.704\% \text{ for 91 days}$$

$$= 6.835\% \text{ annualized (365-day year).}$$

■

Example 7.8 showed that by going short currency futures that expire at T1, long currency futures that expire at T2, and long Eurodollar futures that expire at T1, a firm can create a synthetic long foreign-currency-denominated short-term interest rate futures position. To create a synthetic short position in foreign-currency-denominated interest rate futures, we simply take the opposites of the above positions:

1. Go long currency futures that expire at T1.

2. Go short currency futures that expire at T2.

3. Go short Eurodollar futures that expire at T1.

The appropriate hedge ratios for this strategy are exactly the same as the ratios required to create a long synthetic position.

Forward Covered Interest Rate Parity   Many countries are beginning to develop short-term interest rate futures markets. The returns implied by these contracts are related by arbitrage to the returns implied by synthetic interest rate contracts denominated in the same currencies.

Suppose $r^t_{T1,T2}$ (A) is the rate between T1 and T2 implied by an actual currency-A-denominated short-term interest rate futures contract. Arbitrageurs can trade between a synthetic currency A interest rate futures contract and an actual futures contract. Their trading activity will ensure that

$$1 + \text{Synthetic currency-A-denominated rate between T1 and T2} \qquad (7.31)$$
$$= 1 + r^t_{T1,T2} \text{ (A)}.$$

Using Equations 7.27 and 7.29, Equation 7.31 can be written as

$$\left[\frac{F_{t,T2} \text{ ($/A)}}{F_{t,T1} \text{ ($/A)}}\right] = \left[\frac{1 + r^t_{T1,T2} \text{ (\$)}}{1 + r^t_{T1,T2} \text{ (A)}}\right]. \qquad (7.32)$$

This expression is very similar to the covered interest rate parity formula, Equation 7.13. The only difference is that instead of determining the pricing relationships between dates t and T, it calculates the rate between dates T1 and T2 using prices locked in at date t. This relationship is called **forward covered interest rate parity**. Because of it, even small markets for foreign-currency-denominated short-term futures contracts benefit from the full liquidity of the U.S. markets.

Summary

The foreign exchange futures market allows firms engaged in international trade to hedge the business risk they face due to exchange rate fluctuation. U.S. exporters and U.S. firms with foreign subsidiaries can use short exchange rate hedges to protect against appreciation in the dollar. U.S. importers and foreign firms with U.S. subsidiaries can use long exchange rate hedges to protect themselves against depreciation in the U.S. dollar. They can also use natural hedging strategies that do not involve the futures markets to lock in future foreign currency costs and revenues. The foreign exchange market's fundamental no-arbitrage equation will indicate whether a futures or natural hedge is preferable in a given case. The choice is often determined by the initial position of the hedging firm.

The foreign exchange futures market can be used to create synthetic exchange rate futures that are denominated in currencies other than the dollar. Such cross-rate futures contracts are formed by combining positions in the dollar-denominated contracts of the two currencies to be exchanged. Synthetic interest rate futures denominated in other currencies can also be created with the U.S. futures contracts. These synthetic strategies allow firms that operate in non-U.S. markets to lock in exchange and interest rates in the currencies of their choice.

Problems

For each of the following problems, use the exchange rates from Figures 7.1 and 7.4. Suppose it is currently May 23, 1989. The last day of futures trading is September 18. Also, assume that any funds lent on May 23 will not be paid until May 25.

1. Suppose the cross rate between Deutsche marks and British pounds is 3.1000 (DM/BP) or 0.3226 (BP/DM). How can you earn arbitrage profits?

2. Suppose the short-term lending rate in Germany is 7.50 percent (365-day year). You have $250 million to lend. What synthetic riskless U.S. dollar rate can you earn using a cash-and-carry strategy between May 25 and September 20?

3. Suppose the short-term borrowing rate in Switzerland is 7.50 percent (365-day year). You wish to borrow $100 million. What synthetic riskless U.S. dollar borrowing rate can you create using a reverse cash-and-carry strategy between May 25 and September 20?

4. Suppose a multinational corporation that is based in the United States has a business in Britain. It projects that it will have earnings of 500 million British pounds that it will receive on September 20. The firm wishes to repatriate these British earnings into dollars, but it fears the pound will depreciate.
    a. What futures hedge will allow the firm to lock in a dollar value of earnings?
    b. What natural hedge will accomplish the same thing? Suppose the firm is a net borrower of British pounds at a borrowing rate of 12 percent (365-day year) and the U.S. lending rate 8.50 percent. Construct a quasi-arbitrage table to demonstrate your answer.
    c. Is the natural hedge or the futures hedge preferable? Relate your answer to the fundamental no-arbitrage equation.

■ 5. Recreate Table 7.4. Redo the calculations where the December 18 spot rate for scenarios I and IV is 1.2000 ($/BP).

6. Show how to create a short position in a synthetic short-term British pound interest rate futures contract to lock in a pound-denominated borrowing rate from September 20 through December 20. What borrowing rate can you lock in with this contract assuming you can borrow U.S. dollars at the LIBOR? Assume that on May 23, the Eurodollar futures price is 91.00.

Commodity Futures

In this chapter we will study the metal, petroleum, and agricultural futures markets. Agricultural futures contracts have been trading at the Chicago Board of Trade since the 1800s. The metals futures contracts have also existed for a long time; copper has been traded at the Commodity Exchange Inc. (COMEX) since the 1930s. Now there are major contracts on gold and silver as well. The petroleum futures contracts were introduced after events in the early 1970s initiated a period of upheaval and volatility in the petroleum markets. Trading in a heating oil contract began at the New York Mercantile Exchange in 1978. Today the NYMEX has contracts on crude oil, unleaded gasoline, and propane as well.

The most important difference between financial and commodity futures is that financial assets are always pure assets, but commodities can be pure or convenience assets. The major factors that determine whether a commodity is a pure or convenience asset are the primary use of the asset, market conditions of surplus or shortage, and seasonal production and consumption patterns.

The fundamental no-arbitrage equation for convenience assets is more complicated than that for pure assets. Therefore, pricing commodity futures requires a deeper understanding of the cash market for the underlying asset than does pricing financial futures.

Commodity futures contracts are used widely in risk management. Commodity futures hedging strategies sometimes employ specialized trading arrangements, such as the NYMEX Exchange of Futures for Physicals facility in the petroleum markets and basis trading agreements in the agricultural markets. Hedging strategies in the livestock futures market must adjust for the rate of livestock growth over time.

We begin this chapter by expanding on our discussion of the fundamental no-arbitrage equation, pure and convenience assets, and convenience values in Chapter 2. After covering this section, the reader can move to the section that discusses the commodity of his or her interest.

The Fundamental No-Arbitrage Equation
for Commodity Futures

In Chapter 2, we defined a pure asset as an asset that is held solely for its expected capital gains and explicit payouts.[1] Assets such as stocks and bonds fall into this category. A convenience asset is held only by those who receive a benefit in addition to expected capital gains and explicit payouts. In Example 2.11, we saw that copper is often a convenience asset. Typically people do not hold copper purely for capital gains and explicit payouts; they usually have some other reason, such as to avoid shortages (stockouts) or to ensure easy access during a production process. The extra benefit they receive from holding a convenience asset is called the *convenience value*.

Equation 2.27 in Chapter 2 gives the no-arbitrage relationship for convenience assets. Since the only explicit payouts from holding commodities are storage costs (a negative type of payout), this no-arbitrage relationship takes the following form for commodities:

$$F_{t,T} = P_t(1 + r_{t,T}) + SC_{t,T} - CV_{t,T}, \tag{8.1}$$

where $SC_{t,T}$ and $CV_{t,T}$ are the future values as of time T of storage costs and the convenience value between times t and T. In percentage terms, this relationship is

$$\frac{F_{t,T} - P_t}{P_t} = r_{t,T} + \left(\frac{SC_{t,T}}{P_t}\right) - \left(\frac{CV_{t,T}}{P_t}\right), \tag{8.1a}$$

where the last term is the (nonannualized) convenience yield.

In Chapter 2, we learned that much of the arbitrage that enforces the no-arbitrage relationship in convenience asset markets is quasi-arbitrage. In equilibrium, those holding the commodity are most likely to be the ones who will receive a convenience value. Thus, cash-and-carry arbitrages are most likely to be performed by quasi-arbitrageurs who plan to sell some of their convenience-asset holdings. Further, the difficulty of selling convenience assets short causes most short-selling for reverse cash-and-carry arbitrages to be performed effectively by quasi-arbitrageurs who plan to hold convenience assets.[2] We will see how quasi-arbitrage can enforce the no-arbitrage relationship in the commodities markets by exploring the profit opportunities offered when Equations 8.1 and 8.1a do not hold.

First, suppose the futures price in the copper market is higher than Equation 8.1 indicates so that:

$$F_{t,T} > P_t(1 + r_{t,T}) + SC_{t,T} - CV_{t,T}. \tag{8.2}$$

---

[1] The reader should review the material on pure and convenience assets in Chapter 2.

[2] Recall that an actual short sale would require the borrower to compensate the lender for the lost convenience value and the lender to rebate the storage costs to the borrower. Later we will see how this is achieved in the oil market.

Table 8.1 Cash-and-Carry Quasi-Arbitrage Table for Copper User

Benchmark position: sale of copper out of inventory to raise funds

Cash-and-Carry Pure Arbitrage Components	Cash-and-Carry Quasi-Arbitrage Components	Relevant Price or Rate
1. Buy copper	Refrain from selling copper	Bid
Pay storage	Pay storage	—
Receive convenience value	Receive convenience value	—
2. Short futures	Short futures	Bid
3. Borrow	Borrow	Borrowing rate

Resulting position: synthetic sale of copper

Next, suppose there is a copper user who is receiving the convenience value from storing copper but is considering selling off part of his stocks to raise funds. If he refrains from selling his copper, he can perform a cash-and-carry quasi-arbitrage that will profit from the pricing situation in Equation 8.2. Table 8.1 presents the copper user's cash-and-carry quasi-arbitrage strategy.

If the copper user follows his benchmark plan to sell his copper, his cash flows will be

Copper Sale

Transaction	t	T
Sell copper at t	P_t	

If he retains his copper and makes a synthetic sale through quasi-arbitrage, he will receive the convenience value from holding copper but must borrow and pay storage costs. His cash flows will be

Synthetic Copper Sale

Transaction	t	T
Pay storage		$-SC_{t,T}$
Receive convenience value		$CV_{t,T}$
Go short futures	0	$F_{t,T} - F_{T,T}$
Sell copper at T		$P_T = F_{T,T}$
Borrow	P_t	$-P_t(1 + r_{t,T})$
Net	P_t	$F_{t,T} - SC_{t,T} + CV_{t,T} - P_t(1 + r_{t,T})$

The synthetic copper sale is superior to the actual sale if

$$F_{t,T} - SC_{t,T} + CV_{t,T} - P_t(1 + r_{t,T}) > 0 \tag{8.3}$$

or

$$F_{t,T} > P_t(1 + r_{t,T}) + SC_{t,T} - CV_{t,T} \qquad (\Omega^c > 0).$$

Table 8.2 Reverse Cash-and-Carry Quasi-Arbitrage Table for Copper User

<u>Benchmark position</u>: hold copper inventory

Reverse Cash-and-Carry Pure Arbitrage Components	Reverse Cash-and-Carry Quasi-Arbitrage Components	Relevant Price or Rate
1. Short-sell copper	Sell copper from inventory	Bid
Receive storage	Save storage	—
Refund convenience value	Lose convenience value	—
2. Go long futures	Go long futures	Ask
3. Lend	Lend	T-bill ask

<u>Resulting position</u>: synthetic copper inventory

This condition is exactly the same as that in Equation 8.2. As quasi-arbitrageurs such as this copper user forgo copper sales and take short futures positions, the copper futures price will fall and the spot copper price will rise until Equation 8.1 is restored. We would get a similar result if copper users reacted to the high copper futures price simply by buying copper (and receiving the convenience value), going short futures, and borrowing.

Now suppose the futures price is lower than Equation 8.1 requires so that

$$F_{t,T} < P_t(1 + r_{t,T}) + SC_{t,T} - CV_{t,T}. \tag{8.4}$$

Quasi-arbitrageurs can profit from this situation through reverse cash-and-carry strategies.

Consider another copper user who receives a convenience value on copper held in inventory. She can earn a quasi-arbitrage profit in this situation by selling her copper and replacing it with a synthetic copper position. Table 8.2 presents this reverse cash-and-carry quasi-arbitrage strategy.

If the copper user retains her copper inventories, her cash flows will be

	Hold Physical Copper	
Transaction	t	T
Keep copper at t		
Pay storage		$-SC_{t,T}$
Receive convenience value		$CV_{t,T}$
Net	0	$CV_{t,T} - SC_{t,T}$

If the copper user sells her copper and replaces it with T-bills and a long futures position, she will lose the convenience value from holding the copper but save storage costs. The cash flows from the synthetic strategy will be

Synthetic Copper Position

Transaction	t	T
Sell copper at t	P_t	
Lend proceeds	$-P_t$	$P_t(1 + r_{t,T})$
Go long futures	0	$F_{T,T} - F_{t,T}$
Buy copper at T		$-P_T = -F_{T,T}$
Net	0	$P_t(1 + r_{t,T}) - F_{t,T}$

The synthetic copper position is superior to physical storage if

$$P_t(1 + r_{t,T}) - F_{t,T} > CV_{t,T} - SC_{t,T} \tag{8.5}$$

or

$$F_{t,T} < P_t(1 + r_{t,T}) + SC_{t,T} - CV_{t,T} \qquad (\Omega^r < 0).$$

This condition is exactly the same as that in Equation 8.4. Thus, when Equation 8.4 holds, people with copper inventories will sell their copper and go long futures. This will drive the copper spot price down and the copper futures price up until the equilibrium of Equation 8.1 is established.

The fundamental no-arbitrage equation for commodities futures contracts with different expiration dates is very similar:

$$F_{t,T2} = F_{t,T1}(1 + r_{T1,T2}) + SC_{T1,T2} - CV_{T1,T2} \tag{8.6}$$

or

$$F_{T1,T2} = r_{T1,T2} + \left(\frac{SC_{T1,T2}}{F_{T1,T2}} \right) - \left(\frac{CV_{T1,T2}}{F_{T1,T2}} \right). \tag{8.6a}$$

The storage costs and convenience values in these equations are those expected to hold between times T1 and T2 at time t.

Marginal Convenience Values

Different users of a commodity derive different convenience values from holding it. Thus, those who consider selling copper out of inventory in Tables 8.1 and 8.2 are most likely to lose the least convenience value by selling. The convenience value in Equation 8.1, therefore, represents the lowest, or marginal, convenience value received by all those holding the commodity.[3] If the marginal convenience value equals zero, the futures market is at full carry. Example 2.11 showed that this was the case in the gold market in October 1988.

---

[3] Similarly, the storage costs in Equation 8.1 are those incurred by the marginal holder of the commodity.

Figure 8.1 Marginal Convenience for Copper (Dollars per Pound per Month)

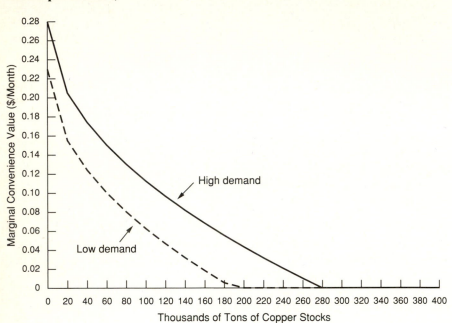

Figure 8.1 graphs two curves, called **marginal convenience value curves**, that could describe the relationship between the level of copper stocks and the marginal convenience value. These curves slope downward, because in equilibrium those with the greatest convenience value will store the metal. Thus, if copper storage is low, the convenience value of the marginal copper holder is likely to be high. If copper storage is high, the convenience value of the marginal holder will likely be low.

The higher marginal convenience value curve represents the relationship between stocks and marginal convenience value when demand for the commodity is high. The lower curve represents this relationship when demand for the commodity is low. Fama and French [1988] provided an indirect test of the relationship between the two curves by documenting the impact of overall demand on marginal convenience values. They showed that marginal convenience values are high during economic expansions and low during economic contractions.

Figure 8.1 also shows that the extent to which the futures market for a commodity is below full carry—that is, how high the marginal convenience value is—depends on the location of the marginal convenience value curve and the level of commodity stocks. For a given marginal convenience value curve, the market moves toward full carry as inventory holdings increase. At some point, there may be so much of a commodity that the marginal convenience value falls to zero. Then the price of the commodity must fall until even those who enjoy no convenience value will hold the asset and the asset becomes (albeit perhaps temporarily) a pure asset. For a given level of stocks, a downward shift in the marginal convenience value curve also moves the market toward full carry, because the marginal convenience value falls.

Example 8.1 shows how we can learn a great deal about the market for a commodity by observing the convenience values implied by its futures prices.

■ **Example 8.1:   Determining Marginal Convenience Values from Futures Prices**   Commodity futures prices can show us the marginal convenience values that the market expects for a commodity over time. These marginal convenience values can provide information about the current market for that commodity and the market's expectations about future supply and demand conditions. If we rearrange Equation 8.6, we see that the marginal convenience value implied by current futures prices for the period from T1 to T2 is

$$CV_{T1,T2} = F_{t,T1}(1 + r_{T1,T2}) + SC_{T1,T2} - F_{t,T2}. \tag{8.7}$$

Let's see what the implied marginal convenience values can reveal about the copper market during October 1988. Figure 8.2 presents the October 12, 1988, metal futures prices. The cost of storing copper at this time was $1.95 per ton per month plus a $3.95-per-ton one-time transfer fee. The annualized December three-month interest rates implied by the Eurodollar and T-bill futures prices were 8.65 and 7.36 percent, respectively (7.22 percent discount yield). If we use the 7.36 percent T-bill yield as our interest rate, the convenience values implied by these prices are as follows:[4]

December 1988–March 1989:

$$CV_{T1,T2} = \$1.2030\left[1 + \left(\frac{3}{12}\right)(0.0736)\right] + \left[\frac{(\$1.95)(3) + \$3.95}{2,000}\right] - \$1.0700$$

$\quad = \$0.1600$ per pound for 3 months

$\quad = \$0.0533$ per pound per month.

March 1989–May 1989:

$$CV_{T1,T2} = \$1.0700\left[1 + \left(\frac{2}{12}\right)(0.0736)\right] + \left[\frac{(\$1.95)(2) + \$3.95}{2,000}\right] - \$1.0250$$

$\quad = \$0.0621$ per pound for 2 months

$\quad = \$0.0311$ per pound per month.

---

[4] If the interest rate structure is upward sloping, it will be appropriate to use higher interest rates as we go further out in time. However, using somewhat higher rates in this calculation will not affect the convenience values significantly.

Figure 8.2 Metal Futures Transactions Prices for October 12, 1988

```
                                          Lifetime     Open
            Open  High Low Settle Change  High Low  Interest
     COPPER-STANDARD (CMX)-25,000 lbs.; cents per lb.
Oct    128.50 129.40 128.50 129.30 -   .20 129.50 108.00     513
Dec    120.90 121.80 118.80 120.30 +   .20 121.80  64.70  25,439
Mr89   107.50 108.60 105.80 107.00 -   .20 108.60  66.50   7,023
May    103.70 103.90 102.00 102.50 -   .30 103.90  73.15   1,058
July   100.70 100.70  98.60  99.40 -   .30 100.70  76.00     567
Sept    99.20  99.20  98.50  97.80 -   .40  99.20  76.00     343
Dec     97.00  98.00  95.90  96.30 -   .40  98.00  77.45     537
     Est vol 6,000; vol Tues 7,171; open int 35,533, -230.
     GOLD (CMX)-100 troy oz.; $ per troy oz.
Oct    405.50 409.00 405.50 408.40 +  4.00 533.50 391.80     502
Dec    409.50 416.00 409.50 412.20 +  3.80 546.00 395.50  82,456
Fb89   415.00 421.00 414.70 417.40 +  3.80 549.50 401.00  12,966
Apr    420.50 426.50 420.50 422.60 +  3.90 550.00 407.00   9,108
June   424.80 431.20 424.80 427.80 +  3.90 570.00 412.00  16,147
Aug     ....   ....   ....  433.20 +  4.00 575.00 419.30   6,994
Oct     ....   ....   ....  438.80 +  4.10 575.50 423.00   8,851
Dec    441.50 446.50 441.50 444.30 +  4.30 514.50 428.00   9,125
Fb90    ....   ....   ....  449.90 +  4.40 516.00 439.70   4,121
Apr     ....   ....   ....  455.50 +  4.50 525.80 443.00   3,021
June    ....   ....   ....  461.30 +  4.60 497.00 447.00   2,168
Aug    470.50 470.50 470.50 467.30 +  4.70 470.50 453.00     665
     Est vol 40,000; vol Tues 31,552; open int 156,124, -2,235.

     PLATINUM (NYM)-50 troy oz.; $ per troy oz.
Oct    516.00 527.00 515.00 520.40 +  7.30 667.50 452.00   1,269
Ja89   512.00 527.50 512.00 519.40 +  9.30 646.00 459.00  13,937
Apr    517.00 530.00 517.00 522.90 +  9.30 643.50 482.00   2,933
July   524.00 524.00 524.00 527.60 +  9.30 640.00 501.00     364
Oct    526.00 535.00 526.00 533.30 +  9.30 564.00 507.00     425
     Est vol 9,739; vol Tues 5,356; open int 18,928, -534.
     PALLADIUM (NYM) 100 troy oz.; $ per troy oz.
Dec    120.75 123.00 120.75 122.50 +  2.40 139.50 104.50   4,074
Mr89   121.00 122.25 120.50 121.65 +  2.40 132.00 115.50   1,513
June   119.75 119.75 119.75 120.65 +  2.40 131.00 114.00     520
     Est vol 892; vol Tues 45; open int 6,198, -28.
     SILVER (CMX)-5,000 troy oz.; cents per troy oz.
Oct    631.0 631.0 631.0 632.0 +  12.0  674.0 616.0       7
Dec    632.5 647.0 632.0 639.5 +  12.0 1082.0 606.0  48,062
Mr89   648.5 662.0 647.0 654.2 +  12.1 1073.0 631.0   8,378
May    658.5 669.5 656.5 664.0 +  12.0  948.0 645.0   4,117
July   678.0 681.0 678.0 674.4 +  11.9  985.0 654.0   6,090
Sept   686.0 686.0 686.0 684.5 +  12.0  861.0 660.0   5,041
Dec    693.0 708.0 693.0 699.9 +  12.0  886.0 680.0   4,600
Mr90    ....  ....  ....  716.1 +  12.0  910.0 700.0   3,207
May    730.0 730.0 730.0 726.4 +  12.0  910.0 727.0   2,701
July    ....  ....  ....  736.8 +  12.0  761.5 740.0   1,911
     Est vol 23,000; vol Tues 15,824; open int 84,204, -379.
     SILVER (CBT)-1,000 troy oz.; cents per troy oz.
Oct    633.0 637.0 631.0 632.0 +  12.0  937.0 607.0      15
Dec    633.0 748.0 632.0 639.5 +  11.5  946.0 616.0  13,592
Fb89   642.0 658.0 642.0 649.0 +  10.5  840.0 627.0     563
Apr    653.0 666.0 653.0 660.5 +  10.5  855.0 640.0     315
June   675.0 677.0 672.0 673.0 +  14.0  865.0 650.0     474
     Est vol 2,000; vol Tues 1,200; open int 15,045, -382.
```

Source: *The Wall Street Journal*, October 13, 1988.

May 1989–July 1989:

$$\text{CV}_{T1,T2} = \$1.0250 \left[1 + \left(\frac{2}{12}\right)(0.0736) \right] + \left[\frac{(\$1.95)(2) + \$3.95}{2,000} \right] - \$0.9940$$

= $0.0475 per pound for 3 months

= $0.0237 per pound per month.

Clearly the market expected copper's marginal convenience value to fall over time. This was because there was a severe copper shortage during the fall of

Table 8.3 Forward Implied Repo Rates Implied by Copper Futures Prices, March 31, 1980

Month	Futures Price	Annualized Forward Implied Repo Rate
April	$0.8550	—
May	0.8710	18.36%
June	0.8860	16.60
July	0.9000	14.97
September	0.9220	12.05
December	0.9470	8.72

Note: These calculations assume $1.95-per-ton-per-month storage costs with a one-time $3.95-per-ton warehouse fee.

1988, so only those with a very high convenience value would have found it worthwhile to hold copper. The copper shortage conditions would be shown in Figure 8.1 by the high demand convenience value curve. The declining implied marginal convenience values show that the market expected the shortage to subside over time so that copper stocks would increase and holders with lower convenience values could begin to store copper.

In Figure 8.1, we saw that the marginal convenience value can actually fall to zero if a glut causes a shift from a high demand convenience value curve to a low demand convenience value curve. In such cases, the commodity becomes a pure asset. This situation in fact occurred in the copper market at the end of March 1980. Table 8.3 shows the futures settlement prices for copper on March 31, 1980. It also provides the annualized forward repo rates implied by these copper futures prices and the 1988 copper storage costs.[5] For example, the annualized forward implied repo rate between April and May of 1980 was

Forward Implied Repo Rate
$$= \frac{\{\$0.8710 - [(\$1.95)(1) + \$3.95]/2,000 - \$0.8550\}}{\$0.8550}$$
$$= 1.53\% \text{ for 1 month}$$
$$= 18.36\% \text{ annualized.}$$

The three-month and one-year T-bill rates during this period were around 15.50 percent and 14.50 percent, respectively. The three-month Eurodollar deposit rate was roughly 19 percent. The fact that the forward implied repo rate on April and May copper futures was between these rates indicates that the copper futures market was at, or close to, full carry for those contracts. This indicates that a copper glut in March led to some storage by parties who stood to receive little or no convenience value.

---

[5] While these costs may be too high because of inflation between 1980 and 1988, they are close enough to demonstrate our point.

The forward implied repo rates fall steadily as we move to contracts expiring later. This implies that the market expected the marginal convenience value to increase over time. The market seemed to expect the stocks held for investment purposes to be worked off over time so that those with positive convenience values would again become the marginal holders of copper. ▪

In Example 8.1, we learned about copper market conditions by looking at the convenience values implied by the futures prices. Conversely, knowledge about a commodity market is crucial for understanding how futures prices are set. Example 8.1 shows that during a period of shortage, the market expected a supply response to lead to a lessening of the shortage and a reduction in the convenience values over time. Similarly, during a glut, the market expected a supply response to lead to a reduction in stocks and an increase in the convenience values over time. Those with superior knowledge about the speed at which commodity stocks adjust can make better estimates of future convenience values. Thus, they can profit by trading on their expertise.[6]

The major determinant of copper's marginal convenience value is whether the copper market is experiencing shortage or glut conditions. For many other commodities, the time of year is the primary factor affecting the marginal convenience value.

We will now study the commodity cash and futures markets individually.

Metal Futures

Cash Market

Metals are generally considered as falling into one of two use categories: precious metals, which are used as a store of value, and industrial metals, which are used in manufacturing. The precious metals include gold, silver, platinum, and palladium.[7] The industrial metals include copper and aluminum. This distinction is only a loose one, however. The precious metals have some industrial uses, and the durability of the industrial metals allows them to serve as stores of value as well. Therefore, we will view metals as forming a use spectrum from primarily precious to primarily industrial rather than rigidly categorizing them as one form or the other. At the extreme precious end of the spectrum is gold, which is used mainly as a store of value and therefore is almost always a pure asset. At the other extreme are copper and aluminum, which are used almost entirely for industrial purposes and thus are usually convenience assets.[8]

---

[6] Many investment banks have models for this.

[7] Precious metals are good stores of value because they have a high per-unit volume and high durability.

[8] See Teweles and Jones [1987] for a detailed description of the various metals spot markets.

Figure 8.3 Commodities Spot Transactions Prices for May 23, 1989

CASH PRICES

Tuesday May 23, 1989
(Quotations as of 4 p.m. Eastern time)

GRAINS AND FEEDS

	Tues	Mon	Yr.Ago
Barley, top-quality Mpls., bu	n3.75-4.0	3.75-4.00	2.32½
Bran, wheat middlings, KC ton	76.00	76.00	54.00
Corn, No. 2 yel. Cent-Ill. bu	bp2.59½	2.60½	2.03
Corn Gluten Feed, Midwest, ton ..	78.-120.	78.-120.	107.50
Cottnsd Meal, Clksdle,Miss. ton	...155.-162½	155.-162½	157.50
Hominy Feed,Cent-Ill. ton	82.00	82.00	75.00
Meat-Bonemeal, 50% pro. Ill. ton.	220.-222½	225.00	265.00
Oats, No. 2 milling, Mpls., bu	n2.00-.35	2.00-.40	209.00
Sorghum, (Milo) No. 2 Gulf cwt ...	4.91	4.93	3.86
Soybean Meal,			
Decatur, Illinois ton.............	202.-208.	201½-205½	242.50
Soybeans, No. 1 yel Cent-Ill. bu ...	bp7.00½	6.91½	7.53½
Wheat, Spring 14%-pro Mpls. bu			
	4.42¾-.50¾	4.42¼-.50¼	3.59¼
Wheat, No. 2 sft red, St.Lou. bu ...	3.94½	3.93½	3.35½
Wheat, No. 2 hard KC, bu	4.48½	4.47¾	3.41¾
Wheat, sft wht, del Portland Ore. .	4.56	4.56	3.46

FOODS

Beef, 700-900 lbs. Mid-U.S.,lb.fob .	n.a.	1.14	1.14
Broilers, Dressed "A" NY lb	x.6994	.7230	.6280
Butter, AA, Chgo., lb.	1.30½	1.30½	1.30½
Cocoa, Ivory Coast, $metric ton ...	g1,539	1,543	2,040
Coffee, Brazilian, NY lb.	n1.35	1.35	1.21
Eggs, Lge white, Chgo doz.	.67-.72	.67-.72	.50
Flour, hard winter KC cwt	11.05	11.05	9.05
Hams, 17-20 lbs, Mid-US lb fob	n.a.	.67	n.a.
Hogs, Iowa-S.Minn. avg. cwt	46.75	46.25	51.00
Hogs, Omaha avg cwt	46.50	45.75	49.50
Pork Bellies, 12-14 lbs Mid-US lb ..	n.a.	.33½	.47
Pork Loins, 14-17 lbs. Mid-US lb ..	n.a.	.99	n.a.
Steers, Tex.-Okla. ch avg cwt	75.25	75.50	76.50
Steers, Feeder, Okl Cty, av cwt ...	87.15	87.50	88.40
Sugar, cane, raw, world, lb. fob ...	.1153	.1177	.0916

FATS AND OILS

Coconut Oil, crd, N. Orleans lb. ...	xxn.28	.28	.24¾
Corn Oil, crd wet mill, Chgo. lb. ...	n.21½	.21½	.22½
Corn Oil, crd dry mill, Chgo. lb.	n.21	.21	.21
Cottonseed Oil, crd Miss Vly lb. ...	a.22	.22	.24½
Grease, choice white, Chgo lb.	.12½	.12½	.14¼
Lard, Chgo lb.	.14	.14	.16¾
Palm Oil, ref. bl. deod. N.Orl. lb. .	n.20½	.20½	.20½
Peanut Oil, crd, Southeast lb.	n.a.	n.a.	.30½
Soybean Oil, crd, Decatur, lb.	.2152	.2170	.2459
Tallow, bleachable, Chgo lb.	.14¾	.14¾	.16¼
Tallow, edible, Chgo lb.	b.16½	.16½	.17½

FIBERS AND TEXTILES

Burlap, 10 oz. 40-in. NY yd	n.2820	.2820	.2830
Cotton 1 1/16 in str lw-md Mphs lb	.6235	.6222	.6367
Wool, 64s, Staple, Terr. del. lb.	3.75	3.75	4.50

METALS

Aluminum ingot lb. del. Midwest	q.99½-1.02	.99½-1.02	1.21½
Copper cathodes lb	p1.13½-.17	1.15½-.23	1.02¼
Copper Scrap, No 2 wire NY lb	k.88¾	.90¾	.75
Lead, lb.	p.36-.37	.36-.37	.35
Mercury 76 lb. flask NY	q295-310	295-310	350.00
Steel Scrap 1 hvy mlt Chgo ton	111.-118.	111.-118.	106.50
Tin composite lb.	q6.2216	6.1778	4.2676
Zinc Special High grade lb p.85-.85½	.85-.85½	.57	

MISCELLANEOUS

Rubber, smoked sheets, NY lb.	n.50½	.51	.62½
Hides, hvy native steers lb., fob ...	.85	.85	.93

PRECIOUS METALS

Gold, troy oz

Engelhard indust bullion	365.77	361.01	458.68
Engelhard fabric prods	384.06	379.06	481.61
Handy & Harman base price	364.50	359.75	457.25
London fixing AM 363.40 PM ...	364.50	359.75	457.25
Krugerrand, whol	a363.00	363.00	458.50
Maple Leaf, troy oz.	a374.75	374.00	474.50
American Eagle, troy oz.	a374.75	374.00	474.50
Platinum, (Free Mkt.)	488.70	497.75	584.50
Platinum, indust (Engelhard)	500.00	495.00	573.45
Platinum, fabric prd (Engelhard)	600.00	595.00	673.45
Palladium, indust (Engelhard) ..	151.00	149.50	125.75
Palladium, fabrc prd (Englhard)	166.00	164.50	140.75

Silver, troy ounce

Engelhard indust bullion	5.235	5.185	6.685
Engelhard fabric prods	5.602	5.548	7.153
Handy & Harman base price	5.182	5.145	6.700
London fixing (in pounds)			
Spot (U.S. equiv. $5.1000)	3.2290	3.2295	3.5760
3 months	3.3380	3.3295	3.6415
6 months	3.4545	3.4415	3.7185
1 year	3.6730	3.6500	3.8880
Coins, whol $1,000 face val	a3,760	3,725	5,400

a-Asked. b-Bid. bp-Country elevator bids to producers. c-Corrected. d-Dealer market. e-Estimated. f-Dow Jones International Petroleum Report. g-Main crop, ex-dock, warehouses, Eastern Seaboard, north of Hatteras. j.-f.o.b. warehouse. k-Dealer selling prices in lots of 40,000 pounds or more, f.o.b. buyer's works. n-Nominal. p-Producer price. q-Metals Week. r-Rail bids. s-Thread count 78x54. x-Less than truckloads. z-Not quoted. xx-f.q.b. tankcars.

Source: *The Wall Street Journal,* May 24, 1989.

All metals are **exhaustible resources** that exist in finite supply and so become scarcer as the years go by.[9] Metals are also relatively homogeneous commodities, so the metals markets are very liquid. All of the metals are traded internationally in markets that resemble the foreign exchange and Treasury securities markets. There is an international network of dealers who stand ready to buy and sell metals. Some exchanges, such as the London Metal Exchange, also trade industrial metals. Because metals are so homogeneous, well publicized, and standard, metals prices are quoted in the financial press and electronic media. Figure 8.3 presents an excerpt

---

[9] Of course, recycling and improvements in the efficiency of mining and refining can increase the supply of metals, but eventually the metals will be used up.

**Figure 8.4 COMEX Gold, Silver, and Copper Futures
Annual Volume, 1983–1989**

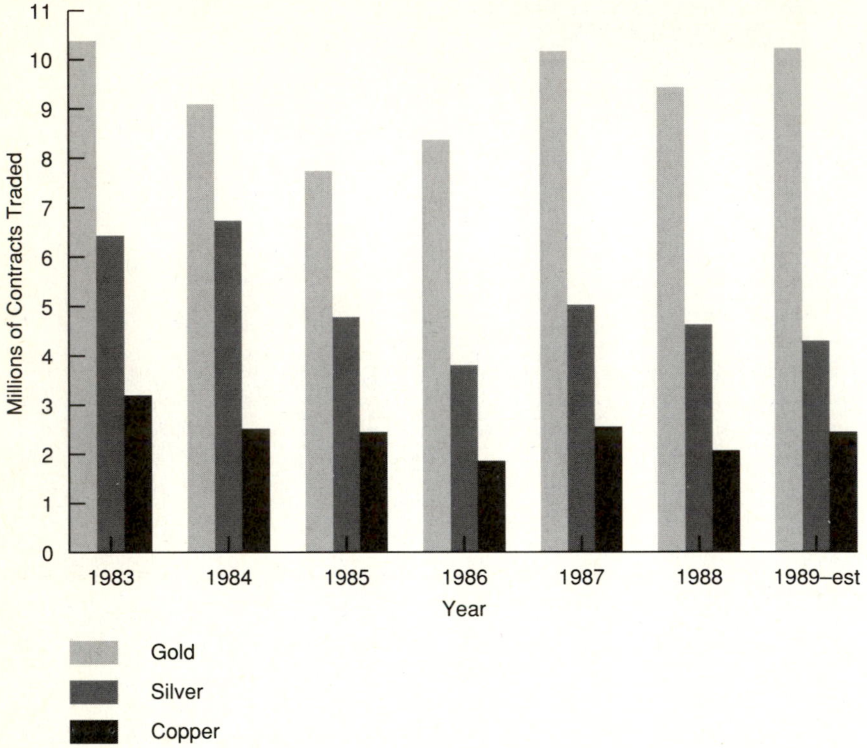

Source: Futures Industry Association.

from *The Wall Street Journal* that gives various spot price quotations for the
different commodities markets, including metals.[10]

Futures Market

The major metals futures contracts in the United States are the gold, silver, and
copper contracts at the Commodity Exchange Inc. (COMEX) and the platinum
and palladium contracts at the New York Mercantile Exchange (NYMEX). The
Chicago Board of Trade also has gold and silver contracts, and the COMEX
has an aluminum contract.[11] Figures 8.4 and 8.5 show the annual trading volume
of the COMEX and NYMEX contracts in the years 1983 through 1989.

[10] With commodities, one must be careful when interpreting a "spot" price. Sometimes these
prices are those "posted" by a particular buyer and may not move as freely as competitive prices.

[11] Other futures exchanges also trade metal futures. For example, gold futures are traded in various
exchanges throughout the world, including the BMF (Brazil), the Hong Kong Futures Exchange, the
Montreal Exchange, the Sydney Futures Exchange, and the Tokyo Commodity Exchange.

Figure 8.5 NYMEX Platinum and Paladium Futures Annual Volume, 1983–1989

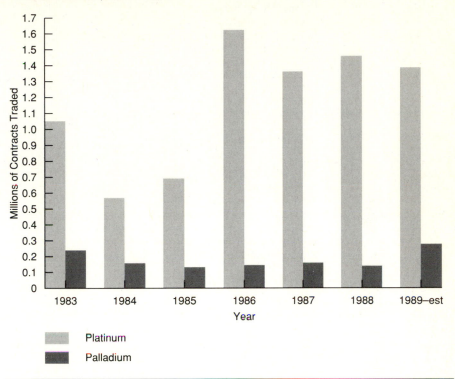

Source: Futures Industry Association.

The terms of all the metals contracts are very similar to those of the COMEX gold futures contract that we discussed in detail in Chapters 1 through 3. Each metals contract specifies an acceptable range of quantities and grades for delivery, adjustments to the futures price for delivery of nonpar grades, and a delivery period that is usually about one month.

Gold Contract Specifications

Contract:	Gold
Exchange:	Commodity Exchange, Inc.
Quantity:	100 troy ounces
Delivery months:	Current calendar month, next two months, and February, April, June, August, October, December
Delivery specifications:	Gold cast in either one bar or three 1-kilogram bars; aggregate weight of 100 troy ounces (5 percent more or less) with specified tolerances and fineness above 99.5 percent; delivery by accepted warehouse or vault receipt
Minimum price movement:	$10.00 per contract, or $0.10 per ounce

Silver Contract Specifications

Contract:	Silver
Exchange:	Commodity Exchange, Inc.
Quantity:	5,000 troy ounces
Delivery months:	Current calendar month, next two months, and January, March, July, September, December
Delivery specifications:	Refined silver cast in bars of 1,000 or 1,100 troy ounces with specified tolerances; aggregate weight of 5,000 troy ounces (6 percent more or less) and fineness above 99.9 percent; delivery by accepted warehouse or vault receipt
Minimum price movement:	$5.00 per contract, or $0.001 per ounce

Copper Contract Specifications

Contract:	Copper
Exchange:	Commodity Exchange, Inc.
Quantity:	25,000 pounds
Delivery months:	All months for one year and then the same cycle as silver
Delivery specifications:	Grade 2 electrolytic cathode copper; aggregate weight of 25,000 pounds (2 percent more or less); other grades deliverable with adjustments; delivery by accepted warehouse receipt
Minimum price movement:	$12.50 per contract, or $0.0005 per pound

Palladium Contract Specifications

Contract:	Palladium
Exchange:	New York Mercantile Exchange
Quantity:	100 troy ounces
Delivery months:	Current calendar month, next two months, and March, June, September, December
Delivery specifications:	100 troy ounces (2 percent more or less) in no more than four pieces of plate or ingots, with no individual piece weighing less than 10 ounces; palladium with minimum of 99.9 percent fineness; some lots or bars of lesser content can be delivered at a discount to the futures price
Minimum price movement:	$5.00 per contract, or $0.05 per ounce

Platinum Contract Specifications

Contract:	Platinum
Exchange:	New York Mercantile Exchange
Quantity:	50 troy ounces
Delivery months:	Current calendar month, next two months, and January, April, July, October
Delivery specifications:	50 troy ounces (2 percent more or less); platinum lots or bars with minimum of 99.9 percent fineness; some lots or bars of lesser content can be delivered at a discount to the futures price
Minimum price movement:	$5.00 per contract, or $0.10 per ounce

Since we have used gold and copper for our examples in Chapters 1 through 3, we will not discuss the metals contracts further. We will now move on to petroleum futures.[12]

---

[12] See Ball, Torous, and Tschoegl [1985], Ma [1986], and Monroe and Cohn [1986] for studies of pricing in the gold market.

Figure 8.6   Petroleum Transactions Prices for May 23, 1989

OIL PRICES

Tuesday May 23, 1989

CRUDE GRADES	Tues	Mon	Yr. Ago
OFFSHORE-d			
European "spot" or free market prices			
Arab lt.	hn17.00	16.80	14.65
Arab hvy.	hn15.80	15.60	14.30
Iran, lt.	hn16.80	16.60	14.55
Forties	hn18.60	18.35	16.10
Brent (Jun)	hn17.75	17.50	16.50
Bonny lt.	hn18.75	18.55	16.50
Urals-Medit.	hn16.90	16.70	15.90
DOMESTIC-f			
Spot market			
W. Tex. Int Cush			
(1925) (Jul)	h19.05	20.95	17.40
W.Tx.sour, Midl (1800-1900)	h17.90-18.00	19.75-.85	16.12
La. sw. St.Ja (1950-1965)	h19.20-.25	20.55-.65	17.33
No. Slope del USGULF	hn17.05	17.15	15.55
REFINED PRODUCTS			
Fuel Oil, No. 2 NY gal.	g.4450	.4975	.5000
Gasoline, lded, reg.			
NY gal.	g.6625	.6635	.5335
Gasoline, unlded, reg.			
NY gal.	g.6425	.6475	.5235
Propane, Mont Belvieu,			
Texas, gal.	g.2025	.2025	.2500

a-Asked. b-Bid. c-Corrected. d-as of 11 a.m. EST in Northwest Europe. f-As of 4 p.m. EST. Refiners' posted buying prices are in parentheses. g-Provided by Oil Buyers Guide. h-Dow Jones International Petroleum Report. n.a.-Not available. z-Not quoted. n-Nominal. r-Revised.

Source: *The Wall Street Journal,* May 24, 1989.

Petroleum Futures

Cash Market

The markets for petroleum and petroleum products are among the most complex cash markets we will study in this book. Petroleum is bought and sold in many forms. First, there is an active market for oil and gas reserves still in the ground. Petroleum companies trade reserves among themselves, and individual investors can purchase shares in companies that consist of nothing more than petroleum reserves. Next, there is active trading in the crude oil and natural gas that are extracted from the ground. Oil companies, refiners, and end users all participate in the cash markets for oil and gas. Recently, investment banks have started to arbitrage and speculate in the oil and gas markets just as they do in many financial markets. Finally, there are very competitive spot markets in the final products, such as heating oil, gasoline, and propane, that are refined from crude oil. Figure 8.6 presents an excerpt from *The Wall Street Journal* that quotes spot prices in the various petroleum markets.

The petroleum markets have undergone a major transformation over the past two decades. Up through the early 1970s, the oil market was characterized by

Figure 8.7 NYMEX Crude Oil, Heating Oil, and Gas Futures Annual Volume, 1983–1989

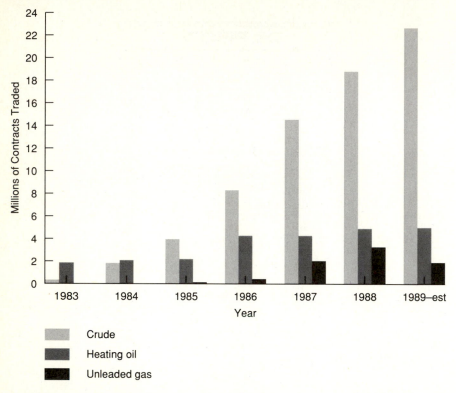

Source: Futures Industry Association.

stable prices, long-term contracts between major petroleum companies, and government price controls. But the era of stability ended with the Middle East oil embargo of 1973 and the subsequent rise in pricing power of the Organization of Petroleum Exporting Countries (OPEC). Petroleum prices became very volatile and have remained among the most volatile of all commodity prices. The deregulation of U.S. oil markets, the political crisis in Iran in the late 1970s, the growth of the petroleum spot markets, and, most recently, the disarray within OPEC have all contributed to the persistence of petroleum price volatility.

Futures Market

The increased volatility of petroleum prices since the early 1970s led to the development of futures trading in oil and oil products. The major petroleum futures exchange in the United States is the New York Mercantile Exchange (NYMEX). It trades contracts on crude oil, gasoline, heating oil, and propane. Figure 8.7 shows the annual trading volume of the NYMEX contracts in the 1983–1989 period.

Figure 8.8 Petroleum Futures Transactions Prices for October 12, 1988

	Open	High	Low	Settle	Change	Lifetime High	Low	Open Interest
CRUDE OIL, Light Sweet (NYM) 1,000 bbls.; $ per bbl.								
Nov	13.45	14.20	13.42	14.11 +	.56	18.42	12.28	37,414
Dec	13.11	13.78	13.07	13.74 +	.54	18.35	12.13	91,900
Ja89	13.03	13.63	12.98	13.61 +	.49	18.20	12.20	46,867
Feb	13.03	13.55	13.00	13.55 +	.43	18.10	12.30	20,285
Mar	13.08	13.56	13.04	13.56 +	.40	18.05	12.45	19,895
Apr	13.20	13.55	13.20	13.59 +	.38	18.25	12.60	9,002
May	13.21	13.60	13.21	13.63 +	.37	17.82	12.70	3,609
June	13.26	13.49	13.25	13.67 +	.36	16.80	12.85	1,963
July	....	....	....	13.71 +	.35	17.60	12.90	1,335
Aug	13.46	13.46	13.46	13.75 +	.34	16.40	13.00	639
Sept	13.50	13.50	13.50	13.79 +	.33	14.90	13.08	107
Est vol 95,612; vol Tues 78,156; open int 233,016, −7,556.								
HEATING OIL NO. 2 (NYM) 42,000 gal.; $ per gal.								
Nov	.3890	.4100	.3885	.4084 +	.0176	.5140	.3700	20,781
Dec	.3975	.4180	.3975	.4167 +	.0175	.5200	.3765	33,286
Ja89	.4040	.4225	.4035	.4224 +	.0166	.5150	.3825	16,508
Feb	.4035	.4225	.4025	.4214 +	.0161	.5150	.3825	12,652
Mar	.3890	.4005	.3885	.4044 +	.0146	.5030	.3700	2,511
Apr	.3730	.3830	.3715	.3884 +	.0126	.5000	.3565	1,488
May	.3655	.3730	.3655	.3784 +	.0116	.4700	.3520	1,200
June	.3610	.3680	.3588	.3724 +	.0106	.4680	.3465	2,083
July	.3660	.3660	.3660	.3714 +	.0101	.4700	.3475	765
Aug	....	....	....	.3764 +	.0101	.4600	.3545	216
Sept	....	....	....	.3834 +	.0101	.4245	.3640	122
Dec	....	....	....	.4049 +	.0101	.4031	.3785	100
Est vol 25,992; vol Tues 16,942; open int 91,867, −335.								
GASOLINE, Unleaded (NYM) 42,000 gal.; $ per gal.								
Nov	.4065	.4295	.4060	.4266 +	.0187	.4960	.3896	17,015
Dec	.3741	.3950	.3741	.3950 +	.0195	.4880	.3600	15,557
Ja89	.3630	.3818	.3630	.3802 +	.0184	.4640	.3465	7,475
Feb	.3650	.3820	.3650	.3802 +	.0172	.4630	.3490	5,050
Mar	.3780	.3900	.3780	.3884 +	.0164	.4680	.3590	2,039
Apr	.3860	.4005	.3860	.3959 +	.0154	.4735	.3680	1,465
May	.4000	.4025	.4000	.4025 +	.0150	.4495	.3740	1,041
June	.4020	.4020	.4020	.4055 +	.0140	.4159	.3850	207
Est vol 9,562; vol Tues 15,327; open int 49,849, −779.								

Source: *The Wall Street Journal,* October 13, 1988.

Figure 8.8 presents the prices of the NYMEX petroleum futures contracts on October 12, 1988.

We will discuss the markets for each of these contracts individually.

Crude Oil Futures   The NYMEX crude oil contract has the following specifications:

Crude Oil Contract Specifications

Contract:	Crude oil
Exchange:	New York Mercantile Exchange
Quantity:	1,000 U.S. barrels (42,000 gallons)
Delivery months:	All months
Delivery specifications:	Par grade is West Texas Intermediate (0.4 percent sulfur, 40 degrees API gravity); other grades are deliverable with price adjustments specified by the exchange; delivery is F.O.B., seller's facility, in Cushing, Oklahoma, using specified techniques; alternative delivery procedures are also available upon agreement of both parties and notification of the exchange
Minimum price movement:	$0.01 per barrel, or $10.00 per contract

The exchange publishes adjustments to invoice prices for delivery of crudes other than the par West Texas Intermediate. The two characteristics that most affect the market value of a crude oil, and therefore its delivery adjustment factor, are its sulfur content and its gravity. High sulfur content is undesirable, because sulfur is a pollutant. Low gravity is desirable, because it allows refiners to produce relatively more of the expensive products such as gasoline and jet fuel.

Because oil is traded internationally, the exchange also allows parties to agree to consummate deliveries at locations and dates other than those specified in the contract.

Convenience Values   Because crude oil is an industrial commodity, the first step in deriving its fundamental no-arbitrage equation is to establish whether it is a pure or convenience asset. First, let us consider how the market uses oil in a very simple model in which there is no uncertainty about the need for oil. In this case, oil producers will extract oil from the ground only as it is needed to postpone extraction costs as long as possible and minimize above-ground storage costs. Therefore, we would not expect to see crude oil stored above ground.

In the real world, of course, we do see above-ground storage of crude oil. One reason for such storage is to protect oil users against supply interruption. It is very costly for refiners to shut down due to temporary shortages. Also, oil supplies are quite vulnerable to interruption. Political turmoil in the Middle East has led to oil shortages, and oil tankers can sink. Thus, oil producers and users may store oil above ground to receive a convenience value.[13] In this case, the futures and spot prices of crude oil will satisfy Equations 8.1 and 8.6 with a positive convenience value, and the crude oil futures market will be at less than full carry.

However, oil, like copper, can become a pure asset at times. Suppose, for example, that oil producers have overestimated the need for oil. This can lead to a glut, in which all those who derive convenience value from storing oil are fully stocked. In this case, some of the oil will be stored by those with a zero marginal convenience value. Before taking on such storage, these people will require an expected rate of return that will cover both interest and physical storage costs. When oil is a pure asset, the futures and spot prices of crude oil will be at full carry. This situation will persist until crude oil users work the oil inventories back down to normal levels.

Example 8.2 demonstrates how to determine whether crude oil is a pure or convenience asset at a given time.

- **Example 8.2: Determining Whether Oil Is a Pure or Convenience Asset**
Oil has acted as both a pure asset and a convenience asset at different times in recent history. In this example, we examine episodes of each kind of behavior.

We obtain the prices of the NYMEX crude oil futures contract on October 12, 1988, from Figure 8.8. Table 8.4 gives the percentage differences among prices of the

---

[13] Crude oil storage below ground is more likely done for investment purposes, because oil in this form is not accessible enough to provide much convenience value.

Table 8.4 Percentage Differential in NYMEX Crude Oil Futures Prices, October 12, 1988

Expiration Dates	Percentage Difference	Percentage Difference Annualized
November 1988–December 1988	– 2.62%	– 31.44%
December 1988–January 1989	– 0.95	– 11.40
January 1989–February 1989	– 0.44	– 5.28
February 1989–March 1989	0.07	0.84
March 1989–April 1989	0.22	2.64
April 1989–May 1989	0.29	3.48
May 1989–June 1989	0.29	3.48

adjacent contracts on that date.[14] It is clear from the price change rates that the market expected crude oil to be a convenience asset through at least May 1989, for the annualized percentage changes in the futures prices up through that date were much lower than the T-bill rates, which at that time were above 7 percent. Since full-carry futures prices must rise to cover both interest and storage costs, these futures price differentials clearly were well below full-carry levels.

This futures price pattern suggests there was a temporary shortage of crude oil around the end of 1988. The marginal convenience value must have been very high to generate a –31 percent annualized futures price differential between November and December. Only those with very large convenience values could afford to hold crude oil under such circumstances. The market appeared to expect the shortage to gradually improve, for the futures price differentials changed from large negative values for the contracts due to expire in late 1988 to a steady positive level for the contracts due to expire in late spring of 1989. This indicates that the market expected the marginal convenience value to drop considerably and then stabilize.

Crude oil appeared to behave as a pure asset for awhile in 1986. On March 25, 1986, the following prices and rates prevailed:

May 1986 crude oil futures	$12.25
June 1986 crude oil futures	$12.62
90-day Eurodollar deposit rate	7.43%
3-month T-bill rate	6.39%

The percentage difference between the May and June futures prices was 3.02 percent over three months, or 36.24 percent annualized. This was much higher than either the Eurodollar deposit or T-bill rate. This indicates that the crude oil futures market was at full carry at this time.

As we discussed earlier, this kind of situation is likely to arise during an oil glut. In this case, the spot price of oil dropped sharply from January to March 1986,

---

[14] These percentages do not represent the implied repo rate, because we have not subtracted storage costs.

indicating that production had far exceeded consumption. The price of West Texas Intermediate, for example, fell from $18.85 on January 31 to $10.40 on March 31. Our evidence that oil was a pure asset during this period suggests that the spot price dropped until those with zero marginal convenience values found it worthwhile to hold the crude oil in inventory. ∎

Exchange Agreements and the Fundamental No-Arbitrage Equations

Earlier in this chapter, we saw that quasi-arbitrage profits are possible if the futures price drops below the levels given by the fundamental no-arbitrage equations, 8.1 and 8.6. Potential quasi-arbitrageurs must make sure that their quasi-arbitrage profits compensate them for the convenience value lost by selling out of inventory.

In the crude oil markets, opportunities for reverse cash-and-carry pure arbitrage also exist, for a contracting process to allow arbitrageurs to effectively sell crude oil short has been developed. This process uses **oil exchange agreements**, which essentially are repurchase agreements similar to those we discussed in Chapter 5. Under an oil exchange agreement, one party agrees to sell another party a given type of oil for a prespecified period and then buy it back. Both the purchase and sale prices are negotiated in advance. Example 8.3 demonstrates how an oil exchange agreement can be used to perform a reverse cash-and-carry pure arbitrage even when oil is not a pure asset.

▪ **Example 8.3: Reverse Cash-and-Carry Arbitrage with Oil Exchange Agreements**   Suppose that on October 12, 1988, an oil trader observed that the NYMEX crude oil futures price for March 1989 delivery was $13.56 and the oil spot price was $14.10. The yield on a five-month T-bill was 7.20 percent annualized, or 1.80 percent over three months. The trader knew he could enter into an oil exchange agreement to buy 42,000 barrels of crude oil immediately at the current spot price and sell the oil back at the end of March 1989 for $13.60. The time line for this agreement was

This oil exchange agreement would allow the trader to execute a pure reverse cash-and-carry arbitrage strategy that would yield the following arbitrage profit:

Transaction	Arbitrage Strategy	
	t	T
Enter exchange agreement	−$14.10	$13.60
Sell oil	$14.10	
Go long March futures	0	$P_T - \$13.56$
Purchase oil and return	0	$-P_T$
Net	0	$0.04

With these transactions, the trader would effectively borrow the oil from the opposite party and use the futures market to lock in a March purchase price ($13.56) lower than the price the opposite party had to pay to receive the oil back in March.

We can examine the origin of this profit by rewriting Equation 8.4, the condition for a reverse cash-and-carry arbitrage, as follows:

$$F_{t,T} - P_t < P_t r_{t,T} + SC_{t,T} - CV_{t,T}. \tag{8.8}$$

In a short sale, the borrower of the commodity must compensate the lender for the lost convenience value, and the lender must rebate the storage costs to the borrower. Further, the borrower receives interest on the proceeds from the short sale. In an exchange agreement, the net of these three transactions comes from the differential between the initial price and the repurchase price:

$$\text{Repurchase price} - \text{Initial price} = P_t r_{t,T} + SC_{t,T} - CV_{t,T}. \tag{8.9}$$

If the convenience value is greater than the total carrying costs (interest + storage costs), the initial purchase price will exceed the repurchase price. If the convenience value is less than the total carrying costs, the initial purchase price will be lower than the repurchase price. If we combine Equations 8.8 and 8.9, we see that there is a reverse cash-and-carry arbitrage if

$$F_{t,T} - P_t < \text{Repurchase price} - \text{Initial price}.$$

In this example,

$$\begin{aligned}
\$13.56 - \$14.10 = -\$0.54 &< \$13.60 - \$14.10 \\
&= -\$0.50.
\end{aligned}$$

A reverse cash-and-carry arbitrage existed as long as the differential between the initial purchase price and the repurchase price was less than $0.54. ∎

Hedging with Crude Oil Futures   As with all futures, one of the main uses of the crude oil futures contract is to hedge the price of its underlying asset—oil. Refiners who have fixed contract prices for their refined products are concerned about rising prices of crude and therefore will use long anticipatory hedges.[15] Crude oil producers and those holding inventories are concerned about falling prices and thus will use short inventory hedges.[16]

As Figure 8.6 suggests, there are many types of crude oil that differ by sulfur content and gravity. The NYMEX contract, however, is the only crude oil futures

---

[15] The general exposure of a refiner is a more complex issue. For example, a refiner is hurt by rising input prices but helped by rising output prices. See Hirshleifer [1988b] and our analysis of the crack spread in the next section.

[16] Producers use inventory hedges because they already own the oil in the ground.

contract available, and its price has become the standard against which other crude prices are quoted. Therefore, an oil hedger must be concerned with the basis risk of using the NYMEX contract to hedge the price of other grades.

In Example 3.3, we saw how to construct a crosshedge with the NYMEX futures contract. Example 8.4 shows how to mitigate basis risk in a crude oil hedge by using the Exchange of Futures for Physicals (EFP) facility of the NYMEX that we described in Chapter 1.

■ **Example 8.4: Controlling Basis Risk with EFPs**   Suppose that on October 12, 1988, a European refiner wishes to lock in the price of North Sea crude for delivery in March 1989. At the same time, a North Sea oil producer wishes to lock in a sale price for North Sea crude for March 1989. Both parties could simply hedge on the NYMEX, but their hedges would be exposed to the risk of the differential between the price of North Sea crude and that of West Texas Intermediate, the underlying crude of the NYMEX oil futures contract. They could also enter into a forward contract for the North Sea crude, but neither side would have a guarantee that the other would meet the contract obligations.

Another possibility, which has gained a great deal of popularity in recent years, is to use the NYMEX Exchange of Futures for Physicals (EFP) facility. With this approach, the two parties would enter into an EFP agreement requiring the producer to deliver North Sea crude in March 1989 at the then prevailing NYMEX futures price adjusted by a given differential. Suppose the EFP agreement in this case stipulates delivery of 100,000 barrels of North Sea crude in March at the NYMEX March futures price less $0.40 per barrel. At the same time, the parties agree to enter immediately into futures positions at the NYMEX. The refiner enters into 100 long NYMEX March contracts to protect against a price rise, and the producer enters into 100 short NYMEX March contracts to protect against a price drop. Each party must put up full margin and will be subject to marking to market.

Suppose the two parties enter into March futures positions at a futures price of $13.56 per barrel. Then each will lock in a price of

$$\text{EFP locked-in price} = \text{Current futures price} - \text{EFP differential}$$
$$= \$13.56 - \$0.40$$
$$= \$13.16 \text{ per barrel.}$$

Thus, the parties are able to use the NYMEX and completely control the risk of the differential between the price of West Texas Intermediate and that of North Sea crude. Most important, perhaps, the futures positions of the two parties are guaranteed by the NYMEX clearinghouse. If the price of crude oil rises and the producer fails to deliver the crude, the refiner will still profit on the long futures position, and this will offset the higher cost of crude. Of course, if the differential between the West Texas Intermediate and North Sea crude drops to $0.30, the refiner will lose $0.10 relative to the original contract. ■

Heating Oil Futures   The NYMEX heating oil contract has the following specifications:

Heating Oil Contract Specifications

Contract:	Heating oil
Exchange:	New York Mercantile Exchange
Quantity:	1,000 U.S. barrels (42,000 gallons)
Delivery months:	All months
Delivery specifications:	No. 2 heating oil; delivery is F.O.B., seller's facility, in New York harbor; alternative delivery procedures are available upon agreement of both parties and notification of the exchange
Minimum price movement:	$0.0001 per gallon, or $4.20 per contract

Like the crude oil contract, the heating oil contract allows the parties to consummate a contract using alternative delivery arrangements and EFPs.

Convenience Values   As with the crude oil contract, the most important issue in the pricing of heating oil futures contracts is whether the underlying asset, heating oil, is a pure or convenience asset. For heating oil, this is determined primarily by seasonal factors. The seasonal pattern of heating oil production and storage causes heating oil to be a pure asset at some times of the year and a convenience asset at others.

Demand for heating oil is high in the winter months and low in the summer months. Heating oil producers adjust their output according to these seasonal swings in demand. However, it would be inefficient for them to maintain refining capacity that could produce large quantities of heating oil during the heating season but would have to lie idle over the rest of the year. Thus, in the summer and fall, the producers accumulate stocks of heating oil to be consumed in the winter along with the winter production.

The producers know the heating oil stocks they build up in the summer and fall will not be used for several more months. This means that they will receive no convenience value from the stored oil during the summer and fall. Thus, heating oil is a pure asset at this time of the year. As winter ends and production can again keep up with consumption, the only reason to store heating oil is to obtain some convenience value. Thus, heating oil becomes a convenience asset in late winter and spring.

To demonstrate these ideas, suppose there is no uncertainty about heating oil demand and production over the year. In this case, there is no need to accumulate precautionary heating oil stocks that receive a convenience value; any storage will be for investment purposes only.

Figure 8.9 shows the effect of seasonal demand on the level of heating oil inventories held throughout the year. Part a shows that consumption equals production between February and July. There is no need for inventories during this period, so stocks of heating oil, shown in part b, are zero. Starting in July, refiners begin to shift their product mix toward heating oil and production exceeds consumption. Inventories build up until consumption begins to exceed production in November, then start to decline. Heating oil is a pure asset between July and February, because there are parties who are willing to store it without receiving convenience value during these months. It is a convenience asset during the remainder of the year.

Figure 8.9 Effect of Seasonal Demand on Heating Oil Inventories

(a) Consumption and Production

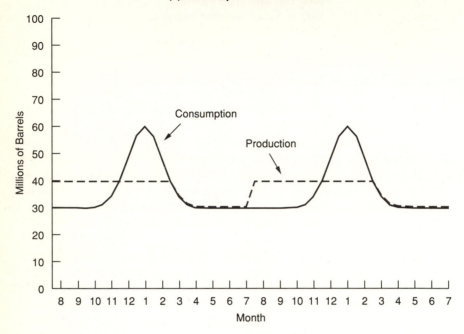

(b) Inventories

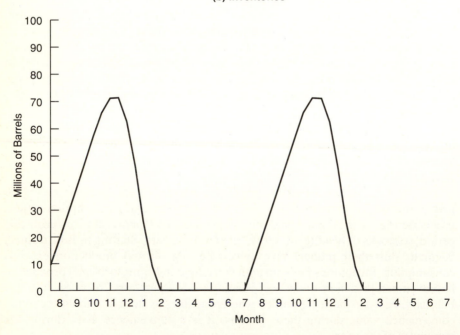

Figure 8.10   Total U.S. Inventories of Heating Oil, July 1985–July 1987

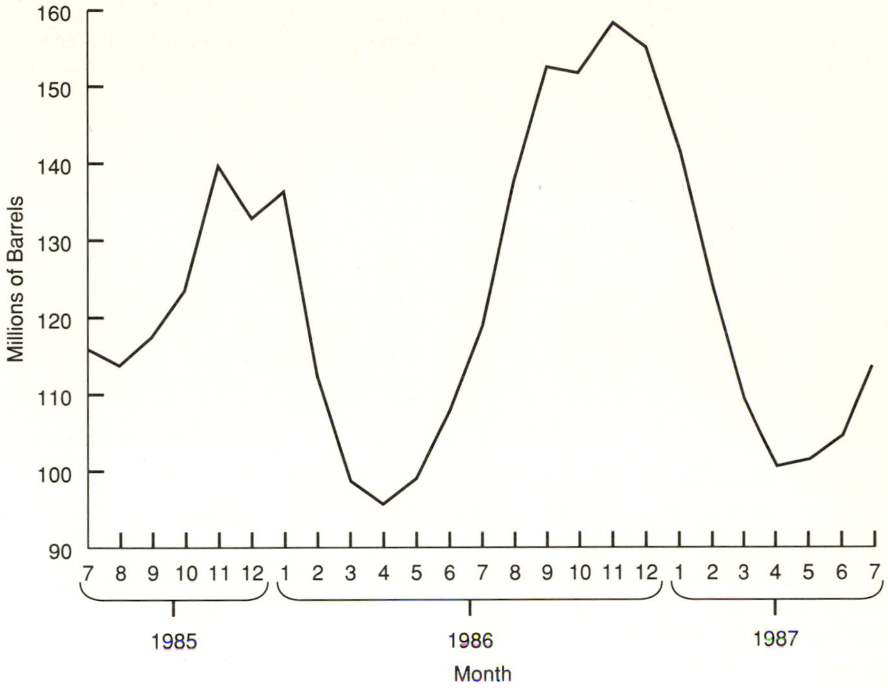

Source: U.S. Department of Energy.

Figure 8.10 graphs actual heating oil inventories between July 1985 and July 1987. As expected, inventories begin to build well before the heating season, peak during the season, and decline as the heating season progresses. In the real world, inventories never drop to zero. Some are held for emergencies and others are stocks awaiting shipment. These inventories, however, provide convenience value. In a normal year, heating oil appears to be held by some as a pure asset only during the summer and the early part of the heating season and becomes a convenience asset over the rest of the year. Of course, if the winter turns out to be less severe than expected, inventories of heating oil will be carried later into the year and heating oil will remain a pure asset for a longer than normal period.

We expect the heating oil futures market to be at full carry when heating oil is a pure asset and at less than full carry over the rest of the year. Further, because the marginal storage cost for heating oil is likely to rise as more heating oil is stored, we expect the term $SC_{t,T}$ in Equation 8.1 and $SC_{T1,T2}$ in Equation 8.6 to increase with the level of inventories.

Example 8.5 demonstrates how the seasonal patterns of heating oil demand and production affect heating oil futures prices.

Table 8.5 Percentage Differentials in NYMEX Heating Oil Futures Prices, October 12, 1988

Expiration Dates	Percentage Difference	Percentage Difference Annualized
November 1988–December 1988	2.03%	24.36%
December 1988–January 1989	1.37	16.44
January 1989–February 1989	– 0.24	– 2.88
February 1989–March 1989	– 4.03	– 48.36
March 1989–April 1989	– 3.96	– 47.52
April 1989–May 1989	– 2.57	– 30.84
May 1989–June 1989	– 1.59	– 19.08
June 1989–July 1989	– 0.27	– 3.24
July 1989–August 1989	1.35	16.20
August 1989–September 1989	1.86	22.32

▪ **Example 8.5: Seasonality and Carry for Heating Oil Futures**   In this example, we will examine the seasonal behavior of the heating oil futures market by studying actual heating oil futures prices. The October 12, 1988, heating oil futures prices shown in Figure 8.8 cover the period from the beginning of the 1988–1989 heating season through the beginning of the 1989–1990 heating season. Table 8.5 presents the nonannualized and annualized percentage price differentials among contracts of successive months. We will compare these differentials with the prevailing market interest rates to determine when the heating oil futures market was at full carry. As in Example 8.1, we will use the 8.65 percent annualized December three-month rate implied by the Eurodollar futures price and the 7.36 percent rate (7.22 percent discount yield) implied by the T-bill futures price as our benchmark market interest rates.

The highest percentage increase among successive futures prices was for the contracts that were due to expire in November and December 1988. At that time, we would expect heating oil to be a pure asset and oil storage to be at its peak so that the futures price must rise enough to cover both interest and the higher storage costs. The high futures price differential we observe tends to support our hypothesis that the market was at full carry during these months. The percentage price differential for the contracts that were due to expire in December 1988 and January 1989 was also high, though lower than the differential for the previous period. This suggests the market was at full carry during these months as well but the implied storage cost was lower as stocks were expected to run down.

The futures prices then fell steadily from January to July 1989. This implies that the market was not at full carry over this period and that the convenience values became very large. Clearly, only those with extreme potential need for heating oil would have stored it during these months.

The market appears to have gone back to full carry in July 1989. The futures prices began to rise again as the market expected producers to build inventories for the next heating season. ▪

Example 8.5 shows that our simple theory of the heating season appears to explain the behavior of heating oil futures prices very well. We will now show that similar forces are at work in the market for the unleaded gasoline futures contract.

Unleaded Gasoline Futures   The NYMEX contract on unleaded gasoline has the following specifications:

Unleaded Gasoline Contract Specifications

Contract:	Unleaded gasoline
Exchange:	New York Mercantile Exchange
Quantity:	1,000 U.S. barrels (42,000 gallons)
Delivery months:	All months
Delivery specifications:	Unleaded gasoline; delivery is F.O.B., seller's facility, in New York harbor; alternative delivery procedures are available upon agreement of both parties and notification of the exchange
Minimum price movement:	$0.0001 per gallon, or $4.20 per contract

Like the crude oil and heating oil contracts, the unleaded gasoline contract allows the parties to use alternative delivery arrangements and EFPs.

Convenience Values   The seasonal consumption and production patterns of unleaded gasoline mirror those of heating oil. The months of greatest demand are in the summer, the time of lowest demand for heating oil. This is fortunate for refiners, because they can adjust their output to produce relatively more heating oil for the winter months and relatively more gasoline for the summer months. In late winter and early spring, refiners begin to produce more gasoline than is consumed to build up inventories for the summer. In the middle of the summer, they start producing less gasoline and more heating oil to prepare for the heating season. Thus, we expect gasoline to be a pure asset from late winter through the beginning of summer and a convenience asset over the remainder of the year. Example 8.6 shows that unleaded gasoline futures price data support this pattern.

▪ **Example 8.6: Seasonality and Carry for Unleaded Gasoline Futures**
We can use the October 12, 1988, futures prices shown in Figure 8.8 to study the behavior of the unleaded gasoline futures market. Table 8.6 presents the non-annualized and annualized percentage price differentials among contracts of successive months. As in Examples 8.1 and 8.5, we will use the 8.65 percent annualized December three-month rate implied by the Eurodollar futures price and the 7.36 percent (7.22 percent discount yield) implied by the T-bill futures price to approximate the interest costs during this period.

Unleaded gasoline futures prices fell for contracts due to expire in the late fall and early winter of 1988 and 1989. This suggests that, as expected, the futures market was well below full carry and unleaded gasoline was not expected to be a pure asset during these months. The prices of the contracts due to expire in late winter and early spring of 1989 rose at rates that exceeded the prevailing market interest rates. The futures market apparently moved to

Table 8.6 Percentage Differentials in NYMEX Gasoline Futures Prices, October 12, 1988

Expiration Dates	Percentage Difference	Percentage Difference Annualized
November 1988–December 1988	−7.41%	−88.92%
December 1988–January 1989	−3.75	−45.00
January 1989–February 1989	0.00	0.00
February 1989–March 1989	2.16	25.92
March 1989–April 1989	1.93	23.16
April 1989–May 1989	1.67	20.04
May 1989–June 1989	0.75	9.00

full carry over this period, because the market expected refiners to increase inventories of unleaded gasoline.[17] ∎

Propane Futures   The NYMEX futures contract on propane has the following specifications:

Propane Contract Specifications

Contract:	Propane
Exchange:	New York Mercantile Exchange
Quantity:	1,000 U.S. barrels (42,000 gallons)
Delivery months:	All months
Delivery specifications:	Liquefied propane gas; delivery is F.O.B., seller's pipeline in Mont Belvieu, Texas; alternative delivery procedures are available upon agreement of both parties and notification of the exchange
Minimum price movement:	$0.0001 per gallon, or $4.20 per contract

This contract also allows parties to form alternative delivery arrangements and to use EFPs.

Hedging

Producers and consumers of heating oil, unleaded gasoline, and propane use futures contracts to hedge the prices they pay and receive for these products.[18] Producers of heating oil and unleaded gasoline often hedge both the prices they pay for crude oil and the prices they receive for heating oil and unleaded gasoline. This allows them to reduce the risk of their **gross refining margins**, which are

---

[17] The percentage price change between the May and June 1989 contracts seems too small to be a full-carry differential. However, the June price is probably unreliable given the small amount of open interest.

[18] See Chen, Sears, and Tzang [1987] for a discussion of hedging with energy futures.

defined as the revenues from selling heating oil and gasoline less the cost of crude oil per barrel. This type of hedge is called a **crack spread**.

Crack Spread The first step in constructing a crack spread hedge is to compute the petroleum gross refining margins. These margins depend primarily on the price of crude oil, the amount of heating oil and unleaded gasoline produced by each barrel of crude oil, and the prices of the refined products. We will consider these factors only in our refining margin calculations. For this discussion, we will assume that each barrel of crude oil produces 14 gallons of heating oil and 28 gallons of unleaded gasoline.

These assumptions about the refining process eliminate some refining cost and revenue factors from our calculation of the gross refining margins. In reality, refiners are reasonably able to adjust the amount of each product they produce from a barrel of crude. Further, crude oil contributes only 80 to 90 percent of refiners' total operating costs, and heating oil and gasoline provide only about 80 percent of total refining revenues.[19] If the prices of other petroleum products, such as jet fuel, are correlated with heating oil and unleaded gasoline prices, refiners can hedge them with heating oil and unleaded gasoline futures. Thus, refiners should be able to hedge almost all of their gross refining margins with NYMEX futures contracts.

We can use our assumptions about the refining process to compute the total revenue from the heating oil and unleaded gasoline produced from one barrel of crude oil. The heating oil revenue per barrel of crude is

> Per-barrel revenue from heating oil
> = (Number of gallons per barrel)(Price per gallon)
> = (14)(Price per gallon of heating oil).

The unleaded gasoline revenue per barrel of crude is

> Per-barrel revenue from unleaded gasoline
> = (Number of gallons per barrel)(Price per gallon)
> = (28)(Price per gallon of unleaded gasoline).

Now we can compute the gross refining margin per barrel of crude:

> Gross refining margin per barrel of crude
> = Per-barrel revenue from heating oil
>   + Per-barrel revenue from unleaded gasoline
>   − Per-barrel cost of crude oil
> = (14)(Price per gallon of heating oil)
>   + (28)(Price per gallon of unleaded gasoline)
>   − Per-barrel price of crude oil.

---

[19] See *NYMEX Energy Hedging Manual* (1986).

Because refining takes time, we determine the gross refining margin by the prices for heating oil and unleaded gasoline at the end of the refining period (T2) and of crude oil at the beginning of the refining period (T1):

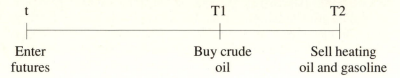

t	T1	T2
Enter futures	Buy crude oil	Sell heating oil and gasoline

Thus, we can represent the gross refining margin as

$$\text{Gross refining margin per barrel} = (14)(P^h_{T2}) + (28)(P^u_{T2}) - P^c_{T1}, \qquad \textbf{(8.10)}$$

where superscripts h, u, and, c refer to heating oil, unleaded gasoline, and crude oil, respectively.

These prices generally move together, because the price of crude oil is strongly influenced by the prices of heating oil and unleaded gasoline. However, because the crude oil is purchased before the heating oil and unleaded gasoline are sold, and because there can be short-term fluctuations in the relationship among the three prices, the refiner can face significant risk. If, for example, there is an unexpected drop in the prices of heating oil and unleaded gasoline between T1 and T2, the gross refining margin will suffer.

A refiner can lock in a gross refining margin by using futures contracts to lock in each of the three prices in Equation 8.10. Since the refiner intends to purchase crude oil, he or she will go long crude oil futures that expire at time T1. Because the refiner intends to sell heating oil and unleaded gasoline, he or she will go short heating oil and unleaded gasoline futures that expire at T2. We can derive the appropriate hedge ratios from the futures contracts' specifications and the crude oil yields of heating oil and unleaded gasoline as follows:

1.   Each crude oil contract represents 1,000 barrels. These 1,000 barrels will produce the following quantity of heating oil:

Gallons of heating oil per crude oil contract
   = (1,000 barrels of crude oil)(14 gallons heating oil per barrel)
   = 14,000 gallons.

Since each heating oil contract represents 42,000 gallons, we can say that each crude oil contract represents $14/42$ heating oil contracts.

2.   The same 1,000 barrels of crude oil will also produce the following quantity of unleaded gasoline:

Gallons of unleaded gasoline per crude oil contract
   = (1,000 barrels of crude oil)(28 gallons unleaded gasoline per barrel)
   = 28,000 gallons.

Since each unleaded gasoline contract also represents 42,000 gallons, one crude oil contract represents $28/42$ unleaded gasoline contracts.

Thus, for every 30 crude oil contracts (30,000 barrels) the refiner goes long, he or she must go short 10 [(14/42)(30)] heating oil contracts and 20 [(28/42)(30)] unleaded gasoline contracts. This is a crack spread position. If the refiner enters into these positions at time t, the hedged gross refining margin per 30,000 barrels of crude oil will be

Hedged gross refining margin per 30,000 barrels **(8.11)**

$$= (30,000 \text{ barrels})(\text{Gross refining margin per barrel}) + \text{Futures profits}$$

$$= (30,000)[(14)(P^h_{T2}) + (28)(P^u_{T2}) - (P^c_{T1})]$$

$$+ 10(42,000)(F^h_{t,T2} - F^h_{T2,T2})$$

$$+ 20(42,000)(F^u_{t,T2} - F^u_{T2,T2})$$

$$+ 30(1,000)(F^c_{T1,T1} - F^c_{t,T1})$$

$$= (30,000)[(14)(F^h_{t,T2}) + (28)(F^u_{t,T2}) - F^c_{t,T1}].$$

We get the final step in Equation 8.11 from the delivery date convergence of spot and futures prices, of crude oil at time T1, and of heating oil and unleaded gasoline at time T2. This crack spread allows the refiner to lock in the gross refining margin implied by the futures prices at time t.

Example 8.7 demonstrates the use of the crack spread.

▪ **Example 8.7: A Crack Spread**   Suppose that on October 12, 1988, a crude oil refiner is planning to buy 30,000 barrels of crude oil on January 31, 1989, and expects to complete refining on February 28, 1989. Current futures prices on October 12 are as given in Figure 8.8. The time line for the refiner's plans is

To hedge his margin, the refiner takes on the crack spread position we calculated earlier. He goes long 30 crude oil futures contracts and goes short 10 heating oil contracts and 20 gasoline contracts.

Table 8.7 shows how variable the refiner's profits from this plan can be. It presents the total gross refining profits and the per-barrel gross refining margin under four different scenarios for the spot prices of crude oil, heating oil, and unleaded gasoline.

Under scenario I, the gross refining cash flows are as follows:

Heating oil revenues
= (Number of barrels)(Gallons per barrel)(Price per gallon)
= (30,000)(14)($0.4700)
= $197,400.

Unleaded gasoline revenues
= (Number of barrels)(Gallons per barrel)(Price per gallon)
= (30,000)(28)($0.4500)
= $378,000.

Table 8.7 Crack Spread, 30,000 Barrels of Crude Oil, October 12, 1988

	Futures Price	Number of Contracts
January crude oil futures	$13.6100 per barrel	30 long
February heating oil futures	$ 0.4214 per gallon	10 short
February gasoline futures	$ 0.3802 per gallon	20 short

	Scenarios			
	I	II	III	IV
Crude spot price	$18.0000	$17.0000	$11.0000	$ 11.0000
Heating oil spot price	0.4700	0.5000	0.2500	0.4500
Gasoline spot price	0.4500	0.4800	0.2500	0.4500
Spot Transaction				
Heating oil revenue	$197,400	$210,000	$105,000	$ 189,000
Gasoline revenue	378,000	403,200	210,000	378,000
Crude cost	540,000	510,000	330,000	330,000
Gross profit	$ 35,400	$103,200	$–15,000	$ 237,000
Per barrel	1.18	3.44	–0.50	7.90
Futures Transactions				
Heating oil profit	$–20,412	$–33,012	$ 71,988	$ –12,012
Gasoline profit	–58,632	–83,832	109,368	–58,632
Crude profit	131,700	101,700	–78,300	–78,300
Futures profit	$ 52,656	$–15,144	$103,056	$–148,944
Per barrel	1.76	–0.50	3.44	–4.96
Net				
Total profit	$ 88,056	$ 88,056	$ 88,056	$ 88,056
Per barrel	2.94	2.94	2.94	2.94

Crude oil costs
   = (Number of barrels)(Price per barrel)
   = (30,000)($18.00)
   = $540,000.

Gross refining margin
   = Revenues – Costs
   = $197,400 + $378,000 – $540,000
   = $35,400
   = $1.18 per barrel.

The refiner's profits vary considerably across the four price scenarios. The refiner can eliminate such profit variability by locking in his gross refining margin with a crack spread. To fully hedge his crude purchase of 30,000 barrels, he must go long 30 crude oil contracts and go short 10 heating oil and 20 unleaded gasoline contracts. This will lock in a gross refining margin of

$$\text{Gross refining margin} = (30,000)[(14)(F^h_{t,T2}) + (28)(F^u_{t,T2}) - F^c_{t,T1}]$$
$$= (30,000)[(14)(\$0.4214) + (28)(\$0.3802) - \$13.61]$$
$$= \$88,056$$
$$= \$2.94 \text{ per barrel.}$$

The unhedged gross refining margin is very low in scenario I because the heating oil and unleaded gasoline prices are low relative to the crude price. However, the refiner can make money in this situation with a crack spread, because he is long the commodity that is relatively expensive and short the commodities that are relatively inexpensive. As with all spreads, only relative price movements matter. ∎

Example 8.7 is based on some important simplifying assumptions. A crack spread can easily be adjusted to account for the more complicated aspects of hedging actual gross refining margins. A refiner can hedge the margins generated as the refining product mix changes over the year by varying the number of heating oil and unleaded gasoline contracts used in a crack spread. Similarly, a refiner can use the heating oil and unleaded gasoline contracts to crosshedge other refining products by employing the techniques for adjusting hedge ratios developed in Chapter 3.

A speculator who believes the prevailing crack spread is too low might enter into a **reverse crack spread** consisting of a short position in crude oil and long positions in heating oil and unleaded gasoline. This position will make money if the speculator's hunch is borne out and the gross refining margin increases.

Grain Futures

Cash Market

Like the cash markets for other commodities, the cash market for grains is a dealer market. The major dealers are grain elevators, who buy, sell, and store grains. The futures markets have become an integral part of the cash market. Cash prices often are quoted as a discount or a premium to a futures price on the Chicago Board of Trade.

Futures Market

Most of the important grain futures contracts are traded at the Chicago Board of Trade.[20] Figure 8.11 shows the annual trading volume of the four major contracts—

---

[20] Other grain contracts are traded on the Kansas City Board of Trade and the Minneapolis Grain Exchange.

Figure 8.11 CBOT Grain Futures Annual Volume, 1983–1989

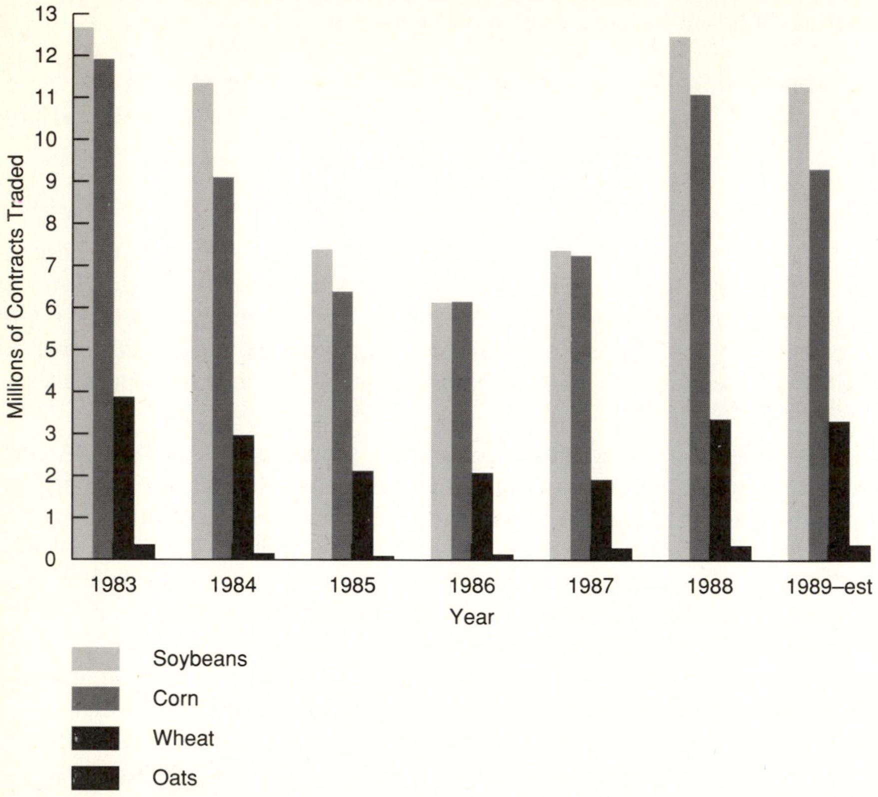

Source: Futures Industry Association.

soybeans, corn, wheat, and oats—in the years 1983 through 1989.[21] Figure 8.12 presents the prices of the CBOT grain futures contracts on October 12, 1988.

The contract specifications are as follows:

Soybean Contract Specifications

Contract:	Soybeans
Exchange:	Chicago Board of Trade
Quantity:	5,000 bushels
Delivery months:	January, March, May, July, August, September, November
Delivery specifications:	No. 2 Yellow and substitutions at differentials established by the exchange; delivery is by warehouse receipt any trading day during the delivery month
Minimum price movement:	$0.0025 per bushel, or $12.50 per contract

[21] See Gray and Peck [1981] for a discussion of the grain futures markets.

Figure 8.12   Grain Futures Transactions Prices for October 12, 1988

	Open	High	Low	Settle	Change	Lifetime High	Low	Open Interest

—GRAINS AND OILSEEDS—

CORN (CBT) 5,000 bu.; cents per bu.

	Open	High	Low	Settle	Change	Lifetime High	Low	Open Interest
Dec	296¼	297¼	295¼	296¼	+ 1¼	370	184	140,310
Mr89	300	300	298¼	299¼	+ 1	370	193½	57,271
May	301	301¼	299¾	300¾	+ 1¼	369	207½	21,501
July	297¼	298¼	296¾	297¼	+ 1¼	360	233	15,879
Sept	273¼	274¼	272½	273	+ 1½	317¾	245	3,387
Dec	258¼	259¼	257¼	257¼	+ ¼	295	234	10,806

Est vol 30,000; vol Tues 35,981; open int 249,179, +2,031.

OATS (CBT) 5,000 bu.; cents per bu.

	Open	High	Low	Settle	Change	Lifetime High	Low	Open Interest
Dec	257	257½	254¼	256¾	+ 2	389½	162	3,788
Mr89	257	258½	255½	257½	+ 2	367¾	161	2,007
May	256½	257½	255	256½	+ 2	340	187	532
July	231½	233	230	233	+ 2	277	221	616

Est vol 1,000; vol Tues 1,603; open int 6,970, +18.

SOYBEANS (CBT) 5,000 bu.; cents per bu.

	Open	High	Low	Settle	Change	Lifetime High	Low	Open Interest
Nov	792	795	789	790¼	− 3¼	1045	499½	57,609
Ja89	806	807½	803	803½	− 2¼	1034	553	25,602
Mar	815	815½	811	811¾	− 2½	1023	579	15,259
May	814	815¼	812	812	− 2¼	1003	647	6,275
July	808	810½	806	806½	− 3¼	986	685	8,395
Aug	798	798	796	797	+ 1	951	725	1,139
Sept	750	752	746	746	− 3	835	701	1,676
Nov	718½	722	717½	719½	+ 1	793	663	6,272

Est vol 30,000; vol Tues 32,663; open int 122,230, −1,759.

SOYBEAN MEAL (CBT) 100 tons; $ per ton.

	Open	High	Low	Settle	Change	Lifetime High	Low	Open Interest
Oct	254.00	254.00	251.50	252.40	− .60	322.00	159.00	2,019
Dec	255.50	256.50	254.10	254.80	− .70	318.70	159.00	37,774
Ja89	255.50	256.00	254.00	254.10	− 1.10	313.00	177.00	14,189
Mar	253.00	254.00	251.50	251.70	− .80	308.00	193.50	11,044
May	249.00	249.00	247.50	248.20	− .30	304.00	200.50	5,745
July	245.00	245.00	243.60	243.70	+ 1.50	300.00	221.00	2,417
Aug	237.50	237.50	235.20	235.20	− 1.30	298.00	217.50	645
Sept	229.00	229.00	227.50	228.40	− .10	290.00	214.00	537
Oct	219.00	219.00	219.00	219.00	− 1.00	237.00	208.00	519
Dec	218.00	219.00	216.60	218.50	− .50	270.00	203.00	462

Est vol 15,000; vol Tues 19,208; open int 75,351, +516.

SOYBEAN OIL (CBT) 60,000 lbs.; cents per lb.

	Open	High	Low	Settle	Change	Lifetime High	Low	Open Interest
Oct	23.70	23.80	23.65	23.69	+ .02	34.20	17.25	1,174
Dec	24.10	24.23	24.03	24.09	+ .05	34.25	18.30	40,615
Ja89	24.40	24.50	24.30	24.35	+ .04	33.95	20.75	15,462
Mar	24.90	24.98	24.80	24.86	+ .06	33.60	21.25	13,789
May	25.25	25.40	25.25	25.27	+ .02	33.00	22.95	5,108
July	25.50	25.50	25.40	25.40	....	32.50	23.00	3,175
Aug	25.50	25.55	25.30	25.30	− .10	32.05	25.05	809
Sept	25.45	25.45	25.35	25.42	− .03	28.70	25.15	815
Oct	24.75	24.85	24.70	24.85	− .10	26.95	24.60	966
Dec	24.60	24.65	24.30	24.30	− .30	28.05	22.80	1,246

Est vol 13,500; vol Tues 10,977; open int 83,159, +13.

WHEAT (CBT) 5,000 bu.; cents per bu.

	Open	High	Low	Settle	Change	Lifetime High	Low	Open Interest
Dec	434	435½	431½	434¾	+ ½	435½	289	46,239
Mr89	437½	439½	434½	438¼	+ 1¼	440¼	323	18,774
May	412	414½	411	413	+ 1	420	330	4,724
July	372	373	370	371¾	− ¼	395	327	6,791
Sept	375½	377	374½	377	+ 2	379	350½	103

Est vol 8,000; vol Tues 19,233; open int 76,646, −1,818.

Source: *The Wall Street Journal*, October 13, 1988.

Corn Contract Specifications

Contract:	Corn
Exchange:	Chicago Board of Trade
Quantity:	5,000 bushels
Delivery months:	March, May, July, September, December
Delivery specifications:	No. 2 Yellow and substitutions at differentials established by the exchange; delivery is by warehouse receipt any trading day during the delivery month.
Minimum price movement:	$0.0025 per bushel, or $12.50 per contract

Wheat Contract Specifications

Contract:	Wheat
Exchange:	Chicago Board of Trade
Quantity:	5,000 bushels
Delivery months:	March, May, July, September, December
Delivery specifications:	No. 2 Soft Red, No. 2 Hard Red Winter, No. 2 Dark Northern Spring, No. 1 Northern Spring, and substitutions at differentials established by the exchange; delivery is by warehouse receipt any trading day during the delivery month
Minimum price movement:	$0.0025 per bushel, or $12.50 per contract

Oats Contract Specifications

Contract:	Oats
Exchange:	Chicago Board of Trade
Quantity:	5,000 bushels
Delivery months:	March, May, July, September, December
Delivery specifications:	No. 2 Heavy, No. 1, and substitutions at differentials established by the exchange; delivery is by warehouse receipt any trading day during the delivery month
Minimum price movement:	$0.0025 per bushel, or $12.50 per contract

Like the metal futures contracts, the grain futures contracts allow delivery at any time during the delivery month. Most of the grain contracts allow for multiple deliverable grades and locations. Unlike the gold, T-bond, and T-note contracts, which use multiplicative factors to adjust for delivery of grades of different quality, the grains use an additive factor, as discussed in Chapter 1. Thus, the grain invoice price is

$$\text{Invoice price} = \text{Quoted futures price} + \text{Adjustment factor.} \qquad (8.12)$$

The adjustment factors are supplied by the exchange before the futures contracts begin trading. Table 8.8 lists the Chicago Board of Trade adjustments for delivery of different grades into the wheat futures contract.

Example 8.8 shows how to determine the invoice prices for the wheat contract.

▪ **Example 8.8: Computing Invoice Prices for Wheat**   Suppose the wheat spot prices and delivery-adjusted spot prices in Chicago are as follows:

Grade	Spot Price	Delivery-Adjusted Spot Price
No. 1 Soft Red	$3.50	$3.49
No. 1 Hard Red Winter	3.49	3.48
No. 1 Dark Northern Spring	3.49½	3.48½
No. 2 Soft Red	3.48½	3.48½
No. 2 Hard Red Winter	3.48½	3.48½
No. 2 Dark Northern Spring	3.49	3.49
No. 1 Northern Spring	3.50	3.50
No. 3 Soft Red	3.47½	3.48½
No. 3 Hard Red Winter	3.48	3.49
No. 3 Dark Northern Spring	3.48½	3.49½
No. 2 Northern Spring	3.49	3.50

Table 8.8   Price Adjustment for Delivery of Different Grades of Wheat, Chicago Board of Trade

$0.01-Per-Bushel Premium

No. 1 Soft Red
No. 1 Hard Red Winter
No. 1 Dark Northern Spring

Par

No. 2 Soft Red
No. 2 Hard Red Winter
No. 2 Dark Northern Spring
No. 1 Northern Spring

$0.01-Per-Bushel Discount

No. 3 Soft Red
No. 3 Hard Red Winter
No. 3 Dark Northern Spring
No. 2 Northern Spring

Note: Delivery in Toledo carries a $0.02-per-bushel discount.

As shown in Chapter 1, the delivery-adjusted spot price is

Delivery-adjusted spot price = Spot price − Adjustment factors.

The grade with the lowest delivery-adjusted spot price is Number 1 Hard Red Winter wheat at $3.48 per bushel. The spot price of Number 1 Hard Red Winter wheat is higher than that of several other grades, but the additional payment the delivering party receives for this premium grade more than covers its higher price. It will become the cheapest grade, and the futures price will adjust such that $QF_{T,T}$ = $3.48 per bushel. ∎

Convenience Values   To see how seasonal patterns in the grain markets affect grain prices, storage, and marginal convenience values, we will briefly study a model in which there is no uncertainty as we did for heating oil.[22]

Certainty   Suppose the wheat harvest begins in late May and extends through November and that wheat is consumed at a constant rate over the year. Suppose also that there is no uncertainty about the size of the harvest or the consumption rate. Part a of Figure 8.13 graphs this wheat production and consumption pattern over several years. Part b shows how wheat inventories behave under these conditions. When production exceeds consumption, wheat inventories increase;

---

[22] Much of this certainty model is adapted from Sharpe [1981].

Figure 8.13 Equilibrium in the Wheat Spot Market

(a) Consumption and Production

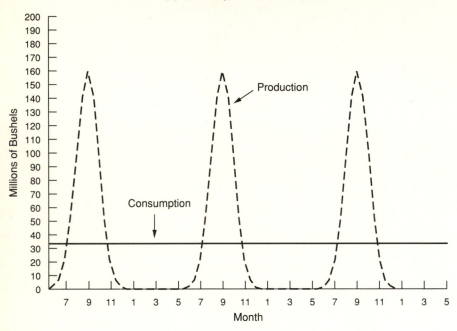

(b) Inventories

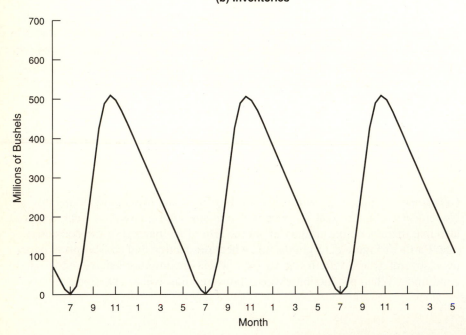

Figure 8.13 (continued)

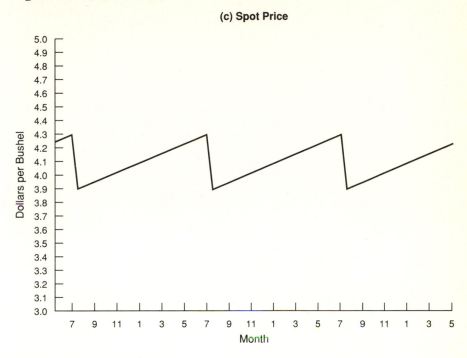

(c) Spot Price

when consumption exceeds production, wheat inventories decrease. Inventories fall to zero just when production begins to exceed consumption at the beginning of the harvest.

Since there is no convenience value in a world of certainty, the only storage will be for pure investment purposes. Thus, in this simple model wheat is a pure asset when it is stored between harvests. The spot price of wheat therefore must rise between harvests at a rate that covers both interest and physical storage costs;[23] this is shown in part c of Figure 8.13. When inventories reach zero during the next harvest, wheat is no longer a pure asset and the wheat price does not have to rise to cover interest and storage costs. In fact, the price will fall back to the level of the previous harvest, because the supply and demand conditions at harvest time are identical every year. This price pattern will repeat itself every year, as part c illustrates.

Uncertainty   In the real world, grain markets are beset by many uncertainties. Weather conditions have a major impact on crop size. Farmers' planting and

[23] One might suspect that the wheat consumption rate would fall between harvests because of the rising prices, but we will ignore this effect for simplicity. Allowing for falling consumption would not change our analysis significantly.

Figure 8.14 Total U.S. Wheat Inventories, 1973–1986

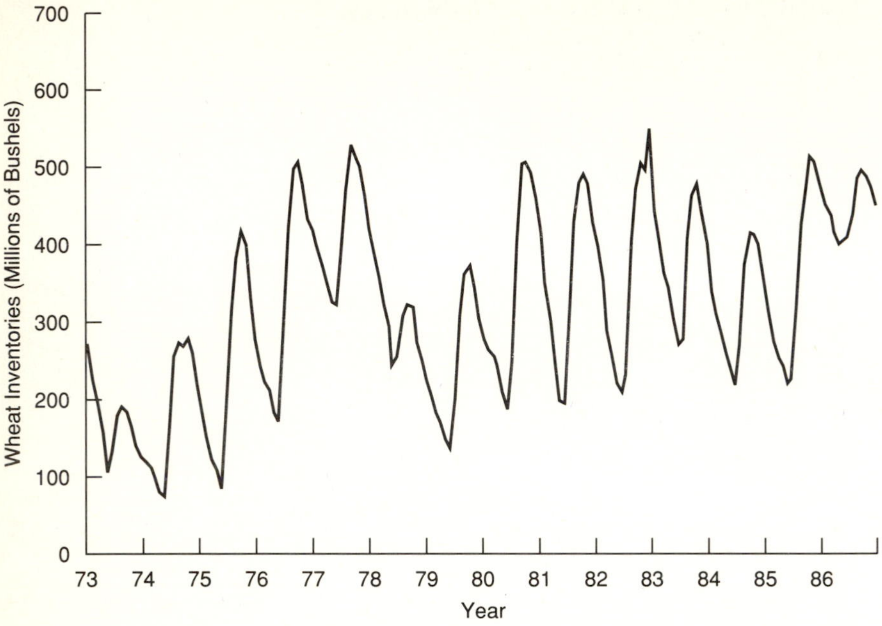

Source: Chicago Board of Trade.

harvesting decisions are not always generally known. Further, demand for grains depends on the general health of the economy. Yet many of the inventory and cash price characteristics of our certainty model still hold in the actual world of uncertainty. In Figure 8.14, we see that actual wheat inventories have followed a pattern very similar to that shown for inventories in the certainty case in Figure 8.13. Actual inventories are lowest during the late spring and early summer, just before the initial harvest of winter wheat. They peak in late summer and early fall as the last major portion of the spring wheat harvest is completed. After that, they decline as consumption outpaces production.

Wheat prices in the real world also behave much like the prices in the certainty case. Figure 8.15 presents a frequency table of the yearly lows (part a) and highs (part b) of wheat prices by month.[24] The lowest prices frequently occur in the summer, during the harvest. The highest prices are more uniformly spread out, although they almost never occur during the harvest. Despite the great uncertainty in the wheat markets, this pattern is similar to that of the certainty case, in which wheat prices reach their lowest levels at harvest time.

[24] Because of the large variability in wheat prices, a plot of actual prices is not very revealing.

Figure 8.15 Lowest and Highest Wheat Prices, Number 2 Winter Wheat, 1883–1985

(a) Month of Lowest Wheat Price

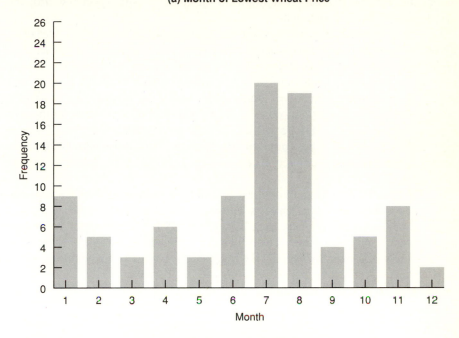

(b) Month of Highest Wheat Price

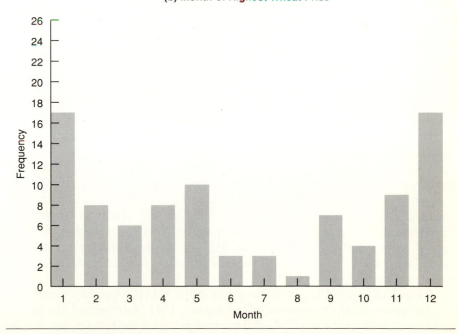

Source: Chicago Board of Trade.

However, the actual wheat market does not completely conform to the patterns of the certainty model. In the real world, there is considerable wheat storage over harvests, which the certainty model does not predict. The certainty model suggests that no one will hold inventories if prices are expected to drop, as they typically do over a harvest.

There are two explanations for the storage we observe over harvests. First, much of the wheat inventory at harvest time is held to comply with U.S. government programs that encourage the accumulation of "surplus" wheat. Second, uncertainty about harvest size prompts wheat users to hold wheat stocks to guarantee themselves continuous access to wheat. For example, millers will suffer significant costs if they must shut down due to temporary wheat shortages. They may be willing to hold precautionary stocks of wheat even if they expect the wheat price to fall. In such cases, those who hold wheat over a harvest receive a convenience value in addition to the expected capital gain (net of storage costs).

This analysis suggests that wheat is usually a pure asset between harvests and a convenience asset over harvests. However, this need not always be the case. Suppose one year there is a very large harvest that cannot be consumed before the next harvest. In order for those who do not receive convenience value to be induced to carry the wheat over the harvest, the marginal convenience value must drop to zero. Wheat will then be a pure asset even over the harvest.

Figure 8.16 shows how these pricing relationships have affected the wheat futures markets. Part a presents total U.S. stocks of wheat for the years 1977 and 1981. In 1976 the wheat crop was exceptionally large, so a significant amount of that crop was carried over through the 1977 harvest. At their lowest point in June 1977, wheat stocks were still at more than 60 percent of the highest point they would reach in September 1977. It is very likely, then, that some of the large wheat inventory held over the harvest of 1977 yielded no convenience value. Thus, we would expect the futures market to have been at full carry even over the 1977 harvest.

Part b of Figure 8.16 shows the relationship among the prices of the March, May, July, September, and December wheat futures contracts at the end of January 1977. As expected, the futures prices rose steadily as the time to expiration increased. This pattern supports our hypothesis that the wheat futures markets was at full carry throughout the year.

Part a of Figure 8.16 shows that wheat inventories behaved in a more normal fashion in 1981. Again stocks reached their lowest point in June, but they were at less than 40 percent of the highest point reached in October. The lower level of inventories held over the 1981 harvest makes us suspect that they were held to receive a convenience value. This suggests that the price spread among futures contracts that expired before and after the harvest should have been consistent with the non-full-carry market characterized by Equation 8.6.

Part c of Figure 8.16 graphs the prices of the March, May, July, September, and December contracts as of the end of January 1981. As expected, the futures price was lower for the contracts that expired just after the harvest than for the

Figure 8.16 Inventory Carryover and Futures Prices

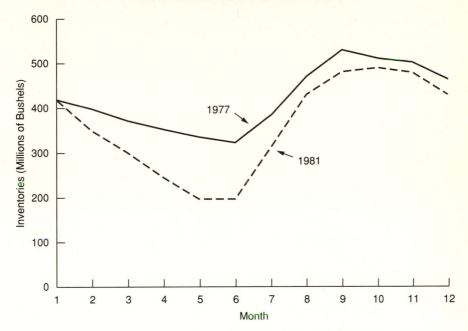

(a) Total U.S. Wheat Inventories, 1977 and 1981

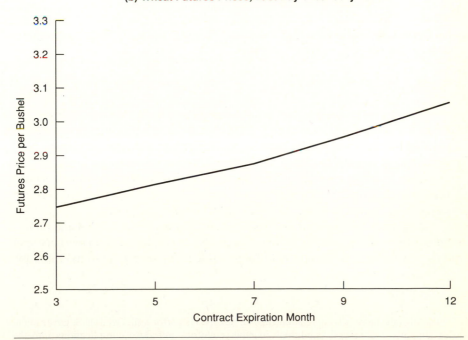

(b) Wheat Futures Prices, Last Day of January 1977

Source: Chicago Board of Trade.

Figure 8.16 (continued)

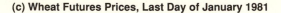

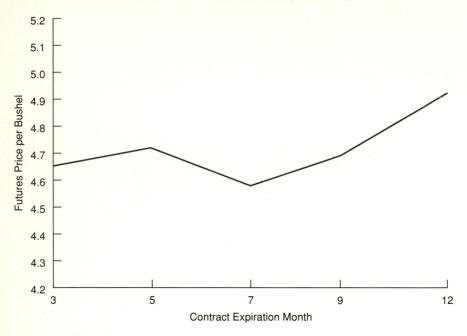

(c) Wheat Futures Prices, Last Day of January 1981

ones that expired just before it. The market returned to full carry for spreads among contracts that expired after the harvest.[25]

Hedging

One of the primary uses of grain futures contracts is to reduce the business risk that results from grain price volatility. Farmers can take short futures positions that will hedge the prices at which they will sell their grain if they adjust for quantity uncertainty, as we demonstrated in Chapter 3. Grain elevator operators can use long futures positions to hedge the prices they pay for grain or short futures positions to hedge the prices they receive for selling grain. Grain processors can also use long futures positions to hedge the cost of buying grain.

In Chapter 3 we learned that basis risk, or the divergence of spot and futures prices, often reduces the effectiveness of futures hedges. In the grain markets, spot prices may behave differently than futures prices for several reasons. First, the

---

[25] Unfortunately, these pricing relationships do not always perform this well. U.S. government price supports and harvest conditions in other countries introduce complications into the observed relationship between inventory levels and wheat futures prices.

grade of grain being hedged may differ from the cheapest grade underlying the futures. Second, the grain may be purchased or sold in a location not specified by the futures contract. Third, the time at which the hedge will be lifted may not be known in advance or may differ from the expiration date of the futures contract. In the first two cases, grain hedges have an asset mismatch; in the third case, they have a maturity mismatch.

Often the basis risk in grain hedges is not severe, because grain prices tend to move together. However, grain hedgers who do face substantial basis risk can eliminate it by using **basis trading** agreements, in which they create contracts that are tied to quoted futures prices. In such arrangements, two parties agree to trade a certain type and grade of grain at a given premium or discount over the price of a particular futures contract. These agreements can then be perfectly hedged with a futures position.

Example 8.9 demonstrates how basis trading affects the basis risk of grain buyers and sellers.

▪ **Example 8.9: Wheat Basis Trading**   Suppose that on May 1, a grain elevator operator wishes to hedge the price she will pay for Number 1 Hard Red Winter wheat in July and the price she will receive when she sells it in November. Assume there is no futures contract with specifications that exactly match her needs. So the elevator operator decides to hedge her purchase and sale prices through basis trading.

She hedges her purchase price by contracting with several wheat farmers to buy 100,000 bushels of Number 1 Hard Red Winter wheat on July 1 at $0.10 below the *current* July futures price of $3.50 per bushel at the Chicago Board of Trade. This contract is a *forward contract* to purchase wheat on July 1 at $3.40 per bushel. It involves the wheat futures market only to establish a forward price. This is a very common type of arrangement between farmers and elevator operators.

Now that the elevator operator has locked in the price of purchasing wheat, her next step is to determine how she will sell the wheat she receives. She enters into a basis trading contract to sell the wheat to a grain processor at a price tied to the futures price when the sale takes place. She agrees to sell her 100,000 bushels to the grain processor at any time the latter chooses between October 17 and October 31 at the then prevailing November Chicago Board of Trade wheat futures price plus $0.05 per bushel.

These positions lock in the elevator operator's wheat costs. But her revenues are still uncertain, for they depend on what the November futures price during the last two weeks of October will be. We will calculate her costs and revenues using the notation on the following time line:

The forward contract between the elevator operator and the farmers locks in a purchase cost on July 1 (date t1) of

Purchase cost
    = (Current July futures price − Discount)(Number of bushels)
    = $(F_{t,T1} − \text{Discount})(\text{Number of bushels})$
    = ($3.50 − $0.10)(100,000)
    = $340,000.

The elevator operator's revenues will be determined by the November futures price on the day the grain processor takes delivery of the wheat. Suppose the grain processor decides to take delivery on date t^*, which is within the contractual sale period between October 17 (t2) and October 31 (t3). The elevator operator's revenues at t^* will be

Revenues
    = (November futures price on t^* + Premium)(Number of bushels)
    = $(F_{t^*,T2} + \text{Premium})(\text{Number of bushels})$
    = $(F_{t^*,T2} + $0.05)(100,000)$
    = $(100,000)(F_{t^*,T2}) + $5,000.$

Now suppose the elevator operator wants to hedge her revenue risk. She does so by going short 100,000 bushels' (20 contracts') worth of November futures at the May 1 futures price of $3.55 per bushel. If the elevator operator closes out her futures positions when she delivers the wheat on date t^*, her hedged revenues will be

Hedged revenues
    = Revenues + Futures profit
    = $(100,000)(F_{t^*,T2}) + $5,000 + (100,000)(F_{t,T2} − F_{t^*,T2})$
    = $(100,000)(F_{t,T2}) + $5,000$
    = (100,000)($3.55) + $5,000
    = $360,000.

By taking the short futures position, the elevator operator has locked in a gross profit of $20,000 ($360,000 − $340,000). She is still exposed to some residual risk, for the rate of return produced by the $20,000 gross profit will depend on when the grain processor takes delivery. A late delivery date will raise the elevator operator's storage costs and postpone her receipt of the gross profit. Thus, her rate of return will be lower the later the delivery date.

Suppose storage costs $0.10 per bushel per year. If the grain processor takes delivery on October 17, the elevator operator must pay storage for 108 days. Her rate of return from her $20,000 gross profit will be[26]

---

[26] As always, we use the 360-day year convention when computing short-term rates of return.

$$\text{Rate of return} = \frac{\text{Gross profit} - \text{Storage}}{\text{Initial cost}}$$

$$= \frac{\$20,000 - (\$0.10)(100,000)(108/360)}{\$340,000}$$

$$= \frac{\$20,000 - \$3,000}{\$340,000}$$

$$= 5.00\% \text{ for } 108 \text{ days}$$

$$= 16.67\% \text{ annually.}$$

Now suppose the grain processor takes delivery of the wheat on October 28. The elevator operator must pay storage for 119 days. Her rate of return will be

$$\text{Rate of return} = \frac{\text{Gross profit} - \text{Storage}}{\text{Initial cost}}$$

$$= \frac{\$20,000 - (\$0.10)(100,000)(119/360)}{\$340,000}$$

$$= \frac{\$20,000 - \$3,306}{\$340,000}$$

$$= 4.91\% \text{ for } 119 \text{ days}$$

$$= 14.85\% \text{ annually.}$$

Clearly, the elevator operator will not do as well if the delivery date is late. The risk to revenues due to uncertainty over the delivery date cannot be eliminated unless the elevator operator negotiates a premium over the futures price that increases if delivery is delayed.

What market forces determine the premiums and discounts used in basis trading arrangements? Suppose the elevator operator faces an interest rate of 10 percent per year. In that case, the returns earned by the elevator operator (and presumably others) in the wheat market will produce excess profits. Competition for these profits will drive $F_{t,T2}$ down until the spread between $F_{t,T1}$ and $F_{t,T2}$ and the premia and discounts negotiated by grain elevator operators yield a normal return. ■

Soybean Product Futures

The preceding section listed the specifications of the raw soybean futures contract. In this section, we will study the futures contracts written on the oil and meal produced from soybeans.

Cash and Futures Markets

Virtually all soybeans are processed to yield soybean oil and soybean meal. Soybean oil is used to produce cooking oil, margarine, and other vegetable-fat

Figure 8.17 CBOT Soybean Oil and Meal Futures Annual Volume, 1983–1989

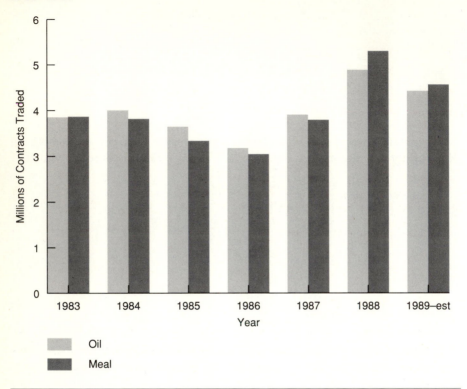

Source: Futures Industry Association.

products. Soybean meal is used as a protein supplement for poultry and livestock and as a component of some nonfood products. The processing of soybeans is called **crushing**.

The Chicago Board of Trade offers futures contracts on soybean meal and soybean oil. Figure 8.17 shows the annual trading volume of the soybean oil and soybean meal contracts from 1983 through 1989. The specifications for these futures contracts are as follows:

Soybean Oil Contract Specifications

Contract:	Soybean oil
Exchange:	Chicago Board of Trade
Quantity:	60,000 pounds
Delivery months:	January, March, May, July, August, September, October, December
Delivery specifications:	Crude soybean oil, deliverable by registered warehouse receipts
Minimum price movement:	$0.0001 per pound, or $6.00 per contract

Soybean Meal Contract Specifications

Contract:	Soybean meal
Exchange:	Chicago Board of Trade
Quantity:	100 tons
Delivery months:	January, March, May, July, August, September, October, December
Delivery specifications:	Minimum protein of 44 percent, deliverable by approved shipping certificates
Minimum price movement:	$0.10 per ton, or $10.00 per contract

Producers and users of soybean oil and meal use these futures contracts to hedge the prices they pay and receive for these products. Producers of oil and meal often hedge both the prices they pay for the raw soybeans and the prices they receive for the oil and meal. This allows them to lock in their **gross processing margins**. This type of hedge is called a **crush spread** and is very similar to the petroleum crack spread hedges we studied earlier.

Crush Spread   Soybean gross processing margins depend on the price of soybeans, the amount of oil and meal produced by each bushel of raw soybeans, and the prices of the soybean products. Typically, each 60-pound bushel of soybeans yields 11 pounds of oil, 48 pounds of meal, and 1 pound of hulls and waste. These ratios may change slightly from year to year as soybean quality varies, but in this discussion we will assume they are fixed.

The prices of soybean oil and meal are quoted in terms of pounds and tons, respectively. We must convert them to prices per bushel to compute the revenue earned on each bushel of soybeans. Therefore, the oil revenue per bushel of raw soybeans is

Per bushel revenue from oil
= (Number of pounds per bushel)(Price per pound)
= (11)(Price per pound of oil).

The 48 pounds of soybean meal produced by a bushel of soybeans is equal to 2.4 percent of a ton. Therefore, the meal revenue per bushel of raw soybeans is

Per bushel revenue from meal
= (Number of tons per bushel)(Price per ton)
= (0.024)(Price per ton of meal).

We can now compute the gross processing margin for a bushel of soybeans:

Gross processing margin per bushel
= Per-bushel revenue from oil + Per-bushel revenue from meal
  − Per-bushel cost of raw soybeans
= (11)(Price per pound of oil) + (0.024)(Price per ton of meal)
  − Per-bushel price of raw soybeans.

Soybean crushing takes several weeks, so the gross processing margin is determined by the prices for oil and meal at the end of the crush (T2) and of raw soybeans at the beginning of the crush (T1), as shown in the following time line:

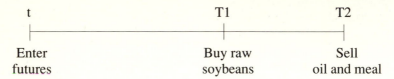

t	T1	T2
Enter futures	Buy raw soybeans	Sell oil and meal

Thus, we can write the gross processing margin formula as

Gross processing margin per bushel   (8.13)
$$= (11)(P_{T2}^o) + (0.024)(P_{T2}^m) - P_{T1}^b$$

where superscripts o, m, and, b refer to oil, meal, and beans, respectively.

The soybean gross processing margin generally is stable, because the soybean price tends to move with the oil and meal prices. Nevertheless, a soybean processor can face significant risk, because the soybeans are purchased before the oil and meal are sold and the relationship among the three prices can experience short-term fluctuations. If, for example, there is an unexpected drop in the price of oil and meal between T1 and T2, the gross processing margin will suffer.

A soybean processor can lock in a gross processing margin by using futures to lock in each of the three prices in Equation 8.13. Since the processor plans to purchase raw beans, he or she will go long soybean futures that expire at time T1. Also, because the processor plans to sell oil and meal, he or she will go short soybean oil and soybean meal futures that expire at T2.

The appropriate ratios for such a hedge depend on the yields of oil and meal from raw soybeans and the specifications of the three futures contracts. Each soybean futures contract covers 5,000 bushels of soybeans. These 5,000 bushels will produce 55,000 pounds of soybean oil:

Pounds of oil per soybean contract
    = (5,000 bushels of soybeans)(11 pounds of oil per bushel)
    = 55,000 pounds.

Since each soybean oil futures contract covers 60,000 pounds of oil, the oil production from the 5,000 bushels of soybeans covered by one soybean contract represents $55/60$, or $110/120$, oil contracts.

The 5,000 bushels of soybeans covered by one soybean futures contract will also produce 120 tons of soybean meal:

Tons of meal per soybean contract
    = (5,000 bushels of soybeans)(48 pounds of meal per bushel)
    = 240,000 pounds
    = 120 tons.

Since each meal futures contract represents 100 tons, the meal produced by 5,000 bushels of soybeans represents $120/100$, or $144/120$ meal contracts.

Thus, for every 120 soybean contracts a processor goes long, he or she must go short 110 oil contracts and 144 meal contracts to hedge the gross processing margin. Such a combination of futures positions is a crush spread hedge. If the processor enters into these positions at time t, his or her hedged gross processing margin per 5,000 bushels will be

$$
\begin{aligned}
\text{Hedged gross processing margin per 5,000 bushels} \qquad & \textbf{(8.14)} \\
= (5,000 \text{ bushels})(\text{Gross processing margin per bushel}) & \\
+ \text{Futures profits} & \\
= (5,000)[(11)(P^o_{T2}) + (0.024)(P^m_{T2}) - (P^b_{T1})] & \\
+ (110/120)(60,000)(F^o_{t,T2} - F^o_{T2,T2}) & \\
+ (144/120)(100)(F^m_{t,T2} - F^m_{T2,T2}) & \\
+ (5,000)(F^b_{T1,T1} - F^b_{t,T1}) & \\
= (5,000)[(11)(F^o_{t,T2}) + (0.024)(F^m_{t,T2}) - F^b_{t,T1}]. &
\end{aligned}
$$

The final step in Equation 8.14 comes from the delivery date convergence of the spot and futures prices of soybeans at time T1 and of the spot and futures prices of oil and meal at time T2. Thus, a crush spread allows processors to lock in the gross processing margins implied by the futures prices at time t.

Example 8.10 demonstrates the use of the crush spread.

▪ **Example 8.10: A Crush Spread**   Suppose that on October 12, 1988, a soybean processor is planning to buy 600,000 bushels of soybeans on November 30 and complete the crush on December 30. He decides to use futures to hedge the gross processing margin he will earn. Current futures prices on October 12 are as given in Figure 8.12. The time line for his planned transactions is

To hedge his margin, the processor takes on the crush spread position we calculated earlier. He goes long 120 soybean futures contracts and goes short 110 oil contracts and 144 meal contracts.

Table 8.9 shows how this crush spread locks in the processor's gross processing margin. It presents the processor's hedged revenues and the revenues he would have earned from an unhedged position under four different scenarios for the spot prices of beans, oil, and meal.

Under scenario I, the revenues from soybean oil and meal and the cost of soybeans are as follows:

Oil revenues
= (Number of bushels)(Pounds per bushel)(Price per pound)
= (600,000)(11)($0.23)
= $1,518,000.

Table 8.9 Crush Spread, 600,000 Bushels of Soybeans, October 12, 1988

	Futures Price	Number of Contracts
November soybean futures	$ 7.9025 per bushel	120 long
December soybean oil futures	$ 0.2409 per pound	110 short
December soybean meal futures	$254.8000 per ton	144 short

	Scenarios			
	I	II	III	IV
Soybean spot price	$ 8.0000	$ 8.7000	$ 6.0000	$ 10.0000
Oil spot price	0.2300	0.3000	0.2000	0.3300
Meal spot price	225.0000	260.0000	225.0000	240.0000
Spot Transactions				
Oil revenue	$1,518,000	$1,980,000	$1,320,000	$2,178,000
Meal revenue	3,240,000	3,744,000	3,240,000	3,456,000
Beans cost	4,800,000	5,220,000	3,600,000	6,000,000
Gross profit	$ –42,000	$ 504,000	$ 960,000	$ –366,000
Per bushel	–0.07	0.84	1.60	–0.61
Futures Transactions				
Oil profit	$ 71,940	$ –390,060	$ 269,940	$ –588,060
Meal profit	429,120	–74,880	429,120	213,120
Beans profit	58,500	478,500	–1,141,500	1,258,500
Futures profit	$ 559,560	$ 13,560	$ –442,440	$ 883,560
Per bushel	0.93	0.02	–0.74	1.47
Net				
Total profit	$ 517,560	$ 517,560	$ 517,560	$ 517,560
Per bushel	0.86	0.86	0.86	0.86

Meal revenues
=   (Number of bushels)(Tons per bushel)(Price per ton)
=   (600,000)(0.024)($225.00)
= $3,240,000.

Soybean costs
=   (Number of bushels)(Price per bushel)
=   (600,000)($8.00)
= $4,800,000.

If the processor does not hedge, his gross processing margin will be

Gross processing margin
$$= \text{Revenues} - \text{Costs}$$
$$= \$1,518,000 + \$3,240,000 - \$4,800,000$$
$$= -\$42,000$$
$$= -\$0.07 \text{ per bushel.}$$

The unhedged gross processing margin is negative, because the prices of oil and meal are low relative to the price of soybeans. However, because the processor has chosen to hedge, his profits on the crush spread will exceed the gross processing loss and his hedged margin (from Equation 8.14) will be

Hedged gross processing margin
$$= (600,000)[(11)(F^o_{t,T2}) + (0.024)(F^m_{t,T2}) - F^b_{t,T1}]$$
$$= (600,000)[(11)(\$0.2409) + (0.024)(\$254.80) - \$7.9025]$$
$$= \$517,560$$
$$= \$0.86 \text{ per bushel.}$$

The unhedged gross processing profits vary considerably under the other three scenarios. But with the hedged position, the soybean processor earns the same profit in every case. ∎

Now suppose a speculator observes the crush spread in Example 8.10 and determines that it is too low given historical levels of the gross processing margin. This speculator might enter into a **reverse crush spread**, which involves a short position in soybeans and a long position in oil and meal. Just as the crush spread makes money if the gross processing margin decreases, the reverse crush spread makes money if the margin increases. The speculator will profit if the hunch about the spread is correct.

Livestock Futures

Another major group of agricultural futures contracts are those written on livestock and livestock products. The most important livestock contracts are those written on young cattle (the **feeder cattle** contract), cattle and hogs of slaughter age and weight (the **live cattle** and **live hogs** contracts), and frozen bacon (the **pork bellies** contract). All these contracts trade on the Chicago Mercantile Exchange.

The livestock contracts differ from the grain contracts in that their underlying assets are **transformable** commodities—commodities that grow and change over time. With contracts on soybeans, corn, wheat, and oats, one can buy the commodity grade that is deliverable today and hold it to deliver in the future. For example, if one buys 5,000 bushels of soybeans on January 1, the same soybeans can be delivered six months later into the July futures contract. But cattle that are of deliverable grade on January 1 will grow over the six months until July and therefore will not have the right specifications for delivery at that time. If one wishes to purchase cattle in January to deliver into the July futures contract, one must select cattle that are much younger and much lighter than the contract requires. Over time, the cattle will transform into the deliverable grade.

Figure 8.18 Cattle Growth Path: Weight versus Time

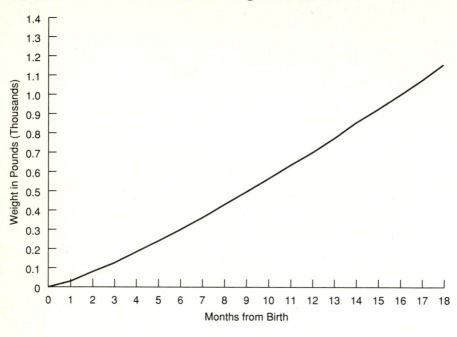

Livestock futures are very similar to T-bill futures in this respect. T-bill futures accept delivery of bills with only three months to maturity. Thus, to buy a T-bill that will be deliverable into a contract that expires in 60 days, one must select a bill with 151 days to maturity. After 60 days, this bill will have 91 days left to maturity and therefore will meet the delivery requirement.

Cash Market

The structure of livestock futures prices is greatly affected by the time required for cattle and hogs to grow to deliverable grade and by the costs of growing them. The following time line and the growth curve in Figure 8.18 depict the growth of beef calves to slaughter weight:[27]

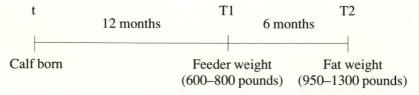

[27] See Chicago Board of Trade, *Commodity Trading Manual* (1985) for a further discussion of the beef market.

Figure 8.19 Cattle Slaughter, Total U.S. Commercial, 1983 and 1985

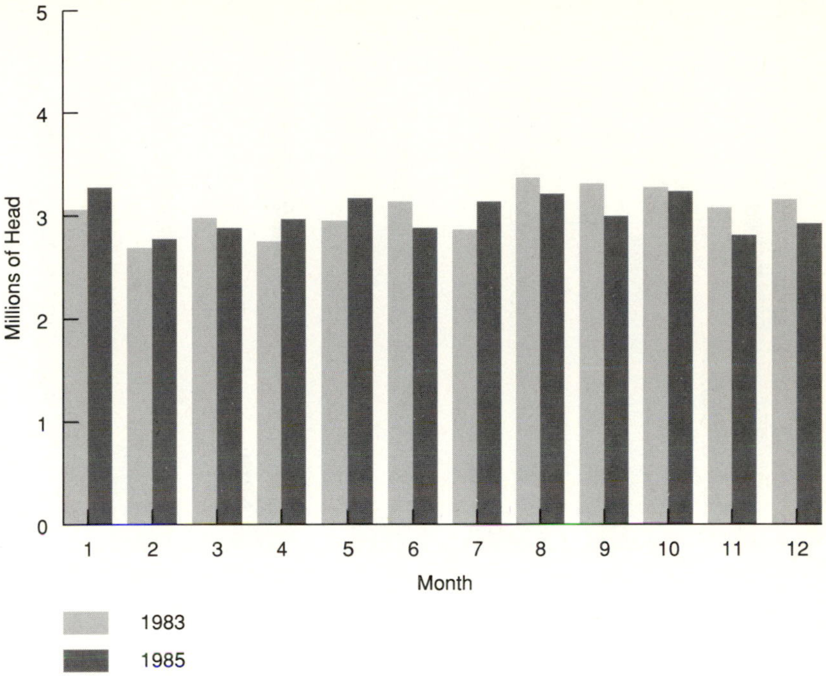

Source: Chicago Mercantile Exchange.

Feeder cattle are roughly one year old and usually below optimal slaughter weight. It takes them another six to nine months to grow to slaughter weight. At this point, they are called **fat cattle**. The growth of **feeder hogs** to slaughter-weight **market hogs** usually takes five to six months. The cost of feeding and otherwise maintaining livestock of different weights determines the overall non-interest-carrying costs of storing livestock. For example, suppose a rancher purchases a 10-month-old head of cattle and wishes to hold it until it reaches fat weight. Figure 8.18 shows that the 10-month-old head weighs about 560 pounds. The cost to the rancher of holding the head is the cost of adding about another 600 pounds to it over an eight-month period.

Convenience Values   Earlier, we saw that the futures market will be at full carry only if some of the underlying commodity in storage does not provide convenience value. In the grain markets, the seasonality of grain harvests creates times of the year when grain prices fall and grain is stored only by those receiving a convenience value. But modern breeding techniques have eliminated much of the production seasonality for livestock.

Figure 8.19 graphs the number of head of U.S. commercial cattle slaughtered by month in 1983 and 1985. Clearly the breeding and slaughter of cattle are spread

Figure 8.20 CME Livestock Futures Annual Volume, 1983–1989

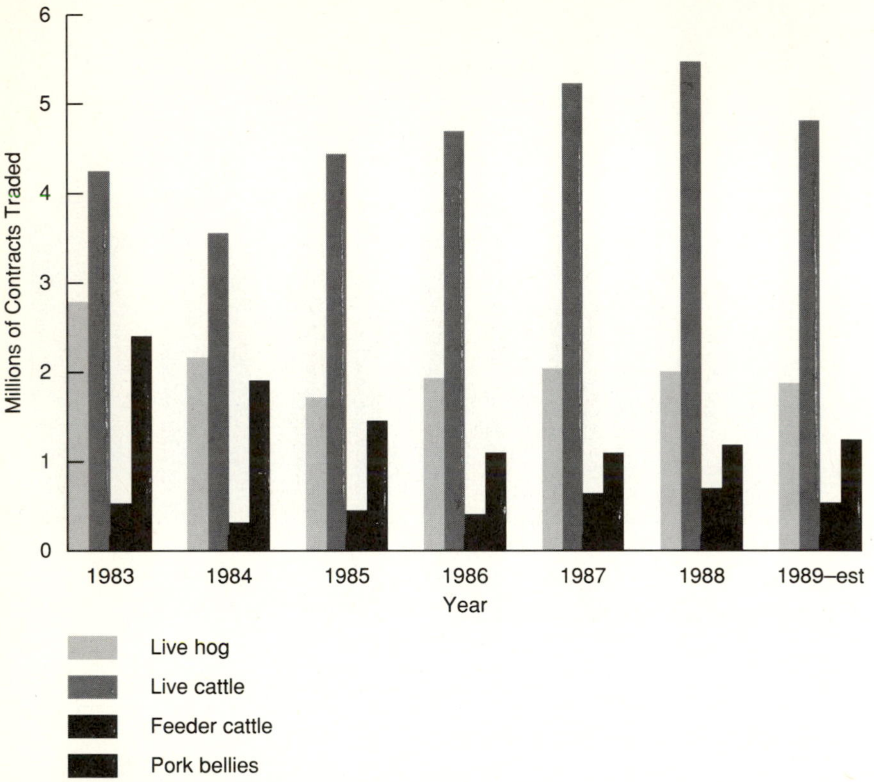

Source: Futures Industry Association.

quite evenly over the year. Hogs also are also slaughtered at a fairly even rate over the year. Therefore, we can safely assume that livestock holdings always include some inventory that receives no convenience value. The livestock futures markets should always be at full carry.

Futures Market

Figure 8.20 graphs the annual trading volume of the four major livestock futures contracts in the years 1983 through 1989.[28] Figure 8.21 presents the prices of the CME futures contracts on October 12, 1988.

The specifications of these contracts are as follows:

[28] See Leuthold [1983] for a general discussion of the uses of the livestock futures markets.

Figure 8.21 Livestock Futures Transactions Prices for October 12, 1988

```
                                        Lifetime      Open
              Open  High  Low Settle Change  High Low Interest
   CATTLE-FEEDER (CME) 44,000 lbs.; cents per lb.
Oct     81.70 81.90 81.50 81.75 +  .20 82.90 69.70  2,501
Nov     82.50 83.20 82.40 83.10 +  .72 84.05 70.25  5,623
Ja89    84.00 84.50 83.90 84.45 +  .57 84.55 74.00  4,702
Mar     82.85 83.40 82.80 83.40 +  .50 83.60 74.00  3,596
Apr     82.00 82.35 82.00 82.35 +  .30 82.45 74.40    945
May     80.85 81.20 80.70 81.20 +  .30 81.25 60.00    511
Aug     79.95 80.00 79.90 80.00 +  .10 80.00 78.50    184
   Est vol 2,023; vol Tues 2,418; open int 18,062, +29.
   CATTLE-LIVE (CME) 40,000 lbs.; cents per lb.
Oct     72.30 72.75 72.25 72.60 +  .25 73.47 58.65  6,762
Dec     74.30 75.30 74.20 75.25 +  .97 75.30 60.25 35,597
Fb89    74.00 74.95 73.85 74.92 + 1.02 74.95 65.10 22,415
Apr     75.00 75.85 74.85 75.80 +  .85 76.00 67.20 10,567
June    73.90 74.70 73.85 74.65 +  .70 75.20 68.75  3,559
Aug     71.50 72.25 71.50 72.20 +  .70 73.20 69.70  1,727
Oct     71.35 71.50 71.30 71.45 +  .70 74.00 69.50    564
   Est vol 18,432; vol Tues 22,693; open int 81,198, +1,492.
   HOGS (CME) 30,000 lbs.; cents per lb.
Oct     40.10 40.45 39.95 40.30 +  .10 46.40 37.40  1,713
Dec     41.55 42.25 41.52 42.07 +  .30 48.50 38.30 14,152
Fb89    45.42 45.85 45.20 45.57 +  .02 52.00 41.80  6,856
Apr     43.95 44.40 43.80 44.15 +  .10 51.65 40.60  4,487
June    48.40 48.65 48.10 48.40  ....  56.25 42.50  1,261
July    48.55 48.90 48.55 48.55 -  .22 56.00 47.07  1,004
Aug     47.60 48.15 47.60 47.85 +  .05 51.00 45.97    150
Oct     44.50 44.95 44.50 44.55  ....  47.00 43.50    107
   Est vol 5,290; vol Tues 6,663; open int 29,730, +1,068.
   PORK BELLIES (CME) 40,000 lbs.; cents per lb.
Feb     47.95 48.40 47.55 48.05 +  .05 67.00 46.40  8,320
Mar     48.55 48.95 48.15 48.65 +  .10 66.35 46.75  2,792
May     49.90 50.40 49.70 50.12 +  .15 65.50 48.50  2,217
July    50.90 51.45 50.70 50.92 +  .17 64.50 49.35  1,957
Aug     49.80 50.30 49.40 49.40 +  .10 58.25 47.00    229
   Est vol 3,409; vol Tues 2,199; open int 15,515, +44.
```

Source: *The Wall Street Journal,* October 13, 1988.

Feeder Cattle Contract Specifications

Contract:	Feeder cattle
Exchange:	Chicago Mercantile Exchange
Quantity:	44,000 pounds
Delivery months:	January, March, April, May, August, September, October, November
Delivery specifications:	Cash settlement against the Seven-Day Cattle-Fax U.S. Feeder Steer Price per pound for 600–800 pounds per steer
Minimum price movement:	$0.00025 per pound, or $11.00 per contract

Live Cattle Contract Specifications

Contract:	Live cattle
Exchange:	Chicago Mercantile Exchange
Quantity:	40,000 pounds
Delivery months:	February, April, June, July, August, October, December
Delivery specifications:	Delivery of USDA Livestock Acceptance Certificate; par grade is number 1, 2, 3, or 4 Choice live steers, averaging between 1,050 and 1,200 pounds; detailed requirements and alternative grades are dictated by the exchange rules
Minimum price movement:	$0.00025 per pound, or $10.00 per contract

Live Hogs Contract Specifications

Contract:	Live hogs
Exchange:	Chicago Mercantile Exchange
Quantity:	30,000 pounds
Delivery months:	February, April, June, July, August, October, December
Delivery specifications:	Delivery of USDA Livestock Acceptance Certificate; par grade is number 1, 2, or 3 barrows and gilts, between 210 and 240 pounds; detailed requirements and alternative grades are dictated by the exchange rules
Minimum price movement:	$0.00025 per pound, or $7.50 per contract

Pork Bellies Contract Specifications

Contract:	Frozen pork bellies
Exchange:	Chicago Mercantile Exchange
Quantity:	40,000 pounds
Delivery months:	February, March, May, July, August
Delivery specifications:	Delivery of Green Square–Cut Clear Seedless Bellies with a USDA Meat Inspection Division Inspection legend; standard grade and differentials established by the exchange
Minimum price movement:	$0.00025 per pound, or $10.00 per contract

The feeder cattle contract is a cash settlement contract. Contracts still open at the end of trading are settled by the average Seven-Day Cattle-Fax U.S. Feeder Steer Price for 600-to-800-pound steers, an index that averages the prices from various auctions held throughout the country over the previous seven days. This price index is applied to the 44,000-pound quantity specified by the futures contract to determine the contract's settlement value.

The live cattle contract is a delivery contract. It calls for delivery of a USDA Livestock Acceptance Certificate that gives title to cattle with specified location, number of head, net weight, quality grade, and estimated yield grade.[29] The par delivery is for 40,000 pounds of live steers of Choice grade 1, 2, 3, or 4 and an average weight of between 1,050 and 1,200 pounds. But a variety of discounts can be applied to the price for delivery of cattle that deviate, within limits, from this standard.

The live hog contract calls for delivery of a USDA Livestock Acceptance Certificate that grants title to market hogs. The par delivery is for 30,000 pounds of hogs (barrows and gilts) that are of grade 1, 2, or 3 and weigh between 210 and 240 pounds. The live hog contract also includes discounts for delivery of nonpar hogs.

The pork bellies contract is also a delivery contract. It requires a warehouse receipt for frozen bellies held in cold storage warehouses that are approved by the exchange.

Fundamental No-Arbitrage Equation

The fundamental no-arbitrage equation for transformable commodities such as livestock is

---

[29] See Purcell and Hudson [1986] for a discussion of the certificate system for live cattle.

$$F_{t,T} = P_t(1 + r_{t,T}) + SC_{t,T}. \tag{8.15}$$

Because livestock purchased at t will grow in size between t and T, P_t is the price of livestock that will grow to become deliverable at T and $F_{t,T}$ is the futures price of the deliverable grade. By convention, spot and futures prices are quoted on a per-pound basis. However, since livestock grow over time, the spot price in the no-arbitrage relationship must apply to livestock of a lower weight than the futures price does. When we calculate the no-arbitrage futures price, we must be sure that the spot and futures prices refer to livestock of the appropriate weights. Therefore, we will use prices per head of livestock to compute the relationship and will convert them back to a per-pound basis later.

The term $SC_{t,T}$ is the future value at time T of all the noninterest costs incurred while transforming the commodity into the deliverable grade between t and T. With T-bill futures, the costs of holding the bills until they become deliverable are negligible. However, the costs of transforming livestock into deliverable grade are substantial, as they include the costs of feeding and holding the livestock between t and T. These costs are driven primarily by feed, labor, yardage, and veterinary expenses. Example 8.11 shows how these costs affect the no-arbitrage price of the live cattle contract.

▪ **Example 8.11: The Fundamental No-Arbitrage Price for Live Cattle**
Suppose we wish to compute the no-arbitrage futures price on May 15 for the August live cattle futures contract. Because the contract's deliverable grade is a steer roughly 18 months of age, the spot price that will determine the no-arbitrage futures price on May 15 is that of a 15-month old steer. By August, this steer will be deliverable into the futures contract.

Figure 8.18 shows that a 15-month steer weighs approximately 920 pounds and an 18-month old steer approximately 1,150 pounds. Suppose the current per-pound price of a 15-month-old steer is $0.75. Then the price of a 15-month-old steer, P_t, will be

   P_t = (Pounds per steer)(Price per pound)
      = (920)($0.75)
      = $690.00.

Next, we must compute the two components of the cost of carry. Suppose interest carrying costs are 8 percent per year and noninterest carrying costs are the costs of bringing a 920-pound steer up to 1,150 pounds. Also, suppose the future value at time T of the noninterest costs is $0.50 per pound gained. Then the total future value of noninterest carrying costs is

   Future value of noninterest carrying costs
      = (Pounds of gain)(Cost per pound of gain)
      = (230)($0.50)
      = $115.00.

The no-arbitrage price for a delivered 18-month-old live steer in August is therefore

$$F_{t,T} = \$690(1.02) + \$115.00$$
$$= \$818.80$$
$$= \$0.7120 \text{ per pound.}$$

The price per pound of the spot cattle is higher than the futures price even though there are positive carrying costs. This is because the futures price applies to a steer of roughly 1,150 pounds while the spot price applies to a steer of only about 920 pounds.

To determine the number of head of cattle we must purchase at time t for delivery at T, we simply take the total number of pounds to be delivered at time T and divide by the weight per head of cattle at time T. Thus, at time t we must purchase

$$\text{Number of head per contract} = \frac{40,000 \text{ pounds/contract}}{1,150 \text{ pounds/head}}$$
$$= 34.78 \text{ head/contract.}$$

The total weight of the cattle purchased at time t is therefore

$$\text{Pounds of steer purchased at } t = (\text{Pounds per head at } t)(\text{Number of head})$$
$$= (920)(34.78)$$
$$= 31,997.60 \text{ pounds.}$$

■

As we discussed earlier, the cattle and hog markets are likely to be at full carry because some of the livestock in inventory probably will receive no convenience value. Due to the high costs of transacting in these markets, most livestock arbitrage is likely to be quasi-arbitrage. If the futures price is too high relative to the spot, farmers and ranchers will add to their stocks or refrain from selling from them. If the futures price is too low relative to the spot, they will sell off some of their stocks or refrain from purchasing new livestock. These actions will enforce the fundamental no-arbitrage price.[30]

Spreads   Because feeder cattle turn into live cattle in about six months, the feeder cattle futures price and the price of the live cattle futures contract that expires six months later have the following no-arbitrage relationship:

---

[30] Another pricing issue, which has generated considerable debate, is how well the live cattle futures price predicts the future spot price. See Leuthold [1974], Helmuth [1981], Palm and Graham [1981], Kolb and Gay [1983], and Koppenhaver [1983].

$$F_{t,T2}^{l} = F_{t,T1}^{f}(1 + r_{T1,T2}) + SC_{T1,T2}, \tag{8.16}$$

where T1 is the expiration date of the feeder futures contract and T2 = T1 + 6 months. Superscripts f and l refer to feeder and live cattle, respectively, and, as before, the futures prices apply to one head of cattle. The holding costs are those incurred as feeder cattle grow into live cattle.

This relationship must hold because one can transform feeder cattle at T1 into live cattle at T2 simply by letting them grow. Forward cash-and-carry and reverse cash-and-carry strategies therefore are feasible between T1 and T2. Since the growing process takes six months, this spread between the feeder and live cattle futures prices can hold only for T2 − T1 = 6 months.

Equation 8.16 suggests that the feeder–live cattle futures price spread is driven largely by the costs of feeding the cattle between T1 and T2. Example 8.12 tests this theory by comparing the cattle spreads and feed costs in two recent years.

▪ **Example 8.12:   Cattle Spreads and Feed Costs**   Suppose we wish to see whether the futures price spread between the October feeder cattle contract and the following April live cattle contract conformed to the no-arbitrage equation, 8.16, in August 1985 and 1988. The following futures prices prevailed on August 19 of 1985 and 1988:

	1985	1988
October feeder futures (per pound)	$0.6195	$0.8157
April live cattle futures, following year (per pound)	0.5925	0.7497
December corn futures (per bushel)	2.2375	2.9575
March corn futures, following year (per bushel)	2.3175	2.9975

Following Figure 8.18, we will assume feeder cattle are 700 pounds and live cattle are 1,150 pounds. Then the prices of buying one head of feeder cattle using the 1985 and 1988 October futures contracts were

1985 head of feeder cattle = ($0.6195)(700) = $433.65
1988 head of feeder cattle = ($0.8157)(700) = $570.99.

The prices received for delivering one head of live cattle six months later with the following years' April futures contracts were

1986 head of live cattle = ($0.5925)(1,150) = $681.38
1989 head of live cattle = ($0.7497)(1,150) = $862.16.

These live cattle prices were the locked-in prices of selling the heads of feeder cattle purchased at locked-in prices six months earlier. As discussed earlier, the differential between the futures prices of feeder cattle and live cattle should reflect six months' carrying costs. Interest rates were roughly 8 percent in both 1985 and 1988. Thus, the interest carrying costs were

1985 interest carrying costs = (0.04)($433.65) = $17.35
1988 interest carrying costs = (0.04)($570.99) = $22.84.

Assuming the fundamental no-arbitrage equation held in both cases, the future values of the six months' noninterest carrying costs were

$$1985 \text{ noninterest carrying costs} = \$681.38 - \$17.35 - \$433.65$$
$$= \$230.38$$
$$= \$0.51 \text{ per pound weight gain}$$

$$1988 \text{ noninterest carrying costs} = \$862.16 - \$22.84 - \$570.99$$
$$= \$268.33$$
$$= \$0.60 \text{ per pound weight gain.}$$

The noninterest carrying costs apparently were higher in 1988 than in 1985. Probably this was due in part to the higher cost of feed in 1988. Corn futures prices were significantly higher in 1988 than in 1985. While the corn futures price does not represent cattle feed grade, the feed grade price moves closely with the price of the deliverable grade for the futures contract. Thus, the futures prices for live cattle and feeder cattle seem to have reflected carrying costs, as our theory predicts.

As another confirmation of our theory, we can look at the costs of carrying feeders and transforming them into fat cattle published by the U.S. Department of Agriculture. For the six months between July 1988 and January 1989, the USDA estimate was \$0.61 per pound of weight gain. This is extremely close to our estimate.

In order to trade on the feeder cattle–live cattle spread, we must calculate the appropriate hedge ratio. In Example 8.11, we saw that each live cattle futures contract represents about 34.78 head of cattle. At the feeder stage, these head of cattle will weigh approximately

Weight of feeder cattle
= (Pounds per head of feeder cattle)(Number of head)
= (700)(34.78)
= 24,346 pounds.

This represents $24,346/44,000 = 0.5533$ feeder cattle futures contracts. Thus, if we wish to perform a forward cash-and-carry strategy between feeder cattle and live cattle futures contracts, we need roughly 55 long feeder cattle contracts for every 100 short live cattle contracts. ∎

Hedging

As with other futures contracts, livestock futures are used extensively for hedging. Livestock growers may wish to hedge the values of their livestock with a short inventory hedge. Growers who purchase feeder cattle or hogs and sell mature cattle or hogs may wish to hedge their margins. Livestock purchasers (who have fixed contracts to sell the processed meat) may wish to hedge their costs with a long anticipatory hedge.[31]

---

[31] See Leuthold and Mokler [1979] and Kenyon and Clay [1987] for a discussion of hedging margins for hog and cattle growers. See Hayenga and DiPietre [1982] and Miller and Luke [1982] for a discussion of hedging wholesale meat prices.

Summary

This chapter covered the pricing and uses of the metals, petroleum, and agricultural futures markets. The pricing relationships in these markets depend on whether the underlying assets of the futures contracts are pure or convenience assets. If the underlying asset is a pure asset, the futures market will be at full carry. If the underlying asset is held only by those who derive some convenience value, the futures market will be at less than full carry. The seasonal pattern of production and consumption in the petroleum and agricultural markets is one of the primary factors determining whether the underlying asset is a pure or convenience asset.

The commodity futures contracts are used largely for hedging. Hedging in the metals markets is similar to that in other markets, but the petroleum and agricultural futures markets employ some unique hedging strategies. The technique of crack spread hedging allows petroleum refiners to lock in their gross refining margins. The NYMEX Exchange of Futures for Physicals facility allows hedgers to lock in futures prices even for crude or petroleum product grades that differ from those underlying the futures contracts. Grain hedgers can eliminate their basis risk by using basis trading agreements that are tied to futures prices. Soybean processors can use crush spread hedges to lock in their gross processing margins. Finally, both hedging and arbitrage strategies that employ livestock futures must account for the fact that the underlying livestock commodities grow and change over time.

Problems

1. Suppose the current spot price of copper is $1.20 per pound. Copper storage is $0.02 per pound per month, and the borrowing and lending rates are 12 percent per annum.
    a. If the futures price for delivery of copper in three months is $1.25 per pound, is copper a pure asset? (Assume the market is in equilibrium.)
    b. Suppose the marginal convenience value for copper is $0.01 per pound per month and the futures price is again $1.25 per pound. Demonstrate a quasi-arbitrage strategy that will earn a profit.
    c. Suppose the marginal convenience value is $0.03 per pound per month and the futures price is again $1.25 per pound. Demonstrate a quasi-arbitrage strategy that will be profitable.

2. Would you more likely expect to see the crude oil futures market at full carry following a rapid increase or a rapid decrease in price?

3. Consider the platinum futures prices in Figure 8.2 assuming a short-term interest rate of 8 percent (ignore storage costs).
    a. What is the implied forward repo rate between April and July 1989? Why is it so much lower than the short-term interest rate?
    b. What is the expected marginal convenience value between April and July 1989?

■ 4.   Reproduce Table 8.7. Use it to analyze the same scenarios using the March and April 1989 futures prices from Figure 8.8.

5.   Suppose two parties enter into an Exchange of Futures for Physicals (EFP) agreement on the NYMEX. On October 12, 1988, they agree that on June 22, 1989, the long party will deliver 10,000 barrels of Arabian Light crude oil at a $2-per-barrel discount from the then prevailing NYMEX crude oil futures price. Today, they both enter into June futures contracts at the June futures settlement price for October 12. Using the information in Figure 8.8, show the cash flows for each party. Use two scenarios for the NYMEX crude oil futures price on June 22: $10 and $16 per barrel. What price have the two parties locked in?

6.   Suppose feeder cattle weigh 700 pounds and live cattle weigh 1,150 pounds. It takes six months to turn feeder cattle into live cattle. Using the prices in Figure 8.21, determine the cost, per pound of weight gain, of turning feeder cattle into live cattle between April and October 1989. Assume a short-term interest rate of 8 percent. Also assume that feeder cattle are pure assets.

■ 7.   Reproduce Table 8.9. Use it to analyze the same scenarios using the July and August 1989 futures price from Figure 8.12.

Options and Options on Futures

Futures and forward contracts are called **derivative securities**, because their payoffs derive from the value of their underlying assets. Another derivative security that has been widely traded over the past two decades is the option. The primary difference between an option and a futures or forward contract is that options confer a *right,* rather than an obligation, to buy or sell the underlying asset. This difference causes options to have payoffs very different from those on futures and forward contracts.

The first options to be traded on exchanges were written on individual stocks. In 1973, the Chicago Board of Trade created the Chicago Board Options Exchange (CBOE). Since then several other markets, such as the American Stock Exchange, the New York Stock Exchange, the Pacific Stock Exchange, and the Philadelphia Stock Exchange, have introduced trading in options on individual stocks. In 1982, the Philadelphia Stock Exchange introduced options on foreign exchange. In 1983, the CBOE began trading options on the Standard and Poor's 100 Index. Several other exchanges followed with their own index options (like index futures, options on indexes are cash settlement contracts). Also in 1982, the Commodity Futures Trading Commission authorized each futures exchange to introduce options on one of its futures contracts as part of a pilot program. The program was a success, and today most futures exchanges trade options on some of their futures contracts. One can now trade options on futures on underlying assets as diverse as foreign exchange, Eurodollar time deposits, Treasury bonds, gold, and oil. Like futures trading, option trading has become worldwide.

This chapter will introduce us to the options markets. We will study a technique, called **payoff analysis**, that allows us to determine the payoff patterns of strategies that use options. Then we will see how to analyze positions that combine several options. Finally, we will see how to use options as an alternative to futures for risk management and will derive the fundamental no-arbitrage equation for options.

Figure 9.1 Stock Option Transactions Prices for May 23, 1989

CHICAGO BOARD

Option & NY Close	Strike Price	Calls—Last Jun	Calls—Last Jul	Calls—Last Aug	Puts—Last Jun	Puts—Last Jul	Puts—Last Aug
I B M	105	5⅞	7½	10⅛	½	1⅛	2 5/16
109⅝	110	2⅜	4¼	6⅞	2	2 13/16	4⅜
109⅝	115	11/16	2	4½	5¾	6	6⅞
109⅝	120	⅛	13/16	2 11/16	10⅜	10¼	10⅞
109⅝	125	s	5/16	1 9/16	s	r	r
109⅝	130	s	3/16	13/16	s	r	r
In Min	45	r	⅜	1⅜	r	r	r
In Pap	40	s	r	11½	s	r	r
49⅞	45	5⅜	5⅞	r	⅛	r	r
49⅞	50	1¼	2	3⅝	1 1/16	1¾	2¼
49⅞	55	¼	½	1½	4¾	r	r

Source: *The Wall Street Journal,* May 24, 1989.

Options on Stocks

We will begin by discussing options on stocks (we will cover options on futures later in the chapter). Most of the techniques we will use to study stock options are also applicable to index options, options on foreign exchange, and options on futures.

A **call option** is a contract between two parties in which the buyer of the option pays a **premium** to acquire the *right* to purchase an underlying asset. The contract specifies an **exercise**, or **strike**, **price** at which the asset can be purchased and a maturity date. The buyer will choose whether or not to exercise the right to purchase according to market conditions.

Figure 9.1 provides an excerpt from *The Wall Street Journal* that gives price information for stock options traded at the Chicago Board Options Exchange on May 23, 1989.[1] Because all the examples in this chapter will focus on IBM stock options, we will consider the price information for those options given in the figure.

Figure 9.1 first shows that the closing market price for IBM stock on that date was $109⅝. Then it gives the premia of the various call options on IBM stock. These options had expiration dates in June, July, and August[2] and exercise prices that ranged from $105 to $130.[3] The call option on IBM stock that was due to expire in June and had an exercise price of $110 per share had a premium of $2⅜. This means that the party who bought the option made an immediate payment of $2⅜ to the seller, or **writer**, of the option.

[1] Each contract on the CBOE represents 100 shares of stock, but option prices are quoted on a per-share basis.

[2] At the CBOE, all the exercise dates fall on the third Friday of the expiration month.

[3] Some of these options may not have been traded or offered on this date. Such cases are denoted by lowercase *r* and *s,* respectively.

Some simple properties of call option pricing are apparent from Figure 9.1. The $110 July call option sold for a higher price than the $110 June call option. This suggests that call options with more distant expiration dates are more valuable. This is because they give the holder a greater "option"—that is, the right to buy at a fixed price is granted over a longer period of time. Figure 9.1 also shows that the $105 June call option sold for a higher price than the $110 June call option. This indicates that call options with lower exercise prices are more valuable, for they give the buyer the right to purchase the underlying asset at a lower price.

A **put option** gives the buyer the *right* to sell an underlying asset. Like a call option contract, a put option contract sells for a premium and specifies an exercise, or strike, price and a maturity date.

Figure 9.1 also gives the May 23, 1989, prices for put options on IBM stock. The June put option with the $110 exercise price had a premium of $2 per share. As with the call option, the buyer paid this premium to the writer of the option when the contract was sold.

These put option prices also demonstrate some simple properties of put pricing. The $110 July put option had a higher premium than the $110 June put option. Thus, as with calls, puts with more distant expiration dates are more valuable.[4] The $105 June put option sold at a lower premium than the $110 June put. Thus, unlike call options, put options are less valuable the lower their exercise prices, for the right to sell at a low price clearly is worth less to an option holder than the right to sell at a high price.

The IBM options traded at the Chicago Board Options Exchange can be exercised at any time up to their expiration dates. Such options are called **American options**. Another type of option, called a **European option**, can be exercised only on the expiration date. This distinction is not geographical, however; both kinds of options are traded throughout the world. American options are worth more than otherwise identical European options because of the value of the right to exercise early.

Payoff Diagrams

Options and futures are complicated instruments. We will use a standard analytical tool called a **payoff diagram** to assess the risks and returns options and futures strategies offer. A payoff diagram shows how strategies involving options and futures will perform under different future market conditions. It graphs the profitability of a given strategy against all possible values for the underlying asset of the derivative security at expiration.

Figure 9.2 presents a payoff diagram for the very simple strategy of going long the hypothetical Standard and Poor's 1 futures contract introduced in Chapter 2. Suppose the futures contract expires in two months and the current futures price is $115 per share. Because the S&P 1 contract is written solely on IBM stock, the

---

[4] Notice that this does not appear to be true for the $120 put options. This is probably so because the $120 put options were not heavily traded, so the quoted prices are not contemporaneous.

Figure 9.2   Long Futures, S&P 1 Contract

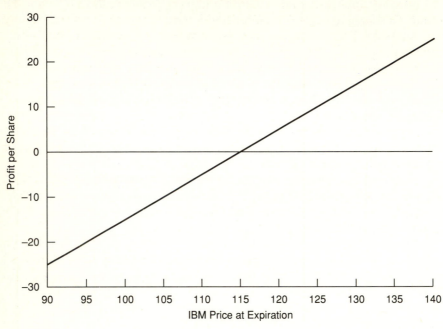

payoff to the long futures position depends on the value of IBM in two months.[5] If the price of IBM is $115, the long futures position has a zero payoff. If the price of IBM is $125, the long futures position yields $10, for the long can buy the stock at a net price of $115 and sell it for $125. If the price is $105, the long futures position loses $10, because the long is obligated to buy the IBM stock at a net price of $115 and can sell it for only $105. The payoff diagram for a long futures position is therefore an upward-sloping, 45-degree line that crosses zero at the initial futures price of $115. Since a short futures position has exactly the opposite payoff from a long position, the payoff diagram for a short position in the S&P 1 futures is the downward-sloping, 45-degree line depicted in Figure 9.3.

Payoff Diagrams for Options

The risk-and-return characteristics that distinguish options from futures are easily illustrated by comparing the payoff diagrams for options positions with the

---

[5] Because of marking to market, the futures payoff can also depend on the borrowing and lending rates.

Figure 9.3 Short Futures, S&P 1 Contract

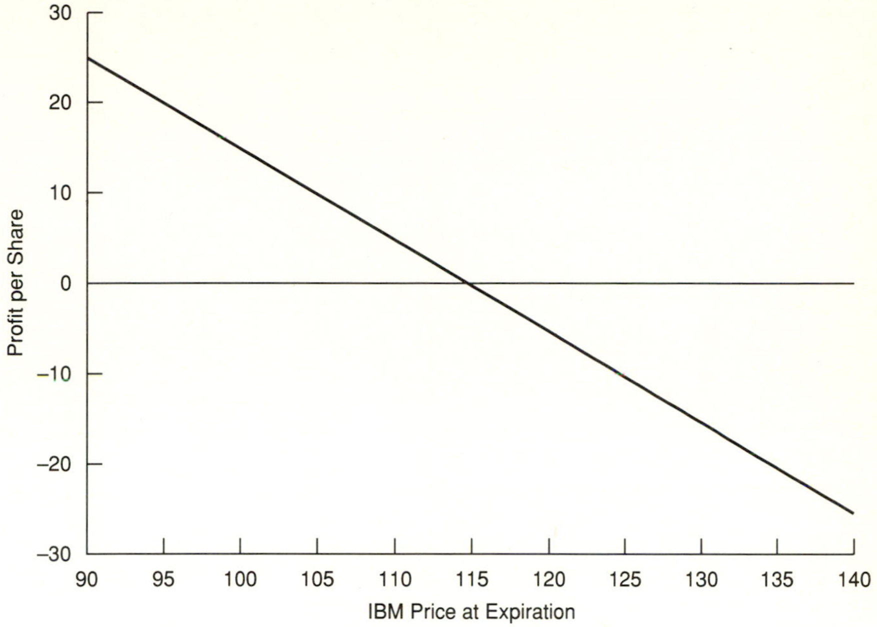

preceding payoff diagrams for long and short futures positions.[6] The option payoff diagrams differ for puts and calls and for the buyers and writers of option positions.

Buying a Call Option   The buyer of a call option will earn a gross profit if the price of the underlying asset rises above the exercise price. If it falls below the exercise price, the call option will not yield a positive payoff and the buyer will choose not to exercise.

Figure 9.4 graphs the payoffs to the buyer of an IBM call option that has an exercise price of $115, expires in two months, and has a premium of $2. If the price of IBM in two months is $115, the right to purchase IBM for $115 is worthless. This option is said to be **at the money.** The option buyer gains nothing but still has paid the $2 premium, so he or she has a net loss of $2. If the price of IBM in two months is $125, the buyer will exercise the option, buy the stock for $115, and sell it at $125 for a gain of $10. Then the option will be **in the money,** because it yields a gross gain. However, the option holder's net gain is only $8 because of the initial $2 premium. If the price of IBM in two months is $105, it will be unprofitable for the buyer to exercise his or her right to buy the stock at

---

[6] If an American option is exercised early, the horizontal axis refers to the price of the stock at the time the option is exercised.

Figure 9.4 Long Call Option, IBM

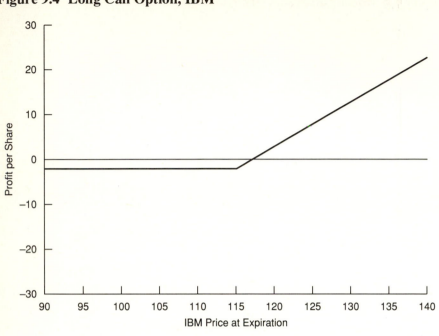

$115, and the option will expire worthless. Then the option will be **out of the money**. The buyer will lose the $2 premium.

The payoff diagram for the buyer of the call is a flat line that turns into a 45-degree line, with the kink occurring at the exercise price.[7] For every dollar by which the price of IBM exceeds the exercise price, the option holder gains a dollar toward paying off the premium. At a stock price of $117, the profit of $2 from exercising the option just pays for the premium. Any further increase in the price of IBM stock will simply add to the profit of the position. On the other hand, because the holder of the call does not have to exercise the option, his or her loss will not exceed $2 no matter how far the price of IBM drops below $115. Thus, a call option offers limited downside risk but unlimited upside potential. This contrasts sharply with the payoff on a long futures position, which offers unlimited upside potential and virtually unlimited downside risk.[8]

---

[7] It is standard practice in drawing payoff diagrams to ignore the timing difference between the payment of the premium and the receipt of profits from exercising the option. We will follow this convention. However, a correct diagram would use the future value of the option premium as of the option's expiration date.

[8] All of these diagrams will be the same for options on indexes except that the horizontal axis will measure the value of the index at the options' expiration.

Figure 9.5 Short Call Option, IBM

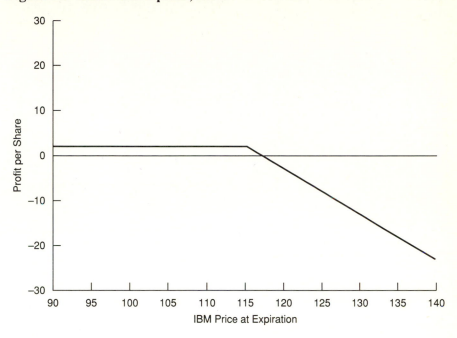

Writing a Call Option   The writer, or seller, of a call option takes a position exactly opposite to that of the buyer, so his or her payoffs are precisely opposite the buyer's. Figure 9.5 plots the payoff diagram of the writer of the call option with the $115 exercise price, the $2 premium, and expiration in two months. If the price of IBM in two months is $115, the option is worthless and the writer will have a net gain of the $2 premium. If the price of IBM falls anywhere below $115, the buyer will not exercise the option and the writer will earn $2 from the premium. If the price is $125, the buyer will exercise the option, and the writer will have to sell the stock for $115 per share when it is really worth $125. He or she will lose $10 on the option but will retain the $2 premium, so the net loss will be $8. At a price of $117, the writer's $2 gain from the premium will be completely canceled by the loss on the option. Net earnings will be negative for all prices above $117.

The payoff diagram thus is constant at the premium for all prices at or below the exercise price. It falls at a 45-degree angle as the price exceeds the strike price, for every dollar by which the price increases above that point is a dollar lost by the writer of the call. Thus, the call writer's position has limited positive potential and unlimited negative potential. Because of the risk incurred by writing a call option, the writer must keep a margin account as collateral.[9]

---

[9] See Cox and Rubinstein [1985] for a discussion of margins for writing call options.

Figure 9.6 Long Put Option, IBM

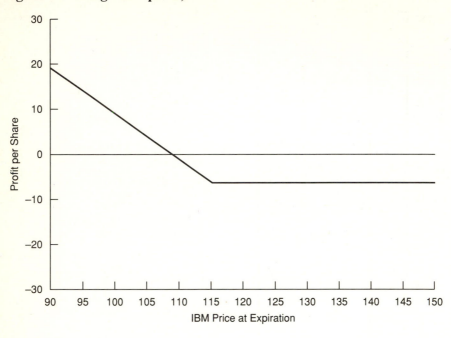

Buying a Put Option   The buyer of a put option will earn a gross profit if the price of the option's underlying asset is below the strike price at expiration, for then the buyer can sell the asset for more than its market value. If the market price is greater than the exercise price, the put holder will not gain by exercising the option.

Figure 9.6 gives the payoff diagram for an IBM put that has a $115 exercise price, expires in two months, and has a $6 premium. If the price of IBM stock in two months is $115, the put option is at the money. The option will be worthless, and the holder will have a net loss of the $6 premium. If the price of IBM is $125, the put option is out of the money. The option holder will not exercise and will suffer a $6 net loss. But if the price of IBM is $105, the option is in the money and the option holder will earn $10 by exercising his or her right to sell a stock that is worth $105 at a price of $115. The net gain after accounting for the premium will be $4. At a $109 price, the put holder will have a zero net gain, for the $6 dollar gain on the option will be offset by the $6 premium payment.

Thus, the payoff diagram for a put option is a downward-sloping, 45-degree line, while the price of the underlying asset is below the exercise price. Once the asset price reaches the exercise price, the payoff diagram flattens out indefinitely at the net loss of the premium. Like a call option, a put option offers virtually unlimited upside potential and limited downside risk.

Writing a Put Option   The payoffs for the writer of a put option are exactly opposite those of the put buyer. Figure 9.7 shows the payoff diagram faced by the

Figure 9.7 Short Put Option, IBM

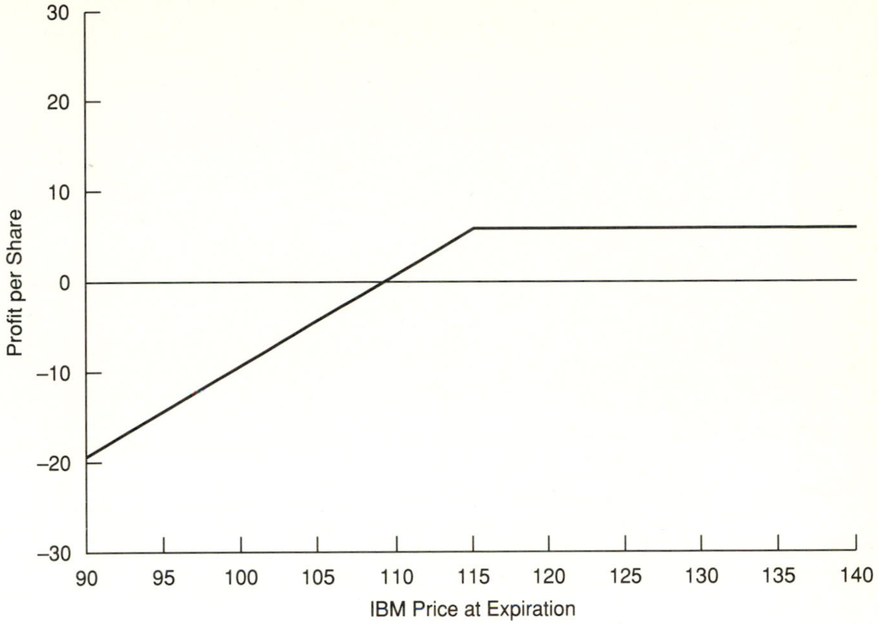

writer of the foregoing IBM put option. If the IBM price in two months is $115 or higher, the writer will have a net gain of the $6 premium, for the put holder will choose not to exercise. If the IBM price is less than $115, the holder will exercise the option and the writer will suffer a gross loss on the option. If the price is $105, the writer must buy the stock for $115 when it is really worth $105. The net loss will be $4: the $10 loss on the option less the premium earnings of $6. At a price of $109, the writer's loss on the option will be exactly offset by his or her gain on the premium and the net earnings will be zero.

Therefore, the put writer's payoff diagram is constant at the premium as long as the price of the underlying asset is equal to or greater than the strike price. It is an upward-sloping, 45-degree line for all prices lower than the strike price. A put writer faces virtually unlimited downside risk and limited upside potential and must establish a margin account just as a call writer must.

Combinations

Investors can use the options markets to create positions whose risk-and-return characteristics can be adjusted with a great deal of flexibility and precision. Thus, options allow investors to fine-tune their strategies in ways that other instruments do not. The strategies that allow such risk-and-return adjustment combine options with one another and with other securities and assets. The great variety of options, even for individual stocks, contributes to the trading flexibility the options markets

Figure 9.8 Long Straddle, IBM

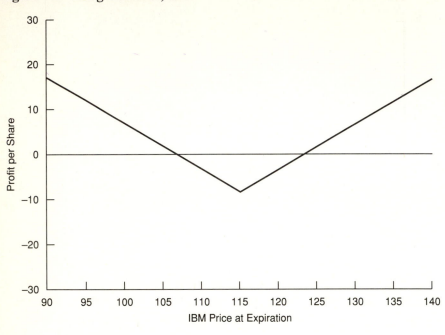

offer. The risk-and-return characteristics of these combinations can be quite complex, so we will use payoff diagrams to analyze them.

We will now study several option combination strategies. Example 9.1 shows how investors can use options to trade on their expectations of future stock price volatility.

▪ **Example 9.1: A Straddle**   Suppose an investor expects the price volatility of a certain stock to shift in some manner in the future. He can trade on his expectations by using an option strategy called a **straddle**. To buy a straddle in the options market, the investor buys an equal number of calls and puts that are written on the same stock and have the same exercise price.

Suppose the straddle involves the IBM calls and puts we have been studying in this chapter. Recall that these options have exercise prices of $115 and are due to expire in two months. The calls cost $2 per share and the puts $6 per share, so the total cost of this straddle is $8 per share.

Figure 9.8 shows the payoff diagram for this straddle. If the price of IBM stock in two months turns out to be $115 per share, both the call and the put will expire at the money. Neither option will have any value, so the investor will suffer a net loss of the $8 premia. If the price of IBM moves to $123 at expiration, the put option will expire worthless but the call option will be in the money, so the investor will exercise it. He will buy the stock at the $115 exercise price and sell it at the market price, thereby earning $123 − $115 = $8. This exactly offsets the

Figure 9.9 Short Straddle, IBM

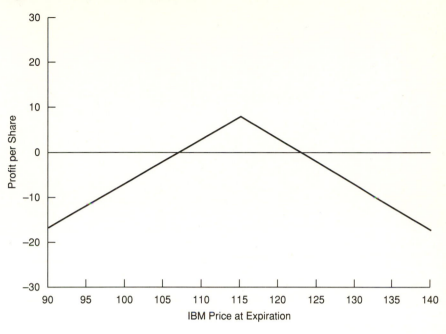

premia paid earlier, so the investor will have zero net earnings. If the price of IBM moves to $107, the call option will expire worthless. However, the put option will be in the money and the investor will exercise it to earn $115 − $107 = $8, which again exactly offsets the premia paid earlier. Thus, the straddle will lose money if the price of IBM is between $107 and $123 at expiration, because the profit from exercising either the call or the put will not cover the cost of buying the two options. The straddle will make a profit if the price is outside of this range.

The expected profitability of buying this straddle depends on the volatility of the IBM stock price. The straddle will make money if the price of IBM is very high or very low, and it will lose money if the price stays relatively stable. It therefore is a desirable strategy for investors who believe the price of IBM will be very volatile. The payoff diagram shows exactly how volatile prices must be for the straddle to pay off. This depends, of course, on the call and put premia. In equilibrium, the call and put premia are set such that the market is satisfied with the risk-return characteristics of the strategy. Thus, the straddle will be undertaken only by investors who think IBM stock will be more volatile than the market believes.

Investors who expect the market to be less volatile than the market does will sell straddles. To sell a straddle, one simply sells both the call and the put. The payoff diagram for this strategy, shown in Figure 9.9, is exactly opposite that of buying a straddle. Short straddle positions profit from stable prices but lose with large price moves.

Figure 9.10 Straddle: Volatility Increase, IBM

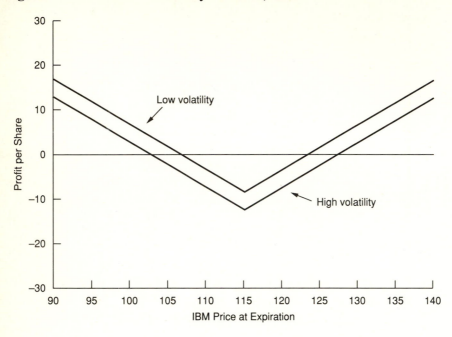

Now suppose there is a general increase in market volatility. The long straddle position in Figure 9.8 becomes very desirable, because the put and call premia were set under conditions of lower perceived volatility. Therefore, investors will buy straddles, and this will drive both call and put prices up until the market reaches a new equilibrium. Suppose, for example, that the call and put prices rise to $4 and $8, respectively, as a result of an increase in volatility. Figure 9.10 shows that under this new equilibrium, prices must move further in either direction for the long straddle position to profit. This reflects the higher level of volatility. Thus, this example shows that increases in volatility tend to raise the prices of both calls and puts. This is a general property of option pricing that we will cover in more detail later. ∎

Example 9.2 demonstrates an option combination strategy that allows investors to not only act on their volatility expectations, as they can with a straddle, but adjust the amount of risk they take in the process.

▪ **Example 9.2: A Strangle**   Suppose an investor wishes to take a position based on her expectations for market volatility but does not wish to incur the full risk of a straddle. She can meet these two goals with a **strangle** position, which combines puts and calls that have different exercise prices and premia that are lower than those of the options used in a straddle.

Figure 9.11 Long Strangle, IBM

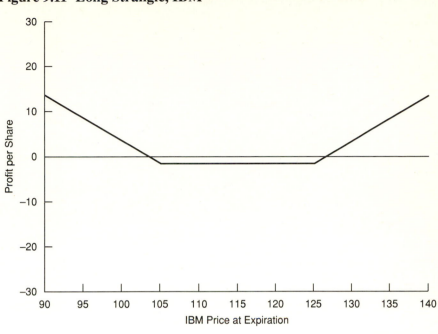

Figure 9.11 presents the payoff diagram for a strangle that involves buying a call with a strike price of $125 and a put with a strike price of $105. Again we assume both options expire in two months. The $125 call will have a lower price than the $115 call used in the straddle in Example 9.1. Suppose its price is $0.25. Likewise, the $105 put will have a lower price than the $115 put—say, $1. The cost of the strangle is therefore $0.25 + $1.00 = $1.25, much lower than the $8 price of the straddle.

The cheaper price of the strangle comes at a cost, however. Figure 9.12 compares the payoff diagrams of this strangle and the straddle in Example 9.1. It shows that prices must move further to create a profit on the strangle than they must on the straddle. Thus, as with all options strategies, there is a trade-off between low premia and high required price moves. ∎

Example 9.3 presents another option combination strategy—the **bull spread**, which allows investors to trade off risk and potential return.

∎ **Example 9.3: A Bull Spread**   Suppose an investor believes the price of IBM will rise but is not confident enough to take a long futures position with its potential for virtually unlimited losses. One strategy is to buy a call option. Another is to enter into a bull spread by buying one call and selling another. The call purchased in a bull spread must have a lower exercise price than that of the call sold.

Figure 9.12 Long Strangle versus Long Straddle, IBM

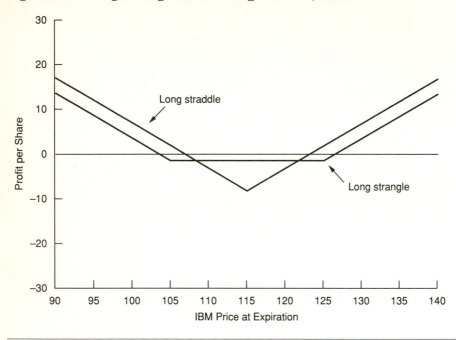

Figure 9.13 shows how a bull spread works. It presents the payoff diagrams for a call option on IBM with a $110 exercise price and a bull spread created by buying a $110-exercise-price call on IBM and selling a $115-exercise-price call on IBM. The $110 call has a $4.25 premium and the $115 call has a $2 premium, so the net cost of the bull spread is $4.25 − $2.00 = $2.25. Both options expire in two months.

The buyer of the $110 call will reap a gross profit of $1 for every dollar by which the IBM price exceeds $110. If the IBM price falls below the call's exercise price, the buyer will lose only the $4.25 premium. If this investor enters into a bull spread by selling a $115 call as well, he can lower the potential downside loss on the $110 call. This is because at an IBM price of less than $115, the call that was sold will be out of the money and will not be exercised, but the $2 premium earned on it will lower the premium paid on the $110 call. The investor can lose at most $2.25.

The cost of a lower potential downside loss is that the bull spread will lose dollar for dollar on the $115 call as the IBM price rises above $115. In that range, the $115 option will be in the money and will be exercised to the call writer's disadvantage. These losses will reduce the gains on the $110 call to a constant level. The bull spread will earn $5 more on the call owned than it will lose on the call sold. This gain less the premium cost of the bull spread yields a $2.75 constant gain.

Figure 9.13 Bull Spread versus Long Call, IBM

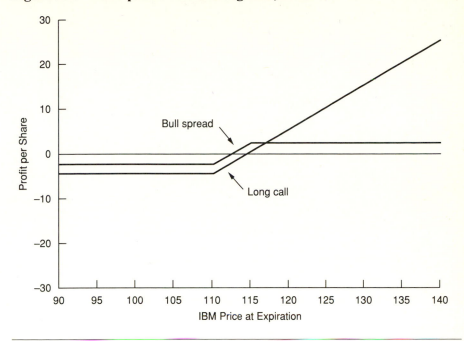

Thus, the bull spread makes money when the price of IBM rises and loses money when the price falls. However, its downside risk is limited, unlike that of a futures position, and its potential loss is smaller than that with a long call position. The cost of this protection from loss is that the bull spread's upside potential is also limited. ■

Put-Call Parity

In equilibrium, the prices of put and call options are related both to each other and to interest rates and the price of the underlying stock. This relationship is called **put-call parity**. It is useful to understand not only because it shows how the values of puts and calls are related but because it can help us evaluate certain option-trading strategies.

We will derive the put-call parity relationship by studying a trading strategy that involves selling a call and buying a put with the same exercise prices. Figure 9.14 presents the payoff diagram when such a strategy is carried out with options that have an exercise price of $115, a maturity of two months, a call premium of $2, and a put premium of $6. This strategy will require a $4 net premium, but for now we will omit the option premia in the payoff diagram. The diagram also assumes the options are European options, written on stocks that will pay no dividends before the options expire. We will relax both of these assumptions later.

Figure 9.14 Long Put–Short Call, IBM (Excluding Premia)

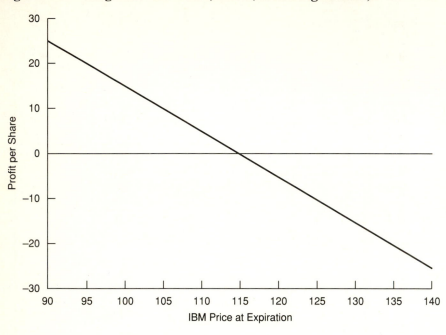

Figure 9.14 is a downward-sloping, 45-degree line that crosses the axis at the $115 exercise price. It is exactly the same as the payoff diagram in Figure 9.3 for a short futures position when the futures price is $115. Thus, by selling a call and buying a put, we can create a payoff pattern identical to that of a short futures position. The one difference is that the option strategy requires a premium payout while the short futures position does not.

In Chapter 2, we saw that

$$\text{T-bill} = \text{Stock} - \text{Futures}, \tag{9.1}$$

where the face value of the T-bill is equal to the futures price. We have just shown that

$$\text{Put} - \text{Call} = -\text{Futures}, \tag{9.2}$$

where the futures price equals the exercise price of the options. Combining Equations 9.1 and 9.2, we get

$$\text{T-bill} = \text{Stock} + \text{Put} - \text{Call}. \tag{9.3}$$

If there are to be no arbitrage opportunities, the cost of a T-bill must equal the cost of buying the stock and the put less the cost of the call. The cost of the T-bill is simply the present value of the face value, which we assume is equal to the options' exercise price. Thus, the put-call parity relationship is

PV(Exercise price) = Stock price + Put premium – Call premium.   **(9.4)**

Example 9.4 shows how put-call parity holds for options on IBM stock.

▪ **Example 9.4: Put-Call Parity**   We can demonstrate put-call parity by calculating the prices and payoffs of the strategies represented by the two sides of Equation 9.4. Consider the case of European IBM call and put options that have an exercise price of $115 and expire in two months. The price of the call is $2,.and the price of the put is $6. Assume IBM is expected to pay no dividend in the next two months. Suppose also that the current price of IBM stock is $109.30 and the bond-equivalent yield on a two-month T-bill is 9 percent annualized or 1.5 percent nonannualized.

Strategy A, prescribed by the right-hand side of Equation 9.4, is

Buy IBM stock, buy a put, and sell a call.

The cost of this strategy is $109.30 + $6.00 – $2.00 = $113.30. Strategy B, prescribed by the left-hand side of Equation 9.4, is

Buy a T-bill with a face value of $115.

The price of the T-bill is the present value of the face value, calculated with a 1.5 percent two-month discount rate:

$$\text{T-bill price} = \frac{\$115}{1.015} = \$113.30.$$

Thus, the two strategies cost the same initially. To show that put-call parity holds, we must now show that they yield the same payout in two months. Strategy B will pay $115 no matter what the price of IBM is in two months. Table 9.1 presents the payoffs from strategy A. It shows that this strategy will also yield $115 in two months regardless of the price of IBM. The two strategies therefore are identical. If Equation 9.4 does not hold and the costs of the two strategies differ, an arbitrage opportunity exists. The trading response to the arbitrage opportunity will quickly drive prices back into line. ▪

Example 9.5 shows how the put-call parity relationship can be used as a conceptual tool to evaluate certain trading strategies.

▪ **Example 9.5: Evaluating a Portfolio Strategy**   Portfolio managers often use a **covered call** strategy in which they sell call options and hold the options' underlying stock. Because call writers receive a premium, this strategy often is promoted as a way to "enhance the yield" of an equity portfolio.

We will consider a specific example to see how the covered call strategy pays off under varying market conditions. Suppose a portfolio manager who owns IBM stock writes a call option on IBM that has an exercise price of $115, a premium of $2, and an expiration date two months in the future. The current price of IBM stock is $115.

Table 9.1 Payoffs from Strategy A

IBM Price	Long Put	Short Call	Total
$ 90	$25	$ 0	$115
95	20	0	115
100	15	0	115
105	10	0	115
110	5	0	115
115	0	0	115
120	0	−5	115
125	0	−10	115
130	0	−15	115

Figure 9.15 presents the potential payoffs for this covered call. The upward-sloping, 45-degree line that crosses zero at $115 is the return from merely holding IBM stock. Any $1 increase in the price of IBM yields a $1 capital gain, while a $1 decrease yields a $1 dollar capital loss. If the portfolio manager enters into a covered call strategy by writing a call on IBM in addition to holding IBM stock, he will earn the payoff represented by the kinked line in Figure 9.15. If the price of IBM stock two months from now is lower than the exercise price of $115, the option will expire worthless and the portfolio manager will add the premium of $2 to his portfolio. The strategy works to the manager's advantage in such cases, for his return on the stock is enhanced by $2. But it works to his disadvantage if the price of IBM rises. After the stock reaches $115, the short call option will lose $1 for every $1 increase in IBM. Thus, the maximum value the covered call portfolio can reach is $117 per share. The covered call therefore offers a trade-off between a boost to portfolio value if prices are low and a $117 cap on the portfolio value. Table 9.2 demonstrates this numerically.

We have seen the shape of the covered call payoff diagram before. It is exactly the same as that of the written put in Figure 9.7. Rewriting the put-call parity equation, 9.3, shows us why this is true:

$$\text{Stock} - \text{Call} = \text{T-bill} - \text{Put.} \tag{9.5}$$

Thus, the portfolio manager could reach the covered call position just as easily by selling his stocks, buying T-bills, and buying puts. The choice between the two strategies depends on which is cheaper, and this can be indicated by the put-call parity relationship. If put-call parity holds, the two strategies will be equivalent. ∎

Put-Call Parity with American Options and Dividends   So far, for simplicity we have derived the put-call parity relationship only for European options written on stocks that do not pay dividends before the options expire. When we relax these assumptions, the put-call relationships become more complicated, but

Figure 9.15 Covered Call versus Long Stock, IBM

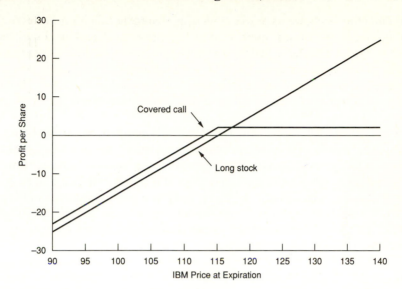

Table 9.2 Payoffs from Covered Call

IBM Price	Short Call	Total
$ 90	$ 2	$ 92
95	2	97
100	2	102
105	2	107
110	2	112
115	2	117
120	−3	117
125	−8	117
130	−13	117

they still carry the same intuition as in Equation 9.3.[10] If the underlying stocks pay dividends but the options are still European, the relationship becomes

$$\text{T-bill} = \text{Put} + \text{Stock} - \text{PV(Dividends)} - \text{Call}. \qquad (9.6)$$

For American options on dividend-paying stocks, the relationship becomes

$$\text{Call} - \text{Stock} + \text{Exercise price} + \text{PV(Dividends)} \geq \text{Put} \geq \qquad (9.7)$$
$$\text{Call} - \text{Stock} + \text{PV(Exercise price)}.$$

[10] See Cox and Rubinstein [1985] for a discussion of the derivation of Equations 9.6 and 9.7.

Options as an Alternative to Futures

Throughout this book, we have seen how firms can reduce their profit uncertainty by using futures or forward contracts to lock in prices or rates. One disadvantage of such hedging strategies is that they do not allow firms to benefit from favorable movements in prices or rates. There is a strong tendency to engage in "20-20 hindsight" and disparage hedging strategies that have locked in a lower price than the firm would have received or a higher price than it would have paid had it not hedged.

One increasingly popular way around this problem is to use options to manage risk. Because options offer downside protection, they allow firms to hedge against adverse price or rate movements but still profit from favorable movements. This is equivalent to insurance against unfavorable movements. Like all insurance it comes at a cost, which in this case is the options premium. Because of the great diversity of options contracts, firms usually have considerable flexibility in choosing the type of insurance they create with options. Example 9.6 illustrates the insurance choices a firm might face.

■ **Example 9.6: Using Options to Hedge a Portfolio**   Consider a portfolio manager who owns 100,000 shares of IBM stock and is concerned that the stock price will drop from its current May level of $113.30 over the next two months. The manager observes the following prices in the futures and options markets:

July S&P 1 futures price	$115 per share
July $115 exercise price, IBM put premium	$6 per share
July $105 exercise price, IBM put premium	$1 per share

The manager is considering four strategies for managing the value of her IBM portfolio over the next two months:

- *Strategy A:* Keep the portfolio unhedged
- *Strategy B:* Hedge the portfolio by going short 100,000 shares worth of S&P 1 futures
- *Strategy C:* Hedge the portfolio by buying 100,000 shares worth of the $115-exercise-price IBM puts at a total price of $600,000
- *Strategy D:* Hedge the portfolio by buying 100,000 shares worth of the $105-exercise-price IBM puts at a total price of $100,000

We will evaluate these four strategies by comparing the effect each would have on the manager's portfolio value under two scenarios for the price of IBM stock in July. Under the first scenario, the IBM price falls to $100 per share in July; under the second, it rises to $130 per share.

Strategy A: No Hedge

Scenario	Portfolio Value	Hedge Payoff	Unhedged Value
$100	$10,000,000	$0	$10,000,000
$130	$13,000,000	$0	$13,000,000

Cost of position = $0

Strategy B: Go Short Futures at $115

Scenario	Portfolio Value	Hedge Payoff	Hedged Value
$100	$10,000,000	($115 – $100) per share = $1,500,000	$11,500,000
$130	$13,000,000	($115 – $130) per share = –$1,500,000	$11,500,000

Cost of position = $0

The short futures position offsets the fall in portfolio value with futures profits under the first scenario but suffers a loss if the portfolio value rises. This strategy therefore locks in the futures price of $115 per share.

Strategy C: Buy $115 Puts

Scenario	Portfolio Value	Hedge Payoff	Hedged Value	Net Hedged Value
$100	$10,000,000	($115 – $100) per share = $1,500,000	$11,500,000	$10,900,000
$130	$13,000,000	$0	$13,000,000	$12,400,000

Cost of positon = $600,000

When the IBM price is low, the put option makes a profit. Excluding the put premium, the portfolio has a *floor* value per share of the $115 exercise price. Under the higher IBM price, the put option expires worthless and the manager's portfolio will be worth $130 per share. The options position provides the floor value for the portfolio at a cost of $6 per share. We can view this cost as a premium for the insurance that the portfolio value will not fall below $11.50 million. The premium effectively lowers the portfolio value to $10.90 million at the $100 IBM price and to $12.40 million at the $130 IBM price.

Strategy D: Buy $105 Puts

Scenario	Portfolio Value	Hedge Payoff	Hedged Value	Net Hedged Value
$100	$10,000,000	($105 – $100) per share = $500,000	$10,500,000	$10,400,000
$130	$13,000,000	$0	$13,000,000	$12,900,000

Cost of positon = $100,000

When the IBM price is low, the put option again makes a profit. Excluding the put premium, the portfolio's *floor* value per share is now the $105 exercise price. When the IBM price is high, the put option expires worthless and again the manager enjoys a portfolio value of $130 per share. The downside guarantee on the portfolio value comes at a cost of $1 per share, which is lower than the $6-per-share cost for the floor of $115 per share. With this strategy, the manager essentially creates an insurance policy with a larger *deductible,* because it lowers her floor by $10 per share. As with all insurance policies, the lower deductible comes with a saving in the premium (of $5 per share). The $1-per-share premium effectively lowers the portfolio value to $10.40 million at the $100 IBM price and to $12.90 million at the $130 IBM price.

Figures 9.16 and 9.17 plot the portfolio value under the four strategies both excluding and including the premia. It is clear from Figure 9.17 that no one strategy is definitely "best." If the price of IBM rises sharply, the unhedged strategy yields the highest portfolio value. If the price of IBM falls sharply, the futures strategy is preferable. Of the two insurance strategies, the $115-exercise-price put performs better if the price of IBM falls, but the $105-exercise-price put performs better if the IBM price rises. The manager must choose the portfolio value structure that will best satisfy her preferences. ∎

The strategies of buying put options in Example 9.6 offer portfolio insurance to the portfolio manager. The put options provide value only if the price of the portfolio stock drops below the put exercise price. If the price rises above the exercise price, the manager will merely lose her premium.

We can evaluate these strategies using put-call parity as in Example 9.5. The two put strategies involve holding the underlying asset and buying puts. Rewriting the put-call parity equation, 9.3, we get

$$\text{Stock} + \text{Put} = \text{T-bill} + \text{Call}. \tag{9.8}$$

Thus, holding the portfolio of IBM stock and buying puts is identical to buying T-bills and buying calls if put-call parity holds. The equivalence of these two strategies is evident from Figure 9.17.

General Rules for Using Options to Hedge   Example 9.6 illustrates some general rules for hedging against falling prices. A firm can *lock in* a price using short futures positions. It can *insure against* falling prices using puts. It can lower the insurance cost by using a *deductible* (with a lower-exercise-price put).

There are similar rules for hedging against rising prices. A firm can *lock in* a price using long futures positions. It can *insure against* rising prices using calls. It can lower the insurance cost by using a *deductible* (with a higher-exercise-price call).

Options therefore provide an attractive hedging alternative to futures. Managers accustomed to buying insurance for other purposes might be more comfortable hedging with options than with futures. Further, the existence of options with several exercise prices on a wide range of commodities and securities allows risk managers to design their options insurance with considerable flexibility.

Option Pricing and Arbitrage

Throughout this book, we have seen how futures contracts are priced by arbitrage. Options too are priced by arbitrage, although the arbitrage trading strategies used in the options markets are more complicated than those used in the futures markets. A full understanding of option pricing relationships requires a level of mathematics that is beyond the scope of this book. However, we can develop some intuition about option pricing and present the formulas arbitrageurs use to price options. To build our intuition about option pricing, we will first study a simple, albeit

Figure 9.16 Portfolio Value: Gross Unhedged, Futures, and Puts

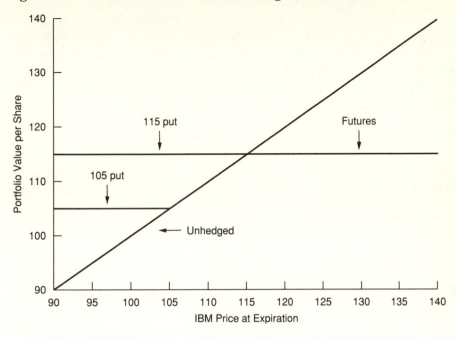

Figure 9.17 Portfolio Value: Net Unhedged, Futures, and Puts

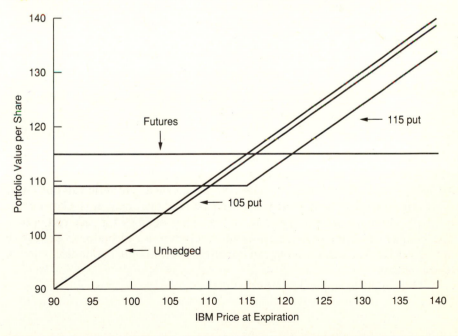

Table 9.3   Payoffs from Strategies And B

Strategy		Cost	Payoff in 1 Year	
			$P_1 = \$100$	$P_1 = \$130$
A:	Buy 2 calls	$ 2C	(2)($0.00) = $ 0.00	(2)($15.00) = $ 30.00
B:	Buy 1 share	$109.30	$100.00	$130.00
	Borrow	–$ 91.74	–$100.00	–$100.00
	Total	$ 17.56	$ 0.00	$ 30.00

Note: $100/1.09 = $91.74.

unrealistic, example. Then we will show how we can use the techniques and intuition learned from this example to understand the famous **Black-Scholes** option pricing model, the most widely used option pricing model today.

Two-State Pricing

To compute the equilibrium price of an option, we will first identify another, equivalent investment strategy. In equilibrium, the price of entering into the equivalent strategy must be equal to the price of the option.

  We will begin with a very simple example in which we assume the price of IBM stock is currently $109.30 and can move only once between now and one year from now.[11] Further, the IBM price one year from now must be either $130 or $100. Finally, we will assume the riskless rate of interest at which we can borrow or lend is 9 percent. We wish to know the price of a call option on IBM under these circumstances.

  Now consider two investment strategies that can be held for exactly one year:

- *Strategy A:* Buy two one-year call options on IBM with an exercise price of $115. The premium on the options is unknown to us at this time, so we will denote it by $C.
- *Strategy A:* Buy one share of IBM stock and borrow $91.74 for one year.

  The payoffs from these strategies are given in Table 9.3. Even though strategy B involves no options, its payoffs are exactly the same as those generated by the options held in strategy A. Thus, we can create a **synthetic call option** by following strategy B. In this example, we must hold one share of stock for every two call options we wish to replicate, or 0.5 shares of stock for each call option. The number of shares of stock we need to replicate a call option is called the option's **delta**. The delta will play an important role throughout our discussion of option pricing.

  Our simple example demonstrates that

---

[11] See Cox, Ross, and Rubinstein [1979] and Rendleman and Bartter [1979] for a further discussion of this two-state model.

Table 9.4 Payoffs from Arbitrage Strategy

Strategy	Cost	Payoff in 1 Year	
		P₁ = $100	P₁ = $130
Buy 1 share	$109.30	$100.00	$130.00
Borrow	–$ 91.74	–$100.00	–$100.00
Sell 2 calls	–$ 18.00	(–2)($0.00) = $ 0.00	(–2)($15.00) = –$ 30.00
Total	–$ 0.44	$ 0.00	$ 0.00

$$\text{Call} = (\text{Delta})(\text{Stock}) - \text{T-bill}, \tag{9.9}$$

where, as usual, – *T-bill* refers to borrowing. Thus, we have a relationship for call options that is very similar to the relationship we derived for futures contracts:

$$\text{Futures} = \text{Stock} - \text{T-bill}. \tag{9.10}$$

The equivalence of the two investment strategies, shown in Equation 9.9, allows us to compute a price for the option. Strategy B replicates two call options for a price of $17.56. Thus, each call option should sell for C = $8.78. If call options sell for any other price, an arbitrage opportunity exists, as Examples 9.7 and 9.8 demonstrate.

- **Example 9.7: Arbitrage Profits from an Overpriced Option**   Suppose that in the simple case presented above, there is a $115-exercise-price call option on IBM stock that expires in one year and can be purchased for $9. We have just seen that we can create a synthetic call option for $8.78. Thus, we can profit by buying synthetic calls for $8.78 and selling actual calls for $9. Table 9.4 presents the payoffs from this strategy.

   The net cost today (for two calls) is –$0.44, or an inflow of $0.44. There are no obligations or cash flows one year from now. Thus, this strategy is a pure arbitrage. Arbitrageurs will buy the stock and drive up its price, increasing the cost of replicating the option. They will sell call options, driving down those options' prices. This process will eliminate the arbitrage opportunity. ▪

Example 9.8 shows how underpriced options also create arbitrage opportunities.

- **Example 9.8: Arbitrage Profits from an Underpriced Option**   Suppose a $115-exercise-price call option on IBM stock that expires in one year costs $8.50. We can still create two synthetic call options for $17.56 ($8.78 each) by buying one share of IBM stock and borrowing $91.74. Thus, we can create two synthetic written calls by selling one share of IBM stock short and lending $91.74. We can earn an arbitrage profit by writing synthetic calls and buying actual calls. Table 9.5 presents the payoffs from this strategy.

   The net cost today (for two calls) is –$0.56, or an inflow of $0.56. As in Example 9.7, there is no obligation one year from now. This strategy therefore is

Table 9.5 Payoffs from Arbitrage Strategy

Strategy	Cost	Payoff in 1 Year $P_1 = \$100$	Payoff in 1 Year $P_1 = \$130$
Short 1 share	–$109.30	–$100.00	–$130.00
Lend	$ 91.74	$100.00	$100.00
Buy 2 calls	$ 17.00	(2)($0.00) = $ 0.00	(2)($15.00) = $ 30.00
Total	–$ 0.56	$ 0.00	$ 0.00

a pure arbitrage. Arbitrageurs will short-sell the stock and drive down its price, reducing the inflow from replicating a written position on the option. They will buy actual call options, driving up those options' prices. As a result, the arbitrage opportunity will disappear. As with futures arbitrage, if selling stock short is costly, quasi-arbitrageurs can carry out the above arbitrage strategy by effectively selling stock short and lending the proceeds. ∎

Examples 9.7 and 9.8 demonstrate that arbitrage will drive the option price in our simple example to the cost of creating a synthetic call option. This synthetic call is easily created with a very small amount of information: We need to know only the current stock price, the option's exercise price, the option's expiration date, the riskless rate of interest, and the possible stock prices when the option expires.

A review of the factors we do *not* need to know in our example will show how simple it is to price an option. A call option makes money if the price of the underlying stock rises and loses money if the price falls. Thus, one might suspect that the option price will depend on the probability that IBM will be $100 or $130 in one year. This is not the case, though, for we can replicate the payoff from the option with our synthetic strategy regardless of whether the IBM price is low or high. Two arbitrageurs might disagree on the relative probabilities that the stock price will rise or fall, but they cannot disagree on the price of the option! Similarly, one might suspect that because options are risky assets, we will need risk-adjusted discount rates to price them. But our strategy requires only the riskless rate of interest.

In Chapter 2, we saw that using arbitrage to price futures contracts also eliminates the need to know much about the underlying asset. The fundamental no-arbitrage equation,

$$F_{t,T} = P_t(1 + r_{t,T}),$$

requires no knowledge of the possible future spot prices, the probability distribution of those prices, or the risk-adjusted discount rate.

The Black-Scholes Formula

The previous section introduced option pricing and arbitrage with a very simple example. We saw that we can compute an option's price using the following intuition: One can replicate a call option on a stock by holding delta shares of the stock and borrowing to partially finance the stock purchase. In 1973, Black and Scholes published a revolutionary paper showing that when the prices of an option's underlying stock shift continuously, as they often do in the real world, the option pricing intuition we developed with our simple example still holds. In this section, we will introduce the Black-Scholes option pricing model and show how to use it to replicate call options in a way very similar to that used in our two-state model. The Black-Scholes model thus will allow us to use our understanding of arbitrage to price options.

The Black-Scholes model applies to European call options on stocks that pay no dividends before the options expire. Later in the chapter, we will discuss how to deal with American options on dividend-paying stocks. At that time, we will also discuss some of the technical assumptions of the model and their validity.

The Black-Scholes formula initially appears quite formidable:

$$\text{Call premium} = P_0 N(d1) - PV(E)N(d2) \qquad\qquad \textbf{(9.11)}$$

$$d1 = \frac{\ln[P_0/PV(E)] + 0.5(V^2)(T)}{V\sqrt{T}}$$

$$d2 = d1 - V\sqrt{T},$$

where

P_0 = current stock price

E = exercise price

T = time to expiration (in years)

$PV(\ )$ = present value using the riskless rate

V = volatility of stock price returns

$N(\ )$ = cumulative normal distribution function

$\ln(\ )$ = natural logarithm

The formula requires only five inputs, three of which—the current stock price, the exercise price, and the option's time to maturity—are directly observable. A fourth input, the riskless rate of interest, is needed to determine the present value of the exercise price. While not directly observable, the riskless rate is easily approximated by the broker call rate or the T-bill rate, so we consider it to be effectively observable.

The only parameter input into the Black-Scholes formula that is not observable is the stock price volatility. The volatility is the (annualized) standard deviation of the rate of change of the stock price over the period until the option expires. Obviously it cannot be observed. However, investors use several techniques to estimate it. We will review one such technique: the historical volatility method.

Historical Volatility   One common technique for estimating stock volatility is to use the volatility of the stock over some past period. This estimate is called the **historical volatility**. The assumption implicit in the historical method is that the stock's past volatility is a good indication of its future volatility. Investors who uses this method must choose a past time period that they feel experienced volatility conditions similar to those expected in the period covered by their options contracts.

Table 9.6 shows how to compute historical volatility. It presents an example in which a stock's historical volatility is computed from hypothetical closing stock prices over the 30-day period before an option purchase is to take place. The third column in the figure gives the daily rates of change in the stock price.[12] The *daily* historical volatility is the standard deviation of the entries in the third column. We calculate the annualized standard deviation as follows:

$$V = \text{Annualized volatility} \tag{9.12}$$
$$= (\sqrt{N})(\text{Daily volatility}),$$

where N is the number of trading days in a year.[13] We assume N is equal to 250.

Other methods of estimating volatility account not only for the stock's historical closing prices but for its past open, high, and low prices. Some investors make intuitive estimates of stock volatility based on their "feel" for the market. Many option traders develop their own techniques for estimating volatility. Determining the correct volatility is both an art and a science.

Implied Volatility   One can determine the market's estimate of volatility by computing the **implied volatility** of the Black-Scholes model. Because four out of the five inputs to the model are essentially observable, one can solve the model for the level of volatility that sets the Black-Scholes theoretical price equal to the market price. This is the implied volatility of the option. Unfortunately, one cannot find arbitrage opportunities in this way. If the implied volatility is used as the volatility estimate in the Black-Scholes model, the model will, by definition, indicate that the option is correctly priced.

Comparison of the Black-Scholes Model and the Two-State Example
The inputs required by the Black-Scholes model are very similar to those of our two-state example. In the latter case, we need to know the current stock price, the exercise price, the time to maturity, the riskless rate, and the range of possible prices during the following year. The Black-Scholes model also requires the first four inputs. The range of possible prices used in the two-state example is the analog of stock price volatility in the Black-Scholes model.

---

[12] This rate of change often is calculated as the difference between the natural logarithms of the current and previous prices.

[13] We use $\sqrt{N}$ because the standard deviation is a square root.

Table 9.6 Computing Historical Volatility

Day	Price	Rate of Change
−30	$130.00	—
−29	126.86	−2.418%
−28	126.61	−0.193
−27	129.23	2.069
−26	131.77	1.960
−25	128.38	−2.572
−24	125.22	−2.459
−23	127.84	2.092
−22	125.60	−1.754
−21	126.35	0.595
−20	127.44	0.869
−19	123.48	−3.110
−18	122.44	−0.838
−17	124.64	1.791
−16	122.17	−1.978
−15	124.33	1.762
−14	121.45	−2.312
−13	118.47	−2.454
−12	114.73	−3.161
−11	117.88	2.748
−10	115.19	−2.279
−9	113.51	−1.460
−8	115.52	1.769
−7	117.98	2.127
−6	116.49	−1.261
−5	117.59	0.950
−4	117.31	−0.246
−3	119.86	2.177
−2	121.40	1.288
−1	123.06	1.366

Daily standard deviation = 1.945%
Annual standard deviation = $(1.945\%)(\sqrt{250}) = 30.752\%$

Note: We assume 250 trading days in a year.

As with the two-state example, the information requirements of the Black-Scholes model are remarkably light. As we noted in the two-state case, it seems plausible, a priori, that the expected future stock price[14] and some risk-adjusted discount rate would be necessary to compute option prices. However, like the two-state example, the Black-Scholes model requires neither of these variables, because it can price the options by arbitrage. We will show how this works later in the chapter.

---

[14] In the two-state example, knowing the probabilities of high and low prices is tantamount to knowing the expected future spot price.

Computing the Black-Scholes Option Price   Anyone who uses the Black-Scholes formula for trading will have programmed Equation 9.11 into a computer or calculator. However, to learn the formula it is useful to work through it once, as we do in Example 9.9.

▪ **Example 9.9: Computing the Value of a Call Option Using Black-Scholes**
Suppose we observe the following parameters for an IBM call option:

$$P_0 = \$109.30$$

$$E = \$115.00$$

$$T = 0.167 \text{ (2 months)}$$

$$r = 9\%$$

$$V = 30\%$$

We wish to determine the equilibrium price for this option. The Black-Scholes model will give us this result in the following four steps:

Step 1: Compute the Present Value of the Exercise Price[15]

$$PV(\$115.00) = \frac{\$115}{1.015}$$
$$= \$113.30.$$

Step 2: Compute d1 and d2   The elements d1 and d2 are simply variables used for intermediate calculations:

$$d1 = \frac{\ln(\$109.30/\$113.30) + (0.5)(0.30)^2(0.167)}{(0.30)(\sqrt{0.167})}$$

$$= -0.2319$$

$$d2 = -0.2319 - (0.30)(\sqrt{0.167})$$
$$= -0.3545.$$

Step 3: Compute N(d1) and N(d2)   N(d1) and N(d2) refer to the area under a standard normal (bell-shaped) curve up to d1 and d2, respectively. Figure 9.18 demonstrates this for N(d1).
One can obtain these areas either from the back of a standard statistics textbook or by using a computer program. The values in this example are

---

[15] Most Black-Scholes computer programs ask for the T-bill rate in an annualized, continuously compounded form. The present value of the exercise price is then Ee^{-rT}. For simplicity, we will avoid continuous compounding here.

Figure 9.18 Computing N(d1), Normal Distribution

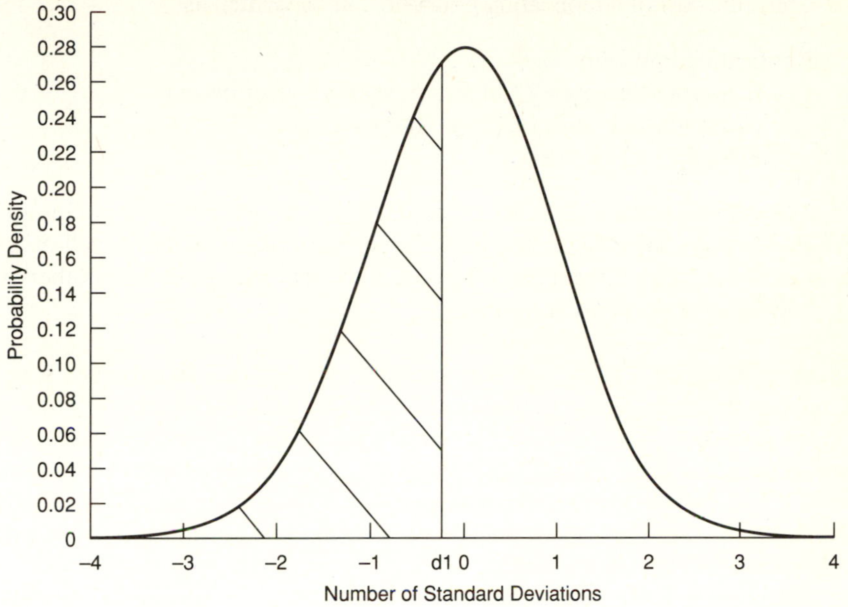

N(d1) = 0.4083
N(d2) = 0.3615.

Step 4: *Compute the Call Option Price*

Call = ($109.30)(0.4083) − ($113.30)(0.3615)
     = $3.67.

                                                                             ■

Logic of the Black-Scholes Formula

The Black-Scholes formula is founded on the same intuition that we developed in our two-state example. In that simple case, we showed that one can create a synthetic call option by buying delta shares of the underlying stock and borrowing to partially finance the purchase. The portion of the purchase cost not covered by the borrowing is the cost of replicating the option. Arbitrageurs make sure that the market price of each call option equals the cost of its replicating portfolio. Black and Scholes showed that when stock prices move continuously, one can still replicate an option using the strategy of buying delta shares of the underlying stock and borrowing to finance part of the purchase. They proved that

Delta = N(d1)
Borrowing = PV(E)N(d2),

where the right-hand-side variables are as defined in the Black-Scholes formula (Equation 9.11).

Thus, the cost of a replicating portfolio can be written as

Replicating Portfolio Cost
= (Current stock price)(Number of shares) – Borrowing
= (Current stock price)(Delta) – Borrowing
= $P_0 N(d1) - PV(E)N(d2)$.

This is exactly the same as the Black-Scholes formula. We therefore can interpret the Black-Scholes formula as the price of a portfolio that replicates a call option. The price of the option should equal the cost of the replicating portfolio; otherwise there will be an opportunity for arbitrage.

Dynamic Hedging   In the two-state example, we replicate an option by simply purchasing the appropriate portfolio and waiting until the option expires. At expiration, the portfolio will have the same value as the option. But when prices move continuously, as in the Black-Scholes case, the appropriate replicating portfolio will change over time as changes in the stock price and volatility alter the delta term. Therefore, the replication portfolio must be adjusted periodically to incorporate changes in the delta.

The option replication strategy that requires such adjustment is called **dynamic hedging**. It involves the following steps:

1.   Purchase delta shares of stock.

2.   Borrow to partially finance the stock purchase.

3.   Recompute the delta periodically using current inputs.
    a.   If the delta has gone up, purchase enough stock to bring the stock holdings up to the current delta. Finance this purchase entirely by borrowing.
    b.   If the delta has gone down, sell enough stock to lower the stock holdings to the current delta. Repay some of the borrowing with the proceeds.

This strategy requires an initial outlay given by the Black-Scholes formula. The subsequent portfolio adjustments require no additional outlays, nor do they generate any income. Black and Scholes showed that the portfolio produced by the dynamic hedging strategy will have exactly the same value as the option when the option expires. Thus, dynamic hedging replicates a call option at a current cost given by the Black-Scholes formula.

Example 9.10 demonstrates a dynamic hedge.

▪ **Example 9.10: Dynamic Hedging Using the Black-Scholes Model**   Suppose an arbitrageur wishes to create a synthetic call option with the same characteristics as the call option on IBM stock in Example 9.9. Using results from that example, we see that

Table 9.7 Dynamic Hedge Using the Black-Scholes Model

Days to Expiration	Stock Price	Delta	Net Purchase	Borrowing	Interest
61	$109.30	0.4083	$44.63	$40.96	—
60	111.30	0.4650	6.31	47.28	$0.010
59	110.50	0.4398	−2.78	44.51	0.012
58	110.00	0.4232	−1.83	42.69	0.011
57	111.00	0.4514	3.13	45.83	0.010
56	112.00	0.4801	3.21	49.05	0.011
55	112.50	0.4939	1.55	50.62	0.012
etc.					

$$\text{Delta} = N(d1)$$
$$= 0.4083$$
$$\text{Borrowing} = PV(E)N(d2)$$
$$= (\$113.30)(0.3615)$$
$$= \$40.96.$$

For each 100 call options the arbitrageur wishes to replicate, he must buy approximately 41 shares of IBM stock. The current cost of the replicating portfolio is

$$\text{Portfolio cost} = (0.4083)(\$109.30) - \$40.96$$
$$= \$3.67,$$

which equals the Black-Scholes price.

Suppose the arbitrageur adjusts this portfolio daily to account for changes in his delta. Table 9.7 presents the daily record of this dynamic hedging strategy.

After the first day, the price moves to $111.30 and the delta rises to 0.4650. This represents a change of

$$\text{Change in delta} = 0.4650 - 0.4083$$
$$= 0.0567.$$

The arbitrageur therefore must purchase 0.0567 more shares of stock for each option he is replicating, at a per-share cost of

$$\text{Cost of balancing} = (\text{Change in delta})(\text{Current stock price})$$
$$= (0.0567)(\$111.30)$$
$$= \$6.31.$$

The arbitrageur borrows to finance this purchase and thus adds $6.31 to his borrowing. With the interest owed from the previous borrowing, the total outstanding debt is now $47.28

After the second day, the price moves down to $110.50 and the delta falls to 0.4398. This represents a change of

$$\text{Change in delta} = 0.4398 - 0.4650$$
$$= -0.0252.$$

The arbitrageur must sell 0.0252 shares of stock for each option he is replicating. This brings in

$$\text{Inflow from rebalancing} = \text{(Change in delta)(Current stock price)}$$
$$= (0.0252)(\$110.50)$$
$$= \$2.78.$$

The arbitrageur pays off some of his debt with this inflow. Adding the interest owed on the previous borrowing, the total outstanding debt is now $44.51.

If the arbitrageur continues this process, the value of his portfolio of stocks and borrowing will equal that of the call option at expiration. ∎

To truly conform to the Black-Scholes model, a dynamic hedge must update the delta continuously. Obviously this is impractical, although it would make one's broker very happy. In real-life applications, traders choose convenient intervals for hedge adjustments as in Example 9.10.[16]

Put Option Pricing   Once we know the Black-Scholes price for a call option, it is easy to price a put option having the same Black-Scholes input variables. Assume that, like the call, the put is a European option on a stock that pays no dividends before it expires. If we rewrite the put-call parity relationship given by Equation 9.4, we get an expression for the put premium:

$$\text{Put premium} = \text{PV(Exercise price)} - \text{Stock price} + \text{Call premium.} \quad \textbf{(9.13)}$$

This equation is easily solved, since we know the Black-Scholes call price as well as the stock price and the present value of the option exercise price.

As with a call option, a dynamic strategy can be used to replicate a put option. This strategy involves going short the stock and lending.

Sensitivity of the Black-Scholes Model to Changes in Inputs

We can use the Black-Scholes formula to see how changes in certain market factors affect option prices. We will show how the Black-Scholes call price changes with variations in each of the model's inputs. We will use the input values from Example 9.9 as our starting values.

Changes in Current Stock Price   Figure 9.19 shows that an increase in the underlying stock price will increase the call option price. Recall that Black and Scholes showed that

---

[16] Usually the interval chosen for hedge adjustments depends on how much the delta changes over time.

Figure 9.19 Black-Scholes Call Price: Effect of Changing Current Stock Price

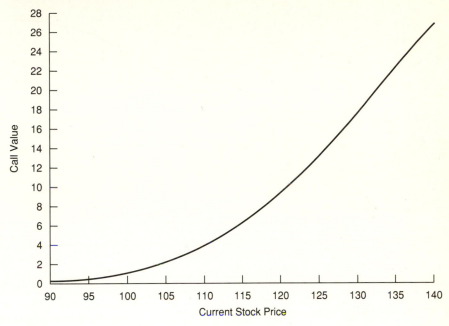

$$\text{Call} = (\text{Delta})(\text{Stock}) - \text{T-bill},\tag{9.14}$$

because one can replicate a call option by holding delta shares of the underlying stock and borrowing. This means that the call should behave just like delta shares of the underlying stock. For each dollar increase in the stock price, the value of the call will go up by delta dollars. Thus, the slope of the curve in Figure 9.19 is simply the delta of the option.

Figure 9.20 graphs the delta of the option as a function of the current stock price. As the stock price drops well below the $115 exercise price, the delta drops toward zero. An option that is way out of the money (and unlikely to be exercised) will not be highly sensitive to changes in the stock price. As the stock price rises well above the exercise price, the delta increases toward 1. An option that is way in the money (and likely to be exercised) is more likely to behave like the stock.

Changes in Exercise Price   Figure 9.21 shows that the call option price is higher the lower the exercise price. Further, a $1 increase in the exercise price decreases the value of the option by less than $1. This relationship is also apparent from the option prices in Figure 9.1. For example, a $115-exercise-price IBM call option that expires in July sells for $2, while a $120-exercise-price call option that expires in July sells for $0 13/16. The difference in option prices is much lower than the $5 difference in exercise prices.

Figure 9.20 Black-Scholes Delta: Effect of Changing Current Stock Price

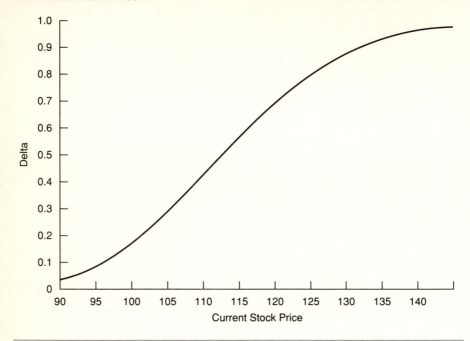

Figure 9.21 Black-Scholes Call Price: Effect of Changing Exercise Price

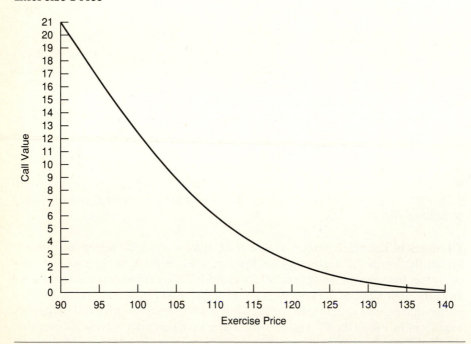

Figure 9.22 Black-Scholes Call Price: Effect of Changing Riskless Rate

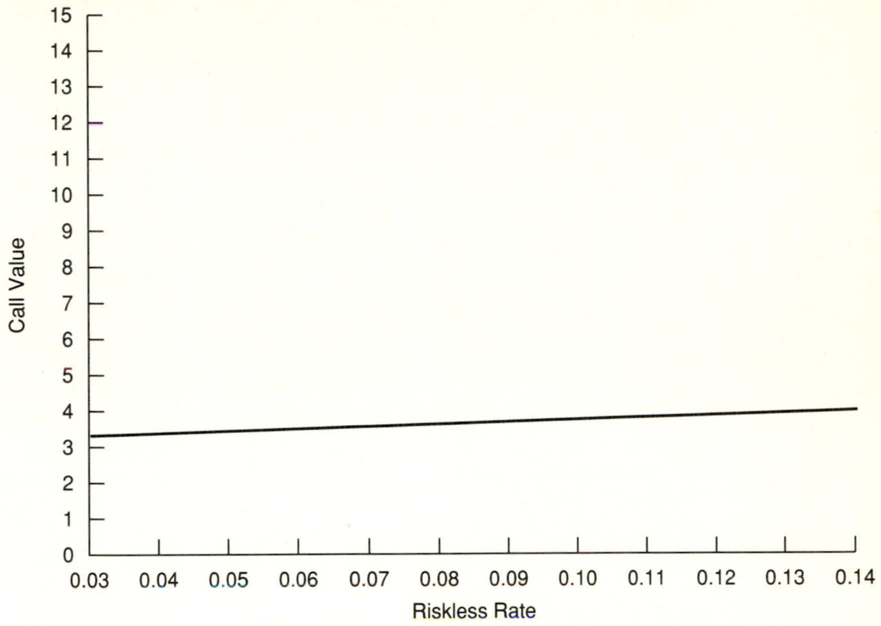

Changes in Riskless Rate   Figure 9.22 shows that call options increase in value if the riskless interest rate rises. This is because the present value of the exercise price falls as the riskless rate increases. The Black-Scholes formula, Equation 9.11, clearly shows that a fall in the present value of the exercise price will increase the value of a call option.

Changes in Volatility   Figure 9.23 shows that call prices will increase if the volatility of the underlying stock increases. We already encountered this relationship in the straddle in Example 9.1. In that case, increases in volatility make straddles more attractive, leading investors to buy both calls and puts. This drives both call and put prices up. More generally, call options become more valuable with increases in volatility because large upward moves in the underlying stock lead to greater profits than do small upward moves, while the downside protection of the option ensures that large downward moves will be no more damaging than small ones.

Changes in Time to Maturity   Figure 9.24 shows that call options are more valuable the longer their times to maturity. The reason is that with longer times to maturity, the effective volatility of the stock price is greater, because there is more time for the price of the underlying stock to make big moves. Further, the present value of the exercise price is lower the longer the time to maturity. Both of these effects contribute to higher call option value.

Figure 9.23 Black-Scholes Call Price: Effect of Changing Volatility

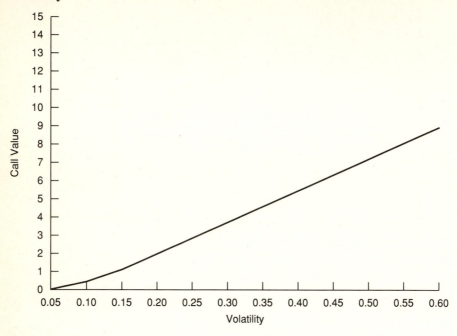

Figure 9.24 Black-Scholes Call Price: Effect of Changing Time to Expiration

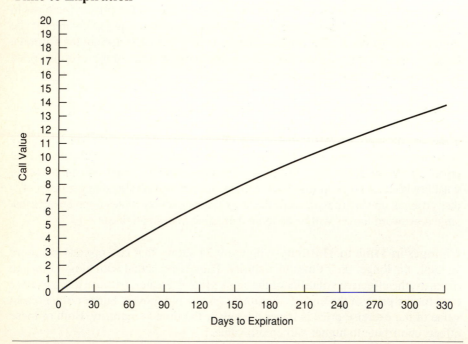

Assumptions of and Adjustments to the Black-Scholes Model

As with any model, the derivation of the Black-Scholes pricing model is based on a number of simplifying assumptions. If these assumptions are reasonable approximations of actual conditions, the model will be a good one. When the assumptions are not reasonable approximations, the model should be adapted. In this section, we will discuss the main assumptions of the Black-Scholes model and show how to adapt the model when these assumptions are violated.

Continuous Price Changes   The Black-Scholes model assumes the option's underlying stock price moves continuously. This means that if we were to graph the stock's price movement over time, we would not need to lift the pen from the paper. A trader performing a dynamic hedge must be able to adjust his or her holdings of the underlying stock as the delta changes in response to price movements. If the stock price does not move continuously but jumps before the trader can adjust the stock holdings, the hedge will not perform properly. This problem led to major losses for firms that attempted to replicate put options with dynamic hedges during the stock market crash of October 1987. Merton [1976] and Jones [1984] have developed option pricing models that account for discontinuous stock price movements.

Constant Riskless Interest Rate   The Black-Scholes model assumes that the riskless interest rate is known and constant. If the rate moves over time, the borrowing and lending rates that will be used in the dynamic hedges are not known over time. Merton [1973] developed a model that accounts for moving riskless rates.

Constant Volatility   The Black-Scholes model assumes that the volatility, or standard deviation of the rate of change of the underlying stock's price, is known and constant. Option pricing models such as the Constant Elasticity of Variance model[17] can account for stock price volatility that moves over time in a known manner. Accounting for volatility that moves in an uncertain way is a current area of research.

European Expiration   The Black-Scholes model assumes that the option being priced is a European call option on a stock that pays no dividend before the option expires. The assumption of European expiration is a good one for call options on stocks that pay no dividends, for Merton [1973] showed that one would never choose to exercise such a call option early.[18] Unfortunately, this is not true

---

[17] This model was developed by John Cox. For a description, see Ritchken [1987].

[18] Merton showed that call options on non-dividend-paying stocks are always worth more "alive" than "dead." Thus, even if owners of call options decided to exercise, there would be people who would pay them more for the options than the owners could receive by exercising them.

for put options or for options on stocks that pay dividends before the options expire. For example, suppose we know that a stock is going to pay a large dividend tomorrow. The price of the stock therefore will drop significantly over the next day, and the expiration value of the call option will go down. In this case, it may pay to exercise the call option early.[19] Jarrow and Rudd [1983] and Cox and Rubinstein [1985] discuss several techniques that account for early exercise and dividends.

Validity of the Black-Scholes Approach   We have just seen that the Black-Scholes model makes a number of assumptions that might be violated and that other models can account for such violations. However, all of these other models are based on the intuition of the Black-Scholes model: that the price of an option should be the same as the cost of a dynamic strategy that replicates the option. All employ the Black-Scholes approach of using a delta to set up dynamic hedges.[20]

Options on Futures

Options on futures are similar to options on "physicals" such as stocks except that they give the option holder the right to enter into a futures contract. A **call option on a futures** gives the holder the right to enter into a long futures position at a prespecified exercise price. A **put option on a futures** gives the holder the right to enter into a short futures position at a predetermined exercise price. To exercise an option on a futures, one enters into the appropriate futures position. The exercise price is the fixed price at which the clearinghouse enters the option holder into the futures position.

   Examples 9.11 and 9.12 demonstrate how to exercise options on the hypothetical S&P 1 futures contract.

▪ **Example 9.11: Exercising a Call Option on an S&P 1 Futures Contract** Suppose that in May an investor holds a $115-exercise-price call option on an S&P 1 futures contract that expires in July. The current July futures price for the S&P 1 is $125. If the investor decides to exercise the option, the clearinghouse will enter her into a long July S&P 1 futures position at the $115 exercise price. Because the current futures price is $125, the clearinghouse will pay the investor $10 in marking-to-market gains. This will bring her long position up to the current $125 futures price. The investor will then be able to close out this position by entering into an offsetting short position, or she can keep the long position open.

   The gross profit from exercising the option will be

---

[19] In general, an option is most likely to be exercised early if it is well into the money, because then the value afforded by the downside protection is worth less.

[20] Black and Scholes [1972], MacBeth and Merville [1979], and Whaley [1982] provided empirical tests of option pricing models.

$$\text{Profit} = \text{(Current futures price)} - \text{(Exercise price)}$$
$$= \$125 - \$115$$
$$= \$10.$$

The net profit will be the $10 gross profit less the premium.

Now suppose the current futures price is $100. If the investor exercises the call option, the clearinghouse will enter her into a long futures position at $115 and then mark her to market at the current $100 futures price. The investor will lose $15 on the transaction. Thus, the owner of a call option on a futures will not exercise if the current futures price is below the exercise price. ∎

■ **Example 9.12: Exercising a Put Option on an S&P 1 Futures Contract**
Suppose that in May an investor holds a $115-exercise-price put option on an S&P 1 futures contract that expires in July. The current July futures price for the S&P 1 is $100. If the investor decides to exercise the put option, the clearinghouse will enter him into a short July S&P 1 futures position at the $115 exercise price. Because the current futures price is $100, the clearinghouse will pay the investor $15 in marking-to-market gains. This will lower the short position to the current futures price of $100. The investor will then be able to close out this position by entering into an offsetting long position, or he can keep the short position open.

The gross profit from exercising the option will be

$$\text{Profit} = \text{(Exercise price)} - \text{(Current futures price)}$$
$$= \$115 - \$100$$
$$= \$15.$$

The net profit will be the $15 gross profit less the premium.

Now suppose the current futures price is $125. If the investor exercises the option, the clearinghouse will enter him into a short futures position at $115 and then mark him to market at the current $125 futures price. The investor will lose $10 on the transaction. Thus, put option owners will not exercise if the futures price is above the exercise price. ∎

Examples 9.11 and 9.12 demonstrate that the payoffs from holding options on S&P 1 futures are very similar to those from holding options on IBM stock. The only difference is that the payoffs from options on futures are computed from the futures price instead of the stock price. The payoff diagrams for options on futures are identical to those for options on stocks except that the futures price rather than the stock price is on the horizontal axis.

The similarity between options and options on futures is even closer because most options on futures expire at about the same time as the underlying futures. Suppose they expire on exactly the same date. We know that the futures price will be equal to the spot price on that date. Thus, if a European call option on IBM and a European call option on the S&P 1 futures have the same exercise prices and expiration dates, they will also have identical payoffs. If the option on futures expires somewhat before the futures, the two contracts will have slightly different payoffs. In practice, however, the expiration dates on the options on futures and the futures are so close that the two types of contracts can be considered almost identical.[21]

Given the similarity between options and options on futures, why do options on futures exist? The next section shows that arbitrage with options on futures can be a little less costly than arbitrage with options on physicals.

Pricing and Arbitrage for Options on Futures

We have seen that options on stocks can be priced by examining the cost of option-replicating portfolios. Such portfolios consist of delta shares of stock and borrowing and require periodic dynamic readjustment. Black [1976] showed that call options on futures can be priced by using similar strategies to construct replicating portfolios. These strategies involve

1. Going long delta futures for each call to be replicated

2. Lending

Investors must also adjust the number of futures positions as the delta changes over time.

Black showed that the cost of such a strategy is

$$\text{Call premium} = PV(F_0)N(d1) - PV(E)N(d2) \qquad \textbf{(9.15)}$$

$$d1 = \frac{\ln(F_0/E) + 0.5(V^2)(T)}{V\sqrt{T}}$$

$$d2 = d1 - V\sqrt{T},$$

where the inputs are the same as those in the Black-Scholes model except that

F_0 = current futures price

V = standard deviation of rate of change of futures price

This formula is called the **Black formula**. The delta for options on futures is

$$\text{Delta} = PV(\$1)N(d1). \qquad \textbf{(9.16)}$$

The dynamic strategy suggested by the Black formula is somewhat easier to implement than the one suggested by the Black-Scholes model.[22] Options on futures usually are traded in pits adjacent to the futures pits, so it is quite easy and inexpensive to arbitrage between the two types of contracts. Arbitrage with options

---

[21] There are some important differences between American options and American options on futures. For example, while we would never exercise an American call option on a non-dividend-paying stock early, we might exercise a call option on a futures early.

[22] This is why many firms use short futures positions rather than short stock positions to replicate put options for portfolio insurance.

on stocks, on the other hand, requires trading across markets. Further, it is easier to get in and out of futures contracts than it is to change positions in the underlying stock. Thus, options on futures are slightly less expensive for arbitrageurs than options on stocks.

Embedded Options

Up to this point we have been examining **traded options**, the formal options on physicals and options on futures that are traded in financial markets. We can also use our analysis to study the options that are implicitly in many types of contracts when one party can terminate the contract at his or her discretion. The classic example of such **embedded options** is the *prepayment option* of a standard mortgage agreement. In a home mortgage contract, the borrower has the option to prepay the loan at the interest rate quoted in the contract. If interest rates fall, the borrower may benefit by repaying the loan and refinancing at a lower rate. If interest rates rise, however, it will not be in the borrower's interest to prepay the loan. Thus, the prepayment option essentially grants the borrower an **embedded call option** on the value of the loan. If rates fall (and hence the present value of the loan payments increases), the borrower will exercise the option. If rates rise (and the present value of the loan payments thus decreases), the borrower will not exercise the option.

Figure 9.25 shows that the prepayment option can significantly affect mortgage values in the secondary market. It plots the market value of a GNMA security backed by a portfolio of 11 percent residential mortgages against the value of T-note futures from January 1985 through May 1989. The T-note futures price represents the effect of interest rate changes on the value of a riskless investment. Figure 9.25 thus shows how the value of a security that includes the prepayment option changes relative to the value of a riskless security without such an option as interest rates fall. The kinked shape of the curve in Figure 9.25 shows that once interest rates fall to a certain level, the GNMA security price does not increase as rapidly as does the price of the security without the prepayment option. This is because the prepayment option places a cap on mortgage values once interest rates fall below a given level.[23]

Owning a GNMA security is thus like writing a covered call. The kinked line in Figure 9.25 is very similar to the covered call option shown in Figure 9.15. To hedge a GNMA security, it is not enough to buy T-note futures to guard against increases in interest rates. One must also buy a call option on T-note futures to offset the option written.

---

[23] Unlike the covered call in Figure 9.15, there is still a slight upward movement in value as rates rise above the "kink." This occurs because some investors do not optimally exercise their embedded call options.

Figure 9.25 GNMA 11 Percent versus T-Note Futures, 1985–1989

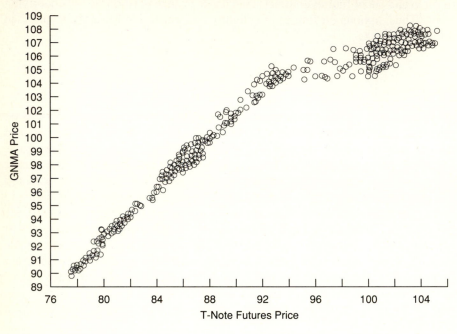

Source: Prudential-Bache.

Summary

The introduction and growth of the options markets have opened up a wide range of trading and hedging strategies for investors and firms. Investors have considerable leeway in adjusting the risk-and-return characteristics of the positions they take by combining options with one another and with other assets. Portfolio managers can use options to create insurance for their portfolios so that the portfolios will benefit from favorable price movements but will not suffer losses from unfavorable movements. The terms of such insurance, the premia and deductibles, can be adjusted by choosing the appropriate options positions. Options on futures are very similar to options on physicals and thus can be used for many of the same purposes.

Like futures contracts, options are priced by arbitrage. The put-call parity relationship derived in this chapter shows how put and call prices relate to each other. This relationship is very useful for investors who wish to evaluate certain option trading strategies. The Black-Scholes option pricing model, which this chapter covered on an intuitive level, determines a call option's price by computing the value of a portfolio that replicates the option. The Black-Scholes model requires that the replicating portfolio be periodically adjusted with a dynamic hedging technique that accounts for the effects of stock price changes. This pricing model is widely used by options traders. There are also several other option pricing

Figure 9.26 Eurodollar Futures and Futures Option Transactions Prices for May 23, 1989

```
EURODOLLAR (IMM)—$1 million; pts of 100%
                                        Yield      Open
       Open  High  Low Settle  Chg  Settle Chg Interest
June   90.72 90.77 90.59 90.65 + .05  9.35 –  .05 209,500
Sept   91.07 91.07 90.89 91.00 + .07  9.00 –  .07 226,609
Dec    91.03 91.05 90.90 91.02 + .11  8.98 –  .11 106,004
Mr90   91.13 91.14 91.00 91.10 + .08  8.90 –  .08 62,561
June   91.11 91.13 90.99 91.06 + .05  8.94 –  .05 34,537
Sept   91.06 91.06 90.92 90.98 + .02  9.02 –  .02 28,890
Dec    90.94 90.94 90.81 90.86 + .01  9.14 –  .01 24,937
Mr91   90.98 91.00 90.88 90.92 + .01  9.08 –  .01 16,290
June   90.95 90.99 90.87 90.91 + .01  9.09 –  .01 14,103
Sept   90.95 90.96 90.86 90.90 + .01  9.10 –  .01 19,281
Dec    90.89 90.92 90.80 90.85 + .01  9.15 –  .01 11,940
Mr92   90.94 90.96 90.84 90.90 + .02  9.10 –  .02 7,012
 Est vol 289,347; vol Mon 183,076; open int 761,664, +205.

EURODOLLAR (CME) $ million; pts. of 100%
Strike      Calls—Settle            Puts—Settle
Price    Jun-c  Sep-c  Dec-c   Jun-p  Sep-p  Dec-p
9025     0.43   0.88   0.98    0.03   0.15   0.24
9050     0.23   0.70   0.82    0.08   0.21   0.32
9075     0.11   0.53   0.67    0.21   0.29   0.41
9100     0.05   0.39   0.54    0.40   0.39   0.51
9125     0.02   0.28   0.41    0.62   0.52   ....
9150     0.01   0.19   0.31    0.85   0.68   0.75
 Est. Vol. 19,007, Mon vol. 12,938 calls, 10,782 puts
```

Source: *The Wall Street Journal*, May 24, 1989.

models in use that follow the same approach as the Black-Scholes model but are based on less restrictive assumptions.

Problems

1. Consider the strategy of writing a July IBM $115-exercise-price straddle on May 23, 1989. Use the prices in Figure 9.1.
    a. Produce a payoff diagram for this strategy.
    b. Over what ranges of July IBM prices does this strategy earn a profit?
    c. When would you undertake this strategy?

2. Consider the strategy of buying one July IBM $115-exercise-price call option and two July IBM $115-exercise-price put options on May 23, 1989. Use the prices in Figure 9.1.
    a. Produce a payoff diagram for this strategy.
    b. Over what ranges of July IBM prices is this strategy profitable?
    c. When would you undertake this strategy?

Use Figure 9.26 to solve Problems 3 through 5. Recall from Chapter 5 that the Eurodollar futures price is 100 minus the LIBOR. (The options prices are quoted in percentage points.)

3. Consider the May 23, 1989, prices for Eurodollar futures and futures options in Figure 9.26.

    a.   Draw a payoff diagram for the strategy of buying one September Eurodollar 91.00-exercise-price call option and going short one September Eurodollar futures contract versus the September Eurodollar futures at the options' expiration. Ignore the cost of the options.

    b.   How does this diagram compare with the strategy of buying one September Eurodollar 91.00-exercise-price put option?

    c.   What does this say about the equilibrium price of the call versus that of the put?

    d.   Do the actual prices accord with your theory in part c?

4.   Repeat Problem 4, but use 91.50-exercise-price options.

5.   Suppose that on May 23, 1989, you know your firm will have $5 million to lend out for three months on September 18. You plan to lend in the Eurodollar market at the LIBOR (with funds paid immediately). You fear that interest rates will fall between now and September 18. Consider these three scenarios for the September 18 LIBOR:

    ▪   I: 6 percent
    ▪   II: 8 percent
    ▪   III: 10 percent

Consider these three strategies:

A: Go long September Eurodollar futures.
B: Buy call options on Eurodollar futures with an exercise price of 91.00.
C: Buy call options on Eurodollar futures with an exercise price of 91.50.

    Figure your net interest rate under each scenario (gross of contract costs) for each strategy. Compute the cost of each strategy. Produce a payoff diagram for net interest versus the LIBOR on September 18. Do this both gross and net of contract costs.

6.   Suppose the current price of IBM stock is $109.30. The riskless rate of interest is 9 percent. One year from now, the stock will be selling for either $96 or $134.

    a.   Using the techniques in Table 9.3, construct a strategy that will replicate the payoff from holding two $115-exercise-price IBM call options that expire in one year.

    b.   In equilibrium, what will be the price of the call option?

    c.   How does the price you derived in part b compare to that when the price of IBM can go only to $100 or $130? How do you explain the difference?

Interest Rate Swaps

The **interest rate swap market** has been one of the most rapidly growing sectors in the international capital markets over the past decade. In a very short time, trading in interest rate swaps has grown from nothing to hundreds of billions of dollars' worth of transactions every year. Interest rate swaps are used primarily by people who wish to convert variable-rate loans into fixed-rate loans and vice versa. They are very similar to short-term interest rate futures contracts and are used in many of the same ways, often as an alternative to futures.

At its simplest level, an interest rate swap involves one party swapping fixed-rate interest payments for another party's floating-rate payments. However, the instruments offered in the swap market have grown in complexity. For example, one can now swap floating-rate payments denominated in German Deutsche marks for fixed-rate payments denominated in Italian lire. In this chapter we will introduce interest rate swaps, provide examples of how they are used, and demonstrate the similarity between interest rate swaps and positions in interest rate futures contracts.

Generic Interest Rate Swaps

The simplest form of interest rate swap is called a **generic swap** or **plain vanilla swap**.[1] The two parties involved are called **counterparties**. One party, the **fixed-rate payer**, agrees to make periodic fixed payments to the other. The fixed amount is known to both parties when the deal is made. In exchange, the other party, the **floating-rate payer**, agrees to make periodic variable payments to the first party. The floating payment varies according to some short-term interest rate index. These payments are quoted as rates that are applied to a **notional principal amount**. No principal actually changes hands in the swap. The standard periodicity of a generic swap is six months, although annual payments are also common. Figure 10.1 illustrates the flow of payments in a generic swap.

---

[1] Much of the material in this section is taken from MacFarlane, Ross, and Showers [1985].

Figure 10.1 Generic Interest Rate Swap

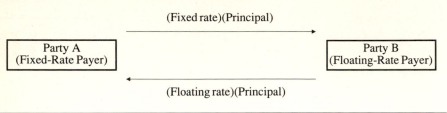

The date on which the counterparties commit to the swap is called the **trade date**. Interest begins to accrue on the **effective date**. The **settlement date** is the date on which any net cash payment is made between the two parties. This might occur if a swap is being traded in the secondary market. The swap is priced on the trade date as of the settlement date. In generic swaps, and when a swap is being entered for the first time, the effective date is usually the same as the settlement date. The **maturity date** of a swap is the date on which the payments cease.

Swap interest payments are made in arrears. The first payment—say, six months after the effective date—is figured according to the short-term interest rate index on the effective date. The next payment, such as in one year, is calculated according to the short-term interest rate index six months from the effective date. Thus, both parties know the next payment in advance.

Example 10.1 presents a generic interest rate swap.

▪ **Example 10.1: Generic Interest Rate Swap**   Suppose that on September 15, 1988, two counterparties enter into a generic interest rate swap that begins on September 22, 1988. The swap has a maturity of five years. Thus, the trade date of the swap is September 15, 1988, the effective date is September 22, 1988, and the maturity date is September 22, 1993.

The notional face value of the swap is $10 million. The swap calls for the fixed-rate payer to pay the current yield to maturity on a five-year, 12 percent Treasury note plus 50 basis points. Assuming the current yield to maturity on this note is 10 percent, the fixed-rate payments are at a 10.5 percent rate. The floating-rate payer agrees to pay the six-month LIBOR. Payments will be swapped every six months. Table 10.1 presents the payments made by each party.

The first swap of payments occurs six months after the effective date, on March 22, 1989. The fixed-rate payment on this date, as on all other payment dates, is

$$\text{Fixed-rate payment} = \frac{(\text{Annualized fixed rate})(\text{Notional principal})}{2}$$
$$= \frac{(0.1050)(\$10 \text{ million})}{2}$$
$$= \$0.5250 \text{ million.}$$

The floating-rate payer will pay interest based on the 8 percent LIBOR that prevailed on the effective date of September 22, 1988. This payment is

Table 10.1 Interest Rate Swap Payments

Fixed rate: 10.50%
Notional principal: $10 million

Date	Six-Month LIBOR	Fixed Payment (Millions)	Floating Payment (Millions)	Net to Fixed-Rate Payer (Millions)
9/22/88	8.00%	—	—	—
3/22/89	8.40	$0.5250	$0.4000	–$0.1250
9/22/89	8.70	0.5250	0.4200	–0.1050
3/22/90	9.10	0.5250	0.4350	–0.0900
9/22/90	9.50	0.5250	0.4550	–0.0700
3/22/91	10.00	0.5250	0.4750	–0.0500
9/22/91	9.70	0.5250	0.5000	–0.0250
3/22/92	10.50	0.5250	0.4850	–0.0400
9/22/92	11.00	0.5250	0.5250	0.0000
3/22/93	11.50	0.5250	0.5500	0.0250
9/22/93	—	0.5250	0.5750	0.0500

Floating-rate payment (March 22, 1989)

$$= \frac{(\text{Annualized 6-month LIBOR})(\text{Notional principal})}{2}$$

$$= \frac{(0.0800)(\$10 \text{ million})}{2}$$

$$= \$0.4000 \text{ million.}$$

The net payment to the fixed-rate payer on March 22, 1989, is

Net payment to fixed-rate payer
= Floating-rate payment – Fixed-rate payment
= $0.4000 million – $0.5250 million
= –$0.1250 million.

The floating-rate payer therefore receives a positive net payment of $0.125 million.
    The second payment of the swap will occur on September 22, 1989. The fixed-rate payer again will pay $0.5250 million, but now the floating-rate payer will pay interest based on the six-month LIBOR that prevailed six months earlier on March 22, 1988:

Floating-rate payment (September 22, 1989)

$$= \frac{(\text{Annualized 6-month LIBOR})(\text{Notional principal})}{2}$$

$$= \frac{(0.0840)(\$10 \text{ million})}{2}$$

$$= \$0.4200 \text{ million.}$$

The swap in Example 10.1 is the simplest type of interest rate swap. Many generic swaps involve slightly more complicated terms, although they retain the same general structure as the one in Example 10.1. For instance, the semiannual payments in Example 10.1 were computed simply by dividing the annual interest rates by 2. Some swaps require the floating payments to be calculated by multiplying the six-month LIBOR by the ratio of the number of days in each six-month period to 360. In other simple swaps, the floating payment is specified as the LIBOR plus or minus a certain number of basis points.

Like futures and options, swaps develop only if two counterparties agree to enter into a swap contract. Thus, the total net supply of swaps is always zero. Another similarity is that the gains on one side of a swap will always equal the losses on the other, as we saw in Example 10.1.

Table 10.1 clearly shows that the fixed-rate payer loses when short-term interest rates fall and gains when interest rates rise. The fixed-rate payer pays a fixed amount in all cases but receives a lower amount when interest rates are low and a higher amount when they are high. The floating-rate payer gains when interest rates fall and loses when they rise. Thus, the fixed-rate payer's position is similar to that of a short short-term interest rate futures position. The floating-rate payer's position is similar to that of a long short-term interest rate futures position. We will define this relationship more precisely in the next section.

Interest Rate Swaps and Eurodollar Strips

If we reinterpret our results from Example 10.1, we can see that interest rate swaps are very similar to a certain hypothetical combination of Eurodollar futures positions. Suppose, for the purposes of argument, that there is a six-month Eurodollar time deposit futures contract. It is just like the actual 90-day contract except that its gains and losses are calculated as $50 per basis point instead of $25 per basis point, because its interest covers a period twice as long. The contract will be settled with cash, and the final settlement futures price will be

Final settlement price = 100 − (6-month LIBOR at expiration).

We can create a position very similar to that of an interest rate swap by combining these hypothetical Eurodollar contracts into a strip. Recall from Chapter 5 that a strip of Eurodollar futures is a collection of Eurodollar futures contracts with different expiration dates, where the number of contracts is the same for each expiration date. Suppose that on September 22, 1988, we enter into a strip that has 10 short six-month Eurodollar time deposit futures contracts for every September 22 and March 22 expiration date over the next 4½ years. Thus, these contracts will cover the next nine expiration dates, so the last group of 10 contracts expires on March 22, 1993. Suppose also that the current futures price for all of the contracts is 89.50. The interest rate reflected by this price, 10.5 percent, is the same as the fixed rate in the swap agreement in Example 10.1.

We will calculate the profits this short strip will yield if the six-month LIBOR follows the scenario in Table 10.1. The first group of 10 contracts in the strip expires on March 22, 1989, with a settlement price of $100 - 8.40 = 91.60$. The futures profit is

> Futures profit (March 22, 1989)
> $=$ (Number of contracts)(Initial futures – Closing futures)($50 per basis point)
> $= (10)(89.50 - 91.60)(100)(\$50)$
> $= -\$105,000$
> $= -\$0.1050$ million.

The second group of 10 contracts expires on September 22, 1989, with a settlement price of $100 - 8.70 = 91.30$. The futures profit is

> Futures profit (September 22, 1989)
> $= (10)(89.50 - 91.30)(100)(\$50)$
> $= -\$90,000$
> $= -\$0.0900$ million.

When we compare these cash flows with those of the swap in Example 10.1, we see that the strip profits equal the net receipts earned by the fixed-rate payer in the swap six months later. The loss on the 10 Eurodollar futures contracts that expire on March 22, 1989, exactly equals the loss to the fixed-rate payer on September 22, 1989. The loss on the 10 futures contracts that expire on September 22, 1989, exactly equals the loss to the fixed-rate payer on March 22, 1990. This pattern continues over the lives of the swap and the strip. Since the strip's cash flows precede those of the swap by six months, the strip never has a payment equal to the very first payment to the fixed-rate party in the swap.

The six-month timing difference between the cash flows of the swap and the strip occurs because the net swap payments are determined by the interest rate at the beginning of each six-month period, while the futures gains and losses are calculated by the interest rate at the end. We saw this distinction in Example 5.4 in Chapter 5, when we showed how to hedge a floating-rate loan with a strip of short Eurodollar time deposit futures contracts. The gains and losses on the strip were set by the interest rates on the futures expiration dates, the same dates that the interest being hedged was determined for the following quarters. One final difference between the swap and the hypothetical strip is that the entire net cash flows on the swap occur on the repricing dates, while the strip cash flows are marked to market over each six-month period.

Except for these minor technical differences, we have shown that the fixed-rate payer in a swap has net cash flows equal to those of a strip of hypothetical six-month short Eurodollar time deposit futures contracts. All the futures contracts in this strip must have the same initial price, and this price must reflect the fixed interest rate of the swap. The floating-rate payer in a swap has net cash flows essentially equal to those of a strip of hypothetical six-month long Eurodollar time deposit futures contracts. Since we saw in Chapter 5 that a firm can hedge a variable-rate loan with a strip of short Eurodollar futures, we are not surprised to learn that an interest rate swap can also hedge a variable-rate loan. Example 10.2 shows how such a hedge works.

Table 10.2 Hedged Interest Costs Using a Swap

Fixed rate: 10.50%
Notional principal: $10 million
Floating spread: 1.00%

Date	Six-Month LIBOR	Interest Payment (Millions)	Net Receipts to Fixed-Rate Payer (Millions)	Interest Payment (Millions)
9/22/88	8.00%	—	—	—
3/22/89	8.40	$0.4500	–$0.1250	$0.5750
9/22/89	8.70	0.4700	–0.1050	0.5750
3/22/90	9.10	0.4850	–0.0900	0.5750
9/22/90	9.50	0.5050	–0.0700	0.5750
3/22/91	10.00	0.5250	–0.0500	0.5750
9/22/91	9.70	0.5500	–0.0250	0.5750
3/22/92	10.50	0.5350	–0.0400	0.5750
9/22/92	11.00	0.5750	0.0000	0.5750
3/22/93	11.50	0.6000	0.0250	0.5750
9/22/93	—	0.6250	0.0500	0.5750

▪ **Example 10.2: Using a Swap to Hedge a Variable-Rate Loan**   Suppose a firm borrows $10 million at a floating rate on September 22, 1988. The loan calls for the firm to pay the six-month LIBOR plus 100 basis points over the next five years. The interest rate for the initial period is set at the current LIBOR plus 100 basis points, and the interest is to be paid in arrears. The interest rate is reset every six months.

The firm wishes to convert this variable-rate loan into a fixed-rate loan. It can do so with an interest rate swap in which it exchanges fixed-rate payments for floating-rate payments. The firm gets the quote for the swap in Example 10.1. This swap allows the firm to exchange the LIBOR payments for 10.5 percent fixed-rate payments. This side of the swap is appropriate for the firm, because the firm wishes to receive floating-rate payments that will cover its loan obligation and to pay a fixed rate.

Table 10.2 shows what the firm's interest payments will be if it does and does not hedge its interest payments by entering into the swap. The fixed-rate payer's net payments under the swap are taken from Table 10.1.

Table 10.2 shows that no matter what happens to the six-month LIBOR over the next five years, the firm's net interest payments will always be $575,000 because of its swap position. Thus, the firm pays a fixed interest rate of

$$\text{Locked-in rate} = \frac{(2)(\text{Interest payment})}{\text{Principal}}$$

$$= \frac{(2)(\$575,000)}{\$10,000,000}$$

$$= 11.50\%,$$

where we multiply by 2 to annualize the rate.

The interest rate swap has allowed the firm to create a fixed-rate loan at the 10.5 percent fixed rate of the swap plus the 100-basis-point spread over the LIBOR required by the firm's loan. The floating-rate payments the firm receives under the swap cover the LIBOR component of its loan obligation, but the firm still must pay the 100-basis-point spread. ∎

Hedging a Swap with Eurodollar Strips

We have seen that the cash flows of an interest rate swap are similar to those of a strip of hypothetical six-month Eurodollar time deposit futures contracts. Now we will see that the hypothetical six-month Eurodollar time deposit contract can be created synthetically with a strip of 90-day Eurodollar time deposit futures. Thus, the cash flows of an interest rate swap are also similar to those of a strip of 90-day Eurodollar futures. As a result, it is possible for traders to hedge their interest rate swaps by combining 90-day Eurodollar time deposit futures contracts.

The hypothetical six-month Eurodollar time deposit futures contract is written on the 180-day LIBOR at the contract's expiration date, time T. It covers the following time line:

To show that the hypothetical six-month Eurodollar futures is equivalent to a strip of 90-day Eurodollar futures, we must determine what strip of the 90-day contracts would have the same cash flows as the hypothetical contract over this period.

We know from Chapter 5 that the following relationship should hold between interest rates at time T:

$$1 + r_{T,T+180} = (1 + r_{T,T+90})(1 + r^T_{T+90,T+180}) \qquad (10.1)$$
$$\approx 1 + r_{T,T+90} + r^T_{T+90,T+180},$$

where

$r_{T,T+180}$ = nonannualized six-month LIBOR that prevails at T

$r_{T,T+90}$ = nonannualized 90-day LIBOR that prevails at T

$r^T_{T+90,T+180}$ = nonannualized 90-day LIBOR implied at time T by the time T + 90 Eurodollar futures contract

Equation 10.1 simply says that at time T, the 180-day rate must equal the rate one could receive by investing for 90 days and then rolling the proceeds into a 90-day investment that carries a rate locked in at time T. The last line of Equation 10.1 reflects the small size of the interest-on-interest term. If we rewrite Equation 10.1, we can approximate the LIBOR implied by the futures that expires at T + 90:

$$r^T_{T+90,T+180} = r_{T,T+180} - r_{T,T+90}. \qquad (10.2)$$

Equation 10.1 shows us how to create a synthetic 180-day Eurodollar time deposit futures contract. First, we can use a 90-day Eurodollar futures contract that expires at time T to lock in the rate $r_{T,T+90}$. Then we can use a 90-day Eurodollar futures contract that expires at time T + 90 to lock in the rate $r^T_{T+90,T+180}$. By definition, the price of the latter contract will be determined by $r^T_{T+90,T+180}$ at time T. The hypothetical six-month Eurodollar time deposit futures contract can be formed synthetically simply by combining these two 90-day Eurodollar time deposit futures contracts.

Example 10.3 demonstrate how to create a synthetic 180-day Eurodollar time deposit futures contract.

▪ **Example 10.3: Creating a Synthetic 180-Day Eurodollar Time Deposit Futures Contract**   Suppose that in 50 days we will have $10 million to lend over a period of 180 days and we wish to lock in an interest rate for this planned lending. Our strategy is to take 10 long positions in 90-day Eurodollar time deposit futures contracts that expire in 50 and 140 days. We will close out the second futures contracts in 50 days, when the first futures contract expires, and we lend out the $10 million. The time line for this strategy is

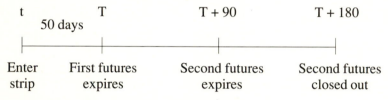

Suppose the prices of these futures contracts at time t are

Eurodollar time deposit futures that expires in 50 days	92.50
Eurodollar time deposit futures that expires in 140 days	92.00

The 90-day interest rates implied by these futures prices are 7.5 and 8 percent, respectively.

Table 10.3 presents four scenarios for the 90- and 180-day LIBOR in 50 days (at time T). It also shows the net 180-day lending rate that can be locked in for our $10 million by the futures positions prescribed above. We will show how to compute this rate by working through scenario I.

Under Scenario I, the 90-day LIBOR in 50 days is 9.5 percent and the 180-day LIBOR is 10 percent. Our futures contracts that expire at T will converge to a price of 90.50 = 100.00 − 9.50 at that time to reflect the current 90-day LIBOR. We know from Equation 10.2 that the 90-day LIBOR implied at time T by the futures that expires at time T + 90 will be the 180-day LIBOR at T minus the 90-day LIBOR at T:

90-day LIBOR implied at T by futures that expires at T + 90

$$= \frac{0.100}{2} - \frac{0.095}{4}$$

$= 2.625\%$ for 90 days

$= 10.50\%$ annualized.

Table 10.3 Creating a Synthetic Six-Month Eurodollar Time Deposit Futures Contract

Principal: $10 million
Futures expiring in 50 days: 92.50
Futures expiring in 140 days: 92.00

	Scenario			
	I	**II**	**III**	**IV**
180-day LIBOR	10.000%	5.000%	9.500%	4.500%
90-day LIBOR	9.500%	4.500%	10.000%	5.000%
Forward 90-day LIBOR	10.500%	5.500%	9.000%	5.000%
Interest received (millions)	$0.5000	$0.2500	$0.4750	$0.2250
Profit on 50-day futures (millions)	–$0.0500	$0.0750	–$0.0625	$0.0625
Profit on 140-day futures (millions)	–$0.0625	$0.0625	–$0.0250	$0.1000
Net interest (millions)	$0.3875	$0.3875	$0.3875	$0.3875
Rate	7.750%	7.750%	7.750%	7.750%

Therefore, the price of the futures that expires at time T + 90 will converge to 89.50 = 100.00 – 10.50 at time T.

Now that we know the prices of our two futures contracts at time T, we can compute the lending rate locked in for our $10 million at T by our position in the two contracts. The actual interest we will receive over the 180 days will be

$$\text{Interest received} = (0.10/2)(\$10 \text{ million})$$
$$= \$0.5000 \text{ million}.$$

The profit at T on the futures that expire at T will be

$$\text{Profit on first futures contracts} = (90.50 - 92.50)(100)(10)(\$25)$$
$$= -\$0.0500 \text{ million}.$$

The profit at T on the futures that expire at T + 90 will be

$$\text{Profit on second futures contracts} = (89.50 - 92.00)(100)(10)(\$25)$$
$$= -\$0.0625 \text{ million}.$$

The net interest on the loan is the interest received plus the futures profits:

$$\text{Net interest received}$$
$$= (\$0.5000 \text{ million} - \$0.0500 \text{ million} - \$0.0625 \text{ million})$$
$$= \$0.3875 \text{ million}.$$

On a percentage basis, this interest is

$$\text{Rate received} = \frac{\$0.3875 \text{ million}}{\$10 \text{ million}}$$

$$= 3.875\% \text{ for 180 days}$$

$$= 7.750\% \text{ annualized.}$$

This rate is the exact average of the 7.5 and 8 percent rates implied by the two futures contracts when we entered into our futures positions at time t.

Thus, by taking long positions in 90-day Eurodollar time deposit futures contracts that expire at times T and T + 90, we have created a synthetic 180-day Eurodollar time deposit futures contract that expires at time T. The interest rate locked in by the synthetic futures contract is the average of the rates implied by the two 90-day Eurodollar time deposit futures at time t.

In practice, this method of creating a synthetic 180-day Eurodollar time deposit futures is less precise than it appears in this example. For one thing, this example uses the approximation in Equation 10.1. Furthermore, we assume here that a futures contract that expires exactly 90 days after time T exists. But these approximations are not very far off, and practitioners generally find that this technique works quite well. ■

Example 10.3 shows that we can create a synthetic 6-month Eurodollar time deposit futures contract using consecutive 90-day Eurodollar time deposit futures contracts. Since we have also shown that an interest rate swap is similar to a strip of 6-month Eurodollar time deposit futures contracts, we now know that a swap is also similar to a strip of 90-day Eurodollar time deposit futures contracts.[2]

This finding shows that we can hedge an interest rate swap with a strip of 90-day Eurodollar futures. Suppose we enter into an interest rate swap as a fixed-rate payer. We face the risk that short-term interest rates will fall. Our swap position has the same risk as a strip of short Eurodollar time deposit futures contracts. To hedge this swap, we can enter into a strip of *long* Eurodollar time deposit futures contracts that extend in time as far as the swap.

The use of strips of Eurodollar time deposit futures to hedge swaps has become a standard technique. This partly explains the large amount of open interest in the Eurodollar time deposit futures market that extends to distant contract months. Figure 10.2 presents a *Wall Street Journal* excerpt showing May 23, 1989, futures prices, volume, and open interest for both the T-bond and Eurodollar time deposit futures contracts. For the T-bond contract, the December open interest was only 9.71 percent of the June open interest. In contrast, for the Eurodollar time deposit contract, the December open interest was 50.60 percent of the June open interest.

Using strips of Eurodollar time deposit futures to hedge swaps does not work well for longer-term swaps that have 5- to 10-year maturities, for active trading in

---

[2] One other technical difference between the swap and the strip of 90-day Eurodollar futures is that the rates implied by the Eurodollar futures will not be the same at all expirations, while the fixed-rate payment of a swap will always be the same. We can approximate the fixed-rate payment as the average of the rates implied by the Eurodollar futures prices today.

Figure 10.2 Transactions of T-Bond and Eurodollar Time Deposit Futures Contracts for May 23, 1989

```
                        FUTURES
                                      Yield        Open
              Open  High  Low Settle  Chg Settle Chg Interest
     TREASURY BONDS (CBT)—$100,000; pts. 32nds of 100%
     June    93-02 93-15 92-19 92-27 − 10 8.765 + .035 201,176
     Sept    92-31 93-09 92-15 92-23 −  9 8.779 + .032  95,031
     Dec     92-25 93-04 92-12 92-18 − 10 8.797 + .036  19,538
     Mr90    92-21 92-28 92-09 92-14 −  9 8.811 + .032   6,693
     June    92-22 92-22 92-04 92-10 −  8 8.825 + .028   4,346
     Sept    92-15 92-15 91-31 92-05 −  8 8.843 + .029   1,999
     Dec     ....  ....  ....  92-00 −  7 8.861 + .025     266
     Mr91    ....  ....  ....  91-26 −  7 8.882 + .025     160
     June    ....  ....  ....  91-20 −  7 8.904 + .025     206
       Est vol 300,000; vol Mon 371,102; op int 329,435, −6,668.

     EURODOLLAR (IMM)—$1 million; pts of 100%
                                      Yield        Open
              Open  High  Low Settle  Chg Settle Chg Interest
     June    90.72 90.77 90.59 90.65 + .05 9.35 − .05 209,500
     Sept    91.07 91.07 90.89 91.00 + .07 9.00 − .07 226,609
     Dec     91.03 91.05 90.90 91.02 + .11 8.98 − .11 106,004
     Mr90    91.13 91.14 91.00 91.10 + .08 8.90 − .08  62,561
     June    91.11 91.13 90.99 91.06 + .05 8.94 − .05  34,537
     Sept    91.06 91.06 90.92 90.98 + .02 9.02 − .02  28,890
     Dec     90.94 90.94 90.81 90.86 + .01 9.14 − .01  24,937
     Mr91    90.98 91.00 90.88 90.92 + .01 9.08 − .01  16,290
     June    90.95 90.99 90.87 90.91 + .01 9.09 − .01  14,103
     Sept    90.95 90.96 90.86 90.90 + .01 9.10 − .01  19,281
     Dec     90.89 90.92 90.80 90.85 + .01 9.15 − .01  11,940
     Mr92    90.94 90.96 90.84 90.90 + .02 9.10 − .02   7,012
       Est vol 289,347; vol Mon 183,076; open int 761,664, +205.
```

Source: *The Wall Street Journal,* May 24, 1989.

Eurodollar time deposit futures extends only 3 to 4 years in the future. Those who wish to hedge longer swaps use either the stack hedge that we introduced in Chapter 5 or longer-term Treasury instruments.

Advantages of Swaps over Strips

People who wish to hedge variable-rate loans can use either interest rate swaps or strips of Eurodollar time deposit futures contracts. Because interest rate swaps often are hedged in the Eurodollar time deposit futures markets, arbitrageurs make sure that the advantage of using one over the other is very small. Many variable-rate borrowers prefer to hedge with swaps, because swaps embody Eurodollar futures strips in a single package and do not involve marking to market. Also, hedging with swaps is simpler, because swap cash flows are paid in arrears while strip cash flows occur at the beginning of each interest period. Therefore, swap cash flows match the interest payments on variable-rate loans more closely than do strip cash flows.

Quasi-Arbitrage

Firms often use interest rate swaps as tools in quasi-arbitrage. In Example 10.2, a firm uses an interest rate swap to convert a variable-rate loan into a fixed-rate loan.

Table 10.4 Creating a Synthetic Variable-Rate Loan

Action	Cash Flow
Pay 10% fixed	– 10.00%
Receive 10.50% fixed	+ 10.50%
Pay LIBOR	– LIBOR
Net	– (LIBOR – 0.50%)

This firm would have a quasi-arbitrage opportunity if the rate it would be charged directly for a fixed-rate loan exceeded the fixed rate it pays under the swap arrangement. Example 10.4 demonstrates how a firm that takes out a variable-rate loan can also use a swap for quasi-arbitrage.

■ **Example 10.4: Creating a Synthetic Variable-Rate Loan**   Suppose a firm wishes to borrow at a variable rate over a period of five years. It can borrow directly at the LIBOR plus 25 basis points, or it can convert a 10 percent, fixed-rate loan into a variable-rate loan by entering as a floating-rate payer into a swap of the six-month LIBOR for 10.5 percent.

Table 10.4 calculates the variable rate the firm will pay under the swap arrangement. It will pay 10 percent fixed to service its loan and pay the six-month LIBOR and receive 10.5 percent under the swap. Its net payment is therefore the LIBOR less the 50-basis-point net profit on its fixed payments. The firm has created a synthetic variable-rate loan at the LIBOR minus 50 basis points. The synthetic variable rate is less than the LIBOR plus the 25 basis points the firm would pay by borrowing directly at a variable rate. The firm thus makes a quasi-arbitrage profit of 75 basis points by choosing the swap strategy. ■

Quasi-arbitrage with swaps can be somewhat riskier than quasi-arbitrage with futures, because swap transactions are not guaranteed by a clearinghouse as futures contracts are. Swaps are guaranteed by large money center banks, however. Before entering into a swap, one must be careful to assess the risk of the guarantor.

Taking Offsetting Positions in Swaps

In Chapter 1, we saw that a futures position can be easily reversed by entering into an offsetting futures position. A forward position is somewhat more difficult to reverse. One must buy oneself out of the position with the opposite party or enter into an opposite position and carry both positions until expiration. Reversing interest rate swap positions is still more complicated, for there are four ways to do it. One could enter into an opposite swap position, assign the swap to another party, buy out the opposite position, or create a synthetic opposite position.

Examples 10.5 and 10.6 show how to reverse a swap with the first method by entering into an offsetting position.

Table 10.5 Offsetting a Swap: Floating-Rate Payer

Action	Cash Flow
1. Initial swap	
Receive 10.50% fixed	+10.50%
Pay LIBOR	– LIBOR
2. Offsetting swap	
Pay 12.00% fixed	– 12.00%
Receive LIBOR	+ LIBOR
Net	– 1.50%

Table 10.6 Offsetting a Swap: Fixed-Rate Payer

Action	Cash Flow
1. Initial swap	
Pay 10.50% fixed	– 10.50%
Receive LIBOR	+ LIBOR
2. Offsetting swap	
Receive 9.00% fixed	+ 9.50%
Pay LIBOR	– LIBOR
Net	– 1.00%

■ **Example 10.5: Offsetting a Swap: Floating-Rate Payer**   Suppose a firm has entered as a floating-rate payer into a swap that exchanges the LIBOR for 10.5 percent fixed interest. The swap has a term of five years and a notional principal of $10 million. Two years later, short-term rates have risen and the firm wishes to reverse its position. It can do so by taking a fixed-rate payer position in a new swap agreement. The new swaps have different terms due to the higher level of interest rates.

Suppose the new three-year swaps require the fixed-rate payer to exchange 12 percent interest for the LIBOR. Table 10.5 presents the firm's net interest payments if it enters into a new three-year swap as a fixed-rate payer. The firm's floating-rate payments will cancel each other, for the firm will pay the LIBOR on its first swap and receive the LIBOR on its new swap. However, the firm must pay 12 percent fixed interest on the new swap and will receive only 10.5 percent fixed interest on the old swap. The net result of the transaction is that the firm must pay 1.5 percent on the notional principal over the next three years. Its semiannual payments will be $75,000 each. ■

■ **Example 10.6: Offsetting a Swap: Fixed-Rate Payer**   Suppose a firm has entered as a fixed-rate payer into a swap that exchanges 10.5 percent fixed interest for the LIBOR. The swap has a term of five years, and its notional principal is $10 million. After two years, short-term rates have fallen and the firm wishes to reverse its swap position. It can do this by entering into a new swap as a floating-rate payer.

Suppose the new three-year swaps require the floating-rate payer to exchange the LIBOR for 9.5 percent interest. Table 10.6 shows the firm's net cash flows if it takes a floating-rate position in a new three-year swap. The firm's floating-rate payments will cancel, for the firm will receive the LIBOR on its old swap and pay the LIBOR on the new one. However, the firm must pay 10.5 percent interest on the old swap and will receive only 9.5 percent interest on the new swap. The net result is that the firm must pay 1 percent on the notional principal for the next three years. This amounts to semiannual payments of $50,000. ∎

A firm can also reverse a swap position by assigning it to another party as long as the initial counterparty agrees. If interest rates have moved against a firm, no one will take the swap without compensation. Swaps that require compensating payments are called **differential swaps**. A firm will be willing to assign the swap if the assignment fee is less than the present value of the cost of reversing the swap by entering into an opposite position. The two firms in Examples 10.5 and 10.6 must make semiannual payments over three years of $75,000 and $50,000, respectively, because they reversed their swaps with opposite positions. These are the costs they must weigh against the cost of reversing a swap through an assignment. Similarly, a firm might choose to buy its initial counterparty out of a swap agreement if the buyout fee is less than the present value of the cost of taking an opposite position.

The final course open to a firm that wishes to offset a swap is to create an opposite position in a synthetic swap. Earlier we saw that one can create a synthetic swap with a strip of Eurodollar time deposit futures. A floating-rate payer who wants to offset his or her swap position can do so by entering a strip of short Eurodollar time deposit futures. A fixed-rate payer can use a strip of long Eurodollar time deposit futures. Of course, the time until expiration of the initial swap must be short enough that existing Eurodollar time deposit contracts can form a synthetic swap of equal maturity.

Foreign Exchange Swaps

A rapidly growing sector of the swap market involves transactions in different currencies. For example, a firm may choose to raise funds using floating-rate borrowing in Italian lire, but wish to pay Deutsche marks. The firm can enter into a swap that will allow it to swap floating-rate payments in the two different currencies. Similarly, a firm may choose to raise funds using fixed-rate borrowing in lire but wish to pay floating-rate Deutsche marks. Again, the firm can enter into a swap that will allow it to swap these payments. Firms that utilize such swaps are searching for quasi-arbitrage opportunities.

Summary

Interest rate swaps are used by firms throughout the world to convert variable-rate loans into fixed-rate loans and vice versa. We have seen that the cash flows of interest rate swaps are very similar to those of certain strips of 90-day Eurodollar time deposit futures contracts. This means that swaps can be used for many of the same purposes as Eurodollar futures. Furthermore, Eurodollar futures can be used to hedge interest rate swap positions. Swaps have some advantages over Eurodollar strips when it comes to hedging loan payments. They are less complicated, and the timing of their cash flows usually matches that of loan interest payments more precisely.

In this chapter, we concentrated on the most simple types of swaps. A variety of more complicated swaps are traded, many of them involving different currencies.

Problems

1. Using Lotus, reproduce Table 10.1. Recalculate with a fixed rate of 10 percent.

2. Using Lotus, reproduce Table 10.2. Recalculate with a floating-rate spread of 1.50 percent.

3. Using Lotus, reproduce Table 10.3. Recalculate with a 50-day futures price of 92.30 and a 140-day futures price of 92.10.

References

Aggarwal, R. "Stock Index Futures and Cash Market Volatility." *Review of Futures Markets* 7 (1988): 290–299.

Aliber, R. "The Interest Rate Parity Theorem: A Reinterpretation." *Journal of Political Economy* 81 (1973): 1451–1459.

Anderson, R. W., and J. P. Danthine. "Cross-Hedging." *Journal of Political Economy* 89 (1981): 1182–1196.

Anderson, R. W., and J. P. Danthine. "Hedger Diversity in Futures Markets." *Economic Journal* 93 (1983): 370–389.

Arak, M., P. Fischer, L. Goodman, and R. Darganani. "The Municipal-Treasury Futures Spread." J*ournal of Futures Markets* 7 (1987): 355–371.

Arak, M., and L. Goodman. "How to Calculate Better Hedge Ratios." *Futures Magazine* 15 (1986): 56–57.

Arak, M., and L. Goodman. "Treasury-Bond Futures: Valuing the Delivery Options." *Journal of Futures Markets* 7 (1987): 269–286.

Bailey, W. "The Market for Japanese Index Futures: Some Preliminary Evidence." *Journal of Futures Markets* 9 (1989): 283–295.

Ball, C., W. Torous, and A. Tschoegl. "The Degree of Price Resolution: The Case of the Gold Market." *Journal of Futures Markets* 5 (1985): 29–43.

Barnhill, T. "Valuation of the Quality and the Switching Options and Their Impact on Treasury Bond Futures Prices." Center for the Study of Futures Markets, Columbia University, WP CSFM-#152, 1987.

Barnhill, T., and W. Seale. "Optimal Exercise of the Switching Option in Treasury Bond Arbitrage." *Journal of Futures Markets* 8 (1988): 517–532.

Bassett, G., V. France, and S. Pliska. "The MMI Futures Spread on October 19, 1987." Working paper, Chicago College of Business Administration, University of Illinois, January 1989.

Batkins, C. "Hedging Mortgage-Backed Securities with Treasury Bond Futures." *Journal of Futures Markets* 7 (1987): 675–693.

Benninga, S., R. Eldor, and I. Zilcha. "The Optimal Hedge Ratio in Unbiased Futures Markets." *Journal of Futures Markets* 4 (1984): 155–160.

Benninga, S., and M. Smirlock. "An Empirical Analysis of the Delivery Option, Marking to Market, and the Pricing of Treasury Bond Futures." *Journal of Futures Markets* 5 (1985): 361–374.

Bierwag, G. *Duration Analysis: Managing Interest Rate Risk.* Cambridge, Mass.: Ballinger, 1987.

Black, F. "The Pricing of Commodity Contracts." *Journal of Financial Economics* 3 (1976): 167–179.

Black, F., and M. Scholes. "The Valuation of Option Contracts and a Test of Market Efficiency." *Journal of Finance* 27 (1972): 399–418.

Black, F., and M. Scholes. "The Pricing of Options and Corporate Liabilities." *Journal of Political Economy* 81 (1973): 637–659.

Bodie, Z., and V. I. Rosansky. "Risk and Return in Commodity Futures." *Financial Analysts Journal* (May–June 1980): 27–39.

Bortz, G. "Does the Treasury Bond Futures Market Destabilize the Treasury Bond Cash Market?" *Journal of Futures Markets* 4 (1984): 25–38.

Boyle, P. "The Quality Option and the Timing Option in Futures Contracts." *Journal of Finance* 44 (1989): 101–113.

Branch, B. "Testing the Unbiasedness Expectations Theory of Interest Rates." *Financial Review* 13 (1978): 51–66.

Brealey, R., and S. Myers. *Principles of Corporate Finance.* 2d ed. New York: McGraw-Hill, 1988.

Breeden, D. T. "An Intertemporal Asset Pricing Model with Stochastic Consumption and Investment Opportunities." *Journal of Financial Economics* 7 (1979): 265–296.

Breeden, D. T. "Consumption Risk in Futures Markets." *Journal of Finance* 35 (1980): 503–520.

Brennan, M. "The Supply of Storage." *American Economic Review* 47 (1958): 50–72.

Brennan, M. "A Theory of Price Limits in Futures Markets." *Journal of Financial Economics* 16 (1986): 213–233.

Brennan, M., and E. Schwartz. "Evaluating Natural Resource Investments." *Journal of Business* 58 (1985): 135–157.

Brennan, M., and E. Schwartz. "Arbitrage in Stock Index Futures." Working paper, University of California–Los Angeles, 1986.

Brodt, A. "Optimal Bank Asset and Liability Management with Financial Futures." *Journal of Futures Markets* 8 (1988): 457–481.

Byrne, B. *The Stock Index Futures Market: A Trader's Insights and Strategies.* Chicago: Probus, 1987.

Campbell, T., and W. Kracaw. "Optimal Managerial Incentive Contracts and the Value of Corporate Insurance." *Journal of Financial and Quantitative Analysis* 22 (1987): 315–328.

Capozza, D., and B. Cornell. "Treasury Bill Pricing in the Spot and Futures Market." *Review of Economics and Statistics* 61 (1979): 513–520.

Carleton, D. W. "Futures Markets: Their Purpose, Their History, Their Growth, Their Successes and Failures." *Journal of Futures Markets* 4 (1984): 237–271.

Carter, C. A., G. C. Rausser, and A. Schmitz. "Efficient Asset Portfolios and the Theory of Normal Backwardation." *Journal of Political Economy* 91 (1983): 319–331.

Chambers, D. "An Immunization Strategy for Futures Contracts on Government Securities." *Journal of Futures Markets* 4 (1984): 173–187.

Chance, D. "Futures Contracts and Immunization." *Review of Research in Futures Markets* 5 (1986): 124–140.

Chance, D., M. Marr, and G. Thompson. "Hedging Shelf Registrations." *Journal of Futures Markets* 6 (1986): 11–27.

Chang, E. "Returns to Speculators and the Theory of Normal Backwardation." *Journal of Finance* 40 (1985): 193–208.

Chang, J., and J. Loo. "Marking to Market, Stochastic Interest Rates, and Discounts on Stock Index Futures." *Journal of Futures Markets* 7 (1987): 15–20.

Chen, K., R. Sears, and D. Tzang. "Oil Prices and Energy Futures." *Journal of Futures Markets* 7 (1987): 501–518.

Chiang, R., G. Gay, and R. Kolb. "Commodity Exchange Seat Prices." *Review of Futures Markets* 6 (1987): 1–12.

Chichilnisky, G. "Manipulation and Repeated Games in Futures." In *The Industrial Organization of Futures Markets,* edited by R. Anderson, 193–214. Lexington, Mass.: Heath, 1984.

Chow, B., and D. Brophy. "The U.S. Treasury Bill Futures Market and Hypotheses Regarding the Term Structure of Interest Rates." *Financial Review* 13 (1978): 36–50.

Chow, B., and D. Brophy. "Treasury-Bill Futures Market: A Formulation and Interpretation." *Journal of Futures Markets* 2 (1982): 25–47.

Chung, Y. P. "A Transactions Data Test of Stock Index Futures Market Efficiency and

Index Arbitrage Profitability." Working paper, Ohio State University, November 1988.

Cicchetti, P., C. Dale, and A. Vignola. "Usefulness of Treasury Bill Futures as Hedging Instruments." *Journal of Futures Markets* 1 (1981): 378–387.

Cook, T. Q. "Treasury Bills." In *Instruments of the Money Market,* edited by T. Q. Cook and T. D. Rowe, 81–93. Richmond, Va.: Federal Reserve Bank of Richmond, 1986.

Cootner, P. "Returns to Speculators: Telser vs. Keynes." *Journal of Political Economy* 68 (1960): 396–404.

Cornell, B. "Taxes and the Pricing of Stock Index Futures: Empirical Results." *Journal of Futures Markets* 5 (1985): 89–101.

Cornell, B., and K. French. "The Pricing of Stock Index Futures." *Journal of Futures Markets* 3 (1983): 1–14.

Cornell, B., and M. Reinganum. "Forward and Futures Prices: Evidence from the Foreign Exchange Markets." *Journal of Finance* 36 (1981): 1035–1045.

Cox, J., J. Ingersoll, and S. Ross. "The Relationship between Forward Prices and Futures Prices." *Journal of Financial Economics* 9 (1981): 321–346.

Cox, J., and M. Rubinstein. *Options Markets.* Englewood Cliffs, N.J.: Prentice-Hall, 1985.

Cox, J., S. Ross, and M. Rubinstein. "Option Pricing: A Simplified Approach." *Journal of Financial Economics* 7 (1979): 229–263.

Dale, C., and R. Workman. "Measuring Patterns of Price Movements in the Treasury Bill Futures Market." *Journal of Business and Economics* 33 (1981): 81–87.

Diamond, B., and M. Kollar. *24-Hour Trading: The Global Network of Futures and Options Markets.* New York: Wiley, 1989.

Dooley, M. and P. Isard. "Capital Controls, Political Risk, and Deviations from Interest Rate Parity." *Journal of Political Economy* 88 (1980): 370–384.

Dubofsky, D. "Hedging Dividend Capture Strategies with Stock Index Futures." *Journal of Futures Markets* 7 (1987): 471–481.

Duffie, D., and M. Jackson. "Optimal Hedging and Equilibrium in a Dynamic Futures Market." Research Paper 814, Graduate School of Business, Stanford University, 1986.

Dusak, C. "Futures Trading and Investor Returns: An Investigation of Commodity Market Risk Premiums." *Journal of Political Economy* 81 (1973): 1387–1406.

Eaker, M. "Covered Interest Arbitrage: New Measurement and Empirical Results." *Journal of Economics and Business* 32 (1980): 249–253.

Easterbrook, F. "Monopoly, Manipulation, and the Regulation of Futures Markets." *Journal of Business* 59 (1986): 103–127 (supplement).

Ederington, L. H. "The Hedging Performance of the New Futures Markets." *Journal of Finance* 34 (1979): 157–170.

Edwards, F. "The Regulation of Futures Markets: A Conceptual Framework." *Journal of Futures Markets* 1 (1981): 417–439.

Edwards, F. "Futures Markets in Transition: The Uneasy Balance between Government and Self-Regulation." *Journal of Futures Markets* 3 (1983): 191–205.

Edwards, F. "The Clearing Association in Futures Markets: Guarantor and Regulator." In *The Industrial Organization of Futures Markets,* edited by R. Anderson, 225–252. Lexington, Mass.: Heath, 1984.

Edwards, F. "Futures Trading and Cash Market Volatility: Stock Index and Interest Rate Futures." *Journal of Futures Markets* 8 (1988): 421–439.

Elton, E., M. Gruber, and J. Rentzler. "Intra-Day Tests of the Efficiency of the Treasury Bill Futures Market." *Review of Economics and Statistics* 66 (1984): 129–137.

Emmet, E., and D. Vaught. "Risk and Return in Cattle and Hog Futures." *Journal of Futures Markets* 8 (1988): 79–87.

Fabozzi, F. *The Handbook of Treasury Securities.* Chicago: Probus, 1988.

Fama, E. "Perspectives on October 1987, or, What Did We Learn from the Crash?" In *Black Monday and the Future of Financial Markets,* edited by R. Kamphuis, R. Kormendi, and J. Watson, 71–82. Homewood, Ill.: Irwin, 1989.

Fama, E., and K. French. "Commodity Futures Prices: Some Evidence on Forecast Power, Premiums, and the Theory of Storage." *Journal of Business* 60 (1987): 55–73.

Fama, E., and K. French, "Business Cycles and the Behavior of Metals Prices." *Journal of Finance* 43 (1988): 1075–1093.

Feder, G., R. E. Just, and A. Schmitz. "Futures Markets and the Theory of the Firm under Price Uncertainty." *Quarterly Journal of Economics* 94 (1980): 317–328.

Figlewski, S. "Margins and Market Integrity: Margin Setting for Stock Index Futures and Options." *Journal of Futures Markets* 4 (1984a): 385–416.

Figlewski, S. "Hedging Performance and Basis Risk in Stock Index Futures." *Journal of Finance* 39 (1984b): 657–669.

Figlewski, S. "Hedging with Stock Index Futures: Theory and Application in a New Market." *Journal of Futures Markets* 5 (1985): 183–199.

Figlewski, S., and S. Kon. "Portfolio Management with Stock Index Futures." *Financial Analysts Journal* (January–February 1982): 52–60.

Finnerty, J., and H. Park. "Stock Index Futures: Does the Tail Wag the Dog? A Technical Note." *Financial Analysts Journal* (March–April 1987): 57–61.

Fischel, D. "Regulatory Conflict and Entry Regulation of New Futures Contracts." *Journal of Business* 59 (1986): 85–102 (supplement).

Fishe, R., and L. Goldberg. "The Effects of Margins on Trading in Futures Markets." *Journal of Futures Markets* 6 (1986): 261–271.

French, K. "A Comparison of Futures and Forward Prices." *Journal of Financial Economics* 12 (1983): 311–342.

French, K. "Detecting Spot Price Forecasts in Futures Prices." *Journal of Business* 59 (1986): S39–S54.

Frenkel, J. A., and R. M. Levich. "Covered Interest Arbitrage: Unexploited Profits?" *Journal of Political Economy* 83 (1975): 325–338.

Frenkel, J. A., and R. M. Levich. "Transactions Costs and Interest Arbitrage: Tranquil versus Turbulent Periods." *Journal of Political Economy* 85 (1977): 1209–1227.

Gammill, J., and T. Marsh. "Trading Activity and Price Behavior in the Stock and Stock Index Futures Markets in October 1987." *Journal of Economic Perspectives* 2 (1988): 25–44.

Garbade, K., and W. Silber. "Cash Settlement of Futures Contracts: An Economic Analysis." *Journal of Futures Markets* 3 (1983): 451–472.

Gay, G., and S. Manaster. "The Quality Option Implicit in Futures Contracts." *Journal of Financial Economics* 13 (1984): 353–370.

Gay, G., and S. Manaster. "Implicit Delivery Options and Optimal Exercise Strategies for Financial Futures Contracts." *Journal of Financial Economics* 16 (1986): 41–72.

Geske, R., and D. Pieptea. "Controlling Interest Rate Risk and Return with Futures." *Review of Futures Markets* 6 (1987): 64–86.

Goodfriend, M. "Eurodollars." In *Instruments of the Money Market,* edited by T. Q. Cook and T. D. Rowe, 53–64. Richmond, Va.: Federal Reserve Bank of Richmond, 1986.

Gramatikos, T., and A. Saunders. "Stability and the Hedging Performance of Foreign Currency Futures." *Journal of Futures Markets* 3 (1983): 295–305.

Grant, D. "A Market Index Futures Contract and Portfolio Selection." *Journal of Economics and Business* 34 (1982): 387–390.

Gray, R. W., and A. E. Peck. "The Chicago Wheat Futures Market: Recent Problems in Historical Perspective." *Food Research Institute Studies* 18 (1981): 89–115.

Greenwald, B., and J. Stein. "The Task Force Report: The Reasoning behind the Recommendations." *Journal of Economic Perspectives* 2 (1988): 3–23.

Gross, M. "A Semi-Strong Test of the Efficiency of the Aluminum and Copper Markets at the LME." *Journal of Futures Markets* 8 (1988): 67–77.

Grossman, S. "The Existence of Futures Markets, Noisy Rational Expectations and Informational Externalities." *Review of Financial Studies* 64 (1977): 431–449.

Grossman, S. "Program Trading and Stock and Futures Price Volatility." *Journal of Futures Markets* 8 (1988): 413–419.

Harris, L. "S&P 500 Cash Stock Price Volatilities." Working paper, School of Business Administration, University of Southern California, 1988.

Harris, L. "The October 1987 S&P 500 Stock-Futures Basis." *Journal of Finance* 44 (1989): 77–99.

Hartzmark, M. "Regulating Futures Margin Requirements." *Review of Research in Futures Markets* 5 (1986a): 242–260.

Hartzmark, M. "The Effects of Changing Margin Levels on Futures Market Activity, the Composition of Traders in the Market, and Price Performance." *Journal of Business* 59 (1986b): 147–180 (supplement).

Hayenga, M., and D. DiPietre. "Hedging Wholesale Meat Prices: Analysis of Basis Risk." *Journal of Futures Markets* 2 (1982): 131–140.

Heaton, H. "On the Possible Tax-Driven Arbitrage Opportunities in the New Municipal Bond Futures Contract." *Journal of Futures Markets* 8 (1988): 291–302.

Hegde, S. "The Impact of Interest Rate Level and Volatility on the Performance of Interest Rate Hedges." *Journal of Futures Markets* 2 (1982): 341–356.

Hegde, S., and B. Branch. "An Empirical Analysis of Arbitrage Opportunities in the Treasury Bill Futures Market." *Journal of Futures Markets* 5 (1985): 407–424.

Hegde, S., and B. McDonald. "On the Informational Role of Treasury Bill Futures." *Journal of Futures Markets* 6 (1986): 629–643.

Helmuth, J. "A Report on the Systematic Downward Bias in Live Cattle Futures Prices." *Journal of Futures Markets* 1 (1981): 347–358.

Hemler, M. *The Quality Delivery Option in Treasury Bond Futures Contracts.* Ph.D. diss., Graduate School of Business, University of Chicago, March 1988.

Herbst, A., J. McCormack, and E. West. "Investigation of a Lead-Lag Relationship between Spot Stock Indices and Their Futures Contracts." *Journal of Futures Markets* 7 (1987): 373–381.

Hieronymous, T. A. *Economics of Futures Trading.* New York: Commodity Research Bureau, 1971.

Hilliard, J. "Hedging Interest Rate Risk with Futures Portfolios under Term Structure Effects." *Journal of Finance* 38 (1984): 1547–1569.

Hirshleifer, D. "Residual Risk, Trading Costs, and Commodity Futures Risk Premia." *Review of Financial Studies* 1 (1988a): 173–193.

Hirshleifer, D. "Futures Market Equilibrium and the Structure of Production in Commodity Markets." *Journal of Political Economy* 96 (1988b): 1206–1220.

Hodrick, R., and S. Srivastava. "Foreign Currency Futures." *Journal of International Economics* 22 (1987): 1–24.

Holthausen, D. M. "Hedging and the Competitive Firm under Price Uncertainty." *American Economic Review* 69 (1979): 989–995.

Howard, C. "Are T-Bill Futures Good Forecasters of Interest Rates?" *Journal of Futures Markets* 1 (1982): 305–315.

Hunter, W. "Rational Margins on Futures Contracts: Initial Margins." *Review of Research in Futures Markets* 5 (1986): 160–173.

Jagannathan, R. "An Investigation of Commodity Futures Prices Using the Consumption-Based Intertemporal Capital Asset

Pricing Model." *Journal of Finance* 40 (1985): 175–192.

Jarrow, R., and G. Oldfield. "Forward Contracts and Futures Contracts." *Journal of Financial Economics* 9 (1981): 373–382.

Jarrow, R., and A. Rudd. *Option Pricing.* Homewood, Ill.: Irwin, 1983.

Johnson, L. L. "The Theory of Hedging and Speculation in Commodity Futures." *Review of Economic Studies* 27 (1960): 139–151.

Jones, E. P. "Option Arbitrage and Strategy with Large Price Changes." *Journal of Financial Economics* 13 (1984): 91–113.

Jones, F. "Spreads: Tails, Turtles, and All That." *Journal of Futures Markets* 1 (1981): 565–596.

Jones, F. "The Economics of Futures and Options Contracts Based on Cash Settlement." *Journal of Futures Markets* 2 (1982): 63–82.

Jones, R. A. "Conversion Factor Risk in Treasury Bond Futures: A Comment." *Journal of Futures Markets* 4 (1985): 115–119.

Judge, G., W. Griffiths, R. C. Hill, H. Lutkepohl, and L. Tsoung-Chao. *The Theory and Practice of Econometrics.* 2d ed. New York: Wiley, 1985.

Kahl, K., R. Rutz, and J. Sinquefield. "The Economics of Performance Margins in Futures Markets." *Journal of Futures Markets* 5 (1985): 103–112.

Kaldor, N. "Speculation and Economic Stability." *Review of Economic Studies* 7 (1939): 1–27.

Kamara, A. "Market Trading Structures and Asset Pricing: Evidence from the Treasury-Bill Markets." *Review of Financial Studies* 1 (1988): 357–375.

Kane, A., and A. Marcus. "Conversion Factor Risk and Hedging in the Treasury-Bond Futures Market." *Journal of Futures Markets* 4 (1984): 55–64.

Kane, A., and A. Marcus. "The Quality Option in the Treasury Bond Futures Market: An Empirical Assessment." *Journal of Futures Markets* 6 (1986a): 231–248.

Kane, A., and A. Marcus. "Valuation and Optimal Exercise of the Wild Card Option in the Treasury Bond Futures Market." *Journal of Finance* 41 (1986b): 195–207.

Kane, E. "Market Incompleteness and Divergences between Forward and Futures Interest Rates." *Journal of Finance* 35 (1980): 221–234.

Kawaller, I. "Hedging with Futures Contracts: Going the Extra Mile." *Journal of Cash Management* (July–August 1986): 34–36.

Kawaller, I., P. Koch, and T. Koch. "The Temporal Price Relationship between S&P 500 Futures and S&P 500 Index." *Journal of Finance* 42 (1987): 1309–1329.

Kawaller, I., and T. Koch. "Cash-and-Carry Trading and the Pricing of Treasury Bill Futures." *Journal of Futures Markets* 4 (1984): 115–123.

Kawaller, I., and T. Koch. "Managing Cash Flow Risk in Stock Index Futures: The Tail Hedge." *Journal of Portfolio Management* (Fall 1988): 41–44.

Kenyon, D., and J. Clay. "Analysis of Profit Margin Hedging Strategies for Hog Producers." *Journal of Futures Markets* 7 (1987): 183–202.

Keynes, J. M. *A Treatise on Money.* Vol. 2. London: Macmillan, 1930.

Khoury, S. *Speculative Markets.* New York: Macmillan, 1984.

Khoury, S., and G. Jones. "Daily Price Limits on Futures Contracts: Nature, Impact, and Justification." *Review of Research in Futures Markets* 3 (1984): 22–36.

Kilcollin, T. "Difference Systems in Financial Futures Markets." *Journal of Finance* 37 (1982): 1183–1197.

Kleidon, A. "Arbitrage, Nontrading, and Stale Prices: October, 1987." Working paper, Graduate School of Business, Stanford University, 1988.

Klemkosky, R., and D. Lasser. "An Efficiency Analysis of the T-Bond Futures Market." *Journal of Futures Markets* 5 (1985): 607–620.

Kochin, L., and R. Parks. "Was the Tax-Exempt Bond Market Inefficient or Were Future Expected Tax Rates Negative?" *Journal of Finance* 43 (1988): 913–931.

Kodres, L. "Tests of Unbiasedness in Foreign Exchange Futures Markets: The Effects of Price Limits." *Review of Futures Markets* 7 (1988): 138–166.

Kolb, R., and G. Gay. "The Performance of Live Cattle Futures as Predictors of Subsequent Spot Prices." *Journal of Futures Markets* 3 (1983): 55–63.

Kolb, R., G. Gay, and J. Jordan. "Are There Arbitrage Opportunities in the Treasury-Bond Futures Market?" *Journal of Futures Markets* 3 (1982): 217–229.

Koppenhaver, G. "The Forward Pricing Efficiency of the Live Cattle Futures Market." *Journal of Futures Markets* 3 (1983): 307–319.

Koppenhaver, G. "Futures Market Regulation." *Economics Perspectives* 11 (1987): 3–15.

Kuberek, R., and N. Pefley. "Hedging Corporate Debt with U.S. Treasury Bond Futures." *Journal of Futures Markets* 3 (1983): 345–353.

Kyle, A. "A Theory of Futures Market Manipulations." In *The Industrial Organization of Futures Markets,* edited by R. Anderson, 141–174. Lexington, Mass.: Heath, 1984.

Laatsch, F., and T. Schwarz. "Price Discovery and Risk Transfer in Stock Index Cash and Futures Markets." *Review of Futures Markets* 7 (1988): 272–289.

Landes, W., J. Stoffels, and J. Seifert. "An Empirical Test of a Duration-Based Hedge: The Case of Corporate Bonds." *Journal of Futures Markets* 5 (1985): 173–182.

Lang, R., and R. Rasche. "A Comparison of Yields on Futures Contracts and Implied Forward Yields." *Federal Reserve Bank of St. Louis Review* (December 1978): 21–30.

Lasser, D. "A Measure of Ex-Ante Hedging Effectiveness for the Treasury Bill and Treasury Bond Futures Markets." *Review of Futures Markets* 6 (1987): 278–295.

Leuthold, R. M. "The Price Performance on the Futures Market of a Nonstorable Commodity: Live Beef Cattle." *American Journal of Agricultural Economics* 56 (1974): 271–271.

Leuthold, R. M. "Commercial Use and Speculative Measures of the Livestock Commodity Futures Market." *Journal of Futures Markets* 3 (1983): 113–135.

Leuthold, R. M., and R. S. Mokler. "Feeding-Margin Hedging in the Cattle Industry." *International Futures Trading Seminar* (Chicago Board of Trade) 6 (1979): 56–68.

Levich, R. "Currency Forecasters Lose Their Way." *Euromoney* (March 1983): 140–147.

Little, P. "Financial Futures and Immunization." *Journal of Financial Research* 9 (1985): 1–12.

Livingston, M. "The Cheapest Deliverable Bond for the CBT Treasury Bond Futures Contract." *Journal of Futures Markets* 4 (1984): 161–192.

Livingston, M. "The Effect of Coupon Level on Treasury Bond Futures Delivery." *Journal of Futures Markets* 7 (1987): 303–309.

Lumpkin, S. A. "Repurchase and Reverse Repurchase Agreements." In *Instruments of the Money Market,* edited by T. Q. Cook and T. D. Rowe, 65–80. Richmond, Va.: Federal Reserve Bank of Richmond, 1986.

Ma, C., R. Rao, and R. Sears. "Limit Moves and Price Resolution: The Case of the Treasury Bond Futures Market." *Journal of Futures Markets* 9 (1989): 321–335.

MacBeth, J., and L. Merville. "An Empirical Examination of the Black-Scholes Call Option Pricing Model." *Journal of Finance* 34 (1979): 1173–1186.

McCormick, F. "Covered Interest Arbitrage: Unexploited Profits? Comment." *Journal of Political Economy* 87 (1979): 411–417.

McCurdy, T., and I. Morgan. "Tests of the Martingale Hypothesis for Foreign Currency Futures." *International Journal of Forecasting* 3 (1987): 131–148.

McDonald, R. "Taxes and the Hedging of Forward Commitments." *Journal of Futures Markets* 6 (1986): 207–222.

McDonald, R., and D. Siegel. "Investment and the Valuation of Firms When There Is an Option to Shut Down." *International Economic Review* 26 (1985): 331–349.

MacDonald S., and S. Hein. "Futures Rates and Forward Rates as Predictors of Near-Term Treasury Bill Rates." *Journal of Futures Markets* 9 (1989): 249-262.

MacDonald S., R. Peterson, and T. Koch. "Using Futures to Improve Treasury Bill Portfolio Performance." *Journal of Futures Markets* 8 (1988): 167–184.

MacFarlane, J., D. Ross, and J. Showers. *The Interest Rate Swap Market: Yield Mathematics, Terminology and Conventions.* New York: Salomon Brothers, June 1985.

MacKinlay, A., and K. Ramaswamy. "Program Trading and the Behavior of Stock Index Futures Prices." *Review of Financial Studies* 1 (1988): 137–158.

McLeod, R., and G. McCabe. "Hedging for Better Spread Management." *The Bankers Magazine* 163 (1980): 47–52.

Maness, T., and A. Senchack. "Futures Hedging and the Reported Financial Position of Thrift Institutions." *Review of Research in Futures Markets* 5 (1986): 142–158.

Marcus, A. "Efficient Asset Portfolios and the Theory of Normal Backwardation: A Comment." *Journal of Political Economy* 92 (1984): 162–164.

Marcus, A., and D. M. Modest. "Futures Markets and Production Decisions." *Journal of Political Economy* 92 (1984): 409–426.

Meisner, J., and J. Labuszewski. "Treasury Bond Futures Delivery Bias." *Journal of Futures Markets* 4 (1984): 569–577.

Merton, R. "Theory of Rational Option Pricing." *Bell Journal of Economics and Management Science* 4 (1973): 141–183.

Merton, R. "Option Pricing When Underlying Stock Returns Are Discontinuous." *Journal of Financial Economics* 3 (1976): 125–144.

Miller, S., and D. Luke. "Alternative Techniques for Cross-Hedging Wholesale Beef Prices." *Journal of Futures Markets* 2 (1982): 121–129.

Modest, D., and M. Sundaresan. "The Relationship between Spot and Futures Prices in Stock Index Futures Markets: Some Preliminary Evidence." *Journal of Futures Markets* 3 (1983): 15–41.

Modigliani, F., and M. Miller. "The Cost of Capital, Corporate Finance, and the Theory of Investment." *American Economic Review* 48 (1958): 261–297.

Monroe, M., and R. Cohn. "The Relative Efficiency of the Gold and Treasury Bill Futures Markets." *Journal of Futures Markets* 6 (1986): 477–493.

Morgan, G. "Forward and Futures Pricing of Treasury Bills." *Journal of Banking and Finance* 5 (1981): 483–496.

Myers, S. "The Determinants of Corporate Borrowing." *Journal of Financial Economics* 5 (1977): 147–176.

Newbery, D. "The Manipulation of Futures Markets by a Dominant Producer." In *The Industrial Organization of Futures Markets,* edited by R. Anderson, 35–62. Lexington, Mass.: Heath, 1984.

Ng, N. "Detecting Spot Price Forecasts in Futures Prices Using Causality Tests." *Review of Futures Markets* 6 (1987): 250–267.

Palm, L., and J. Graham. "The Systematic Downward Bias in Live Cattle Futures: An Evaluation." *Journal of Futures Markets* 1 (1981): 359–366.

Park, H., and A. Chen. "Differences between Futures and Forward Prices: A Further Investigation of Marking-to-Market Effects." *Journal of Futures Markets* 5 (1985): 77–88.

Parker, J., and R. Daigler. "Hedging Money Market CDs with Treasury-Bill Futures." *Journal of Futures Markets* 1 (1981): 597–606.

Peck, A. E. "Hedging and Income Stability: Concepts, Implications, and an Example." *American Journal of Agricultural Economics* 57 (1975): 410–419.

Poole, W. "Using T-Bill Futures to Gauge Interest-Rate Expectations." *Economic Review* (Spring 1978): 7–15.

Puglisi, D. "Is the Futures Market for Treasury Bills Efficient?" *Journal of Portfolio Management* 4 (1978): 64–67.

Purcell, W., and M. Hudson. "The Certificate System for Delivery in Live Cattle: Conceptual Issues and Measures of Performance." *Journal of Futures Markets* 6 (1986): 461–475.

Raynauld, J., and J. Tessier. "Risk Premiums in Futures Markets: An Empirical Investigation." *Journal of Futures Markets* 4 (1984): 189–211.

Rendleman, R. "Commentary on the Effects of Stock Index Futures Trading on the Market for Underlying Stocks." *Review of Research in Futures Markets* 5 (1986): 174–186.

Rendleman, R., and B. Bartter. "Two State Option Pricing." *Journal of Finance* 34 (1979): 1093–1110.

Rendleman, R., and C. Carabini. "The Efficiency of the Treasury Bill Futures Market." *Journal of Finance* 34 (1979): 895–914.

Rentzler, J. "Trading Treasury Bond Spreads against Treasury Bill Futures: A Model and Empirical Test of the Turtle Trade." *Journal of Futures Markets* 6 (1986): 41–61.

Resnick, B. "The Relationship between Futures Prices for U.S. T-Bonds." *Review of Research in Futures Markets* 3 (1984): 88–104.

Resnick, B., and E. Henninger. "The Relationship between Futures and Cash Prices for U.S. Treasury Bonds." *Review of Research in Futures Markets* 2 (1983): 287–299.

Richard, S., and M. Sundaresan. "A Continuous-Time Equilibrium Model of Forward Prices and Futures Prices in a Multigood Economy." *Journal of Financial Economics* 9 (1981): 347–371.

Ritchken, P. *Options: Theory, Strategy, and Applications.* Glenview, Ill.: Scott, Foresman, 1987.

Rolfo, J. "Optimal Hedging under Price and Quantity Uncertainty: The Case of a Cocoa Producer." *Journal of Political Economy* 88 (1980): 100–116.

Roll, R. "The International Crash of October 1987." In *Black Monday and the Futures of Financial Markets,* edited by R. Kamphuis, R. Kormendi, and J. Watson, 35–70. Homewood, Ill.: Irwin, 1989.

Ruder, D., and A. Adkins. "Automation of Information Dissemination and Trading in U.S. Securities Markets." In *Innovation and Technology in the Markets: A Reordering of the World's Capital Market System,* edited by D. Siegel. Chicago: Probus, 1990.

Rutledge, D. J. "Hedgers' Demand for Futures Contracts: A Theoretical Framework with Applications to the United States Soybean Complex." *Food Research Institute Studies* 11 (1972): 237–256.

Saloner, G. "Self-Regulating Commodity Futures Exchanges." In *The Industrial Organization of Futures Markets,* edited by R. Anderson, 261–273. Lexington, Mass.: Heath, 1984.

Sandor, R. L. "Innovation by an Exchange: A Case Study of the Development of the Plywood Futures Contract." *Journal of Law and Economics* 16 (1973): 119–136.

Schroeder, T., and M. Hayenga. "Comparison of Selective Hedging and Options Strategies in Cattle Feedlog risk Management." *Journal of Futures Markets* 8 (1988): 141–156.

Senchack, A., and J. Easterwood. "Cross Hedging CDs with Treasury Bill Futures." *Journal of Futures Markets* 3 (1983): 429–438.

Sharpe, W. *Investments.* 2d ed. Englewood Cliffs, N.J.: Prentice-Hall, 1981.

Silber, W. "Innovation, Competition and New Contract Design in Futures Markets." *Journal of Futures Markets* 1 (1981): 123–155.

Simpson, W., and T. Ireland. "The Impact of Financial Futures on the Cash Market for Treasury Bills." *Journal of Financial and Quantitative Analysis* 20 (1985): 371–379.

Slentz, J. "The TED Spread." *Market Perspectives* (Chicago Mercantile Exchange) 5 (1987): 1–4.

Smith, C., and R. Stulz. "The Determinants of Firms' Hedging Policies." *Journal of Financial and Quantitative Analysis* 20 (1985): 391–405.

Stein, J. L. "The Simultaneous Determination of Spot and Futures Prices." *American Economic Review* 51 (1961): 1012–1025.

Stigum, M. *Money Market Calculations: Yields, Break-Evens and Arbitrage.* Homewood, Ill.: Dow Jones-Irwin, 1983.

Stoll, H. "Index Futures, Program Trading, and Stock Market Procedures." *Journal of Futures Markets* 8 (1988): 319–412.

Stoll, H., and R. Whaley. "Expiration Day Effects of Index Options and Futures." *Financial Analysts Journal* (March–April 1987): 16–28.

Stoll, H., and R. Whaley. "Futures and Options on Stock Indexes: Economic Purpose, Arbitrage, and Market Structure." *Review of Futures Markets* 7 (1988): 224–248.

Stone, J. "Principles of the Regulation of Futures Markets." *Journal of Futures Markets* 1 (1981): 117–121.

Stulz, R. "Optimal Hedging Policies." *Journal of Financial and Quantitative Analysis* 19 (1984): 127–140.

Stulz, R. "Program Trading, Portfolio Insurance, and the Crash of 1987." *Financial Markets and Portfolio Management* 1 (1988): 11–22.

Summers, L., and V. Summers. "When Financial Markets Work Too Well: A Cautious Case for a Securities Transaction Tax." In *Innovation and Technology in the Markets: A Reordering of the World's Capital Market System,* edited by D. Siegel. Chicago: Probus, 1990.

Swinnerton, E., R. Curcio, and R. Bennett. "Index Arbitrage, Program Trading, and the Prediction of Intraday Stock Price Changes." *Review of Futures Markets* 7 (1988): 300–323.

Telser, L. G. "Futures Trading and the Storage of Cotton and Wheat." *Journal of Political Economy* 66 (1958): 233–255.

Telser, L. G. "Margins and Futures Contracts." *Journal of Futures Markets* 1 (1981): 225–253.

Teweles, R., and F. Jones. *The Futures Game: Who Wins, Who Loses, Why?* New York: McGraw-Hill, 1987.

Toevs, A., and D. Jacob. "Futures and Alternative Hedge Ratio Methodologies." *Journal of Portfolio Management* (Spring 1986): 60–70.

Turnovsky, S. J. "The Determination of Spot and Futures Prices with Storage Commodities." *Econometrica* 51 (1983): 1363–1387.

Vignola, A., and C. Dale. "Is the Futures Market for Treasury Bills Efficient? An Analysis of Alternative Specifications." *Journal of Financial Research* 3 (1980): 169–188.

Whaley, R. "Valuation of American Call Options on Dividend Paying Stocks: Empirical Tests." *Journal of Financial Economics* 10 (1982): 29–58.

Whaley, R. "Expiration-Day Effects of Index Futures and Options: Empirical Results." *Review of Research in Futures Markets* 5 (1986): 292–304.

Williams, J. *The Economic Function of Futures Markets.* Cambridge: Cambridge University Press, 1986.

Witt, H., T. Schroeder, and M. Hayenga. "Comparison of Analytical Approaches for Estimating Hedge Ratios for Agricultural Commodities." *Journal of Futures Markets* 7 (1987): 135–146.

Working, H. "The Theory of the Inverse Carrying Charge in Futures Markets." *Journal of Farm Economics* 30 (1948): 1–28.

Working, H. "The Theory of Price of Storage." *American Economic Review* 39 (1949): 1254–1262.

Zeckhauser, R., and V. Niederhoffer. "The Performance of Market Index Futures Contracts." *Financial Analysts Journal* (February 1983): 59–65.

Name Index

Subject Index